Windows NT®
Registry

New
Riders

New Riders Professional Library

Windows NT®
Registry

New
Riders

201 West 103rd Street,
Indianapolis, Indiana 46290

Sandra Osborne

with a Foreword by
Jerold Schulman

Windows NT® Registry

Sandra Osborne

Trademark Acknowledgments

Warning and Disclaimer

Publisher
Jim LeValley

Executive Editor
Linda Ratts Engelman

Managing Editor
Caroline Roop

Acquisitions Editor
Karen Wachs

Development Editor
Lisa M. Gebken

Project Editor
Leah D. Williams

Copy Editor
Nancy E. Sixsmith

Indexer
Kevin Fulcher

Technical Reviewers
Brien C. Boland
Jerold Schulman
David Navarro
Jerry Pournelle
Emil Varona

Team Coordinator
Amy Lewis

Manufacturing Coordinator
Brook Farling

Book Designer
Ruth Lewis

Cover Designer
Brainstorm Design

**Production Team
Supervisor**
Daniela Raderstorf

Production
Louis Porter, Jr.
Megan Wade

About the Author

Sandra Osborne is a senior technical developer for a large international organization in Washington, D.C., where she leads a team that uses Registry manipulation and answer files to create automated installations. Sandra was responsible for migrating the organization's network from Windows 3.1 to Windows 95, which involved 6,000+ users, 60 servers in three central locations, and over 150 field offices worldwide. She is currently involved in evaluating the implementation of Windows NT 5.0 and Windows Terminal Server as a possible migration strategy. Sandra has more than 20 years of computer experience, including stints in the U.S. Navy, the Tennessee Valley Authority, and various computer firms. An experienced programmer and analyst, Sandra has used all flavors of Windows since its inception. She holds a Bachelor of Science degree in Physics from the University of North Alabama, and has associate degrees in Computer Science, Mathematics, and Nuclear Engineering. This is her first book.

About the Technical Reviewers

These reviewers contributed their considerable practical, hands-on expertise to the entire development process for *Windows NT Registry*. As the book was being written, these folks reviewed all the material for technical content, organization, and flow. Their feedback was critical to ensuring that *Windows NT Registry* fits our readers' need for the highest quality technical information.

Brien C. Boland has more than 15 years of professional IT experience. During the 1980s, he was founder and president of two computer companies located in Washington D.C. During that time, he provided hardware, software, programming, networking, and consulting services to the federal government and to companies worldwide. During the 1990s, he has been a consultant to the World Bank and IMF. He was also vice-president of Systems Engineering for a large Wall Street investment/brokerage firm. Brien has written several in-depth articles published by *Computer World*. He has spoken at national conferences, such as the International NetWare User's Conference and has been a guest lecturer at several local colleges.

Jerold Schulman is president of JSI, Inc., a Windows NT Platform Products reseller and has more than 30 years of information technology experience. After graduating from Drexel University in 1964, Jerold held various corporate IT positions, culminating in becoming vice-president of Information Services for the Americas with a major international transportation conglomerate. Jerold publishes the Windows NT Tips, Tricks, and Registry Hacks site at `http://www.jsiinc.com/reghack.htm`. Jerold and his wife live in Alpharetta, Georgia, where they enjoy community service, travel, and cooking; but mostly each other.

Dedication

This book is dedicated to my brother Michael Osborne, and to my friends David Quinby, Anna Gibson, and Mike Gibson. Thanks for always believing in me and being there when I needed you.

Contents

xi

Foreword

When Macmillan Publishing approached me to act as a technical editor for this book, my first reaction was "Thank you, but no thank you." Do we need yet another dry, lifeless, dissertation on editing the Windows NT Registry—The Secret of Life with Windows NT Revealed? Who is Sandra Osborne? I don't have the time for this! Do I need the work? (As a matter of fact, I did.)

I have been using Windows NT since the first version 3.1 release. In 1994, it became the focus of my business. In January 1997, I first published the Windows NT Tips, Tricks, and Registry Hacks site as a marketing tool. It has since assumed a life of its own. I spend countless hours researching new tips, answering newsgroup queries, and researching customer support issues. The vast majority of queries I receive fall into the "I know how to configure Windows NT by using this or that GUI (graphical user interface), but how do I that in a batch job?" category.

Osborne's book is unique in that it answers that question. In a series of well-organized chapters, Sandra takes us from the familiar GUI, with its check boxes, radial buttons, text boxes, and drop-down lists, to the underlying Registry entries they create and maintain. Sprinkled throughout are author notes, troubleshooting, tips, and warnings, which bring you the benefit of her "I've been there, done that" experience.

Who is Sandra Osborne? Someone who saw the need and had the skills necessary to allow me to answer a resounding YES, we do need another Windows NT Registry book. When you read it, I am sure you will agree.

Jerold Schulman
JSI, Inc.
Alpharetta, Georgia—USA
July 26, 1998

Acknowledgments

Well, it looks like I have finally reached the end of this book. It has been a long, involved process of writing and rewriting. Of course, it would have been an altogether impossible task without the help of a great editorial staff. The staff associated with this book was just that, starting with Linda Engelman, who, from the very start, never stopped believing that this would be a great book. She also had the faith to begin this project with an unproven author who never would have survived without a shoulder to lean on. Thanks, Linda!

Next, I would like to thank Jane Brownlow and Karen Wachs, who took over for Jane when she moved elsewhere within the company. These two women were my mother hens and they tried their best to meet deadlines that moved like the morning sun. They are the best. Thanks, guys.

I also want to express my appreciation to the book's development editor, Lisa Gebken. She spent tireless hours reading, editing, rereading, and re-editing the book. Her tips and experience were invaluable and they certainly went a long way in making this book possible. Thanks, Lisa.

Thanks also go out to Brien Boland and Jerold Schulman for the superb technical editing that found all the technical mistakes and omissions. Great job, guys!

I want to also thank the following friends and colleagues who suffered through the last six months, never tiring of hearing me talk about book, book, book, book, book: Suzanne Blanchette, Wendy Brooks, Diane Nelson, Paula and David Perry, Tom Prosch, Frank Ries, John Michael Scott, Debbie Scrugs, Lori Thaler, and my parents, Jordan and Sheila Osborne.

I also have to mention my cats Brutus and "Little Cat," who stared at me from various perches and provided company as the keyboard clicked late into the night. And to my dogs, Dana, Skully, and Stonewall, who kept my feet warm and provided the needed diversions of chewing and playing.

Finally, as important as all of these people are, I am most thankful to you, the reader, because without you there would be no need for this book.

Sandra Beth Osborne
June 22, 1998
Washington, DC

Introduction

Having bought this book, you must already be familiar with the concept of the Windows Registry. So you already know that the Registry dates back to Windows 3.1, when OLE information was kept in the REG.DAT file as a way for multiple applications to share the same information. And, although there were other settings, such as some file associations, Windows 3.1 did little to exploit the Registry.

With the advent of Windows 95, and continuing with Windows NT 4.0, the Registry has become the primary source for hardware, software, and networking information. It is also the source of thousands of other settings, including most of the Windows 3.1 WIN.INI and SYSTEM.INI files. The Registry has evolved into the central component that Windows NT 4.0 was built around.

Who Is This Book For?

Windows NT Registry is for anyone who wants to learn how to use the Windows NT Registry to solve a wide range of hardware issues. If you want to learn how to find out where the CD-ROM settings can be found inside the Registry or configure your new network adapter, this is the book you want.

Second, this book is for those who want to learn how to configure Windows NT through modification of the Registry. If you want to learn how to manage users or network services by making changes to the Windows NT Registry, this book is for you.

Whether you are an experienced Windows NT guru or just want to finally see what all the Registry murmur is about, this book will become one of your most valued resources.

Who Is This Book Not For?

This book is not for those who want to learn how to use Windows NT or its components. If you want to learn how to use the Windows NT Explorer, User Manager, Server Manager, RAS, or other Windows NT components, this book is not for you.

If you want to learn NT Server or network administration, this book is not for you.

Finally, if you seek to learn how to program the Windows NT Registry via the use of programming languages such as Microsoft Visual Basic or Visual C++, this book is not for you.

However, if you want to learn about the innermost workings of the operating system and how this knowledge can help solve a wide range of issues, you have found the right source.

Skills Required

Because this book is targeted at Windows NT configuration specialists, including both server administrators and workstation technicians, you are presumed to possess the following skills:

- Familiarity with Windows NT Workstation 4.0 and Windows NT Server 4.0
- Knowledge of REGEDIT.EXE to view and modify the Registry
- Familiarity with REGEDT32.EXE for hive manipulation and Registry modification

With these skills and this book, you will be able to solve a wide array of problems, ranging from hardware conflicts to communications solutions.

How This Book Is Organized

Arranged in a topical fashion, *Windows NT Registry* enables you to turn to any chapter and receive valuable advice and troubleshooting techniques that can be applied immediately. Where possible, Control Panel applet settings are also discussed.

This book is intended as a topical reference for Registry troubleshooting. To this end, the book is divided into four parts. Each part groups chapters by subject, and each chapter deals with a specific aspect of that subject. To make your troubleshooting woes a little easier, chapters can be read in any order or skipped entirely.

Part I: Managing Hardware

Part I consists of nine chapters that step you through the HKEY_LOCAL_MACHINE Registry key, showing you how to use the Registry to help solve hardware-related issues.

Chapter 1, "Disk Drives," discusses floppy drives, hard drives, and CD-ROM drives. Attention is given to the Registry settings, what they mean, and how to manage them.

Chapter 2, "Configuring Display Settings," discusses Registry settings for video cards, screen savers, fonts, video resolution, colors, and other display settings.

Chapter 3, "Settings for Mice and Keyboards," discusses the settings for the serial mouse, PS/2 mouse, and keyboards.

Chapter 4, "Settings for Sound," discusses sound card settings, including hardware settings and windows sound settings, including schemes.

Chapter 5, "Settings for Memory," discusses memory settings, including memory management.

Chapter 6, "Settings for Configuring Network Adapters," discusses network adapters and their settings. Only ISA and PCI cards are discussed here; PCMCIA (PC Cards) are discussed in Chapter 9.

Chapter 7, "Configuring Printers," discusses settings for local and network printers.

Chapter 8, "Other Hardware Issues," involves configuring scanners, tape backups, and Iomega Zip drives.

Chapter 9, "Configuring Notebook Computers," discusses the settings for configuring PCMCIA Cards (PC Cards), including PCMCIA modems and network cards, the PC or PCMCIA bus, and standalone versus network-configuration settings.

Part II: Managing NT Workstation Components

Part II talks about the Windows NT components that can be modified via the Registry.

Chapter 10, "Modifying the Windows NT Workstation Boot Process," discusses what happens to the Registry during the Windows NT boot process and shows you how to run applications and services.

Chapter 11, "Managing the Desktop," discusses non-hardware components of the Windows NT desktop, including accessibility options.

Chapter 12, "System Components," discusses Microsoft ODBC and file extensions.

Chapter 13, "Windows NT Profiles," discusses hardware and software profiles.

Chapter 14, "Security," discusses security issues from a Registry point of view, particularly user accounts, passwords and protection, objects, and permissions.

Chapter 15, "Settings Created by the User Manager Tool," discusses how to use the Registry to manage the User Manager Tool.

Part III: Managing Network Clients

Part III deals with Dial-Up Networking, computer identification, network services, and network protocols.

Chapter 16, "Settings for Dial-Up Networking," discusses RAS and other Dial-Up Networking components of Windows NT and shows you how to use the Registry to modify and troubleshoot issues concerning remote computer access.

Chapter 17, "Configuring Network Services," shows you how to manage PC identification through the Registry, including the Server Service, the Workstation Service, and the Client Service for NetWare.

Chapter 18, "Configuring Network Communications," discusses Net BIOS, WINS, DNS, and other Windows NT communications.

Chapter 19, "Configuring TCP/IP," discusses TCP/IP, DHCP, NWLink, and settings for Point-to-Point Tunneling.

Part IV: Appendixes

Appendix A, "Windows NT Workstation Registry Keys," contains a complete listing and explanation of the Windows NT Workstation Registry keys (without hardware-specific keys). This appendix was produced from a clean installation of Windows NT 4.0 Workstation and contains all the keys, values, and settings as they are originally installed. Use this appendix to troubleshoot problems that occur when the Registry is changed by applications and hardware.

Appendix B, "Windows NT Server Registry Issues," explains the differences between the Windows NT Server Registry keys and the Windows NT Workstation Registry keys.

On the Web

New Riders Publishing established a Web site to provide further information not included in this book: `http://www.newriders.com`. Topics such as managing various software applications and working with other operating systems are included, as well as managing the Internet and working with settings for DCOM, Active Server Pages, ActiveX, Visual InterDev, Internet Explorer, Web servers, and Netscape.

Conventions Used

The following table lists the special conventions that are used in this book.

Special Text	Meaning
"Text in quotes"	References and quotes
Text in italics	Emphasis

The following features are found throughout this book and relate important information about a particular topic.

This format also shows the value name and possible setting. The data type may also be included for some values in front of the setting. This format is used when writing a .REG file and also when REGEDIT.EXE is used to export part of the Registry.

Tip

Tips provide methods and techniques that can be used to explore topics and issues.

Troubleshooting

Troubleshooting tips provide ways to modify the Registry that help you solve hardware and software problems.

Warning

Warnings highlight areas where problems may arise if the wrong steps are taken, including hardware, software, and (most importantly) Registry errors.

Author Note

Author notes discuss my personal experiences in the real world of computers. These areas include little-known aspects of components, and how they can help solve troubleshooting and other issues.

Most Registry entries are formatted as follows:

```
    Value Name      Data Range
    Data Type       Example Setting
```

Others are formatted as follows:

```
    "Value Name"="Setting"
```

Registry Data Types and Editors

Next, I discuss the Registry data types and the Registry editors. So, you can either skip to your favorite Registry topic or refresh your Registry skills with the following discussion on the Registry tools of the Windows NT operating systems.

Hives

The Windows NT Registry consists of five main HKEYs or hives and numerous sub-keys, entries, and values.

The five (5) top-level or main HKEYs are:

- HKEY_LOCAL_MACHINE. This key contains the hardware information, as discovered by NTDETECT. The ControlSet subkeys are found here.

- HKEY_CURRENT_USER. This key stores all of the current user information, and it is actually contained under the HKEY_USERS key (see Figure I.1). The number for this key is the Security ID (SID) for the current user. All changes made to either of these keys appear in both places.

- HKEY_USERS. This key contains a subkey for each user that is listed in the User Manager for this PC. The .Default key listed under this key is copied when new users are created, becoming a new subkey. This is also the key that is used during boot time, before a user logs on.

- HKEY_CLASSES_ROOT. This HKEY is a copy of the [HKEY_LOCAL_MACHINE\ SOFTWARE\Classes] key, as with the HKEY_CURRENT_USER key. This key holds settings for file extensions and ODBC.

- HKEY_CURRENT_CONFIG. Like the previous two keys, this key points to [HKEY_LOCAL_MACHINE\SYSTEM\CurrentControlSet\Hardware Profiles\Current] and holds the hardware settings that Windows NT uses to boot the computer.

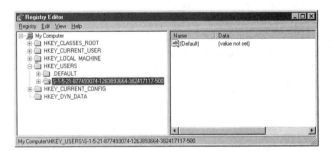

Figure I.1 Actual location of HKEY_CURRENT USER.

Each of the previous keys constitutes a *hive* under Windows NT, which is stored as a file on a hard disk. The hive files for the Default, SAM, Security, Software, and System keys are stored in the %SystemRoot%\System32\Config directory.

Data Types

Almost all settings in the Registry have values associated with them. *Values* are the actual entries found under a key that holds specific data; they can be static data or executable files. The following data types are used:

- REG_BINARY. This data type holds binary data that may be displayed as either a binary or hexadecimal number.
- REG_DWORD. This data type holds data that is four bytes long. This value can be shown as binary, decimal, or hexadecimal data.
- REG_DWORD_BIG_ENDIAN. This data type holds a 32-bit number that has its highest ordered byte first.
- REG_EXPAND_SZ. This data type holds a string that can be appended to (expandable) and hold environment variables.
- REG_FULL_RESOURCE_CONNECTOR. This data type is found only under the [HKEY_LOCAL_MACHINE\HARDWARE] key and holds a hardware resource descriptor.
- REG_LINK. This data type holds symbolic links that are stored in Unicode format.
- REG_MULTI_SZ. This data type holds multiple data strings.
- REG_NONE. This data type holds data that is either unknown or encrypted.
- REG_RESOURCE_LIST. This data type is found only under the [HKEY LOCAL MACHINE\HARDWARE] key and holds hardware resource lists.
- REG_RESOURCE_REQUIREMENTS_LIST. This data type holds resource requirements.
- REG_SZ. This data type holds a string value in Unicode format, which is terminated with either a character or NULL.

Editing the Registry

The Registry can be edited using a variety of tools. The easiest way to view and modify the Registry is to use the Registry editors that are supplied with Windows NT 4.0: REGEDIT.EXE and REGEDT32.EXE.

The other way to modify the Registry is to use programming tools that access the Registry directly. These tools, such as WinBatch, Visual C++, Visual Basic, and others, are not discussed as a part of this book.

Two Editors—When to Use Which

Although the Registry holds a vast amount of information about any given system, its arrangement into hives, keys, subkeys, and values makes Registry troubleshooting a forthright endeavor. Fortunately, Windows NT 4.0 comes with two utilities to search the Registry. The first Registry editor in Windows NT is REGEDT32.EXE; the second is REGEDIT.EXE.

Figures I.2 and I.3 are views of the two different Windows NT 4.0 Registry editors. Although the interfaces of these two programs are different, both can be used to access the Registry.

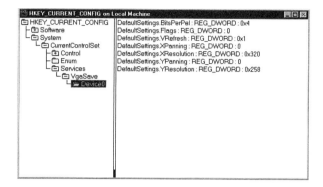

Figure I.2 REGEDT32.EXE.

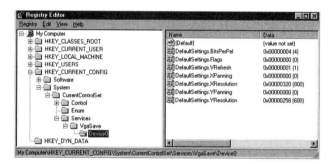

Figure I.3 REGEDIT.EXE.

Table I.1 shows the differences between the two programs. These differences should be considered when you decide which program to use to access the Registry.

Table I.1 **Differences between REGEDT32.EXE and REGEDIT.EXE**

REGEDT32.EXE

Option	Description
Read Only setting	This option prevents inadvertent changes from occurring while you view keys and settings.
Security menu	This menu has three options:
	Permissions—Allows different users to access the Registry in different ways. Administrators may be given full control; the user may be allowed to view only the Registry.

continues

Table I.1 **Continued**

Option	Description
	Auditing—Allows the auditing of certain Registry events. This option can only be used by a user who is a member of the Administrators local group or one who has been assigned the Audit right. Figure I.4 shows the Registry events that can be audited.
	Ownership—Shows which user owns a specific key. The key's owner may permit another user to take ownership of a key. A system administrator can assign a user the right to take ownership or can take ownership of any key personally.
Loading and unloading hives	This option is Active when either the HKEY_USERS or HKEY_LOCAL_MACHINE key is selected. *Hives* are sections of the Registry that are stored as a file on a hard disk. The hive files for the Default, SAM, Security, Software, and System keys are stored in the %SystemRoot%\ System32\Config directory. Hive files can be moved from one computer to another, but can only be accessed and used via the Registry editors. When you move hives across platforms, always back up the present hives because the new one may not be compatible with the new computer.
Three string value	Although both Registry editors allow for the creation of string values, REGEDIT.EXE allows single static strings to be created. The REG_SZ data type identifies single static string entries. REGEDT32.EXE allows for the creation of two more string values: the multiple string with a *REG_MULTI_SZ* prefix, and the expandable string with a *REG_EXPAND_SZ* prefix. Both Registry editors display all string value types.
REGEDIT.EXE	
Find tool	Although both programs have a Find tool, only the REGEDIT.EXE Find tool allows searching for key *values* and *settings*. REGEDT32.EXE allows searching on keys only. REGEDT32.EXE allows searching only for keys.
Importing and exporting	Both programs allow for the importing and exporting of Registry files. REGEDT32.EXE does this through hives and text files; REGEDIT.EXE does it through .REG files. .REG files always begin with the single line: REGEDIT4. The information in `filename`.REG can be incorporated

Option	Description
	into the Registry by executing the file or running reged-it.exe *filename*.REG. Appending A "is" when executing this line will cause REGEDIT.EXE to operate in silent mode. Figures I.5 and I.6 show the format differences between files exported with the two Registry editors. Both files show the first two settings of the System\CurrentControlSet\Services\VgaSave\Device0 key. Only .REG files can be easily edited and imported back into the Registry. These files cannot be imported if they contain values of data types REG_MULTI_SZ, REG_EXPAND_SZ, or REG_BINARY.
The HKEY_DYN_DATA Registry key	Because the REGEDIT.EXE Registry editor was originally included with Windows 95, HKEY_DYN_DATA appears as the sixth major key of the Registry, even when run under Windows NT 4.0. Because this key holds the dynamic Plug and Play (PnP) data that is the basis for Windows 95 PnP settings and because Windows NT 4.0 has limited PnP functionality, this key is blank when viewed by REGEDIT.EXE and does not appear in REGEDT32.EXE.

Knowing When to Use the Right Tools

If you have ever worked on an old car, repaired some plumbing, hunted down an electrical problem, or assembled computer hardware, you know that you need to use the correct tool. This applies equally well to the use of the different Registry editors.

There are two reasons to turn to the Registry to help with a solution:

- To determine the value of a specific setting.
- To modify or troubleshoot certain settings.

Because REGEDT32.EXE has a Read Only setting, it is generally considered to be preferable to REGEDIT.EXE when you simply view the Registry, especially when all that is needed is a known key. REGEDIT.EXE, having superior import and export functions, is preferable for finding values, exporting keys, and modifying the Registry for REG_SZ and REG_DWORD data types.

Finally, as Microsoft says, and you knew this would be here somewhere…

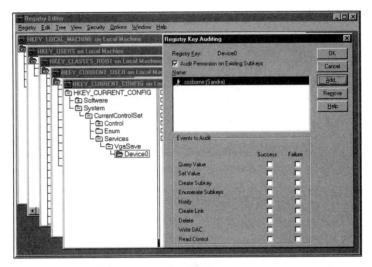

Figure I.4   REGEDT32.EXE auditing option.

Figure I.5   Registry file exported from REGEDT32.EXE.

Figure I.6   Registry file exported from REGEDIT.EXE.

Warning

"Using Registry Editor incorrectly can cause serious, system-wide problems that may require you to rein-stall Windows NT to correct them. (Macmillan Publishing, Sandra Osborne, and) Microsoft cannot guar-antee that any problems resulting from the use of Registry Editor can be solved. Use (these) tools at your own risk."

I

Managing Hardware

1

Disk Drives

- **Floppy drives**

  The Registry settings for floppy drives are discussed, with an emphasis on enabling floppy drives and their enumeration.

- **Hard drives**

  The Registry settings for hard drives are discussed, including CMOS settings, disk partition settings, disk administrator settings, and hive locations.

- **CD-ROM Drives**

  The Registry settings for CD-ROM drives are discussed, covering hardware settings, driver settings, and the use of Autorun files.

Floppy Drives

All entries for hardware are listed under the [HKEY_LOCAL_MACHINE] key. Under this key is the SYSTEM subkey, which lists all hardware that was found by the system at bootup. Because different hardware may or may not be attached, several subkeys, called ControlSet00# (where # is an integer starting at 1), are created to hold configurations that are different due to attached hardware. The ControlSet00# may or may not be numbered consecutively. Every hardware change causes a change to the ControlSet00# keys.

The Hardware key is also found under the [HKEY_LOCAL_MACHINE] key, and contains all of the hardware-specific entries, as detected by the NTDETECT program at boot time. This will be discussed further in Chapter 10, "Modifying the Windows NT Workstation Boot Process."

Examples of different ControlSet00# can be seen in the following floppy drive entries for a Toshiba Satellite Pro 410CDT notebook, showing first ControlSet002 and then ControlSet001.

```
[HKEY_LOCAL_MACHINE\SYSTEM\ControlSet002\Services\Floppy]
"Type"=dword:00000001
"Start"=dword:00000001
"Group"="Primary disk"
```

```
"ErrorControl"=dword:00000000
"Tag"=dword:00000002

ControlSet001
[HKEY_LOCAL_MACHINE\SYSTEM\ControlSet001\Services\Floppy]
"Type"=dword:00000001
"Start"=dword:00000001
"Group"="Primary disk"
"ErrorControl"=dword:00000000
"Tag"=dword:00000002
[HKEY_LOCAL_MACHINE\SYSTEM\ControlSet001\Services\Floppy\Enum]
"0"="Root\\LEGACY_FLOPPY\\0000"
"Count"=dword:00000001
"NextInstance"=dword:00000001
```

Notice that under the [HKEY_LOCAL_MACHINE\SYSTEM\ControlSet001\
Services\Floppy] key, there is also an ENUM (Enumerated) key, which exists only for
hardware found at or before bootup. Because the floppy was not enabled the first time
Windows NT booted, the ControlSet001 key does not have an ENUM key, showing
that no floppy drive was detected.

The ControlSet001 entries were exported after enabling the floppy drive via the
system BIOS and rebooting Windows NT. This time the floppy was detected and
enumerated as "0"="Root\\LEGACY_FLOPPY\\0000". The LEGACY_FLOPPY part of this key
reflects the fact that Windows NT 4.0 has little PnP capability. If this floppy drive
were part of the Windows NT 4.0 PnP, the LEGACY_FLOPPY entry would be replaced
with an entry starting with *PnP.

This enumeration is reflected in the following keys and values:

```
[HKEY_LOCAL_MACHINE\SYSTEM\CurrentControlSet\Enum\Root\LEGACY_FLOPPY]
"NextInstance"=dword:00000001
[HKEY_LOCAL_MACHINE\SYSTEM\CurrenControlSet\Enum\Root\LEGACY_FLOPPY\0000]
"Service"="Floppy"
"FoundAtEnum"=dword:00000001
"Class"="Unknown"
"ClassGUID"="{4D36E97E-E325-11CE-BFC1-08002BE10318}"
"Problem"=dword:00000000
"StatusFlags"=dword:00000008
"BaseDevicePath"="HTREE\\ROOT\\0"
"DeviceDesc"="Floppy Device"
[HKEY_LOCAL_MACHINE\SYSTEM\CurrenControlSet\Enum\Root\LEGACY_FLOPPY\0000\
Control]
"ActiveService"="Floppy"
```

Author Note

Because Windows NT 4.0 does not have full Plug-and-Play capability, several ControlSets may be listed.
The ControlSet currently in use is found at HKEY_LOCAL_MACHINE\SYSTEM\CurrentControlSet\.

Hard Drives

This section discusses the settings for hard drives that are attached to the system, as reported by NTDETECT at boot time. Although the entries shown here cannot be modified, they can help show that drives have been detected and what their resources are.

CMOS Settings

If you have ever installed a hard drive on a computer that does not have a Plug and Play BIOS, you are aware that you must know the number of cylinders and the number of heads to install a replacement drive if the C drive fails. It is also useful to know which version of the manufacturer's firmware is installed on your drive. These values can be seen in this exported TESTDEC.REG file:

```
[HKEY_LOCAL_MACHINE\HARDWARE\DEVICEMAP\AtDisk\Controller 0]
01. HKEY_LOCAL_MACHINE\HARDWARE\DEVICEMAP\AtDisk\Controller          0]
02. "Controller Address"=dword:000001f0"                          (496)
03. "Controller Interrupt"=dword:0000000e                          (14)

04. [HKEY_LOCAL_MACHINE\HARDWARE\DEVICEMAP\AtDisk\Controller 0\Disk 0]
05. "Identifier"="TOSHIBA MK1926FCV                   "
06. "Firmware revision"="S0.11 A "
07. "Serial number"="95B32407                "
08.
09. "Identify - Number of cylinders"=dword:0000062b              (1579)
10. "Identify - Number of heads"=dword:00000010                   (16)
11. "Identify - Sectors per track"=dword:0000003f                 (63)
12.
13. "Apparent - Number of cylinders"=dword:00000314               (788)
14. "Apparent - Number of heads"=dword:00000020                   (32)
15. "Apparent - Sectors per track"=dword:0000003f                 (63)
16.
17. "Actual - Number of cylinders"=dword:0000062b               (1579)
18. "Actual - Number of heads"=dword:00000010                     (16)
19. "Actual - Sectors per track"=dword:0000003f                   (63)
```

Three hard drive parameters are listed under three qualifiers:

Author Note

The Windows NT Registry can be used to record hard drive and other hardware parameters that must be reported when replacing parts. This is particularly useful for corporations that have large numbers of computers that are the same.

- `Identify` settings state the values that are reported by the firmware of the hard drive, as seen in lines 9–11.

- `Apparent` settings state the values that are used when a BIOS does not support drives greater than 512 MB, as seen in lines 13–15.

- `Actual` settings state the parameter values reported by the computer's BIOS, as seen in lines 17–19.

Among the other information that can be found here is the controller's base address and interrupt (IRQ) value, which in this case are 496 and 14, respectively, as seen in lines 2 and 3.

System Partition

Windows NT can be set to boot on any given partition. The boot partition can be discovered by viewing this key and value:

```
1. [HKEY_LOCAL_MACHINE\System\Setup]
2. "SystemPartition"="\\Device\\Harddisk0\\Partition1"
```

On this PC, Windows NT is set up to run off of HardDisk 0, Partition 1.

Windows NT can migrate and/or use any of the following file systems on the system partition:

- *FAT.* The File Allocation Table file system format is in the old DOS format, but it supports long file names under Windows NT 4.0

- *NTFS.* The NT File System is the 32-bit file system that is included with Windows NT as a migration option. The main advantage of this file system is that it uses less hard drive space to store the same information than the FAT file system.

- *HPFS.* This file system can be migrated to NTFS at install time, but Windows NT 4.0 no longer uses this file system as a valid operating format.

Note

Windows NT 4.0 cannot be installed on a volume that uses the Windows 95 or Windows 98 FAT32 file system.

Tip

If you use REGEDT32.EXE to view this key, or if you view the .REG file created by exporting this key with REGEDIT.EXE, you see only the REG_DWORD hexadecimal values. If this key is viewed with REGEDIT.EXE, the decimal values appear in parentheses next to the hex values. I have added the decimal values to the previous TESTDEC.REG printout.

Disk Administrator

Figure 1.1 shows the Registry settings that govern the aspects of the Disk Administrator program. These settings are representative of the Window size, Toolbar settings, and program-specific settings that can be found under the key:

```
[HKEY_CURRENT_USER\Software\Microsoft]
```

This is one of the most important keys in the Registry—it holds more information about Microsoft applications than any other portion of the Registry. The subkeys under this key are discussed throughout this book.

Hive List

A listing of the location and name of all the hives that can be loaded into a computer's Registry are listed under the key:

```
[HKEY_LOCAL_MACHINE\SYSTEM\ControlSet001\Control\hivelist]
```

For example, if the C drive is on HardDisk 1, Partition 1; the Security hive can be found at C:\win\system32\config\Security, as is shown in the key:

```
"\\REGISTRY\\MACHINE\\SECURITY"="\\Device\\Harddisk0\\Partition1\\WIN
\\System32\\Config\\SECURITY"
```

CD-ROM Drives

Many parameters for CD-ROM drives can also be found by viewing the Registry. In addition to hardware settings, the Registry also has drivers, INF file setup, and other software-related issues.

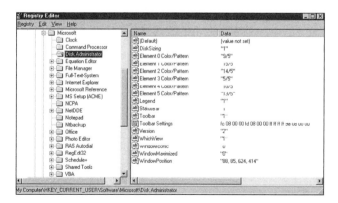

Figure 1.1   The Disk Administrator Registry key.

CD-ROM Drivers

This key holds information about CD-ROM controllers, their associated .INF files, and driver descriptions.

```
01. [HKEY_LOCAL_MACHINE\SYSTEM\ControlSet001\Control\Class\
    {4D36E97B-E325-11CE-BFC1-08002BE10318}]
02. @="SCSI controllers"
03. "Class"="SCSIAdapter"
04. "Icon"="-10"
05. "Installer32"="SysSetup.Dll,ScsiClassInstaller"
06. "LegacyInfOption"="SCSI"
07.
08. [HKEY_LOCAL_MACHINE\SYSTEM\ControlSet001\Control\Class\
    {4D36E97B-E325-11CE-BFC1-08002BE10318}\0000]
09. "InfPath"="scsi.inf"
10. "InfSection"="atapi_Inst"
11. "ProviderName"="Microsoft"
12. "DriverDesc"="IDE CD-ROM (ATAPI 1.2)/Dual-channel PCI IDE Controller"
```

From this key (in line 8, where {4D36E97B-E325-11CE-BFC1-08002BE10318} is the classGUID of the SCSI controller), you can see that the controller is installed via the SCSI.INF file and that the CD-ROM uses an ATAPI PCI/IDE controller. Most of the .INF files used by Windows NT 4.0 on any given system can be found in the %SystemRoot% \INF directory. So, if you look at the atapi_Inst section of the SCSI.INF file, you see:

```
1. [atapi_Inst]
2. CopyFiles = @atapi.sys
```

This gives you the CD-ROM driver for this PC, which is the ATAPI.SYS driver, supplied by Microsoft. Also, the following key confirms the ATAPI.SYS to be the CD-ROM driver, and it also shows the Interrupt (IRQ) and Base address:

```
1. [HKEY_LOCAL_MACHINE\HARDWARE\DEVICEMAP\Scsi\Scsi Port 0]
2. "DMAEnabled"=dword:00000000    (0)
3. "Interrupt"=dword:0000000f     (15)
4. "IOAddress"=dword:00000170     (360)
5. "Driver"="atapi"
```

The following key gives the specific CD-ROM ID:

```
1. [HKEY_LOCAL_MACHINE\HARDWARE\DEVICEMAP\Scsi\Scsi Port 0\
2. Scsi Bus 0\Target Id 0\Logical Unit Id 0]
3. "Identifier"="TOSHIBA CD-ROM XM-1202B 1635"
4. "Type"="CdRomPeripheral"
```

For these entries, the CD-ROM identified as a TOSHIBA CD-ROM XM-1202B 1635 has its IRQ at Interrupt 15 with a Base Address of 360. As said before, the numeric entries can only be seen when using REGEDIT.EXE to view the Registry. SCSI CD-ROM information can also be found under the `[HKEY_LOCAL_MACHINE\`
`HARDWARE\RESOURCEMAP\ScsiAdapter\]` key.

Autorun CDs

The CD-ROMs that include an AUTORUN.INF file automatically start when inserted. This Autorun feature can be turned off by setting the Autorun value to 0.

1. `[HKEY_LOCAL_MACHINE\SYSTEM\CurrentControlSet\Services\Cdrom]`
2. `"Autorun"=dword:00000001`

Configuring Display Settings

- **The Display applet**

  This section discusses the Registry settings that are created or modified by the Control Panel's Display applet. This includes setting the display's resolution, colors, and fonts.

- **Configuring video cards**

  This section discusses the issues and associated Registry settings used when configuring display adapter cards.

- **The Font key**

  This section discusses the Font key that is used to set menu and toolbar fonts.

The Display Applet

The Display applet is used to set a variety of options and settings that affect the video adapter, the video display, and the way the desktop is presented to the user. When you launch the display applet, you see the Display Properties dialog box shown in Figure 2.1.

Figure 2.1 shows the applet that is produced after the Windows Explorer 4.0 Web browser is installed. The Background tab is used to set the options for the display of the Desktop's background. First, the Wallpaper frame shows a list box that is used to select an HTML document or picture file to use as the Desktop's wallpaper. This list of available files is read from the ACCESSOR.INF file found in the %SYSTEMROOT%\INF directory. If you select a file from this list, the following value is set under the [HKEY_CURRENT_USER\Control Panel\Desktop] key.

```
Wallpaper           Bitmap Path and Filename
REG_SZ
```

This value is set to the path and file name of the bitmap chosen in the wallpaper list box. The path of the file is included if the file's location is other than

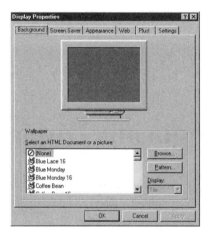

Figure 2.1 The Display Properties dialog box.

%SYSTEMROOT% or %SYSTEMROOT%\SYSTEM32. The default setting is
(None), which is the first selection shown in the list box. This value can be set using
the Policy Editor.

Tile Wallpaper

When you select a Wallpaper from the list box, the Display list box becomes enabled.
You can use this list box to select to either tile the wallpaper or to display it in the
center of the desktop. Depending on your choice, the TileWallpaper value is set as
follows:

```
TileWallpaper        0 or 1
REG_SZ
```

If this value is set to 1, the Tile option in the Display list box is selected. If set to 0,
the Center option is set. The default setting is 0. This value can be set using the Policy
Editor.

Pattern

The Pattern button is used to either select or create the pattern to be displayed on the
Desktop. If you do not select Wallpaper, the pattern covers the entire desktop.

Author Note

The Policy Editor, POLEDT.EXE, can be used to conFigure many of the Desktop options available with the
Display applet. These values, of which the Wallpaper value is one, are noted as they are previously. These
values, and the way they are set with the Policy Editor, are discussed in Chapter 13, "Windows NT Profiles."

If Wallpaper is selected, the pattern fills the space from around the wallpaper to the edges of the Desktop. If this button is grayed out, the selected wallpaper fills the entire Desktop, which leaves no display room for a pattern. When you click this button, you see the Pattern dialog box shown in Figure 2.2.

The options that are available in this box are read from the values found under the [HKEY_CURRENT_USER\Control Panel\Patterns] key. The name of each value listed here appears as one entry in the Pattern list box. Changing the names of these values changes the name of the associated pattern listed in the list box. All of these values are of data type REG_SZ, and are shown in Figure 2.3, as viewed with REGEDT32.EXE.

All of these values are set to a string of eight hexadecimal numbers that represent the pattern's overlay. New values can be created by adding a new value, Sandra Pattern for example, and setting it to a string of zeroes with spaces between them. This pattern can then be edited using the Edit Pattern button of Figure 2.2, as shown in Figure 2.4.

Now, if you select a pattern using the Pattern dialog box, the following Registry value is set under the [HKEY_CURRENT_USER\Control Panel\Desktop] key.

```
Pattern               Hexadecimal Sting
REG_SZ
```

Figure 2.2   The Pattern dialog box.

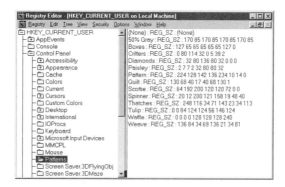

Figure 2.3   The Patterns key.

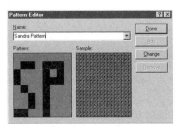

Figure 2.4   Editing a new pattern.

This value is set to the same string of eight hexadecimal numbers as the corresponding value under the Patterns key, shown in Figure 2.3. The default setting is " ", which is the same as selecting None.

The Screen Saver Tab

The options available on this tab, shown in Figure 2.5, are used to set the Desktop's screen saver and its operation.

Although you can add options for some of the screen savers under their own key, discussed in the "Screen Saver.Name Key" section, all screen savers set the following values under the [HKEY_CURRENT_USER\Control Panel\Desktop] key.

Screen Saver List Box

This drop-down list box contains the names of all the screen savers that are available to be installed. When you select a screen saver, the following values are set:

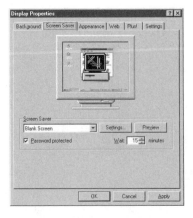

Figure 2.5   The Screen Saver tab.

```
ScreenSaveActive            0 or 1
REG_SZ
```

When a screen saver is selected, this value is set to 1, it displays the selected screen saver as specified by the `SCRNSAVE.EXE` value, and it is displayed. If this value is set to 0, no screen saver is displayed. The default setting is 0.

```
SCRNSAVE.EXE                FileName
REG_SZ
```

This value is set to the name of the executable file that runs the selected screen saver. If the previous value is set to 0, this file is not run. There is no default setting.

Password Protected

Checking the Password Protected check box sets this value:

```
ScreenSaverIsSecure         0 or 1
REG_SZ
```

When the check box is checked this value is set to 1 and the screen saver will not allow access to the desktop until the user's standard Windows NT password is entered. If this value is set to 0 then pressing any key will cancel the screen saver. The default setting is 0.

Wait Text Box

Setting a number in the Wait text box determines how long the system must remain idle before the screen saver is launched. This text box sets this value:

```
ScreenSaveTimeOut           Seconds
REG_SZ
```

This value is set to the number of seconds that corresponds to the number of minutes set in the text box. The default is 900 seconds, or 15 minutes.

The Settings Button

Some of the available screen savers have additional settings that are available from the dialog box produced by clicking the Settings button. If no settings are available, you see the message box of Figure 2.6.

This message box appears for all screen savers that do not correspond to a separate Registry key, [`HKEY_CURRENT_USER\Control Panel\Desktop\Screen Saver.Name`] where *Name* corresponds to a screen saver in the list box. This key is discussed in the next section.

The Screen Saver.Name Key

This key, as mentioned previously, contains values that are available to be set from the Settings button's dialog box. Each screen saver that has options available with this

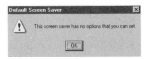

Figure 2.6   No available options.

button has a Screen Saver.Name key associated with it. The option dialog boxes and
the values that they set are discussed in the next sections.

The Flower Box Dialog Box

If you select the 3D Flower Box (Open GL) screen saver, you see the 3D FlowerBox
Setup dialog box of Figure 2.7.

The Coloring frame sets these values under the [HKEY_CURRENT_USER\
Control Panel\Screen Saver.3DFlowerBox] key.

- Checkerboard, Per Side, and One Color radial Buttons—These buttons set the
  following value:
  ```
  ColorPick          500, 501 or 502
  REG_SZ
  ```
  This value is set differently, depending on the radial button selected:

Setting	Button Selected
500	Checkerboard
501	Per Side
502	One Color

- Smooth, Slanted, and Cycle check boxes—These check boxes set the following
  values:

Figure 2.7   The 3D FlowerBox Setup dialog box.

```
Smooth                  0 or 1
REG_SZ
```

The Smooth check box sets this value to 1 when checked and 0 when cleared.

```
Slanted                 0 or 1
REG_SZ
```

The Slanted check box sets this value to 1 when checked and 0 when cleared.

```
Cycle                   0 or 1
REG_SZ
```

The Cycle check box sets this value to 1 when checked and 0 when cleared.

- The Spin, Bloom, and Two-Sided check boxes—These boxes set the following values:

```
Spin                    0 or 1
REG_SZ
```

The Spin Check box sets this value to 1 when checked and 0 when cleared.

```
Bloom                   0 or 1
REG_SZ
```

The Bloom Check box sets this value to 1 when checked and 0 when cleared.

```
TwoSided                1028 or 1032
REG_SZ
```

The Two-Sided Check box sets this value to 1032 when checked and 1028 when cleared.

- The Shape list box sets the following value.

```
Geom                    0, 1, 2, 3, or 4
REG_SZ
```

This value is set to the following, depending on the list box selection:

Setting	Selection
0	Cube
1	Tetrahedron
2	Pyramids
3	Cylinder
4	Spring

The Complexity and Size slide bars set these values:

```
Subdiv                  2 to 10
REG_SZ
```

This value is set between 2 and 10, depending on the position of the Complexity slide bar.

```
ImageSize              2 to 10
REG_SZ
```

This value is set between 2 and 10, depending on the position of the Size slide bar.

The 3D Flying Objects Dialog Box

If you select the 3D Flying Objects (Open GL) screen saver, you see the 3D Flying Objects Setup dialog box of Figure 2.8.

This dialog box sets these values under the [HKEY_CURRENT_USER\Control Panel\ Screen Saver.3DFlyingObj] key.

- The Style list box—This list box sets this value:
  ```
  Type              0, 1, 2, 3, 4, 5 or 6
  REG_SZ
  ```

  This value is set differently, depending on the selected option in the list box, as follows.

Setting	Selection
0	Windows Logo
1	Explode
2	Ribbon
3	Two Ribbons
4	Splash
5	Twist
6	Textured Flag

- The Color Usage frame—This frame contains two check boxes, Color Cycling and Smooth Shading, which set the following value:
  ```
  Options              0, 1, 2, 3 , 4, 5 or 6
  REG_SZ
  ```

Figure 2.8   3D Flying Objects Setup dialog box.

This value is set differently, depending on the status of these check boxes, as follows:

Setting	Color Check Box	Smooth Check Box
0	Cleared	Cleared
1	Cleared	Checked
2	Checked	Cleared
3	Checked	Checked

■ The Resolution and Size slide bars—These slide bars set the following values:

```
Tesselation          0 to 200
REG_SZ
```

This value is set between 0 and 200, depending on the position of the Resolution slide bar.

```
Size                 0 to 200
REG_SZ
```

This value is set between 0 and 100, depending on the position of the Size Slide bar.

The 3D Maze Dialog Box

If you select the 3D Maze (Open GL) screen saver, you see the Maze Setup dialog box of Figure 2.9.

This dialog box sets these values under the [HKEY_CURRENT_USER\Control Panel\ Screen Saver.3DMaze] key.

■ The Walls, Floor, and Ceiling buttons—When you click one of these buttons, you see the Configure Texture dialog box of Figure 2.10.

If you choose the Default radial button, the texture is set by using the up and down arrow buttons, which are discussed in the next section. Choosing the User

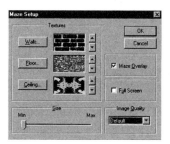

Figure 2.9   3D Maze dialog box.

Figure 2.10   The Configure Texture dialog box.

radial button and then selecting a .BMP file by using the Choose button grays out the up and down arrow buttons for the selected button; and sets the following values, depending upon the button selected (Walls, Floor, or Ceiling), as follows:

```
DefaultTextureEnable        2 to 7
REG_SZ
```

This value is set differently, depending upon the radial buttons selected for each button in the Configure Texture dialog box, as follows:

Setting	Wall	Floor	Ceiling
0	User	User	User
1	Default	User	User
2	User	Default	User
3	Default	Default	User
4	User	User	Default
5	Default	User	Default
6	User	Default	Default
7	Default	Default	Default

```
WallTextureFile        Path and Filename
REG_SZ
```

This value is set to the path and file name of the selected bitmap when the Wall button is set to the User radial button.

```
FloorTextureFile        Path and Filename
REG_SZ
```

This value is set to the path and file name of the selected bitmap when the Floor button is set to the User radial button.

```
CeilingTextureFile        Path and Filename
REG_SZ
```

This value is set to the path and file name of the selected bitmap when the Ceiling button is set to the User radial button.

The previous values do not have a default setting.

- Texture buttons—To the right of each of the previous buttons are one set each of up and down arrow buttons. These buttons are used to select a texture for the Wall, Floor, or Ceiling and set the following values:

  These values are set from 0 to 6, depending upon the image selected by using the up and down arrow buttons. If the Red Brick image is selected, the value is set to 0. Each time the up arrow is clicked, the new image adds the value of 1 to the value's setting (the down arrow subtracts 1) until the Red Brick image is reached again; the image previous to the Red Brick image sets these values to 6.

  ```
  DefWallTexture              0 to 6
  REG_SZ
  DefFloorTexture             0 to 6
  REG_SZ
  DefCeilingTexture           0 to 6
  REG_SZ
  ```

- The Maze Overlay check box sets this value.

  ```
  Overlay             0 or 1
  REG_SZ
  ```

  This value is set to 1 when the Maze Overlay check box is checked and 0 when it is cleared.

- Full Screen check box—This check box enables the Size slide bar and the Image Quality check box when it is cleared; it also sets this value:

  ```
  TurboMode           0 or 1
  REG_SZ
  ```

  This value is set to 1 when checked and 0 when cleared.

- Size slide bar

  When the TurboMode value is set to 0, this value can be set as follows:

  ```
  Size                0 to 100
  REG_SZ
  ```

  This value will be set from 0 to 100, depending on the setting of the slide bar.

- The Image Quality list box sets this value.

  ```
  ImageQuality            0 or 1
  REG_SZ
  ```

  This value is set to 1 if the High selection from the list box is selected and to 0 if the default is selected.

The 3D Pipes Dialog Box

If you select the 3D Pipes (Open GL) screen saver, you see the 3D Pipes Setup dialog box of Figure 2.11.

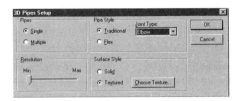

Figure 2.11   3D Maze Pipes Setup dialog box.

This dialog box sets these values under the [HKEY_CURRENT_USER\Control Panel\ Screen Saver.3DPipes] key.

- The Pipes frame's radial buttons set this value.

  ```
  MultiPipes              0 or 1
  REG_SZ
  ```

  This value is set to 0 if the Single radial button is selected and to 1 if the Multiple radial button is selected.

- The Pipe Style frame—If the Flex radial button is selected, the Joint Type list box is grayed out; if the Traditional radial button is selected, the list box is enabled. These buttons also set these values:

  ```
  JointType               0 to 3
  REG_SZ
  ```

  When the Traditional radial button is selected, this value is set from 0 to 4, depending upon the selected entry in the Joint Type list box, as follows:

Setting	Selection
0	Elbow
1	Ball
2	Mixed
3	Cycle

  ```
  Flex                    0 or 1
  REG_SZ
  ```

  This value is set to 0 when the Traditional radial button is selected and to 1 when the Flex radial button is selected. Also, setting this value to 1 disables the Joint Type list box.

- The Resolution slide bar sets this value:

  ```
  Tesselation             0 or 1
  REG_SZ
  ```

  This value is set from 0 to 200, depending upon the slide bar's setting.

- The Surface Style frame—This frame contains the radial buttons Solid and Textures. This frame also contains the Choose Texture button that is used to select a texture when the Textures button is selected. This button is grayed out if the Solid button is selected. These buttons also set these values:
  ```
  SurfStyle                0 or 1
  REG_SZ
  ```

This value is set to 1 if the Solid button is selected and 0 if the Textured button is selected.
  ```
  Texture                  Path and Filename
  REG_SZ
  ```

This value contains the path and file name of the texture file selected with the Choose Texture button.

The 3D Text Dialog Box

If you select the 3D Text (Open GL) screen saver, you will see the 3D Text Setup dialog box of Figure 2.12.

This dialog box sets these values under the [HKEY_CURRENT_USER\Control Panel\ Screen Saver.3DText] key

- The Display frame—This frame contains the Text and Time radial buttons. The frame also contains a text box, which is only enabled when the Text radial button is selected. These options set the following values:
  ```
  DemoType          0 or 1
  REG_SZ
  ```

This value is set to 1 if the Time radial button is selected and 0 if the Text radial button is selected.
  ```
  Text              Text
  REG_SZ
  ```

This value contains the text entered into the Text text box when the previous value is set to 0.

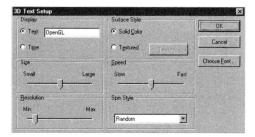

Figure 2.12   3D Text Setup dialog box.

- The Surface Style frame—This frame contains the Solid Color and Textured radial buttons. The frame also contains the Texture button, which is only enabled when the Textured radial button is selected. These options set the following values:

```
SurfStyle          0 or 1
REG_SZ
```

This value is set to 1 if the Textured radial button is selected and 0 if the Solid Color radial button is selected.

```
Texture            Path and File Name
REG_SZ
```

This value is set to the path and file name of the bitmap file selected by using the Texture button.

- The Size, Speed, and Resolution slide bars set these values:

```
Size          0 to 100
REG_SZ
```

This value is set between 0 and 100, depending on the position of the Size slide bar.

```
Speed         0 or 100
REG_SZ
```

This value is set between 0 and 100, depending on the position of the Speed slide bar.

```
Tesselation   0 or 100
REG_SZ
```

This value is set between 0 and 100, depending on the position of the Resolution slide bar.

- The Spin Style list box sets this value:

```
RotStyle      0, 1, 2 or 3
REG_SZ
```

This value is set differently, depending upon the selected entry in the list box, as follows.

Setting	Selection
0	None
1	See Saw
2	Wobble
3	Random

The Bézier Dialog Box

If you select the Bézier screen saver, then you see the Bézier Screen Saver Setup dialog box of Figure 2.13.

Figure 2.13 The Bézier dialog box.

This dialog box sets these values under the [HKEY_CURRENT_USER\Control Panel\ Screen Saver.Bezier] key.

■ Length frame

    Length   1 to 10
    REG_SZ

This value is set to the selected entry of the Béziers in each loop (1–10) text box.

■ Width frame

    Width   1 to 100
    REG_SZ

This value is set to the selected entry of the Repeat each loop (1–100) text box.

■ Speed frame

    LineSpeed   2 to 20
    REG_SZ

This value is set from 2 to 20, depending upon the setting of the Speed slide bar.

The Marquee Setup Dialog Box

If you select the Marquee Setup screen saver, you see the dialog box of Figure 2.14.

This dialog box sets these values under the [HKEY_CURRENT_USER\Control Panel\ Screen Saver.Marquee] key:

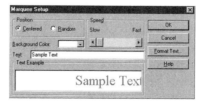

Figure 2.14 The Marquee Display dialog box.

- The Position frame—This frame contains one set of radial buttons that set this value.

  ```
  Attributes            00000 0r 00010
  REG_SZ
  ```

  This value is set to the following, as long as the Font Style is set to Regular, and the Strikeout and Underline check boxes, located on the Format Text dialog box, are cleared.

  `00000`: The Centered radial button is selected.

  `00010`: The Random radial button is selected.

  This value is further modified by the font style of the text set with the Format Text dialog box as well as the Strikeout and Underline check boxes, which are discussed later in this section under the "Font Style Text and List box" bullet.

- The Speed slide bar sets this value:

  ```
  Speed              1 to 30
  REG_SZ
  ```

  This value is set from 1 to 30, depending upon the setting of the Speed slide bar.

- The Background Color list box sets this value:

  ```
  BackgroundColor        0 0 0 to 255 255 255
  REG_SZ
  ```

  This color is set to the hexadecimal representation of the color chosen in the Background Color list box, as follows (the colors are listed in the same order as they appear in the list box).

Setting	Color
0 0 0	Black
128 0 0	Maroon
0 128 0	Green
128 128 0	Orange
0 0 128	Navy
128 0 128	Purple
0 128 128	Teal
192 192 192	Gray 1
192 220 192	Silver
166 202 240	Gray 2
255 251 240	White 1
160 160 164	Gray 3
128 128 128	Dark Gray

255 0 0	Red
0 255 0	Lime
255 255 0	Yellow
0 0 255	Blue
255 0 255	Fuscia
0 255 255	Aqua
255 255 255	White 2

■ The Text text box—If you enter text into the Text text box, this value is set.

```
Text            Text String
REG_SZ
```

This value holds the text string that the screen saver displays.

■ The Format Text button—This button is used to format the font of the string entered into the Text text box and sets the following value:

```
Font               Font Name
RE_SZ
```

This value is set to the font name selected from the Font list box.

■ Font Style text and list box—This combination of text and list box sets the same Attributes value as was discussed previously. This value is set as follows, as long as the Strikeout and Underline check boxes, discussed next, are not checked.

```
Attributes    00000, 00100, 00001, and 00101   or
              00010, 00110, 00011, and 00111
REG_SZ
```

The setting of this value depends both upon the Font Style selected from the Font Style list box and upon the radial button selected in the Position frame, discussed in the Position Frame bullet earlier in this section. Table 2.1 shows the relationship between these two options and the attributes value settings.

Table 2.1 **Attributes Value Settings**

Radial Button		**Font**		
	Regular	**Italic**	**Bold**	**Bold Italic**
Center	00000	00100	00001	00101
Random	00010	00110	00011	00111

■ Size text and list box—This combination of text and list box sets this value:

```
Size 8 - 12,14,16,18,20,22,24,26,28,36,48 or 72
REG_SZ
```

This value is set to the selected number shown in the Font Size text box.

- The Effects frame—The set of check boxes shown in this frame also affect the Attributes value. If the Strikeout check box is selected, the value 11000 is added to the current Attributes value setting. If the Underline check box is selected, the value 10000 is added to the current Attributes value setting. If both check boxes are selected, the value 11010 is added to the current Attributes value setting.

- The Color drop-down list box sets the same value that is set with the Background Color list box.

- The Script list box sets this value:
  ```
  CharSet              Character Set Decimal
  REG_SZ
  ```

This drop-down list box shows the available character sets installed on the computer. This value is set to the decimal representation of this character set. A few examples are:

Setting	Character Set
0	Western
161	Greek
162	Turkish
186	Baltic
204	Cyrillic
238	Central European

The Mystify Dialog Box

If you select the Mystify screen saver, then you see the Mystify dialog box, shown in Figure 2.15.

This dialog box sets these values under the [HKEY_CURRENT_USER\Control Panel\ Screen Saver.Mystify] key.

- The Shape text box and Active check box—The Shape text box is used to

Figure 2.15   The Mystify dialog box.

select the polygon that the screen saver displays. You can select either Polygon 1 or Polygon 2. Each selection sets its own set of Registry entries, which are determined by the state of the Active check box. When this check box is selected, both the Lines text box and the options available within the Colors to Use frame are enabled. Depending on the polygon selected, the following Registry values are set:

```
Active1          0 or 1
REG_SZ
```

This value is set for Polygon 1; it is set to 1 when the Active check box is checked and to 0 when it is cleared.

```
Active2          0 or 1
REG_SZ
```

This value is set for Polygon 2; it is set to 1 when the Active check box is checked and to 0 when it is cleared.

■ The Lines list box sets the following values, depending on the selected polygon:

```
Lines1          Decimal Number
REG_SZ
```

This value is set for Polygon 1 and is set to the selected setting of the Lines list box.

```
Lines2          Decimal Number
REG_SZ
```

This value is set for Polygon 2 and is set to the selected setting of the Lines list box.

■ The Colors To Use frame—This frame has one set of radial buttons that are used to set the polygon's colors. If you select the Two Colors radial button, the drop-down list boxes to the right are enabled. These list boxes determine the starting and ending colors for the selected polygon and set the following values:

```
WalkRandom1          0 or 1
REG_SZ
```

This value is set for Polygon 1, and is set to 1 if the Multiple Random Colors radial button is selected and 0 if the Two Colors radial button is selected.

```
WalkRandom2          0 or 1
REG_SZ
```

This value is set for Polygon 2, and is set to 1 if the Multiple Random Colors radial button is selected and 0 if the Two Colors radial button is selected.

```
StartColor1          0 0 0 to 255 255 255
REG_SZ
```

This value is set for Polygon 1, and is set to the numerical value of the color selected in the first list box (see "The Background Color list box" for a list of color settings).

```
EndColor1          "0 0 0" to "255 255 255"
REG_SZ
```

This value is set for Polygon 1, and is set to the numerical value of the color selected in the second list box.

```
StartColor2          0 0 0 to 255 255 255
REG_SZ
```

This value is set for Polygon 2, and is set to the numerical value of the color selected in the first list box.

```
EndColor2            0 0 0 to 255 255 255
REG_SZ
```

This value is set for Polygon 2, and is set to the numerical value of the color selected in the second list box.

■ The Clear Screen check box sets this value:

```
Clear Screen         0 or 1
REG_SZ
```

This value is independent of the polygon selected, and is set to 1 when the Clear Screen check box is checked and to 0 when it is cleared.

The Marquee Display Dialog Box

If you select the Marquee Display screen saver then you will see the Starfield Simulation Setup dialog box of Figure 2.16. This dialog box sets these values under the [HKEY_CURRENT_USER\Control Panel\Screen Saver.Stars] key.

■ The Warp Speed slide bar sets this value:

```
WarpSpeed            0 to 10
REG_SZ
```

This value is set from 0 to 10, depending upon the setting of the Warp Speed slide bar.

■ The Starfield Density frame—This frame contains the Number of stars (10–200) list box that sets this value:

```
Density              10 to 200
REG_SZ
```

This value is set from 10 to 200, depending upon the selected entry of the setting of the Number of stars (10–200) list box.

Figure 2.16   The Starfield Simulation Setup dialog box.

Figure 2.17   The Appearance tab.

The Appearance Tab

This tab, shown in Figure 2.17, is used to set color scheme and font options for the windows that appear on the Desktop.

These options set the following Registry values under the keys discussed next.

- Schemes—Desktop color schemes are set by the selection of the Scheme list box that contains one entry for each value listed under the [HKEY_CURRENT USER\ Control Panel\Appearance] key. The default colors that this scheme uses are shown in the display box at the top of the Appearance tab and are defined by the values under this key. The values have the same name as the entries in the Scheme list box. If you create a new scheme using the Save As button, a new value is created under this key with the name supplied by the user. If you click the Delete key, the scheme's value is deleted from this key. The scheme that you select sets the following value under the [HKEY_CURRENT_USER\Control Panel\ Current] key:

    Color Schemes   Desktop Scheme
    REG_SZ

    This value is set to the name of the scheme selected in the Scheme list box.

- Item list box—This list box contains a list of Windows items that can be configured using the Size, Color, and Font list boxes. These items set various values

---

Troubleshooting

Always create a backup of these keys and the Appearance key by using the REGEDT.EXE's Export feature. This backup ensures that you can re-create the Desktop scheme if it becomes corrupt.

under the [HKEY_CURRENT_USER\ControlPanel\Desktop], [HKEY_CURRENT_USER\
ControlPanel\Desktop\WindowMetrics], and [HKEY_CURRENT_USER\ControlPanel\
Colors] keys.

The Web Tab

This tab is installed with the Microsoft Internet Explorer 4.0 and is discussed in
Chapter 25, which is available at www.macmillantech.com/Osborne.

The Plus! Key

This tab, shown in Figure 2.18, sets the following values under the
[HKEY_CURRENT_USER\Control Panel\Desktop] key:

- The Use large icons check box:
  ```
  IconSpacing           131 or 147
  REG_SZ
  ```
  This value is set to 147 when the previous check box is set and to 131 when it is
  not.
  ```
  IconVerticalSpacing          75 or 91
  REG_SZ
  ```
  This value is set to 75 when the previous check box is set and to 91 when it is
  not.

- The Show windows contents while dragging check box sets this value:
  ```
  DragFullWindows      0 or 1
  REG_SZ
  ```
  This value is set to 1 when the previous check box is set and to 0 when it is not.

Figure 2.18   The Plus! Tab.

- The Smooth edges of screen fonts check box sets this value:
  ```
  FontSmoothing        0 or 1
  REG_SZ
  ```

  This value is set to 1 when the previous check box is set and to 0 when it is not.

- The Show icons using all possible colors check box sets this value:
  ```
  WallpaperStyle        0 or 2
  REG_SZ
  ```

  This value is set to 2 when the previous check box is set and to 0 when it is not.

- The stretch desktop wallpaper to fit the screen check box sets this value:
  ```
  WallpaperStyle        0 or 2
  REG_SZ
  ```

  This value is set to 2 when the previous check box is set and to 0 when it is not.

The last tab of the display applet, Settings, is discussed in the "Display Applet's Settings Tab" section later in this chapter.

Configuring Video Cards

Some Windows NT errors are difficult to track because one component generates the error but it is caused by a different component. Most of these errors are memory- or IRQ-related, but some can be conflicts with the BIOS or video driver.

In some PCs with high-resolution video cards, Windows NT may stop responding, which requires a hard boot, when you use the Windows NT drag-and-drop feature to copy files to or from a floppy drive. At first, this looks like a problem with the floppy drive, but the problem is actually a memory conflict with the system BIOS and the video card —*not* the floppy drive. To correct this, start REGEDT32.EXE and open the [HKEY_LOCAL_MACHINE\system\CurrentControlSet\Control\GraphicsDrivers] key.

From the Edit menu, choose Add Key, and enter the following: **DisableUSWC**, leaving the Class entry blank. This disables the miniport from using USWC (Uncached Speculative Write Combining) memory, which then solves the memory conflict.

Detecting Video Cards

When Windows NT is installed, it uses the DISPLAY.INF file, located in the %SYSTEMROOT%\INF directory, to install video cards. If you view this file and scroll down to the [detect. Services] section, you see the following list:

```
[detect.Services]
ati         = ATI_COMPAT
cirrus      = CIRRUS_COMPAT
dell_dgx    = DELL_DGX_COMPAT
et4000      = ET4000_COMPAT
mga         = MGA_COMPAT
mga_mil     = MGA_MIL_COMPAT
ncr77c22    = NCR77C22_COMPAT
qv          = QV_COMPAT
s3          = S3_COMPAT
v7vram      = V7VRAM_COMPAT
wdvga       = WDVGA_COMPAT
weitekp9    = WEITEKP9_COMPAT
Xga         = XGA_COMPAT
```

When Windows NT is installed, this section is read into the Registry key shown in 2.19. However, these values may not always be read into the CurrentControlSet001 key as shown. The actual display class used by the computer is found in the same key position that is shown in Figure 2.19, except that it is under the CurrentControlSet key.

The Display Applet's Settings Tab

If you go to the Settings tab of the Display applet, you see Figure 2.20.

This tab is used to set the display type. The options and the Registry settings that this tab creates are discussed in the next section.

Figure 2.19   The display class key.

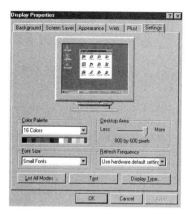

Figure 2.20   The Display applet's Settings tab.

Figure 2.21   The Display Type dialog box.

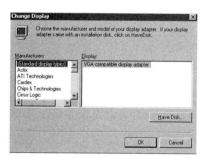

Figure 2.22   The Change Display dialog box.

Display Type

You can use the Display Type button, shown in Figure 2.20, to install a video card. When you click this button you see the Display Type dialog box shown in Figure 2.21.

Finally, to change the adapter, click the Change button, which produces the Change Display dialog box shown in Figure 2.22.

This dialog box shows all of the available display adapters, as listed in the DISPLAY.INF file. Windows NT uses this file when Windows NT is installed to set the values for your type of card.

If your card is not listed in DISPLAY.INF, you must use a separate installation disk that is usually provided by the manufacturer.

Detecting the Video Driver

Several sections of the Registry contain information concerning the computer display and how it is set up and/or changed. The following values are found under the `[HKEY_LOCAL_MACHINE\HARDWARE\DEVICEMAP\VIDEO]` key:

```
\Device\Video0        Registry Path
REG_SZ
```

This value contains the Registry path, which may be a different ControlSet00# than ControlSet001, where the current video adapter information is stored. There is no default setting, but an example is: `\\REGISTRY\\Machine\\System\\ ControlSet001\\Services\\VgaSave\\Device0`.

```
VgaCompatible         \\Device\\Video0"
REG_SZ
```

Like many of the settings in the Registry, the `VgaCompatible` setting is defined as another setting that in turn is defined as a Registry value, and is found under the

> **Warning**
>
> When writing this key in a .REG file, the \\ (double backslashes) should be preserved because without them this key does not work properly after it is imported. In fact, when Registry keys are listed as setting values within .REG files, double backslashes should always be used.
>
> Further, if the key value is a directory path using the Universal Naming Convention (UNC), four backslashes should be used at the start of the path, with double backslashes between directories, as in the following:
>
> > \\\\NTSERVER\\RESOURCE\\FILENAME
>
> As can be seen in Figure 2.23, the backslashes appear normal when viewed with REGEDIT.EXE.

Figure 2.23 The Hardware/DeviceMap/Video key.

[HKEY_LOCAL_MACHINE\SYSTEM\ControlSet001\Services\VgaSave\Device0] key. These values are:

```
VgaCompatible              0 or 1
REG_DWORD
```

This value states whether the video driver is VGA-compatible. If it is set to 1, the driver is VGA-compatible; if set to 0, it is not.

```
InstalledDisplayDrivers         Hexadecimal Numbers
REG_MULTI_SZ
```

This value contains the video drivers currently installed for the video card.

```
HardwareInformation.Crc32       Hexadecimal Numbers
REG_BINARY\
```

This value contains hardware information on the video card.

Setting the Display Resolution and Color

The values that store the resolution settings made via the Control Panel Display applet are found under the [HKEY_LOCAL_MACHINE\SYSTEM\ControlSet003\HardwareProfiles\0001\System\CurrentControlSet\Services\VgaSave\Device0] key. These values are discussed in the next sections.

Bits for Pixel

```
DefaultSettings.BitsPerPel         Number of Bits per Pixil
REG_DWORD
```

Author Note

If you open REGEDIT.EXE to this value, highlight it, and then right-click the mouse to edit the entry, you see that the vga.dll driver is installed.

This value contains the number of colors for the video mode requested by the user, usually 16 or 256 colors.

Default Resolution Values

These values set the resolution of the video display.

Bits Per Pixel

```
DefaultSettings.BitsPerPel          Number of bits per pixel
REG_DWORD
```

This value determines the number of colors for the video mode set by the user.

Interlaced

```
DefaultSettings.Interlaced          0 or 1
REG_DWORD
```

This value determines whether the previous user mode is interlaced.

Refresh Rate

```
DefaultSettings.Vrefresh            Number in Megahertz (MHz)
REG_DWORD
```

This value contains the refresh rate of the user's selected video mode.

Resolution Width

```
DefaultSettings.Xresolution         Number of Pixels
REG_DWORD
```

This value determines the width of the video mode.

Tip

If you have more that two profiles, and you want the new resolution to appear for them, the other profiles need to also be changed. If you want only one profile to use, these settings then change the values only under one profile. This is useful when configuring notebooks for external monitors that can display greater resolutions than the notebook itself.

Author Note

You can refresh your video settings by placing this key in a VIDEOSET.REG file and executing it. This comes in handy if the video settings become corrupt.

Resolution Height

```
DefaultSettings.Yresolution          Number of Pixels
REG_DWORD
```

This value determines the height of the video mode.

Panning

To enable panning (either up and down or left to right), set the following values under the same key as before.

```
DefaultSettings.Xpanning        0 or 1
REG_DWORD
```

Set this value to 1 to enable left to right panning of the desktop.

```
DefaultSettings.Ypanning        0 or 1
REG_DWORD
```

Set this value to 1 to enable up and down panning of the desktop.

The Font Key

The values and settings under the [HKEY_LOCAL_MACHINE\SYSTEM\CurrentControlSet\ HardwareProfiles\0002\Software\Fonts] key governs the way that the hardware pro-file sets display fonts. (This is discussed further in Chapter 13, "Windows NT Profiles.") These values, discussed in the following sections, are also found under the [HKEY_CURRENT_CONFIG\Software\Fonts] key, the [HKEY_LOCAL_MACHINE\SOFTWARE\ Microsoft\WindowsNT\CurrentVersion\GRE_Initialize] key, and the [HKEY_LOCAL_MACHINE\SOFTWARE\Microsoft\Windows NT\CurrentVersion\WOW\boot] key. These values are used by some applications to set menu and toolbar fonts.

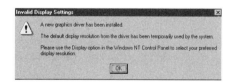

Figure 2.24   Invalid display settings error message.

Warning

Be sure to set the resolution to a setting that can be displayed with your monitor. If you set it to an unsupported resolution, you receive the system message displayed in Figure 2.24 when you restart Windows NT.

System Fixed Font

```
FIXEDFON.FON        Font Filename String
REG_SZ              vgafix.fon
```

This value sets the system fixed font. This is the same entry that was found in Windows 3.1 SYSTEM.INI file under the [boot] section.

Default System Font

```
FONTS.FON           Font Filename String
REG_SZ              vgasys.fon
```

This value specifies the file name of the default system font.

Desktop Font Size

```
LogPixels           Hexadecimal Number - 0x78 or 0x60
REG_DWORD
```

This value sets the desktop font size. A setting of **0x78**, or 120 dpi (dots per inch) yields large fonts; a setting of **0x60**, or 96 dpi, which is also the default, yields small fonts. If this setting is changed, the computer must reboot before it takes effect. This value can also be set from the Display applet in the Control Panel.

Console Font

```
OEMFONT.FON         Font Filename String
REG_SZ              vgaoem.fon
```

This value sets the file name of the default console font.

Settings for Mice and Keyboards

- **The Mouse key**

  The Registry key that holds the majority of mouse-related settings is discussed.

- **The Mouse applet**

  The Registry settings for the Mouse applet found in the Control Panel are discussed, covering all tabs and options available from the applet.

- **Other Mouse Registry**

  Other mouse-related settings are discussed here, including the `ClassGUID` and INF file location.

- **The Keyboard applet**

  The Registry settings for the Keyboard applet found in the Control Panel are discussed in this chapter.

The Mouse Key

The settings for the mouse are listed under the `[HKEY_CURRENT_USER\Control Panel\ Mouse]` key. Because most of the settings in this chapter are listed under this key, I will refer to this key as the *Mouse key*.

The other subkeys under the `[HKEY_CURRENT_USER\Control Panel]` key hold the settings and options, as viewed with the various applets in the Control Panel. These applets are discussed throughout this book.

The Mouse Applet

The mouse applet in the Control Panel is the first place to look when issues concerning the mouse arise. This applet makes changes that are stored in the Registry. The mouse settings can also be directly manipulated with the Registry editors.

If you open the Mouse applet, you see the dialog box shown in Figure 3.1.

The Buttons Tab

In the Button configuration area on the Buttons tab are two radial buttons. One is labeled Right-handed; the other is Left-handed. These buttons determine the following SwapMouseButtons value:

```
1. [HKEY_CURRENT_USER\Control Panel\Mouse]
2. "SwapMouseButtons"="0"
```

If the Right-handed radial button is selected, this value is 0; if Left-handed is chosen, the value is 1.

In the Double-click speed area, you see a slide bar that allows the double-click speed of the mouse to be set to Slow or Fast. The slide bar sets the following value under the Mouse key:

```
"DoubleClickSpeed"="100"
```

This value can be set from 100 to 900 (100 is fastest).

The Pointers Tab

Click the Pointers tab to see the Scheme drop-down list box. This list box, as seen in Figure 3.2, contains all entries under the [HKEY_CURRENT_USER\Control Panel\Cursors\Schemes] key.

These entries have the following form:

```
01. "Dinosaur"="
02. C:\\WIN\\Cursors\\3dgarro.cur,
03. ,
04. C:\\WIN\\Cursors\\dinosaur.ani,
05. C:\\WIN\\Cursors\\dinosau2.ani,
06. C:\\WIN\\Cursors\\cross.cur,
```

Figure 3.1   The Mouse Properties dialog box.

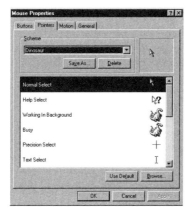

Figure 3.2   The Pointers tab.

```
07. ,
08. ,
09. C:\\WIN\\Cursors\\banana.ani,
10. C:\\WIN\\Cursors\\3dsns.cur,
11. C:\\WIN\\Cursors\\3dgwe.cur,
12. C:\\WIN\\Cursors\\3dsnwse.cur,
13. C:\\WIN\\Cursors\\3dgnesw.cur,
14. C:\\WIN\\Cursors\\3dsmove.cur,
15. "
```

Notice that I have separated the values so that there is one value on each line. If you write this setting into an .REG file, however, write it all on one line. Notice that there are 13 values listed under the Dinosaur setting, which correspond to the 13 values shown in the large scroll box that lists the way the mouse appears. This scroll box can be seen in Figure 3.2, with a starting entry of `Normal Select`. The settings follow:

- Normal Select
- Help Select
- Working in Background
- Busy
- Precision Select
- Text Select
- Handwriting
- Unavailable
- Vertical Resize

- Horizontal Resize

- Diagonal Resize 1

- Diagonal Resize 2

- Move

- Alternate Select

Each setting under this key maps a .CUR or .ANI file to the appropriate setting.

If you now look at the [HKEY_CURRENT_USER\Control Panel\Cursors] key, you see that this key is defined as @="Dinosaur" in my Registry. Therefore, the settings that show up in the large scroll box are retrieved from the key:

1. [HKEY_CURRENT_USER\Control Panel\Cursors\Schemes]
2. "Dinosaur"="

The Motion Tab

Moving onto the Motion tab, as seen in Figure 3.3, you see another slide bar in the Pointer speed area.

This slide bar sets the following values under the Mouse key:

1. MouseThreshold1   0,1 or 2
    REG_SZ
2. MouseThreshold2   0,1,2,3 or 4
    REG_SZ
3. MouseSpeed   0 to 6
    REG_SZ

Figure 3.3   The Motion tab.

The other setting on this tab is the Snap to default check box, which sets the following Boolean value under the Mouse key:

```
SnapToDefaultButton          0 or 1
REG_SZ
```

If the check box is not checked, this value is set to 0; if checked, the value is set to 1.

The General Tab

The last tab on the Mouse applet screen is the General tab (see Figure 3.4). There is only one item on this page—the Name drop-down list box, which contains one or two entries. These entries are listed under the following key as `\1_0_21_0_31_0` and `\1_1_21_0_31_0`:

```
1. [HKEY_LOCAL_MACHINE\SYSTEM\CurrentControlSet\Enum\Root\*PNP0F03]
```

This Plug-and-Play key indicates that Windows NT has found this hardware at bootup. Only two entries are found under this key (Microsoft PS/2 Port Mouse and Microsoft Serial Mouse), and these entries match the ones in the Name list box, as seen in Figure 3.4:

```
1. [HKEY_LOCAL_MACHINE\SYSTEM\CurrentControlSet\Enum\Root\*PNP0F03
2. "DeviceDesc"="Microsoft Serial Mouse"
3.
4. [HKEY_LOCAL_MACHINE\SYSTEM\CurrentControlSet\Enum\Root\*PNP0F03
5. "DeviceDesc"="Microsoft PS/2 Port Mouse"
```

Now, if you look at the values under these two subkeys, you see this:

```
1. [HKEY_LOCAL_MACHINE\SYSTEM\ControlSet001\Enum\Root\*PNP0F03\1_0_21_0_31_0]
```

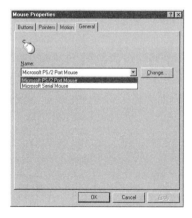

Figure 3.4 The Serial Mouse Registry key.

```
2. "Service"="sermouse"
3. "ClassGUID"="{4D36E96F-E325-11CE-BFC1-08002BE10318}"
4. "Class"="Mouse"
5. "Driver"="{4D36E96F-E325-11CE-BFC1-08002BE10318}\\0001"
```

This key gives you the `ClassGUID` for this device and the location in the Registry where you can find its driver, plus the name of the service under the `[HKEY_LOCAL_MACHINE\SYSTEM\CurrentControlSet\Services]` key, which in this case is Sermouse. The Sermouse key is shown in Figure 3.5

Other Mouse Registry Settings

If you search the Registry for the `ClassGUID`, you see what appears in Figure 3.6.

Now, from the entry for `INFPath`, `INFSection`, and the previous `PNP0F03` key, you can look at the MSMOUSE.INF file and see these values:

```
1. [LegacyXlate.DevId]
2. MICROSOFT_PS2_MOUSE=*PNP0F03; MS PS/2 mouse i8042prt
```

The i8042prt driver governs this mouse, which is also the keyboard driver.

If you search the Registry for i8042prt, you see the contents of Figure 3.7.

Figure 3.5 Mouse parameter values.

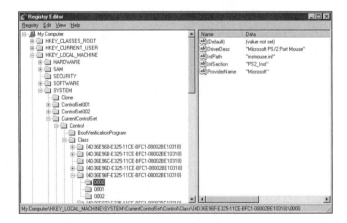

Figure 3.6 The Mouse `ClassGUID`.

The highlighted Parameters key is where you change those aspects of the mouse that are not available from the Control Panel Mouse applet (such as the number of buttons), which is set by the following value:

```
Number of Buttons          2 or 3
REG_DWORD
```

If this value is set to 2, then 2 buttons will be active on the mouse and if it's set to 3, 3 buttons will be active.

Keyboards

As with the mouse, the Registry settings for the keyboard can be set from the Keyboard applet in the Control Panel. These and other keyboard settings are discussed in the following sections.

Setting Up the Keyboard

Keyboards are Plug-and–Play devices that must be found by the system BIOS before the PC can boot. Most PCs give a Keyboard 101 error if a keyboard is not detected.

Author Note

The other services where mice may be found are under the [HKEY_LOCAL_MACHINE\SYSTEM\ Current ControlSet\Services\] key: Sermouse (refer to Figure 3.5) and Busmouse.

Tip

If you use a Microsoft IntelliMouse, the wheel may stop functioning after some types of software are installed. Try deleting the following keys:

```
[HKEY_LOCAL_MACHINE\System\CurrentControlSet\Services\VxD\VRCHSYS]
[HKEY_LOCAL_MACHINE\System\CurrentControlSet\Services\VxD\VRCHDOS]
[HKEY_CURRENT_USER\Software\Microsoft\Windows\Current Version\
Explorer\Cabinet State]
```

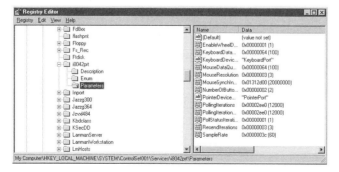

Figure 3.7   Mouse parameters.

One feature of the keyboard that is set by the Registry at bootup is the NumLock key. The value that determines whether NumLock is on or off is found under the [HKEY_CURRENT_USER\Control Panel\Keyboard] key:

    InitialKeyboardIndicators   0 or 2

If you want to change the status of NumLock when Windows NT boots so that NumLock is on, change the value of this setting from 0 to 2. If you turn NumLock off and shut the computer down, however, this value is reset from 2 to 1.

The Keyboard Applet

If you open the Control Panel and launch the Keyboard applet, you see the Keyboard Properties dialog box, shown in Figure 3.8.

The Speed Tab

There are two slide bars on the Speed tab: Repeat delay and Repeat rate. The settings for these slide bars are held in the following values under this Registry key:

Troubleshooting

If you have a serial mouse on COM1 or COM2 that occasionally fails to be detected by NTDETECT at startup, you can fiddle with the connector without rebooting by adding the following value to the [HKEY_LOCAL_MACHINE\System\CurrentControlSet\Services\Sermouse\Parameters] key:

    OverrideHardwareBitstring   0 or 1
    REG_DWORD

A data value of 1 indicates that the mouse is installed on COM1; a data value of 2 specifies COM2.

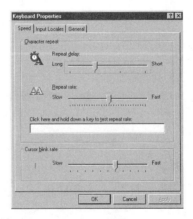

Figure 3.8   The Keyboard Properties dialog box.

```
KeyboardDelay              0 to 3
REG_SZ
KeyboardSpeed              0 to 31
```
A setting of 31 yields the fastest speed.

The other slide bar on this tab controls the Cursor blink rate. Its value is stored in this key: [HKEY_CURRENT_USER\Control Panel\Desktop]
```
CursorBlinkRate            200 – 1200
REG_SZ
```
A setting of 200 is the fastest.

The Input Locales Tab

The next tab in the Keyboard applet is the Input locales tab (see Figure 3.9). The first item on this tab is the Installed input locales and layouts area, which lists all of the country keyboard layouts that are loaded into memory by Windows NT at bootup.

The information in this area is stored in several Registry keys. First, the listings in this box correspond to the values under this key:

1. `[HKEY_CURRENT_USER\Keyboard Layout\Preload]`
2. `"1"="00000409"`
3. `"2"="00000436"`
4. `"3"="00000423"`

My Registry lists three entries, and as Figure 3.9 shows, there are three entries in the Input locales area.

If you search the Registry for the value `00000409`, you find that this is the code page for the U.S.:

Figure 3.9   The Input Locales tab.

1. `[HKEY_LOCAL_MACHINE\SYSTEM\ControlSet001\Control\Keyboard Layout\`
   `DosKeybCodes]`
2. `"00000409"="us"`

Listed under this key are values for all of the keyboards you see when you press the Add button. But you also find this next key, which gives you the keyboard driver for the `00000409`, or U.S., keyboard layout:

1. `[HKEY_LOCAL_MACHINE\SYSTEM\CurrentControlSet\Control\`
   `Keyboard 1. 1. 1. 2. Layouts\00000409]`
2. `"Layout Text"="US"`
3. `"Layout File"="KBDUS.DLL"`

The driver is given in the Layout File setting; for this keyboard it is the KBDUS.DLL file. All of the keyboard layouts available in Windows NT have similar entries under this key.

This tab also has three radial buttons in the Switch locales area that control this key:

1. `[HKEY_CURRENT_USER\Keyboard Layout\Substitutes]`
2. `"00000436"="00040409"`

The two numeral values here are keyboard layouts; in this case, they show that the Belarus and U.S. keyboard layouts will switch in and out if Ctrl+Shift is pressed.

The last entry on this screen is the Enable indicator on taskbar check box. When this box is checked, a "Hotkey" value is added to this key:

```
[HKEY_CURRENT_USER\Keyboard Layout\Toggle]
    Hotkey                  1 or 2
    REG_SZ
```

This setting's value is set to either 1 or 2. 1 indicates that the Left Alt+Shift button is set; 2 shows if Ctrl+Shift is set. If either the box is not checked or the None button is set, there is no Hotkey setting under this key.

The General Tab

The last tab on the Keyboard applet is the General tab, as seen in Figure 3.10.

There is only one item on this page: a drop-down list box that displays the current keyboard. Most computers will list the PC/AT Enhanced Keyboard (101/102-Key). If you search the Registry for this keyboard, you find this:

1. `[HKEY_LOCAL_MACHINE\SYSTEM\ControlSet001\Control\Class\`
2. `{4D36E96B-E325-11CE-BFC1-08002BE10318}\0000]`
3. `"InfPath"="keyboard.inf"`
4. `"InfSection"="STANDARD_Inst"`
5. `"ProviderName"="Microsoft"`
6. `"DriverDesc"="PC/AT Enhanced Keyboard (101/102-Key)"`

The values give you the .INF file and section from which this keyboard is set up. If you open this .INF file and look at the [`STANDARD_Inst`] section—note that this keyboard is the default Windows NT Keyboard—you see this:

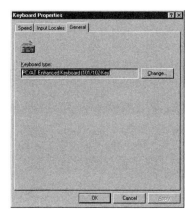

Figure 3.10   The General tab.

```
%*PNP030b.DeviceDesc%    = STANDARD_Inst,*PNP030b    ;Default keyboard
```

This gives you the Plug-and-Play value that Windows NT uses for this device. Searching the Registry for this value gives these results:

```
01. [HKEY_LOCAL_MACHINE\SYSTEM\CurrentControlSet\Enum\Root\
02. *PNP030b\1_0_22_0_32_0]
03. "HardwareID"=hex(7):2a,50,4e,50,30,33,30,62,00
04. "BaseDevicePath"="HTREE\\ROOT\\0"
05. "FoundAtEnum"=dword:00000001
06. "Service"="i8042prt"
07. "ClassGUID"="{4D36E96B-E325-11CE-BFC1-08002BE10318}"
08. "Class"="Keyboard"
09. "Driver"="{4D36E96B-E325-11CE-BFC1-08002BE10318}\\0001"
10. "Mfg"="(Standard keyboards)"
11. "DeviceDesc"="PC/AT Enhanced Keyboard (101/102-Key)"
12. "ConfigFlags"=dword:00000000
13. "Problem"=dword:00000000
14. "StatusFlags"=dword:00000008
```

This key holds the values that Windows NT has read from the firmware for this device.

4

Settings for Sound

- ● **The Keyboard applet**

  The Registry settings for the Keyboard applet found in the Control Panel are discussed, covering all tabs and options available from the applet.

- ● **The Multimedia applet**

  The Registry settings for the Multimedia applet found in the Control Panel are discussed, covering all tabs and options available from the applet.

- ● **Other Sound Registry keys and their values**

  Other sound-related Registry settings are discussed, including 32-bit drivers and associated DLLs, 16-bit drivers, and wave channels.

Installing Sound

As you probably already know, with Windows NT 4.0 as with previous versions of NT, sound cards are not automatically detected by the operating system at install time. The one exception to this is when you upgrade from a previous version of Windows NT to version 4.0—the previous settings for any existing sound card are retained.

Most often, you install sound cards via the Multimedia applet in the Control Panel. Open this applet, and you see the Multimedia Properties dialog box shown in Figure 4.1.

The list of multimedia drivers is generated from the driver definitions under the `[Installable.Drivers]` section of the MMDRIVER.INF file located in the %SYSTEMROOT%\INF directory.

Figure 4.1 shows that, although this PC does not have any audio devices installed, it does have other audio components, as evidenced by the components listed under Media Control Devices and Video Compression Codecs. Actually, all of the components appearing under the top-level items on this screen are listed under the following Registry key:

```
1. [HKEY_LOCAL_MACHINE\SOFTWARE\Microsoft\Windows NT\CurrentVersion\
drivers.desc]
2. "mciwave.dll"="(MCI) Sound"
```

Figure 4.1 The Multimedia Properties dialog box.

3. `"mciseq.dll"="(MCI) Midi Sequencer"`
4. `"mcicda.dll"="(MCI) CD Audio"`
5. `"mciavi32.dll"="(MCI) Microsoft Video for Windows"`

This partial listing is like the old [drivers.desc] section in the Windows 3.1 CONTROL.INI file and shows the installed components under the Media Control Devices item, as shown in Figure 4.1.

Click the Add button; the Add dialog box appears. If you select the Creative Labs Sound Blaster 1.X, Pro, 16 entry and click OK, you may see the warning box shown in Figure 4.2.

This is not a Registry error; it can be automated by deleting all SNDBLST.DLL and SNDBLST.DL_ files from the %SYSTEM% drive. If you get this message, click New and proceed to install the card by selecting the appropriate I/O address and interrupt. Reboot to restart your PC.

After your PC restarts, open the Registry using REGEDIT.EXE; you see that a new value has been added to the [HKEY_LOCAL_MACHINE\SOFTWARE\Microsoft\ Windows NT\CurrentVersion\drivers.desc] key:

`"SNDBLST.DLL"="Creative Labs Sound Blaster 1.X, Pro, 16"`

Figure 4.2 Sound driver warning screen.

Now that you have confirmed the installation of the sound card, you can modify its properties. Most of these properties can be modified from the Multimedia applet of the Control Panel.

Installing Multimedia Devices

This tab is discussed first because it lists all of the audio devices available. On the Devices tab, click the plus sign on the Audio Devices branch, select an audio device, and click the Properties button. If you select the Sound Blaster audio device that you just installed, you see the dialog box shown in Figure 4.3.

The Do not map through this device check box is set by the following Registry value found under the [HKEY_LOCAL_MACHINE\SOFTWARE\Microsoft\Windows NT\ CurrentVersion\Wave Mapper\SNDBLST.DLL] key:

```
Mappable          0 or 1
REG_DWORD
```

This value may not be present on all computers.

A setting of 0 indicates that the box is not checked.

If you now click the Settings button, the dialog box shown in Figure 4.4 appears.

This screen shows a text message with the I/O address of the card; two text boxes, labeled Interrupt and DMA Channel; and three buttons, one labeled Advanced.

Figure 4.3 Sound Blaster properties dialog box.

> **Tip**
>
> If you want to hear sounds through the internal PC system speaker on you may need to disable your sound card. Select the Do not use audio features on this device radial button to disable the selected device.
>
> Changing the following value to 00000004 also disables the card. The key shown here disables the Sound Blaster card you installed:
>
> 1. [HKEY_LOCAL_MACHINE\SYSTEM\CurrentControlSet\
> 2. Services\sndblst]
> 3. "Start"=dword:00000001

Although there is not a text box to change the I/O address, it can be changed (along with the interrupt, DMA channel, and DMA buffer size—set via the Advanced button) by modifying values found under this Registry key:

```
[HKEY_LOCAL_MACHINE\SYSTEM\CurrentControlSet\Services\sndblst\Parameters\
Device0]
```

First, the preceding subkey name `sndblst` indicates that the kernel driver for the card just installed is SNDBLST.SYS. The values that need to be modified to change the dialog box settings in Figure 4.4 follow:

- I/O Base Address
  ```
  Port         I/O address in Decimal Form
  REG_DWORD
  ```
  Specifies the I/O port start address that has been assigned to this sound card. The Sound Blaster default setting is `0x220` (I/O Address 220).

- Interrupt
  ```
  Interrupt    Hexadecimal
  REG_DWORD    0xa
  ```
  Specifies the hexadecimal value of the interrupt that is assigned to this sound card. The Sound Blaster default setting is `0xa` (Interrupt 10). Sound cards can usually be set to IRQs 5, 7, 9, 10, and 11.

- DMA channel and DMA buffer size
  ```
  1. "DmaChannel"=dword:00000001        Channel 1
  2. "DmaChannel16"=dword:00000005      Channel 5
  3.
  4. "Actual Dma Buffer Size"=dword:00001000   4K
  5. "Dma Buffer Size"=dword:00001000          4K
  ```
  The four Registry values define the DMA channel settings for transferring digitized sound. The buffer size is usually set to 4KB, which can be seen in line 4 of the previous Registry example. The DMA channel is usually set to 1, 2, or 3; the DMAChannel16 is set to 4, 5, 6.

Other values that are found under this key follow:

- Configuration Error
  ```
  Configuration Error      Hexadecimal Value
  REG_DWORD
  ```
  Written by the install program to indicate an error; a value of `ffffffff` means that the driver was installed correctly. This value is only used if the sound driver fails to load. Other possible settings for this value follow:

Warning

If you set this value to an interrupt that the sound card cannot use, you see the dialog box shown in Figure 4.5 when you reboot.

Figure 4.4   Sound Blaster hardware parameters.

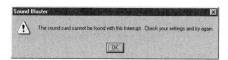

Figure 4.5   Sound Blaster error dialog box.

Setting	Meaning
0	Unspecified error; setup did not find the sound card hardware interrupt conflict
3	DMA channel conflict
4	Found hardware, unspecified error

■ Digital Signal Processor (DSP) Version

```
DSP Version          Digital Number
REG_DWORD
```

Specifies the version of the DSP used for this sound card's programmable logic array (PLA), which is the on-card lookup table used by the card internally.

■ MIDI Port Base Address

```
MPU401 Port       Decimal Address
REG_DWORD           00000330
```

Specifies the base address of the MIDI port used by this sound card; the previous example address is 330.

■ MIDI File Format

```
Synth Type        1 or 2
REG_DWORD
```

Specifies the MIDI file format. If set to 1, the card uses an FM chip; if set to 2, the card uses an MPU-401 port. The name of the MIDI Synth driver can also be found under the [HKEY_LOCAL_MACHINE\SOFTWARE\Microsoft\WindowsNT\ CurrentVersion\Midimap] key; for the installed card, this is the value:

```
"Mapping Name"="SNDBLST OPL3"
```

Setting Playback and Recording Options

Select the Audio tab to see the dialog box shown in Figure 4.6.

Although the values of the slide bars are not set in the Registry, the other properties set by this screen are set in the Registry. Three of the settings are governed by the following values under the [HKEY_CURRENT_USER\Software\Microsoft\Multimedia\ Sound Mapper] Registry key:

■ Preferred device list box in the Playback area:

```
Playback        String Value
REG_SZ          "Sound Blaster Playback"
```

■ Preferred device list box in the Recording area:

```
Record    String Value
REG_SZ          Sound Blaster Record"
```

■ Use preferred devices only check box:

```
PreferredOnly    1 or 2
REG_DWORD
```

A setting of 1 indicates that the box is checked.

The third list box, Preferred quality, is set by this value under the [HKEY_CURRENT_USER\Software\Microsoft\Multimedia\Audio] key:

```
DefaultFormat    String Value
REG_SZ           CD Quality"
```

The possible formats available in the Preferred quality drop-down list box are defined by this value:

```
SystemFormats    String Value
REG_SZ           CD Quality,Radio Quality,Telephone Quality"
```

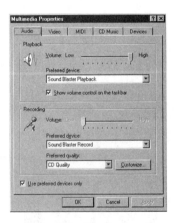

Figure 4.6   The Audio tab.

These formats are further defined by the hexadecimal settings of the values found under the [HKEY_CURRENT_USER\Software\Microsoft\Multimedia\Audio\WaveFormats] key:

1. "CD Quality"=
2. hex:01,00,02,00,44,ac,00,00,10,b1,02,00,04,00,10,00
3.
4. "Radio Quality"=
5. hex:01,00,01,00,22,56,00,00,22,56,00,00,01,00,08,00
6.
7. "Telephone Quality"=
8. hex:01,00,01,00,11,2b,00,00,11,2b,00,00,01,00,08,00

The Show Volume Control on the Taskbar check box is set via the Service value found under the [HKEY_CURRENT_USER\Software\Microsoft\Windows\CurrentVersion\Applets\SysTray] key:

Services   3 or 7
REG_DWORD

A setting of 3 indicates that the box is not checked; a setting of 7 indicates that the box is checked.

Setting Video File Display Options

The radial buttons on the Video tab, as seen in Figure 4.7, define the screen size in which a video runs.

These buttons are defined by the following values found under the [HKEY_CURRENT_USER\Software\Microsoft\Multimedia\Video For Windows\MCIAVI] key:

DefaultOptions   0 or 2
REG_DWORD

A setting of 0 selects the Window button, and a setting of 2 selects the Full screen button.

The drop-down list box for the Window radial button sets the size of the Window that the video file runs in. This list box sets the following value under the [HKEY_CURRENT_USER\Software\Microsoft\Multimedia\Video For Windows\MCIAVI] key:

DefaultOptions   Decimal Number
REG_DWORD

The decimal numbers for the list box options are:
Double Original Size: 0x00000100 (256)

1/16 of Screen Size: 0x00010000 (65536)

1/4 of Screen Size: 0x00020000 (131072)

1/2 of Screen Size: 0x00040000 (262144)

Maximized: 0x00080000 (524588)

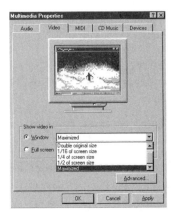

Figure 4.7 The Video tab.

If you click the Advanced button, you see the AdvancedVideo Options dialog box shown in Figure 4.8.

The Maximum 16-bit compatibility check box is set by the following Registry value found under the [HKEY_CURRENT_USER\Software\Microsoft\Multimedia\MCIAVI] key:

```
RejectWOWOpenCalls    0 or 1
REG_DWORD
```

A setting of 1 indicates that the box is checked.

Setting MIDI Options

The MIDI tab properties (see Figure 4.9) are set by the following values under the [HKEY_CURRENT_USER\Software\Microsoft\Windows\CurrentVersion\Multimedia\ MIDI Map] key:

```
CurrentScheme         String Value
REG_SZ                Sandra"
```

The Configure button, shown in Figure 4.9, defines the CurrentScheme as set when selecting the Custom configuration button. In this case, I used the Configure button

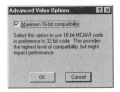

Figure 4.8 The AdvancedVideo Options dialog box.

to create a scheme called Sandra, to which the preceding value is set. The Single instrument button does not affect this value.

```
UseScheme          0 or 1
REG_DWORD
```

This value is set to 0 if the Single instrument button is selected and set to 1 if the Custom configuration button is selected.

```
CurrentInstrument      String Value
REG_SZ                 SNDBLST.DLL<0000>"
```

This value determines the instrument that is selected in the list box under the Single instrument button. The previous setting is for the Sound Blaster FM Synthesis selection. A setting of `MMDRV.DLL<0000>` sets the Creative Labs Sound Blaster 1.5 selection.

Further settings for the selected MIDI instrument can be found under the Registry keys: [HKEY_LOCAL_MACHINE\SYSTEM\CurrentControlSet\Control\MediaResources\MIDI\mmdrv.dll<0000>]

and

[HKEY_LOCAL_MACHINE\SYSTEM\CurrentControlSet\Control\MediaResources\MIDI\SNDBLST.DLL<0000>]

Some of the settings under these keys follow:
1. "Active"="1"
2. "Description"="Creative Labs Sound Blaster 1.5"
3. "Driver"="mmdrv.dll"

These values indicate that this MIDI device is available for use, that it is called *Creative Labs Sound Blaster 1.5*, and that it uses the *mmdrv.dll* driver.

Figure 4.9   The MIDI tab.

Setting CD Music Options

Options for CD-ROMs are set from the CD Music tab, as seen in Figure 4.10.

The CDROM list is actually set with the Disk Administrator and is read from the `\Device\CdRom0` value under the `[HKEY_LOCAL_MACHINE\SYSTEM\DISK]` key:

```
\Device\CdRom0      Drive Letter
REG_SZ              D:
```

This setting assigns the drive letter D to the CD-ROM drive.

The Volume slide bar is set with the following value found under the `[HKEY_LOCAL_MACHINE\SYSTEM\CurrentControlSet\Control\MediaResources\mci\cdaudio\unit 0]` key:

```
Volume Settings     Hexadecimal Values
REG_BINARY
```

This value has a range of `hex:00,00,00,00,00,00,00,00` at the Low setting and `hex:00,00,00,00,ff,00,00,00` at the High setting.

Other Sound Registry Keys and Their Values

Not all settings for sound can be found using the Multimedia applet as a guide. Here are some more areas where Sound Registry values are stored.

32-Bit Drivers and Associated DLLs

The values under the `[HKEY_LOCAL_MACHINE\SOFTWARE\Microsoft\WindowsNT\CurrentVersion\Drivers32]` Registry key could have been found under the [drivers] section of the Windows 3.1 SYSTEM.INI file. These include the values for 32-bit drivers associated with wavemapper, msacm.imaadpcm, msacm.msadpcm, msacm.msgsm610, and vidc.msvc. Other values under this key are definitions for all Windows NT .DLL associations, installed for all sound applications.

Figure 4.10 The CD Music tab.

Some of the driver values under this key are
1. `"wavemapper"="msacm32.drv"`
2. `"msacm.msadpcm"="msadp32.acm"`
3. `"msacm.imaadpcm"="imaadp32.acm"`

Other entries added by the Sound Blaster card are
1. `"wave1"="SNDBLST.DLL"`
2. `"MIDI1"="SNDBLST.DLL "`
3. `"aux1"="SNDBLST.DLL "`
4. `"mixer"="SNDBLST.DLL "`

The values under the Registry key `[HKEY_LOCAL_MACHINE\SOFTWARE\Microsoft\ Windows NT\CurrentVersion\MCI32]` define the 32-bit MCI sound drivers:
1. `"WaveAudio"="mciwave.dll"`
2. `"Sequencer"="mciseq.dll"`
3. `"CDAudio"="mcicda.dll"`
4. `"AVIVideo"="mciavi32.dll"`

16-Bit Drivers

The values under the Registry key `[HKEY_LOCAL_MACHINE\SOFTWARE\Microsoft\ WindowsNT\CurrentVersion\Drivers]` could have been found under the `[drivers]` section of the Windows 3.1 SYSTEM.INI file, but they are the 16-bit drivers used by the sound applications. The timer value is defined under this key:

`"timer"="timer.drv"`

The values under the Registry key `[KEY_LOCAL_MACHINE\SOFTWARE\Microsoft\ Windows NT\CurrentVersion\MCI]` could have been found under the `[mci]` section of the SYSTEM.INI and define 16-bit sound drivers such as these:
1. `"WaveAudio"="mciwave.drv"`
2. `"Sequencer"="mciseq.drv"`
3. `"CDAudio"="mcicda.drv"`
4. `"AVIVideo"="mciavi.drv"`

Wave Channel

Every sound card uses a wave channel. These channels are associated with a sound card through these wave values. A Sound Blaster card that uses Wave Channel 1 has this value under the `[HKEY_LOCAL_MACHINE\SOFTWARE\Microsoft\WindowsNT\ CurrentVersion\Userinstallable.drivers]` key:

`"wave1"="SNDBLST.DLL"`

Other options associated with the installed sound card's driver are found under this key. There are no other options listed under this key for the Sound Blaster card installed previously.

Author Note

The values under the key [HKEY_LOCAL_MACHINE\SOFTWARE\Microsoft\WindowsNT\ CurrentVersion\MCI] are discussed in Chapter 12, "System Components."

5

Settings for Memory

- **Managing memory with the System applet**

  This section discusses the Registry settings for the System applet used for memory management.

- **The Memory Management key**

  This section discusses the Memory Management Registry key and its values.

Managing Memory with the System Applet

With the advent of Windows NT 4.0 and Windows 95, memory management has been largely left to the operating system. Gone are the days when you used memory managers such as QEMM to do tedious *hole management* (placing device drivers into *upper memory addresses*—UMAs).

Because Windows NT does most of this tweaking of upper memory for you, however, memory management by the user is limited to the properties of the Windows NT page file and a few other settings.

The size and other properties of the Windows NT page file are set from the System applet of the Control Panel. When you open this applet, you see the System Properties dialog box. Figure 5.1 shows the Performance tab selected.

A slide bar sets the performance boost of the foreground application. The Change button (found in the Virtual Memory area) changes the properties of the page file.

The Registry value set by the Boost slide bar is found under the
`[HKEY_LOCAL_MACHINE\SYSTEM\CurrentControlSet\Control\PriorityControl]` key and is
```
Win32PrioritySeparation    0 to 2
REG_DWORD
```

This value can be set to 0, 1, or 2:

- **0. Short processor interval.** A setting of 0 gives the same processing time to threads for foreground processes, background processes, and processes with a priority class of `Idle`.

- **1. Medium processor interval.** This setting gives more processor time to threads for foreground processes than to threads for background processes each time they are scheduled.

Figure 5.1 The Performance tab of the System applet.

- 2. Long processor interval. This setting gives much more processor time to threads for foreground processes than to threads for background processes each time they are scheduled.

When you click the Change button, you see the Virtual Memory dialog box shown in Figure 5.2.

The list box displays all of the page files that are currently used by Windows NT. You cannot see the path of the actual page file, however. To discover this, open the Registry using the REGED32.EXE editor. Find the [HKEY_LOCAL_MACHINE\SYSTEM\ CurrentControlSet\Control\Session Manager\Memory Management] key and look at the PagingFiles Value. There should be an entry with this form:

```
PagingFiles    Page File String
REG_MULTI_SZ   Example: C:\PageFile\pagefile.sys 51 100
```

This example entry gives the path of the page file, PAGEFILE.SYS, as C:\PageFile. The numbers at the end of this example value are the minimum and maximum sizes of the page file. These values are set in the Paging File Size for Selected Drive area when you click the Set button.

Author Note

When using Windows NT Server 4.0, the processor time assigned to each thread is greater, albeit fixed, than the time assigned to threads when using Windows NT Workstation 4.0. Windows NT Server 4.0 uses the value of Win32PrioritySeparation to calculate a brief priority boost for foreground processes. The higher the value, the greater the boost.

Figure 5.2   The Virtual Memory dialog box.

Finally, at the bottom of this screen in the Registry Size area is a text box where you can enter a value for the Maximum Registry Size. The value that this option sets in the Registry is found under the [HKEY_LOCAL_MACHINE\SYSTEM\ControlSet001\Control] key and is

RegistrySizeLimit   Decimal Number
REG_DWORD

This value, if set to 00700000, would set the Registry to a maximum size of 7MB.

The Memory Management Key

In the previous section, you were introduced to the Memory Management key located at [HKEY_LOCAL_MACHINE\SYSTEM\CurrentControlSet\Control\Session Manager\Memory Management]. If you open the Registry to this key, you see the window shown in Figure 5.3.

Warning

If you use the NTFS File System, and you place the PAGEFILE.SYS in a directory other than C:\, C:\WINNT, or some other directory that the system does not have full access to, then you will receive the following error message at logon:

        Limited virtual memory

This message means that your system is running without a properly sized paging file. Use the Virtual Memory option of the System applet in the Control Panel to create a paging file or to increase the initial size of your paging file.

Use the Registry to eliminate this error by modifying the paging files value to set the path to C:, C:\WINNT, or another directory to which the system has full rights.

The values listed under this key have the following explanations and values.

Page Pool Values

```
PagedPoolSize        Decimal Number
REG_DWORD            Example: 02000000

NonPagedPoolSize     Decimal Number
REG_DWORD            Example: 00000000
```

Windows NT has two memory pools that it automatically adjusts: the *paged memory pool* and the *nonpaged memory pool*. Although Windows NT usually determines the sizes of these files, the file size can also be changed by using the Registry and setting the previous values.

```
PagedPoolQuota       Decimal Number
REG_DWORD            Example: 00000000

NonPagedPoolQuota    Decimal Number
REG_DWORD            Example: 00000000
```

These two settings govern the way that Windows NT allocates memory. If these values are not zero, Windows NT Server or Workstation cannot dynamically allocate memory, which can then cause this error message:

```
Not enough server storage is available to process this command.
```

Set these values to zero to solve this problem.

Figure 5.3   The Memory Management key.

Author Note

Although the minimum and maximum numbers for this value can be different, I recommend that you use the same numbers for these settings. If the numbers are different, unnecessary fragmentation can occur, especially when using the NTFS File System.

The pagefile should not be set to a size greater than twice the amount of RAM, or Windows NT's performance will suffer. Also, a memory dump will not be written if the **PageFile** size is not at least 12MB greater than the amount of RAM.

Finally, if possible, span the pagefile across more than one disk because Windows NT load balances the pagefile when it spans multiple disks.

Locked Bytes

```
IoPageLockLimit    Decimal Number representing less than Physical Memory
REG_DWORD
```

This value indicates the number of locked bytes for input/output operations. If this value is zero, the default value of 512KB is used. This value's maximum setting is determined by the amount of physical memory, and it should be set according to Table 5.1.

Table 5.1 **Maximum Lock Limits**

Amount of Physical Memory (RAM)	Maximum Lock Limit
RAM < 64MB	RAM–7MB
64MB < RAM < 512MB	RAM–16MB
RAM > 512MB	RAM–64MB

The Large System Cache Value

```
LargeSystemCache    0 or 1
REG_DWORD
```

If this value is set to nonzero, the system favors the system-cache working set over the processes working set. This value is set to a nonzero value if it is a Windows NT Server or Advanced Server installation. This value also influences how often paged data is written to the disk:

- **0.** When set to **0**, a file system cache of approximately 8MB is set. Changed pages stay in memory until the number of available pages drops to about 1,000. This setting is useful for servers that run applications that perform their own memory caching, such as Microsoft SQL Server; as well as applications that perform best with ample memory, such as Internet Information Server.

- **1.** When set to 1, a large system cache working set is created that can be expanded to the size of physical memory minus 4MB, when required. Changed pages stay in memory until the number of available pages drops to about 250. Use this setting for all computers running Windows NT Server or Advanced Server on large networks.

Further information on using large system caches can be found in Chapter 17, "Configuring Network Services."

Warning

If any of the previous four pool values is set to a nonzero number, the Windows NT performance is degraded.

The System Page Value

```
SystemPages    0 to Number of Entries
REG_DWORD
```

This value gives the number of system page table entries reserved for mapping input/output buffers and other settings into the system address space. The default setting is 0. This value should be set as shown here:

- 0. When set to 0, Windows NT calculates the optimal number of page table entries using information for the type of platform and available system memory. Windows NT adjusts this setting upon reboot if the amount of system memory changes.

- *Nonzero entry*. When set to a nonzero number, the number of system page table entries that Windows NT calculates is overridden and replaced with this setting. Further, Windows NT does not recalculate this value if the amount of system memory changes.

Clearing the Pagefile

```
ClearPageFileAtShutdown    0 or 1
REG_DWORD
```

Setting this value to 1 clears the inactive pages that Windows NT uses upon reboot. This is useful if you have a dual-boot system and you want to protect sensitive information that may have been cached by the system.

Executive Paging

```
DisablePagingExecutive    0 or 1
REG_DWORD
```

This value determines the paging properties for the user-mode and kernel-mode drivers, as well as kernel-mode system code, and determines whether this data can be paged to the disk drive when the data is not in use. This value should be set as follows:

- 0. The previous drivers and kernel code must remain in physical memory.
- 1. The previous drivers and kernel code may be paged to the disk drive.

Tip

For computers running Windows NT Server 4.0, you can change this value by using the Control Panel. Open the Network applet, choose the Services tab, and then double-click Server. For a large file system cache, click Maximize Throughput for File Sharing; for a standard file system cache, click Maximize Throughput for Network Applications.

Setting the L2 Cache (Secondary RAM Cache)

```
SecondLevelDataCache     0 to Cache Size
REG_DWORD
```

This value informs Windows NT about the size of any L2 cache installed on the system. If the Windows NT *Hardware Abstraction Layer* (HAL) does not recognize the correct amount of installed L2 cache, this value can be set to force Windows NT to see the cache as follows:

- **0.** This setting sets the L2 cache at 256KB.

- *Other value.* If your cache is greater than 256KB, modify this entry with REGEDIT.EXE and set this entry to the size of your cache using a decimal number.

6

Settings for Configuring Network Adapters

- **Installing network cards via the Network applet**

  Network adapters are added through the use of the Control Panel Network applet. This section shows how this is done.

- **Adding network card .INF files**

  This section discusses adding a network card's .INF file to the Registry so that the card will appear in the Network applet.

- **The Service Name key**

  This section discusses the network card Service Name key and its use in the Registry.

- **The NetRules key**

  This section discusses the NetRules Registry key, which holds network driver information.

- **The Network Card Description key**

  This section shows where network protocol information is found in the Registry. Also covered here is the Network # key that holds the information that describes the network card.

- **The Network Adapter Service key**

  This section discusses Windows NT services associated with network adapters and the Registry values that control them.

- **The Network Card Parameters key**

  This section discusses where to find network configuration parameters, such as an IRQ, within the Registry.

Installing Network Cards via the Network Applet

Like the hardware components discussed in the previous chapters, network adapter cards are installed from the Control Panel by using the Network applet.

Figure 6.1 The Adapters tab of the Network applet.

For a computer that does not have any network adapters installed, the Adapters tab on the Network applet screen looks like the one shown in Figure 6.1 if no adapters are installed.

To add a network adapter, click the Add button. You see a list of network adapters, as shown in Figure 6.2.

Adding Network Card .INF Files

This list is generated from the Registry key [HKEY_LOCAL_MACHINE\SOFTWARE\ Microsoft\Ncpa\InfOptions], which lists all of the OEMNAD★.INF files found in the %SYSTEMROOT%\SYSTEM32 directory. To add entries to this list, rename your OEMSETUP.INF file **OEMAD★.INF**, where ★ is a number, letter, or a pair consisting of either or both. Further, the added character(s) must not already exist in other OEMNAD★.INF files. When you reboot the PC, Windows NT adds a subkey for this .INF file, which is listed alphabetically under the [HKEY_LOCAL_MACHINE\ SOFTWARE\Microsoft\Ncpa\InfOptions] key.

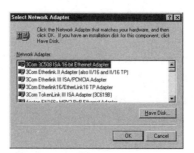

Figure 6.2 Adding a network adapter.

To install the Compaq Integrated NetFlex-3 network adapter, copy the OEMSETUP.INF to a temporary directory and rename the file **OEMNADSS.INF**.

Now, you need to open the new OEMNADSS.INF and change the adapter name that is displayed in Figure 6.2 to a unique name. Do this by changing the following Registry entry:

```
1. [OptionsTextENG]
2. NetFlex3          =          "Compaq NetFlex-3 Controller - New"
```

For this adapter, I have modified `Compaq NetFlex-3 Controller` to `Compaq NetFlex-3 Controller – New`. This adapter can now be seen in the Select Network Adapter dialog box, as shown in Figure 6.3.

If you reboot the PC and use REGEDT32.EXE, you see that Windows NT has added a new key, as shown in Figure 6.4.

Now, looking more closely at this key, you see one value and one subkey. It is the subkey that is important here: [HKEY_LOCAL_MACHINE\SOFTWARE\Microsoft\Ncpa\InfOptions\Oemnadss.inf\NetAdapter.PCI]

Opening REGEDT32.EXE and looking at this key, you see two values:

```
OptionList          String List
REG_MULTI_SZ
```

The setting for this value is a multiple string that can be read from REGEDT32.EXE. If this value is viewed with REGEDIT.EXE, however, numbers are seen instead of the string list. This list contains the service name used by this card,

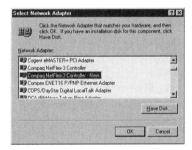

Figure 6.3   Displaying the new adapter entry.

Tip

If the lists for services, protocols, and adapters in the Network applet are blank after components are installed, a new Registry key has probably been added under [KEY_LOCAL_MACHINE\SOFTWARE], which means that the current user does not have the correct read rights to this key.

To fix this, use REGEDT32.EXE to add read rights for this key for all network users. Also, if a restriction to any data under this key is needed, place this key at least three levels down from the [HKEY_LOCAL_MACHINE\SOFTWARE] key.

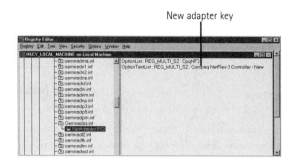

Figure 6.4 .INF File Registry key.

which is copied from the card's .INF file from the `ProductSoftwareName` entry in the .INF file. For the Compaq card, the name is `CpqNF3`.

```
OptionTextList         String List
REG_MULTI_SZ
```

The setting for this value is a multiple string and can be read from REGEDT32.EXE. If this value is viewed with REGEDIT.EXE, however, numbers are seen instead of the string list. This list contains the name shown in the Network Applet Adapter tab and is copied from the . INF file section:

```
1. [OptionsTextENG]
2. NetFlex3           =          "Compaq NetFlex-3 Controller - New"
```

The Service Name Key

If you open REGEDIT.EXE and search the Registry for the service name, which for this card is `CPQNF3`, the first key found is [`HKEY_LOCAL_MACHINE\HARDWARE\`
`RESOURCEMAP\OtherDrivers\CpqNF3`]. The existence of this key shows that the adapter has been installed by the system.

The next key you find is [`HKEY_LOCAL_MACHINE\SOFTWARE\Compaq\CpqNF3`], which has a subkey called `CurrentVersion`. The values under this key contain information gathered by Windows NT from the adapter's .INF file. The values here are

```
Description          Miniport Driver String Descriptor
REG_SZ
```

This value shows the name of the miniport driver used by this network card and is read from the following section of the .INF file:

> **Tip**
>
> When performing a company-wide migration, network parameters for IRQ, base address, and other settings may need to be modified at the .INF file level. The .INF file settings govern the Registry parameters installed by Windows NT.

1. [FileConstantsENG]

2. ProductSoftwareDescription= Miniport Driver String Descriptor

```
InstallDate          Hexadecimal Number
REG_DWORD
```

This value shows the date that the adapter was installed in hexadecimal form. A decimal number for this value can be seen with REGEDIT.EXE, but the value does not represent a standard date.

```
MajorVersion and MinorVersion        Hexadecimal Numbers
REG_DWORD
```

These two separate values show the version of the network driver installed for this card

```
RefCount             Hexadecimal Number
REG_DWORD
```

The value of the NETWORKCARD# can be found under the [HKEY_LOCAL_MACHINE\ SOFTWARE\Microsoft\WindowsNT\CurrentVersion\NetworkCards\] key. This value is 1 if only one card is installed. This key is described in more detail later in this chapter.

```
ServiceName          Service Name String
REG_SZ
```

This value shows the service name under the [HKEY_LOCAL_MACHINE\SYSTEM\ CurrentControlSet\Services\] key. This value is usually set to the same name as the value OptionList.

```
SoftwareType         String
REG_SZ
```

This value specifies the type of file used to operate this card. This will usually be of the type driver.

```
Title                Driver Name String
REG_SZ
```

This value shows the name found in the following .INF file section:

1. [FileConstantsENG]

2. ProductSoftwareTitle= Driver Name String

The NetRules Key

The next Registry values to look at are found under the [HKEY_LOCAL_MACHINE\ SOFTWARE\Compaq\CpqNF3\CurrentVersion\NetRules] key. Because Windows NT adds one set of Registry values for the network card driver file and another set for the adapter itself, a specific subkey called NetRules is added under the driver or adapter key.

The NetRules subkey shows network components that are a part of the network installation, which include network bindings and specific driver files. The values under this key are discussed in the following sections.

The *Bindable* Value

```
Bindable      fromClass toClass  String1  String2  Decimal Number
REG_MULTI_SZ
```

This value, when viewed with REGEDT32.EXE, shows whether the card is bound to any network protocols that are listed on the Protocols tab of the Network applet. This value can have several settings; the example for the Compaq card follows:

```
bindable = CpqNF3Driver CpqNF3Adapter non exclusive 100
```

The first two variables, fromClass and toClass, are components of class CpqNF3Driver and are available to be bound to components of class CpqNF3Adapter.

The String1 variable non shows that the components of class CpqNF3Driver have at least one binding. The String2 variable exclusive shows that the components of class CpqNF3Adapter cannot accept additional bindings.

The decimal number 100 states the "weight" given to this binding by Windows NT. Bindings with higher weights are enabled before those with lower weights, up to the number of bindings that the adapter will accept.

Also, because this value is of data type REG_MULTI_SZ, several different bindings can be listed here. Finally, remember that all binding rules defined anywhere within the Registry apply to all network component classes.

The *Bindform* Value

```
Bindform ObjectName Yes¦No Yes¦No [container¦simple¦streams]
REG_SZ
```

This value contains naming information about how bindings are made to this adapter. The example for the Compaq card follows:

```
"bindform"="\"CpqNF3Sys\" yes no container"
```

The ObjectName variable field, \CpqNF3Sys\, shows the name (in some cases the name prefix, CpqNF3) that identifies the component to Windows NT. The name prefix, CpqNF3, is the same as that seen in the OptionList and is also found under the CurrentControlSet\Services subkey.

The first Yes¦No pair states that the component can or cannot have binding information sent directly to its Linkage subkey. The second Yes¦No pair states that the component's name does or does not appear in any binding strings generated by Windows NT.

The [container¦simple¦streams] variable determines how binding names are constructed.

The *Class* Value

```
Class             NewClassName            OldClassName¦basic [Yes¦No]
REG_MULTI_SZ
```

This value is where the network component defines a new class. Multiple classes can be specified. The example for the Compaq card follows:

```
Class REG_MULTI_SZ : CpqNF3Driver Basic
```

The `NewClassName` variable is optional—it is used only when the `OldClassName` has been renamed via programming functions such as this:

```
1. RENAME CLASS <OldClassName> ;
2.    OF <ClassLibrary> ;
3.    TO <NewClassName>
```

The `OldClassName¦basic` variable is the class originally assigned by Windows NT. For this Compaq card, this value is `CpqNF3Driver Basic`.

The `[Yes¦No]` variable is also optional, and it shows that the class is a logical endpoint associated with the bindings protocol; the default is `No`.

The *INF* Value

```
InfName        INF File Name String (oemnadss.inf)
REG_SZ
```

This value shows the .INF file that was used to install this adapter. The example for the Compaq card follows:

```
InfName="oemnadss.inf"

InfOption INF File Section Name String (CPQNF3)
REG_SZ
```

This value shows the section of the previous .INF file that was used to install this adapter. The example for the Compaq card follows:

```
InfOption"="CPQNF3"
```

The *Component Type* Value

```
Type           component className [lowerClass]
REG_SZ
```

Tip

The classes listed by this value are not related to the OLE and DDE classes found under the [HKEY_LOCAL_MACHINE\SOFTWARE\Classes Registry] key.

Tip

A *logical endpoint* informs the protocol that it should stop searching for bindable adapters. If you want the binding protocol to stop searching for adapter bindings, set the first [Yes¦No] parameter to Yes, making this a logical endpoint.

This value states the component type by defining it as network component classes. The example for the Compaq card follows:

```
type="CpqNF3Sys ndisDriver CpqNF3Driver"
```

The `component` variable shows the name of the component to be defined as `CpqNF3Sys`.

The `className` variable shows the upper class that is assigned to the component `ndisDriver`.

The `[lowerClass]` variable shows the lower class that is assigned to the component `CpqNF3Driver`.

The *Predefined Class* Value

```
Predefined class      NewClassName      OldClassName¦basic [Yes¦No]
REG_SZ
```

This key follows the same convention for the class value and is read from the adapter's .INF file. It may or may not exist, depending on the network adapter.

Values That Can Be Added for Control

```
Hidden                0 or 1
REG_DWORD
```

You can add this value and set it equal to 1 to prevent the adapter from appearing in the list shown in the Adapters tab of the Network applet. This value prevents users from being able to modify this card.

```
Review        0 or 1
REG_DWORD
```

Add this value and set it equal to 1 to enable bindings review. When set to 1, Windows NT reads the component's .INF file, if any bindings are changed. This value enables network components to modify binding information and/or obtain information for new or modified connections.

Sharing Capabilities

```
Interface     InterfaceName UpperClass "objectName" NamingMethod
REG_MULTI_SZ
```

This value allows one component's capabilities to be made available to other system components.

The `InterfaceName` variable is the token name for the secondary interface.

Tip
The lower class name may be missing; in this case, the first (or upper level) class type name is used to define both upper and lower classes.

The UpperClass variable is the interface belonging to this class. (LowerClass is the primary interface.)

The ObjectName variable is the name that Windows NT uses when creating the device name.

The namingMethod variable determines how the bindings appear.

This is an optional key and is not used for the sample Compaq card.

Components Role

```
Use
REG_SZ service¦driver¦transport¦adapter [Yes¦No]  [Yes¦No]
```

This value shows the role assigned to the component. If the entry is missing, a setting of service is assumed. The example for the Compaq card follows:

```
use"="driver"
```

service. Exists for end user support. An EventLog entry is made if the service exists but has no available transport (bindings are 0).

driver. Supports the associated driver/card. If no bindings are included for a given driver, that driver is not loaded. No error appears because no "denial of service" occurred.

transport. Is used only to support services. As with the Driver entry, it does not load unless necessary.

adapter. Hardware devices are always assigned as an adapter. Network components can be assigned to be a driver, transport, or service.

The first Yes¦No variable is optional. If it exists, it must be defined as Yes or No (stating whether driver group names are to be used in place of the specific driver dependencies). The second Yes¦No value is also optional and must also be set to Yes or No (stating whether transport group names are to be used in place of the specific transport dependencies). If either of these Yes¦No values is present and set to Yes, Windows NT creates dependency references based on group names instead of specific service names.

The Ncpa Key

The next place you find the value CpqNF3 is under the [HKEY_LOCAL_MACHINE\ SOFTWARE\Microsoft\Ncpa] key. This key was discussed briefly earlier in this chapter and will be discussed in depth in Chapter 19, "Configuring TCP/IP."

The Registry search utility finds one more entry for CpqNF3 under the Ncpa key; the next key found that contains this name is [HKEY_LOCAL_MACHINE\SOFTWARE\ Microsoft\WindowsNT\CurrentVersion\NetworkCards]. All installed network cards are found under this key.

Also found under this key is a subkey named 1; this is the NETWORKCARD# that you found under the RefCount value. There are several values under this 1 subkey, which are described in the following sections.

The *ServiceName* Value

```
ServiceName          Service Name String
REG_SZ
```

This is the same value as discussed previously, except that it gives the service name found in the \Device\CpqNF31 value listed under the [HKEY_LOCAL_MACHINE\HARDWARE\ RESOURCEMAP\OtherDrivers\CpqNF3] key. Thus, the example for the Compaq card follows:

```
"ServiceName"="CpqNF31"
```

You will take a closer look at this Service key in the Service key section later in this chapter.

The *Manufacturer* Value

```
Manufacturer         Manufacturer String
REG_SZ
```

This value shows the manufacturer of the card as read from the Manufacturer entry in the adapter's .INF file. The example for the Compaq card is, of course

```
"Manufacturer"="Compaq"
```

The *Description* Value

```
Description          Network Card Description String
REG_SZ
```

This value gives the complete description of the network card, as discovered by Windows NT from the adapter's .INF file. As shown in Figure 6.5, this is also the text string that can be seen in the Item Notes section of the Network applet's Adapters tab. The example for the Compaq card follows:

```
"Description"="Compaq Integrated NetFlex-3 10 T UTP Module Network
Adapter"
```

Figure 6.5 The Network dialog box's Item Notes area.

The *ProductName* Value

```
ProductName          Product Name String
REG_SZ
```

This is the product name as read from the `ProductSoftwareNameSection` of the .INF file. An example for the Compaq card follows:

```
"ProductName"="CpqNF3"
```

The *Title* Text String

```
Title    Title String
REG_SZ
```

This text string is seen in the Network Adapters section of the Network applet's Adapters tab (refer to Figure 6.5). An example for the Compaq card follows:

```
"Title"="[1] Integrated NetFlex-3 10 T UTP Module PCI Bus 0"
```

The Service Key

The last key found during the Registry search is the Service key, which appears in the subkey `[HKEY_LOCAL_MACHINE\SYSTEM\CurrentControlSet\Services\CpqNF31]`. The values under this key are described in the following sections.

The *Type* Value

```
Type       1 or 4
REG_DWORD
```

`Type` specifies that the service is for a driver or an adapter. `0x1` means driver and `0x4` means adapter, so an example for the Compaq card follows:

```
"Type"=dword:00000004
```

The *Start* Value

```
Start
REG_DWORD
```

`Start` is used to load this service on demand. A value of `0x3` means that it can be loaded. An example for the Compaq card follows:

```
"Start"=dword:00000003
```

Author Note

The subkey `[HKEY_LOCAL_MACHINE\SOFTWARE\Microsoft\WindowsNT\CurrentVersion\NetworkCards\1\NetRules]` follows the same convention as the `NetRules` section, discussed earlier in this chapter.

The *ErrorControl* Value

```
ErrorControl          0 or 1
REG_DWORD
```

This is a Service key default. A value of `0x1` means normal error handling. An example for the Compaq card follows:

```
"ErrorControl"=dword:00000001
```

There are two subkeys found under this key. The Parameters key is described in the next section; the Linkage key and its subkeys are discussed in Chapter 19.

The Parameters Key

The last key discussed in this chapter is `[HKEY_LOCAL_MACHINE\SYSTEM\ CurrentControlSet\Services\CpqNF31\Parameters]`. This key determines the hardware-specific settings for the network card. All values may not be present for every card.

The values under this key are discussed in the following sections.

The *CableType* Value

```
CableType             1 or 2
REG_DWORD
```

This value shows the cable type as either an unshielded twisted pair (`UTP=1`) or a shielded twisted pair (`STP=2`). This value is used only for Proteon 1390 adapter cards.

The *CardType* Value

```
CardType              Decimal Number
REG_DWORD
```

This value shows the card type installed by Windows NT. If a manufacturer uses the same driver for all of its network cards, the driver checks the `CardType` value to find the installed card's model number. This value cannot be changed using the Network applet. Some settings for this value follow:

Value	Setting	Equals
DEC	1	DEC100
	2	DEC20x
	3	DEC PC
	4	DEC Station
	5	DEC422
	7	DEC101
Proteon	1	Proteon 1390
	2	Proteon 1990

Value	Setting	Equals
Ungermann–Bass	2	UB PC
	3	UB EOTP
	4	UBPS

The *CardSpeed* Value

```
CardSpeed              4 or 16 Mps
REG_DWORD
```

This value shows the speed of the card as 4 or 16 megabits per second in hexadecimal form (0x4 or 0x10), and is used only for Proteon 1390 adapter cards.

The *DMAChannel* Value

```
DMAChannel             5, 6, or 7
REG_DWORD
```

This value shows the DMA channel that the card is using.

The *Duplex* Value

```
Duplex                 1 or 2
REG_DWORD
```

This value shows whether the card can use duplexing. The value for the Compaq card follows:

```
"Duplex"=dword:00000001
```

The *NetworkAddress* Value

```
NetworkAddress
REG_SZ                 Number
```

Some network cards have the network address permanently set in the adapter's EPROM. If the card has this burned-in address, but the address is not available on the system, the card will use this value instead of the burned-in address. The Network applet can be used to change this value for Token-Ring adapters, but it cannot be used for Ethernet adapters.

Author Note

Some routers do not support duplexing with some cards. If you turn on duplexing and experience router problems, turn duplexing off via this Registry value and try again.

The *Transceiver* Value

```
Transceiver          1 or 2
REG_DWORD
```

This value shows whether the transceiver is external (1) or on board (2). If using a DEC/Intel/Xerox (DIX) connection, set this value to 1.

This value can also be blank, as in the case of the Compaq card:

```
"NetworkAddress"=""
```

The *SlotNumber* Value

```
SlotNumber           Hex Value
REG_DWORD
```

This value shows the number of the computer's adapter slot in which the card is installed, in hexadecimal format. The value for the Compaq card follows:

```
"SlotNumber"=dword:ffffffff
```

The *BusNumber* Value

```
BusNumber            Number
REG_DWORD
```

This value defines the bus number, and its starting value is 0 for computers with one bus type. If the computer has more than one bus, such as an ISA bus and a PCI bus, the second bus is 1, the third 2, and so on. The general case is given by this formula:

```
BusNumber = (Number of Busses)-1
```

The default for this value is usually 0, but the value depends on the installation of the card.

An example for the Compaq card follows:

```
"BusNumber"=dword:00000000
```

The *BusType* Value

```
BusType              0 to 11
REG_DWORD
```

This value states the type of bus for the PC. Like the BusNumber value, it cannot be changed from the Control Panel.

> **Tip**
>
> If an ISA network card is being installed on a PC with a PCI bus, and the card or network is not recognized, set BusNumber to 0; the PC should then recognize the card.
>
> Also, this is one of the few network values that cannot be changed via the Network applet in the Control Panel.

The valid numbers and their meanings follow:

Number	Meaning
0	MIPS (Jazz-Internal bus)
1	ISA bus
2	EISA bus
3	MCA bus
4	TcChannel bus
5	PCI
6	VMEBus
7	NuBus
8	PCMCIABus
9	CBus
10	MPIBus
11	MPSABus

An example for the Compaq card follows:
```
"BusType"=dword:00000005
```

The *MediaType* Value

```
MediaType        1 to 5
REG_DWORD
```

The value shows what type of network the card is using. The values and their meanings follow:

Value	Meaning
1	Ethernet
2	Token-Ring
3	ARCnet
4	FDDI network
5	Apple LocalTalk

An example for the Compaq card follows:
```
"MediaType"=dword:00000001
```

The *MaximumPacketSize* Value

```
MaximumPacketSize    Number
REG_DWORD
```

If using an IBM Token-Ring, this value states the maximum packet size that the adapter may transmit. If the card is used to send data across a bridge that uses smaller packet sizes on the destination network than are used on the card's home network, set this value to the smaller size.

The *MemoryMapped* Value

```
MemoryMapped      0 or 1
REG_DWORD
```

This value equals 1 if it is memory-mapped, and 0 if it is not. If the card cannot be memory-mapped, then this value will not exist.

The *MemoryMappedBaseAddress* Value

```
MemoryMappedBaseAddress    Hexadecimal Memory Address
REG_DWORD
```

If the card has memory address settings set by the manufacturer, this value shows the base memory (I/O) address that is used by the card. This value must match the manufacturer's setting.

The *IRQ* Value

```
InterruptNumber    IRQ Number
REG_DWORD
```

This value shows the interrupt request number (IRQ), in hexadecimal form, that the installed card is using.

An example for the Compaq card follows:

```
"InterruptNumber"=dword:0000000b
```

This translates to IRQ 11.

The *IoBaseAddress* Value

```
IoBaseAddress        Hexadecimal Number
REG_DWORD
```

This value is an optional one that shows the I/O port base address in hexadecimal form. For some adapters, this entry means that the card is a primary card (1) or a secondary card (2).

> **Author Note**
>
> The InterruptNumber value may appear as Irq for some network cards. These values hold the same information for their specific cards.

7

Configuring Printers

- **The Printer applet**

  The Registry settings produced by the Printer applet are discussed here. This applet is available from the Control Panel or from the Settings selection of the Start menu.

- **The Printer Properties dialog box**

  This dialog box is where you configure printer properties. It is accessed by executing one of the icons in the Printer applet or by pressing the right mouse button while highlighting a Printer applet icon and selecting Properties.

- **User settings for printers**

  This section discusses Printer Registry keys and values that can be set by the user, as well as other values found under the Print key.

- **Other printer settings in the Registry**

  This section discusses the printing keys and values associated with Windows debugging and Windows 3.1.

The Printer Applet

Open the Control Panel and launch the Printers applet. If no printers have been added to Windows NT, you see only the Add Printer Wizard. Launch this wizard; first choose to install a network or local printer, and then select a port (see Figure 7.1).

The Printers listing is read from the NTPRINT.INF file located in the %SYSTEMROOT%\INF directory. Choose the printer that you want to install from this list and click the Next button. Now enter a name for your printer, which will be listed as a subkey under the [HKEY_LOCAL_MACHINE\SYSTEM\CurrentControlSet\ Control\Print\Printers] key.

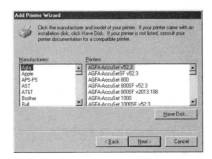

Figure 7.1   The Add Printer Wizard.

This Print key and its subkeys contain information about supporting DLLs, drivers, and all installed printers. These subkeys—Environments, Forms, Monitors, Printers, and Providers—will be discussed later in the chapter. If an OEM printer manufacturer adds its own keys, this is where you find them.

Click the Next button; you are asked if you want this printer to be shared. If you choose to share the printer, enter a share name for the printer, as shown in Figure 7.2.

This name is stored in two places—first in the following Registry value under the `[HKEY_LOCAL_MACHINE\SYSTEM\CurrentControlSet\Services\LanmanServer\Shares]` key:

```
DeviceName    MaxUses, Path, Permissions, Remark, Type
MultiSZ
```

`MaxUses` indicates the maximum number of computers that can be simultaneously connected to this printer. Although the upper limit is infinite (`0xffffffff`), the practical limit is determined by the network hardware over which the printer is shared.

Figure 7.2   Sharing a printer.

`Path` indicates the path of the printer on the network—for example, `Path=\\\$WksName$\\Brother HJ-770`. `Permissions` is not used; the default is `0`. `Remark` refers to the manufacturer's name and/or printer model name. `Type` indicates a hardware or software device. A `1` indicates a hardware device.

The second place where this name is stored is in the Printer Properties dialog box, as described in the next section. Click the Next button, choose to print a page, and click Finish.

The Printer Properties Dialog Box

After Windows NT finishes copying files, a printer icon with the printer name that you assigned with the Add Printers Wizard shows up in the Printers applet screen. Highlight this printer icon and press the right mouse button; you see the Printer Properties dialog box, as shown in Figure 7.3. All of the settings on this dialog box are set in values that can be found under the `[KEY_LOCAL_MACHINE\SYSTEM\CurrentControlSet\Control\Print\Printers\HPLaserJet 5]` key.

The General Tab

The settings for the General tab, as seen in Figure 7.3, are stored in these values:

- Comment box:
  `"Description"=REG_SZ "HP 5 Printer"`
- Location box:
  `"Location"=REG_SZ "Sandra's Desktop PC"`
- Driver drop-down list box:
  `"Printer Driver"=REG_SZ "HP LaserJet 5"`
- Separator Page Button dialog box:
  `"Separator File"="C:\\WIN\\system32\\pcl.sep"`
- Print Processor screen:
  `Default data Type : "Datatype"="RAW"`
  `Print Processor : "Print Processor"="winprint"`

> **Tip**
>
> Although SystemRoot\SYSTEM32 is the default spool directory, a different path can be created for spool print jobs. Create the value `DefaultSpoolDirectory`, with a REG_SZ data type, and set it to the path of the new spool directory under the `[HKEY_LOCAL_MACHINE\SYSTEM\CurrentControlSet\Control\Print\Printers]` key. This value creates a new spool area for all printers.
>
> If you do not want to use this spool setting for every printer, however, you can create a printer-specific spool path by adding the value `SpoolDirectory`, typing **REG_SZ**, and setting it to the new spool path under the key `[HKEY_LOCAL_MACHINE\SYSTEM\CurrentControlSet\Control\Print\Printers\` *[printer name]*.

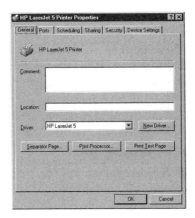

Figure 7.3 The General tab of the Printer Properties dialog box.

The Ports Tab

The Ports tab, shown in Figure 7.4, is used to assign printer ports to the specified printer.

The setting for the LPT1 value corresponds to the box that is checked. This value can have more than one entry.

■ Port column check boxes:

```
"Port"="LPT1:"
```

The Scheduling Tab

The Scheduling tab is used to set spooling priorities for the specified printer (see Figure 7.5).

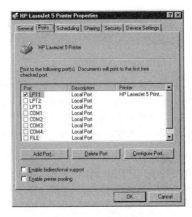

Figure 7.4 The Ports tab of the Printer Properties dialog box.

The first set of radial buttons is in the Available frame. If the Always button is selected, each of the following values is set to 0:

```
"StartTime"=dword:00000000
"UntilTime"=dword:00000000
```

If the From button is selected, the previous values have this range:

```
From "0" (7PM) to "1439" (6:59 PM)
```

The next set of radial buttons determines spooling attributes and directs the printer to either spool print documents or to print directly to the printer. If the radial button for spooling is selected, two additional radial buttons are enabled. All four of these buttons are encapsulated within the hexadecimal number of the following value:

```
"ChangeID"=dword:005f58b1
```

The setting for this value has a wide range of settings, in hexadecimal form, depending on the combinations of the selected radial buttons.

The Sharing Tab

The Sharing tab, as seen in Figure 7.6, determines how the selected printer is shared across the network.

As mentioned earlier in the chapter, the value that stores the Share Name field follows:

```
"Share Name"="HP LaserJet 5"
```

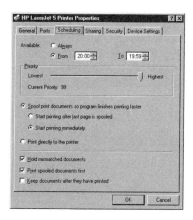

Figure 7.5   The Scheduling tab of the Printer Properties dialog box.

Author Note

Selecting the Always radial button is the same as setting the From and To fields to the same number. This in effect yields a range of zero, which is the setting for the Always button.

User Settings for Printers

This section discusses Registry keys and values that hold printing preferences, which can be set by the user.

Printer Listing

All printers installed by the user are listed as string values under the key
`[HKEY_CURRENT_USER\Software\Microsoft\Windows NT\CurrentVersion\Devices]`:

```
  Deviceoutput           device-name, device-driver, port-connection
  REG_SZ
```

`device-name` is the printer name as it appears in the Printers applet screen. `device-driver` is the filename of the device driver; the default `winspool`. `port-connection` is the output device to which the printer sends a file. This will be one of the values listed in the port screen of the Add Printers Wizard. The default is `LPT1`.

Setting a Default Printer

Open the Printers applet, select a printer, and press the right mouse button. The third menu item that appears is Set as Default. Selecting this item sets the Device value under this key: `[HKEY_CURRENT_USER\Software\Microsoft\WindowsNT\CurrentVersion\Windows]`. This value is formatted the same as the preceding Device value. The other printer-related value under this key is

```
  DosPrint      Yes or No
  REG_SZ
```

Set this value to `Yes` to use MS-DOS interrupts; if set to `No`, data is sent directly to the printer's assigned printer port.

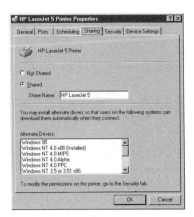

Figure 7.6   The Sharing tab of the Printer Properties dialog box.

Other Values under the Print Key

The subkeys of the Print key [`HKEY_LOCAL_MACHINE\SYSTEM\CurrentControlSet\`
`Control\Print`] are Environments, Forms, Monitors, Printers, and Providers. Before I
discuss these subkeys, however, you must first look at the values found under the main
Print key:

```
BeepEnabled   0 or 1
REG_DWORD
```

When this value is set to 1 and a remote printer job receives an error on a certain
print server, the computer beeps each time a job is retried every 10 seconds. The
default is 0 (disabled).

```
DisableServerThread   0 or 1
REG_DWORD
```

When this value is set to 1, the browse thread on the current machine is disabled.
This thread is used to call and notify other printer servers to announce that this
printer exists. The default is 0 (false).

Fast Printer Threshold Values

The following values determine the time that a computer's printer waits before timing
out:

```
FastPrintSlowDownThreshold    Setting in Milliseconds
REG_DWORD
```

```
FastPrintThrottleTimeout    Setting in Milliseconds
REG_DWORD
```

If your printer pauses with spooling enabled, it probably did not receive data within
a certain timeout period. Now, because the spooler throttles back on sent data when
the `FastPrintSlowDownThreshold` setting is reached, it should be set to a large enough
number to prevent printer timeouts. Also, because the `FastPrintThrottleTimeout`
value causes one byte of data per period to be sent to the printer until the
`FastPrintSlowDownThreshold` threshold is passed, the number of the
`FastPrintSlowDownThreshold` value should not be set higher than about five seconds.

The default for `FastPrintSlowDownThreshold` is 2,000 (two seconds).

The `FastPrintSlowDownTheshold` default is given by taking the
`FastPrintWaitTimeout` setting and dividing it by the `FastPrintThrottleTimeout`
setting.

```
FastPrintWaitTimeout Setting in Milliseconds
REG_DWORD
```

With spooling enabled, the port thread must be in sync with the spooling application.
This setting defines how long the port thread waits before it pauses the current print job
and moves on to the next one. The default is 24,000 milliseconds or 4 minutes.

```
NetPrinterDecayPeriod            Setting in Milliseconds
REG_DWORD
```

This value gives the time, in milliseconds, that the PC caches a network printer. This cache presents the list of printers if the Browse dialog box is used. The default is 600,000 milliseconds or 1 hour.

```
PortThreadPriority    Priority values
REG_DWORD
```

This value sets the priority of the port threads, which send output to the printer. Possible settings are

```
THREAD_PRIORITY_ABOVE_NORMAL
```

```
THREAD_PRIORITY_NORMAL
```

```
THREAD_PRIORITY_BELOW_NORMAL
```

The default is `THREAD_PRIORITY_NORMAL`.

```
PriorityClass
REG_DWORD
```

Although Windows NT 4.0 does not support this value, you do not have to remove it from the Registry. Windows NT ignores it and uses `SpoolerPriority` instead, described in the following sections.

```
SchedulerThreadPriority      0, 1, or 0xFFFFFFFF
REG_DWORD
```

This value sets the scheduler thread priority that is used by Windows NT to assign print jobs to ports. This setting determines the order in which the processor runs this thread.

Possible settings:

`0`	Normal
`1`	Above Normal
`0xFFFFFFFF`	Below Normal

```
SpoolerPriority    Priority value
REG_DWORD
```

This value defines the print spooler's priority class and normally does not appear in the Registry. If it is not present, the spooler's priority class is set to the default for this key, `NORMAL_PRIORITY_CLASS`.

Possible settings:

```
IDLE_PRIORITY_CLASS
```

```
NORMAL_PRIORITY_CLASS
```

```
HIGH_PRIORITY_CLASS
```

If there are any other values listed under this key, they are ignored.

Environment Keys and Values

The settings for a printer's environment can be found under the [HKEY_LOCAL_MACHINE\ SYSTEM\CurrentControlSet\Control\Print\Environments] key. Listed under this key are subkeys for several different operating systems. These subkeys are:

Windows 4.0   Windows NT Alpha_AXP

Windows NT PowerPC   Windows NT R4000

Windows NT x86

Each of these keys has, in turn, several subkeys; these are \Drivers and \Print Processors. \Drivers, in turn, may have subkeys with the name of each installed printer, listing values for printer drivers and other files needed to operate the printer. \Print Processors lists the Windows NT print service used to manage the Windows NT print services.

Under the \Drivers subkey, there may be a PrinterDriverName subkey that may list these values:

```
Configuration FileFile Name String
REG_SZ
```

This value states the filename of the configuration DLL that is used for the selected printer environment. The default is the filename of the installed DLL.

```
Data FileFile Name String      Filename
REG_SZ
```

This value states the name of the printer datafile used for the selected print environment. The default is the installed .PPD filename.

```
DriverFile Name String
REG_SZ
```

This value states the name of the driver DLL for the selected print environment. The default is the filename of the installed DLL.

```
VersionVersion Number
REG_DWORD
```

Author Note

You may remember the PriorityClass value in previous versions of Windows NT. This value is replaced by the SpoolerPriority value in Windows NT 4.0.

Tip

Most printers are installed with a setting under the Windows NT x86 key.

Author Note

A subkey named \Version-2 may exist between the \Drivers subkey and the PrinterDriverName subkey.

This value states the installed print driver's version number.

The \Print Processors subkey may list the following value:

```
DriverFileName.DLL
REG_SZ
```

This shows the DLL used by Windows NT to manage printer services. The default is winprint.dll.

Print Monitor Keys and Values

The Print Monitor values are found in the subkeys listed under the
[HKEY_LOCAL_MACHINE\SYSTEM\CurrentControlSet\Control\Print\Monitors\] key.
These keys are:

\Digital Network Port

\Local Port

\PJL Monitor Port

Although the Digital Network Port key has several subkeys listed under it, there is only one value found here:

```
DriverDLL FileName
REG_SZ
```

This states the DLL used for the network printer port.

The subkeys of the Digital Network Port key are discussed in the following sections.

The Options Key

The following REG_DWORD values, with defaults, may be found under this key:

```
Adapter=0
ConnectionType=0x1
DlcBufferSize=0x27100
DlcT1Timer=0x5
DlcT2Timer=0x2
DlcTiTimer=0x3
EventLogging=0x7
LinkStationsUsed=0x40
StatusUpdateInterval=0x3c
```

The Files Key

This key lists files used by the Windows NT print system. The values found under this key are:

```
RootDLL File
REG_SZ
```

This value shows the print service DLL and path.

```
NumberSYS File
REG_SZ
```

This value shows other files used by the print service and their path. There may be more than one of these entries.

The Ports Key

There may be a \Ports subkey, with a *<portname>* subkey under it, containing the following value:

```
PrintSwitchControl character string
REG_SZ
```

This value states the format control character that the LPR Print Monitor sends to the print server using the print control file. If this value is not found in the Registry, a lowercase 1 is sent as the control character. This value can be set to any string; thus, there is no default for this value. The first letter of the string is used as the control character, ignoring the rest of the string. Depending on your printer, an f may need to be used instead of a 1.

Print Providers Keys and Values

The print service providers have subkeys under the [HKEY_LOCAL_MACHINE\SYSTEM\CurrentControlSet\Control\Print\Providers\Print Services Name] key.

LanMan Print Services is the default key found under the previous key. The print and point features of Windows NT can be controlled by the values listed under this key. You can enable the drivers so that they can be loaded only from a trusted print server rather than from the user's server.

```
NameDLL filename
REG_SZ
```

This states the name of the DLL used by this print provider. The default DLL is win32spl.dll.

```
LoadTrustedDrivers    0 or 1
REG_DWORD
```

If this value is set to 1 (enabled), the printer drivers are not installed from the remote print server but instead are installed from the path specified in TrustedDriverPath. The default setting is 0.

```
TrustedDriverPathDriver Install Path String
REG_DWORD
```

This states the printer driver install path. This path also states the trusted print server shares. Just connecting to a print server does not mean that the printer drivers will be installed from that server, however. In fact, only the driver settings will be installed from that server because printer drivers are always copied only from the `TrustedDriverPath` setting.

Other Printer Settings in the Registry

The Windows debugging and Windows 3.1 printing keys and their values may or may not be found on your computer. This section discusses other settings that affect printing under Windows NT.

Windows Debugging

The values found under the `[HKEY_CURRENT_USER\SOFTWARE\Microsoft\WindowsNT\CurrentVersion\Windows]` key control the display and printing of any error and/or warning messages when running the debug build of Windows NT. These entries have meaning only when you debug Windows Manager code. These values are

```
fPrintError          0 or 1
REG_SZ
```

If this value is set to 1, error messages generated during debugging are printed. A setting of 0 suppresses the printing of error messages. The default is 1, or true.

```
FPrintFileLine       0 or 1
REG_SZ
```

If this value is set to 1, the file and line numbers that generated the error during debugging are printed. A setting of 0 suppresses the printing of file and line numbers. The default is 0, or false.

```
FprintVerbose        0 or 1
REG_SZ
```

Tip

Network popups for remote print jobs are controlled by adding the value `NetPopup` under the subkey [HKEY_LOCAL_MACHINE\SYSTEM\CurrentControlSet\Control\Print\Providers]:

```
        NetPopup          0 or 1
        REG_DWORD
```

If set to 1, this value enables the display of a pop-up message for remote network print jobs. If this key is present, its default setting is 1.

This value states the level of detail to be printed if warnings and/or error messages are generated during debugging.

    0 Standard debugging data is displayed.

    1 All data is displayed.

The default is 0, or false.

```
FprintWarning          0 or 1
REG_SZ
```

If this value is set to 1, warnings generated during debugging are printed. A setting of 0 suppresses the printing of warnings. The default is 1, or true.

```
FpromptOnError              0 or 1
REG_SZ
```

If this value is set to 1, the user is prompted by the debugger if error messages are generated during debugging. If set to 0, there is no prompting.

The default is 1, or true.

```
FpromptOnVerbose            0 or 1
REG_SZ
```

This value sets the level of user prompts if warnings and errors are generated during debugging.

    0 Standard data is displayed.

    1 All data is displayed.

The default is 0, or false.

```
FpromptOnWarning            0 or 1
REG_SZ
```

This value determines users' notification by the debugger if warnings are generated during debugging.

    0 Do not prompt.

    1 Prompt.

The default is 0, or false.

16-Bit Windows 3.x Application Values

These values are used by 16-bit applications that were designed to run under Windows 3.1. These values are found under the same [HKEY_CURRENT_USER\SOFTWARE\Microsoft\ Windows NT\CurrentVersion\Windows] key. The values listed here follow:

```
DeviceNotSelectedTimeout    Time in Seconds
REG_SZ
```

This value states the time that the system waits for a device to be turned on. If a printer is not turned on during this time, Windows NT does not print to it. Depending on the printer, Windows NT may post an error message if the printer is not already switched on. The default is 15.

```
SpoolerTrue or False          Boolean
REG_SZ
```

If this value is set to False, the output is not sent through the Print Manager. This setting turns the Print Manager off; the default is Yes.

```
TransmissionRetryTimeoutTime in Seconds
REG_SZ
```

This value states the amount of time, in seconds, that Windows NT attempts transmission retries. If a successful transmission does not happen within this amount of time, then the Print Manager displays a message stating that the printer is not receiving characters (the system default value). The default is 45.

8

Other Hardware Issues

● **HP ScanJet 4c**

This section discusses Registry settings used by the Hewlett-Packard HP ScanJet scanner.

● **Tape backups**

This section discusses how to use the Registry to solve problems that can occur when using tape backup drives with Windows NT 4.0. Also discussed are settings for the Sytos Plus tape backup drive.

● **Iomega Zip drives**

This section discusses Registry settings used by Iomega Zip drives.

HP ScanJet 4c

The HP ScanJet 4c is a SCSI device that must be attached to a SCSI controller card. You need to use a SCSI adapter that allows for changing the IRQ and base address settings.

The Registry values that can be used to manipulate the IRQ and base address of SCSI adapter cards are found under the [`HKEY_LOCAL_MACHINE\SYSTEM\`
`CurrentControlSet\Services\`*AdapterCard*`\Parameters\Device`] key, where *AdapterCard* is the name of the adapter, as read from the adapters .INF file, such as sym53416. These values follow:

```
DriverParameter     /IRQ /Base Address
REG_Multi_SZ
```

Both the IRQ and base address are contained in this value and are formatted:
IRQ: `/IRQ=10`

base address: `/IO=0x220`

This Registry value can also be set by using the HPRESSET.EXE program provided with the scanner.

Another item provided with the scanner is the HP ScanJet Scanners applet in the Control Panel, as seen in Figure 8.1.

This applet is registered in the Control Panel with the following value under the key [HKEY_CURRENT_USER\Control Panel\MMCPL], where the DLL path will be C:\\WINNT\\System32\\hpscnmgr.dll:

```
ScanJet          DLL Path
REG_SZ
```

If you now launch this applet and choose the SCSI tab, the HP ScanJet Properties dialog box shown in Figure 8.2 appears.

The SCSI tab includes a drop-down list box that lists all of the SCSI adapters installed on the system. This information is read from values found under the subkey(s) of the [HKEY_LOCAL_MACHINE\HARDWARE\RESOURCEMAP\ScsiAdapter\] key.

Figure 8.1 The HP ScanJet Scanners applet.

Troubleshooting

You may experience hardware problems if you are using older SCSI boards under Windows NT 4.0 that do not allow for changes in IRQ (such as the HP SYM53400 SCSI adapter, which can only use IRQ 5). You have to upgrade this adapter to the HP SYM53416, which will allow a wider choice of IRQ settings. If you have problems with other old SCSI boards, try upgrading them.

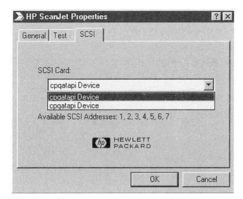

Figure 8.2   The HP ScanJet Properties dialog box.

Tape Backups

Tape backups have historically had problems when used under Windows NT. A few general and specific issues are discussed here.

General Problems

Some problems that can occur when you use tape backups with Windows NT 4.0 are common across manufacturers. Some of these problems are discussed in the following sections.

Verify Backup

If you use the Windows NT 4.0 native backup software (BACKUP.EXE) to back up the SystemRoot%\System32\Config directory and then choose the Verify After Backup option, the software will not verify these files. This is because the Verify option is designed to skip the files in the %SystemRoot%\System32\Config directory. This directory is where the volatile log and Windows NT Registry files are kept. These files are almost always being written to and the files can actually change between the time they are backed up and when they are verified. Although the files in this directory can not be verified as being backed up, all files are actually backed up on the tape.

You can use the registry to back up these files by setting the following value, found under the [HKEY_CURRENT_USER\Software\Microsoft\Ntbackup\Backup Engine] key:

```
Backup files inuse        0 or 1
REG_DWORD
```

Set this value to 1 to back up files that are still in use, and to the default of 0 to skip the backup of files that are still in use.

Another value that controls the backup of these types of files is the following value found under the [`HKEY_CURRENT_USER\Software\Microsoft\Ntbackup\User Interface`] key:

```
Skip Open Files      0, 1, or 2
REG_SZ
```

This value determines the action that Windows NT Backup will take when it tries to back up files that are either open or unreadable:

Setting	Action
0.	Wait, do not skip file.
1.	Skip opened or unreadable files.
2.	Wait to back up files, as specified by the `Wait time` value.

```
Wait Time            0 to 65535 seconds
REG_SZ
```

This value specifies the time to wait when it tries to open files that are in use or unreadable. This value is only used when `Skip Open Files` is set to 2. The default setting is 30 seconds.

Using RDISK.EXE to Back Up Files

The best way to back up system files is to use the Windows NT 4.0 *Emergency Repair Disk* (ERD) program, RDISK.EXE. This backup method is particularly useful when you need to restore an NTFS partition that has become unbootable. You can also use this method to replace mirrored partition files without breaking the mirror.

You can create an ERD disk and then use it to replace any Windows NT 4.0 system file.

Old Firmware

If you use a tape backup with Windows NT and you experience any of the following problems, the firmware of your tape backup controller card needs to be upgraded, or the card must be replaced with a newer one:

- Your SCSI internal tape drive works fine for a few days and the following error message appears while running the tape backup software:

  ```
  The tape device has been detected and the tape driver started.
  However, the tape device is not responding.
  ```

Tip

If you want to increase the reliability of the backup data, use a higher-end tape drive with *Error Correction Control* (ECC) . These drives actually check for errors on the tape. This feature can cause problems with some drives, however, as discussed later in this chapter.

If you reboot Windows NT, the tape drive works for another few days with the same results.

■ The tape cartridge does not always eject correctly, generating this error message:
```
Tape device reported error on request to get device status. Error
reported: Hardware failure.
```

To view the firmware version number in the Registry, open a registry editor and find the key [HKEY_LOCAL_MACHINE\HARDWARE\DEVICEMAP\SCSI\ScsiPort#\ ScsiBus#\TargetID#\LogicalUnitId0\], where the # symbol is the Scsiport#, Bus#, and SCSI-ID# where the tape drive is connected. Look at this value:
```
Identifier         vendor Model# firmware version number.
REG_MULTI_SZ
```

The firmware section of this string shows the firmware revision number. Use this number when you get an upgrade from the tape drive's manufacturer.

The Sytos Plus Tape Backup Drive

If you have Sytos Plus Tape Backup, you may experience a few bugs when you use it with the Windows NT 4.0 Tape Backup software. These bugs and their fixes follow:

■ *Restore problem.* If you use a Sytos Plus tape backup drive, the Windows NT Backup program may not be able to restore files from the tape if the file that is being restored spans more than one tape, or if the entire file is on the second tape. If you have this problem, find the [HKEY_CURRENT_USER\SOFTWARE\ Microsoft\Ntbackup\Backup Engine\] key, add the *Use Fast File Restore* value, and set it to 0. Restart Windows NT and try the backup again.

■ *Translation error.* If you are trying to restore or catalog a Sytos Plus tape, you may see the error An error occurred during translation of data to or from the tape in the drive. This error occurs because data on the current tape has set the ECC flag value in the Windows NT Registry to the wrong value. To correct this, find the [HKEY_CURRENT_USER\SOFTWARE\Microsoft\Ntbackup\ Translators] key, and set the following value to 0:
```
Sytos Plus ECC flag      0, 1, or 2
REG_DWORD
```

Troubleshooting
Before you can use the Windows NT 4.0 RDISK.EXE program, you must have the correct version of the SETUPDD.SYS file. Install Service Pack 2 or later. For new installations, copy the SETUPDD.SYS file from the service pack to your Windows NT 4.0 Setup disk number 2 (created during setup), and then use this disk to install Windows NT.

Possible settings follow:

0   Off   The NTBACKUP searches the tape for a software ECC.
1   On   The NTBACKUP searches the tape for a software ECC.
2   Auto   NTBACKUP finds whether an ECC is on the tape by
              checking the data on the tape.

Also, depending on the type of tape that you are using, this value needs to be set differently. Use these values for the following tapes:

Tape	Type
4mm DAT	0
8mm DAT	0
1/4 in. 525	0
1/4 in. 150	1

The default for this value is 2.

Iomega Zip Drives

Although Windows NT supports various removable hard disks and magnetic-optical disk drives, all of these drives are treated as hard disks by Windows NT 4.0, and they must be partitioned and given a drive letter.

Because Windows NT treats removable drives as fixed hard drives, and because Windows NT assigns a drive letter to a physical drive first and to logical partitions second, removable drives are assigned drive letters before any logical partitions.

Iomega makes several types of removable disk drives. The following sections discuss the Parallel, IDE, ATAPI, and SCSI Zip drives.

Iomega Parallel Port Zip Drive

This drive is not listed in the Windows NT 4.0 *Hardware Compatibility List* (HCL). There is a driver for this drive available for Windows NT 4.0 that can be downloaded from the Iomega Web site at www.iomega.com. Look for a section called Tech Stuff, then Software, then Iomega FTP, and finally Windows NT Tools.

Tip
Be sure to reset this value back to 1 after restoring the file, or you will experience problems when you restore files that exist entirely on the first tape.

Tip
If the Windows NT 3.x version of the tape backup software was previously installed on your PC, you need to remove this software *before* upgrading it to Windows NT 4.0, or the ECC value cannot be used.

Iomega IDE and ATAPI Zip Drives

If you do not know whether the Iomega Zip drive that you use is an ATAPI or IDE drive, look at the `identifier` value under the `[HKEY_LOCAL_MACHINE\HARDWARE\DEVICEMAP\Scsi\ScsiPort0\ScsiBus0\TargetID0]` key, which was discussed earlier in the "Tape Backups" section. Find the `LogicalUnitId0` key, as shown in Figure 8.3. (The identifier shown in Figure 8.3 is for a Western Digital SCSI hard drive.)

```
Identifier          Drive Identifier Revision Number
REG_MULTI_SZ
```

This value has at least two entries: the first specifies the manufacturer; the second specifies the firmware revision number. An Iomega drive has `IOMEGA ZIP` as the drive identifier. The revision number depends on the type of Iomega drive installed. An ATAPI drive's firmware revision number is `100 23.D`; the IDE firmware revision number is `100 B.29`.

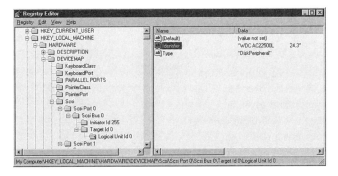

Figure 8.3 The Firmware identifier.

Warning

If the Windows NT system files are installed on a logical partition, and you then add a removable drive to the system, a new drive letter is assigned to the partition that contains the boot partition after Windows NT reboots. This action generates the following error message at startup:

```
ARC path needs to be changed.
```

If a correction is not made for the new drive letter in the BOOT.INI file, Windows NT cannot boot. Even if you modify the BOOT.INI file, however, after Windows NT boots, it won't find many system files and directories because the Registry contains the old drive letter for the boot partition.

You need to open the Registry, find the system-related file entries (application entries are OK), and manually search and replace the old drive letter with the new one. This is why Windows NT system files should always be placed on the C: drive.

Tip

If you use the ATAPI version of the Iomega Zip drive, it will not work initially with Windows NT 4.0. This is because Windows NT identifies this type of Zip drive as a floppy drive and assigns the first available floppy type drive letter (usually B:) to this drive.

Installing the Zip-Fix HotFix available from Microsoft can solve this problem; use FTP to download it from

```
ftp://ftp.microsoft.com/bussys/winnt/winntpublic/fixes/usa/nt40/
hotfixes-postSP3/zip-fix
```

9

Configuring
Notebook Computers

- **PC Cards**

  The support included with Windows NT 4.0 Workstation for PC Cards is limited to
  basic PC Card enabling. This support does not include the PC Card features that are
  available with Windows 95, such as dynamic Plug-and-Play configuration and hot swap-
  ping. There are still many settings that can be used to install and recognize PC Cards with
  Windows NT, however.

- **Standalone versus network configuration**

  Find out how network-connection issues for docked and undocked notebook computers
  are addressed with Registry settings. Although hardware profiles are often used with
  notebook computers, they will be discussed in Chapter 13, "Windows NT Profiles."

PC Cards

PC Cards (formerly known as *PCMCIA cards*) consist of all cards that are connected to
a computer system through the use of a PCMCIA bus. Almost all PCMCIA busses
that you encounter are on notebook computers. These cards are detected during the
execution of NTLDR. *NTLDR* is the NT loader executable that loads and runs
NTDETECT.COM (which reports connected hardware to Windows NT) when
Windows NT boots. These programs are fully discussed in Chapter 10, "Modifying the
Windows NT Workstation Boot Process."

   Installing and configuring PC Cards under Windows NT 4.0 consists of a series of
automatic and manual steps, as discussed in the following sections.

The PCMCIA Applet

One way to determine whether Windows NT has properly detected and configured
your PCMCIA bus and installed PC Cards is to open the Control Panel and look for
a PC Card (PCMCIA) applet, as seen in Figure 9.1.

The information that is displayed by this applet is gathered by NTLDR during the Windows NT boot process. This information is displayed on two tabs: the Socket Status tab and the Controller tab.

The Socket Status Tab

The Socket Status tab contains two items, as seen in Figure 9.2.

The PC cards and sockets are listed below list box shows all of the installed PC Cards, their status, and the socket in which they are installed. The socket number that the card uses is found to the right of the PC Card name.

A Properties button is also on this tab. When this button is clicked, you see another dialog box, shown in Figure 9.3, that contains three tabs: one for PC Card information, one for the PC Card driver, and another for the resources assigned to the card.

The CardInfo Tab

The Manufacturer entry on the CardInfo tab of Figure 9.3 shows the PC Card's manufacturer, as listed under the *ManufacturerID* subkey and the [HKEY_LOCAL_MACHINE\ SYSTEM\CurrentControlSet\Services\Pcmcia\DataBase] key. The *ManufacturerID* is the name of the card's manufacturer—for example, 3COM Corporation for 3COM cards. See Figure 9.4. This key is discussed later in the chapter.

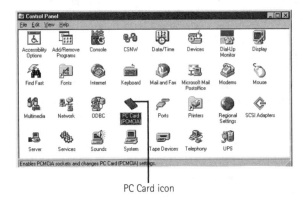

PC Card icon

Figure 9.1 The PC Card (PCMCIA) applet.

> **Troubleshooting**
>
> If you are trying to determine why a particular PC Card is not configured, the presence of the PCMCIA applet's icon, shown in Figure 9.1, will first tell you that the computer has detected the PCMCIA bus. You can then use this applet, along with the following Registry settings, to determine the configuration problem.

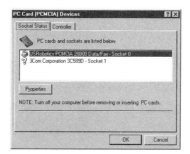

Figure 9.2 PC Card status and socket number.

Figure 9.3 The PC Card Properties dialog box.

The manufacturer's PCMCIA Database key has several ManufacturerID subkeys under it, as seen in Figure 9.4. Find the keys that correspond to your manufacturer's. Under these keys are PC Card-specific keys that have the following `REG_SZ` values under them:

`Driver`   Name of the driver file. Example: Elnk3

`Option`   Name of the .INF file section used to install this card. Example: ELNK3ISA509

Tip

A red X appears if you have not yet set up the card using the Network applet for network cards or the Modem applet for modems. If you set up the card and it still shows an X, remove the card from the PC Card Manager using the Remove button, and then restart Windows NT and reinstall the card. If this does not work, try to adjust the IRQ and base address settings, either through the following Registry settings or from the applet. If the card still does not work, download a new driver or a new .INF file from the Web.

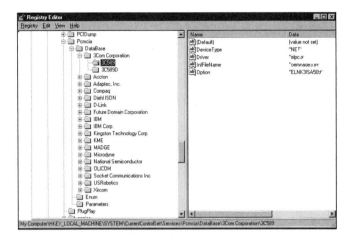

Figure 9.4   The ManufacturerID subkey.

InfFileName   Name of the .INF file used to install this card. Example: oemnade3.inf

DeviceType   Type of PCMCIA device. Possibilities include NET and SCSI.

This information can also be found in the .INF file stated in the `InfName` value found under the `[HKEY_LOCAL_MACHINE\SOFTWARE\Microsoft\WindowsNT\CurrentVersion\NetworkCards\1\NetRules]` key.

Driver   The name of the PC Card's device driver, which is on the Driver tab shown in Figure 9.5.

The Driver Tab

The Driver tab, shown in Figure 9.5, shows the driver file that this card uses, as well as information on the driver's status. This filename is read from the previous `Driver` value.

Author Note

The driver name shown here does not have to have the exact name as the driver filename. If this name and the device driver's actual name are different, the PC Card's resources are read from the Service key, as defined by the `REG_FULL_RESOURCE_DESCRIPTOR` value under the `[HKEY_LOCAL_MACHINE\HARDWARE\DESCRIPTION\System\PCMCIA PCCARDS]` key (created by PCMCIA.SYS).

Figure 9.5 The Driver tab.

The Resources Tab

The Resources tab displays the resources that this card uses. These resources can be found under the `[HKEY_LOCAL_MACHINE\SYSTEM\CurrentControlSet\Services\ServiceName\Parameters]` key, where `ServiceName` is the service name found in the *ServiceName* value under the `[HKEY_LOCAL_MACHINE\SOFTWARE\Microsoft\WindowsNT\CurrentVersion\NetworkCards\1\NetRules]` key.

These resources are written here from the resource list given by the `REG_FULL_RESOURCE_DESCRIPTOR` value under the `[HKEY_LOCAL_MACHINE\HARDWARE\DESCRIPTION\System\PCMCIA PCCARDS]` key, which is created by PCMCIA.SYS.

The Resources tab of the PC Card applet shows the settings in Figure 9.6, which are read by the *interrupt request* (IRQ) and `MemoryMappedBaseAddress` settings.

The values found under this key are

```
Pcmcia        0 or 1
REG_DWORD
```

This is sort of a master PC Card setting, which will enable or disable PCMCIA.SYS from using the other values found under this key. A setting of 1 enables PCMCIA.SYS to use these values.

Figure 9.6 The Resources tab.

Table 9.1 **Registry settings for PC Card resources**

Value	Data Type	Resource
InterruptNumber	REG_DWORD	Interrupt value.
IoBaseAddress	REG_DWORD	I/O port base address.
IoLength	REG_DWORD	I/O port length.
IoBaseAddress_1	REG_DWORD	I/O port base address.
IoLength_1	REG_DWORD	I/O port length.
MemoryMappedBaseAddress	REG_DWORD	Host base memory.
MemoryMappedSize	REG_DWORD	Host base memory length.
PCCARDMemoryWindowOffset	REG_DWORD	Card base (host base offset).
Address_16	REG_DWORD	0 or 1; a setting of 1 shows that this card uses 16-bit memory access.
MemoryMappedBaseAddress_1	REG_DWORD	Host base memory.
MemoryMappedSize_1	REG_DWORD	Host base memory length.
PCCARDMemoryWindowOffset_1	REG_DWORD	Card base (host base offset).
PCCARDMemoryWindowOffset_2	REG_DWORD	Card base (host base offset).
MemoryMappedBaseAddress_3	REG_DWORD	Host base memory.
MemoryMappedSize_3	REG_DWORD	Host base memory length.
PCCARDMemoryWindowOffset_3	REG_DWORD	Card host base offset.
PCCARDAttributeMemoryAddress	REG_DWORD	Attribute memory.
PCCARDAttributeMemorySize	REG_DWORD	Attribute memory length.
PCCARDAttributeMemoryOffset	REG_DWORD	Attribute memory offset.
PCCARDAttributeMemoryAddress_1	REG_DWORD	Attribute memory.
PCCARDAttributeMemorySize_1	REG_DWORD	Attribute memory length.
PCCARDAttributeMemoryOffset_1	REG_DWORD	Attribute memory offset.
AttributeMemory1_16	REG_DWORD	0 or 1; a setting of 1 shows that the card uses 16-bit memory access.
ModemFunction	REG_DWORD	0 or 1; a setting of 1 shows that the modem is a multi-function modem device.
CcrBase	REG_DWORD	Configuration register base.
PortWidth16	REG_DWORD	1=16 bit accesses to I/O space.
CardMemorySize	REG_DWORD	Card memory length.
CardMemorySize_1	REG_DWORD	Card memory length.
AttributeMemorySize	REG_DWORD	Attribute memory length.
AttributeMemorySize_1	REG_DWORD	Attribute memory length.

The Controller Tab

This tab, shown in Figure 9.7, has one list box that displays the resources used by the PCMCIA controller as it was reported by NTLDR.

The PCMCIA controller is described by the values under the [HKEY_LOCAL_MACHINE\SYSTEM\CurrentControlSet\Enum\Root\LEGACY_PCMCIA] key.

Installing PC Cards

Now that you have seen the PC Cards detected by Windows NT, you must now install the software drivers and other files that operate these files. There are several types of PC cards; you'll look at modems and network cards here.

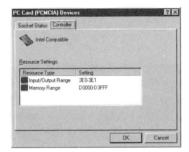

Figure 9.7 The Controller tab.

Troubleshooting

If there is no resource list found under the [HKEY_LOCAL_MACHINE\HARDWARE\DESCRIPTION\ System\PCMCIA PCCARDS] key, there is a problem with the PCMCIA Card because PCMCIA.SYS did not create a resources key. Some of these possible problems follow:

- The PC Card may not be inserted correctly in the socket.

- There may be multiple resource list values listed under this key.

- The card may need an override added to the Registry before PCMCIA.SYS can correctly configure the card, as discussed here.

Overrides need to be added if a new card cannot use the settings given by the manufacturer's .INF file. This override key can be created by adding another key with a name composed of the ServiceName plus a digit from 1 to 9. Next create a Resources Parameters key as discussed in Table 9.1 and add as many of the table values as needed.

Modems

All modems, including PC Card modems, are installed by using the Modems applet found in the Control Panel. If your computer does not have any modems installed, the Install New Modem Wizard is launched (see Figure 9.8).

This wizard is one of the few available with Windows NT 4.0 that is Plug-and-Play enabled. The wizard processes all MDM*MFR*.PNF files located in the %SYSTEMROOT%\INF directory, where *MFR* is a manufacturer's abbreviation, such as BOCA for Boca Research, Inc.

After you install a modem and restart your computer, launch the Modem applet again; this time you see the Modems Properties dialog box, as shown in Figure 9.9.

If you click the Add button, you launch the Install New Modem Wizard shown in Figure 9.8. Clicking the Remove button produces a dialog box that asks whether you are sure you want to remove the modem. The other two buttons, Properties and Dialing Properties, produce their own dialog boxes.

Figure 9.8   The Install New Modem Wizard.

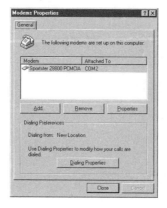

Figure 9.9   The Modems Properties dialog box.

The Properties button produces the dialog box shown in Figure 9.10. The settings in this dialog box—as well as those in the dialog boxes produced by the Dialing Properties button (see Figure 9.11), the Connection tab (see Figure 9.12), and the Advanced button (see Figure 9.13)—set values found under the
`[HKEY_LOCAL_MACHINE\SYSTEM\CurrentControlSet\Control\Class\`
`{4D36E96D-E325-11CE-BFC1-08002BE10318}\XXXX]` key, where `XXXX` will be 0000, 1111, and so on, depending on the number of modems installed.

This key has the following values:

```
AttachedTo    COM Port
REG_SZ        Example: COM1
```

This entry specifies the COM port to which the modem is connected. (It can be seen in Figure 9.9, in the Attached To column; and in Figure 9.10, beside Port.)

Figure 9.10 The PCMCIA Properties dialog box.

Figure 9.11 The Dialing Properties dialog box.

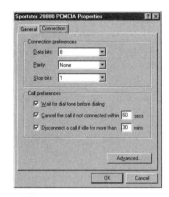

Figure 9.12 This dialog box appears after clicking the Connection tab.

Figure 9.13 The Advanced Connection Settings dialog box.

```
FriendlyName        INF File String
REG_SZ              Example: Sportster 28800 PCMCIA
```

This is the name that is seen in the Modem column shown in Figure 9.9:

```
Manufacturer        INF File String
REG_SZ              Example: U.S. Robotics, Inc.

Model        INF File String
REG_SZ       Example: Sportster 28800 PCMCIA

ID           Hex Value
REG_BINARY

PortSubClass        Hex Value
REG_BINARY

ConfigDialog        DLL File Name
REG_SZ              Example: modemui.dll
```

```
InactivityScale      Hex Value        (REG_BINARY)
Reset        AT Command String
REG_SZ          Example: ATZ<cr>
Properties    Hex Value
REG_BINARY
PortDriver    VXD File Name
REG_SZ          Example: Serial.vxd
DeviceType    Hex Value
REG_BINARY
InfPath        INF File Name
REG_SZ          Example: mdmusrsp.inf"
InfSection    Install Section of the INF File
REG_SZ          Example: Modem17
ProviderName   INF File String
REG_SZ          Example: U.S. Robotics, Inc.
DriverDesc    INF File String
REG_SZ          Example: Sportster 28800 PCMCIA
ResponsesKeyName    INF File String
REG_SZ     Example: Sportster 28800 PCMCIA::U.S. Robotics, Inc.::U.S.
                     Robotics, Inc.
DCB           Hex Value
REG_BINARY
UserInit      User Created String
REG_SZ
```

This is the string that is added in the Extra Settings text box shown in Figure 9.13:

```
Logging       Hex Value
REG_BINARY
LoggingPath   Log File path and Name
REG_SZ     Example: C:\\WIN\\ModemLog_Sportster 28800 PCMCIA.txt
VoiceSwitchFeatures    Hex Value
REG_BINARY
```

Network PC Cards

Network PC Cards are installed the same way as ISA or PCI network cards: by using the Network applet from the Control Panel, as discussed in Chapter 6, "Settings for Configuring Network Adapters." The Registry difference between PCMCIA network cards and other types of network cards is the PCMCIA value found under the

`[HKEY_LOCAL_MACHINE\SYSTEM\ControlSet001\Services\Elnk31\Parameters]` key:

```
Pcmcia
DWORD    1 or 0
```

A setting of 1 means that this adapter is a PC Card.

Standalone Versus Network Configuration

If you sometimes connect your notebook to a network, and also use it when it is not connected to the network, you probably receive some error messages saying that the network is not available. You can use the Registry to eliminate some of these messages. Use the Run key, discussed in Chapter 10, along with REGEDIT.EXE `FILE.REG` `/S` to incorporate different changes into the Registry, based on the presence of a network.

Persistent Connections

If you create network connections that are added by Windows NT at boot time, these connections are referred to as *persistent connections*. They are network drive mappings that are created in addition to those created by the login script. To clear persistent network connections from attempting to attach while the computer is used in local mode, set the following value found under the `[HKEY_CURRENT_USER\Software\`
`Microsoft\WindowsNT\CurrentVersion\Network\Persistent Connections]` key:

```
SaveConnections    Yes or No
REG_SZ
```

A value of `Yes` causes Windows NT to try to connect to this resource during logon; setting this value to `No` prevents persistent connections.

File Paths

File paths are paths for programs that are executed from the network while the user is logged in. These paths are found under various keys and values, and should be replaced with local paths or removed completely while the computer is used in local mode.

File Extensions

Another way to redirect network programs is to change the program paths that a file's associated file extension launches.

Managing NT Workstation Components

10

Modifying the Windows NT
Workstation Boot Process

- **The Windows NT pre-Registry boot process**

  This section discusses the steps that Windows NT takes before it can access the system Registry files.

- **The role of the Registry**

  Learn how to use the Registry during the Windows NT boot process and how to load the various sections of the Registry.

- **Troubleshooting and modifying the boot process**

  Learn some troubleshooting tips and techniques that you can use if the boot process fails.

The Windows NT Pre-Registry Boot Process

As you already know, Windows NT is able to run on several different types of hardware. Although the boot process is different for each platform, these differences do not affect how the Registry is later accessed; this Registry access happens at a point in the boot process that is platform-independent. In light of this, we will examine only the X86 or Intel boot process.

As shown in Figure 10.1, Windows NT processes 12 steps, starting with the *Power On Self Test* (POST) test and ending with the loading of the *Hardware Abstraction Layer* (HAL), before the Windows NT Registry is first used. These steps are discussed in the following sections.

Initializing the Computer

The first step in the boot process is to turn the computer on. As soon as the PC is powered up, the computer's CPU is configured to operate in *real memory mode*, which uses segments and offsets.

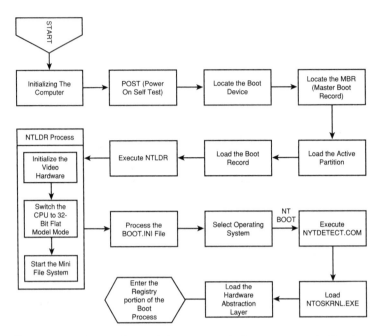

Figure 10.1 The Windows NT boot process before you access the Registry.

Next, the CPU's instruction pointer is set to
`0xffff:0x0000`

This is the memory address that holds the first command of the computer's POST routine.

The Power On Self Test (POST)

This routine inspects the computer's hardware via the system BIOS, and first determines the amount of memory, which you can see as it is counted onscreen, and the presence of a keyboard.

Next, any adapters present are initialized. The initialization of these cards may or may not be displayed on the screen. These messages are presented by the adapter's on-board POST routine, which runs after the computer's POST has completed. Some common messages you see here are video and network adapter initialization messages.

After these POST routines finish, the CPU's instruction pointer is set to run any software interrupts found at 19 hex (`19h`).

Locating the Boot Device

The software interrupt 19h is called the *reboot computer interrupt;* it attempts to find any boot drives attached to the system. The system first tries to locate the A: drive; if there is no boot drive there, it then checks the C: drive.

If the system finds a C: drive, it uses a two-step process to determine whether the found C: drive is a boot device. The next two steps encompass this process.

Locate the Master Boot Record (MBR)

The first sector of the C: drive is searched to find the *Master Boot Record* (MBR), which starts on the first logical sector of the active partition. For FAT file systems, the MBR is one sector long. Once the MBR is found, it is loaded into memory.

Locate the Active Partition

The MBR includes a routine that executes and searches the *partition table,* which is a part of the MBR. This program executable is the first layer of programs necessary to boot the operating system. This program attempts to find a flag showing that a given partition has been set to be the active partition.

Load the Boot Record

Finally, the active partition's boot record is loaded into memory. Up to now, the boot process for MS-DOS and for Windows NT were the same. After an active partition is found, these two operating systems boot differently. If you were to boot MS-DOS, the MBR program would load the file IO.SYS into RAM at memory address 700h, and then the MSDOS.SYS file would pass control of the operating system to the SYSINIT portion of IO.SYS.

However, because Windows NT is installed and the setup process has modified the MBR to boot Windows NT instead of loading the IO.SYS file, the MBR program finds, loads into memory, and executes the NTLDR file (no extension). This file must be located at the C:\ root directory or Windows NT will not boot.

> **Tip**
> Most computers can be set to boot off the C: drive first. This is usually an option that can be set in the system BIOS.

> **Note**
> The MBR is modified when Windows NT is installed so that it executes NTLDR. The MBR that was on the system when Windows NT was installed is saved as the file BOOTSECT.DOS. This file must be present if a dual boot is configured to run the operating system that was present prior to installing Windows NT.

Execute NTLDR

NTLDR is the file that controls the user operating system selection process. For NTLDR to function properly, it needs the following files, which must be located in the root directory of the active partition:

- NTDETECT.COM
- BOOT.INI
- BOOTSECT.DOS

If your PC boots using a SCSI drive, the NTBOOTDD.SYS file also needs to be located in the root directory. The Windows NT setup process creates this file, NTBOOTDD.SYS, by detecting the SCSI device driver, copying it to the root directory, and renaming it to NTBOOTDD.SYS.

NTLDR then performs these steps:

1. *NTLDR initializes the video hardware.* NTLDR initializes the video hardware by a BIOS call, which sets the video card to the 80×25 16-color alphanumeric mode.

2. *The processor switches into 32-bit flat model mode.* Because Intel computers are based on the old 8088 architecture, the CPU boots first into real-mode processing, which can execute only 8- and 16-bit programs. But because NTLDR is almost entirely a 32-bit executable, the CPU must be switched into 32-bit flat model mode before NTLDR can execute completely. Therefore, after NTLDR initializes the video, it switches the CPU into 32-bit flat model mode.

> **Tip**
>
> If the MBR program does not find an active partition on the C: drive, the CPU's instruction pointer goes to the software interrupt 18h. This interrupt is where the ROM BASIC is located on the old IBM XT/AT. If you are using a clone or newer PC, and there is no active partition, you receive a message similar to the following:
>
>   Cannot locate operating system.
>
> If you load Windows NT from a network, as with a net PC, this interrupt is redirected by the POST routine for the computer's network card to point to the network adapter card's ROM. This process enables the operating system to be loaded from a network server.

> **Author Note**
>
> If Windows NT is used on a computer that has the SCSI BIOS enabled, the NTBOOTDD.SYS is not automatically created by the installation of Windows NT 4.0. You should rename your SCSI device driver **NTBOOTDD.SYS,** and place it on a boot floppy to enable you to boot your computer from the A: drive.

3. *The mini file system* is started. In order for NTLDR to access files on the boot drive, it first determines the type of file system being used on the boot partition, and then loads a pared-down version of the detected operating system. If NTLDR detects other file systems installed on other partitions, it loads mini-file systems for those formats as well. These mini-file systems exist only within NTLDR; they support file systems of type FAT, HPFS, or NTFS.

Processing the BOOT.INI file

The BOOT.INI file contains the entries seen during the boot process when you are asked to select an operating system. This system file is in text format, located in the root directory of the boot partition, and marked System, Hidden, and Read Only. Opening the Control Panel, launching the System applet, and selecting the Startup/Shutdown tab, as seen in Figure 10.2, enables you to modify this file. You can also run the Dos attrib -h -r -s command, which enables you to edit this file with any text editor (just be sure to reset the attributes when you finish).

The BOOT.INI entries that can be changed from this applet are timeout and default (see Figure 10.3); these entries are discussed next. Now go to the boot partition's root directory (usually the C: drive), locate the BOOT.INI file, highlight it, and click the right mouse button to open it; you then see a file like the one shown in Figure 10.3.

Looking at this file, you see two bracketed sections for [Boot Loader] and [operating systems].

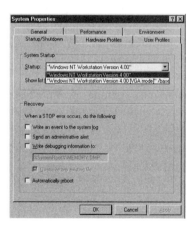

Figure 10.2   Modifying the BOOT.INI via the Control Panel.

```
[Boot Loader]
timeout=30
default=scsi(0)disk(0)rdisk(0)partition(1)\nt

-OR-

default=multi(0)disk(0)rdisk(0)partition(1)\WINNT

[operating systems]
scsi(0)disk(0)rdisk(0)partition(1)\
nt = "Windows NT (from c:\nt)" /NODEBUG

c:\ = "MS-DOS"

multi(0)disk(0)rdisk(0)partition(1)\
WINNT="Windows NT Workstation Version 4.00"

multi(0)disk(0)rdisk(0)partition(1)\
WINNT="Windows NT Workstation Version 4.00 [VGA mode]"/
basevideo /sos
```

Figure 10.3   Sample BOOT.INI file.

The [Boot Loader] section of the BOOT.INI file contains the following:
timeout=

This is the number of seconds before the default operating system listed in
default= (shown next) automatically starts.
default=

This lists the path of the default operating system, written in *Advanced RISC
Computer* (ARC) format. This format has the following form:
<path> = "<menu option>" [optional parameters]

In this format, <path> is the operating system path and "<menu option>" is the text
that displays in the Boot menu screen.

This format, including [optional parameters], is discussed in the following
section.

Selecting the Operating System to Boot

This section lists the possible operating systems that can be booted by selecting the
appropriate entry. As mentioned previously, Windows NT selections are formatted
using the ARC convention. A sample ARC path, with explanations, follows:
scsi(0)disk(0)rdisk(0)partition(1)\winnt = "Windows NT" /NODEBUG

- `scsi(0)` or `multi(0)`. Refers to the primary controller that is used to boot Windows NT. The `scsi`/`multi` portion of this first entry shows that the controller is either a SCSI type controller (`scsi`), or an IDE or other type of controller (`multi`). The number portion (`0`) shows which controller is used if there is more than one controller of that type installed on the PC.

- `disk(0)`. Refers to the physical disk attached to the appropriate controller; `0` refers to disk 1.

- `rdisk(0)`. Refers to the SCSI *logical unit* (LUN) that the SCSI controller uses. There is usually only one LUN per SCSI ID.

- `partition(1)`. Refers to the partition on the drive that is used to boot Windows NT.

- `\winnt`. Refers to the directory that a multiboot uses if booting from a specified disk and partition.

Some [optional parameters] follow:

- `/DEBUG` and `/NODEBUG`. Shows that there is or is not debugging information that needs to be monitored. This is used mostly by Windows NT administrators; if set to `/DEBUG`, it slows down the execution of Windows NT.

- `/SOS`. Displays the names of any drivers that are loaded by Windows NT during the boot process. If this option is not present, the default dots are displayed.

- `c:\ = "MS-DOS"`. Path entries in the BOOT.INI, not written in ARC format, which indicate operating systems other than Windows NT that can be booted. These entries are determined during setup from files that exist on the PC, and usually reflect the operating system that was present before Windows NT was installed. If the MSDOS.SYS or IBMDOS.COM files are found, MS-DOS is then an alternate selection. If the OS2 file is found, OS/2 is an alternate selection.

Using NTLDR to Boot Operating Systems Other than Windows NT

If MS-DOS, OS/2 1.x, or OS/2 2.0 is selected from the NTLDR user selection menu, NTLDR loads the hidden file, BOOTSECT.DOS, into RAM at memory address `700h`. NTLDR switches the CPU back to real mode and then starts the boot sector program contained in the BOOTSECT.DOS file mentioned previously. This other operating system then boots normally.

Windows NT Boot

If the selection is Windows NT, the NTDETECT.COM program begins to execute, and the files NTOSKRNL.EXE and HAL.DLL are loaded into RAM memory. These files are not initialized until later in the boot process.

Executing NTDETECT.COM

This program performs a hardware inventory that is passed to NTLDR and eventually written to the System Registry. The following hardware is currently detected by NTLDR: machine ID, bus/adapter type, video, keyboard, communication port, parallel port, floppy drives, and the mouse.

Loading the Operating Kernel and the Hardware Abstraction Layer

These are the last two steps in the Windows NT boot process that occur before the Registry is accessed. These steps are included in the kernel load phase (when the System Registry first comes into play), which occurs after NTLDR starts executing the NTDETECT.COM program. During this stage, the Windows NT kernel (NTOSKRNL.EXE) and the HAL are loaded into memory but are not initialized.

The Role of the Registry

The Registry first enters the Windows NT boot process during the initialization of the operating kernel and the loading into RAM of the NTOSKRNL.EXE and HAL.DLL files.

Figure 10.4 shows the steps that Windows NT uses to create and process the System Registry during the boot process.

As seen in Figure 10.4, Windows NT uses 24 steps when creating and processing the Windows NT Registry. The first of these steps is finding, loading, and starting system services.

Settings for Running Services

At this point in the boot process, Windows NT needs to load device drivers to operate disk drives and other operating-system components. These device drivers are Windows NT services and are found in the System Registry. The following two sections describe the boot process steps that use the Registry to load and run these services.

Loading the Registry's System Hive

The System Registry hive [HKEY_LOCAL_MACHINE\SYSTEM] is located and is loaded into memory. The NTOSKRNL.EXE file then scans the Registry for all hardware drivers that have a start value equal to zero. This start value can be found in the Registry under all subkeys of the [HKEY_LOCAL_MACHINE\SYSTEM\CurrentControlSet\Services] key, as seen in Figure 10.5.

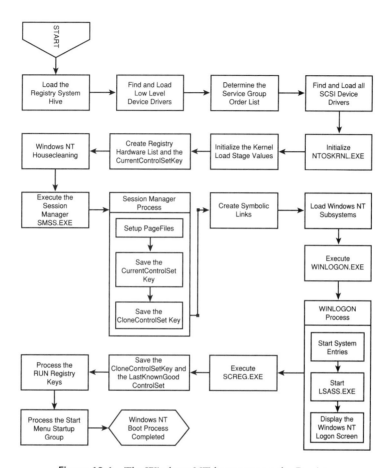

Figure 10.4 The Windows NT boot process: the Registry.

Figure 10.5 System services `start` and `type` values.

Finding and Loading the Low-Level Device Drivers

These system services, whose `start` values are set to zero, are loaded before the system kernel loads, but are not initialized. Also found under each service's subkey is the `type` value. When this value is set to `1`, the subkey shows that the driver associated with this service is a kernel device driver. These services are usually low-level device drivers, such as the ATAPI disk driver shown in Figure 10.5.

The *ServiceGroupOrder* List Value

Service groups are collections of services that load together at boot. The service groups are loaded in a linear fashion, and services that do not belong to a group are loaded after all service groups load. The services identified previously are not loaded into RAM memory as they are detected; they are loaded according to their position in the list value found under the key `[HKEY_LOCAL_MACHINE\SYSTEM\CurrentControlSet\Control\ServiceGroupOrder]`, as seen in Figure 10.6. This key has the following values:

```
List            Services# TAG, TAG, [el]  (ServiceGroup Order)
REG_MULT_SZ
```

The first entry in this value shows the number of services included with the service group. This value determines the load order for the services that are included in a service group. All services included by a service group have an associated tag assigned to them. Each tag has a unique numeric that determines the given services load order within the service group. The entries in this value define this load order.

Finding and Loading All SCSI Device Drivers

In Figure 10.6, you see that the System Port Extender SCSI miniport is loaded first, port services are loaded next, and so on.

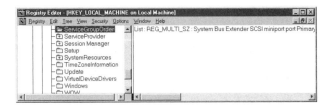

Figure 10.6   The `ServiceGroupOrder` list.

Author Note

The drivers in this list are all loaded into RAM by using BIOS INT 13 calls in real mode. However, if the boot drive does not support BIOS INT 13, such as a SCSI drive, the Windows NT SCSI device driver NTBOOTDD.SYS is used to load these services.

Also during this loading process, NTLDR switches the CPU between real and protected mode. NTLDR can then use the BIOS INT 13 to load services and still be able to load the executive, HAL.DLL, and other 32-bit drivers into extended memory. This loading process is similar to the way memory managers such as QEMM were used with Windows 3.1.

The Blue Screen Appears

At this stage of the boot process, the screen turns blue, signifying that NTOSKRNL.EXE is initialized and system control is passed to it. Also, all of the drivers that were discovered in the kernel load phase are initialized.

Initializing the Kernel Load Stage Drivers

At this point, the Registry is scanned again, this time for services that have a start value of 1. As with the kernel load phase, the services are loaded according to the `SeviceGroupOrder` list. These drivers, which are initialized as soon as they are loaded, load by using the drivers that were identified in the kernel load phase, not with BIOS INT 13.

Creating the Registry Hardware List and the *CurrentControlSet* Key

During this stage, the Registry Hardware list is created by using the information passed to NTLDR by the NTDETECT.COM file.

It is also at this stage that the `[HKEY_LOCAL_MACHINE\SYSTEM\CurrentControlSet]` key and its subkeys are created by adding a pointer to the `[HKEY_LOCAL_MACHINE\ SYSTEM\ControlSet00X]` key, where X is given by the `Default` value located under the `[HKEY_LOCAL_MACHINE\SYSTEM\Select]` key.

The `[HKEY_LOCAL_MACHINE\SYSTEM\Clone]` is also created, and both this key and the `CurrentControlSet` key are initialized.

Windows NT Housecleaning

Some device drivers, such as some Novell network drivers, use a larger memory space to initialize their drivers than the drivers use after they are initialized. For these drivers, NTOSKRNL.EXE frees the memory space used by these drivers.

Settings for File Systems

Windows NT 4.0 supports three types of file systems, which were discussed in Chapter 1, "Disk Drives."

Execute SMSS.EXE

After the `CurrentControlSet` and the Hardware list are created, Windows NT starts the executable SMSS.EXE, which is called the *Session Manager.* When this program executes, it searches the Registry for [`HKEY_LOCAL_MACHINE\SYSTEM\ CurrentControlSet\Control\Session Manager`] and reads the `BootExecute` value that contains a list of programs to launch.

The Autocheck Program

It is this list that contains the AUTOCHK.EXE program. Windows NT uses this program, which is similar to the DOS executable CHKDSK.EXE, to perform system checks on a disk's partition.

When you see the disk check information on the Windows NT blue screen, you know that the Session Manager file, SMSS.EXE, has started. If this information does not appear on the screen, the `autochk*` entry has been removed from the `BootExecute` value.

NTFS Partitions

System partitions that are converted to the NTFS file format add another entry to this `BootExecute` value:

```
autoconv \DosDevices\x: /FS:ntfs
```

This entry is usually added after the `autocheck` entry.

Session Manager and Pagefiles

At this point in the boot process, the Session Manager sets up pagefiles, which Windows NT uses to swap memory pages from RAM to disk after autocheck finishes running. The page files are defined under the [`HKEY_LOCAL_MACHINE\SYSTEM\ CurrentControlSet\Control\Session Manager\Memory Management`] key (refer to Chapter 5, "Settings for Memory").

> **Author Note**
>
> The `BootExecute` value is usually set to autocheck autochk*. If you change this value to autocheck autochk /p, the /p option instructs the AUTOCHK.EXE program to perform the equivalent of a CHKDSK /F on all system partitions each time the computer boots.
>
> Also, the `BootExecute` value can have multiple entries because it is of data type REG_MULTI_SZ. So, if you add another entry after autocheck autochk*, such as **\DosDevices\c:**, AUTOCHK.EXE performs the CHKDSK /f functions only on the C: drive partition.
>
> Finally, if you schedule CHKDSK for use on multiple disks, an `autocheck` entry is created for each disk. If you do not want one of these disks checked, delete the associated string from the `BootExecute` value.

Saving the *CurrentControlSet* and the *Clone ControlSet*

Next, because the partitions have been checked and the paging files are set up, the `CurrentControlSet` and the clone `ControlSet` are written to the Registry.

Creating Symbolic Links

The next step in the Windows NT boot process is the creation of *symbolic links.* These links allow old MS-DOS commands to be associated with the right file or file-system component. These links are found in the Registry under the key `[HKEY_LOCAL_MACHINE\SYSTEM\CurrentControlSet\Control\Session Manager\ DOS Devices]`. Values that may be found here are `AUX`, defined as COM1; and `PRN`, defined as LPT1.

Settings for Subsystems and the Windows Logon Process

After Windows NT completes the setup of the Registry services and hardware keys and determines the operating system's file format, the boot process can load the communicating subsystems and start the Windows NT logon process.

Loading Subsystems

The last step in the boot process before the Windows NT logon is the loading of the Win32 subsystem listed under the `[HKEY_LOCAL_MACHINE\SYSTEM\ CurrentControlSet\Control\Session Manager\SubSystems]` key in the `Required` value. The Win32 subsystem controls all of the computers' input and output routines, as well as the video display. Running the CSRSS.EXE executable found in the %SYSTEMROOT%\SYSTEM32 directory starts this subsystem, which then starts the WinLogon process, the first step of which is running the executable WINLOGON.EXE.

WINLOGON.EXE

The WinLogon step of the Windows NT boot process performs these steps:

1. *Starting systems entries.* After the boot process begins the Win32 subsystem, the WINLOGON.EXE automatically starts. This, in turn, starts the system entries in the *System Value* found under the `[HKEY_LOCAL_MACHINE\Software\Microsoft\ WindowsNT\Current Version\Winlogon]` key.

2. *Starting the Local Security Authority subsystem LSASS.EXE.* Next, WINLOGON.EXE starts the Local Security Authority subsystem file LSASS.EXE.

3. *Starting the print spooler SPOOLSS.EXE.* After the Local Security Authority subsystem begins, WINLOGON.EXE starts the print spooler file SPOOLSS.EXE.

4. *The Windows NT logon screen.* At this point in the Windows NT boot process, the welcome screen is displayed, showing the familiar Ctrl+Alt+Del logon message.

Bypassing the Logon Screen

The Registry can be used to bypass the Windows NT logon screen and log on automatically to Windows NT. This procedure is very useful when running updates and retrofits on systems that may not have users logged on. To bypass this screen, perform the following steps:

1. Run the Registry Editor REGEDIT32.EXE and find the following key:

   `[HKEY_LOCAL_MACHINE\SOFTWARE\Microsoft\WindowsNT\CurrentVersion\Winlogon]`

2. There are several values under this key. You need to modify these values with entries specific to your network. The values that you need to modify, and how to do so, follow:

   `DefaultDomainName`. Modify this value to show your default logon domain name.

   `DefaultUserName`. Modify this value to show which default user you want to logon to Windows NT as. You usually want to give administrator rights to this account.

   `DefaultPassword`. Enter the Windows NT password for this default account.

3. Under the same key as the previous values, choose the Edit, Add Value menu selection to add a value called `AutoAdminLogon`, set the data type to `REG_SZ`, and set it equal to `1`.

When the system reboots, the Windows logon screen is bypassed and the system automatically logs on the default user set.

Completing the Boot Process

After a user successfully logs onto Windows NT, the following final steps of the boot process are completed.

> **Tip**
>
> If you set the password to be blank, autologon only occurs once because Windows NT sets the `AutoAdminLogon` value to `0` after it boots. You can also skip the autologon process by holding down the Shift key as Windows NT boots. Also, if you use AutoLogon, do not set the `DontDisplayLastUserName` value to 1.

The Service Controller (SCREG.EXE)

Immediately after the Windows logon screen displays, the Service Controller executable, SCREG.EXE, runs. This program makes one last scan of the Registry, searching for systems that have a `start` value of `2`.

In the section about loading services with a `start` value of `0` or `1`, you learned how the load order for these services is determined. The load order for services with a `start` value of `2` also has an associated load order. This load order is determined by the `DependOnGroup` and/or the `DependOnService` value, which is found under the Services key, as seen in Figure 10.7.

Although the device driver services discussed previously were loaded serially, these later services are loaded in parallel for better operating-system performance. Of course, all services to be loaded must load the dependencies listed in the previous values first, if they exist, or the service does not load. In this case, you see the error message in Figure 10.8. Not all services have dependencies.

Two other types of `start` values are also run at this time: the `start` values `10` and `20`.

Services that have a `start` value of `10` allow only one service to run in any given memory space. Configuring the service to run in this way allows the same executable to start several different times, having a different name and memory space in each instance. One example of this type of service is the EventLogger service.

The second type of services, those with start values of `20`, contain multiple services in each executable. So, when these multiple parts of the same executable run, each has a new thread created for it, but does not run in a separate memory space. One example of this type of service is the LanmanWorkstation service.

Figure 10.7   Service dependencies.

Figure 10.8   The service controller error message.

The *Clone* ControlSet and the *LastKnownGood* ControlSet

After all of the services have been started and a user is successfully logged onto Windows NT, the `Clone` ControlSet key is copied into the `LastKnownGood` ControlSet key. The `LastKnownGood` key is the ControlSet that is loaded if you press the spacebar when Windows NT displays the possible boot options.

The CurrentUser Key

The current user is loaded at this point from information based on the Windows login and the user keys found under the HKEY_USERS key. Windows NT copies the logged-in user's settings to the HKEY_CURRENT_USERS key.

This completes the Windows NT boot process.

The Run Keys

After the boot process is completed, Windows NT processes any programs that it finds under the Run keys. These keys follow:

- *The Run key.* This key is found at [HKEY_LOCAL_MACHINE\SOFTWARE\Microsoft\ Windows\CurrentVersion\Run], and is used to run programs each time Windows NT is booted. You always find one value here:

    `"SystemTray"="SysTray.Exe"`

    This runs the Windows NT system tray. And, although the same effects can usually be obtained by placing the executable in the Start menu's StartUp group, placing them in the Run key is more secure.

- *The Run Once key.* This key is found at [HKEY_LOCAL_MACHINE\SOFTWARE\ Microsoft\Windows\CurrentVersion\RunOnce], and is used to run a program once the next time Windows NT boots.

Any executable that runs under Windows NT can be placed in these Run keys.

Troubleshooting and Modifying the Boot Process

The final section of this chapter addresses error messages that may be seen during the Windows NT boot process. Most errors are generated during the NTLDR and BOOT.INI boot phases.

> **Tip**
> The Registry entries that were discussed in the "Bypassing the Logon Screen" section can be placed in a .REG file, which is then incorporated into the Registry through a batch file that is placed in the Run Once key. This process can be used to boot, logon, reboot, upgrade, and reset the logon. In this way, the Run Once keys can be used to place entries into the Run keys, which can produce dramatic results.

Troubleshooting NTLDR

■ *NTLDR is missing.* If the NTLDR file is missing or cannot be found on the root partition, you see this error message:
```
BOOT: Couldn't find NTLDR. Please insert another disk.
```
Boot the computer with a DOS boot disk and be sure that NTLDR is located on the C: drive.

■ *Missing NTDETECT.COM.* If you see the following error message after the Windows NT blue screen appears, the NTDETECT.COM is missing:
```
Fatal System Error: 0x00000067[sr]
Configuration Initialization error
```
Boot the computer with a DOS boot disk and be sure that NTDETECT.COM is located on the C: drive.

■ *Dual boot errors—Missing BOOTSECT.DOS.* If you are using a dual-boot configuration to boot operating systems other than Windows NT, and you try to boot this other operating system, you see the following error message:
```
Couldn't open boot sector file
multi(0)disk(0)rdisk(0)partition(1):\bootsect.dos
```
The BOOTSECT.DOS is missing.

Boot the computer with a DOS boot disk and be sure that BOOTSECT.DOS is located on the C: drive.

Modifying the BOOT.INI

■ *No Boot menu.* If you boot Windows NT and you do not see the Boot selection menu appear, the BOOT.INI file is corrupted, cannot be found, or the `time=` value in the `[Boot Loader]` section of BOOT.INI is set to `0` or another low value. If it is just set to a low value, pressing the down-arrow key repeatedly displays the menu.

■ *Wrong Windows NT path.* If NTLDR cannot find Windows NT at the ARC path given by the BOOT.INI file, you see this message:
```
OS Loader V2.10
loading file scsi(0)disk(0)rdisk(0)partition(1)\nt\system32
\ntoskrnl.exe.
```
Boot the computer with a DOS boot disk and be sure that ntoskrnl.exe is located on the boot partition.

Troubleshooting

If you are using the NTFS file system, you will not be able to read the NTFS partition if you boot the computer with a floppy disk that is using the FAT file system. To solve this problem, perform the following steps to create an NTFS boot floppy:

1. Use DISKCOPY to make a copy of the Windows NT Setup Disk 1; this is the first disk that Windows NT creates when it is installed.

2. Delete all of the files on the copied disk.

3. Find the NTDETECT.COM and BOOTSECT.DOS files on your system partition and copy them to the floppy. You may have to set the View All attributes of the Windows NT Explorer or use `attrib` to set the file options of these files.

4. Find the NTLDR file on your system partition, copy it to the floppy, and rename it to SETUPLDR.BIN.

5. Find the NTBOOTDD.SYS file on your system partition and copy it to the floppy.

6. Either copy the BOOT.INI file from your system partition to the floppy or create a new one on the floppy, as shown here:

```
[boot loader]
timeout=10
default= scsi(0)disk(0)rdisk(0)partition(1)\WINNT

[operating systems]
scsi(0)disk(0)rdisk(0)partition(1)\WINNT="Windows NT Server Version
4.0"
```

Tip

If you have enough room on your computer, it is a good idea to install a second bootable installation of Windows NT that can be used to troubleshoot the main system if it fails to boot.

Managing the Desktop

- **Accessibility options**

  Learn which settings can be modified to configure the Registry to set the accessibility options found in the Accessibility applet of the Control Panel.

- **Regional settings**

  This section discusses settings that can be modified to configure the Registry to set the regional options found in the Regional applet of the Control Panel.

Accessibility Options

Windows NT 4.0 includes a Control Panel applet that can be used to configure Windows NT as a friendlier operating system for persons who may be disabled. This applet can help configure the keyboard, mouse, alarm sounds, and serial key devices. If you open the Control Panel and launch the Accessibility Options applet, you see the dialog box shown in Figure 11.1.

This screen has four tabs on it. These tabs and their settings create Registry subkeys and values under the [HKEY_CURRENT_USER\Control Panel\Accessibility] key, which I will refer to as the *Accessibility key*. The four tabs of this screen and the values that they set are described in the following sections.

The Keyboard Tab

This tab sets various values under three different Registry subkeys, all of which are found under the Accessibility key. These subkeys and their values are described next.

The ...\StickyKeys Subkey

The Flags value under this key is set to a different hexadecimal number, depending on which check boxes are selected on the dialog box shown in Figure 11.2.

Figure 11.1   The Accessibility Options applet dialog box.

This screen pops up when you choose the Settings button within the StickyKeys frame. The value found under this key follows:

```
Flags        Hex Value
REG_SZ
```

Table 11.1 shows how the `Flags` value is set when different check boxes of Figure 11.2 are checked.

Figure 11.2   The Settings for StickyKeys dialog box.

Table 11.1   **The StickyKey *Flag* value settings**

Numerical Value	Turns Off Accessibility Features After Idle For	Makes a Sound When Turning a Feature On or Off
0		
1	X	
2		X
3	X	X

The ...\Keyboard Response Subkey

The values under this subkey are set from the Keyboard tab of the Accessibility Options applet. There are three frames on this tab; the ...\Keyboard Response subkey is associated with the Settings button located in the FilterKeys frame. If you click this button, you see the screen shown in Figure 11.3.

This screen has a Filter options frame, which includes two radial buttons. If you select the ignore repeated keystrokes button and click the Settings button that is enabled as a result, you see the screen shown in Figure 11.4.

This screen has one slide bar, which creates the settings for the following two Bounce values:

```
BounceTime                 500 to 2000
REG_SZ

Last BounceKey Setting      500 to 2000 (Hex)
REG_DWORD                   000001f4
```

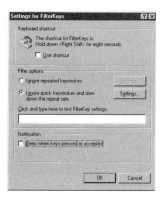

Figure 11.3   The Settings for FilterKeys dialog box.

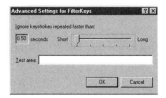

Figure 11.4 The BounceKey value dialog box.

If you select the second radial button and click its associated Settings button, you see the screen shown in Figure 11.5.

The RepeatKeys Values

This screen has two frames on it. The first frame, RepeatKeys, has two radial buttons and two slide bars within it. If the No keyboard repeat button is selected, the first four of the following values are set to zero (0); if the Slow down keyboard repeat rates button is selected, the two slide bars affect the four values as shown here:

```
AutoRepeatDelay          300 - 2000
REG_SZ

Last Valid Delay         300 - 2000 (Hex)
REG_DWORD
```

The Repeat delay slide bar sets these two values from a range of .3 seconds (**300**) to 2 seconds (**2000**).

```
Last Valid Repeat        300 - 2000 (Hex)
REG_DWORD

AutoRepeatRate           300 - 2000
REG_SZ
```

Figure 11.5 The Repeat, Delay, and Wait values dialog box.

The Repeat rate slide bar sets these two values from a rage of .3 seconds (**300**) to 2 seconds (**2000**).

The Slow Key Values

These values are set from the slide bar located in the SlowKeys frame:

```
DelayBeforeAcceptance      0 - 2000
REG_SZ

Last Valid Wait            0 - 2000 (Hex)
REG_DWORD
```

The Flags Value

```
Flags                  Hex Value
REG_SZ
```

Table 11.2 shows how the Flags value is set when different check boxes of Figure 11.3 are checked.

Table 11.2 **The FilterKey** *Flag* **value settings**

Numerical Value	Use FilterKeys	Use Shortcut	Beep When Keys Pressed or Accepted
26			
27	X		
30		X	
31	X	X	
90			X
91	X		X
94		X	X
95	X	X	X

The ...\ToggleKeys Subkey

The Flags value under this key is set to a different hexadecimal number, depending on whether the Use shortcut check box in Figure 11.6 is checked. Table 11.3 shows the different hexadecimal settings for this value.

Tip
Be sure to test these rates by holding down a key if these settings are manually set in the Registry. These values can be set from 0 to 2000 seconds.

Figure 11.6   The ToggleKeys values dialog box.

This screen pops up after you choose the Settings button within the StickyKeys frame. The value found under this key is

```
Flags                   Hex Value
REG_SZ
```

Table 11.3   **The StickyKey *Flag* value settings**

Numerical Value	Use ToggleKeys	Use Shortcut
26		
27	X	
30		X
31	X	X

The Sound Tab

If you select the Sound tab of the Accessibility Options applet, you see the dialog box shown in Figure 11.7.

The ...\SoundSentry Key

This key has several values under it that are set by the Use ShowSounds check box and the Settings button, as seen in Figure 11.7. These values, and how they are set, are as follows:

```
Flags                   Numerical Value
REG_SZ
```

This value behaves like the other `Flag` values discussed in previous sections and has the following settings:

```
Hex Value "2"
```

This Hex setting indicates that the Use SoundSentry check box is not checked.

```
Hex Value "3"
```

Figure 11.7   The Sound tab.

This hexadecimal setting indicates that the Use SoundSentry check box is checked.

```
WindowsEffect              Numerical Value
REG_SZ
```

If you click the Settings button, as seen in Figure 11.7, the dialog box shown in Figure 11.8 appears.

This dialog box has one drop-down list box on it that sets the `WindowsEffect` value as follows, depending on the list box selection:

None   0

Flash active caption bar   1

Flash active window   2

Flash desktop   3

Figure 11.8   The Settings for SoundSentry dialog box.

The ...\ShowSounds Key

This key has one value under it, which is set by the Use ShowSounds check box seen in Figure 11.7.

```
On                      0 or 1
REG_SZ
```

If the check box is checked, this value is set to 1; if it is not checked, the value is set to 0.

The Mouse Tab

If you select the Mouse tab of the Accessibility Options applet, you will see the dialog box shown in Figure 11.9.

The ...\MouseKeys Key

This tab sets various values under the ...\MouseKeys subkey, which is found under the Accessibility key. These values follow:

```
Flags                   Numerical Value
REG_SZ
```

This value behaves the same as the other Flags values discussed in this section. Its settings are shown in Table 11.4.

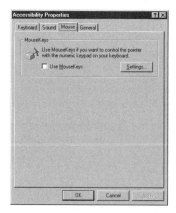

Figure 11.9   The Settings for Mouse tab.

Table 11.4 **The MouseKeys *Flags* value settings**

Numerical Value	Use MouseKeys	Use Shortcut	Use MouseKeys When Numlock Is	
			On	Off
26			X	
27	X		X	
30		X	X	
31	X	X	X	
154				X
155	X			X
158		X		X
159	X	X		X

```
MaximumSpeed            10 to 360
REG_SZ
```

This value is set by the Top speed slide bar, as seen in Figure 11.10.

```
TimeToMaximumSpeed      5000 (slow) to 1000 (fast)
REG_SZ
```

This value is set by the Acceleration slide bar, shown in Figure 11.10.

The General Tab

If you select the General tab of the Accessibility Options applet, you see the dialog box shown in Figure 11.11.

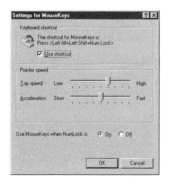

Figure 11.10   The Settings for MouseKeys dialog box.

Figure 11.11 The General tab.

The ...\TimeOut Key

This key has two values under it: the `Flags` value and the `TimeToWait` value. These values can be set as the following:

```
Flags                        Numerical Setting
REG_SZ
```

This value behaves the same as the other `Flags` values discussed in this section and has settings shown in Table 11.5.

Table 11.5 **The TimeOut *Flags* value settings**

Numerical Value	Use StickyKeys	Use Shortcut	Make Sounds...	Press Modifier...	Turn StickyKeys Off
26					
27	X				
30		X			
31	X	X			
90					X
91	X				X
94		X			X
95	X	X			X
158		X	X		
159	X	X	X		
218			X		X
219	X		X		X
222		X	X		X
223	X	X	X		X

Numerical Value	Use StickyKeys	Use Shortcut	Make Sounds...	Press Modifier...	Turn StickyKeys Off
282				X	
283	X			X	
286		X		X	
287	X	X		X	
346				X	X
347		X		X	X
414		X	X	X	
415	X	X	X	X	
474			X	X	X
475	X		X	X	X
478		X	X	X	X
479	X	X	X	X	X

```
TimeToWait    300000(5 Minutes) to 1800000 (30 Minutes)
REG_SZ
```

This value is set by the Minutes drop-down list box, which is enabled when the Turn off accessibility features after idle for check box is checked.

Accessibility Key

This main key has the following value created under it if the Make a sound when turning a feature on or off check box, seen in Figure 11.11, is checked. The value is set to 1 if the check box is checked; it is set to 0 if it is not checked.

```
Sound on Activation          0 or 1
REG_DWORD
```

The ...\SerialKeys Key

If you click the Settings button seen in Figure 11.11, you see the dialog box shown in Figure 11.12.

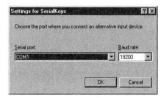

Figure 11.12 The SerialKeys dialog box.

This screen contains two drop-down list boxes that are used to set the following values:

```
ActivePort     COM1, COM2, COM3, or COM4
REG_SZ
```

This value is set by the Serial port drop-down list box.

```
Baud           300 - 19200
REG_DWORD
```

This value is set by the Baud rate drop-down list box.

```
Flags          2 0r 3
REG_DWORD
```

This `Flags` value is different from the previous `Flags` value because it is a `REG_DWORD` data type. It is set to `3` if the Support SerialKey devices check box is checked; it is set to `2` if it is not checked.

Regional Settings

If you open the Control Panel and launch the Regional Settings applet, you see the screen shown in Figure 11.13.

This screen has six tabs, which set Registry values found under the `[HKEY_CURRENT_USER\ControlPanel\International]` key. These values and the tabs that are used to set them are described in the following sections.

The Regional Settings Tab

```
sCountry          Country Name
REG_SZ
```

This value is set from the drop-down list box showing the country list.

The Set as system default locale check box on this tab sets font settings (refer to the section called "The Font Key" in Chapter 2).

Figure 11.13   The Regional Settings Properties dialog box.

The Number Tab

This tab contains nine drop-down list boxes that set the following values:

```
SDecimal          . (Period)
REG_SZ
```

This value is set by the Decimal Symbol drop-down list box.

```
IDigits           0 to 9
REG_SZ
```

This value is set by the No. of Digits after Decimal drop-down list box.

```
SThousand         , (Comma)
REG_SZ
```

This value is set by the Digit Grouping Symbol drop-down list box.

```
SGrouping         0 t0 9; 0 to 9
REG_SZ             Example 8;0
```

This value is set by the No. of Digits in Group drop-down list box, and it may not exist if it was originally set to 3 and never changed.

```
SNegativeSign     - (Minus Sign)
REG_SZ
```

This value is set by the Negative Sign Symbol drop-down list box, and it may not exist if it was originally set to - and never changed.

```
INegNumber        0 to 5
REG_SZ
```

This value is set by the Negative Number Format drop-down list box.

```
IZero             0 (.7) or 1 (0.7)
REG_SZ
```

This value is set by the Display Leading Zeros drop-down list box.

```
IMeasure          0 (Metric) or 1 (US)
REG_SZ
```

This value is set by the Measurement System drop-down list box.

```
SList             , (Comma)
REG_SZ
```

This value is set by the List Separator drop-down list box.

The Currency Tab

This tab contains seven drop-down list boxes that set the following values:

```
sCurrency         $ (Dollar Sign)
REG_SZ
```

This value is set by the Currency Symbol drop-down list box.

```
ICurrency         0 to 3
REG_SZ
```

This value is set by the Positive Currency Format drop-down list box.

```
INegCurr            0 to 15
REG_SZ
```

This value sets the Negative currency format drop-down list box.

```
ICurrDigets     0 to 9
REG_SZ
```

This value sets the No. of Digits in Group drop-down list box.

```
SList           ,
REG_SZ
```

This value sets the Digit Grouping Symbol drop-down list box.

```
sdecimal
REG_SZ          .
```

This value sets the Decimal Symbol drop-down list box.

```
sMonGrouping            0 to 9; 0 to 9
REG_SZ
```

This value is similar to the sGrouping value and is set by the No. of Digits in Group drop-down list box.

The Time Tab

This tab contains five drop-down list boxes that set the following values:

```
STimeFormat             Values from the List Box
REG_SZ
```

This value is set by the Time Style drop-down list box, and it may not be present if it was originally set to HH.MM.SS and never changed.

```
STime                   : (colon)
REG_SZ
```

This value is set by the Time Separator drop-down list box.

```
s1159               AM
REG_SZ
```

This value is set by the AM Symbol drop-down list box.

```
s2359               PM
REG_SZ
```

This value is set by the PM Symbol drop-down list box.

Note

The Decimal Symbol drop-down list box on the Currency tab sets the same Decimal value as the one shown on the Number tab.

The Date Tab

This tab contains six drop-down list boxes, but only three of these boxes are active. The active boxes and the values that they set follow:

```
SShortDate              Values from the List Box
REG_SZ
```

This value is set by the Short Date Style drop-down list box.

```
SDate                   / (Forward Slash)
REG_SZ
```

This value is set by the Date Separator drop-down list box.

```
sLongDate               Values from the List Box
REG_SZ
```

This value is set by the Long Date Style drop-down list box.

The Input Locales Tab

This tab sets the same Registry keys and values for keyboards that were discussed in Chapter 3, "Settings for Mice and Keyboards."

12

System Components

- **File extensions**

  This section discusses the use of file extensions and the way that the Registry can be used to manage these extensions.

- **Settings for ODBC**

  Object Database Connectivity (ODBC) is used to connect to various types of databases, either locally or on a network. This section discusses the role that the Registry plays when using and setting up ODBC.

File Extensions

File extensions are the last three (sometimes four) letters at the end of a filename, after the dot operator(.). An example is the .DOC extension of a Word document. When a file is either run from the Start menu's Run command or launched from the Windows NT Explorer or another file manager, Windows NT 4.0 uses the file's extension to determine what program to launch to view the file. For the Word document example, the .DOC extension tells Windows NT to use Word to open and view the file. You can also use the Windows NT Open With command by either pressing the Shift+F2 keys, or by selecting a file in Explorer and holding down the Shift key while clicking the right mouse button. This action displays the dialog box seen in Figure 12.1, which lets you choose a program that opens the file.

This dialog box also displays if you try to launch a file that has an extension that Windows NT does not recognize, such as an .SAN extension.

If you select the Notepad application to open the .SAN file, and check the Always use this program to open this file check box, Windows NT creates the Registry entries described in the following sections, which enable all future launches of a .SAN file to be opened with the Notepad application.

The File Extension Registry Keys

The first key created for a newly recognized extension is the Root extension key, which has the same name as the extension of the file that you are opening. The keys found under the [HKEY_CLASSES_ROOT] key are copied from the subkeys under the

Figure 12.1   Unknown extension Open With dialog box.

[HKEY_LOCAL_MACHINE\SOFTWARE\Classes] key. These keys, described in upcoming sections, hold file extension information for all users, including file type and file extension information for Windows Explorer. File extensions are associated with a specific file type by specifying the file type with a file extension using the Registry. For this example, use an unknown (to Windows NT) file extension called .SAN.

The *[HKEY_CLASSES_ROOT\.san]* Key

This key has at least one value, the @ default value. This key also may have other values and/or subkeys:

```
@            Autofile Key Pointer
REG_SZ       Example: san_auto_file
```

This value is simply a pointer to the Registry key that is given by the @ value setting. I will refer to this as the *extension pointer*.

```
Content Type       File Description
REG_SZ             Example: Text/Plain
```

This value shows the location of the associated MIME Database key and describes the use of the file (discussed in the "MIME Extensions" section, later in this chapter).

The *[HKEY_CLASSES_ROOT\.san\ShellNew]* Subkey

This key usually has one value and may have additional subkeys. The Quattro Pro extension .wb2 is an example of an extension that has subkeys to handle the launch of different program versions.

```
NullFile     String Handler
REG_SZ       Example: " "
```

This value is usually blank and shows the action that should be taken if a null file has the listed extension.

The *[HKEY_CLASSES_ROOT\san_auto_file]* **Key**

This key is the extension pointer. It also has one or more values, and will usually have subkeys beneath it:

```
@              User-Supplied String
REG_SZ         Example: Example of an Unknown File Extension
```

This string can be entered by the user in the Open With dialog box's Description of '.san' Files text box, as seen in Figure 12.1.

```
EditFlags      Comma-Separated Number Entries
REG_BINARY
```

These flags are added by an application's setup program, are application-specific, and instruct the program how to open files.

The *[HKEY_CLASSES_ROOT\batfile\DefaultIcon]* **Key**

```
@                        Icon Information
REG_EXPAND_SZ
```

This value includes the file path for the default icon, the icon filename, and the icon marker. If this value is viewed with REGEDT32.EXE, the default icon information can be seen, as shown in Figure 12.2. This information shows that the default icon used for .BAT files is the 153rd icon found in the %SYSTEMROOT%\ SYSTEM32\SHELL32.DLL file. In addition to the Windows NT Registry editors, you can also use third-party icon view programs to view this icon information.

The *[HKEY_CLASSES_ROOT\batfile\shell]* **Subkey**

Entries under this key are used to populate the pop-up menu produced by right-clicking on a file in Windows NT Explorer. The subkeys here have the following form:

```
[HKEY_CLASSES_ROOT\batfile\shell\menu item\command]
```

The *menu item* entry is the entry that is seen on the pop-up menu; *command* lists a path and filename for the program to launch in order to perform the given *menu item* (see Figure 12.3).

Figure 12.2   The DefaultIcon key.

Author Note

This key can be added to any extension key that is pointed to by a root extension. This value can then be used to set the icon that is displayed for any given file.

Other Extension Keys

There are a few other places in the Registry that deal with extensions and the way files are opened and processed.

Document Preferences

The key `[HKEY_CURRENT_USER\Software\Microsoft\WindowsNT\CurrentVersion\Extensions]` associates personal preferences for documents with particular command lines. This key enables the automatic opening of the file type with the associated application. The value, with examples, that holds this key's information follows:

```
File Extension    Application and Extension
REG_SZ    Example: pbrush.exe ^.bmp
```

MIME Extensions

Some applications do not record their file extension information in the `[HKEY_CLASSES_ROOT]` key, but instead write this information to an application-specific subkey under the `[HKEY_CLASSES_ROOT\MIME\Database\Content Type]` key, as seen in Figure 12.4. This application-specific subkey can be found in the `Content Type` value, shown at the start of this chapter.

Figure 12.4 also shows the MIME `Extension` value, which follows:

```
Extension    File Extension
REG_SZ    Example: .avi
```

This value holds the file-extension descriptions for MIME applications or for applications that use MIME to determine how to handle files. This example can be found under the `[HKEY_CLASSES_ROOT\MIME\Database\Content Type\video\avi]` key.

Figure 12.3 The `menu item` launch command.

> **Tip**
>
> Some common menu items used in these entries are Edit, Open, and Print.

Figure 12.4 The Content Type value.

Class ID Pointers

Some programs need to know the Registry *Class ID* (CLSID) for certain files. These class IDs are found in the extension pointer keys in the following format:

[HKEY_CLASSES_ROOT*Extension Pointer*\Extensions*File Extension*]

Extension Pointer is the extension pointer, as discussed earlier, and *File Extension* is the file extension itself. An example of the .avi extension is

[HKEY_CLASSES_ROOT\AVIFile\Extensions\AVI]

This key has one value that holds the CLSID for the program that is associated with this file extension.

Property Sheet Handler Class IDs

There may be a subkey listed under the key pointed to by the Root key called [HKEY_CLASSES_ROOT\batfile\shellex\PropertySheetHandlers\PifProps] or [HKEY_CLASSES_ROOT\batfile\CLSID], each having a default @ value listing a CLSID. If this key is present, it shows the CLSID for the program that launches this type of file.

Settings for ODBC

Object Database Connectivity (ODBC) is the way that some programs connect to and use various databases. Using the ODBC32 applet in the Control Panel, you can configure ODBC. If you launch this applet, you see the screen displayed in Figure 12.5.

You can add a user DSN (system DSNs are discussed in "The Data Source Name Key" section) by selecting either the User DSN or System DSN tab, clicking the Add button, selecting a Microsoft Access database, and clicking Next. You see the screen shown in Figure 12.6, which also shows the information displayed when clicking the Options button.

Figure 12.5   The ODBC32 applet.

The ODBC.INI Key

This key contains the information from the old Windows 3.1 ODBC.INI file. There are several keys, subkeys, and associated values found under this key, which are described in the next few sections.

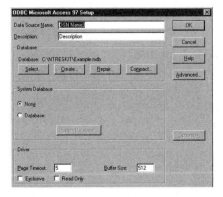

Figure 12.6   The ADD Microsoft Access 97 DSN dialog box.

Tip

Depending on what database you select, you may see a different DSN dialog box. Figure 12.6 shows the Microsoft Access 97 setup screen. All of these screens work the same way and also appear if you select a user DSN and click the Configure button.

The ODBC Key

This key, [HKEY_LOCAL_MACHINE\SOFTWARE\ODBC\ODBC.INI\ODBC], holds values that are specific to ODBC. These values follow:

```
TraceFile    Log File Name
REG_SZ       Example: \\SQL.LOG
```

This value gives the name of the logfile used by ODBC to trap errors and other settings.

```
TraceDll     Trace File and Path
REG_SZ       Example: C:\\WINNT\\System32\\odbctrac.dll
```

This value shows the .DLL file and path used to perform SQL traces.

The ODBC Data Sources Key

This key, [HKEY_LOCAL_MACHINE\SOFTWARE\ODBC\ODBC.INI\ODBC Data Sources], lists values that correspond to the System DSNs that are added the same way that user DSNs are added, except that you use the System DSN tab from the Add DSN dialog box.

```
DSNName      Driver File Name
REG_SZ       Example: Microsoft Excel Driver (*.xls)
```

This key collates a DSNName with an ODBC drive file.

The Data Source Name Key

The string that you enter into the Data Source Name text box shown in Figure 12.6 becomes the key name that is created in the Registry for this DSN. This key is created at [HKEY_LOCAL_MACHINE\SOFTWARE\ODBC\ODBC.INI*DSNName*], where *DSNName* is the data source name string. The Description text box string is stored in the Description value listed under the newly created key. Other values found under this key follow:

```
DBQ    Database and Path
REG_SZ       Example: C:\\NTRESKIT\\Example.mdb
```

This entry is the database and path that appear in the Database area shown in Figure 12.6. This entry is created when a database is selected or created using the Select and Create buttons. The database you select here is used to access the ODBC connection:

```
Driver    Driver DLL File
REG_SZ       Example: @System\Odbcjt32.dll
```

@System refers to the Windows System32 directory, and the Driver DLL File refers to the file shown in the ODBC Drivers tab of the ODBC32 Applet.

```
DriverId     Hex Value
REG_DWORD    Example: 00000019
```

This value shows the fileID of the Driver File shown in the Driver value.

```
FIL                 Database File Type
REG_SZ              Example: MS Access
```

This shows the database type for the database given by the DBQ value (explained previously).

```
Exclusive           0 or 1
REG_BINARY
```

If this value is set to 1, the database given by the DBQ value cannot be shared and is locked when any user is connected to it.

```
ReadOnly            0 or 1
REG_BINARY
```

If this value is set to 1, the database given by the DBQ value cannot be written to and is accessed in read-only mode.

```
SafeTransactions    0 or 1
REG_DWORD           Example: 00000000
```

When this value is set to 1, transactions written to the database are verified for accuracy and are not changed if an error occurs during processing. If this value is 0, changes are made immediately and are not rolled back when an error occurs.

```
SystemDB    System Database and Path
REG_SZ      Example: C:\Win\system32\system.mdw
```

This value shows the name and location of the system database used in conjunction with the database given by the DBQ value. SystemDB is set from the System Database area's radial buttons on the ADD DSN dialog box (refer to Figure 12.6).

```
UID    User Login ID
REG_SZ

PWD    User Login Password
REG_SZ
```

If you click the Advanced button from the ADD DSN dialog box, you see the screen in Figure 12.7.

Figure 12.7   The Set Advanced Options dialog box.

The strings entered into two text boxes, Login name and Password, are stored in the Registry in the values UID and PWD.

SQL-Specific Values

If the DSNName (as described in the previous section) refers to a SQL database, you may see these additional values:

```
Server      SQL Server Name
REG_SZ      Example: SONT2D
```

This value contains the name of the SQL server that has SQL Server installed on it.

```
UseProcForPrepare    Yes or No
REG_SZ
```

If this value is set to Yes, stored procedures are generated to support the SQLPrepare ODBC function.

```
OEMTOANSI    Yes or No
REG_SZ
```

This value determines how text pages are stored by the SQL server. A setting of 1 enables AnsitoOEM conversions.

```
Trusted_Connection    Yes or No
REG_SZ
```

These values show whether a Windows NT trusted domain can be used to access the SQL Server. A setting of 1 means that trusted domains can be used to connect to the SQL Server.

The Database Engines Key

Different database engines can be associated with an ODBC connection, depending on the type of database that it is connected to. All of these engine keys may have one or more values listed under them. Specific values will be discussed under each engine, and common values will be discussed in the "Common Database Engine Values" section.

The types of database engines used by ODBC, their subkeys, and their values are described in the following sections.

Microsoft Access Jet Database Engines

This is the Microsoft Access database engine; if used, it is found under the [HKEY_LOCAL_MACHINE\SOFTWARE\ODBC\ODBC.INI*DSNName*\Engines\Jet] key. There are no specific Access Jet values under this key.

> **Author Note**
>
> Although the password that is entered on this screen is not visible from the applet, it is plainly visible within the Registry editor. For this reason, these ODBC connections are not completely secure because any user can log into the database using the UID and PWD value settings.

dBASE, xBase, and Microsoft FoxPro Database Engines

This Excel Database engine, if used, is found under the [HKEY_LOCAL_MACHINE\
SOFTWARE\ODBC\ODBC.INI*DSNName*\Engines\Xbase] key. The specific dBASE, Xbase,
and FoxPro values under this key follow:

```
CollatingSequence    ASCII or International
REG_SZ
```

This value sets the collating sequence for any Microsoft FoxPro tables that will be
created or opened by using the Microsoft Jet database engine. This value's default is
ASCII.

```
Deleted    0 or 1
REG_BINARY
```

This value determines how records are treated when they are marked to be deleted.
A setting of 1 is similar to the Microsoft FoxPro command SET DELETED ON, which
instructs the Jet database engine to never reposition or retrieve a deleted record. A setting of 0 is similar to the Microsoft FoxPro command SET DELETED OFF, which
instructs the Jet database engine to treat deleted records the same as other records. This
value's default is 0.

```
Statistics    0 or 1
REG_BINARY
```

This value determines whether the SQL engine uses SQL Monitor to run and
store SQL runtime statistics.

Microsoft Excel Database Engines

This is the Excel database engine, and if used is found under the
[HKEY_LOCAL_MACHINE\SOFTWARE\ODBC\ODBC.INI*DSNName*\Engines\Excel] key.
The specific Excel values under this key follow:

```
MaxScanRows    Numerical Value
REG_DWORD
```

This value shows the number of rows that are scanned when the Excel database
engine is guessing the column types. If this value is set to 0, the entire file is searched.
This value's default is 25.

```
FirstRowHasNames    0 or 1
REG_BINARY
```

Troubleshooting

If you are using the production version of the Microsoft Jet Engine 3.0, you need to pay specific attention to the OEMTOANSI and Trusted_Connection values discussed previously. This is because the
3.0 version of this product reverses the meaning of the Boolean settings, interpreting a Yes setting as
No and a No setting as Yes. Keep this in mind when manipulating these settings.

Also, these settings are discussed here as if this error were not present. Other versions of the Microsoft
Jet Engine do not have this problem.

This value shows whether or not column names are to be imported using the table's first row. A setting of 1 indicates that names are present. This value's default is 1.

Text Database Engines

This is the Text database engine, and if used is found under the
`[HKEY_LOCAL_MACHINE\SOFTWARE\ODBC\ODBC.INI\`*DSNName*`\Engines\Text]` key. There are no specific text values under this key.

Common Database Engine Values

The values listed in this section are common to all database engine keys. These values follow:

```
ImplicitCommitSync          Yes or No
REG_SZ
```

This value governs how and when control is returned to a given executable statement when changes are made outside of the database. In other words, the value controls whether the Jet Engine can process other requests that are not acting on this specific database. A setting of `No` (the default) allows the processing to continue.

```
UserCommitSync              Yes or No
REG_SZ
```

This value governs how and when control is returned to a given executable statement when changes that are part of an explicit change are being processed by the Jet engine. A setting of `Yes` (the default) waits to return control until the changes are committed to the database.

```
ExclusiveAsyncDelay         Hex Value
REG_DWORD
```

If the database is opened exclusively, this value gives the maximum time that the Jet engine waits before committing asynchronous changes to the database. This value's default is 2000 ms.

```
SharedAsyncDelay            Hex Value
REG_DWORD
```

If the database is opened as shareable, this value gives the maximum time that the Jet engine waits before committing asynchronous changes to the database. This value's default is 50 ms.

```
MaxBufferSize               Setting >= 512KB
REG_DWORD
```

This value can be set from the Add DSN dialog box by using the Options button. The Jet 3.0 engine allocates memory for its memory buffer up to this setting, which enables the engine to efficiently manage memory without having to change Registry settings. Although this value can be calculated by using the following formula, any number that is at least equal to 512 can be used:

(Total RAM in MB - 12)/4 + 512 KB

```
PageTimeout          Numeric Value
REG_DWORD
```

This value shows the time between when non-read-only data is initially stored in an internal memory cache and the time that it should be invalidated. This value's default is 5000 ms, or 5 seconds.

```
LockRetry            Numeric Value
REG_DWORD
```

This value gives the amount of time that the Jet engine will repeatedly try to open a locked page before it returns an error message. This value's default is `20`.

```
Threads              Numeric Value
REG_DWORD
```

This value shows the number of background threads that Windows NT 4.0 makes available to the Jet engine.

```
Extensions           File Extensions
REG_SZ
```

This value holds the names of the file extensions that should be scanned when searching for text-based data. This value's defaults are `.txt`, `.csv`, `.tab`, and `.asc`.

The ODBCINST.INI Key

The [`HKEY_LOCAL_MACHINE\SOFTWARE\ODBC\ODBCINST.INI`] key holds information found in the Windows 3.1 ODBCINST.INI file. This key has several subkeys and values listed under it, which are described in the following sections.

The Driver Key

The [`HKEY_LOCAL_MACHINE\SOFTWARE\ODBC\ODBCINST.INI\`*DriverName*] key contains several subkeys under it, one for each driver installed for ODBC. Driver keys that may be found here, along with others not listed, follow:

- Microsoft Access Driver (*.mdb)
- SQL Server (Scripts *.sql; Master Database, .dat)
- Microsoft Excel Driver (*.xls)
- Microsoft FoxPro Driver (*.dbf)
- Microsoft Text Driver (*.txt, *.csv)

These driver keys contain several values that describe the installed ODBC drivers. A key can be found here for each driver available to ODBC. All keys contain the following set of values, which may have different settings, depending on the Driver key under which they are found. These values follow:

```
UsageCount      Numeric Value
REG_DWORD
```

This value contains installation information for the applications that use ODBC and the number of instances that an ODBC component has been installed on Windows NT. This count value is maintained for the three components that make up ODBC:

- ODBC drivers
- ODBC core components
- ODBC translators

For the ODBC translator and driver usage counts, a separate usage count is maintained for each installed component. The following functions increment the UsageCount value when called:

```
SQLInstallDriverManager
```

```
SQLInstallDriver
```

```
SQLInstallTranslator
```

Also, when ODBC components are removed, the UsageCount is decremented. Each time an ODBC component is uninstalled, a removal function is called and the component UsageCount is decremented. The removal functions are SQLRemoveDriverManager, SQLRemoveDriver, and SQLRemoveTranslator.

This value is created the first time one of the ODBC components is installed. If UsageCount reaches 0, this value is removed automatically.

```
Driver          Driver File and Path
REG_SZ          Example: C:\\WINNT\\System32\\odbcjt32.dll
```

This value shows the filename and path for the driver used by this DSN.

```
Setup           Driver File and Path
REG_SZ          Example: C:\\WINNT\\System32\\odbcjt32.dll
```

This value contains the filename and path used by the SETUP.EXE utility when ODBC is initially set up.

```
APILevel        1 or 2
REG_SZ
```

This value indicates whether the driver is accessed from the 32-bit or 16-bit API. A setting of 1 means that it is accessed by the 16-bit API; a setting of 2 means that it uses the 32-bit API.

```
DriverODBCVer   Version Number
REG_SZ
```

This value shows the version number of the driver.

```
FileExtns       File Extension
REG_SZ          Example: *.mdb
```

This value shows the file extensions that this database uses.

Microsoft Code Page Translator

This key shows the Microsoft Code Page Translator information. This translator may be installed or uninstalled one at a time; and its usage is tracked by its own `UsageCount` value, which behaves as explained in the previous section. The key is `[HKEY_LOCAL_MACHINE\SOFTWARE\ODBC\ODBCINST.INI\MS Code Page Translator]`. In addition to a `UsageCount` value, the key contains the following:

```
Translator    Translator File and Path
REG_SZ     Example: C:\\WINNT\\System32\\MSCPXL32.DLL
```

This value specifies the translator file and path.

```
Setup    Setup DLL and Path
REG_SZ     Example: C:\\WINNT\\System32\\MSCPXL32.DLL
```

This value contains the filename and path used by the setup.exe utility when ODBC is initially set up.

The ODBC Translator

This key shows the installed ODBC translators. These translators may be installed or uninstalled one at a time; their usage is tracked by the `UsageCount` value found under the specific translator's key, such as the Microsoft Code Page Translator key, which behaves as explained in the previous section. The ODBC Translator key is `[HKEY_LOCAL_MACHINE\SOFTWARE\ODBC\ODBCINST.INI\ODBC Translators]`, and it contains a value for each translator installed. A sample value for the Microsoft Code Page Translator is

```
Microsoft Code Page Translator        Installed
REG_SZ
```

If the specific translator is installed, the value for it found under this key has the same name as the translator, and it will be set to `Installed,` as seen in the previous example. If a translator is not installed, there is no value found here, and there is no translator key found under `[HKEY_LOCAL_MACHINE\SOFTWARE\ODBC\ODBCINST.INI]`.

ODBC Core Components

The `[HKEY_LOCAL_MACHINE\SOFTWARE\ODBC\ODBCINST.INI\ODBC Core]` key contains a `UsageCount` value that indicates that the core ODBC components are installed. Because all ODBC core components—including the Driver Manager, Cursor Library, Language Library, Administrator, any 16- or 32-bit thinking files, and so on—are uninstalled, as a whole this value indicates that the core components are installed.

13

Windows NT Profiles

- **The Hardware Profiles tab of the System applet**

  This part of the System applet is used to set boot options for Windows NT. Using this applet, you can create boot options that enable the use of hardware such as the notebook docking state, the monitor used, and other hardware.

- **The User Profiles tab of the System applet**

  This tab is used to set a user profile to either local or roaming mode. You can also use this tab to copy and export user profiles so that they can be used on other computers.

- **System policies and the System Policy Editor, POLEDIT.EXE**

  System policies are used by network administrators to configure and control individual users and their computers. Administrators use POLEDIT.EXE to set Windows NT profiles that are either network- or user-based. Using this application, you can create policies, which are either local or network-driven, that can affect Registry settings for both hardware and users.

The Hardware Profiles Tab of the System Applet

If you open the Control Panel and launch the System applet, you see several tabs. Select the Hardware Profiles tab and you see the screen shown in Figure 13.1.

On this tab, you see options, listed just under Available Hardware Profiles, for all profiles that are available for this computer. Each of these profiles is listed as a boot choice under the Hardware Configuration Boot menu that is displayed after NTDETECT for all computers that have more than one possible hardware profile.

The Registry entries made by this tab can be found under the Registry key `[HKEY_LOCAL_MACHINE\SYSTEM\CurrentControlSet\Hardware Profiles\####]`, where #### is the number that Windows NT assigns to the profiles, based upon the order listed in the previous tab. The hardware profile that is in use is listed under the key where #### is equal to *Current*. I will use `0001` for #### when discussing the following keys, but these settings also apply to the other numbered keys.

Figure 13.1 The Hardware Profiles tab of the System applet.

The Hardware Profiles Key

This key has several subkeys under it, which contain the hardware profile information for each of the profiles listed in the Hardware Profiles tab. These keys and their values are discussed in the following sections.

The Font Key

The values and settings under the [HKEY_LOCAL_MACHINE\SYSTEM\CurrentControlSet\ HardwareProfiles\0001\Software\Fonts] key govern the way each profile desktop is displayed. These values are copied to the [HKEY_CURRENT_CONFIG\Software\Fonts] key when Windows NT boots. This is how the hardware profile governs the desktop display. (These values are discussed in the Fonts section of Chapter 2.)

The following four values are used by some applications to set menu and toolbar fonts:

```
FIXEDFON.FON        Font Filename String
REG_SZ              vgafix.fon

FONTS.FON           Font Filename String
REG_SZ              vgasys.fon

LogPixels           Hexadecimal Number - 0x78 or 0x60
REG_DWORD

OEMFONT.FON         Font Filename String
REG_SZ              vgaoem.fon
```

Enabling Network Cards for Profiles

The use of network cards with hardware profiles can be enabled or disabled from the Hardware Profiles tab of the System applet by selecting a profile and clicking the Properties button. When you do this, you see the Docked Properties dialog box shown in Figure 13.2.

The network tab of this dialog box has one check box on it, labeled Network-disabled hardware profile. This check box is set through the following value under the `[HKEY_LOCALMACHINE\SYSTEM\CurrentControlSet\HardwareProfiles\Current\System\CurrentControlSet\Enum\ROOT\LEGACY_ELNK3\0000]` key:

    CSConfigFlags   0 or 1
    REG_DWORD

Setting this value to 1 enables network cards for the Current profile.

The VGA Save key

The values under the `[HKEY_LOCAL_MACHINE\SYSTEM\CurrentControlSet\Hardware Profiles\0001\System\CurrentControlSet\Services\VgaSave\Device0]` key are used to set video options such as resolution, panning, refresh, and so on. These values, which are discussed in Chapter 2, "Configuring Display Settings," are copied to the `[HKEY_CURRENT_CONFIG\System\CurrentControlSet\Services\VgaSave\Device0]` key, where they are used to set the desktop display. The values found here are:

    DefaultSettings.BitsPerPel
    REG_DWORD

    DefaultSettings.Flags
    REG_DWORD

    DefaultSettings.Vrefresh
    REG_DWORD

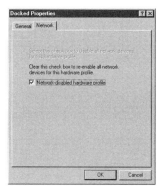

Figure 13.2 Enabling network cards from the Docked Properties dialog box.

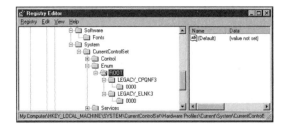

Figure 13.3   The \ROOT\ subkeys.

```
DefaultSettings.Xpanning
REG_DWORD

DefaultSettings.XResolution
REG_DWORD

DefaultSettings.Ypanning
REG_DWORD

DefaultSettings.Yresolution
REG_DWORD
```

Each hardware profile has these values.

The User Profiles Tab of the System Applet

Before we can talk about this tab we must first discuss the way that Windows NT 4.0 uses profile folders to create and store information for user profiles. These folders are the Default User folder and the ALLUSERS folder.

The Default User Folder

All user profiles are generated from the default user folder located at %SYSTEMROOT%\Profiles. This folder contains a separate folder for each profile available to the Windows NT computer. Not all computers have the same user profiles.

> **Tip**
>
> This value is found under each hardware profile key, where Current is replaced with **0001, 0002**, and so on. The value is also found under each network card that is found for the system. Each network card installed has a subkey under the [HKEY_LOCAL_MACHINE\SYSTEM\CurrentControlSet\Hardware Profiles\Current\System\CurrentControlSet\Enum \ROOT] key. Figure 13.3 shows two installed cards.

Furthermore, all folders under the Profiles folder that have users created for them using the User Manager contain a separate NTUSER.DAT file, discussed later in this chapter. These folders contain a link-list directory—a directory with pointers to other directories—that points to the profiled user's desktop components. Table 13.1 shows the folders and contents of the link-list directory, seen in Figure 13.4.

Table 13.1   **User Profile Folders**

User Profile Folder	Contents
Application Data	Application data. Items that this directory may contain are a customer dictionary and application configuration files. Items in this directory are usually placed there by application rules written into the application by the vendor.
Desktop	Shortcut and other items that appear on the desktop when Windows NT boots, except for the Network Neighborhood folder.
NetHood	Shortcuts that appear in the Network Neighborhood folder found on the desktop.
Personal	Shortcuts to program items.
PrintHood	Shortcuts to printer folder items.
Recent	Shortcuts to the most recently used items.
SendTo	Shortcuts to document items.
Start menu	Shortcuts to program items.
Templates	Shortcuts to template items.

Troubleshooting

If you have installed Windows NT 4.0 by upgrading a previous Windows NT 3.51 installation and you are using an old Matrox video card, the **VgaSave** part of the key may be labeled mga instead:
`[HKEY_CURRENT_CONFIG\System\CurrentControlSet\Services\mga\Device0]` key.

Warning

If you are using the NTFS file system, be sure that the user's profile directory has the correct read/write permissions for the specified user or you will see the `Can't open user profile` error message when the user tries to log in. This message can occur if you restrict the %SystemRoot% rights by using NTFS, but then do not exempt the user's profile directory because subdirectories inherit rights from the parent directory unless specified differently.

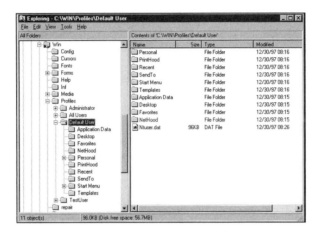

Figure 13.4 Default User profile folders, as seen with Explorer.

The ALLUSERS Folder

The ALLUSERS folder, shown in Figure 13.4, contains settings that are used when creating new user profiles. Stored under this folder are the Common Program Groups. These folders are available to all users that log onto the computer; and can only be created, modified, or deleted by users who are members of the Administrators group.

The NTUSER.DAT File

Windows NT 4.0 also uses the NTUSER.DAT file to manage user profiles. This file, which can be seen in Figure 13.4, is found under the root of each profile folder. This file contains the Registry keys, values, and settings that make up the Registry part of a user profile. This file is actually a copy of the HKEY_CURRENT_USER subkey that is cached on the computer's local hard drive. This subkey contains the settings used to control the logged-in user's Windows NT environment, including the items shown in Table 13.2.

> **Author Note**
> The SendTo folder can be used to extend the Send To menu that pops up when using the right mouse button. Items that you may want to add here are SendTo CommandLine and SendTo Microsoft Word, Excel, and so on.

Table 13.2 **NTUSER.DAT Registry Components**

Registry Component	Contains
Windows NT Explorer settings	All of the Windows NT Explorer settings that are user-definable. This component also includes all of the persistent network connections that are set by the user within Explorer.
Taskbar	Personal program groups, including group properties; program items, including item properties; plus all user settings for the Taskbar.
Printer settings	Network printer settings, but not local printer settings.
Control Panel	All Control Panel settings that are allowed to be set by the user.
Accessories	Settings that affect the user in terms of the Windows NT environment, including applications such as Calculator, Clock, Notepad, Paint, and HyperTerminal.
Help bookmarks	Bookmarks that the user placed in the Windows help files.

Registry Values Set from the User Profiles Tab

Certain values are set from the User Profiles tab of the System applet, as seen in Figure 13.5.

Open this applet and select the User Profiles tab. First, you see a dialog box that lists all of the users that are allowed to log on to this computer. Each of these users has a Registry key created under the [`HKEY_LOCAL_MACHINE\SOFTWARE\Microsoft\ WindowsNT\CurrentVersion\ProfileList\`] key. This subkey has the following form, which is the SID (security ID) for the user:

S-1-5-21-877493074-1263893664-382417117-1000

The values under this key, their settings, and where they are set from are:
```
UserPreference        0,1 or 3
REG_DWORD
```

This value is set from the Change Type dialog box, which you can reach by clicking the Change Type button shown in Figure 13.5. This dialog box has one set of radial buttons on it. If you select the Local Profile button, this value will either not exist or be set to `0`. If the second button, Roaming Profile, is selected, this value is set to `1`. When the Roaming Profile button is selected, the check box for slow connections is enabled. If you check this box, this value is set to `3`.

Author Note

You may not see the NetHood, PrintHood, Recent, or Templates folders on your computer. To see them, click the Explorer's Options menu, select View, and click the Show All Files radial button. You may also want to deselect the Hide File Extensions check box so that all extensions are displayed. Repeat this process if the folders are hidden again.

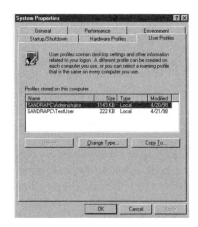

Figure 13.5   The User Profiles tab of the System applet

```
ProfileImagePath        Profile Path String
REG_EXPAND_SZ
```

This value holds a string that shows the path and filename of the profile. If the profile is a local profile, this path is of the form %SYSTEMROOT\PROFILES*USER*, where *USER* is the name of the user. If the profile is a roaming profile on a Windows NT network, the path points to the WINLOGON directory; and if you use a Novell network, the path points to the PUBLIC directory.

```
Sid
REG_BINARY
```

This is the SID that is assigned to each user by Windows NT 4.0.

```
CentralProfile     Template Path and Filename
REG_SZ             "c:\\poledit\\example.adm"
```

This value shows the name of the template that is used by the System Policy Editor to create user profiles. The System Policy Editor, POLEDIT.EXE, is discussed in the next section.

System Policies and the System Policy Editor

Administrators can use the System Policy Editor to create system policies, including both network and local policies. This application is found on the Windows NT 4.0 Server CD, in the CLIENTS\SRVTOOLS\WINNT\I386 directory for Intel machines. Copy the executable to your computer, find the COMMON.ADM and WINNT.ADM files from the CLIENTS\ directory, and copy them to your %SYSTEMROOT%\INF directory.

Now, launch POLEDIT.EXE and choose New Policy from the File menu. You should now see the screen in Figure 13.6.

Two icons of particular interest are the Default User and Default Computer parts of the policy file; they are discussed later in this section.

Double-click the Default Computer icon and click the + sign next to Windows NT Printers, and you will see the screen in Figure 13.7 (note that all three boxes will be gray when you open the icon).

In Figure 13.7, there are three boxes, each with a different setting:

- The first box with a check means that this feature is enabled.

- The second box, grayed out, means that this feature may be enabled, depending on other constraints that are discussed in the following sections.

- The third box is cleared, which means that this feature is not enabled.

Each policy feature can be set to any three of these values.

Before we can discuss the Registry values and settings that are set by this application, we must first have a brief discussion of policies and how they are implemented.

Policy Files

Windows NT 4.0 uses policies to define the Windows NT environment used by a user or a group of users. If POLEDIT.EXE is used to create the policy, it contains a collection of users and computers that is controlled by the policy. This control can be either from the network or the local PC. Group policies always take precedence over user profiles.

If you want the policy to be automatically downloaded from a Windows NT domain, you must name the file NTCONFIG.POL. If you want to change the path and/or name for this file, either use POLEDIT.EXE, discussed later, or change the

Warning

If you are using Novell 4.1 and your users are authenticated by the tree, you should replicate the policy file to the PUBLIC directory of all servers that can be used as an entry authentication point for the NDS tree.

Author Note

You can find out which SID is associated with which user by using the SID value to see the user name, which can then be associated with the SID subkey.

Author Note

The COMMON.ADM file contains the Registry settings that apply to both Windows NT 4.0 and Windows 95. The WINNT.ADM file contains the Registry settings that apply only to Windows NT 4.0. The Windows 95 file is WINDOWS.ADM and applies only to Windows 95.

Figure 13.6   POLEDIT.EXE, the System Policy Editor.

following values under the [HKEY_LOCAL_MACHINE\System\CurrentControlSet\Control\Update] key:

```
UpdateMode      0, 1, or 2
REG_DWORD
```

If this value is set to 0, then no policies are applied; if set to 1, policies are automatically downloaded from the validating domain controller's NETLOGON share if an NTCONFIG.POL file exists there. If this value is set to 2, manual policies are in effect, and the computer checks the setting of the following value to determine whether a policy is in effect:

```
NetworkPath        Manual Policy Filename and Path
REG_SZ             C:\POLICY\MyPolicy.pol
```

This value sets the path for manual updates.

```
Verbose             0 or 1
REG_DWORD
```

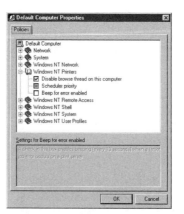

Figure 13.7   Settings for Default Computer.

When this value is set to 1, error messages associated with the location and loading of the policy file are displayed. A setting of 0 suppresses error messages from being displayed.

```
LoadBalance            0 or 1
REG_DWORD
```

When this value is set to 1 on Windows NT Server, the policy download uses network load balancing to help prevent network bottlenecks.

If you are using a Windows NT domain, and you want to use the automatic download feature of policy files, place this NTCONFIG.POL file in the NETLOGON share of the validating domain controller (DC). If you are using a Novell network, you have to place the NTCONFIG.POL file in the PUBLIC directory of every server that authenticates the user's login. After a Windows NT 4.0 workstation locates a policy, it is applied, as discussed in the following sections.

User Preference

If the policy file contains settings that affect the logged-in user (for example, the Sandra icon shown in Figure 13.6), these settings are written to the HKEY_CURRENT_USER key and all group settings are ignored. This is because user settings take precedence over group settings.

Author Note

If the Network Path value is set to a local path such as C:\Policy\MyPolicy.pol, it affects only the local computer. Any change to the policy needs to be made on all computers that have this local policy.

Warning

When you create shortcuts on a Windows NT computer, a UNC (Universal Naming Convention) path is embedded in the .lnk file (for example, \\SandraPC\Admin$). These embedded UNC paths are a problem if the link files are copied to the server and then used as part of the server-based policy. If this shortcut file is downloaded to a different computer than the one that it is created for, the path will be resolved to the local PC and the user will be asked for the original computer's administrator password. This problem can be fixed by applying the Microsoft Windows NT 4.0 Service Pack 3 and then following these steps:

1. Open REGEDIT.EXE and find the
    [HKEY_Current_User\Software\Microsoft\Windows\CurrentVersion\Policies\Explorer] Key.

    Add the following value and set it to 1:

    ```
    LinkResolveIgnoreLinkInfo     1
    REG_DWORD
    ```

Also, the Windows NT Server Resource Kit, Supplement 2 contains the executable SHORTCUT.EXE, which can also be used to correct this problem.

Applying the Default User

If Windows NT Workstation finds a policy file, but it does not contain settings for the logged-in user, then the Default User settings are applied to the HKEY_CURRENT_USER key, even if the user has logged on as administrator. However, if the user is a member of a group that has a policy defined for it, the group settings are applied to the HKEY_CURRENT_USER key instead of the default user settings.

If any policy setting has been grayed out for a group but enabled for the default user, the Default user settings are used. Default user settings take precedence over group settings only when the Group setting is not enabled.

User Group Membership

If Windows NT Workstation finds the policy file, but it does not have specific settings for the logged-in user and the user is a member of one or more groups with settings defined for it (for example, the NTGroup in Figure 13.6), the group settings are applied to the HKEY_CURRENT_USER key, beginning with the lowest priority group and ending with the highest priority group.

The Default Computer

All policy files contain computer information in addition to user information. And if the policy contains settings for a specific computer—for example, the SandraPC icon shown in Figure 13.6—these settings are applied to the HKEY_LOCAL_MACHINE key. If no settings are found for the specific computer, any settings enabled for the default computer are applied to the HKEY_LOCAL_MACHINE key.

Using POLEDIT.EXE to Control the Registry

You can use the System Policy Editor to control and modify the Registry. There are two ways to do this:

■ Open the application and use the Registry mode.

■ Create a new policy that will be downloaded when the user logs in.

Author Note

The default user for policy files should not be confused with the Default User folder mentioned in the last section. This default user is located within the policy file.

Author Note

Policy files do not use Novell groups. Only Windows NT groups can have policy settings enabled for them.

Using Registry Mode

You can use the System Policy Editor to modify the Registry. First, open POLEDIT.EXE; and then select File, Open Registry.

When you do this, you see the dialog box shown in Figure 13.8. This dialog box shows two icons: one for the local user and one for the local computer.

System Policy Templates

System Policy templates are the .ADM files that POLEDIT.EXE uses to determine which Registry entries can be changed. Two standard templates, COMMON.ADM and WINNT.ADM, are supplied with Windows NT Server. These are the files that you copied to the %SYSTEMROOT%\INF directory at the start of this chapter. This file can contain Registry locations, values, and default settings. You can select a template file by choosing Options, Policy Templates from the toolbar. This brings up the Policy Template Options dialog box shown in Figure 13.9.

Notice that there are no icons present in the dialog box. This is because all policies must be closed before new template files can be loaded. If the policies are not closed, the Add and Remove buttons are disabled.

Default User Settings

The following values are set by the options found when the System Policy Editor's Default User icon is launched using the default template.

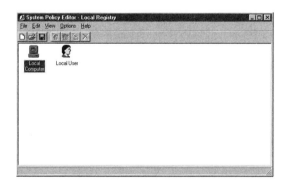

Figure 13.8 Opening the Registry with POLEDIT.EXE.

Author Note

System Policy Editor can only modify Registry settings that are available from the loaded template. This template can contain only User and Hardware information.

The Control Panel—Restrict Display Option

This setting, shown in Figure 13.10, removes or enables tabs in the Control Panel Display applet by setting the following values under the [HKEY_CURRENT_USER\ Software\Microsoft\Windows\CurrentVersion\Policies\System] key.

```
NoDispCPL                0 or 1
REG_DWORD
```

When this value is set to 1 or the Deny access to display icon box is checked (see Figure 13.10), the Display applet of the Control Panel does not display. If set to 0 or the box is cleared, the applet is displayed.

```
NoDispBackgroundPage     0 or 1
REG_DWORD
```

When this value is set to 1 or the Hide Background tab box is checked (see Figure 13.10), the Background tab on the Display applet does not display. If set to 0 or the box is cleared, the tab is displayed.

```
NoDispScrSavPage         0 or 1
REG_DWORD
```

When this value is set to 1 or the Hide Screen Saver tab box is checked (see Figure 13.10), the Screen Saver tab on the Display applet does not display. If set to 0 or the box is cleared, the tab is displayed.

```
NoDispAppearancePage     0 or 1
REG_DWORD
```

When this value is set to 1 or the Hide Appearance tab box is checked (see Figure 13.10), the Screen Saver tab on the Display applet does not display. If set to 0 or the box is cleared, the tab is displayed.

```
NoDispSettingsPage       0 or 1
REG_DWORD
```

When this value is set or the Hide Settings tab box is checked (see Figure 13.10), the Screen Saver tab on the Display applet does not display. If set to 0 or the box is cleared, the tab is displayed.

The Desktop Options

The Desktop option has two boxes under it: Wallpaper and Color scheme, as seen in Figure 13.11.

Figure 13.9   Loading a policy template.

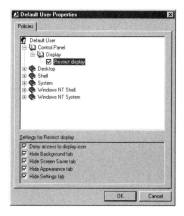

Figure 13.10 The Restrict Display option.

The Wallpaper box sets the following values under the [HKEY_CURRENT_
USER\Control Panel\Desktop] key, which sets the wallpaper file path and denotes
whether it should be tiled.

```
Wallpaper              Wallpaper Filename and path
REG_SZ
```

If the Wallpaper check box is checked, this value exists and will be set to the path
and filename shown in the Wallpaper text box in Figure 13.11. If the box is not
checked, there is no wallpaper value under this key.

```
TileWallpaper          0 or 1
REG_SZ
```

If this value is set to 1 or the Tile Wallpaper box is checked, the wallpaper given by
the value is tiled.

The Color scheme box sets the following values under the [HKEY_CURRENT_USER\
Control Panel\Appearance] key.

```
Current                Color Scheme Name
REG_SZ
```

If the Color scheme box is checked, this value exists and is set to the Color scheme
name. If the box is cleared, this value does not exist.

The Shell Restrictions Options

These options, shown in Figure 13.12, restrict certain properties of the Windows NT
desktop.

Figure 13.11 The Desktop options.

These options set values under more than one Registry key. The values set under the [HKEY_CURRENT_USER\Software\Microsoft\Windows\CurrentVersion\Policies\ Explorer] key are:

```
NoRun           0 or 1
REG_DWORD
```

When this value is set to 1 or the Remove Run Command from Start menu box is checked, the Run command shown on the Start menu is removed.

```
NoSetFolders            0 or 1
REG_DWORD    Off
```

Figure 13.12 The Shell Restrictions options.

When this value is set to 1 or the Remove folders from Settings on Start menu box is checked, the Control Panel and Printers folders, found under the Start menu's Settings option, are removed.

```
NoSetTaskbar              0 or 1
REG_DWORD
```

When this value is set to 1 or the Remove Taskbar from Settings on Start menu box is checked, the Taskbar folder, found under the Start menu's Settings option, is removed.

```
NoFind                    0 or 1
REG_DWORD
```

When this value is set to 1 or the Remove Find command from Start menu box is checked, the Find command, found on the Start menu, is removed.

```
NoDrives             3fffffff
REG_DWORD
```

If this value exists or if the Hide drives in My Computer box is checked, no drives are displayed in the My Computer folder.

```
NoNetHood                 0 or 1
REG_DWORD
```

When this value is set to 1 or the Hide Network Neighborhood box is checked, the Network Neighborhood icon is removed from the Windows NT desktop.

```
NoDesktop                 0 or 1
REG_DWORD
```

When this value is set to 1 or the Hide all items on desktop box is checked, all icons are removed from the Windows NT desktop.

```
NoClose                   0 or 1
REG_DWORD
```

When this value is set to 1 or the Disable Shut Down command box is checked, the Shut Down command is removed from the Start menu.

```
NoSaveSettings            0 or 1
REG_DWORD
```

Author Note

Although removing the Run command does not allow the running of applications using this command prompt, users can still launch applications from Explorer, the DOS command, Internet browser, and so on. To lock down the running of applications further, see the Run only allowed Windows applications setting, discussed in a later section.

Author Note

If both the NoSetFolders and NoSetTaskbar values are set to 1, the Settings option on the Start menu is removed entirely.

If this value is set to 1 or if the Don't save settings at exit box is checked, the user cannot save any changes made to the Windows NT system.

The following values are found under the [HKEY_CURRENT_USER\Software\ Microsoft\Windows\CurrentVersion\Policies\Network] key:

```
NoEntireNetwork              0 or 1
REG_DWORD
```

When this value is set to 1 or the No Entire Network in Network Neighborhood box is checked, the Network Neighborhood icon exists, but the Entire Network option is not displayed in the Network Neighborhood folder.

```
NoWorkgroupContents          0 or 1
REG_DWORD
```

When this value is set to 1 or the No workgroup contents in Network Neighborhood box is checked, the Network Neighborhood icon exists, but the Workgroup option is not displayed in the Network Neighborhood folder.

The System Restrictions Options

These options, shown in Figure 13.13, restrict access to the Windows NT Registry.

The values that are set by these options can be found under several different Registry keys. These keys and their values are:

- [HKEY_CURRENT_USER\Software\Microsoft\Windows\CurrentVersion\ Policies\System]

```
    DisableRegistryTools         0 or 1
    REG_DWORD
```

When this value is set to 1 or the Disable Registry editing tools box is checked, the user cannot run either REGEDIT.EXE or REGEDT32.EXE because each of these programs check this value when they launch.

> **Tip**
>
> You do not have to remove all of the drives in the My Computer folder. The **NoDrives** value can be used to selectively hide drives because the rightmost bit of this hexadecimal value represents the A: drive, and the leftmost bit represents the Z: drive. To hide a specific drive, turn on its bit. Use the following decimal numbers to hide the given drive:
>
> A: 1, B: 2, C: 4, D: 8, E: 16, F: 32, G: 64, H: 128, I: 256, J: 512, K: 1024, L: 2048, M: 4096, N: 8192, O: 16384, P: 32768, Q: 65536, R: 131072, S: 262144, T: 524288, U: 1048576, V: 2097152, W: 4194304, X: 8388608, Y: 16777216, Z: 33554432, ALL: 67108863.

> **Author Note**
>
> Removing the Shut Down command does not prevent the user from pressing Ctrl+Alt+Delete to restart the computer via the Task Manager. If you want to prevent this, remove the user's Shut Down the System right by using the User Manager.

■ [HKEY_CURRENT_USER\Software\Microsoft\Windows\CurrentVersion\Policies\
  Explorer\RestrictRun]
      1   Application Name
      REG_SZ

This value determines what applications can run if the Run only allowed
Windows applications box is checked.

If more than one application was added to the dialog box produced when you click
the Show button, there will be a numerical value listed under the previous key for
each application. These values always start at 1.

The Windows NT Shell—Custom Folders Options

These options, shown in Figure 13.14, are used to customize the programs setting on
the Start menu.

The values that are set by these options can be found under several different
Registry keys. These keys and their values are:

Key: [HKEY_CURRENT_USER\Software\Microsoft\Windows\CurrentVersion\
Explorer\User Shell Folders]
    Programs   UNC Path to the New Programs Folder
    REG_SZ

When this value is set to a pathname, or the Custom Programs folder box is
checked and a path is entered into the text box, the programs shown under the

Figure 13.13 Restricting Registry access.

Tip

If you restrict applications by using the RestrictRun values, be sure to add the SYSTRAY.EXE and
SETUP.EXE programs found in the %SystemRoot%\System32 directory, or else the Start button will not
appear and no programs will run.

Programs setting of the Start menu are read from this new location. The default for this setting is %USERPROFILE%\Start Menu\Programs.

```
Desktop          UNC path for the new Desktop folder
REG_SZ
```

When this value is set to 1 or the Custom desktop icons box is checked, the Desktop icons are read from this new location. The default for this setting is %USERPROFILE%\Desktop.

```
Startup          UNC path to the new Start folder
REG_SZ
```

When this value is set to 1 or the Custom Startup folder box is checked, the Start folder, found under the Programs setting on the Start menu, is read from this new location. The default for this setting is %USERPROFILE%\Start Menu\Programs\Startup.

```
NetHood             UNC Path to the new folder
REG_SZ
```

When this value is set to 1 or the Custom Network Neighborhood box is checked, the Network Neighborhood folder found is read from this new location. The default for this setting is %USERPROFILE%\NetHood

```
Start Menu          UNC Path to the new folder
REG_SZ
```

When this value is set to 1 or the Custom Start menu box is checked, the Start menu folders are read from this new location. The default for this setting is %USERPROFILE%\Start Menu.

```
Key: [HKEY_CURRENT_USER\Software\Microsoft\Windows\CurrentVersion\
Policies\Explorer]
NoStartMenuSubFolders        0 or 1
REG_DWORD
```

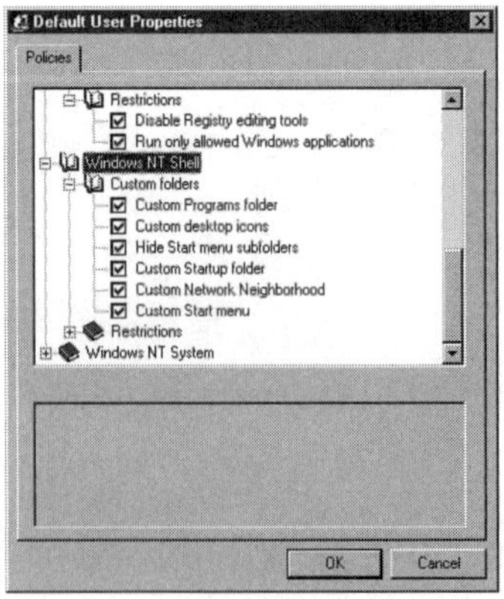

Figure 13.14 Restricting custom folders.

If this value is set to 1, or the Hide Start menu subfolders box is checked, and the `Programs` value is set to a path, the normal Start menu folders are hidden.

The Windows NT Shell—Restrictions Options

These options, shown in Figure 13.15, restrict program settings on the Start menu.

The values that are set by these options can be found under several different Registry keys. These keys and their values are:

Key: [HKEY_CURRENT_USER\Software\Microsoft\Windows\CurrentVersion\
Policies\Explorer]

EnforceShellExtensionSecurity   0 or 1
REG_DWORD

When this value is set to 1 or if the Only use approved shell extensions box is checked, only the extensions listed under the [HKEY_ROOT] key can be created.

NoFileMenu   0 or 1
REG_DWORD

When this value is set to 1 or if the Remove File menu from Explorer box is checked, the File menu option is removed from Microsoft Explorer. (This option was added with Windows NT Service Pack 2 and is not shown in Figure 13.15.)

NoCommonGroups   0 or 1
REG_DWORD

Figure 13.15 Restricting program settings.

Troubleshooting
Always set the NoStartMenuSubFolders value to 1 when the **Program** value is in use.

When this value is set to 1 or if the Remove common program groups from Start menu box is checked, common groups found under the Programs setting on the Start menu do not display.

```
NoTrayContextMenu              0 or 1
REG_DWORD
```

When this value is set to 1 or if the Disable Context Menus for the Taskbar box is checked, then the content menus on the Taskbar will be removed. (This option was added with Windows NT Service Pack 2 and is not shown in Figure 13.15.

```
NoViewContextMenu              0 or 1
REG_DWORD
```

When this value is set to 1 or if the Disable Explorer's default Context menu box is checked, the content menus that appear when the right mouse button is clicked are removed. (This option was added with Windows NT Service Pack 2 and is not shown in Figure 13.15.)

```
NoNetConnectDisconnect              0 or 1
REG_DWORD
```

When this value is set to 1 or if the Remove the Map Network Drive and Disconnect Network Drive options box is checked, the Map Network Drive and Disconnect Network Drive buttons, along with the Tools menu, are removed from Microsoft Explorer. The context menu for My Computer is also removed, which prevents the user from creating new network drive mappings. (This option was added with Windows NT Service Pack 2 and is not shown in Figure 13.15.)

```
LinkResolvedIgnoreLinkInfo
REG_DWORD
```

When this value is set to 1 or if the Disable link file tracking box is checked, link file tracking is disabled. This value is also set to 1 if sharing is not used. (This option was added with Windows NT Service Pack 2 and is not shown in Figure 13.15.)

The Windows NT System Options

These options, shown in Figure 13.16, are used to set Windows NT system options.

The values that are set by these options can be found under several different Registry keys. The following two values are found under the
`[HKEY_CURRENT_USER\Software\Microsoft\Windows NT\CurrentVersion\Winlogon]` key.

```
ParseAutoexec              0 or 1
REG_SZ
```

Author Note

When you right-click a shortcut and choose Properties, you see the path that the shortcut points to—the *absolute path*. When the LinkResolvedIgnoreLinkInfo value is set to **1**, the absolute path is used. Use this setting when copying links to different computers.

When this value is set to 1 or if the Parse Autoexec.bat box is checked, environment variables that are declared in the computer's AUTOEXEC.BAT file are included in the user's Windows NT environment.

```
RunLogonScriptSync          0 or 1
REG_DWORD
```

When this value is set to 1 or if the Run logon scripts synchronously box is checked, the logon script finishes processing before the items in the startup group can execute.

```
Key: [HKEY_CURRENT_USER\Software\Microsoft\Windows\CurrentVersion\Policies\
System]
DisableTaskMgr              0 or 1
REG_DWORD    Off
```

When this value is set to 1 or if the Disable Task Manager box is checked, the Task Manager execution is disabled. (This option was added with Windows NT Service Pack 2 and is not shown in Figure 13.16.)

```
Key: [HKEY_CURRENT_USER\Software\Microsoft\Windows\CurrentVersion\
Explorer\Tips]
Show                        0 or 1
REG_DWORD
```

When this value is set to 1 or if the Show welcome tips at logon box is checked, the welcome screen appears when the user logs in. (This option was added with Windows NT Service Pack 2 and is not shown in Figure 13.16.)

Default User Settings

The following values are set by the options found when the System Policy Editor's Default Computer icon is launched. The options that are available for the default computer are shown in Figure 13.17.

Figure 13.16   Windows NT System options.

Network—System Policies Update

The first of the Default Computer options, System Policies Update, was discussed at the start of this chapter. Listed here are the values discussed earlier, with the Default Computer options that set them.

```
UpdateMode    0, 1, or 2
REG_DWORD
```

Checking the Remote update box shown in Figure 13.17, along with setting the Update mode text box sets this value as follows:

- 0 if the Remote update box is cleared.

- 1 if the Remote update box is checked and the Update mode text box is set to automatic.

- 2 if the Remote update box is checked and the Update mode text box is set to manual.

```
NetworkPath      Manual Policy Filename and Path
REG_SZ           C:\POLICY\MyPolicy.pol
```

The setting for this value, which is read from the text shown in the path for manual update text box, is only used when the UpdateMode value is set to 2.

```
Verbose          0 or 1
REG_DWORD
```

If the Display error messages check box is checked, this value is set to 1.

```
LoadBalance      0 or 1
REG_DWORD
```

If the Load balancing check box is checked, this value is set to 1.

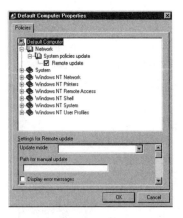

Figure 13.17   The Default Computer options.

System—SNMP Options

The next group of options, shown in Figure 13.18, set options for Windows NT Simple Network Mail Protocol (SNMP).

These options set values found under subkeys of the [HKEY_LOCAL_MACHINE\System\ CurrentControlSet\Services\SNMP\Parameters] key. These subkeys and their values are:

- \ValidCommunities

  ```
  1                    Text of Valid Community
  REG_SZ
  ```

  The values found under this key start with 1 and are incremented by 1; they are set by checking the Communities check box, clicking the Show button, and using the Show dialog box to add SNMP communities. There is one value here for each community listed in the Show dialog box. This value is similar to the value set by the Run only allowed Windows applications check box in the Default User options.

- \PermittedManagers

  ```
  1                    Text of Permitted Manager
  REG_SZ
  ```

  The values under this key are created in the same manner as the previous value: by checking the Permitted managers check box, clicking the Show button, and using the Show dialog box to add SNMP permitted managers. There is one value for each permitted manager listed in the Show dialog box.

- \TrapConfiguration\Public

  ```
  1                    Text for Public Communities Traps
  REG_SZ
  ```

Figure 13.18   Default Computer System options.

2g5674‑ 53habmcde

The values under this key are created in the same manner as the previous values: by checking the Traps for Public community check box, clicking the Show button, and using the Show dialog box to add SNMP public communities traps. There is one value for each public community trap listed in the Show dialog box.

System—Run Options

The next option, also shown in Figure 13.18, sets options for SNMP. This option sets one value found under the [HKEY_LOCAL_MACHINE\Software\Microsoft\Windows\CurrentVersion\Run] key. This value is:

```
Application   Text Name
REG_SZ
```

Checking the Run check box, clicking the Show button, and adding programs with the Show Contents dialog box sets this value. There is one value listed under this key for each application added. The value is set to the text entered into the Value text box of the Add dialog box. If the Run check box is cleared, then this value is removed from the Registry.

Windows NT Network—Sharing Options

The next group of options, shown in Figure 13.19, sets Sharing options for Windows NT shared drives.

These options set values under the [HKEY_LOCAL_MACHINE\System\CurrentControlSet\Services\LanManServer\Parameters] key. These values are:

```
AutoShareWks              0 or 1
REG_DWORD
```

This value is Windows NT Workstation-specific and, if set to 1 or the Create hidden drive shares (workstation) check box is checked, <Drive>$ and <Admin>$ shares are created automatically when Windows NT Workstation starts.

```
AutoShareServer           0 or 1
REG_DWORD
```

This value is Windows NT Workstation-specific and, if set to 1 or the Create hidden drive shares (server) check box is checked, <Drive>$ and <Admin>$ shares are created automatically when Windows NT Server starts.

Windows NT Printing Options

The next group of options, shown in Figure 13.20, sets Windows NT Printing options for Windows NT.

These options set values under the [HKEY_LOCAL_MACHINE\System\CurrentControlSet\Control\Print] key. These values are:

```
DisableServerThread       0 or 1
REG_DWORD
```

Figure 13.19 Drive Sharing options.

If this value is set to 1 or the Disable browse thread on this computer check box is checked, the print spooler does not send print jobs to other print servers.

```
SchedulerThreadPriority          0, 1 or ffffffff
REG_DWORD
```

This value can be set by checking the Settings for Scheduler priority check box and then setting the Priority text box to either Above Normal or Below normal. This value is set as follows:

- **0**. The Settings for Scheduler Priority check box is cleared.

- **1**. The Settings for Scheduler Priority check box is checked and the Priority text box is set to Below Normal.

- **ffffffff**. The Settings for Scheduler Priority check box is checked and the Priority text box is set to Above Normal.

Figure 13.20 Windows NT printing options.

```
BeepEnabled                    0 or 1
REG_DWORD
```

If this value is set to 1 or the Beep for error enabled check box is checked, beeping will occur every 10 seconds when a remote print job error is produced on a print server.

Windows NT Remote Access

The next group of options, shown in Figure 13.21, sets Windows NT Remote Access.

These options set values under the [HKEY_LOCAL_MACHINE\System\ CurrentControlSet\Services\RemoteAccess\Parameters] key. These values are:

```
AuthenticateRetries            Hexadecimal Number (1 - 10)
REG_DWORD
```

Checking the Max number of unsuccessful authentication retries check box, and setting the Number of Retries text box to a number between 1 and 10 sets this value. This value sets the number of retries that are attempted to authenticate a user onto the Windows NT network. If the Max number of unsuccessful authentication retries check box is cleared, this value does not exist. The default value is 2.

```
AuthenticateTime               Hexadecimal Number (20 - 600)
REG_DWORD
```

Checking the Max time limit for authentication check box and setting the Length in Seconds text box to a number between 20 and 600 sets this value. This value sets the maximum time, in seconds, to wait for Windows NT to authenticate the user on the network. If the Max time limit for authentication check box is cleared this value does not exist. The default value is 120.

```
CallbackTime                   Hexadecimal Number (2 - 12)
REG_DWORD
```

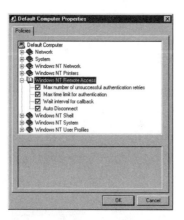

Figure 13.21   Windows NT Remote Access.

Checking the Wait interval for callback check box and setting the Length in Seconds text box to a number between 2 and 12 sets this value. This value sets the time, in seconds, that Windows NT waits before performing a callback from a RAS dial-in user. The default is 2.

```
AutoDisconnect                    Hexadecimal Number (0 - 20)
REG_DWORD
```

Checking the Auto Disconnect and setting the Disconnect After (Minutes) text box to a number between 0 and 20 sets this value. This value sets the time, in minutes, that Windows NT waits before disconnecting a RAS client. The default is 20.

Windows NT Shell—Custom Shared Folders Options

The group of options, shown in Figure 13.22, sets options for Windows NT Custom Shared Folders.

These options set values under the [HKEY_LOCAL_MACHINE\Software\Microsoft\ Windows\CurrentVersion\Explorer\User Shell Folders] key. These values are:

```
Common Programs    Path to location of shared programs items
REG_EXPAND_SZ
```

Checking the Custom shared Programs folder check box and then setting the Path to Location of Shared Programs Items text box sets this value. The default is %SystemRoot%\Profiles\All Users\Start Menu\Programs.

```
Common Desktop              UNC Folder Path
REG_EXPAND_SZ
```

Checking the Custom shared desktop icons check box and then setting the Path to Location of Shared Desktop Icons text box sets this value. The default is %SystemRoot%\Profiles\All Users\Desktop.

```
Common Start Menu              UNC Folder Path
REG_EXPAND_SZ
```

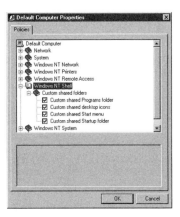

Figure 13.22   Windows NT Custom Shared Folders options.

Checking the Custom shared Start menu check box and then setting the Path to Location of Shared Start Menu Items text box sets this value. The default is %SystemRoot%\Profiles\All Users\Start Menu.

```
Common Startup             UNC Folder Path
REG_EXPAND_SZ
```

Checking the Custom shared Startup folder check box and then setting the Path to Location of Shared Startup Items text box sets this value. The default is %SystemRoot%\Profiles\All Users\Start Menu\Programs\Startup.

Windows NT System—Logon Options

The next group of options, shown in Figure 13.23, sets Windows NT Logon options.

These options set values under the [HKEY_LOCAL_MACHINE\Software\Microsoft\ Windows NT\CurrentVersion\Winlogon] key. These values are:

```
LegalNoticeCaption         Caption Text
REG_SZ
```

Checking the Logon banner check box and then entering text into the Caption text box sets this value to the entered text. If the Logon Banner check box is cleared, this value is removed.

```
LegalNoticeText            Notice Text
REG_SZ
```

Checking the Logon banner check box and then entering text into the Text text box sets this value to the entered text. You can control the display of the Notice by adding a LF/CR (line feed/carriage return) character to your text. If the Logon Banner check box is cleared, this value is removed.

```
ShutdownWithoutLogon       0 or 1
REG_SZ
```

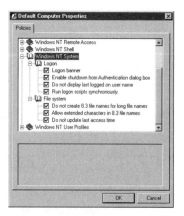

Figure 13.23 Windows NT Custom Logon options.

When this value is set to 1 or the Enable shutdown from Authentication dialog box check box is checked, the Shutdown button found on the Windows NT login screen is removed.

```
DontDisplayLastUserName          0 or 1
REG_SZ
```

When this value is set to 1 or the Do not display last logged on user name check box is checked, the name of the last user to be authenticated to the network does not display in the logon box when Ctrl+Alt+Delete is pressed.

```
RunLogonScriptSync               0 or 1
REG_SZ
```

When this value is set to 1 or the Run logon scripts synchronously check box is checked, the Windows NT shell, including the programs in the startup group, delays initializing until the login script finishes processing. This value takes precedence over the setting for this value in the Default User options.

Windows NT System—File System Options

The next group of options, shown in Figure 13.23, sets Windows NT File System Options. These options set values under the [HKEY_LOCAL_MACHINE\System\ CurrentControlSet\Control\FileSystem] key. These values are:

```
NtfsDisable8dot3NameCreation     0 or 1
REG_DWORD
```

When this value is set to 1 or the Do not create 8.3 filenames for long filenames check box is checked, the 8.3 filename is not created for long filenames.

```
NtfsAllowExtendedCharacterIn8dot3Name   0 or 1
REG_DWORD
```

When this value is set to 1 or the Allow extended characters in 8.3 filenames check box is checked, extended characters are allowed when creating 8.3 filenames.

```
NtfsDisableLastAccessUpdate      0 or 1
REG_DWORD
```

When this value is set to 1 or the Do not update last access time check box is checked, a user can read a file without updating the last access time property of the file. This increases the performance of file open utilities.

Windows NT User Profiles Options

The next group of options, shown in Figure 13.23, sets Windows User Profiles options.

These options set values under the [HKEY_LOCAL_MACHINE\Software\Microsoft\ Windows NT\CurrentVersion\Winlogon] key. These values are:

```
DeleteRoamingCache               0 or 1
REG_DWORD
```

When this value is set to 1 or the Delete cached copies of roaming profiles check box is checked, if a user logs onto an interactive session and uses a roaming profile, the roaming user profile (which is cached locally) is deleted when the user logs off.

```
SlowLinkDetectEnabled          0 or 1
REG_DWORD
```

When this value is set to 1 or the Automatically detect slow network connections check box is checked, then Windows NT detects the existence of slow networks. This value should be set to 1 when connecting with RAS.

```
SlowLinkTimeOut     Hexadecimal Number (1 - 20000)
REG_DWORD
```

When this value is set to 1, or the Automatically detect slow network connections check box is checked and the Time in Milliseconds text box is set from 1-20000; Windows NT waits the given number of milliseconds when determining if a slow network exists. The default is 2000.

```
Show                Hexadecimal Number (0 - 600)
REG_DWORD
```

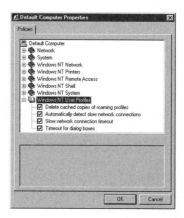

Figure 13.24   Windows NT User Profiles options.

> **Warning**
>
> Setting the NtfsDisable8dot3NameCreation value to **1** can cause DOS programs and some Windows programs to not be able to find files with long filenames.

> **Warning**
>
> When the NtfsAllowExtendedCharacterIn8dot3Name value is set to **1**, computers that do not have the same character code page installed may not be able to read 8.3 filenames that were created with extended characters from a different character code page.

When this value is set to 1, or the Timeout for dialog boxes check box is checked and the Time (Seconds) text box is set from 1-600, Windows NT waits the given number of seconds before closing the User Profile Request dialog box. After the dialog box is automatically closed, Windows NT uses the default user profile values. If this value is set to 0, the user profile defaults are accepted. The default is 30.

14

Security

- **The Windows NT security model**

  This section briefly covers the Windows NT security model and its components. The Registry keys and values that affect these components are discussed in the following sections.

- **Settings for user security**

  This section covers the Registry keys and values that allow Windows NT users to have secure identities. The identities are secured when authenticated by networks and network groups; these groups then grant access to resources.

- **Settings for permissions**

  This section discusses Registry restrictions in terms of the rights and permissions that can be set on certain Registry keys to prevent operating system changes.

- **The C2 Security Manager**

  This section discusses the Registry settings involved in making Windows NT 4.0 C2 security-compliant.

The Windows NT Security Model

The Windows NT Security Model guarantees that each Windows NT user is uniquely identified to the operating system. To a large extent, the Windows NT security model uses the Registry to store and manipulate user security data.

Before we look at the Registry's role in the Windows NT security model, we must first discuss the structure of this model; we start with the Windows NT user logon process.

The Logon Process

Although this process was discussed in Chapter 10, "Modifying the Windows NT Workstation Boot Process," this section discusses the security issues associated with the boot process. This security process includes the generation of the Login dialog box and uses the login name to identify the user, and the login password to validate the user. This part of the login is interactive and involves the following components:

- *Logon process:* This is the logon dialog box.

- *Security subsystem:* This system defines the access-validation and audit-generation policy for the system.

- *Authentication package:* This component checks the user accounts database and determines whether the user has a local account. If the user is a local user, the username and password are authenticated to the local user accounts database. If the user is not found locally, authentication passes to the alternate user accounts database.

- *Security Account Manager (SAM) database:* Once the user is authenticated, the SAM, which is the owner of the user accounts database, returns the security identifier (SID, or security ID) for the user and any global groups that the user belongs to. The SID is one of the most important aspects of Windows NT security and is discussed in the next section.

The Security Identifiers

SIDs are associated with all Windows NT-named objects, token objects, threads, and named and unnamed processes; and are used by Windows NT to identify uniquely a user or group. Once a SID is assigned to a user, it is never subsequently used to identify a different user. The SID is composed of the user's login, password, domain information, and system time and date. This information is represented in binary form in the following cryptic format:

$$S-1-X-Y^1-Y^2-Y^3...(RID) \text{ to } Y^n$$

> **Note**
>
> Because Windows NT 4.0 can support multiple authentication packages, developers of commercial software can create a DLL that contains their own custom authentication package. This DLL is called the *Microsoft Graphical Identification and Authentication DLL*, or MSGINA.DLL, and it is located in the %SYSTEMROOT%\SYSTEM32 directory. This DLL can be used to authenticate users to more than one network simultaneously.
>
> Care should be taken to prevent unauthorized access or replacement of this DLL. The easiest way to do this is to implement the NTFS file system and restrict access to the SYSTEM32 directory to the Administrator account only.

The prefix S-1 shows that the SID is Revision 1. The X value represents the SID creator's authority identifier. The authority value identifier is 48 bits long and is probably the most important information contained in a SID. This value identifies the agency that issued the SID; typically, it represents a corporation or large organization if a domain is in use, or the local Windows NT system for standalone installations.

The Y values represent the SID authority subidentifiers, and the last Y value represents the relative identifier (RID). A domain server uses RID values to create unique SIDs for workstations from the server's base SID. User and group RIDs start at 1,000 and increase by 1 for each user or group that is added to the domain.

The Owner SID

SIDs can be either an owner SID or the owner's group SID. Owner SIDs can belong to either the group or user that owns the object. Only the owner of an object can change its access permissions.

The Group SID

The group SID shows the object's associated group. This is different from the group owner' SID because the associated group is allowed access only to the object, but cannot change its permissions. This SID is only used by the POSIX (Portable Operating System Interface for Computing Environments) subsystem and is ignored by all other Windows NT components.

SIDs are stored in the Registry and are discussed later in this chapter. After the SAM assigns the SIDs, a logon session is created and the SIDs associated with the user are passed to the Local Security Authority (LSA), as described in the next section.

The Local Security Authority (LSA)

This component is the workhorse of the Windows NT security model because it validates the user's permission to use the operating system; it assigns access tokens, manages the local security policy, and provides the interactive user authentication services. This component also manages the audit policy and determines how the audit messages generated by the Security Reference Monitor are logged.

The Security Reference Monitor

This component is the Windows NT security enforcer. It compares the user's permissions with an object's access rights and determines whether the user can access the object. This component is active in the kernel and user mode, and it guarantees that the users who try to access objects have the correct permissions and rights.

The Access Token

Once the LSA authenticates the user, an *access token* is generated for the user that contains all the SIDs and the user rights that belong to the SIDs. This access token is then passed to the Win32 subsystem with a success flag set.

The Win32 Subsystem

At this point in the interactive logon process, the Win32 subsystem starts the Windows NT desktop. Finally, an access token is created for this desktop (the Windows NT shell) that contains all the information related to every object that the user attempts to access or run.

The Security Descriptor

All Windows NT-named objects have a security data structure associated with them called the *security descriptor*. This structure holds the object's security information as it is reported to Windows NT. This descriptor contains system-wide permissions that are applied to all users when they are created with the Windows NT Workstation User Manager or Windows NT Server's User Manager for Domains tool.

This information comprises the standard Windows NT security set that is specific to each instance of an object, and contains the following:

- SIDs. The security descriptor contains all owner and group SID information created for a user.

- Access Control Lists (ACLs). ACLs can include the discretionary and/or system ACL. These ACLs contain Access Control Entries (ACEs) that contain a user's or a group's access permissions. Each ACE in turn contains an Access Mask defining the actions for object types.

There are two types of ACLs:

- Discretionary Access Control Lists (DACLs) contain discretionary protection information. If an object has an associated DACL that is empty, no access is granted to the user. However, if an object does not have a DACL associated with it, any user is granted access.

- System ACLs are controlled by the security administrator and are used to control audit message generation.

Access Control Entries (ACE) determine the access or audit permissions that are granted to users or groups for specific objects. Table 14.1 describes the three ACE types.

Note
If you use the NTFS file system, all objects that are created or stored under directories inherit the parent folder ACL that defines directory permissions, unless inheritance has been turned off on the folder.

Table 14.1 **ACE Types**

ACE	Security
AccessAllowed	Used with Discretionary ACLs, this ACE allows access to an object or resource by comparing a user's or a group's SID to the list of SIDs contained in an ACE. If the SID exists in the ACE, the user or group is granted the rights and permissions, as listed within the same ACE.
AccessDenied	Used with Discretionary ACLs, this ACE works similarly to the previous one, except that if the SID exists in the ACE, the user or group is not given access to the object or resource, as stated by the ACE.
SystemAudit	Used with System ACLs, this ACE produces a log or audit of security events.

Each ACE includes an Access Mask that contains all possible actions or permissions associated with the object. Each ACE grants rights to a user of the object, which are grouped as follows:

- *Specific types:* Each mask has an object associated with it and contains the object's access mask information. The rights that can be assigned with this type are called an object's *Specific Access Mask,* and may include such rights as ReadData, WriteData, Execute, ReadAttributes, and others. These types, as many as 16 per object, are defined when the object is created.

- *Standard types:* All objects can have Standard types defined for them; they consist of the access permissions SYNCRONIZE, WRITE_OWNER, WRITE_DAC, READ_CONTROL, and DELETE

- *Generic types:* When a user requests access to an object the three Generic types are mapped from the Specific and Standard types. The three types are FILE_GENERIC_READ, FILE_GENERIC_WRITE_, and FILE_GENERIC_EXECUTE.

The Security Descriptor Format

The information contained in the security descriptor can be formatted in the following two ways:

- *Absolute Format:* This method is used if the security components are to be allocated separately. In this case, the security descriptor contains memory-offset pointers to the security components. Using this format decreases authentication time. The C programming language uses `InitializeSecurityDescriptor` to return a security descriptor in absolute format.

- *Self-Relative Format:* This method is used when the storing or transmission of security descriptors will cause the relative pointers of the absolute format to fail. Instead of using memory offset, this format stores the descriptor as a single contiguous block of memory, with offsets that point to the beginning of this memory block. The C programming language uses the `MakeSelfRelativeSD()` API call to convert absolute security descriptors to self-relative format.

Settings for User Security

The Registry settings that hold the security information for the user can be found under the [`HKEY_LOCAL_MACHINE\SECURITY\Policy\Accounts\SID`] key, where *SID* is the SID of the user's account. If you open REGEDT32.EXE and find the [`HKEY_LOCAL_MACHINE\SECURITY`] key, you see that it is grayed out, as shown in Figure 14.1.

If you highlight this key and then choose Permissions from the **S**ecurity menu, you see the dialog box shown in Figure 14.2.

To unhide the Security key, check the R**e**place Permission on Existing Subkeys check box, highlight the user that you want to give access to in the **N**ame list, and change the access using the **T**ype of Access list box. Now click OK and click Yes to see the dialog box shown in Figure 14.3.

If you click **Y**es, this dialog box resets all permissions on all subkeys of the Security key to the chosen user's access rights. If you give the logged-in user full access rights with the User Manager tool, you should see the full Security key, as shown in Figure 14.4.

In Figure 14.4, you see three main subkeys under the Security key: Policy, RXACT, and SAM. These keys, their subkeys, and values are described in the following sections.

Figure 14.1   The Security key is hidden.

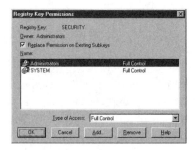

Figure 14.2   The Registry Key Permissions dialog box.

Figure 14.3   The Subkey Permissions dialog box.

The Policy Key

The [HKEY_LOCAL_MACHINE\SECURITY\Policy] key is the largest subkey found under the Security key. It holds information for user and group SIDs under the Accounts subkey, information for group security descriptors under the SecDesc key, and domain information under the Domain key. There are also several policy keys found here that define access to resources. The values and subkeys under these keys are described in the next few sections.

The Accounts Key

The [HKEY_LOCAL_MACHINE\SECURITY\Policy\Accounts] key contains subkeys for all user SIDs created on the system. Each of the SID keys has the following form, where *S-1-5-32-544* is the user account's SID:

[HKEY_LOCAL_MACHINE\SECURITY\Policy\Accounts*S-1-5-32-544*]

This SID can be broken down, as follows:

- *S-1:* This prefix shows that this SID is Revision 1.
- *5:* This value represents the SID creator's authority identifier.
- *32:* This value represents the SID authority subidentifier.
- 544: This value represents the RID.

Each of the SID keys has the following subkeys found under it, which include only one value under each key. These are the default values that appear differently, depending on the Registry editor that you use to view them. If you use REGEDT32.EXE, you see a value name of *<no name>*, REGEDIT.EXE shows (Default), and an exported .REG file shows @. The Data type is REG_NONE, and it appears as REG_BINARY in REGEDIT.EXE. Neither editor is capable of adding values with data type REG_NONE. Some information on these value settings can be seen if you open REGEDIT.EXE, select a value, right-click it, and choose Modify. The resulting screen shows you the settings for this value, such as domain and user names.

```
(No Name, default, or @)     Hexadecimal Number
REG_NONE
```

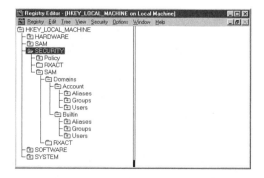

Figure 14.4   The entire Security key.

These subkeys are:

- *Account System Access:* This key, [HKEY_LOCAL_MACHINE\SECURITY\Policy\
  Accounts*SID*\ActSysAc], where *SID* is the user's account SID and defines the
  SID user's access to the Windows NT operating system.

- *Account Privileges:* This key, [HKEY_LOCAL_MACHINE\SECURITY\Policy\Accounts\
  SID\Privilgs], defines the SID user's privileges for accessing network and local
  system resources.

- *Security Descriptor:* This key, [HKEY_LOCAL_MACHINE\SECURITY\Policy\Accounts
  SID\SecDesc], holds the security descriptor of the user.

- *Sid:* This key, [HKEY_LOCAL_MACHINE\SECURITY\Policy\Accounts*SID*\Sid], contains the SIDs of the user's primary group.

- *Domains:* This key, [HKEY_LOCAL_MACHINE\SECURITY\Policy\Domains], holds the
  security information for the user's domain that is set in the Network applet, as
  seen in Figure 14.5.

Policy Keys

These keys define resource policy rights that define access to the specific resource.
There are several keys found here, as shown in Figure 14.6. Figure 14.6 also shows the
information contained in the default value of the PolAcDmN key, which, in this case,
holds the PC Name information.

The Security Descriptor Key

This key, [HKEY_LOCAL_MACHINE\SECURITY\Policy\SecDesc], contains the security
descriptor that creates the security descriptors discussed in the previous section on the
SID key.

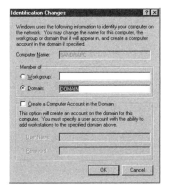

Figure 14.5   The user's domain.

The Secrets Key

This key, [HKEY_LOCAL_MACHINE\SECURITY\Policy\Secrets], may contain subkeys on Internet Services security, as well as third-party application security.

The RXACT (Transaction) Key

This key, [HKEY_LOCAL_MACHINE\SECURITY\RXACT], is the Registry transaction package, and its default value states the rules that Windows NT uses when committing transactions. This key generates the following Windows NT 4.0 error codes:

- 1369L ERROR_RXACT_INVALID_STATE. This error code is generated if Windows NT tries to perform a transaction on a Registry key that does not allow it. This can happen if a new transaction is started when one is in progress or if a transaction is attempted and there is no transaction available.

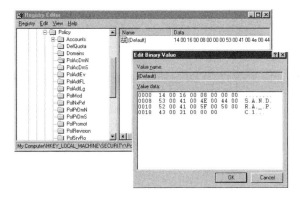

Figure 14.6   Policy keys.

- 1370L ERROR_RXACT_COMMIT_FAILURE. This error code is generated if Windows NT tries to perform a transaction COMMIT to a Registry key and an error occurs.

The SAM Key

This key, [HKEY_LOCAL_MACHINE\SECURITY\SAM], is copied to the [HKEY_LOCAL_MACHINE\SAM] key in the same way that the [HKEY_Current_User] key is copied from the [HKEY_USER\SID] key. All changes to one of these keys are copied to the other key. This key contains the information for the Security Account Manager (SAM) database located on the local computer. If the computer is a Windows NT domain controller, this key also contains domain information. Open the User Manager, select a user, and choose User, Properties; you see the information contained in this key's default value, as seen in Figure 14.7. The SAM key has the following subkeys and values, as described in the following sections.

The Domains Key

This key, [HKEY_LOCAL_MACHINE\SECURITY\SAM\Domains], contains information for the user's domain and has two subkeys under it:

- The Account key contains information for user and group accounts that were added to Windows NT by one of the User Manager tools.

- The Builtin key contains the same type of information as the Account Key, but contains the user and group accounts that are native to Windows NT, such as the Administrator account.

Each of these keys in turn have one each of the Aliases, Groups, and Users subkeys found under them:

- The Aliases subkey contains information on local groups to which the user belongs.

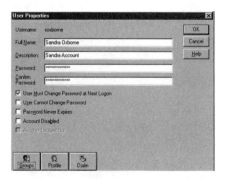

Figure 14.7   User information, as displayed in the User Manager.

- The Groups subkey contains information on network groups to which the user belongs.

- The Users subkey contains a subkey for each user listed in the User Manager tool.

These subkeys, their subkeys, and values are described in the next few sections.

The Account Key

This key, [`HKEY_LOCAL_MACHINE\SECURITY\SAM\Domains\Account`], contains two values of the following form:

```
F    Hexadecimal Number
REG_BINARY
```

This value contains domain login information for the current user.

```
V    Hexadecimal Number
REG_BINARY
```

This value contains information about the type of access allowed for the current user.

The Aliases key, [`HKEY_LOCAL_MACHINE\SECURITY\SAM\Domains\Account\Aliases`], contains group information for the local groups, created by the administrator, that the user belongs to. Users are added to these groups through the Group Memberships dialog box, shown in Figure 14.8.

This key contains a subkey, in hexadecimal form, for each local group that was added by the administrator. This key has the following form and values:

```
Key: 000003EA

C    Hexadecimal Number
REG_BINARY
```

This value contains the group name and other information, as seen in Figure 14.9. The next two keys are subkeys of the Aliases key:

- The Aliases Members key: This key, [`HKEY_LOCAL_MACHINE\SECURITY\SAM\Domains\Account\Aliases\Members`], has a subkey for each of the previous groups that the current user is a member. This subkey is the user's ID of the

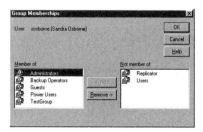

Figure 14.8   The Group Memberships dialog box.

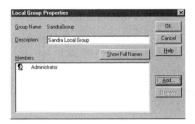

Figure 14.9   Group membership information.

following form, and is the same key found under the [HKEY-USERS] key.:
S-1-5-21-877493074-1263893664-382417117

- The Aliases Names Key: This key, [HKEY_LOCAL_MACHINE\SECURITY\SAM\Domains\
Account\Aliases\Names], contains a subkey for each local group added by the
administrator. The subkeys have the same name as the added group.

The Groups key, [HKEY_LOCAL_MACHINE\SECURITY\SAM\Domains\Account\Groups],
has a subkey for each network group that the user belongs to (this is similar to the
Aliases key). The following subkey is always found here:

`Key: 00000201`

This is the Ordinary Users Network group, and all users created by the User
Manager are members of this group. This key has one value under it, which describes
this group.

`C    Hexadecimal Number`
`REG_BINARY`

The Group Names key, [HKEY_LOCAL_MACHINE\SECURITY\SAM\Domains\Account\
Groups\Names], contains a subkey for each user that is a member of the Network
Groups. Users who do not belong to any other groups except the Ordinary User
group do not have a key listed here.

The Users key, [HKEY_LOCAL_MACHINE\SECURITY\SAM\Domains\Account\ Users],
contains a subkey for each user listed in the User Manager, as shown in Figure 14.10,
as well as a Names subkey.

The User Information keys, one for each user, contain values that store the information displayed by the User Manager (refer to Figure 14.10). These keys have the following form and values:

`Key: 000001F4`

`F    Hexadecimal Number`
`REG_BINARY`

This value contains user logon information.

`V    Hexadecimal Number`
`REG_BINARY`

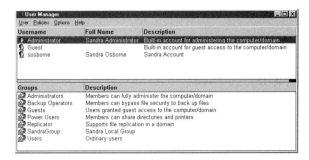

Figure 14.10   Existing users.

This value contains the information shown in Figure 14.10 under the Full Name and Description columns.

The User Names key, [HKEY_LOCAL_MACHINE\SECURITY\SAM\Domains\Account\ Users\Names\], contains a subkey for each user shown in Figure 14.10. These keys have the same names as the users.

The Builtin Key

This key contains the subkeys and values for the users and groups that are built into Windows NT. These subkeys and values have the same format as the ones shown for the Accounts key.

Settings for Permissions

Permissions for Registry access are set through the REGEDT32.EXE program by selecting Security, Permissions, as shown in Figure 14.11.

The security of the Registry is controlled from the Registry Key Permissions dialog box, shown in Figure 14.11. If you click the **T**ype of Access list box, you see the following three permissions.

Read

This permission allows the user selected in the **N**ame dialog box to query a value, view all subkeys of the key, receive audit information about the key, and view the key's security information.

Full Access

This option allows the user selected in the **N**ame dialog box to access the key completely, including delete, add, modify and read; as well as have all of the permissions discussed in the next section.

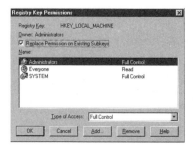

Figure 14.11 Registry Key Permissions.

Special Access

When you select this option, or double-click one of the entries shown in the **N**ame text box of Figure 14.11, you see the Special Access dialog box, shown in Figure 14.12.

The following permissions are available to be set from this dialog box:

- *Query Value:* permits the specified users and groups to read the values found under the given key.

- *Set Value:* permits the specified users and groups to set the values found under the given key.

- *Create Subkey:* permits the specified users and groups to create subkeys under the given key.

- *Enumerate Subkey:* permits the specified users and groups to see all of the sub-keys under the given key.

- *Notify:* permits the specified users and groups to receive audit information for the given key.

- *Create Link:* permits the specified users and groups to create symbolic links to this key.

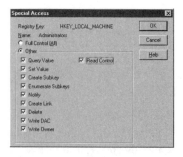

Figure 14.12 The Special Access dialog box.

- *Delete*: permits the specified users and groups to delete this key.
- *Write DAC:* permits the specified users and groups to read the DACL (Discretionary Access Control List) for this key.
- *Write Owner:* permits the specified users and groups to take ownership of this key.
- *Read Control*: permits the specified users and groups to read the security information for this key.

The C2 Security Manager

This security definition, also called *Orange Book security*, was defined by the National Computer Security Center, and any software claiming C2 security must first receive permission from this government authority. Before this agency grants permission, it evaluates the new software by using the criteria defined in the "Department of Defense Trusted Computer System Evaluation Criteria" manual, which is also called the *Orange Book*.

Warning

Do not use the C2 utility found on the Windows NT Resource kit to implement C2 security on your Windows NT Server. This utility uses the C2REGACL.INF file located in the %SYSTEMROOT%\INF directory to modify the permissions set on the Registry. However, after this utility is run, administrators no longer have full access to the Registry; they have Read-Only access.

To fix this problem, assign Full Control on the [HKEY_LOCAL_MACHINE\software] key to a user who is a member of both the Local and the Domain Administrator's groups. This solution only works until NT is rebooted. To fix it permanently, NT must be completely reinstalled (not with an update install).

15

Settings Created by the User Manager Tool

- **The Windows NT Workstation 4.0 User Manager**

  The Windows NT Workstation 4.0 User Manager tool is called *MUSRMGR.EXE* and is shipped with Windows NT 4.0 Workstation. This file is found in the %SystemRoot%\ system32 directory, and it adds, modifies, or removes users from Windows NT. This section discusses the Registry values that are associated with this tool.

- **The Windows NT Server 4.0 User Manager for Domains**

  The Windows NT Workstation 4.0 User Manager tool is shipped with Windows NT 4.0 server and is found in the same directory as the Workstation tool. This section discusses the Registry values that are associated with this tool.

The Windows NT Workstation 4.0 User Manager

The Windows NT Workstation 4.0 User Manager tool adds, removes, or modifies users that are authenticated to log on to the local Windows NT Workstation. Domain users are added by using the Windows NT Server 4.0 User Manager for Domains tool, discussed in the next section.

If you launch the Workstation User Manager, you see the window shown in Figure 15.1.

When a new user is created, there are no Registry entries that correspond to the new user as long as the user is not logged into Windows NT. When the new user logs into Windows NT, a specific key is created. This key is found under [HKEY_USERS], and has the following form:

    S-1-5-21-877493074-1263893664-382417117-500

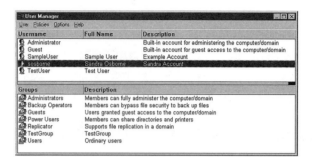

Figure 15.1   The Windows NT Workstation 4.0 User Manager window.

This number is the SID for the logged-in user, and this key is called the *SID key*. There is one SID and one SID key per user (refer to Chapter 14, "Security"). There is only one key found here, even if there is more than one user shown in the User Manager window. This key is the only user-related key initiated by the User Manager; there are several other keys and values that govern the way the User Manager behaves. These keys and their values are described in the next section.

The User Manager Key

The User Manager key, [HKEY_CURRENT_USER\Software\Microsoft\WindowsNT\ CurrentVersion\Network\User Manager], governs the way the User Manager screen is presented. The values found under this key and their settings are:

```
SaveSettings        0 or 1
REG_SZ
```

This value is set from the User Manager window by choosing **O**ptions, **S**ave Settings on Exit, as seen in Figure 15.2.

```
ListboxSplit        0 - 1000
REG_SZ
```

This value reflects the screen division between the User Names window and the Groups window. A value of **0** reflects no Groups window; a setting of **1000** reflects no User Names window.

```
Window    Windows Dimensions
REG_SZ    111 130 495 274 0
```

This value shows the Window Metrics for the User Manager window. *Windows Metrics* are the window's location on the monitor as well as minimize/maximize information. You see four pixel settings in the previous example that state the window's size

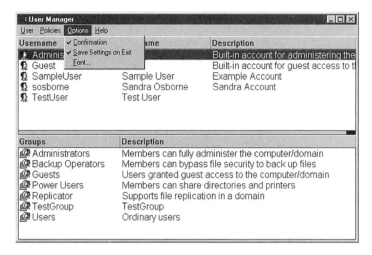

Figure 15.2 Saving User Manager settings.

and position. These settings determine the position of each corner of the User
Manager window and are given as an offset to the 0,0 position. The trailing Boolean
setting, 1 or 0, determines whether the window should be minimized.

```
Confirmation          0 or 1
REG_SZ
```

This value is set by using the **C**onfirmation setting in the **O**ptions menu (refer to
Figure 15.2), and it determines whether the User Manager tool requests user confirmation when it performs user changes such as additions or deletions. If set to 0, confirmation is not required; if set to 1, confirmation is required. The default setting is 1.

The following four values contain font information for the information presented
by the User Manager. The Font dialog box launched from the **O**ptions menu determines these settings (see Figure 15.3).

```
FontFaceName          Font Name
REG_SZ
```

This value determines the font used by the main User Manager window when the
User Manager tool launches. This value is blank by default, and only contains a setting
if the program window shown in Figure 15.3 is used to change the font.

```
FontHeight    0 to Point Size (Decimal)
REG_SZ
```

This value determines the point size of the font specified by the FontFaceName
value. The default setting is 0; if it is set to this setting, the font uses the standard
default point size setting for the given font.

```
FontWeight        0, 400, 700, or 900
REG_SZ
```

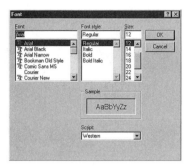

Figure 15.3 User Manager font settings.

This value determines the thickness of the font specified by the `FontFaceName` value. The default setting is `0`.

```
FontItalic          0 Or 1
REG_SZ
```

This value determines whether the font specified by the `FontFaceName` value is italicized. A setting of `1` italicizes the font; the default setting of `0` does not italicize the font.

The Windows NT Server 4.0 User Manager for Domains

The settings for this program are the same as the ones for the Windows NT Workstation User Manager program and can be found under the `[HKEY_CURRENT_USER\Software\Microsoft\WindowsNT\CurrentVersion\Network\ User Manager for Domains]` key. Another value is found here, in addition to the ones found under the User Manager key discussed in the previous section:

```
SortOrder               0 or 1
REG_SZ
```

The View menu of the User Manager for Domains screen determines this value. If Sort by User Name is checked, this value is set to `1`; if Sort by Full Name is checked, this value is set to `0`. The default setting is `1`.

Other Registry Values Used by the User Manager for Domains Tool

The values in the following sections are found under the [HKEY_LOCAL_MACHINE\ SOFTWARE\Microsoft\Windows NT\CurrentVersion\Network\World Full Access Shared Parameters] key and are used by the User Manager for Domains tool.

```
Slow Mode        String
REG_SZ
```

This value states the servers and domains that are accessed over low-speed connections. If you do not specify a low-speed connection, the User Manager for Domains, Server Manager, and Event Viewer use this value to determine connection speed.

```
SortHyphens        0 or 1
REG_DWORD
```

This value determines whether the User Manager ignores hyphens when it sorts lists alphabetically by using any of the following utilities:

- Event Viewer
- Remoteboot Manager
- Server Manager
- User Manager
- User Manager for Domains

This value also affects the base sort order of lists as viewed from the Network, Server, Services, or Devices applets found in the Control Panel. When this value is set to 1, hyphens are sorted and appear before all words starting with A in the previous lists. The default setting of 0 ignores hyphens when sorting lists.

Note
This value's setting applies to all local users of this computer. This means that when any user changes the Low Speed Connection option, the new setting applies to all users.

Note
Further information on the settings for users and groups can be found in Chapter 14, "Security."

Managing Network Clients

16

Settings for Dial-Up Networking

- ● **Launching the Dial-Up Networking applet**

  This section discusses the different ways that the My Computer folder's Dial-Up Networking applet starts.

- ● **The Dial-Up Networking screen**

  This section discusses the Registry values that are used by the main Dial-Up Networking dialog box.

- ● **The More drop-down list box**

  This section discusses the phone book file and Registry values that are set for the preferences of your Dial-Up Networking connections. These preferences are set through the use of the More drop-down list box.

Launching the Dial-Up Networking Applet

Dial-Up Networking is configured by using the Dial-Up Networking applet found in the My Computer folder, located on the Desktop. When you launch this applet after you set up entries in the phone book, you see the screen shown in Figure 16.1.

If you have not set up any Dial-Up Networking phone book entries, you see the dialog box shown in Figure 16.2.

When you click OK, the screen that you see is determined by the `NewEntryWizard` value found under the `[HKEY_CURRENT_USER\Software\Microsoft\RAS Phonebook]` key.

```
NewEntryWizard     0 or 1
REG_DWORD
```

Set this value to `1` to start the New Phonebook Entry Wizard when the phone book is empty (see Figure 16.3). This value is set to `0` if the I know all about phonebook entries and would rather edit the properties directly check box, shown in Figure 16.3, is checked. If this value is set to `1`, then you see the screen shown in Figure 16.4.

If this value is set to `0`, you see the screen shown in Figure 16.4, which is the same screen you see when you click the More button shown in Figure 16.1, and then select Edit entry and modem properties from the drop-down list shown in Figure 16.5. The screen displayed in Figure 16.4 is discussed later in this chapter, under the "The Edit Entry/Clone Entry/New Entry Dialog Box" section and its subsections.

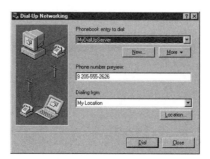

Figure 16.1   The Dial-Up Networking applet.

This list box and the screens that can be produced from it are discussed in the "The More Drop-down List Box" section later in this chapter. Next, we discuss the other settings of the Dial-Up Networking applet.

The Dial-Up Networking Screen

If there is only one entry in the phonebook file, RASPHONE.PBK, the entry name text box becomes the name of the Dial-Up Networking server listed in the Phonebook entry to dial drop-down list box shown in Figure 16.1. This entry is stored in the DefaultEntry value found under the [HKEY_CURRENT_USER\Software\ Microsoft\RAS Phonebook] key. This value and the other values that affect this screen are described in the next sections.

Default Entry Value

```
DefaultEntry        Dial-Up Server Name
REG_SZ              MyDialUpServer
```

As discussed previously, this value holds the dial-up server name shown in the entry name text box shown in Figure 16.3. This value is set to the setting of the entry name text box when you exit the Dial-Up Networking applet.

Phone Number Preview

```
PreviewPhoneNumber   0 or 1
REG_DWORD
```

Figure 16.2   Empty phone book message.

Figure 16.3   New Phonebook Entry Wizard.

When this value is set to 0, the Phone number preview text box is removed from the Dial-Up Networking applet shown in Figure 16.1. The default is 1.

Dialing From Selection

```
UseLocation      0 or 1
REG_DWORD
```

When this value is set to 0, the Dialing from text box and the Location button are removed from the Dial-Up Networking applet shown in Figure 16.1. The default is 1.

The Location Button

If you click the Location button shown in Figure 16.1, you see one of two dialog boxes. If the Use Telephony dialing properties check box, located on the Edit Entry dialog box (this dialog box is discussed later in the chapter) is checked, you see the Dialing Properties dialog box shown in Figure 16.6.

If the previous check box is not checked, you see the Location Settings dialog box shown in Figure 16.7.

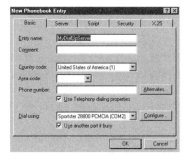

Figure 16.4   The New Phonebook Entry dialog box.

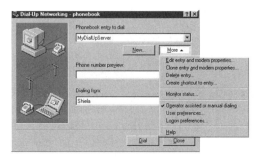

Figure 16.5   The More drop-down list box.

The Dialing Properties Dialog Box

The Dialing Properties dialog box, which can also be displayed by launching the Telephony applet in the Control Panel, sets the dialing properties that the selected dial-up connection uses when dialing from different locations. The Registry values that this screen sets are found under the [HKEY_LOCAL_MACHINE\SOFTWARE\Microsoft\ Windows\CurrentVersion\Telephony\Locations\Location#] key, where # is an integer greater than or equal to 0. Creating these integers is based upon the total number of locations created, not the number of existing locations. There are as many keys as there are locations to dial from. Every Location# key has the following values found under it:

```
Name    Location Name
REG_SZ
```

This is the name of the location that appears in the I am dialing from list box of Figure 16.6 and the Location text box of Figure 16.7.

```
AreaCode    Area Code to Dial
REG_SZ    205
```

This is the number shown in the area code is text box of Figure 16.6.

```
Country    Country Code
REG_DWORD
```

Author Note

These entries and other Dial-Up Networking options are also listed in the RASPHONE.PBK file, located in the %SYSTEMROOT%\System32\ras directory. If an alternate Phonebook file is used, the settings are written there. The Phonebook file settings are discussed throughout this chapter because some Dial-Up Networking options set values in the Registry and others set entries in the Phonebook file.

Tip

When you travel with your notebook, set the PreviewPhoneNumber value to 0 to prevent anyone from viewing your dial-up server connection number. This helps secure your dial-up networking connections.

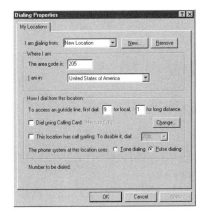

Figure 16.6 The Dialing Properties dialog box.

This value is set to the code of the country selected in the I am in list box. These country codes are read from the `CountryCode` value found under the `[HKEY_LOCAL_MACHINE\SOFTWARE\Microsoft\Windows\CurrentVersion\Telephony\Country List\#]` key, shown in Figure 16.8, where # is 1 to 995.

Figure 16.6 shows the How I dial from this location frame. The following values are set by the To access an outside line, first dial…sentence at the top of this frame. This sentence has two text boxes that set the following values.

```
OutsideAccess     Outside Line Access Number
REG_SZ
```

This is the first text box in the To access an outside line, first dial… sentence and it is included in the phone number to be dialed when dialing from this location.

```
Long Distance Access     Long Distance Access Number
REG_SZ
```

This is the second text box in the sentence and it is included in the phone number to be dialed when dialing from this location.

Also seen in the How I dial from this location frame are the Dial using Calling Card and This location has call waiting check boxes. The state of these check boxes sets the following value, as shown in Table 16.1.

```
Flags     1, 3, 5 or 7
REG_DWORD
```

Author Note

The dialog box shown in Figure 16.4 and the Edit Phonebook Entry screen dialog box, seen with the Script tab shown in Figure 16.13, are launched differently. The dialog box in Figure 16.4 is used to add new entries; the dialog box in Figure 16.12 is used to edit these entries. Both of these dialog boxes set the same Registry values, and are discussed later in this chapter in the "The Edit Entry/Clone Entry/New Entry Dialog Box" section.

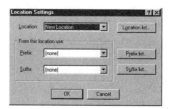

Figure 16.7   The Location Settings dialog box.

Table 16.1   **The *Flags* value**

Setting	Calling Card Box	Call Waiting Box
1	Cleared	Cleared
3	Checked	Cleared
5	Cleared	Checked
7	Checked	Checked

The "This location has call waiting. To disable it, dial" list box is in the same frame. The settings that are available in this list box are found under the `[HKEY_LOCAL_MACHINE\SOFTWARE\Microsoft\Windows\CurrentVersion\Telephony\Locations]` key in the following value:

```
DisableCallWaiting#    *70, 70#, 1170
REG_SZ
```

There are three of these values, which are installed with Windows NT by default. They are named the same, except that the # is **0**, **1**, and **2**, respectively; and they are set to the previous settings.

When you choose one of these values in the list box, it sets this value under the `[HKEY_LOCAL_MACHINE\SOFTWARE\Microsoft\Windows\CurrentVersion\Telephony\Country List\#]` key.

```
DisableCallWaiting    *70, 70#, 1170
REG_SZ
```

This number is dialed, along with any number dialed from this location.

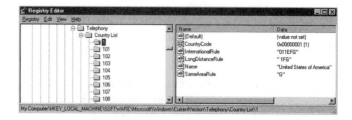

Figure 16.8   Country list Registry key.

The Location Settings Screen

The Location Settings dialog box, shown in Figure 16.7, a holdover from previous Windows NT versions of Dial-Up Networking, is used to add locations to the locations list as well as set dialing prefixes and suffixes. In Windows NT 4.0, this dialog box is included with the Dialing Properties dialog box and can be seen by using the My Locations tab, as shown in Figure 16.9.

The Registry values that are set by this screen are found under the `[HKEY_LOCAL_MACHINE\SOFTWARE\Microsoft\Windows\CurrentVersion\Telephony\Locations\Location#]` key and are discussed next.

The Location text box allows you to select the dialing location and sets the `Name` value discussed in the previous section. These locations are added by clicking the Location Lists button to produce the Locations dialog box; you can view location lists, add locations, delete locations, and replace locations.

The Prefix drop-down list box shows all of the dialing prefixes that can be added to the number dialed by using this location. This selection shows up in the Phone number preview box of Figure 16.1. The setting of a prefix is determined by the following value, found under the `[HKEY_CURRENT_USER\Software\Microsoft\RASPhonebook\Location\#]` key.

```
Prefix     0 to No of Entries in List
REG_DWORD
```

If this value is set to `0`, the Prefix box of Figure 16.7 shows `(None)` and no `Prefix` setting appears in the Phone Number Preview box of Figure 16.1. If this value is not zero, it is set to the number of the entry chosen from the Prefix list box. These entries are numbered sequentially, starting at 1.

```
Prefixes   Prefix String
REG_MULTI_SZ
```

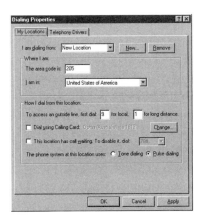

Figure 16.9 The My Locations tab of the Dialing Properties dialog box.

The `Prefixes` value is set to the settings shown in the Prefix drop-down list box. If viewed with REGEDIT.EXE, you see only hexadecimal numbers. If viewed with REGEDT32.EXE, you see the Prefixes list; and if you use a .REG file to add prefixes to this list, you write it in this form:

```
[HKEY_CURRENT_USER\Software\Microsoft\RAS Phonebook]
"Prefixes"=Edit(MultiSZ):/Find "Last Prefix" or end /Insert "New Prefix"
after
```

Executing this .REG file inserts the `New Prefix` into the Prefix list after the `Last Prefix` entry. The `(None)` entry, produced by setting the previous `Prefix` value to `0`, is not included in the `Prefixes` value.

The Suffix drop-down list box shows the dialing suffixes that can be added to the number dialed by using this location. This selection shows up in the Phone number preview box of Figure 16.1. The existence of a suffix is determined by the following value.

```
Suffix     0 to No. of entries in List
REG_DWORD
```

If this value is set to `0`, the Suffix box of Figure 16.7 shows `(None)` and no `Suffix` setting appears in the Phone number preview box of Figure 16.1. If this value is not zero, it is set to the number of the entry chosen from the Suffix list box. These entries are numbered sequentially, starting at `1`, and can be counted as such when viewing the `Suffixes` value found under the `[HKEY_CURRENT_USER\Software\Microsoft\RAS Phonebook]` key with REGEDT32.EXE. This value acts the same as the `Prefixes` value, but it affects the Suffixes list.

The Telephony Applet

The Telephony applet can be used to set the same properties as the Dialing Properties dialog box.

This applet has an extra tab, the Telephony Drivers tab (see Figure 16.10), which the Dialing Properties dialog box does not have and which can be used to set modem properties.

The More Drop-down List Box

You can set most of the preferences of your dial-up networking connection by using the entries on the drop-down list box shown in Figure 16.5. This list box can set several Dial-Up Networking options by using the screens discussed in the next few sections.

The Edit Entry/Clone Entry/New Entry Dialog Box

This dialog box (refer to Figure 16.4, which shows the New Entry dialog box) can be produced in several different ways. If you select Edit Entry and Modem Properties from the More menu, the dialog box shown in Figure 16.4 has a caption of `Edit`

`Phonebook Entry`. If you select Clone entry and modem properties from the More menu, the screen shown in Figure 16.4 has a caption of `Clone Phonebook Entry`. Finally, if you start dial-up networking with no existing phonebook entries, this dialog box is titled `New Phonebook Entry`, as shown in Figure 16.4.

All of these screens are the same dialog box and set the same Registry values. Of course, the Clone Entry and Add Entry dialog boxes create new keys, and the Edit Entry dialog box modifies existing keys. The five tabs of this screen and the Registry values associated with them are discussed in the following sections.

The Basic Tab

This tab configures the basic dial-up networking options for your connection. These options and the Registry items that they set are:

Entry Name Text Box

If there is only one entry in the phonebook, the Entry Name text box tab becomes the name of the Dial-Up networking server listed in the Phonebook entry to dial drop-down list box (refer to Figure 16.1). The phonebook entries are also listed in the RASPHONE.PBK file, located at %SYSTEMROOT%\System32\ras directory. This entry is stored in the `DefaultEntry` value found under the `[HKEY_CURRENT_USER\ Software\Microsoft\RAS Phonebook]` key.

```
DefaultEntry    Dial-Up Server Name
REG_SZ    MyDialUpServer
```

This value is set to the setting of the Entry Name text box when you exit the Dial-Up Networking applet.

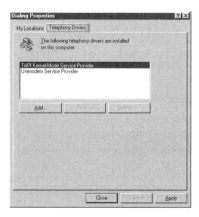

Figure 16.10   The Telephony Drivers tab.

Comment Text Box

The Comment text box does not write to the Registry, but it is stored in the .PBK file (called the *Phonebook file*), and it can be found under the Entry Name section in the `Description` value. The path and file name of the Phonebook file is given in the `AlternatePhonebookPath` value under the `[HKEY_CURRENT_USER\Software\Microsoft\RAS Phonebook]` key.

```
AlternatePhonebookPath    Alternate Phonebook Path\Filename
REG_SZ    C:\Phonebook
```

The Filename section of this path appears in the title bar of Figure 16.1.

Country Code Text Box

Unlike the country code of the Locations dialog box, the setting for this text box is not stored in the Registry, but in the Phonebook file. This text box sets the `CountryCode=` value in the [*MyDialUpServer*] section of the Phonebook file, where *MyDialUpServer* is the name of the dial-up connection. This value is equal to the # subkey of the `[HKEY_LOCAL_MACHINE\SOFTWARE\Microsoft\Windows\CurrentVersion\Telephony\Country List\#]` key.

Area Code Text Box

This entry is not stored in the Registry, but in the Phonebook file. This entry is set with the `AreaCode` value in the [*MyDialUpServer*] section of the Phonebook file, where *MyDialUpServer* is the name of the dial-up connection. The value is set to the area code selected from the Area Code list box or to the area code entered into the text box.

Phone Number

This entry is also stored in the Phonebook file, not in the Registry. This entry is set with the `Phone_Number` value in the [*MyDialUpServer*] section of the Phonebook file, where *MyDialUpServer* is the name of the dial-up connection, and is set to the number shown in the Phone Number text box, including dashes or spaces.

Use Telephony Dialing Properties

This check box sets the `NewEntryWizard` value found under the `[HKEY_CURRENT_USER\Software\Microsoft\RAS Phonebook]` key and determines what screen you see when you launch the Dial-Up Network applet if the address book is empty. This value was discussed at the start of the "Launching the Dial-Up Networking Applet" section at the start of the chapter.

Dial Using

This drop-down list box contains a modem list for the modem installed on your computer, plus a list for multiple lines. This selection is also set in the Phonebook file. This entry is set with the `Device` value. If this value is set to `MultiLine`, the Phone Number box is grayed out.

Configure Button

When you click this button, you see the screen shown in Figure 16.11.

This screen sets the following values in the same Phonebook file and section as the previous options, which are discussed in Table 16.2.

Table 16.2 **Modem Configuration Options**

Option	Description
Initial speed (bps)	This value sets the modem connection speed and is set with the `ConnectBPS` value. This value can be set to any of the settings in the drop-down list box that shows `11512` (refer to Figure 16.11).
Enable hardware flow control	This check box sets the `HwFlowControl` value to 1 when checked and 0 when cleared.
Enable modem error control	This check box sets the `Protocol` value to 1 when checked and 0 when cleared.
Enable modem compression	This check box sets the `Compression` value to 1 when checked and 0 when cleared. If this value is set to 1, the previous `Protocol` value must be set to 1. If this check box is checked, the previous check box is automatically checked.
Disable modem speaker	This check box sets the `Speaker` value to 1, which turns off the modem speaker when checked; and 0, which turns the speaker on when cleared.

Figure 16.11 The Modem Configuration dialog box.

The Server Tab

This tab, shown in Figure 16.12, sets the server connection type as well as network protocols.

The Dial-up server type list box has three dial-up server types that are available for selection. Depending on your choice, different check boxes below the list box are available to set. When you choose a server type, the `BaseProtocol` value in the phonebook file is set differently, depending on the protocol to be used, as follows:

Setting	Protocol	Description
PPP	Windows NT, Windows 95 Plus! Internet	Setting this value to 1 enables all of the check boxes shown in Figure 16.12.
SLIP	Internet	Setting this value to 2 enables only the TCP/IP check box and button. Setting this value to 2 and the `ExcludedProtocols` to 0 is the same as setting this value to 1 and the `ExcludedProtocols` value to 7.
NetBEUI	Windows NT 3.1, Windows for Workgroups 3.11	Setting this value to 3 enables the NetBEUI and Enable Software Compression check boxes. Setting this value to 2 and the `ExcludedProtocols` to 0 is the same as setting this value to 1 and the `ExcludedProtocols` value to 7.

Figure 16.12 The Server tab.

Troubleshooting

If you try to connect to a remote computer but have trouble establishing the connection, set the `ConnectBPS` value to a lower number until the connection completes.

The Network Protocols frame contains three check boxes that set the ExcludedProtocols setting of the Phonebook file. This value is set according to Table 16.3. If you do not select a protocol, then you see an error message instructing you to select at least one protocol.

Table 16.3 **The *ExcludeProtocols* Value**

Setting	TCP/IP	SPX/IPX Box	NetBEUI Box	Server Type
0	X	X	X	PPP
1	X	X	Cleared	PPP
2	X	Cleared	X	PPP
3	X	Cleared	Cleared	PPP
4	Cleared	X	X	PPP
5	Cleared	X	Cleared	PPP
6	Cleared	Cleared	X	PPP
7	Disabled	Disabled	X	Windows NT 3.1

If the Enable software compression check box is checked, the SwCompression value in the Phonebook file is set to 1. If the check box is cleared, the value is set to 0.

The Enable PPP LCP extensions check box sets the LcpExtensions value to 1 if checked, and 0 if cleared. If selected, the enhanced features of PPP are enabled.

The Script Tab

This tab, shown in Figure 16.13, sets scripting options for the connection.

You can set post-dial options by using the After dialing (login) frame, and you can set pre-dial options by pressing the Before dialing button. The dialog box produced by the Before dialing button is the Before Dialing Script dialog box shown in Figure 16.13. If you set pre-dialing options, the Phonebook file lists a DEVICE=Switch section immediately before the DEVICE=Modem section. Post-dialing options are set in a DEVICE=Switch section immediately after the DEVICE=Modems section, unless there are X.25 options set. If X.25 options are set, the postscript DEVICE=Switch is located after the X.25 section.

Finally, depending on the settings of the pre- and post-dialing radial buttons, each of the DEVICE=Switch sections contain a Type value that is set as follows:

Tip

If you want to disable this connection without removing it, you can set the BaseProtocol to 0 and the ExcludeProtocols value to 7. This is the same as unselecting all of the protocols in the Network Protocols frame that cannot be done from the frame itself.

- None: If this radial button is selected, there is no pre- or post- `DEVICE=Switch` section, depending on the None radial button selected. If both None radial buttons are selected, there are no `DEVICE=Switch` sections in the Phonebook file.

- Pop up a terminal window: If this radial button is selected, the `Type` value is set to `Terminal`.

- Run this script: If this radial button is selected, the type value is set to:

(None)—if the (none) option is selected. This has the same effect as selecting the None radial button.

Generic—The Generic Login script is selected.

Path/File name—The path and filename of the script to run. Example: %SYSTEMROOT%\System32\ras\CIS.SCP.

The Security Tab

This tab, shown in Figure 16.14, is used to set security options for the connection.

There are two items to discuss on this screen, first is the Authentication and encryption policy frame and second is the Unsave password button.

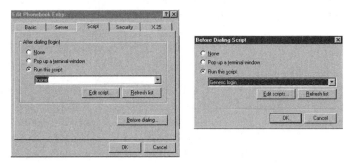

Figure 16.13   The Script tab.

Troubleshooting
If you add 8 to these settings in Table 16.3, the setting repeats itself. For example, 0 and 8 yield the same settings.

Warning
If you are connecting to a server that has older PPP software, such as Windows NT 3.51, set the LcpExtensions value to 0. Setting this to 0 prevents the Time-Remaining and Identification packets from being set to the server, as well as disabling callback while connecting to the server. If you continue to have problems, set the SkipDownLevelDialog value to 0.

The Authentication and Encryption Policy Frame

This frame has one set of three radial buttons. These buttons set the `AuthRestrictions` value by selecting each radial button as follows:

Setting	Description
3	Selects the Accept any authentication including clear text button.
2	Selects the Accept only encrypted authentication button.
1	Selects the Accept only Microsoft authentication button.

When you check the option for Microsoft authentication, the two check boxes shown in Figure 16.14 are enabled. These check boxes set the following values of the Phonebook file:

- `DataEncryption`: Checking the Require data encryption check box sets this value to `1`. Clearing it sets this value to `0`.

- `AutoLogon`: Checking the Use current username and password check box sets this value to `1`. Clearing it sets this value to `0`.

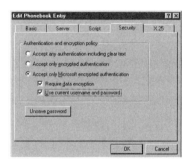

Figure 16.14   The Security tab.

Troubleshooting
The terminal window is useful when you try to troubleshoot connectivity issues.

Author Tip
If you want to set either pre- or post-dialing options for a certain script, but you do not want to use these options all the time, add the `DEVICE=Switch` section and set the type to `(none)`. You can then use a string replacement batch file to replace the `(none)` setting with Terminal or another script setting, as needed.

The Unsave Password Button

When you first create a Dial–Up Networking entry and then go to the Security dialog box to set security options, this button is disabled. To enable this button, launch Dial–Up Networking, select a Phonebook entry to dial, and then click the Dial button, as shown in Figure 16.1. When you do this the first time, you see the dialog box in Figure 16.15.

You use this dialog box to specify a username, password, and domain to connect to. The Registry settings that these fields set are discussed next.

Checking the Save password check box enables the Unsave password button of Figure 16.14. Checking this item also modifies the password Registry key. These keys, shown in Table 16.4, are set with the text boxes shown in Figure 16.15, which set binary values under these subkeys of the [HKEY_LOCAL_MACHINE\SECURITY\Policy\Secrets\RasCredentials!*SID*] key, where *SID* is the SID of the current user.

Table 16.4   **Password Registry Key Settings**

Key	Description
CupdTime	The default value under this key holds the time that you connected to the dial-up network.
CurrVal	The default value under this key holds the current user login information, as well as the state of the Save password button.
OldVal	The default value under this key holds the previously connected user login information, as well as the state of the Save password button for that user.
OupdTime	The default value under this key holds the time that you disconnected from the dial-up network.
SecDesc	The default value under this key holds the information in the Domain text box.

Figure 16.15   The Connect to dialog box.

Troubleshooting

If you have trouble logging on, you can delete either the CurrVal key or the SecDesc key. This deletes all login settings for all of your dial-in server connections.

The X.25 Tab

This tab, shown in Figure 16.16, is used to set X.25 server-connection options.

This screen has four text boxes on it. These values are found under the Device=Pad section of the Phonebook file and are set as follows:

- Network: This is a drop-down list box that shows all of the X.25 connections available, as read from the PAD.INF file located in the %SYSTEMROOT\ System32\Ras directory. Selecting a network sets the `X25Pad` value. This value is set to the item selected from the Network list box, CompuServe, for example.

- Address: This text box holds the address of the X.25 server to connect to. This sets the `X25Address` value and is set to the address entered into the Address text box.

- User Data: This text box holds any additional connection data needed by the X.25 server being connected to. This sets the `UserData` value and is set to the entry of the User Data text box.

- Facilities: This text box holds any facility parameters that you may want to use to request from the X.25 server. This sets the `Facilities` value and is set to the entry of the Facilities text box.

The Dial-Up Monitor Dialog Box

Selecting Monitor Status from the More list produces the dialog box shown in Figure 16.17.

This dialog box has three tabs but only one of them, the Preferences tab shown in Figure 16.17, stores settings in the Registry. The next few sections discuss these settings.

Play a Sound

This frame has four check boxes contained within it. The way these boxes are set, as well as the setting of the Include Dial-Up Networking Monitor button in the task list

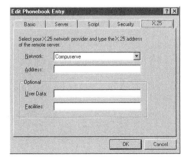

Figure 16.16   The X.25 tab.

check box, determine the setting of the Flags value found under the
[HKEY_CURRENT_USER\Software\Microsoft\RAS Monitor] key. This value is set
according to Table 16.5.

Table 16.5 *Flags* **Value Settings**

Setting	Box 1	Box 2	Box 3	Box 4
0				
1	X			
2		X		
3	X	X		
4			X	
5	X		X	
6		X	X	
7	X	X	X	
8				X
9	X			X
10		X		X
11	X	X		X
12			X	X
13	X		X	X
14		X	X	X
15	X	X	X	X

Checking the Include Dial-Up Networking Monitor button check box adds a
value of 64 to these settings.

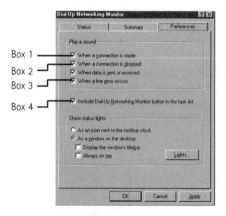

Figure 16.17 The Dial-Up Networking Monitor dialog box.

Show Status Lights

This frame has one set of radial buttons; the second radial button has two check boxes. This frame also includes a Lights button. The radial button sets the following value under the same key as the value in the previous section:

```
Mode    0 or 1
REG_DWORD
```

This value is set to 1 if the first radial button, As an icon next to the taskbar clock, is set; it is set to 0 if the second radial button, As a window on the desktop, is set. The default is 1.

If the second radial button is selected and then the Windows title bar check box is checked, 32 is added to the settings in Table 16.5. Checking the Always on top check box adds 16 to the settings in Table 16.5.

When you click the Lights button, you see the Status Lights dialog box shown in Figure 16.18.

This dialog box shows at least two check boxes within the Show lights for list box and one check box below it. Checking the box for the modem yields the settings for the `Flag` value shown in Table 16.5 and sets the `DeviceList` value under the `[HKEY_CURRENT_USER\Software\Microsoft\RAS Monitor]` key, as shown here:

```
DeviceList    Hexadecimal Number
REG_SZ
```

This is the hexadecimal representation of your installed modem device.

Checking the All Devices check box adds 256 to the settings in Table 16.5 and sets the `DeviceList` value to 0. Checking both check boxes sets the `DeviceList` value to the modem setting and adds 256 to the Table 16.5 settings. Checking Show resizable columns adds 128 to the `Flags` setting.

The base setting for the `Flag` value is set between 0 to 16 if the Status Lights dialog box (shown as the Sportster check box in Figure 16.18) is the only check box selected in this dialog box. Checking the other check boxes add the following decimal values to this base setting:

Always on top	16
Disable the Windows title bar	32
Include Monitor button	64
Show resizable columns	128
All devices	256

Operator Assisted and Manual Dialing

Selecting this More list entry does not produce a dialog box, but it does affect the following value under the `[HKEY_CURRENT_USER\Software\Microsoft\RAS Phonebook]` key:

```
OperatorDial    0 or 1
REG_DWORD
```

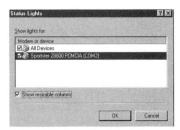

Figure 16.18   The Status Lights dialog box.

This value is set to 1 when the Operator assisted or manual dialing selection on the drop-down list shown in Figure 16.5 is selected. The default is **0**.

The User Preferences Dialog Box

Selecting this More list entry produces the User Preferences dialog box shown in Figure 16.19.

This screen has four tabs that set Registry values, as described in the following sections.

The Dialing Tab

The first item on the Dialing tab, shown in Figure 16.19, is the Enable auto-dial by location list box. (These locations were set up in the previous section.) When you check the box next to a location, RAS AutoDial is enabled for this location, and any network mappings needed to access the phonebook are maintained.

Checking the previous boxes sets the following value under the
`[HKEY_CURRENT_USER\Software\Microsoft\RAS Autodial\Control\Locations]` key:

```
#    0 or 1
REG_DWORD
```

There is a value of the above form located here for each location that was created on this machine. Even if a location has been removed, a value for it remains here. If the check box is checked, this value is set to **0**, and it will be set to 1 if the check box is cleared. To see which of these values correspond to current locations, refer to the previous section on the Dialing Properties dialog box.

The other options of the Dialing tab set values under the `[HKEY_CURRENT_USER\`
`Software\Microsoft\RAS Phonebook]` key and are:

- Number of redial attempts: This setting defines the number of redials that Dial-Up Networking automatically attempts if the connection fails. The following value controls this setting.

  ```
  RedialAttempts     Number of Attempts
  REG_DWORD
  ```

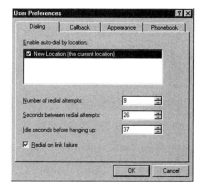

Figure 16.19   The User Preferences dialog box.

This value is set to the number entered into the Number of redial attempts list box.

- Seconds between redial attempts: This setting defines the number of seconds that Dial-Up Networking waits between each redial attempt. The following value controls this setting:

  ```
  RedialSeconds      Number of Redial Delay Seconds
  REG_DWORD
  ```

- Idle seconds before hanging up: This setting defines the number of seconds that Dial-Up Networking waits between hanging up the connection and attempting a redial. The following value controls this setting:

  ```
  IdleHangUpSeconds    Number of Hang-Up Delay Seconds
  REG_DWORD
  ```

- Redial on link failure: Checking this check box causes Dial-Up Networking to automatically redial the connection if the connection is broken inadvertently. This check box sets this value:

  ```
  RedialOnLinkFailure    0 or 1
  REG_DWORD
  ```

  This value is set to 1 if the previous check box is checked and 0 if it is cleared.

Author Note

In order for this auto-dial feature to work, you must start the Remote Access AutoDial Manager service by using the Services applet in Control Panel.

The Callback Tab

This tab, shown in Figure 16.20, sets the server callback options that can reduce a user's phone bill by having the server call back the user after a successful connection is made. This is useful when calling the United States from another country.

This tab has one group of radial buttons on it that sets the `CallbackMode` value under the `[HKEY_CURRENT_USER\Software\Microsoft\RAS Phonebook]` key:

```
CallbackMode    0, 1, or 2
REG_DWORD
```

This value is set to a different number, depending upon the selected radial button:

0   No, skip call back

1   Maybe, ask me during dial when server offers

2   Yes, call me back at the number(s) below

If the `CallBackMode` value is set to 2, the number that is set with the `Number` value under the `[HKEY_CURRENT_USER\Software\Microsoft\RAS Phonebook\Callback\Device]` key, where *Device* is the string shown under Modem or Device, is called by the server.

```
Number     Phone Number to Call Back
REG_SZ
```

The Appearance Tab

This tab, shown in Figure 16.21, sets the appearance options that govern the display of the Dial-Up Networking applet, as well as other display options.

This tab has seven check boxes that set values under the `[HKEY_CURRENT_USER\Software\Microsoft\RAS Phonebook]` key. These check boxes and the values that they set are:

■ Preview phone numbers before dialing: This check box sets the `PreviewPhoneNumber` value, which was discussed in the Phone Number Preview section earlier in this chapter.

Figure 16.20 The Callback tab.

■ Show location setting before dialing: This check box sets the `UseLocation` value, which was discussed in the Dialing From Selection section earlier in this chapter.

■ Start dial-up networking monitor before dialing: This check box sets the `ShowLights` value:

```
ShowLights    0 or 1
REG_DWORD
```

When this value is set to 1 or the check box is checked, the Dial-up monitor starts when the connection is dialed. The monitor does not start when the value is set to 0.

■ Show connection progress while dialing: This check box displays the progress of the connection so that you can see the components that occur during a connection. Use this during AutoDial connections to see the connection occur. If this is not used, a failed connection still shows the point at which it failed. The check box sets this value:

```
ShowConnectStatus    0 or 1
REG_DWORD
```

Checking the check box sets this value to 1, clearing it sets it to 0.

Figure 16.21   The Appearance tab.

Author Tip

The Windows NT RAS client can command the Windows NT RAS Server to wait a specified amount of time before calling back the RAS client. To configure this option, enable the Callback feature and add the following value under the [HKEY_LOCAL_MACHINE\SYSTEM\CurrentControlSet\Services\RasMan\PPP] key:

```
DefaultCallbackDelay      0 to 255 (Seconds)
REG_DWORD
```

Set this value to any number between 0 and 255 seconds, which causes the RAS Server to wait this amount of time before calling back the RAS client.

- Close on dial: Checking this box closes the Dial-Up Networking dialog box when the connection succeeds. It sets this value:
  ```
  CloseOnDial    0 or 1
  REG_DWORD
  ```
  Checking the check box sets this value to 1, clearing it sets it to 0.

- Use wizard to create new phonebook entries: This check box sets the `NewEntryWizard` value, which was discussed in the Use Telephony Dialing Properties section earlier in this chapter.

- Always prompt before auto-dialing: Checking this check box causes AutoDial connections to display a prompt that asks for confirmation before they are dialed. It sets the `DisableConnectionQuery` value under the
  `[HKEY_CURRENT_USER\ Software\Microsoft\RAS Autodial\Control]` key:
  ```
  DisableConnectionQuery    0 or 1
  REG_DWORD
  ```
  Checking the check box sets this value to 1, clearing it sets it to 0.

The Phonebook Tab

This tab, shown in Figure 16.22, sets the Phonebook file location.

This tab has one set of radial buttons that set the following values under the `[HKEY_CURRENT_USER\Software\Microsoft\RAS Phonebook]` key:
```
PhonebookMode    0,1, or 2
REG_DWORD
```
This value is set to a different number, depending on the radial button selected:

Setting	Button	Description
1	The system phonebook	Selecting this option causes Dial Up Networking to use the system phonebook, which is also the default phonebook file, rasphone.pbk, located in the %SYSTEMROOT%\SYSTEM32 directory.
2	My personal phonebook	Selecting this option causes Dial-Up Networking to use a personal phonebook that uses Password Protection mode if it is using an NTFS file system, to prevent other users of the same computer from being able to see your phonebook.
3	This alternate phonebook	Selecting this option causes Dial Up Networking to use a system phonebook that is located outside the %SDYSTEM ROOT%\SYSTEM32 folder. Use this selection to access a phonebook on a remote computer.

- My personal phonebook: When this radial button is selected and you have not created a personal phonebook, you see the dialog box displayed in Figure 16.23 when you click OK.

  Clicking OK creates the C:\%SYSTEMROOT%\Syatem32\ RAS\Administ.pbk file.

- This alternate phonebook: When this radial button is selected, an alternate phonebook file is created for new entries, or an existing phonebook is opened when Dial-Up Networking starts. The phonebook list shown in the drop-down list box below this button is contained in the `Phonebooks` value of the `[HKEY_CURRENT_USER\Software\Microsoft\RAS Phonebook]` key:

  ```
  Phonebooks     List of Phonebooks
  REG_MULTI_SZ
  ```

  This value is a string that lists all of the phonebooks that were created on this system.

  The `AlternatePhonebookPath` that is set to the selection of the drop-down list box is also found under this key. (This value was discussed in the Basic Tab section earlier in this chapter.)

The Logon Preferences Dialog Box

If you have administrator privileges, selecting this More list entry produces the Logon Preferences dialog box shown in Figure 16.24.

Figure 16.22   The Phonebook tab.

Warning

Because Password Protection mode only works when the NTFS file system is being used, personal phonebooks can be read if other users of the same computer use the FAT or FAT32 file system.

This entry does not appear in the More list if the logged–in user does not have administrator rights. This dialog box has four tabs, which are the same as those found in the User Preferences dialog box. In fact, this dialog box is used to copy all subkeys and values found under the [HKEY_USERS\.DEFAULT\Software\Microsoft\RAS Phonebook] key to the [HKEY_CURRENT_USER\Software\Microsoft\RAS Phonebook] key. This is done when the user logs in if the user does not have the [HKEY_CURRENT_USER\Software\Microsoft\RAS Phonebook] key. This sets the default settings the first time Dial–Up Networking is launched. This is also the key that determines which Dial–Up Networking options appear if a user chooses to log on to Windows NT by using Dial–Up Networking.

The tabs and options in this dialog box set the same values as the tabs and options in the User Preferences dialog box, except that they are written to the [HKEY_USERS\.DEFAULT\Software\Microsoft\RAS Phonebook] key.

This dialog box also does not have all of the options that the User Preferences key does, plus it has two additional settings. These additional settings are related to logging onto Windows NT by using Dial–Up Networking, and are located on the Appearance tab shown in Figure 16.26. These settings are discussed next.

Allow Location Edits During Login

Checking this check box allows the new user to make location edits as well as create new locations when they log on to Windows NT by using Dial–Up Networking. This check box sets this value:

```
AllowLogonLocationEdits     0 or 1
REG_DWORD
```

This value is set to 1 when the check box is checked and to 0 when it is cleared.

Allow Phonebook Edits During Login

Checking this check box allows the new user to make Phonebook file edits and create new phonebooks when they log on to Windows NT by using Dial–Up Networking. This check box sets this value:

```
AllowLogonPhonebookEdits     0 or 1
REG_DWORD
```

This value is set to 1 when the check box is checked and to 0 when it is cleared.

Figure 16.23 The add personal phonebook dialog box.

Figure 16.24   The Logon Preferences dialog box.

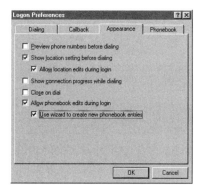

Figure 16.25   The Appearance tab.

17

Configuring Network Services

- **Computer identification**

  Registry entries associated with the computer's identification as well as the identification of workgroups and domains.

- **Windows NT Services**

  These services are set to automatically start when Windows NT is initially installed. These include the Server and Workstation Services.

Computer Identification

If you open the Control Panel, launch the Network applet, and then choose the Identification tab, you see the screen shown in Figure 17.1.

This dialog box is used to set the computer's identification. Next, we discuss the Registry settings that hold this information.

Computer Name

In Figure 17.1, the Computer Name text box is shown grayed out. This is because the Domain radial button is selected, and it cannot be changed and still be able to allow the computer access to the domain. The Computer Name text box sets the following Registry values, as described in the following sections.

ActiveComputerName and *ComputerName*

The `ComputerName` is stored first in these two values under these two keys.

- `[HKEY_LOCAL_MACHINE\SYSTEM\CurrentControlSet\Control\ComputerName\`
  `ActiveComputerName]`
    `ComputerName     Active Name`
    `REG_SZ`

  This value holds the string for the active computer name, which is the name that the computer is known as on the network. If you change the computer name by using the Network applet, this value's setting does not change until you reboot the computer.

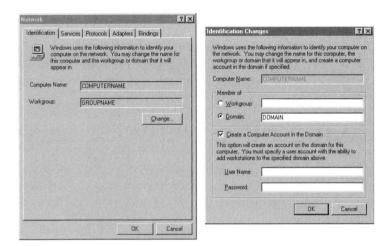

Figure 17.1 The Network applet's Identification tab.

■ [HKEY_LOCAL_MACHINE\SYSTEM\CurrentControlSet\Control\ComputerName\
ActiveComputerName]

    ComputerName   Future Name
    REG_SZ

This value holds the future value of the computer name that the computer is set to at rebooting if the computer name has changed using the network applet.

LOGONSERVER

This value is found under the [HKEY_CURRENT_USER\Volatile Environment] key and it is set to a string that is limited to 15 characters.

    LOGONSERVER   Computer Name
    REG_SZ   \\ComputerName

Host Name

The text box string is also written to the Hostname value under the [HKEY_LOCAL_MACHINE\SYSTEM\CurrentControlSet\Services\Tcpip\Parameters] key:

    Hostname   Computer Name
    REG_SZ   ComputerName

This value is set to the ComputerName string and identifies this computer to the Internet with this host name.

Security Key

The `ComputerName` is stored for use by the Windows NT Security system in the default value of the `[HKEY_LOCAL_MACHINE\SECURITY\Policy\PolAcDmN]` key:

```
@       Hexadecimal Numbers
REG_BINARY
```

To see this value's setting, open REGEDIT.EXE, select the value, right-click, and choose Modify. You see the screen shown in Figure 17.2, which shows the computer name, COMPUTERNAME.

Workgroup

The Workgroup text box sets the default value under the `[HKEY_LOCAL_MACHINE\ SECURITY\Policy\PolPrDmN]` key:

```
@       Hexadecimal Number
REG_BINARY
```

This is a binary entry that contains the workgroup name, as listed in the Workgroup text box when the Workgroup radial button is selected. You can view this value in the same way as the `ComputerName` value.

Domain

The Domain text box can only be set if the domain controller can be found. Also, the computer must either have an existing account in the domain; or the logged-on user must be a member of either the Administrators local group or the Domain Administrators global group, and, therefore, has the right to create a Computer account in the domain. Select the Create a Computer Account in the Domain check-box, and enter a login name and the password of an account that is a member of the Administrators group to also create this account. As with the Workgroup text box, the Domain text box setting can be seen in the default value under the `[HKEY_LOCAL_MACHINE\SECURITY\Policy\PolPrDmS]` key:

```
@       Hexadecimal Number
REG_BINARY
```

This is a binary entry that contains the domain name, as listed in the Domain text box, when the Domain radial button is selected. This value can be viewed as the `ComputerName` value is viewed.

> **Tip**
> When writing this value in a .REG file, remember that all UNC entries must be written with four back-slashes (for example, `\\\\ComputerName`). This value is set to the string listed in the Computer Name text box.

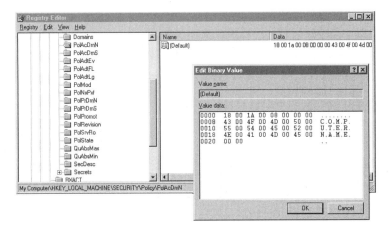

Figure 17.2 Viewing the ComputerName value.

Using Applets to Configure Windows NT Services

The next tab of the Network applet is the Services tab; it can be seen in Figure 17.3.

This tab is used to add, remove, or configure Windows NT Network Services. Most of these services affect values under the [HKEY_LOCAL_MACHINE\SYSTEM\CurrentControlSet\Services\Service] key and subkeys. Some of the values under these keys, such as the service's startup—including the start value, were discussed in Chapter 10, "Modifying the Windows NT Boot Process." The values listed here cover other configuration options for these services.

Finally, to start, stop, or automatically launch these services, you must use the Services applet of the Control Panel shown in Figure 17.4. If you use the Network applet's Services tab to remove services, then they are also removed from the Services applet.

The network services available for installation using the Services tab and those present in the Services applet are discussed next, including the Registry values that they configure.

Automatic Services

When you install Windows NT, several services are installed to start automatically. These services, which can be configured to start and stop by using the Services applet, the files that they reference, and the Registry entries that they create, are discussed next.

Figure 17.3   The Network applet's Services tab.

Alerter Service

This service, which depends on the Workstation Service and cannot be started without it, is configured through the Services applet and is responsible for alerting a list of users about operating system alerts. The Alerter Service does this by notifying the Windows NT Messaging Service of the users to whom alerts should be sent, using NetBIOS names. These names are located in the `AlertNames` value under the

`[HKEY_LOCAL MACHINE\SYSTEM\CurrentControlSet\Services\Alerter\Parameters]` key.

```
AlertNames     NetBIOS Name list
REG_MULTI_SZ
```

This is a binary setting that contains a listing of NetBIOS names for alerts to be sent to.

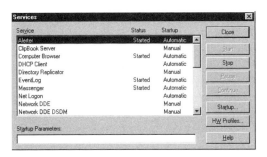

Figure 17.4   The Services dialog box.

Computer Browser

This service, which depends on the Workstation Service and the configuration of the NetBIOS interface, and cannot start without them, is the way that Windows NT notifies other computers on a Windows NT network that it is available for communication. The Browser Service is governed by the following values under the [HKEY_LOCAL_MACHINE\SYSTEM\CurrentControlSet\Services\Browser\Parameters] key.

Backup Period

```
BackupPeriodicity    300 to 4,294,967 Seconds
REG_DWORD
```

If the computer is configured to be a backup browser, the computer must contact the Master Browser to update the browser list. This value sets the time limit between these contacts. The maximum setting equates to 49 days and 8 hours. The default setting is 720 seconds.

Cache Hit Limit

```
CacheHitLimit    0 to 256
REG_DWORD
```

The Master Browser may receive more requests from the client than can be addressed. Set this value to a number that instructs the Browser Service to cache all requests with the same parameters after this number of tries. The default setting is 1.

Cache Response Size

```
CacheResponseSize    0 to 0xFFFFFFFF
REG_DWORD
```

The Master Browser only accepts this many responses for each transport. If you do not want to limit the number of responses, set this value to 0. The default setting is 10.

Direct Host Binding

```
DirectHostBinding    IPX/SPX Binding
REG_MULTI_SZ
```

This value enables Windows for Workgroups (WFW) computers to access Windows NT servers using only IPX/SPX. Setting this value eliminates the use of NetBIOS when connecting with WFW computers. This value affects Windows NT Server, and it can be changed with the Network applet by selecting the server choice of the Show Bindings for list box shown in Figure 17.5.

Choose the NWLink IPX/SPX Compatible Transport entry, which was installed with the IPX/SPX service, and click the Disable button. Check OK and select OK again to exit the applet and restart Windows NT. If you look in the Registry after Windows NT starts, notice that this value is no longer present.

Master Browser Value

```
IsDomainMasterBrowser     TRUE or FALSE
REG_SZ
```

All Windows NT machines can be set to be the Master Browser of the network. The Master Browser queries the network to see what computers are available on the network. This value should be set on at least 15% of the computers on the network to ensure the existence of a Master Browser. If this value is set to True, this computer acts as a Master Browser if one is not already present on the network.

Maintain Server List

```
MaintainServerList     TRUE, FALSE or AUTO
REG_SZ
```

Setting this value to True configures the computer as a backup browser. This setting also causes the computer to communicate with the Master Browser to back up the Browser list, and initiates a Master Browser election if no Master Browser is found. This computer may or may not be promoted to the Master Browser. If this value is set to False, it cannot be a backup server or initiate elections. The default setting is Auto, which means that the computer communicates with the server, which in turn instructs the computer to become a browser server or not.

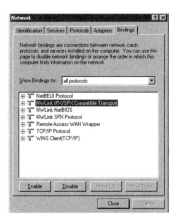

Figure 17.5 Server bindings.

Master Period

```
MasterPeriodicity    300 to 4,294,967 Seconds
REG_DWORD
```

This value acts like the `BackupPeriodicity` value because it sets the time interval for a Master Browser to communicate with the Domain Master Browser. This value also exists on the `DomainMaster` value and, if set, determines the interval that the Master Domain Browser uses when communicating with the WINS server.

Query Driver

```
QueryDriverFrequency    0 to 900
REG_DWORD
```

When a Master Browser determines the computer's presence in the Browser list, it caches this information. After awhile, this information becomes out-of-date, so this value is used to help prevent this. It does this by instructing the Master Browser to dump the cached browser list at the time interval set with this value. The Master Browser then creates a new browser list.

Event Log

This service controls the three kinds of event logs:

- Application
- Security
- Service

These event logs have a subkey for each one found at [HKEY_LOCAL_MACHINE\ SYSTEM\CurrentControlSet\Services\EventLog*LogFile*] key, where *LogFile* is either Application, Security, or Service.

The Windows NT Event Log Files listed under these LogFile keys are controlled by the following values:

Categories

```
CategoryCount    Number
REG_DWORD
```

This value states the number of categories that this log file supports.

Troubleshooting

Be sure to set the `MasterPeriodicity` value large enough to prevent excess network traffic.

Warning

The higher the `QueryDriverFrequency` values setting, the faster browsing occurs; however, the larger this value, the more the risk that the computers listed in the browser list will not be available.

Path and Filename

```
File     Path and filename
REG_SZ
```

This value holds the path for the log file that can be set with Event Viewer and defaults to %SYSTEMROOT%\system32\config\filename.

Category Message File

```
CategoryMessageFile     Path and Filename
REG_EXPAND_SZ
```

This value holds the path and file name of the category message file. This can be the same file as is set with the `EventMessageFile` value below.

Event Message File

```
EventMessageFile     Path and Filename
REG_EXPAND_SZ
```

This value holds the path and file name of the event identifier message file.

Maximum Logfile Size

```
MaxSize     Size in KB
REG_DWORD
```

This value states the maximum size of the log file. The default setting is 512.

Record Management

```
Retention     Time in seconds
REG_DWORD
```

This value causes records older than this value to be discarded. If this value is set to a large number, the Event Log may become filled and generates a Log Full Event. The default setting is 04800 or 7 days.

Other Log File Values

Other Registry values that affect the log files are found under the [HKEY_CURRENT_USER\Software\Microsoft\WindowsNT\CurrentVersion\Network\ Event Viewer] key. These values are:

```
Filter          Filter Scheme for Data
REG_SZ
```

This value stores the filter scheme used to display the data present when the log file was last closed. There is no default setting.

```
Find            Filter Scheme for Data
REG_SZ
```

This value stores the filter scheme used for find when the log file was last closed.

There is no default setting.

```
IfNT              0 or 1
REG_SZ
```

If this value is set to 1, the Event Viewer was monitoring an NT computer when it was closed. If set to 0, it was not monitoring one. The default setting is 1.

```
LogType            0, 1, 2, or 4
REG_SZ
```

This value is set to a different setting, depending on the log file that was being viewed when the Event Viewer was closed; these settings are as follows:

Setting	File
0	System File
1	Security Log File
2	Application File
3	Custom Log File

The default setting is 0.

```
Module          Log File Name, System, Security, Application
REG_SZ
```

This value stores the log file name or type of file. The default setting is System.

NetLogon Service

This service is used to provide the logged-in user a single access point of access to the domain's PDC and to any BDCs. It also synchronizes the changes made to the directory database stored on the PDC to the databases of all of the domain controllers. This service has the following values found under the [HKEY_LOCAL_MACHINE\ SYSTEM CurrentControlSet\Services\Netlogon\Parameters] key.

Change Log Size

```
ChangeLogSize    64KB to 4MB
REG_DWORD
```

This value states the size of the change log, found at %STSTEMROOT%\NET LOGON.CHG, which determines what directories are replicated by the Replicator Service. This setting's default is 64KB.

Mailslot Messages

The Netlogon service uses the following values to configure mailslot messages:

```
MaximumMailslotMessages    1 to 0xFFFFFFFF
REG_DWORD
```

This value sets the maximum number of mailslot messages that the Netlogon service can queue. Because each mailslot message uses almost 1500 bytes of nonpaged pool memory while it is processed, the Netlogon service may become backed up with messages. To prevent this backup, set this value to a low number. However, set it high enough to prevent the Netlogon service from missing incoming mailslot messages. The default setting is 500.

```
MaximumMailslotTimeout    5 to 0xFFFFFFFF
REG_DWORD
```

This value determines the age of mailslot messages that are ignored by the Netlogon Service. Netlogon ignores all received messages that are older than the setting for this value. Set this value high enough to prevent missing messages. This value is useful when the Windows NT server is overloaded. The default setting is 10.

```
MailslotDuplicateTimeout    0 to 5 (Seconds)
REG_DWORD
```

Sometimes duplicate messages are received by the NetLogon service. This service determines duplicates by comparing all newly received messages with the last message received during the time interval specified by this value. Duplicate messages that are received within this time are ignored. To disable the discarding of duplicate messages, set this value to 0. The default setting is 2.

The Pulse Values

Windows NT PDCs iterate a pulse to each of the BDCs on the network to determine whether the BDC needs to update its User Accounts database. The following values are used by the Netlogon service to control this pulse traffic between the PDC and the BDCs.

```
Pulse    60 to 172,800 (Seconds)
REG_DWORD
```

This value sets the pulse frequency, in seconds, for the PDC to update the domain's BDCs. All User Accounts database changes that are committed during this time are collected together. When this time limit expires, the PDC sends a pulse to each BDC that needs the changes. BDCs that are up-to-date do not receive a pulse. If this value is not set, the NetLogon service determines optimal settings based on the domain controller's load. The default setting is 300 seconds, or 5 minutes.

```
PulseConcurrency    1 to 500
REG_DWORD
```

Author Note

The setting of the ChangeLog Size value does not affect the system, so it should be set to 4MB, which prevents the domain's database from being completely replicated when large changes are made. You should set this value to the same setting for all PDCs and BDCs, so this value does not change the replication process when a BDC is promoted.

This value sets the maximum number of simultaneous pulses that the PDC sends to the BDCs. When the BDCs respond to these pulses to receive database changes, a large load can be placed on the PDC if these responses are received concurrently. To control this load, this value sets the number of concurrent BDC responses to the setting of this value. The higher this value is set, the higher the load on the PDC; the lower the setting, the longer it takes to change to all of the BDCs. The default setting is 20.

```
PulseMaximum    60 to 172,800 seconds
REG_DWORD
```

This value sets the maximum pulse frequency time in seconds. The PDC sends each BDC a pulse at this frequency, even if the BDCs database is current. The default setting is 7200 seconds, or 2 hours.

```
PulseTimeout1    1 to 120 seconds
REG_DWORD
```

When a PDC sends a pulse to a BDC, it waits for a response for the amount of time set in this value. If the BDC does not answer within this time, it is considered to be nonresponsive. All nonresponsive BDCs are exempted from the limit specified by the `PulseConcurrency` value. This allows the PDC to send additional pulses to other BDCs in the domain. If you set this value to high, nonresponsive BDCs take a long time to complete a partial replication. If set to low, slow BDCs are misidentified as nonresponsive, which increases the replication load on the PDC. The default setting is 5 seconds.

Replication Timeout

```
PulseTimeout2    60 to 3600 seconds
REG_DWORD
```

This value determines how long a BDC can wait to complete a partial replication. If a BDC responds to a pulse but it does not continue to make progress in the replication of its database within this values time limit, it is considered nonresponsive. If this number is set too high, slow BDCs are allowed to control one of the `PulseConcurrency` slots, which is a waste of resources. If this number is set to low, PDC's replication load increases. The default setting is 300 seconds, or 5 minutes.

BDC Wait Period

```
Randomize    0 to 120 seconds
REG_DWORD
```

This value sets the time that a BDC waits after it receives a pulse before it answers the PDC. This is called the *BDC back-off period*. Always take care to set this value lower than the setting for the `PulseTimeout1` value. The default setting is 1.

Data Transfer Size

```
ReplicationGovernor     0 to 100 percent
REG_DWORD
```

This value sets both the size of the data transferred to the BDC with each call to the PDC and the frequency of these calls. For example, setting this value to 25 percent defines a call to the PDC to use a 32K buffer instead of a 128K buffer. This also means that the BDC has an outstanding replication call from the PDC a maximum of 75 percent of the time. If this value is set to low, replication might never complete. If you set this value to 0, replication never completes, and the BDC and PDC become out of sync. The default setting is 100.

Scripts
```
Scripts     Script File and Pathname
REG_SZ
```

This value states the path and file name to any logon scripts. You can set this value by using the Services applet of the Control Panel. This value can be set by using the Server Manager. This value has no default setting.

Author Note

If a BDC can commit all of the User Accounts database changes within the time limit of a single pulse, the PulseTimeout2 value does not affect it. BDCs usually only fail to perform these changes during one pulse when there have been large changes to the database.

Tip

The time required to replicate changes to the User Accounts database to all the BDCs in a domain is always greater than:

[(Randomize value/2) * No. of BDCs in domain] \ PulseConcurrency value

Author Note

Different replication rates can be established at different times of the day by using a script file with the AT commands net start and net stop:

```
        net stop netlogon, regini scriptfile, net start netlogon
```

The script file must contain the path to the ReplicationGovernor value, as well as any new Registry settings. You can find the REGINI.EXE file in the Windows NT Resource Kit.

Update Database

```
Update      Yes or No
REG_SZ
```

This value, if set to Yes, instructs the Netlogon Service to synchronize the User Accounts database each time it starts. The default setting is No.

Disable Changing the Password

```
DisablePasswordChange    0 or 1
REG_DWORD
```

Windows NT Workstation is initially configured to change machine Account Passwords every 7 days. To disable these password changes, set this value to 1. The default setting for this value is 0. A setting of 1 prevents both client and domain replication traffic.

Refuse Password Changes

```
RefusePasswordChange    0 or 1
REG_DWORD
```

Machine passwords can also be refused at the server level by setting this value on all domain controllers to 1. This does not prevent the client from attempting to change the password every week, but it does prevent replication traffic from the server.

> **Tip**
>
> If you want to set up more than one installation on the same computer using one machine account, you can set the DisablePasswordChange value to 1 and follow these steps:
>
> 1. Install Windows NT. Using the Network applet's Identification tab, set up the computer as a member of a workgroup.
>
> 2. Set the DisablePasswordChange Registry value to 1.
>
> 3. Reboot the system.
>
> 4. Go to the domain controller and use the Server Manager to configure the machine account.
>
> 5. Configure the workstation to join the previous domain using the Network applet's Identification tab.
>
> 6. Install a new copy of Windows NT Workstation in a separate directory, and set up the computer as a workgroup member.
>
> 7. Repeat steps 2 and 3.

The Server Service

This service allows Windows NT client computers to access shared network resources. This service sets the following values found under the [`HKEY_LOCAL_MACHINE\SYSTEM\ CurrentControlSet\Services\LanmanServer`] key.

Scheduled Alerts

```
AlertSched    1 - 65,535 minutes
REG_DWORD
```

This value states the length of time that Microsoft LAN Manager and Windows NT servers check for alert conditions and then send out any required alert messages. The default setting is 5.

Automatic Disconnection

```
AutoDisconnect    0 - 0xFFFFFFF (Minutes)
REG_DWORD
```

This value sets the amount of time that a shared network resource is allowed to be idle before it is disconnected. However, if this time limit expires while the connection has open files or searches, the connection is preserved until these operations finish. Also, be sure to set this value high enough to save server resources without incurring performance problems because of client reconnections. The default setting is 15.

Enabling AutoShare for Servers

```
AutoShareServer    0 or 1
REG_DWORD
```

This value either enables or disables the server's AutoShare feature. A setting of 1 enables this feature; a setting of 0 disables it. When set to 1, Windows NT 4.0 servers automatically create hidden shares for local drives to be used by administrators. This value does not affect local shares that have been created manually. The default setting is 1.

Enabling AutoShare for Workstations

```
AutoShareWks    0 or 1
REG_DWORD
```

This value either enables or disables the Workstation's AutoShare feature. A setting of 1 enables this feature; a setting of 0 disables it. When set to 1, Windows NT 4.0 Workstations automatically create hidden shares for local drives to be used by administrators. This value does not affect local shares that have been created manually. The default setting is 1.

Author Tip

Set the AutoShareServer value to 0 if you want to limit access to a server's local drives.

Blocking Threads

```
BlockingThreads    1 - 9999 (Windows NT Server)
REG_DWORD
```

This value was used only on Windows NT versions prior to 3.51 to prevent the blocking of threads. This value is not used in Windows NT 4.0.

Server Comment

```
Comment      Text String
REG_SZ
```

This value holds the server's comment that is sent in announcements and returned to `NetServerGetInfo` requests.

Disconnect Time

```
ConnectionlessAutoDisc     Integer > 14
REG_DWORD
```

This value states the disconnect time for clients that use direct-hosted IPX. If the client computer fails to send a request to the server during this time limit, the client is automatically disconnected, regardless of the status of open files or pipes. The default setting is `15`.

Critical Threads

```
CriticalThreads    1 - 9999
REG_DWORD
```

This value was used for special-purpose threads concerned with time-critical tasks and is not used in Windows NT 4.0.

Free Disk space

```
DiskSpaceThreshold    0 - 99 percent
REG_DWORD
```

This value states the percentage of free disk space that must remain before an alert is sent. The default setting is `10` percent.

Direct IPX Hosts

```
EnableWFW311DirectIpx     True or False
REG_DWORD
```

This setting allows direct-hosted IPX clients to connect to the Windows NT server. Do not set this value to `True` if the connected client provides inadequate named pipe support when it runs over direct-hosted IPX. Doing so can cause named pipe applications to hang. Set this value to `True` only if the user does not need named pipe support. The default setting is `False`.

Initial Tree Connections

```
InitConnTable    1 - 128
REG_DWORD
```

This value determines the initial number of tree connections to be allocated in the connection table by Windows NT Server. Although the server automatically increases the table as necessary, a higher setting improves performance. The default setting is 8.

Initial File Entries

```
InitFileTable    1 - 256
REG_DWORD
```

This value determines the initial number of file entries that Windows NT Server allocates in the file table of each server connection. The default setting is 16.

Initial Search Entries

```
InitSearchTable    1 - 2048
REG_DWORD
```

This value determines the initial number of entries in the connection's search table. The default setting is 8.

Initial Sessions Entries

```
InitSessTable    1 - 64
REG_DWORD
```

This value determines the initial number of session entries that Windows NT Server allocates in the session table of each server connection. The default setting is 4.

Initial Receive Buffers

```
InitWorkItems    1 - 512
REG_DWORD
```

This value determines the initial number of receive buffers, or work items, used by the server. However, the allocation of work items costs an initial amount of memory, but not as much as having to allocate additional buffers later. The default setting depends upon the server configuration.

MS-DOS File Control Blocks

```
EnableFCBopens    0 or 1
REG_DWORD
```

This value determines whether MS-DOS File Control Blocks (FCBs) are folded together. If set to 1, multiple remote opens are performed as a single open on the server, which saves server resources. The default setting is 1, or True.

Enable Opportunistic Locking

```
EnableOplocks      0 or 1
REG_DWORD
```

This value determines whether the server allows clients to use *opportunistic locking*, or *oplocks*, on files. Although oplocks are a significant performance enhancement, they have the potential to cause lost cached data on some networks, particularly on wide area networks. The default setting is 1, or True.

Opportunistic Locking

```
EnableOplockForceClose      0 or 1
REG_DWORD
```

The setting for this value determines the behavior of a client that has an oplock, but does not respond to an oplock break, as follows:

- 0 or False: The second open request from this client fails, which effectively limits access to the file. LAN Manager version 2.0 clients behave this way.

- 1 or True: This forces the open instance of the client to close, which has the oplock that may result in the loss of cached data. LAN Manager version 2.1 behaves in this fashion.

Maximum Free Connection Blocks

```
MaxFreeConnections      2 - 8 items
REG_DWORD
```

This value sets the maximum number of free connection blocks maintained per endpoint. The default setting depends upon the configuration.

Maximum Link Delay

```
MaxLinkDelay      0 - 100,000 seconds
REG_DWORD
```

This value sets the maximum time allowed for a link delay. If this time limit expires, the server disables raw I/O for this connection. The default setting is 60.

Maximum MS-DOS Search Time

```
MaxKeepSearch      10 - 10,000 seconds
REG_DWORD
```

> **Warning**
>
> If you are using versions of Novell NetWare that are older than version 4, setting the EnableOplocks value to 1 may cause file-locking problems.

This value sets the maximum time during which the server keeps an incomplete MS-DOS search active. Setting a higher time limit causes better interoperability with MS-DOS utilities, such as tree-copy and delete-node. However, higher settings can cause unusual local behavior and higher memory use on the server. The default setting is 1800.

Maximum Simultaneous Requests

```
MaxMpxCt    1 - 100 requests
REG_DWORD
```

This value sets a suggested maximum for the number of simultaneous client requests that are outstanding on the server. Higher settings increase server performance, but require higher use of server work items. The default setting is 50.

Maximum Nonpaged Memory Size

```
MaxNonpagedMemoryUsage    < 1 MB
REG_DWORD
```

This value sets the maximum size of nonpaged memory that the server can allocate at any given time. If you want to administer memory quota control, increase or decrease this setting. The default setting depends on the configuration.

Maximum Paged Memory Size

```
MaxPagedMemoryUsage    < 1 MB
REG_DWORD
```

This value sets the maximum size of pageable memory that the server can allocate at any given time. Increase or decrease this setting to administer memory quota control. The default setting depends on the computer's configuration.

Maximum Nonpaged Memory Size

```
MaxNonpagedMemoryUsage    < 1 MB
REG_DWORD
```

This value sets the maximum size of pageable memory that the server can allocate at any given time. Increase or decrease this setting to administer memory quota control. The default setting depends on the computer's configuration.

Maximum Receive Buffers

```
MaxWorkItems    NTW 1 - 64 ; NTS 1 - 65,535
REG_DWORD
```

This value sets the maximum number of receive buffers, or work items, that the server (NTS) or workstation (NTW) can allocate. If this time limit expires, the transport must initiate flow control, which decreases performance. The default setting depends on the computer's configuration.

Idle Queue Time

```
MaxWorkItemIdleTime    10 - 1800 (Seconds)
REG_DWORD
```

This value sets the amount of time that a work item can stay on the idle queue before it is freed. The default setting is 300.

Minimum Free Connections

```
MinFreeConnections    2 - 5 items
REG_DWORD
```

This value sets the minimum number of free connection blocks maintained per endpoint. The default setting depends on the computer's configuration.

Minimum Free Work Items

```
MinFreeWorkItems    0 - 10 items
REG_DWORD
```

This value sets the minimum number of available receive work items that are needed for the server to begin processing a potentially blocking Server Message Block (SMB). Setting this value to a large value ensures that work items are available more frequently for nonblocking requests, but it also increases the likelihood that blocking requests will be rejected. The default setting is 2.

Minimum MS-DOS Search Time

```
MinKeepSearch    5 - 5000 seconds
REG_DWORD
```

This value sets the minimum amount of time that the server keeps incomplete MS-DOS searches. This value is only used when the server is near the maximum number of open searches. The default setting is 480.

Minimum Link Throughput

```
MinLinkThroughput    > 0 Seconds
REG_DWORD
```

This value sets the minimum link throughput allowed by the server before it disables raw and oplocks for this connection. The default setting is 0.

Minimum Work Items

```
MinRcvQueue    0 - 10 items
REG_DWORD
```

This value sets the minimum number of free receive work items needed by the server before it begins allocating more. A higher setting ensures that there will always be work items available, but settings that are too large are inefficient.

NetWare Shares

```
EnableSharedNetDrives    0 OR 1
REG_DWORD
```

If this value is set to 1, and Client Services for NetWare (CSNW) has been installed, any drives that were connected using NWCS are reshared as Windows NT shares. Windows NT shares are not reshared. The default setting is 1, or `True`.

Mapping Requests

```
EnableSoftCompat    0 or 1
REG_DWORD
```

This value determines that when the server receives a compatibility open request with read access from the client, it maps the request to a normal open request with shared-read access. The mapping of these requests allows multiple MS-DOS–based computers to open one file that can be used for read access by all of the MS-DOS computers. If you set this value to 1, some MS-DOS applications may not function correctly. The default setting is 1, or `True`.

Number of Errors

```
ErrorThreshold    1 - 65535
REG_DWORD
```

This value sets the number of errors that are allowed to occur within the time limit specified by the `AlertSched` value before the server sends an alert message. The default setting is `10`.

Comment Access

```
Hidden    0 or 1
REG_BINARY
```

If this value is set to 1, the server's name and comment value are announced to the client computer. If this value is set to `0`, the server's name and comment are not announced and other domain users cannot view it. The default setting is 1.

Number of Stack Locations

```
IRPstackSize    1 - 12
REG_DWORD
```

This value states the number of stack locations in I/O request packets (IRPs) used by the server. This value may need to be increased for MAC drivers or local file system drivers. The total memory costs of these increases are given by this formula:

No of work items $\star$ 36 bytes = Total memory cost

The default setting is 4.

Valid Link Time

```
LinkInfoValidTime    0 - 100,000 (Seconds)
REG_DWORD
```

This value states the amount of time that the transport link information is valid. If this time limit expires before the last query, the server will require transport link information. The default setting is 60.

Active Core Searches

```
MaxGlobalOpenSearch    Integer > 0
REG_DWORD
```

This value sets the maximum number of resource searches that can be active on the server at any given time. This value is used to limit the server resources used by active searches. Setting this value to high allows more searches to be active, but also uses up more server resources. Setting this value to low saves server resources, but it can affect clients that need a lot of active searches. The default setting is 4096.

Maximum Raw Work Items

```
MaxRawWorkItems    1 - 512 items
REG_DWORD
```

This value sets the maximum raw work items that the server can allocate. The server rejects all raw I/O operations from the client if this time limit is reached. This value's default depends on the configuration of the server.

Network Error Threshold

```
NetworkErrorThreshold    1 - 100 %
REG_DWORD
```

The setting of this value causes an alert to be issued if the percentage of failing network operations, relative to total network operations, exceeds this setting during the AlertSched interval setting. The default setting is 5%.

Non-Blocking Threads

```
NonBlockingThreads    1 - 9999
REG_DWORD
```

This value was used in a previous version of Windows NT to specify the number of threads set aside by the server to service requests that cannot block the thread for a significant amount of time. This value is not used with Windows NT 4.0

Pipe Access

```
NullSessionPipes     Pipe Listing
REG_SZ
```

This value contains a list of all pipes that the client is allowed to access during a null session. If a pipe does not appear on this list, the request to access it is denied. This value does not have a default, and it is used in conjunction with the `RestrictNullSessionAccess` and `NullSessionShares` values.

Null Session File Shares

```
NullSessionShares    Listing of Shares
REG_SZ
```

This value contains a list of all file shares that the client is allowed to access by using a null session. If a share does not appear on this list, the request to access it is denied. This value does not have a default, and it is used in conjunction with the `RestrictNullSessionAccess` and `NullSessionPipes` values.

Open Searches

```
OpenSearch    1 - 2048 searches
REG_DWORD
```

This value states the maximum number of outstanding searches on the server, per connection. Each client can have as many active searches as this value allows. This includes MS-DOS, OS/2, and Windows NT searches. The default setting is `2048`.

Op Break Request Limit

```
OplockBreakWait    10 - 180 seconds
REG_DWORD
```

This value sets the time limit that the server waits for a client to respond to an oplock break request. If this value is set to low, the detection of crashed clients occurs more quickly, but it can potentially cause loss of cached data. The default setting is `35`.

Raw Server Message Blocks

```
EnableRaw    0 or 1
REG_DWORD
```

This value determines whether the server processes raw SMBs. If set to `1`, more data is transferred per transaction, and performance increases. However, if you set this value to 1 and performance decreases, your network has trouble processing raw SMBs. This value entry is automatically tuned by the server. The default setting is `1`, or `True`.

Raw Work Items

```
RawWorkItems    1 - 512 items
REG_DWORD
```

This value states the number of special work items for raw I/O that the server can use. Setting this value to a high setting can increase performance, but it uses more memory.

Maximum Tree Connections

```
SessConns    1 - 2048 connections
REG_DWORD
```

This value sets the maximum number of tree connections that can be made on the server with a single virtual circuit. The default setting is **2048**.

Maximum Files

```
SessOpens    1 - 2048 files
REG_DWORD
```

This value sets the maximum number of files that can be open on a single virtual circuit. The default setting is **2048**.

Maximum Users

```
SessUsers    1 - 64 users
REG_DWORD
```

This value sets the maximum number of users that can be logged on to a server via a single virtual circuit. The default setting is **32**.

Worker Thread Count Per Process

```
ThreadCountAdd    0 - 10 threads
REG_DWORD
```

This value is not used with Windows NT 4.0; it was used in previous Windows NT versions to determine whether the server uses one worker thread per processor for the computer it is running on. This setting states how many additional threads that the server should use. Setting a higher number improves performance but costs memory. Too many threads can hurt performance by causing excessive task-switching. The default depends on the Windows NT configuration.

Author Note

A *virtual-circuit connection* is any logical link between two computers that are identified by their unique network interface card (NIC) addresses.

Server Thread Priority

```
ThreadPriority    0, 1, 2, or 15
REG_DWORD
```

This value is not used with Windows NT 4.0; it was used in previous Windows NT versions to determine the server threads in relation to the base priority of the process. The default setting is 1.

Maximum Threads Per Queue

```
MaxThreadsPerQueue    1 - 65535
REG_DWORD
```

This value determines whether the server dynamically adjusts the number of threads available for the servicing of client requests. The server always uses the smallest number of threads possible to achieve maximum server throughput. The server maintains a queue of client requests for each processor in the system. The default setting is 30.

Duplicate Searches

```
RemoveDuplicateSearches    TRUE or FALSE
REG_DWORD
```

This value determines whether the server should close duplicate searches received from the same client. This helps the server avoid the limit specified with the MaxGlobalOpenSearch value by closing identical searches. Set this value to False if the client needs multiple identical searches to be active. The default setting is True.

Null Session Access

```
RestrictNullSessionAccess    TRUE or FALSE
REG_DWORD
```

This value determines whether the server limits access to requests coming in through the null session. When this value is set to True, the NullSessionPipes and NullSessionShares values are used. The default setting is True.

Sharing Violation Retries

```
SharingViolationRetries    0 - 1000
REG_DWORD
```

This value sets the number of times the server retries an operation after the file system returns a sharing violation. These operations can include open commands, renames, and deletes. Setting this value to a low number prevents network traffic in cases where the client always retries the operations whenever it gets a sharing violation. The default setting is 5.

Sharing Violation Delay

```
SharingViolationDelay    0 - 1000 milliseconds
REG_DWORD
```

This value sets the number of milliseconds that the server delays retrying an operation. Setting this value to low causes sharing violation errors to occur upon the server's next retry. Setting it to high may cause the server's response to the client to be delayed longer than necessary, which negatively affects performance. The default setting is 200.

Request Buffer Size

```
SizReqBuf    512 - 65536 bytes
REG_DWORD
```

This value sets the size of request buffers used by the server. Although a low setting uses less memory, a larger setting increases performance. The default setting is 4356.

Maximum Users

```
Users    Integer > 0
REG_DWORD
Range:    Default:
```

This setting controls the maximum number of users that can be simultaneously logged on to the server. The default setting is 0xFFFFFFFF (infinite).

Xactsrv Virtual Memory Size

```
XactMemSize    64K - 16 MB
REG_DWORD
```

This value is associated with the Xactsrv service that supports remote net API calls from MS-DOS and OS/2, and is a part of the Server Service. The setting determines the maximum amount of virtual memory used by the Xactsrv service. If this value is set to high, memory is available for down-level clients, but this consumes virtual address space and can potentially use pageable memory. The default setting is 1MB.

The Workstation Service

This service controls a number of other services on the local Windows NT machine and sets the Registry values that allow Windows NT client computers to access shared network resources. This service sets the following values found under the [HKEY_LOCAL_MACHINE\SYSTEM\CurrentControlSet\Services\LanmanServer] key.

Read Share File Cache

```
BufFilesDenyWrite     0 or 1
REG_DWORD
```

This value determines whether the redirector should cache files that are opened with FILE_SHARE_READ sharing access only. If a file is opened with the FILE_SHARE_READ access specified, the file cannot be buffered because other processes might be accessing the file. Setting this value to 1 allows the redirector to buffer such files. The default setting is 1.

Buffer Character Mode Pipes

```
BufNamedPipes     0 or 1
REG_DWORD
```

This value determines whether the redirector should buffer character-mode named pipes. Setting this value to 0 guarantees that all pipe write operations are flushed to the server immediately and that read ahead on character-mode named pipes are disabled. The default setting is 1.

Read-Only File Cache

```
BufReadOnlyFiles     0 or 1
REG_DWORD
```

This value determines whether the redirector should cache files that are read-only. If a read-only file is opened, the file cannot be buffered because other processes might be reading the file. Setting this value to 1 allows the redirector to buffer such files. If it is set to 1, other users can still modify the file rights to enable writing to the file, which causes data loss. The default setting is 1.

Counting Illegal Datagram Events

```
IllegalDatagramResetTime     Seconds
REG_DWORD
```

This value determines the time limit during which the number of illegal datagram events is counted. Because Windows NT logs all illegal datagrams by default, the event log can become filled with a multitude of these events in a short amount of time. This value works in conjunction with the NumIllegalDatagramEvents value to limit the number of illegal datagrams that are recorded in the log within the time limit set with this value. The default setting is 60.

Logging Datagram Events

```
NumIllegalDatagramEvents    Number of events
REG_DWORD
```

This value determines the maximum number of datagram events that are logged within the time limit set by the IllegalDatagramResetTime value. Because Windows NT logs all illegal datagrams by default, the event log can become filled with a multitude of these events in a short amount of time. This value works with the IllegalDatagramResetTime value, as before. The default setting is 5.

Lock Increment

```
LockIncrement    Number
REG_DWORD
```

This value is only used by OS/2 applications. If these applications request a lock operation to wait forever, and the lock cannot be immediately granted on a non–LAN Manager version 2.0 server, the setting of this value controls the rate at which the redirector ramps back the failed lock operations. If you do not use OS/2 applications, do not change this value. The default setting is 10.

Lock Maximum

```
LockMaximum    Milliseconds
REG_DWORD
```

This value determines the configuration of the lock backoff package. If this value exists, it can be used to prevent an errant application from "swamping" a server with nonblocking requests. The default setting is 500.

Maximum Data Read

```
LockQuota    Bytes of data
REG_DWORD
```

This value determines the maximum amount of data that is read for each file if the UseLockReadUnlock value is enabled. Set this value higher if the application performs a significant number of lock-and-read style operations. If you set this value to high, you can cause the system to run out of paged memory, but only by increasing this value to a few megabytes and by using an application that locks millions-of-byte ranges. The default setting is 4096.

Maximum Work Buffers

```
MaxCmds    0 - 255
REG_DWORD
```

This value determines the maximum number of work buffers that the redirector reserves. The number of buffers reserved affects performance. Increasing this setting increases your network throughput. The default setting is 15.

Also, if your application performs more than 15 simultaneous operations, increase this value. Because this setting controls the number of execution threads that can be simultaneously outstanding at any given time, your network performance does not always improve when this setting is increased. Each additional execution thread takes about 1K of nonpaged memory if you actually load up the network. These resources are not consumed unless the user makes use of them. The default setting is 15.

Maximum Collection Count

```
MaxCollectionCount    0 - 65535 bytes
REG_DWORD
```

This value determines the threshold where character-mode named pipes initiate writes. If the write is smaller than this setting, the write will be buffered. Although adjusting this setting may improve performance for a named pipe application, it does not affect SQL Server applications. The default setting is 16.

512 Byte Transfer Value

```
Use512ByteMaxTransfer    0 or 1
REG_DWORD
```

This value determines whether the redirector should send a maximum of 512 bytes in a request to an MS-Net server, regardless of the server's negotiated buffer size. If this value is set to 0, request transfers from the Windows NT redirector can cause the MS-Net server to crash. The default setting is 0, or False.

Redirector Performance Enhancements

```
UseLockReadUnlock    0 0r 1
REG_DWORD
```

This value determines whether the redirector uses the lock-and-read and write-and-unlock performance enhancements.

When this value is set to 1, it provides significant performance increases. However, database applications that lock a range and then do not allow data within that range to be read suffer performance degradation unless this value is set to 0. The default setting is 1, or True.

Raw Read Use

```
UseRawRead    0 or 1
REG_DWORD
```

This value determines whether the raw-read enhancement is used. Set this value to 1 to enable the enhancement, which increases performance on a local area network. The default setting is 1, or True.

Raw Write

```
UseRawWrite     0 or 1
REG_DWORD
```

This value determines whether the raw-write enhancement is used. Set this value to 1 to enable the enhancement, which increases performance on a local area network. The default setting is 1, or True.

Unlock Operation

```
UseUnlockBehind    0 or 1
REG_DWORD
```

This value determines whether the redirector will complete an unlock operation before it receives confirmation from the server that the unlock operation is completed. If this value is set to 0, all unlock operations will complete on the server before completing the application's unlock request. The default setting is 1, or True.

Raw Write with Data Enhancement

```
UseWriteRawData    0 or 1
REG_DWORD
```

This value determines whether the raw–write–with data enhancement is used. Setting this value to 1 allows the redirector to send 4K of data with each write-raw operation, which increases performance on a local area network. The default setting is 1, or True.

Opening pipe wait

```
CharWait    0 - 65,535 Milliseconds
REG_DWORD
```

This value sets the time to wait for an instance of a named pipe to become available after opening the pipe.

Increasing this value increases the performance of the pipe server if the application is very busy. The default setting is 3600.

Write Behind data

```
CollectionTime    0 - 65,535,000 Milliseconds
REG_DWORD
```

This value sets the maximum time that write-behind data remain in a character-mode pipe buffer. Increasing this value's setting may cause a named pipe application's performance to improve but does not affect SQL Server applications. The default setting is 250.

Back Off Rate

```
PipeIncrement    Milliseconds
REG_DWORD
```

This value determines the rate at which the redirector "backs off" on failing non-blocking pipe reads. Setting this value prevents an errant application from "swamping" a server with nonblocking requests if there are no data available for the application. You can use the backoff statistics to tune this value entry to cause an application that uses nonblocking named pipes to be more efficient. The default setting is 10.

Maximum Back Off Time

```
PipeMaximum      Milliseconds
REG_DWORD
```

This value determines the maximum time that the redirector starts to "backs off" if nonblocking pipe reads fail.

Setting this value prevents an errant application from "swamping" a server with nonblocking requests if there are no data available for the application. You can use the backoff statistics to tune this value entry to cause an application that uses nonblocking named pipes to be more efficient. The default setting is 500.

Maximum Character Buffer

```
SizCharBuf       64 - 4096 bytes
REG_DWORD
```

This value sets the maximum number of bytes that are written into a character-mode pipe buffer. The default setting is 512.

File Cache Time

```
CacheFileTimeout    Seconds
REG_DWORD
```

This value sets the maximum time that a file is left in the cache after the application has closed it. Increasing this setting causes server operations to reopen files more than 10 seconds after the application has closed them. For example, if you are performing a build over the network, you should increase this setting. The default setting is 10.

Session Timeout

```
SessTimeout      10 - 65535 Seconds
REG_DWORD
```

This value sets the maximum amount of time that the redirector allows a non-long-term operation to be outstanding. The redirector uses this setting to determine how much extra time to wait for the SMB response after the expected length of time has timed out. The time that the redirector waits for a server to respond to an SMB is given by this formula:

```
[(SMB size + size of data sent or received) /
bytes per second] + SessTimeOut
```

This system-wide value is used for all protocols, including TCP/IP. This value does not apply to some types of SMBs, such as transaction commands, that have their own time-out variable in the SMB. The default setting is 45.

Dormant Open Files

```
DormantFileLimit     Number of files
REG_DWORD
```

This value sets the maximum number of files that can be left open on a shared resource after the application has closed the file. This setting is used to increase the default configuration of LAN Manager servers, which allows 60 open files from remote clients and 50 open files from each client workstation. Because the redirector can keep files open in the cache after an application has closed the file, the redirector can overload a LAN Manager server. To correct this, either reduce this setting or increase the maxSessopens and maxOpensvalues for the server. The default setting is 45.

Maximum Dormant Connection Time

```
KeepConn     1 - 65,535 Seconds
REG_DWORD
```

This value sets the maximum amount of time that a connection can be left dormant. This setting is the redirector equivalent of the Disc value in the [HKEY_LOCAL_ MACHINE\SYSTEM\CurrentControlSet\Services\LanmanServer\Parameters] key. The default setting is 600.

Election Packet Events

```
LogElectionPackets     0 or 1
REG_DWORD
Default: 0 (false)
```

This value determines whether the browser should generate events when election packets are received. The default setting is 0, or False.

> **Author Note**
>
> If you have an application running that closes and opens UNC files to a server less than 10 minutes apart, try increasing the KeepConn value. This reduces the number of reconnections made to the server and increases the remaining applications' performance.

Maximum Mailslot Buffers

```
MailslotBuffers    Number of buffers
REG_DWORD
```

This value sets the maximum number of buffers available to process mailslot messages. Setting this to a high number helps to avoid losing mailslot messages for applications that use a high number of mailslot operations. The default setting is 5.

Domain Browsing List

```
OtherDomains    DomainNames
REG_SZ
```

This value sets the Microsoft LAN Manager domains to be listed for browsing. This value does not have a default setting.

Throughput Value

```
ReadAheadThroughput    KB per second
REG_DWORD
```

This value sets the throughput required for connections before the Cache Manager enables read-ahead. The default setting is 0xffffffff.

Maximum Announcement Buffers

```
ServerAnnounceBuffers    Number
REG_DWORD
```

This value sets the maximum number of buffers used to process server announcements and is found under the \Static subkey of the Workstation Service Parameters key. Increasing this setting minimizes the loss of server announcements on a network with several servers. The default setting is 20.

Transport List

```
Transports    List
REG_MULTI_SZ
```

This value lists the transports that the redirector services and is found under the \Linkage subkey of the Workstation service Parameters key. This value does not have a default setting.

File Content Cache

```
UtilizeNtCaching    0 or 1
REG_DWORD
```

This value determines whether the redirector uses the cache manager to cache a file's content. Setting this value to 1 guarantees that all data is flushed to the server immediately after it is written by the application. The default setting is 1, or True.

The Replicator Service

This service controls the automatic duplication of files and directories from the Windows NT server to other Windows NT servers or workstations. If you experience problems using this service, set the following values found under the `[HKEY_LOCAL_MACHINE\SYSTEM\CurrentControlSet\Services\Replicator\ Parameters]` key.

Replication Value

```
Replicate     1, 2, or 3
REG_DWORD
```

This value sets the operation of the Replicator service by specifying the Replicator action as follows:

- 1 or Export: The server maintains a master tree of files to be replicated.
- 2 or Import: The server imports files when it receives an update notice from the export server.
- 3 or Both: The server acts as an export and an import server for the replication of directories or files, as before.

The default setting is 3.

Export List

```
ExportList     List
REG_MULTI_SZ
```

This value contains an unlimited number of servers or domains that receive notices when the export directory is updated. These servers subsequently replicate from the export server. If this value does not exist, the export server sends a notice to its domain requesting replication.

This value can contain multiple list names, separated with a semicolon. If the setting for the `Replicate` value is 2, this value is ignored. There is no default for this setting.

Export Path

```
ExportPath
REG_SZ or REG_EXPAND_SZ
```

This value sets the export path for replication. All files to be replicated must be located in a subdirectory of this export directory. If the setting for the `Replicate` value is 2, this value is ignored. Use the Replicator controls in Server Manager or Server in the Control Panel to set this value, which cannot be a UNC name. This value's default is %SYSTEMROOT%\System32\Repl\Export.

Import List

```
ImportList     List
REG_SZ
```

This value contains an unlimited number of servers or domains that receive notices when the import directory is updated. These servers subsequently replicate from the import server. If no List value is specified, updates come from the import server's domain.

This value can contain multiple list names separated with a semicolon. If the setting for the Replicate value is 1 this value will be ignored. There is no default for this setting.

Import Path

```
ImportPath     Import path
REG_SZ or REG_EXPAND_SZ
```

This value determines the path on the import server that receives replicas from the export servers. If the setting for the Replicate value is 1, this value is ignored. This value's default is SYSTEMROOT%\System32\Repl\Import.

Temporary Crash Directory

```
CrashDir     First-level directory name
REG_SZ
```

This value stores the name of the top-level directory that existed before a replication. It is temporarily recorded in the Registry by the Replicator Service and should be deleted if you see it in the Registry after you use the System Repair Disk.

Replication Stable Time

```
GuardTime     0 to one-half of the Interval value
REG_DWORD
```

This value sets the number of minutes that an export directory must be stable, without any changes to files, before import servers can replicate the files. This option applies only to directories with tree integrity. This value's default is 2 minutes.

Replication Change Interval

```
Interval     1-60 Minutes
REG_DWORD
```

This value determines how often an export server checks the replicated directories for file changes. This option is ignored on import servers. This value's default is 5 minutes.

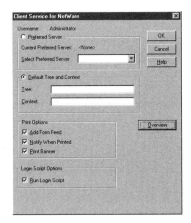

Figure 17.6 The CSNW applet.

Pulse Value

```
Pulse     1 - 10 cycles
REG_DWORD
```

This value determines how often the export server repeatedly sends the last update notice. These repeat notices are sent, even when no changes have occurred, so that import servers that missed the original update notice can receive the notice. The server waits the equivalent of (Pulse ★ Interval) minutes before sending each repeat notice. This value's default is 3.

Replication Update Wait

```
Random     1 - 120 seconds
REG_DWORD
```

This value determines the maximum time that the import servers wait before requesting an update. An import server uses the export server's Random value setting to generate a random number of seconds, ranging from 0 to the value's setting. The import server waits this long after receiving an update notice before it requests the replica from the export server. This prevents the export server from being overloaded by simultaneous update requests. This value's default is 60.

> **Author Note**
>
> If you do not want the user to choose Novell login options, you can add this value under the same key as before:
>
> ```
> DefaultLocation    Server or Tree\Context
> REG_SZ
> ```
>
> This allows the user to log in to this resource only.

Client Services for NetWare

CSNW is a service included with Windows NT that can add support for Novell file and print services. Add this service with the Network applet and reboot the computer. After the computer boots, open the Control Panel and you see an applet called CSNW (Client Services for NetWare). When you launch this applet, you see the screen shown in Figure 17.6.

The Registry values that are set with this screen are found under the [HKEY_LOCAL_ MACHINE\System\CurrentControlSet\Services\NWCWorkstation\Parameters] key. These values are discussed next.

Preferred Server Value

Select the first set of radial buttons shown in Figure 17.6 and enter a server name into the Select Preferred Server text box. This sets the following value under the [HKEY_ LOCAL_MACHINE\SYSTEM\ControlSet001\Services\NWCWorkstation\Parameters\Option *SID*] key, where *SID* is the SID of the currently logged-in user, as displayed in the [HKEY_USERS/*SID*] key:

```
PreferredServer     Server Name
REG_SZ
```

This value is set to the entry of the previous text box.

This entry is set to the tree and context, as follows, if the Default Tree and Context radial button is selected.

```
PreferredServer     Tree\Context
REG_SZ     NetwareTree\ou=Sandra. o=Macmillan
```

This value is set to the concatenated string from the Tree and Context text boxes.

Print Options

These three check boxes set the following value according to Table 17.1. This value is located under the same SID key as the `PreferredServer` value.

```
PrintOption     Number
REG_DWORD
```

> **Author Note**
>
> If you want to run the same login script, independent of the user, add this value to the above SID key:
>
> ```
>         DefaultScriptOptions     0, 1, 0r 3
>         REG_DWORD
> ```
>
> This value uses the same settings as before.

Table 17.1   **The *PrintOption* Value**

Setting	Add Form Feed	Notify When Printed	Print Banner
0	Checked	Not Checked	Not Checked
8	Not Checked	Not Checked	Not Checked
16	Checked	Checked	Not Checked
24	Not Checked	Checked	Not Checked
128	Checked	Not Checked	Checked
136	Not Checked	Not Checked	Checked
144	Checked	Checked	Checked
152	Not Checked	Checked	Checked

The Login Script

If you check the Run Login Script check box displayed in Figure 17.6, the following value is set under the same SID key as the `PreferredServer` value.

```
LogonScript    0, 1 or 3
REG_SZ
```

If the check box is selected and you are using NetWare 3.X (as defined by setting a preferred server), this value is set to 1. If you are using a default tree and context, this value is set to 3 when checked. It is set to 0 when cleared.

18

Configuring Network Communications

- **NetBIOS names and the NetBIOS gateway**

  This section discusses the NetBIOS, Network Basic Input/Output System, and Registry values that are used with the Remote Access Service.

- **AsyncMac and NisWan keys**

  This section discusses values that can be set to synchronize the remote client with the Windows NT RAS Server.

- **RAS and NWLink**

  This section discusses the NWLink protocol Registry values that affect RAS.

- **Remote Access TCP/IP**

  This section discusses the TCP/IP options of the RAS Server.

- **Point-To-Point Protocol**

  This section discusses the RAS Point-To-Point Protocol.

- **Other Remote Access Service (RAS) parameters**

  This section discusses Registry settings that affect RAS but were not included in the previous sections.

NetBIOS Names and the NetBIOS Gateway

NetBIOS defines a client/server programming interface and the NetBIOS naming convention. And, although NetBIOS is not a transport protocol, it can communicate over NetBEUI, NWLink NetBIOS, and NetBIOS over TCP/IP or NetBT. These protocols are discussed in Chapter 19, "Configuring TCP/IP." Before we can discuss the NetBIOS RAS Registry values, we must first talk about NetBIOS names, which are set as shown in Figure 18.1.

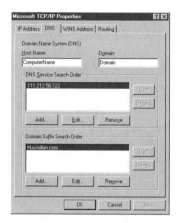

Figure 18.1   The DNS tab of the TCP/IP Properties dialog box.

Figure 18.1 is produced by opening the Control Panel, launching the Network applet, selecting the Protocols tab, selecting the TCP/IP protocol, clicking the Properties button, and choosing the DNS tab in the resulting window.

NetBIOS Names

Because all NetBIOS names, which are limited to 16 characters, must be unique, NetBIOS is said to have a *flat namespace*. However, NetBIOS names can be registered for one user only, for multiple users, or for *groups*. These names, which are registered automatically when computers start, when services start, or when users log on, identify network resources available to the computer. These resources can be located by resolving the name to a TCP/IP address by using cache, broadcasts, LMHOSTS files, or the WINS (Windows Internet Name Service) server.

NetBIOS Name Cache

The NetBIOS name cache, which contains the name-to-address mappings of other computers, caches the entries of the LMHOSTS files. It can be viewed from the Windows NT command line by running NBTSTAT.EXE, as well as allowing for the removal or correction of preloaded entries.

Note

This section discusses some TCP/IP parameters as they relate to NetBIOS. See Chapter 19 for complete TCP/IP information.

This program has the following syntax and performs according to the following switches:

Syntax:

```
nbtstat [-a RemoteName] [-A IP_address] [-c] [-n] [-R] [-r] [-S] [-s]
[interval]
```

- ■ -a <RemoteName>. This switch, where *name* is a ComputerName, runs the NetBIOS adapter status command against the computer specified by *RemoteName*. This command returns the local NetBIOS name table of the remote computer, including the computer network adapter card's MAC address.

- ■ -A <IP address>. This switch produces a list that shows the remote computer's NetBIOS name for the given <IP address>, which should be specified in dotted decimal notation.

- ■ -c. This switch shows the NetBIOS name cache.

- ■ -n. This switch displays the NetBIOS names that were registered locally by Windows NT services, such as the Server or Redirector Service. If you see Registered in this list, the name is registered on this network node by b-node broadcast or by a WINS server.

- ■ -R. This switch causes the NetBIOS name cache to be purged and reloads it from the LMHOSTS file.

- ■ -r. This switch produces a list containing NetBIOS name-resolution statistics for Windows NT networks. If the computer is configured to use WINS, this option returns the number of names.

- ■ -S. This switch generates a list of the current NetBIOS workstation and server sessions, and their stat uses, showing the remote computers with their TCP/IP addresses.

- ■ -s. This switch also displays workstation and server sessions, but it also tries to convert the remote computer's TCP/IP address to its ComputerName by using the remote LMHOSTS file.

Note

By looking at the NetBIOS name cache on a remote computer, you can track down a ComputerName if duplicate addresses are found.

Note

If you use the –a switch, but NBTSTAT.EXE does not produce a response, the computer is either a router or one that does not use NetBIOS over TCP/IP, usually a non-Microsoft computer. Also, if there are multiple network adapters in your computer, NBTSTAT.EXE runs over the first adapter card in the binding list.

- *interval*. This switch redisplays selected statistics, pausing *interval* seconds between each display. Press Ctrl+C to stop the display. If you do not specify this parameter, NBTSTAT.EXE prints the current configuration information only once.

Broadcasts

Using this resolution method results in additional network traffic. As the number of computers on the network increases, large amounts of additional network traffic are generated.

The LMHOSTS File

If this file, located in the %SYSTEMROOT%\system32\drivers\etc directory, is used to resolve a NetBIOS Name, the network administrator must continually maintain this file. The file is a list of NetBIOS Names and their associated TCP/IP addresses. Using this method can require a large amount of administration to keep the file current. Plus, every time that the file changes, each computer on the network must download it. Administrators use the LMHOSTS file when broadcasting fails to resolve the name.

The Domain Name System Server

Using DNS to resolve NetBIOS names implements a distributed database with a hierarchical naming system. The DNS database uses a structured naming convention that must be followed exactly. An example of this is `Osborne.Macmillan.com`, where `Osborne` is the computer name and `Macmillan.com` is the domain name. Using this method is not as flexible as the broadcast and LMHOSTS file methods.

DNS is configured using the screen shown in Figure 18.1, which sets the following values under the `[HKEY_LOCAL_MACHINE\SYSTEM\CurrentControlSet\Services\Tcpip\Parameters]` key.

Host Name

```
Hostname                    NetBIOS or Host Name
REG_SZ
```

This entry is the name that the computer is identified within the DNS database, and is set by the **H**ost Name text box (refer to Figure 18.1). This name is usually the same as the Computer Name shown in Figure 18.2.

Warning

If you use LMHOSTS and also use the Dynamic Host Configuration Protocol (DHCP), as discussed in Chapter 19, additional maintenance is required to maintain the correct names with the correct addresses because LMHOSTS is a static file. Therefore, you should use WINS or DNS when you implement DHCP.

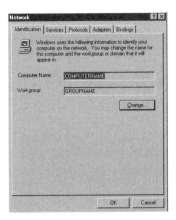

Figure 18.2   Network applet Identification tab.

If these names are not the same, you see the error message shown in Figure 18.3.

Clicking OK identifies your computer with one NetBIOS Name over the Internet (this one) and another NetBIOS name on the local network (the one shown in Figure 18.2).

Domain

```
Domain                  Domain Name
REG_SZ
```

This entry is the domain that this computer connects to and is set by the Domain text box shown in Figure 18.1.

DNS Service Search Order

```
NameServer              DNS Server TCP/IP Address
REG_MULTI_SZ
```

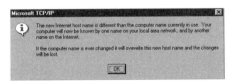

Figure 18.3   NetBIOS name error.

This value sets the search order that the computer uses to find the DNS server. If more than one server is listed here, this value contains all of the TCP/IP addresses for the servers that are set in the DNS **S**ervice Search Order list box, shown in Figure 18.1. The **U**p and Do**w**n buttons on the right of this text box change the search order for these servers, as well as the order in which these addresses are listed in the `NameServer` setting.

Domain Suffix Search Order

```
SearchList          DNS Server TCP/IP Address
REG_MULTI_SZ
```

This value contains a list of the available domain suffixes. A domain suffix, such as `Macmillan.com`, is used, along with the host name, to identify your computer on the Internet. The `HostName` value joins this value to create the DNS database entry. DNS searches for the resolution of these names in the order listed. As with the `NameServer` value, clicking the **U**p and Do**w**n buttons changes the DNS search order, as well as the order in which these addresses are listed in the `SearchList` setting.

WINS Server

Like DNS, the WINS Server—the Windows NT Server NetBIOS Name server—maintains a database that maps the TCP/IP addresses of WINS clients to their NetBIOS Name. Using this service, a user can log onto the network and resolve NetBIOS Name resources by requesting the name's TCP/IP address from the WINS server, which looks up the name and associated address in its database. WINS is configured by using the WINS Address tab of the Microsoft TCP/IP Properties dialog box, shown in Figure 18.4.

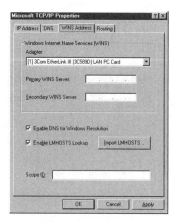

Figure 18.4   The WINS Address tab.

Using this tab to configure WINS sets several Registry values found under two different keys, as follows.

Primary WINS Server

The following values are set with the WINS frame shown in Figure 18.4. They are found under the [HKEY_LOCAL_MACHINE\System\SurrentControlSetServices\NetBt\ Adapters*AdapterName*] key, where *Adapter* name is the name of your adapter card.

```
NameServer            TCP/IP Address
REG_SZ
```

This value contains the TCP/IP address for the primary WINS server that the computer tries to communicate with to resolve NetBIOS names. This value is set with the Primary WINS Server text box.

Secondary WINS Server

```
NameServerBackup        TCP/IP Address
REG_SZ
```

This value contains the TCP/IP address for the secondary WINS server that the computer tries to communicate with to resolve NetBIOS names if the primary WINS server is not available. This value is set with the **S**econdary WINS Server text box.

Primary and Secondary Server Parameters

The following values are set with the two check boxes and the Scope **ID** text box shown in Figure 18.4. They are found under the [HKEY_LOCAL_MACHINE\SYSTEM\ CurrentControlSet\Services\NetBT\Parameters] key.

```
EnableDNS             0 or 1
REG_DWORD
```

This value is set to 1 if the Enable DNS for Windows Resolution check box is checked, and 0 if it is cleared. Setting this value to 1 causes DNS to be used to resolve NetBIOS names.

```
EnableLMHOSTS           0 or 1
REG_DWORD
```

This value is set to 1 if the Enable LMHOSTS Lookup check box is checked, and 0 if it is cleared. Setting this value to 1 causes the LMHOSTS file to be used to resolve NetBIOS names.

```
ScopeID               Scope ID
REG_SZ
```

This value contains the computer's scope identifier, set with the Scope **ID** text box. This value is used only if you use DNS and the DNS server cannot be found. This value is usually not specified.

The NetBIOS Gateway

Windows NT Server or Workstation can be configured to be a RAS Server. If you use NT Workstation you are limited to 10 concurrent connections; Windows NT Server is limited to 256 concurrent connections. This RAS Server can be configured to be a NetBIOS gateway if clients connect by using the NetBEUI protocol. Configuring RAS in this way enables the RAS Server to translate packets to IPX or TCP/IP, enabling the client to share network resources on a multiprotocol LAN. However, the client cannot run applications that rely on IPX or TCP/IP.

To set up RAS as a NetBIOS gateway, set this value under the `[HKEY_LOCAL_MACHINE\System\CurrentControlSet\Services\RemoteAccess\Parameters]` key:

```
NetbiosGatewayEnabled          0 or 1
REG_DWORD
```

Setting this value to 1 makes the RAS Server emulate the NetBIOS gateway. If this value is set to 0, remote NetBEUI clients cannot access the LAN, and other clients can only access it by using a point-to-point connection. This default setting is 1, or enabled.

After the previous value is set and RAS can behave as a NetBIOS gateway, the following values are set under the `[HKEY_LOCAL_MACHINE\System\CurrentControlSet\Services\RemoteAccess\Parameters\NetbiosGateway]` key.

Multicast Datagram Priority

```
DisableMcastFwdWhenSessionTraffic        0 or 1
REG_DWORD
```

Setting this value to 1 gives NetBIOS session traffic (such as Windows NT applications) priority over multicast datagrams (such as server messages). This means that multicast datagrams are transferred only when there is no session traffic. Always set this value to 1 unless you use applications that depend on multicast datagrams. The default setting is 1, or enabled.

Datagram Forwarding

```
EnableBroadcast                 0 or 1
REG_DWORD
```

Setting this value to 1 causes the RAS Server to forward datagram messages to the remote computers, where the forwarding rate is set by the `MultiCastForwardRate` value. Also, because forwarding these messages consumes the bandwidth needed by the remote computer, this value is usually set to its default setting of 0, or disabled.

Warning
You should not change the Netbios Gateway Enabled value's setting directly because this setting affects network bindings.

Datagram Forwarding Rate

```
MultiCastForwardRate      -1 or 0 to 32,767 Seconds
REG_DWORD
```

If the previous `EnableBroadcast` value is set to 1 and this value is set to an integer between 1 and 32,7667, group name multicast datagrams are forwarded to all remote computers. The default setting is 5, and datagrams are forwarded by using the time interval set with this value, as follows:

-1	This setting disables datagram forwarding.
0	This setting guarantees delivery of group name datagrams.
1 to 32,767	This setting forwards datagrams every n seconds, where n is this setting.

Maximum Datagrams Sent

```
MaxBcastDgBuffered                16 to 255
REG_DWORD
```

This value determines the number of datagrams that the gateway buffers for a remote computer. Increase this setting if you use applications that communicate extensively through multicast or broadcast datagrams. The default setting is 32.

Datagrams per Group Name

```
MaxDgBufferedPerGroupName         1 to 255
REG_DWORD
```

This value determines the number of datagrams that can be buffered for each group name. And, although increasing this setting buffers more datagrams per group name, the extra datagrams use additional virtual memory. The default setting is 10.

Enable Remote Access Auditing

```
EnableNetbiosSessionsAuditing     0 or 1
REG_DWORD
```

Setting this value to 1 turns on remote access auditing for the establishment of NetBIOS sessions between remote clients and Windows NT servers. Turning on auditing helps the administrator track NetBIOS resources accessed on the LAN. Setting this value to its default of 0 turns off RAS Auditing.

> **Note**
>
> If the `EnableBroadcast` value is set to 0, forwarding is turned off, even if the `MultiCastForwardRate` value is set to 1 or greater. If the `MultiCastForwardRate` value is set to 1, forwarding is turned off, even if the `EnableBroadcast` value is set to 1.

Virtual Memory Size

```
MaxDynMem      131072 to 4294967295
REG_DWORD
```

This value sets the amount of virtual memory used to buffer NetBIOS session data for each remote client. The default setting is `655350`.

Number of NetBIOS Names

```
MaxNames                    1 to 255
REG_DWORD
```

This value sets the number of unique NetBIOS names that each client can have (a maximum limit of 255 names is allowed for all clients together). The default setting is `255`.

Simultaneous Settings

```
MaxSessions                 1 to 255
REG_DWORD
```

This value sets the maximum number of simultaneous NetBIOS sessions that each client can establish. There is a cumulative limit of 255 for all client sessions. If you use

Note

When the Remote Access Server is a gateway between slow connection lines and the LAN, RAS stores data from the LAN in the server's memory before it is forwarded to the slow line. RAS minimizes the use of the server's physical memory by locking a small set of pages, about 64K per client; and uses the remaining pages, up to the MaxDynMem value setting, to buffer the rest of the data.

Before you can increase this setting, you must ensure that you have disk space available on your hard disk for the PAGEFILE.SYS, which increases as this setting increases.

Warning

If you use a client application that uses a fast LAN sender and a slow receiver, you can have problems if the sender transmits more data than the RAS server can buffer, as set by MaxDynMem. This causes RAS to apply NetBIOS level flow control by not submitting Ncb.receive on the session until it has created enough buffer space to hold the incoming data. Increasing the application servers' NetBIOS SEND/RECEIVE time-outs cause the application server to wait for all data to be transmitted over the slow link to the remote client before proceeding.

Warning

If you use clients that run Windows NT or Windows for Workgroups to dial in to servers that run Remote Access version 1.1 or earlier, set the MaxNames value to 8 or greater.

multiple clients that connect simultaneously, and run 4 or 5 sessions each, be sure to decrease this setting to avoid exceeding the 255 limit. The default setting is 255.

Multiple Network Connections

```
NumRecvQueryIndications          1 to 34
REG_DWORD
```

This setting determines whether a remote access client can initiate multiple network connections simultaneously. Increase this setting if you use a remote client that runs a NetBIOS application that does multiple NCB.CALL commands simultaneously to improve performance. The default setting is 3.

Receive Datagram Commands

```
RcvDgSubmittedPerGroupName       1 to 32
REG_DWORD
```

This value determines the number of NetBIOS receive datagram commands, per group name, that can be submitted simultaneously to the LAN stack. Set this value low to conserve memory because each datagram command that is received locks about 1.5 KB of physical system. The default setting is 3.

Resource Access Level

```
RemoteListen                     0, 1, or 2
REG_DWORD
```

This value sets the LAN client's level of access to a remote client's resources. Setting this value to 1 or 2 posts NCB.LISTEN commands on the NetBIOS names of the client. This value's default is 1, and it performs as follows:

0   No Resource Access - All remote listens consume one session, set this value to 0 to save sessions.

Note

The remote client must be running the Server service to make its resources, disks, and printers available to the LAN users. The remote client must also be running the Messenger service to receive messages from LAN users.

Warning

If you set the RemoteListen value to a number other than the default, NCB.LISTEN is enabled for remote clients who can significantly drain system resources. Also, if this value is set to 2, RAS posts NCB.LISTEN on all RAS client NetBIOS Names. This means that because the average Windows NT client has seven or eight NetBIOS names assigned to it, NCB.LISTEN would post 7 or 8 * 256 NetBIOS names, which is the maximum number of clients allowed per server.

1   Server and Messenger services available to the client.

2   Enables NCB.LISTEN on all remote client NetBIOS names. Setting
                      this value to 2 allows client NetBIOS applications to answer
                      NCB.CALL commands issued by LAN applications.

Work Buffers Size

```
SizWorkBufs                 1024 to 65536
REG_DWORD
```

This value determines the size of work buffers. Use the default setting of 4500 when
you use the SMB or server message block (SMB) protocol.

The AsyncMac and NisWan Keys

The values under the AsyncMac key synchronize the RAS server with the remote
client; the NisWan values define the rules for binding Dial-Up Networking phone
book entries to the transport protocols. This synchronization is accomplished by the
following Registry values, found under the [HKEY_LOCAL_MACHINE\System\
CurrentControlSet\Services\AsyncMacn\Parameters] key. If you change these
settings, you must reboot the computer before they effect.

```
MaxFrameSize                576 to 1514
REG_DWORD
```

This value determines the maximum frame size. Decrease this setting if you encounter
noisy links. Of course, lower settings send less data per frame, which degrades performance. Do not change this setting if you use RAS version 1.1 or earlier; the setting is
negotiated between the RAS server and Windows NT clients. The default setting is
1514.

```
TimeoutBase                 500 - 1000
REG_DWORD
```

This value determines the time limit that a NetBIOS gateway connection is allowed
to connect. The default setting is 500.

> **Note**
> If you use a NetBIOS gateway and experience an abnormal number of time-out errors; and your comput-
> er has a security device, or your modem has hardware compression or error control enabled, increase
> the TimeoutBase setting to 1000. If you still have problems, your network is too slow to use this setting;
> try to connect with the Point-To-Point Protocol (PTPP).

RAS and NWLink

NWLink is the transport protocol used with Novell networks, and is installed with Windows NT by default. The Registry values that affect the RAS server are found under two different Registry keys, as follows.

NWLink and the Routing Information Protocol

The following value, found under the [HKEY_LOCAL_MACHINE\System\ CurrentControlSet\Services\NwlnkRip\Parameters] key, determines the forwarding of Novell Network IPX packets.

```
NetbiosRouting              0, 2, 4, or 6
REG_DWORD
```

This value determines the forwarding of IPX NetBIOS broadcast packets to and from the LAN. When this value is set to non-zero, the RAS server forwards NetBIOS broadcast packets (IPX type-20) between the remote clients and the local network. The default setting is 2, and it performs as follows:

0	Disables NetBIOS routing.
2	Enables forwarding of NetBIOS broadcast packets from the remote client to the LAN.
4	Enables forwarding of NetBIOS broadcast packets from the LAN to the remote client.
6	Enables two-way forwarding of NetBIOS packets between remote clients and the LAN.

Global NWLink IPX Values

These values are used globally by the NWLink protocol and are found under the [HKEY_LOCAL_MACHINE\System\CurrentControlSet\Services\NwLnkIpx\Parameters] key.

Probe Count

```
ConnectionCount             1 to 65535
REG_DWORD
```

This value determines the number of times a probe is sent when SPX tries to connect to a remote node. An error occurs if the probe is sent and no response is received. This value works in conjunction with the ConnectionTimeout value. The default setting is 10.

Connection Time Out

```
ConnectionTimeout                    1 to 65535 Half-Seconds
REG_DWORD
```

This value determines the amount of idle time between connection probes if SPX tries to connect to a remote node. This value works in conjunction with the ConnectionCount value. The default setting is 2, or 1 second.

A dedicated Router

```
DedicatedRouter            0 or 1 (Boolean)
REG_DWORD
```

Setting this value to 1 causes the Windows NT computer to act as a dedicated router; it does not have services, such as the Browser Service, running on it. The computer must have two network interface cards (NICs) installed for this setting to work. After you reboot the computer, you may have to reconfigure the transport protocols to bind to the new adapter card. The default setting is 0, or false.

Dial In IPX Forwarding

```
DisableDialinNetbios               0, 1, 2 or 3
REG_DWORD
```

This value determines the forwarding of IPX type-20 packets between the remote computer, the LAN, using the RAS IPX router; and the RAS server running an IPX NetBIOS application. This value only affects dial-in lines on RAS servers. The default setting is 1, and performs as follows:

0	Enables the broadcasting of IPX type-20 packets from the RAS server to remote clients, from the remote clients to the RAS server; and through the IPX router to the LAN, but only if the router is configured to forward IPX NetBIOS packets.
1	Enables the broadcasting of IPX type-20 packets from remote clients to the internal net and the RAS IPX router. This setting disables broadcasts from the LAN to the remote clients. This is the default setting.
2	Enables the broadcasting of IPX type-20 packets from the LAN to the remote clients.
3	Disables all IPX type-20 broadcasting.

SAP Announcements

```
DisableDialoutSap          0 or 1 (Boolean)
REG_DWORD
```

If this value is set to 1, IPX disables SAP announcements and responses on dial-out WAN lines. This setting prevents the WAN line from being overwhelmed with router-to-router SAP traffic, and enables either the RAS Servers Gateway Service for NetWare (GSNW) or the Client Service for NetWare (CSNW) to correctly identify and find other servers on the WAN. The default setting is 0, or false.

Even Ethernet Sends

```
EthernetPadToEven              0 or 1 (Boolean)
REG_DWORD
```

If this value is set to 1, Ethernet sends are padded to an even length to accommodate ODI card drivers that receive only even-length frames. The default setting is 1, or true.

IPX Datagrams

```
InitDatagrams          1 to 65535
REG_DWORD
```

This setting determines the number of datagrams initially allocated by IPX, and works in conjunction with the MaxDatagrams value. The default setting is 10.

```
MaxDatagrams           1 to 65535
REG_DWORD
```

This setting determines the maximum number of datagrams that IPX allocates, and works in conjunction with the InitDatagrams value. The default setting is 50.

Keep Alive Count

```
KeepAliveCount         1 to 65535
REG_DWORD
```

This setting determines how many times to send a keep-alive probe before timing out when there is no response from the remote node. This value works in conjunction with the KeepAliveTimeout value. The default setting is 8.

Keep Alive Timeout

```
KeepAliveTimeout       1 to 65535 half-seconds
REG_DWORD
```

This setting determines the amount of time that the RAS Server waits before sending a probe to the remote node to verify that the SPX connection is still alive. This value works in conjunction with the KeepAliveCount value. The default setting is 12, or six seconds.

RIP Cache Age

```
RipAgeTime                    1 to 65535 Minutes
REG_DWORD
```

This setting determines the amount of time that the IPX cache, used to locate computers on a remote network, waits before requesting an RIP entry update. If an RIP announcement is received, the timer count is reset and the count starts again. The default setting is 5 minutes.

RIP request Count

```
RipCount                      1 to 65535
REG_DWORD
```

This setting determines the number of times that the RIP protocol layer tries to send a request to find a route on the network before giving up. This value works in conjunction with the `RipTimeout` value. The default setting is 5.

RIP Time Out

```
RipTimeout                    1 to 65535 Half-Seconds
REG_DWORD
```

This setting determines the time-out between RIP request packets that are transmitted when the RIP protocol layer is trying to send a request to find a route on the network. This value works in conjunction with the `RipCount` value. The default setting is 1, or a half-second.

RIP Hash Table

```
RipTableSize                  1 to 65535
REG_DWORD
```

This setting determines the number of buckets in the RIP hash table. The default setting is 7.

RIP Cache Delete Time

```
RipUsageTime                  1 to 65535 Minutes
REG_DWORD
```

This value determines how many minutes IPX waits before deleting an entry from the RIP cache. The setting timer is reset when a packet is sent to the remote computer. The default setting is 15 minutes.

```
SingleNetworkActive           0 or 1 (Boolean)
REG_DWORD
```

If this value is set to 1, either the LAN or the WAN line can be set as active on the computer; however, both cannot be active at the same time. The default setting is 0, or false.

IPX Socket Start Range

```
SocketStart              0 to 65535
REG_DWORD
```

This value determines the start range that IPX uses to auto-assign sockets. This value works in conjunction with the SocketEnd and SocketUniqueness values. The default setting is 0x4000.

IPX Socket End range

```
SocketEnd                1 to 65535
REG_DWORD
```

This value determines the end range that IPX uses to auto-assign sockets. This value works in conjunction with the SocketStart and SocketUniqueness values. The default setting is 0x8000.

Socket Uniqueness

```
SocketUniqueness         1 to 65535
REG_DWORD
```

This value determines the number of sockets that IPX sets aside when auto-assigning sockets. For instance, if this setting is 10 and the SocketStart setting is 0x4000, IPX sets aside the range 0x5000-0x4009. The default setting is 8.

IBM Token Ring Cache

```
SourceRouteUsageTime     1 to 65535 Minutes
REG_DWORD
```

This value determines the number of minutes unused entries can remain in the IBM Token Ring source routing cache before it is flushed. The default setting is 10.

Window Size

```
WindowSize               1 to 10 SPX packets
REG_DWORD
```

This value determines the window used with SPX packets. SPX places this setting into the Allocation field of the SPX packet to tell the remote how many packets are available for receiving data. The default setting is 4.

Remote Access TCP/IP

The values discussed in this section override the values discussed in the WINS and DNS sections at the start of the chapter and exist only during an RAS connection. These values are found under the [HKEY_LOCAL_MACHINE\System\CurrentControlSet\Services\RemoteAccess\Parameters\IP] key, and are discussed next.

DNS Override

```
DNSNameServers          TCP/IP Address
REG_MULTI_SZ
```

When this value is added to the Registry of the RAS Server and an active RAS connection exists, this setting overrides the automatic assignment of the RAS server's DNS servers to the RAS client. The default setting is the TCP/IP address of the DNS server.

Primary WINS Server Override

```
WINSNameServer          TCP/IP Address
REG_SZ
```

When this value is added to the Registry of the RAS Server and an active RAS connection exists, this setting overrides the automatic assignment of the RAS server's WINS server to the RAS client. The default setting is the TCP/IP address of the primary WINS server.

Secondary WINS Server Override

```
WINSNameServerBackup          TCP/IP Address
REG_SZ
```

When this value is added to the Registry of the RAS Server and an active RAS connection exists, this setting overrides the automatic assignment of the RAS server's backup WINS server to the RAS client. The default setting is the TCP/IP address of the secondary WINS server.

Point-To-Point Protocol

This protocol sets most of its values under the [HKEY_LOCAL_MACHINE\System\Current ControlSet\Services\Rasman\PPP] key, as well as several subkeys of this key. These keys and values are discussed next.

Main PPP Key Values

The values in this section are set under the [HKEY_LOCAL_MACHINE\System\Current ControlSet\Services\Rasman\PPP] key, and are discussed here.

RAS Modem wait

```
DefaultCallbackDelay          0 to 255 Seconds
REG_DWORD
```

When added to the RAS client computer, this value determines how long the RAS server's modem waits when returning a call to the RAS client. The default setting is 12.

Enable Software Compression

```
DisableSoftwareCompression          0 or 1
REG_DWORD
```

When this value is set to 0, software compression is enabled; when the value is set to 1, it is disabled. The default setting is 0, or enabled.

The Crypto-Handshake Autication Protocol (CHAP)

```
ForceEncryptedPassword          0 or 1
REG_DWORD
```

This value is used only on RAS servers; if it is set to 1, the server uses the Crypto-Handshake Authentication Protocol (CHAP) during authentication. Setting this to 1 forces the RAS server to use CHAP when authenticating clients. This prevents the Cleartest password from being transmitted during authentication. If it is set to 0, the server negotiates by using the Password Authentication Protocol (PAP). The default setting is 1, or enabled.

PPP Event Logging

```
Logging          0 or 1
REG_DWORD
```

This value determines whether PPP events are written to a transaction log file. If set to 1, all PPP events are logged in the PPP.LOG file found in the %SYSTEMROOT%\System32\Ras directory. Set this value to 1 if you experience problems connecting to RAS with PPP. The default setting is 1, or enabled.

Configure-Request Packets

```
MaxConfigure          Positive Integer
REG_DWORD
```

This value determines the number of Configure-Request packets that are sent when a valid Configure-Ack, Configure-Nak, or Configure-Reject has not been received; before assuming that the peer is unable to respond. The default setting is 10.

Configure-Nak Packets

```
MaxFailure        Positive Integer
REG_DWORD
```

This value determines the number of Configure-Nak packets that are sent when a Configure-Ack has not been sent, before assuming that the configuration is not converging. The default setting is 10.

Config-Rejects Packets

```
MaxReject         Positive Integer
REG_DWORD
```

This value determines the number of Config-Rejects packets that are sent before assuming that the PPP negotiation will not converge. The default setting is 5.

Terminate-Request Packets

```
MaxTerminate      Positive Integer
REG_DWORD
```

This value determines the number of Terminate-Request packets that are sent without receiving a Terminate-Ack, before assuming that the peer is unable to respond. The default setting is 2.

PPP Negotiation Time

```
NgotiateTime      0 - 0xFFFFFFFF Seconds
REG_DWORD
```

This value determines the time limit for a PPP negotiation to converge successfully before the line is disconnected. Setting this value to 0 prevents the line from being disconnected. The default setting is 150.

Packet Transmission Time

```
RestartTimer      0 - 0xFFFFFFFF seconds
REG_DWORD
```

This value determines the time limit for the transmission of Configure-Request and Terminate-Request packets. If this time limit expires, a time-out event occurs, and retransmission of the corresponding Configure-Request or Terminate-Request packet is retransmitted. The default setting is 3.

PPP Subkeys

In addition to the values discussed above, the PPP Protocol also sets values under several subkeys of the main PPP key, as seen in Figure 18.5.

Figure 18.5   PPP subkeys.

These keys may have a `Path` value containing the path to dynamic-link libraries used by the PPP service. These keys are discussed next.

The CBCP Key

```
Path        DLL Path and filename
REG_EXPAND_SZ
```

This value contains the path of the Callback Control Protocol DLL. The default setting is %SYSTEMROOT%\System32\Rascpcp.dll.

The CHAP Key

```
Path        DLL Path and filename
REG_EXPAND_SZ
```

This value contains the path of the Crypto-Handshake Authentication Protocol (CHAP) DLL. The default setting is %SYSTEMROOT%\System32\Raschap.dll.

The CCP Key

```
Path        DLL Path and filename
REG_EXPAND_SZ
```

This value contains the path of the Compression Control Protocol (CCP) DLL. CCP is used to negotiate compression with the remote client. The default setting is %SYSTEMROOT%\System32\Rasccp.dll.

The IPCP Key

This subkey stores the Registry values used by the Internet Protocol Control Protocol (IPCP). The following value is the only value found under this key, unless others are added manually.

Path Value

```
Path          DLL Path and filename
REG_EXPAND_SZ
```

This value contains the path of the Internet Protocol Control Protocol (IPCP) DLL. This value exists in the Registry if RAS is configured to use TCP/IP and TCP/IP is installed. The default setting is %SYSTEMROOT%\System32\Rasipcp.dll.

Additional IPCP Subkey Values

This section discusses values that are not found in the Registry by default, and must be added if the features that they set need to be used. These values are found under the same IPCP subkey, and are discussed next.

```
AcceptVJCompression        0 or 1
REG_DWORD
```

If this value does not exist, it has the same effect as adding it and setting it to 1; in either case, RAS allows RAS clients to accept Van Jacobson (VJ) compression. If you set it to 0, IPCP does not accept VJ header compression.

```
RequestVJCompression       0 or 1
REG_DWORD
```

This value determines whether IPCP requests the IPCP standard option 0x02, VJ compression. If the value of this entry is 1 (or if it is not in the Registry), RAS clients request VJ compression. If the value of this entry is 0, it does not request VJ compression.

```
PriorityBasedOnSubNetwork          0 or 1
REG_DWORD
```

This value determines whether packets are sent over the LAN or a RAS connection when a computer is connected to a LAN by both a network card and a RAS connection set to the same network number. When set to 1, all packets are sent over RAS, which is the same as not having the value in the Registry. If set to 0, the RAS connection is used to send packets from the TCP/IP address set for RAS, other packets are sent over the network card. This value is used in conjunction with the DisableOtherSrcPackets value discussed in the "RAS Address Resolution Protocol Values" section later in this chapter.

```
RequestNameServerAddresses         0 or 1
REG_DWORD
```

This value determines whether IPCP requests Microsoft extension options for WINS and DNS server address negotiation (IPCP options 0x81, 0x82, 0x83, and 0x84). If this

> **Troubleshooting**
>
> If you set the network adapter card to IP address 10.3.3.1 (subnet mask 255.255.0.0) and set the RAS connection to 10.4.3.1, and you do not set the Priority Based On Sub Network value to 0 all packets are sent over the RAS connection. If the value is set to 1, RAS sends 10.4.x.x packets using the RAS connection and all 10.3.x.x packets using the network adapter card.

value is set to 1, or if it is not present in the Registry, the client requests the addresses. If set to 0, IPCP does not request Microsoft extension options for WINS and DNS server address negotiation.

The IPXCP Key

```
Path     DLL Path and filename
REG_EXPAND_SZ
```

This value contains the path of the Internetwork Packet eXchange Control Protocol (IPXCP) DLL. This subkey exists in the Registry when RAS is configured to use IPX, and the CSNW or GSNW has been installed. The default setting is %SYSTEMROOT%\System32\Rasipxcp.dll.

The NBFCP Key

```
Path     DLL Path and filename
REG_EXPAND_SZ
```

This value contains the path of the NetBEUI Framing Control Protocol (NBFCP) DLL. This subkey exists in the Registry when RAS is configured to use NetBEUI and NetBEUI is installed. The default setting is %SYSTEMROOT%\System32\ Rasnbfcp.dll.

The PAP Key

```
Path     DLL Path and filename
REG_EXPAND_SZ
```

This value contains the path of the Password Authentication Protocol (PAP) DLL. The default setting is %SYSTEMROOT%\System32\Raspap.dll.

Other Remote Access Service Parameters

The values discussed here are those that do not belong in the previous sections, but still affect RAS. These parameters are found under different Registry keys, as follows.

Parameters Key Values

These values are found under the [HKEY_LOCAL_MACHINE\SYSTEM\CurrentControlSet\ Services\RemoteAccess\Parameters] key, and are discussed next.

Authenticate Retries

```
AuticateRetries          0, 1, or 2
REG_DWORD
```

This value determines the maximum number of unsuccessful retries that can be attempted if the original connection attempt failed. This value's default is 2.

Authenticate Time

```
AuticateTime          20 to 600 Seconds
REG_DWORD
```

This value sets the maximum time limit, in seconds, in which a user must be authenticated to the network. The user is disconnected from the server if authentication does not occur within this time. If your connections are timing out, increase this value. The default is 120 seconds.

Automatic Disconnection

```
Autodisconnect                0 to 1000 Minutes
REG_DWORD"=dword:00000014
```

This value determines how long an inactive connection is allowed to exist before it is disconnected. A connection is deemed inactive if it does not have any NetBIOS session data transfers. This includes operations such as file manipulation, server access, and messaging. If you want to create a permanent connection that will not be disconnected, no matter what the length of inactivity is, set this value to 0 to turn off Automatic Disconnection. The default is 20 minutes.

Enable Audit

```
EnableAudit               0 or 1
REG_DWORD
```

This value turns on Remote Access auditing if set to 1, and turns it off if set to 0. If turned on, the audit log is written to the Windows NT event log. The default is 1.

Call Back Time

```
CallbackTime             2 to 12 Seconds
REG_DWORD
```

If the Call Back feature of Dial-Up Networking is enabled, this value determines how long the server waits before calling back the client. The default is 2 seconds.

Troubleshooting Tip

When a client computer calls a Remote Access Server, it may communicate a Call Back value through the MODEM.INF file located in %SYSTEMROOT%\System32\Ras directory. This `CallBackTime` value determines how long the server waits.

RAS Address Resolution Protocol Values

These values are found under the [HKEY_LOCAL_MACHINE\System\CurrentControlSet\ Services\RasArp\Parameters] key, and are discussed next.

PPP Packet Forwarding

```
DisableOtherSrcPackets              0 or 1
REG_DWORD
```

This value determines whether a RAS computer, while performing as a simple dial-up router, forwards packets from LAN clients over the PPP link. This value is not used by systems using Windows NT Server Multi-Protocol Routing.

When this value is set to 1 or if this value entry is not in the Registry, the packets header sent by the RAS computer over PPP links lists the IP address of the RAS computer as the source. If set to 0, packets from LAN clients, which do not originate from the RAS computer, are forwarded over the PPP link. This value does not appear in the Registry, by default.

Broadcast Filtering

```
FilterBroadcasts                    0 or 1
REG_DWORD
```

When this value is set to 1 RAS transmits broadcast packets and subnet multicasts. Set this value to 0 for clients calling in to third-party RAS routers that support broadcast/multicast forwarding. Windows NT RAS servers do not forward broadcasts or multicasts. The default setting is 1.

Redirector Values

This value is found under the [HKEY_LOCAL_MACHINE\SYSTEM\CurrentControlSet\ Services\Rdr\Parameters] key.

```
RawIoTimeLimit                      0, 5, or 9
REG_DWORD
```

This value is only used by configurations that use the NetBIOS gateway. This value directs the redirector to send data in 64KB blocks. Also, when this value is set to 5 or 9, throughput increases by 10 to 15 percent. No other simultaneous data transfers are allowed at this speed. By default, this feature is disabled for slow links (14,400 bps or slower) and enabled for faster links, as follows:

0	Raw I/O is disabled when connecting through one or two 64KB channels.
5	Raw I/O is disabled when connecting through one 64KB channel, but enabled when connecting through two 64KB channels.

9   Raw I/O is enabled when connecting through one or two 64K
              channels.

Serial Port Values

This value is found under the [HKEY_LOCAL_MACHINE\SYSTEM\CurrentControlSet\
Services\Serial] key, and is discussed next.

Force Fifo

```
ForceFifoEnable          0 or 1
REG_DWORD
```

This value is set to 1 if the hardware supports a FIFO buffer and the device's driver
enables FIFO. Not all FIFOs are reliable, however, so if the application or the user
notices lost data or no data transmission, set this value to 0. The default setting is 1.

19

Configuring TCP/IP

● **TCP/IP**

This section discusses the settings that can be specified using the TCP/IP Properties dialog box.

● **Other TCP/IP settings**

This section discusses Registry values that affect performance and other issues of TCP/IP that are not configurable from the Properties interface.

● **DHCP Values**

This section discusses the settings that are related to DHCP.

TCP/IP

To install TCP/IP, launch the Network applet in Control Panel, click the Add button, and choose the Protocols tab in the Network dialog box.

On this tab, click the Add button and then select the TCP/IP Protocol entry shown in Figure 19.1. When you do this, you receive the message box shown in Figure 19.2.

Clicking Yes enables DHCP. The settings for this choice are discussed in the "DHCP Values" section at the end of this chapter. If you click the No button, you can specify the TCP/IP addresses to use. These settings are discussed next.

You can modify TCP/IP properties using the TCP/IP Properties dialog box. To see this dialog, launch the Network applet, choose the Protocols tab, select TCP/IP Protocol, and then click the Properties button. You should see a screen like that shown in Figure 19.3.

The IP Address and Routing tabs of this screen are discussed next; the DNS and WINS Address tabs were discussed in Chapter 18.

The TCP/IP Address Tab

The TCP/IP Address tab is used to configure the TCP/IP address settings, including the use of DHCP, and sets the following values under the [HKEY_LOCAL_MACHINE\
SYSTEM\CurrentControlSet\Services\Adapter\Parameters\Tcpip] key.

Figure 19.1 The Network applet's Select Network Protocol dialog box.

The first drop-down list box simply lists the adapters available for use with TCP/IP and determines the Adapter key that the following values are listed under. These values may exist for each available adapter.

DHCP Radial Buttons

The set of radial buttons on this screen determines the use of DHCP for this adapter. These buttons set the following value:

```
EnableDHCP                    0 or 1
REG_DWORD
```

When the first radial button, Obtain an IP Address from a DHCP Server, is selected, this value is set to 1. If the second button, Specify an IP Address, is selected, this value is set to 0. A setting of 1 grays out the three text boxes under the second radial button; a setting of 0 enables them.

The Advanced Button

All of the text boxes shown in Figure 19.3 can also be set through the use of the Advanced button. When you click this button, you see the dialog box shown in Figure 19.4.

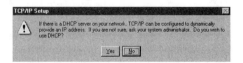

Figure 19.2 DHCP message box.

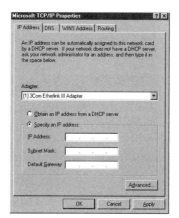

Figure 19.3   The Microsoft TCP/IP Properties dialog box.

Although this screen is useful when adding more than one IP address, it sets the same values as the text boxes shown in Figure 19.3. These values are discussed in the next few sections.

The IP Address Text box

The IP Address is set through the IP Address text box, but it can also be set with the Advanced IP Addressing dialog box by clicking the Add button and using the resulting dialog box shown in Figure 19.5.

The entries that you use for the IP Addresses list box shown in this dialog box also appear in the IP Address text box if this is the first address listed in the IP Addresses list box; regardless, they set this value:

```
IPAddress              Hexadecimal number
REG_MULTI_SZ
```

This value contains a hexadecimal representation of the addresses shown in the IP Addresses list box (refer to Figure 19.4). The first numbers of this list represent the first address listed, with other addresses being listed to the right.

Subnet Mask

As shown in Figure 19.5, the subnet mask is also added through the Add button and is listed in the Subnet Mask text box (refer to Figure 19.3). This sets the following value.

```
SubnetMask             Hexadecimal number
REG_MULTI_SZ
```

This value contains the subnet entry, in the same way that the IPAddress value holds the IP address, and it can be changed in the same manner as before.

Figure 19.4 The Advanced IP Addressing dialog box.

Default Gateway

Gateways can be added through the Add button (refer to Figure 19.4) and the first entry in the list box is listed in the Default Gateway text box (refer to Figure 19.3). These entries are contained in the following value:

```
DefaultGateway          Hexadecimal number
REG_MULTI_SZ
```

This value contains the subnet entries similar to the `IPAddress` and `SubnetMask` values and can be changed in the same manner as before. Using the up and down buttons moves the gateways left and right, respectively, in this value.

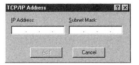

Figure 19.5 The Add Button dialog box.

Author Note

If you want to programmatically add IP addresses to the `IPAddress` value you can create a .REG file with the following entry, where *OLD ADDRESS* refers to the address that the new address should be placed after (use end to append to the list), and *NEW ADDRESS* refers to the address to be added:

```
"IPAddress    "=Edit(MultiSZ):/Find "OLD ADDRESS" or end /Insert
"NEW ADDRESS" after
```

Add one entry for each address added and write the entire entry on one line.

Enable PPTP Filtering

This check box enables Point-to-Point Tunneling Protocol (PPTP) filtering and sets the following value:

```
PPTPFiltering              0 or 1
REG_DWORD
```

If the check box is checked, this value is set to 1 and the network adapter shown in the Adapter list box is disabled for all other protocols, allowing only the reception of PPTP packets. If the check box is cleared, this value is set to 0.

Enable Security

Checking this check box enables TCP/IP security and allows you to control the types of TCP/IP traffic that can communicate with your Windows NT Servers. Use this check box when using your computer as an Internet server. The value that this check box sets is found under the [HKEY_LOCAL_MACHINE\SYSTEM\CurrentControlSet\ Services\Tcpip\Parameters] key, as follows.

```
EnableSecurityFilters           0 or 1
REG_DWORD
```

This value is set to 1 when the check box is checked; it is set to 0 when it is cleared.

The Configure Button

This button is used to limit TCP/IP traffic and is only enabled when the Enable Security check box is checked. When you click this button, you see the screen shown in Figure 19.6.

This screen has three sets of radial buttons and three sets of list boxes, which set the following values:

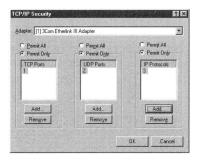

Figure 19.6   TCP/IP Security dialog box.

Warning

A security bug was recently discovered with PPTP. Microsoft is currently working on this issue by tweaking the settings. Take care when using this protocol.

```
TCPAllowedPorts                         0 or Hexadecimal Number
REG_MULTI_SZ
```

This value is set to **0** if the Permit Only radial button is selected, but no ports are listed in the list box. This value is set to hexadecimal number **30** when the Permit All radial button is selected. Also, when you add ports using the Add button, an additional hexadecimal number of **3X** is added to this value for each port added, where **X** is the number of the port. For example, if you add port 3 and port 5, this value is set to **33 00 35**; each port is separated with an **00** entry.

```
UDPAllowedPorts                         0 or Hexadecimal Number
REG_MULTI_SZ
```

This value is set with the second set of radial buttons and with the UDP Ports list box. This value is set with hexadecimal numbers in the same way as the **TCPAllowedPorts** value.

```
RawIPAllowedProtocols                   0 or Hexadecimal Number
REG_MULTI_SZ
```

This value is set with the third set of radial buttons and with the IP Protocols list box. This value is set with hexadecimal numbers in the same way as the **TCPAllowedPorts** value.

The Routing Tab

This tab, shown in Figure 19.7, has only one check box, Enable IP Forwarding, which sets the following value under the **[HKEY_LOCAL_MACHINE\SYSTEM\CurrentControlSet\ Services\Tcpip\Parameters]** key:

```
IPEnableRouter              0 or 1
REG_DWORD
```

This value is set to **1** when the check box is checked and **0** when it is cleared.

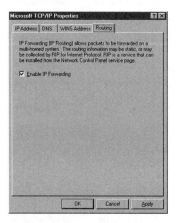

Figure 19.7 The Routing tab.

Other TCP/IP Settings

There are many TCP/IP Registry settings that are not set by using the TCP/IP Properties interface discussed in the previous section. These values are discussed in the following sections.

Using TCP/IP with Remote Clients

The following Registry values are found under the [HKEY_LOCAL_MACHINE\System\ CurrentControlSet\Services\Tcpip\Parameters] key.

Connect Request Retransmit

```
TcpMaxConnectRetransmissions            0 - 0xFFFFFFFF
REG_DWORD
```

This value determines the number of times that TCP retransmits a connect request (SYN) before it aborts the attempt. This value uses the retransmission time-out setting, starting at three seconds, each time a SYN is sent. This time-out setting is doubled for each connection attempted during the same connection attempt. The default setting is 3.

Individual Data Retransmit

```
TcpMaxDataRetransmissions               0 - 0xFFFFFFFF
REG_DWORD
```

This value determines the number of times that TCP retransmits an individual data segment before it aborts the connection. The retransmission time-out is also doubled for this value in the same way as before and is reset when a response is received. The time-out setting is determined dynamically by measuring the round-trip connection time. The default setting is 5.

Maximum Simultaneous Connections

```
TcpNumConnections          0 - 0xFFFFFE
REG_DWORD
```

This value determines the maximum number of connections that TCP can open simultaneously. The default setting is 0xFFFFFE (64).

TIME_WAIT State

```
TcpTimedWaitDelay          0x1E - 0x12C (30 - 300 Seconds)
REG_DWORD
```

This value determines the length of time that a connection remains in the TIME_WAIT state, also known as the *2MSL state*, while it is being closed. Remember that the socket pair cannot be reused during the time that the connection is in the TIME_WAIT state. Also, this value is usually set to be twice that of the network's maximum segment lifetime. The default setting is 0xF0 or 240.

Urgent Data Mode

```
TcpUseRFC1122UrgentPointer                    0 or 1
REG_DWORD
```

This value determines which mode TCP uses for urgent data. If this value is set to 1, TCP uses the RFC 1122 specification for urgent data. If set to 0 or if the value is absent from the Registry, TCP uses the mode used by BSD-derived systems. These two settings interpret the urgent pointer in the TCP header and the urgent data length, and are not interoperable. The default setting is 0.

Receive Window Size

```
TcpWindowSize                       0 - 0xFFFF bytes
REG_DWORD
```

This value determines the maximum TCP receive window size that can be offered to the system. This sets the number of bytes a sender may transmit before receiving an acknowledgment (ACK).

For maximum efficiency, this setting should be an even-numbered multiple of the TCP *Maximum Segment Size* (MSS). The default setting for this value depends on the larger of four times the maximum TCP data size on the network; or 8192, rounded up to an even multiple of the network TCP data size. The default is the smaller of the two. The default Ethernet setting is 8760.

Other Parameters Key Values

The following values are also found under the [HKEY_LOCAL_MACHINE\System\ CurrentControlSet\Services\Tcpip\Parameters] key.

Author Note

If you connect to a slow WAN, increase the TCP TimedWaitDelay value to allow a client to connect. Because this setting affects the time-out setting, and the time-out setting doubles with each connection attempt. However, this setting should be increased slowly to ensure that a connection attempt times out if no connection is available.

ARP Queries with Source Routing

```
ArpAlwaysSourceRoute              0 or 1
REG_DWORD
```

This value determines whether TCP/IP transmits the first ARP queries with source routing enabled on Token Ring networks. If this value is set to 1, TCP/IP is forced to enable source routing; if set to 0, source routing is disabled. By default, the stack first transmits ARP queries without source routing; then it retries with source routing enabled if no reply is received. The default setting is 0, which means that the stack transmits ARP queries without source routing; if no reply is returned, the stack tries again with source routing enabled.

ARP Cache Lifetime

```
ArpCacheLife                      Seconds
REG_DWORD
```

This value determines the lifetime of entries in the ARP cache table. When an entry is placed into the ARP cache, it can either remain there until its lifetime expires or until it's reused because it's the oldest entry. This value can have two different default settings: 120, or 2 minutes, for unused entries, and 600 or 10 minutes for used entries.

Single-Route Broadcasts

```
ArpTRSingleRoute                  0 (false) or 1 (true)
REG_DWORD
```

This value determines whether source-routed (Token-Ring) ARP broadcasts are sent as single-route broadcasts. When set to 1, they are sent as single-route broadcasts; when set to 0, they are sent as all-routes broadcasts. The default setting is 0.

Author Tip

Use larger settings over high-delay or high-bandwidth networks to increase performance.

Troubleshooting

The maximum receive window size is 64KB.

Author Note

Change the setting of the TcpWindowSize value if your clients experience connectivity problems from the timing out of the received data transmission. Reducing the setting causes received data to be sent to the sender more quickly. This decreases the possibility that the sender will time out while waiting for an acknowledgment, but it also increases the amount of network traffic and causes slower throughput.

802.3 SNAP Encoding

```
ArpUseEtherSNAP                 0 (false) or 1 (true)
REG_DWORD
```

This value determines whether TCP/IP is forced to transmit Ethernet packets by using 802.3 SNAP encoding. When set to 1, 802.3 SNAP encoding is used; when set to 0, the stack transmits packets in DIX Ethernet format. It always receives both formats. The default setting is 0.

Standard Internet Database File Path

```
DatabasePath                    File Path
REG_EXPAND_SZ
```

This value sets the path to the standard Internet database files (HOSTS, LMHOSTS, networks, protocols), which is used by the Windows Sockets interface. The default setting is %SYSTEMROOT%\System32\Drivers\Etc.

Default TOS Value

```
DefaultTOS                      0 - 255
REG_DWORD
```

This value sets the default *Type of Service* (TOS) setting in the header of outgoing IP packets. The default setting is 0. See RFC 791 for a definition of the TOS values at www.internic.net.

Default TTL

```
DefaultTTL                      Seconds:   1 - 255
REG_DWORD
```

This value sets the default *Time To Live* (TTL) value of the header of outgoing IP packets. The TTL determines the maximum time limit that an IP packet can live in the network without reaching its destination. This setting determines the limit for the number of routers that an IP packet can pass through before it is discarded. The default setting is 128 for Windows NT 4.0, and 32 for Windows NT 3.5 and 3.51.

DNS Name Servers

```
DhcpNameServer                  IP Address(es)
REG_SZ
```

This value sets the DNS name servers, which are queried by Windows Sockets to resolve names. Of course, the valid settings in the NameServer value, discussed in Chapter 18, take precedence over the settings for the DhcpNameServer value. The DHCP client service, if enabled, writes this value. There is no default setting.

Dead Gateway Detection

0 (false) or 1 (true)

THE MUSIC OF THE NIGHT AWAITS.

TCP performs dead gateway detection. When this
hange to a backup gateway if it retransmits a segment
response, as discussed in the "TCP/IP" section, earli-
ing is 0.

0 (false) or 1 (true)

TCP will try to detect black-hole routers while
set to 1 and several retransmissions of a segment go
d segments without the Don't Fragment bit set. If
, the MSS decreases and the Don't Fragment bit is
value to 1 increases the maximum number of
iven segment. The default setting is 0.

0 (false) or 1 (true)

TCP will use a fixed, default *maximum transmission*
d the actual MTU. When this value is set to 0, TCP
for all connections to computers outside of the
attempts to discover the MTU, or largest packet size,

and TCP segments are limited to this size, TCP can
along the path that connects networks with
is fragmentation reduces network congestion and
efault setting is 0.

rt the use of this value. The system ignores it if it is
present in the Registry.

Packet Data Memory

```
ForwardBufferMemory              Number of Bytes
REG_DWORD
```

This value, which is always a multiple of 256, determines the amount of memory that IP allocates to store packet data in the router packet queue. If this buffer space becomes full, the router begins to discard packets at random from its queue. Multiple buffers are chained together for larger packets. If no buffers are allocated or if the IP router is not enabled, this value entry is ignored. The default setting is 74240, which is enough for fifty 1480-byte packets, and then is rounded to the nearest multiple of 256.

IP Multicasting Support

```
IGMPLevel                        0, 1, or 2
REG_DWORD
```

This value determines the extent to which the system supports IP multicasting and participates in the Internet Group Management Protocol (IGMP). The default setting is 0 and performs as shown here:

0. No multicast support.

1. Send only IP multicast packets.

2. Send and receive IP multicast packets; this setting is for participation in IGMP.

Keep-Alive Retransmission Interval

```
KeepAliveInterval                1 - 0xFFFFFFFF milliseconds
REG_DWORD
```

This value determines the time-out interval that is allowed between keep-alive retransmissions until a response is received. Once a response is received, this setting determines the delay time until the next keep-alive transmission. If the number of retransmissions specified by TcpMaxDataRetransmissions is reached, the connection is aborted. The default setting is 1000, or 1 second.

Author Note

Black-hole routers do not return ICMP destination unreachable messages when the router needs to fragment a TCP packet with the Don't Fragment bit set. TCP must receive these messages to perform path MTU discovery.

Idle Connection Verification

```
KeepAliveTime                    1 - 0xFFFFFFFF milliseconds
REG_DWORD
```

This value determines how often TCP sends a keep-alive packet to verify whether an idle connection is still intact. If the connection is still intact, it acknowledges the keep-alive transmission. By default, keep-alive packets are not sent, and applications can enable the sending of these packets to prevent disconnection during idle periods. The default setting is 7,200,000, or 2 hours.

Maximum Forward Buffer Memory

```
MaxForwardBufferMemory           Network MTU - 0xFFFFFFFF
REG_DWORD
```

This value sets the maximum number of memory bytes that IP allocates in the router packet queue to store packet data. This value works with the ForwardBufferMemory value and must be greater than or equal to its setting. The default setting is 0xFFFFFFFF.

Maximum IP Packet Headers

```
MaxNumForwardPackets             1 - 0xFFFFFFFF
REG_DWORD
```

This value sets the maximum number of IP packet headers that can be allocated for the router packet queue. This value works with the NumForwardPackets value and must be greater than or equal to its setting. The default setting is 0xFFFFFFFF.

Maximum Port Number

```
MaxUserPort                      0x1388 - 0xFFFE
REG_DWORD
```

This value determines the maximum port number used when an application requests an available user port from the system. If you are using ephemeral ports, or short-lived ports, they are usually allocated to port numbers 1024 through 5000 (0x1388). The default setting is 0x1388.

IP Packet Headers

```
NumForwardPackets                1 to < 0xFFFFFFFF
REG_DWORD
```

This value determines the number of IP packet headers that are allocated for the router packet queue. If all of the headers are in use, the router begins to discard packets from the queue at random. This value works with the ForwardBufferMemory value, and it should be at least as large as the number given by dividing the ForwardBuffer Memory setting by the maximum IP data size of the router's connected networks.

This setting cannot be larger than the `ForwardBufferMemory` value divided by 256, because each packet uses at least 256 bytes of forward buffer memory.

The optimal number of forward packets given a `ForwardBufferMemory` size depends on the type of traffic carried on the network; it is somewhere between the previous two settings. If no headers are allocated and routing is not enabled, this value is ignored. The default setting is `50`.

Adapter Card Values

These TCP/IP values, discussed next, are specific to individual network adapter cards, as discussed at the start of this section. These values are found under the
`[HKEY_LOCAL_MACHINE\System\CurrentControlSet\Srvices\Adapter\Parameters\Tcpip]`
key, where `Adapter` refers to the Services subkey for the adapter card.

Zeroes Versus Ones Broadcasts

```
UseZeroBroadcast            0 or 1
REG_DWORD
```

This value determines whether IP uses zeros broadcasts instead of ones broadcasts. When this value is set to `1`, or true, it uses zeroes broadcasts; it uses ones broadcasts when set to `0`, or false. Although most systems use ones broadcasts, some systems, derived from BSD implementations, use zeros broadcasts. Systems using different broadcasts do not interoperate well on the same network. The default setting is `0`, or false.

Maximum Number of Packets

```
MaxForwardPending           Packets, 1 - 0xFFFFFFFF
REG_DWORD
```

This value sets the maximum number of packets that the IP forwarding engine submits to a specific network interface for transmission at one time. Additional packets to be sent are queued in IP until all outstanding transmissions on the interface are completed. Although the default setting of `20` is usually sufficient because most network adapters transmit packets very quickly, a single RAS interface may multiplex many slow serial lines. Using a larger setting may improve the performance of the RAS interface. The optimal setting depends on the number and characteristics of all outgoing lines.

Maximum Transmission Unit (MTU)

```
MTU         68 - MTU (of the underlying network) Bytes
REG_DWORD
```

This value sets the maximum transmission unit (MTU) for a network interface. Because each interface used by TCP/IP can have a different MTU value, the MTU is usually determined through negotiation with the lower driver, and then that lower driver's value is used for the MTU. This value's setting overrides the default MTU for the network interface found. When this setting is greater than the default value of the underlying network, however, the transport uses the network default MTU. If the value of this entry is less than `68`, a value of `68` is used as the MTU.

The MTU should be set large enough to hold any datagram in one frame. This can be limited, however, by the technology making the transfer. Although some technologies limit the maximum size to as few as 128, Ethernet limits the transfers to 1500; and proNet-10 allows up to 2044 octets per frame.

If a datagram is larger than this MTU setting, it is automatically divided into smaller pieces called *fragments,* whose size is a multiple of 8 octets. This fragmentation occurs when the traffic must determine whether the MTU is smaller than the encapsulated datagram. If fragmentation is required, the fragments must travel separately to the destination computer, where they are automatically reassembled before the datagram can be processed. The default setting is `0xFFFFFFFF`.

Disabling the Default Route

```
DontAddDefaultGateway              0 or 1
REG_DWORD
```

This value determines whether the default route for a LAN adapter is disabled. When set to `0`, or if this value entry is not present in the Registry when PPTP is installed, the system installs default routes for each LAN adapter. When set to `1`, the default routes are not installed. (See the RAS subkey PPTPE, discussed in Chapter 18.) The default setting is `0`, but the value is not present in the Registry unless it is added.

Persistent Routes Values

These values contain persistent IP routes. Using the ROUTE.EXE program can configure these values, and using this program with the -p parameter makes the route persistent. These values are found under the `[HKEY_LOCAL_MACHINE\System\CurrentControlSet\Services\Tcpip\Parameters\PersistentRoutes]` key. These values are set with the following comma-delimited format:

```
Destination, SubnetMask, Gateway, PrimaryRouteMetric
```

Author Note
The ones local broadcast address is 255.255.255.255 and the zeros local broadcast address is 0.0.0.0.

Warning
Excessive fragmentation degrades performance.

Furthermore, all of these values are of the REG_SZ data type and do not have a setting; the value is, in effect, the setting. For example, a value entry representing a host route to destination 55.102.26.15, with subnet mask 255.255.0.0, through gateway 133.123.0.2, and with a primary route metric of 4, appears in the Registry, as this:

```
Value Name:     55.102.26.15,255.255.0.0,133.123.0.2,4
Data Type:      REG_SZ
Setting:        (None)
```

NetBT Values

These values contain settings for NetBT (NetBIOS over TCP/IP) that are common to all NetBT services. These values are found under the [HKEY_LOCAL_MACHINE\System\CurrentControlSet\Services\NetBt\Parameters] key.

Repeat Name Broadcasts

```
BcastNameQueryCount                 1 - 0xFFFF
REG_DWORD
```

This value determines the number of times that NetBT broadcasts a query for a given name without receiving a response. The default setting is 3.

Broadcast Name Interval

```
BcastQueryTimeout                   100 - 0xFFFFFFFF milliseconds
REG_DWORD
```

This value determines the time interval between successive broadcast-name queries for the same name. The default setting is 0x2EE, or 750 milliseconds.

Troubleshooting

Windows NT TCP/IP uses *Path Maximum Transfer Unit* (PMTU) detection to request the locally supported MTU from the NIC driver. So, the MTU value usually does not need to be changed; if changed, it can cause decreased performance.

Author Note

If you use Point-to-Point Tunneling Protocol (PPTP), you must add the DontAddDefaultGateway Registry entry to the Registry for each adapter that is not connected to the Internet.

Author Note

NetBT values that are established separately for each adapter card are stored in the subkey for the adapter card. These are described in the next section, "NetBT Values."

Specific Broadcast Address

```
BroadcastAddress    4 byte, little-endian encoded IP address
REG_DWORD
```

This value forces NetBT to use a specific address for all broadcast-name–related packets. When this value is set to the default, NetBT uses the ones-broadcast address appropriate for each network (that is, for a network of 10.101.0.0 with a mask of 255.255.0.0, the subnet broadcast address is 10.101.255.255).

This value is set if the network uses the zeroes-broadcast address, as set with the UseZeroBroadcast value. Using this, the appropriate subnet broadcast address is 10.101.0.0 in the previous example. This value is then set to 0x0b650000. This value is global and is used on all subnets to which NetBT is bound. The default setting is the ones-broadcast address for each network.

Name Cache Timeout

```
CacheTimeout       60000 - 0xFFFFFFFF milliseconds
REG_DWORD
```

This value determines the time interval during which names are cached in the remote name table. The default setting is 0x927C0, or 10 minutes.

Proxy Name Server

```
EnableProxy           0 (disabled) or 1 (enabled)
REG_DWORD
```

This value determines whether the system will act as a proxy name server for the networks to which NetBT is bound. When set to 1, the server acts as a proxy name server that answers broadcast queries for names that it has resolved through WINS. Setting this value to 1 allows a network of B-node implementations to connect to servers on other subnets that are registered with WINS. When set to 0, the server does not act as a proxy server. Always use NCPA when changing this value instead of using the registry editor. The default setting is 0.

Broadcast Name Registration Response

```
EnableProxyRegCheck          0 or 1
REG_DWORD
```

This value determines whether the proxy name server sends a negative response to a broadcast name registration, if the name is already registered with WINS or is in the proxy's local name cache with a different IP address. When set to 1, the server sends a negative response; if set to 0, it does not. The default setting is 0, or false.

Initial Refresh Time Out

```
InitialRefreshT.O.          960000 - 0xFFFFFFF milliseconds
REG_DWORD
```

This value sets the initial refresh time-out used by NetBT during name registration. NetBT tries to contact the WINS servers at one-eighth of this value setting when it first registers names. If it receives a successful registration response, the response contains a new refresh interval, and this value is set to it. The default setting is 960,000, or 16 minutes.

Datagram Send Memory

```
MaxDgramBuffering        0 - 0xFFFFFFFF Bytes
REG_DWORD
```

This value sets the maximum amount of memory that NetBT dynamically allocates for all outstanding datagram sends. If this limit is reached, further sends fail because of insufficient resources. The default setting is 0x20000, or 128K.

RPC Value

```
NbProvider               TCP
REG_SZ
```

This value is used by the Windows NT Executive component, RPC. Do not change this value. The default setting is TCP.

Random IP Address Name Queries

```
RandomAdapter                0 or 1
REG_DWORD
```

This value determines whether NetBT randomly chooses the IP address to use with a name query response from all of its bound interfaces. When set to 1, or true, a random address is used.

The response contains the address of the interface on which the query arrived. Setting this value to one load balances a server with two interfaces on the same network. This value works with the SingleResponse value and is ignored if the SingleResponse value is not set to 1 (this affects multihomed machines only). The default setting is 0.

> **Warning**
>
> If the EnableProxyRegCheck value is set to 1, a system is prevented from changing its IP address, as long as WINS has a mapping for the name.

Opcode Name Refresh

```
RefreshOpCode              8 or 9
REG_DWORD
```

This value determines whether NetBT is forced to use a specific opcode in name refresh packets. Although Microsoft implementations use a setting of 8, some other implementations, such as those by Ungermann-Bass, use 9. Be sure that two implementations use the same opcode, or else they will not interoperate. The default setting is 8.

Keep Alive Time Interval

```
SessionKeepAlive      60,000 - 0xFFFFFFFF milliseconds
REG_DWORD
```

This value determines the time-out interval between keep-alive transmissions on a session. A setting of 0xFFFFFFFF disables keep-alive transmissions. The default setting is 3600000 or 1 hour.

Single Response

```
SingleResponse             0 or 1
REG_DWORD
```

This value determines whether NetBT supplies an IP address from one of its bound interfaces for name query responses. When set to 1, a single response is used; if set to 0, NetBT supplies the IP addresses of all bound interfaces. This value works with the RandomAdapter value, and it must be set to 1 for it to be used. This value applies only to multihomed computers. The default setting is 0, or false.

Name Table Size

```
Size                    1, 2, or 3
REG_DWORD
```

This value determines the size of the name tables that are used to store local and remote names. The small setting, 1, is usually adequate. If the server is acting as a proxy name server, however, the value is automatically set to large, or 3, which increases the size of the name cache hash table. The default setting is 1 and performs as shown here.

1	Small	Up to 16 hash buckets
2	Medium	Up to 128 hash buckets
3	Large	Up to 256 hash buckets

Transport Bind Name

```
TransportBindName              \Device \
REG_SZ
```

This value entry is used by the system during product development. Do not change this value. The default setting is \Device \.

Streams Values

The TCP/IP streams values are found under the [HKEY_LOCAL_MACHINE\System\ CurrentControlSet\Services\Streams\Parameters] key.

```
MaxMemoryUsage                 Number of Bytes
REG_DWORD
```

This value sets the maximum amount of memory that can be allocated to the streams environment. If this limit is reached, stream values fail allocation requests made by streams-based drivers. The default setting is unlimited.

Windows Sockets Values

The TCP/IP Windows sockets values are found under several different subkeys on the [HKEY_LOCAL_MACHINE\System\CurrentControlSet\Services] key. These values are discussed in the following sections, grouped by key name.

\Winsock\Parameters Subkey

This key has one value that is common to the Windows Sockets service and is discussed next.

```
Transports               Strings
REG_Multi_SZ
```

This value contains the Registry key names of installed transports that support Windows Sockets. If TCP/IP is the only installed transport that supports Windows Sockets, this value is Tcpip. The Windows Sockets DLL uses the strings in Transports to find information about each transport. The default setting depends on the installation.

\Tcpip\Parameters\Winsock

This subkey stores Windows Sockets values for TCP/IP and is discussed next.

Helper DLL

```
HelperDllName              Path and Filename
REG_EXPAND_SZ
```

This value sets the name of the Windows Sockets helper DLL used with the TCP/IP transport. The Windows Sockets DLL sets this value's setting, and it cannot be set by a user. The default setting depends on the transport; for TCP/IP, it is %SYSTEMROOT%\System32\Wshtcpip.dll.

Address Families, Socket Types, and Protocols

```
Mapping
REG_BINARY
```

This value identifies the address families, socket types, and protocols supported by the transport. This value is set by the Windows Sockets DLL and cannot be set by a user. The default setting depends on the transport used.

Socket Address Maximum Length

```
MaxSockAddrLen             Octets
REG_DWORD
```

This value sets the maximum length of socket addresses used with the INET sockets family. This value is set by the Windows Sockets DLL and cannot be set by a user. There is no default setting.

Socket Address Minimum Length

```
MinSockAddrLen             Octets
REG_DWORD
```

This value sets the minimum length of socket addresses for the INET Sockets family. This value is set by the Windows Sockets DLL and cannot be set by a user. There is no default setting.

Tcpip\ServiceProvider

This subkey stores values that are used for resolving names. In particular, it stores values used by the GetHostByName() and GetAddressByName() APIs when resolving names.

Class

```
Class                8
REG_DWORD
```

This value determines whether TCP/IP is a name service provider. Do not change this value. The default setting is 8.

Name Resolution Order

```
DnsPriority
REG_DWORD
```

This value sets the priority value that determines the order of name resolution. Low-priority mechanisms are used first, meaning that the default order is local, HOSTS, DNS, and NetBT. If you want to change this order, read the priority values, as needed. Because settings under 1000 decimal are considered to be "fast" name resolution providers, however, setting network-based resolution mechanisms such as DNS and NetBT at values under 1000 can have unwanted results. The default setting is 0x7D0 in hexadecimal, or 2000 in decimal.

Hosts Priority

```
HostsPriority
REG_DWORD
```

This value performs and is set in the same manner as the DnsPriority value. The default setting is 0x1F4 hexadecimal, or 500 decimal.

Local Priority

```
LocalPriority
REG_DWORD
```

This value performs and is set in the same manner as the DnsPriority value. The default setting is 0x1F3 hexadecimal, or 499 decimal.

Netbt Priority

```
NetbtPriority
REG_DWORD
```

This value performs and is set in the same manner as the DnsPriority value. The default setting is 0x7D1 hexadecimal, or 2001 decimal.

Transport Service Name

```
Name                    Name
REG_SZ
```

This value sets the name of the transport service. Do not change this value. The default setting is TCP/IP.

Provider Path and Filename

```
ProviderPath            Path and Filename
REG_SZ
```

This value sets the path and filename of the DLL that is used for TCP/IP name resolution. Do not change this value. The default setting is %SYSTEMROOT%\ System32\Wsock32.dll.

\ServiceProvider\Order Subkey

This key stores the values used by the Winsock Service *Resolution and Registration* (RNR) APIs. These values are pointers to other items in the Registry.

Excluded Providers

```
ExcludedProviders      Name Space Provider Numbers
REG_MULTI_SZ
```

This value sets the name space providers to be excluded when performing name resolution. Set this value to the number (in decimal) from the following table that represents the name space provider(s) that you want to exclude. More than one of the following numbers can be included in this setting by using a single space to separate the numbers. The default setting is `No Entries`.

Number	Name Space Provider
1	NS_SAP
2	NS_NDS
10	NS_TCPIP_LOCAL
11	NS_TCPIP_HOSTS
12	NS_DNS
13	NS_NETBT
14	NS_WINS
20	NS_NBP
30	NS_MS
31	NS_STDA
32	NS_CAIRO
40	NS_X500
41	NS_NIS

CurrentControlSet\Services Key Value

```
ProviderOrder          String
REG_MULTI_SZ
```

This value contains strings that correspond to keys under the CurrentControlSet\Services key. All of these keys must have a ServiceProvider subkey that provides information about the name space provider, particularly `Class` and `ProviderPath` values. Do not change this value. The default setting varies with installed protocols.

\Afd\Parameters Subkey

This subkey stores the values used by AFD.SYS, which is the kernel-mode driver that supports Windows Sockets applications for TCP/IP.

Buffer Multiplier

```
BufferMultiplier                Multiplier
REG_DWORD
```

This value works with the `DefaultReceiveWindow` and `DefaultSendWindow` values that are divided by this value to determine how many messages can be sent/received before flow control is used. The default setting is 512.

Buffered Received Bytes

```
DefaultReceiveWindow            Bytes
REG_DWORD
```

This value sets the number of receive bytes that the AFD.SYS file buffers on a connection before using flow control with some applications. Using a larger setting slightly increases performance, but this increase is at the expense of increased resource utilization. Applications can modify this value on a per-socket basis by using the `SO_RCVBUF` socket option. The default setting is 8192.

Default Send Window

```
DefaultSendWindow               Bytes
REG_DWORD
```

This value performs and is set the same way as the `DefaultReceiveWindow` value, but it is used for the connections' send side. The default setting is 8192.

Buffered Datagram Size

```
FastSendDatagramThreshold       Bytes
REG_DWORD
```

Author Note

Some of the following values have three different defaults, depending on the amount of physical RAM available on the computer:

RAM Category	Amount of RAM
Small	12.5MB or less
Medium	12.5–20MB
Large	More than 20MB

This value sets the maximum size of datagrams that are buffered on send. If a datagram is smaller than or equal to this value, it is buffered on send; larger datagrams are pended, which means that the datagram is locked down in memory and held until it is actually sent. Do not change this value. The default setting, which is set for optimum performance, is `1024`.

Setting the Push Bit

```
IgnorePushBitOnReceives     0 (disabled) or 1 (enabled)
REG_DWORD
```

This value determines whether AFD.SYS treats all incoming packets as if the Push bit is set. Setting this value to `1` treats all incoming packets as if the Push bit is set. If set to `0`, Windows NT completes a Windows Sockets `receive()` when any of the following occurs:

- Data arrives with the Push bit set.
- The user `recv()` buffer is full.
- 0.5 seconds have elapsed since the data arrived.

Change this value to work around client TCP/IP implementations that do not push data properly. The default setting is `0`.

Large Buffer Allocation

```
InitialLargeBufferCount          Buffer Count
REG_DWORD
```

This value determines the initial count for large buffers allocated by AFD.SYS at system boot. Although you can add more buffers to increase performance, this costs physical memory. The default setting is `0` (small), `2` (medium), or `10` (large), depending on the RAM category.

Medium Buffer Allocation

```
InitialMediumBufferCount          Buffer Count
REG_DWORD
```

This value determines the initial count for medium buffers. The default setting is `2` (small), `10` (medium), or `30` (large), depending on the RAM category.

Small Buffer Allocation

```
InitialSmallBufferCount          Buffer count
REG_DWORD
```

This value determines the initial count for small buffers. The default setting is `5` (small), `20` (medium), or `50` (large), depending on the RAM category.

IRP Stack Locations

```
IrpStackSize              Number
REG_DWORD
```

This value sets the number of IRP stack locations needed by AFD.SYS. Although the default setting of 4 is usually sufficient for the existing transports, new transports that need more IRP stack locations can be developed.

Large Buffer Size

```
LargeBufferSize           Bytes
REG_DWORD
```

This value determines the size, in bytes, of the large buffers used by AFD.SYS. Although smaller settings use less memory, a larger setting improves performance. The default setting is 4096.

Medium Buffer Size

```
MediumBufferSize          Bytes
REG_DWORD
```

This value determines the size, in bytes, of the medium buffers used by AFD.SYS. Although smaller settings use less memory, a larger setting improves performance. The default setting is 1504.

Priority Boost

```
PriorityBoost             0 to 16
REG_DWORD
```

This value sets the priority boost that AFD.SYS gives to a thread that completes I/O. This setting is added to the base priority, and the resulting priority should be high enough to enable the thread to run, especially because it was delayed by the I/O operation. Reduce this setting if threads of multithreaded applications are not getting sufficient processor time. The default setting is 2.

Small Buffer Size

```
SmallBufferSize           Bytes
REG_DWORD
```

This value sets the size, in bytes, of the small buffers used by AFD.SYS. Although smaller settings use less memory, a larger setting improves performance. The default setting is 64.

TDI Address Length

```
StandardAddressLength          TDI Address Length
REG_DWORD
```

This value sets the length of the TDI addresses used for the computer. If the customer uses a transport protocol that uses very long addresses, such as TP4, increase this setting to increase performance. The default setting is 24.

Transmit IO Length Defaults

```
TransmitIoLength               Size in Bytes
REG_DWORD
```

This value sets the transmit IO length defaults, depending on the system type. The following shows the defaults :

Windows NT Workstation—page size

Windows NT Server, Small—page size

Windows NT Server, Medium—2 × page size

Windows NT Server, Large——64KB

DHCP Values

This section discusses the values that are used for *Direct Host Connectivity Protocol* (DHCP). These values are discussed in the next two sections.

DHCP Entries for Adapter Cards

The value entries described in this section store data about a DHCP client service for TCP/IP. These values are configured separately for each adapter installed in the computer. These values are found under the [HKEY_LOCAL_MACHINE\System\ CurrentControlSet\Services\Adapter\Parameters\Tcpip] key and are discussed next.

Default DHCP Gateways

```
DhcpDefaultGateway             IP Address(es)
REG_MULTI_SZ
```

This value contains the list of default gateways used to route packets that are not destined for a subnet that the computer is directly connected to, and for which no specific route exists.

This setting is written by the DHCP client service if the service is enabled, and can be overridden by the DefaultGateway value setting. There is no default setting for this value.

DHCP IP Address

```
DhcpIPAddress                    IP address(es)
REG_SZ
```

This value sets the IP address that is used for the interface configured by the DHCP server. The setting for the IPAddress value overrides the DhcpIPAddress setting, unless the first setting for IPAddress is 0.0.0.0. There is no default setting for this value.

DHCP Server Address

```
DhcpServer                       IP address(es)
REG_SZ
```

This value sets the IP address of the DHCP server that configured the IP address for the interface. The DHCP-configured IP address is stored in the DhcpIPAddress setting. There is no default setting for this value.

DHCP Subnet Mask

```
DhcpSubnetMask                   Subnet Mask
REG_SZ
```

This value sets the DHCP-configured subnet mask for the IP address specified with the DhcpIPAddress setting. There is no default setting for this value.

IP Interface Context

```
IPInterfaceContext               0 - 0xFFFFFFFF
REG_DWORD
```

This value is written by the TCP/IP driver for the DHCP client service. There is no default setting for this value.

IP Lease Time Limit

```
Lease                            1 - 0xFFFFFFFF Seconds
REG_DWORD
```

This value sets the time, in seconds, that the computer's lease of the IP address is valid for this adapter. This value entry is used by the DHCP client service. There is no default setting for this value.

IP Lease Start Time

```
LeaseObtainedTime       Time (in seconds) since 12:00 a.m. on
                        January 1, 1970

REG_DWORD
```

This value sets the time that the lease of the IP address for this adapter starts. This value entry is used by the DHCP client service. There is no default setting for this value.

IP Lease End Time

```
LeaseTerminatesTime   Time (in seconds) since 12:00 a.m. on
                      January 1, 1970
REG_DWORD
```

This value sets the time that the lease of the IP address for this adapter ends. This value entry is used by the DHCP client service. There is no default setting for this value.

IP Bind Device

```
LLInterface              Device Name
REG_SZ
```

This value sets the name of the Windows NT device that IP binds to. This value entry is used by services, such as RAS, to direct IP to bind to a different link-layer protocol from the built-in ARP module. The default setting is no string or a blank setting.

Renew Lease Time

```
T1   Time (in seconds) since 12:00 a.m. on January 1, 1970
REG_DWORD
```

This value sets the renew lease time that the service first tries to renew the lease of the adapter's IP address by contacting the server that granted the lease. This value entry is used by the DHCP client service. There is no default setting for this value.

Broadcast Renewal Time

```
T2   Time (in seconds) since 12:00 a.m. on January 1, 1970
REG_DWORD
```

This value sets the renewal lease time that the service attempts to renew the adapter's leased IP address by broadcasting a renewal request. This setting is reached only when the service cannot renew the lease with the original server. This value entry is used by the DHCP client service. There is no default setting for this value.

DHCP Client Request Options

These values are found under the [HKEY_LOCAL_MACHINE\System\CurrentControlSet\ Services\DHCP\Parameters\Option#], where Option# refers to keys that list DHCP options that the client can request from the DHCP server. For each of the default options, the following values are defined.

Registry Location

```
RegLocation                    Location
REG_SZ
```

This value sets the location in the Registry where the option value is written when it is obtained from the DHCP server. Adding a ? character expands the key to include the adapter name that this option is obtained for. The default setting depends on the option's location in the Registry.

Key Type

```
KeyType                  Type
REG_DWORD
```

This value sets the type of Registry key for the previous option. The default setting is 0x7.

IV

Appendixes

A

Windows NT Workstation Registry Keys

This appendix contains a complete listing of the Windows NT Workstation Registry keys, except for the HKEY_LOCAL_MACHINE key. The listed keys were exported from an installation of Windows NT that had all options installed during setup and had no other software installed after setup. The keys listed here are arranged into the following sections:

- HKEY_CLASSES_ROOT subkeys and their values
- HKEY_CURRENT_CONFIG subkeys and their values
- HKEY_CURRENT_USER subkeys and their values
- HKEY_USERS subkeys and their values

The HKEY_LOCAL_MACHINE subkeys and their values are not listed here due to the specific hardware nature of this key. Also, only the Default user key is shown under HKEY_USERS.

Author Note

Values that appear as @ are the default values for the given key.

Tip

This appendix is intended to be used to discover an original Windows NT 4.0 Workstation setting that has become unusable. The keys, values, and settings in this appendix can be copied directly into a .REG file and incorporated into its Registry using REGEDIT.EXE. An electronic version of this file is located at www.macmillan.com\osborne.

HKEY_CLASSES_ROOT
Subkeys and Their Values

[HKEY_CLASSES_ROOT]
[HKEY_CLASSES_ROOT*]
[HKEY_CLASSES_ROOT*\shellex]
[HKEY_CLASSES_ROOT*\shellex\ContextMenuHandlers]
[HKEY_CLASSES_ROOT*\shellex\ContextMenuHandlers\BriefcaseMenu]
@="{85BBD920-42A0-1069-A2E4-08002B30309D}"
[HKEY_CLASSES_ROOT*\shellex\ContextMenuHandlers\ExplorerCompression
Menu]
@="{764BF0E1-F219-11ce-972D-00AA00A14F56}"
[HKEY_CLASSES_ROOT*\shellex\PropertySheetHandlers]
[HKEY_CLASSES_ROOT*\shellex\PropertySheetHandlers\BriefcasePage]
@="{85BBD920-42A0-1069-A2E4-08002B30309D}"
[HKEY_CLASSES_ROOT*\shellex\PropertySheetHandlers\{1F2E5C40-9550-
11CE-99D2-00AA006E086C}]
[HKEY_CLASSES_ROOT*\shellex\PropertySheetHandlers\{3EA48300-8CF6-
101B-84FB-666CCB9BCD32}]
[HKEY_CLASSES_ROOT\.386]
@="vxdfile"
[HKEY_CLASSES_ROOT\.ai]
"Content Type"="application/postscript"
[HKEY_CLASSES_ROOT\.aif]
@="aifffile"
"Content Type"="audio/aiff"
[HKEY_CLASSES_ROOT\.aifc]
@="aifffile"
"Content Type"="audio/aiff"
[HKEY_CLASSES_ROOT\.aiff]
@="aifffile"
"Content Type"="audio/aiff"
[HKEY_CLASSES_ROOT\.ani]
@="anifile"
[HKEY_CLASSES_ROOT\.au]
@="aufile"
"Content Type"="audio/basic"
[HKEY_CLASSES_ROOT\.avi]
@="AVIFile"
"Content Type"="video/avi"
[HKEY_CLASSES_ROOT\.bat]
@="batfile"

[HKEY_CLASSES_ROOT\.bfc]
@="Briefcase"
[HKEY_CLASSES_ROOT\.bfc\ShellNew]
"Command"=hex(2):25,53,79,73,74,65,6d,52,6f,6f,74,25,5c,73,79,73,74,65,6d,33,32,
5c,72,75,6e,64,6c,6c,33,32,2e,65,78,65,20,25,53,79,73,74,65,6d,52,6f,6f,74,25,5c,73,
79,73,74,65,6d,33,32,5c,73,79,6e,63,75,69,2e,64,6c,6c,2c,42,72,69,65,66,63,61,73,65,
5f,43,72,65,61,74,65,20,25,31,21,64,21,20,25,32,00
[HKEY_CLASSES_ROOT\.bfc\ShellNew\Config]
"NoExtension"=""
[HKEY_CLASSES_ROOT\.bmp]
@="Paint.Picture"
[HKEY_CLASSES_ROOT\.bmp\ShellNew]
"NullFile"=""
[HKEY_CLASSES_ROOT\.cda]
@="cdafile"
[HKEY_CLASSES_ROOT\.clp]
@="clpfile"
[HKEY_CLASSES_ROOT\.cmd]
@="cmdfile"
[HKEY_CLASSES_ROOT\.com]
@="comfile"
[HKEY_CLASSES_ROOT\.cpl]
@="cplfile"
[HKEY_CLASSES_ROOT\.cur]
@="curfile"
[HKEY_CLASSES_ROOT\.dcx]
@="DCXImage.Document"
[HKEY_CLASSES_ROOT\.dll]
@="dllfile"
[HKEY_CLASSES_ROOT\.doc]
@="WordPad.Document.1"
[HKEY_CLASSES_ROOT\.doc\ShellNew]
[HKEY_CLASSES_ROOT\.doc\Word.Document.6]
[HKEY_CLASSES_ROOT\.doc\Word.Document.6\ShellNew]
"FileName"="winword.doc"
[HKEY_CLASSES_ROOT\.doc\WordDocument]
[HKEY_CLASSES_ROOT\.doc\WordDocument\ShellNew]
"FileName"="winword2.doc"
[HKEY_CLASSES_ROOT\.doc\WordPad.Document.1]
[HKEY_CLASSES_ROOT\.doc\WordPad.Document.1\ShellNew]
"NullFile"=""
[HKEY_CLASSES_ROOT\.drv]
@="drvfile"

[HKEY_CLASSES_ROOT\.eps]
"Content Type"="application/postscript"
[HKEY_CLASSES_ROOT\.exe]
@="exefile"
[HKEY_CLASSES_ROOT\.fif]
"Content Type"="application/fractals"
[HKEY_CLASSES_ROOT\.fnd]
@="fndfile"
[HKEY_CLASSES_ROOT\.fon]
@="fonfile"
[HKEY_CLASSES_ROOT\.gif]
@="giffile"
"Content Type"="image/gif"
[HKEY_CLASSES_ROOT\.grp]
@="MSProgramGroup"
[HKEY_CLASSES_ROOT\.gz]
"Content Type"="application/x-gzip"
[HKEY_CLASSES_ROOT\.hlp]
@="hlpfile"
[HKEY_CLASSES_ROOT\.hqx]
"Content Type"="application/mac-binhex40"
[HKEY_CLASSES_ROOT\.ht]
@="htfile"
[HKEY_CLASSES_ROOT\.htm]
@="htmlfile"
"Content Type"="text/html"
[HKEY_CLASSES_ROOT\.html]
@="htmlfile"
"Content Type"="text/html"
[HKEY_CLASSES_ROOT\.ico]
@="icofile"
[HKEY_CLASSES_ROOT\.inf]
@="inffile"
[HKEY_CLASSES_ROOT\.ini]
@="inifile"
[HKEY_CLASSES_ROOT\.job]
@="JobObject"
[HKEY_CLASSES_ROOT\.jpe]
@="jpegfile"
"Content Type"="image/jpeg"
[HKEY_CLASSES_ROOT\.jpeg]
@="jpegfile"

"Content Type"="image/jpeg"
[HKEY_CLASSES_ROOT\.jpg]
@="jpegfile"
"Content Type"="image/jpeg"
[HKEY_CLASSES_ROOT\.latex]
"Content Type"="application/x-latex"
[HKEY_CLASSES_ROOT\.lnk]
@="lnkfile"
[HKEY_CLASSES_ROOT\.lnk\ShellNew]
"Command"="RunDLL32 AppWiz.Cpl,NewLinkHere %1"
[HKEY_CLASSES_ROOT\.log]
@="txtfile"
[HKEY_CLASSES_ROOT\.man]
"Content Type"="application/x-troff-man"
[HKEY_CLASSES_ROOT\.mid]
@="MIDFile"
[HKEY_CLASSES_ROOT\.mmm]
@="MPlayer"
[HKEY_CLASSES_ROOT\.mov]
"Content Type"="video/quicktime"
[HKEY_CLASSES_ROOT\.movie]
"Content Type"="video/x-sgi-movie"
[HKEY_CLASSES_ROOT\.mpe]
"Content Type"="video/mpeg"
[HKEY_CLASSES_ROOT\.mpeg]
"Content Type"="video/mpeg"
[HKEY_CLASSES_ROOT\.mpg]
"Content Type"="video/mpeg"
[HKEY_CLASSES_ROOT\.msg]
@="msgfile"
[HKEY_CLASSES_ROOT\.pbk]
@="pbkfile"
[HKEY_CLASSES_ROOT\.pcx]
@="PCXImage.Document"
[HKEY_CLASSES_ROOT\.pfm]
@="pfmfile"
[HKEY_CLASSES_ROOT\.pif]
@="piffile"
[HKEY_CLASSES_ROOT\.pma]
@="PerfFile"
[HKEY_CLASSES_ROOT\.pmc]
@="PerfFile"

[HKEY_CLASSES_ROOT\.pml]
@="PerfFile"
[HKEY_CLASSES_ROOT\.pmr]
@="PerfFile"
[HKEY_CLASSES_ROOT\.pmw]
@="PerfFile"
[HKEY_CLASSES_ROOT\.pnf]
@="pnffile"
[HKEY_CLASSES_ROOT\.ppt]
[HKEY_CLASSES_ROOT\.ppt\PowerPoint.Show.4]
[HKEY_CLASSES_ROOT\.ppt\PowerPoint.Show.4\ShellNew]
"FileName"="powerpnt.ppt"
[HKEY_CLASSES_ROOT\.ps]
"Content Type"="application/postscript"
[HKEY_CLASSES_ROOT\.qt]
"Content Type"="video/quicktime"
[HKEY_CLASSES_ROOT\.que]
@="QueueObject"
[HKEY_CLASSES_ROOT\.reg]
@="regfile"
[HKEY_CLASSES_ROOT\.rmi]
@="MPlayer"
[HKEY_CLASSES_ROOT\.rnk]
@="rnkfile"
[HKEY_CLASSES_ROOT\.rtf]
@="rtffile"
[HKEY_CLASSES_ROOT\.rtf\ShellNew]
"Data"="{\\rtf1}"
[HKEY_CLASSES_ROOT\.sam]
[HKEY_CLASSES_ROOT\.sam\AmiProDocument]
[HKEY_CLASSES_ROOT\.sam\AmiProDocument\ShellNew]
"FileName"="amipro.sam"
[HKEY_CLASSES_ROOT\.scp]
@="txtfile"
[HKEY_CLASSES_ROOT\.scr]
@="scrfile"
[HKEY_CLASSES_ROOT\.shb]
@="DocShortcut"
[HKEY_CLASSES_ROOT\.shs]
@="ShellScrap"
[HKEY_CLASSES_ROOT\.shw]
[HKEY_CLASSES_ROOT\.shw\Presentations31.Show]

[HKEY_CLASSES_ROOT\.shw\Presentations31.Show\ShellNew]
"FileName"="presenta.shw"
[HKEY_CLASSES_ROOT\.sit]
"Content Type"="application/x-stuffit"
[HKEY_CLASSES_ROOT\.snd]
@="aufile"
"Content Type"="audio/basic"
[HKEY_CLASSES_ROOT\.sys]
@="sysfile"
[HKEY_CLASSES_ROOT\.tar]
"Content Type"="application/x-tar"
[HKEY_CLASSES_ROOT\.tgz]
"Content Type"="application/x-compressed"
[HKEY_CLASSES_ROOT\.tif]
@="TIFImage.Document"
"Content Type"="image/tiff"
[HKEY_CLASSES_ROOT\.tiff]
"Content Type"="image/tiff"
[HKEY_CLASSES_ROOT\.ttf]
@="ttffile"
[HKEY_CLASSES_ROOT\.txt]
@="txtfile"
"Content Type"="text/plain"
[HKEY_CLASSES_ROOT\.txt\ShellNew]
"NullFile"=""
[HKEY_CLASSES_ROOT\.url]
@="InternetShortcut"
[HKEY_CLASSES_ROOT\.wav]
@="SoundRec"
"Content Type"="audio/wav"
[HKEY_CLASSES_ROOT\.wav\ShellNew]
"NullFile"=""
[HKEY_CLASSES_ROOT\.wb2]
[HKEY_CLASSES_ROOT\.wb2\QuattroPro.Graph.6]
[HKEY_CLASSES_ROOT\.wb2\QuattroPro.Graph.6\ShellNew]
"FileName"="quattro.wb2"
[HKEY_CLASSES_ROOT\.wb2\QuattroPro.Notebook.6]
[HKEY_CLASSES_ROOT\.wb2\QuattroPro.Notebook.6\ShellNew]
"FileName"="quattro.wb2"
[HKEY_CLASSES_ROOT\.wk4]
[HKEY_CLASSES_ROOT\.wk4\123Worksheet]
[HKEY_CLASSES_ROOT\.wk4\123Worksheet\ShellNew]
"FileName"="lotus.wk4"

[HKEY_CLASSES_ROOT\.wpd]
[HKEY_CLASSES_ROOT\.wpd\WPWin6.1File]
[HKEY_CLASSES_ROOT\.wpd\WPWin6.1File\ShellNew]
"FileName"="wordpfct.wpd"
[HKEY_CLASSES_ROOT\.wpg]
[HKEY_CLASSES_ROOT\.wpg\TextArt.Document]
[HKEY_CLASSES_ROOT\.wpg\TextArt.Document\ShellNew]
"FileName"="wordpfct.wpg"
[HKEY_CLASSES_ROOT\.wpg\WPDraw30.Chart]
[HKEY_CLASSES_ROOT\.wpg\WPDraw30.Chart\ShellNew]
"FileName"="wordpfct.wpg"
[HKEY_CLASSES_ROOT\.wpg\WPDraw30.Drawing]
[HKEY_CLASSES_ROOT\.wpg\WPDraw30.Drawing\ShellNew]
"FileName"="wordpfct.wpg"
[HKEY_CLASSES_ROOT\.wri]
@="wrifile"
[HKEY_CLASSES_ROOT\.wtx]
@="txtfile"
[HKEY_CLASSES_ROOT\.xbm]
@="xbmfile"
"Content Type"="image/x-xbitmap"
[HKEY_CLASSES_ROOT\.xif]
@="XIFImage.Document"
[HKEY_CLASSES_ROOT\.xls]
[HKEY_CLASSES_ROOT\.xls\Excel.Sheet.5]
[HKEY_CLASSES_ROOT\.xls\Excel.Sheet.5\ShellNew]
"FileName"="excel.xls"
[HKEY_CLASSES_ROOT\.xls\ExcelWorksheet]
[HKEY_CLASSES_ROOT\.xls\ExcelWorksheet\ShellNew]
"FileName"="excel4.xls"
[HKEY_CLASSES_ROOT\.z]
"Content Type"="application/x-compress"
[HKEY_CLASSES_ROOT\.zip]
"Content Type"="application/x-zip-compressed"
[HKEY_CLASSES_ROOT\aifffile]
@="AIFF Format Sound"
[HKEY_CLASSES_ROOT\aifffile\DefaultIcon]
@="MPlayer.exe,2"
[HKEY_CLASSES_ROOT\aifffile\shell]
[HKEY_CLASSES_ROOT\aifffile\shell\open]
[HKEY_CLASSES_ROOT\aifffile\shell\open\command]
@="\"C:\\Program Files\\Plus!\\Microsoft Internet\\IExplore.exe\" -nohome"

[HKEY_CLASSES_ROOT\aifffile\shell\open\ddeexec]
@="\"file:%1\",,-1,,,,,"
[HKEY_CLASSES_ROOT\aifffile\shell\open\ddeexec\Application]
@="IExplore"
[HKEY_CLASSES_ROOT\aifffile\shell\open\ddeexec\Topic]
@="WWW_OpenURL"
[HKEY_CLASSES_ROOT\anifile]
@="Animated Cursor"
[HKEY_CLASSES_ROOT\anifile\DefaultIcon]
@="%1"
[HKEY_CLASSES_ROOT\AppID]
[HKEY_CLASSES_ROOT\AppID\{00020C01-0000-0000-C000-000000000046}]
@="Sound Recorder"
[HKEY_CLASSES_ROOT\AppID\{00022601-0000-0000-C000-000000000046}]
@="Media Player"
[HKEY_CLASSES_ROOT\AppID\{D3E34B21-9D75-101A-8C3D-
00AA001A1652}]
@="Paintbrush"
[HKEY_CLASSES_ROOT\AudioCD]
@="AudioCD"
"EditFlags"=hex:02,00,00,00
[HKEY_CLASSES_ROOT\AudioCD\DefaultIcon]
@=hex(2):25,53,79,73,74,65,6d,52,6f,6f,74,25,5c,73,79,73,74,65,6d,33,32,5c,73,68,
65,6c,6c,33,32,2e,64,6c,6c,2c,34,30,00
[HKEY_CLASSES_ROOT\AudioCD\shell]
@="play"
[HKEY_CLASSES_ROOT\AudioCD\shell\play]
@="&Play"
[HKEY_CLASSES_ROOT\AudioCD\shell\play\command]
@=hex(2):25,53,79,73,74,65,6d,52,6f,6f,74,25,5c,73,79,73,74,65,6d,33,32,5c,63,64,
70,6c,61,79,65,72,2e,65,78,65,20,2f,70,6c,61,79,20,25,31,00
[HKEY_CLASSES_ROOT\aufile]
@="AU Format Sound"
[HKEY_CLASSES_ROOT\aufile\DefaultIcon]
@="MPlay32.exe,2"
[HKEY_CLASSES_ROOT\aufile\shell]
[HKEY_CLASSES_ROOT\aufile\shell\open]
[HKEY_CLASSES_ROOT\aufile\shell\open\command]
@="\"C:\\Program Files\\Plus!\\Microsoft Internet\\IExplore.exe\" -nohome"
[HKEY_CLASSES_ROOT\aufile\shell\open\ddeexec]
@="\"file:%1\",,-1,,,,,"
[HKEY_CLASSES_ROOT\aufile\shell\open\ddeexec\Application]
@="IExplore"

[HKEY_CLASSES_ROOT\aufile\shell\open\ddeexec\Topic]
@="WWW_OpenURL"
[HKEY_CLASSES_ROOT\AVIFile]
@="Video Clip"
"EditFlags"=hex:00,00,01,00
[HKEY_CLASSES_ROOT\AVIFile\CLSID]
@="{00022602-0000-0000-C000-000000000046}"
[HKEY_CLASSES_ROOT\AVIFile\Compressors]
[HKEY_CLASSES_ROOT\AVIFile\Compressors\auds]
@="{0002000F-0000-0000-C000-000000000046}"
[HKEY_CLASSES_ROOT\AVIFile\Compressors\vids]
@="{00020001-0000-0000-C000-000000000046}"
[HKEY_CLASSES_ROOT\AVIFile\DefaultIcon]
@="mplay32.exe,3"
[HKEY_CLASSES_ROOT\AVIFile\Extensions]
[HKEY_CLASSES_ROOT\AVIFile\Extensions\AU]
@="{00020003-0000-0000-C000-000000000046}"
[HKEY_CLASSES_ROOT\AVIFile\Extensions\AVI]
@="{00020000-0000-0000-C000-000000000046}"
[HKEY_CLASSES_ROOT\AVIFile\Extensions\WAV]
@="{00020003-0000-0000-C000-000000000046}"
[HKEY_CLASSES_ROOT\AVIFile\Insertable]
@=""
[HKEY_CLASSES_ROOT\AVIFile\protocol]
[HKEY_CLASSES_ROOT\AVIFile\protocol\StdExecute]
[HKEY_CLASSES_ROOT\AVIFile\protocol\StdExecute\server]
@="mplay32.exe /avi"
[HKEY_CLASSES_ROOT\AVIFile\protocol\StdFileEditing]
[HKEY_CLASSES_ROOT\AVIFile\protocol\StdFileEditing\Handler]
@="mciole16.dll"
[HKEY_CLASSES_ROOT\AVIFile\protocol\StdFileEditing\Handler32]
@="mciole32.dll"
[HKEY_CLASSES_ROOT\AVIFile\protocol\StdFileEditing\PackageObjects]
@=""
[HKEY_CLASSES_ROOT\AVIFile\protocol\StdFileEditing\server]
@="mplay32.exe /avi"
[HKEY_CLASSES_ROOT\AVIFile\protocol\StdFileEditing\verb]
[HKEY_CLASSES_ROOT\AVIFile\protocol\StdFileEditing\verb\0]
@="&Play"
[HKEY_CLASSES_ROOT\AVIFile\protocol\StdFileEditing\verb\1]
@="&Edit"
[HKEY_CLASSES_ROOT\AVIFile\protocol\StdFileEditing\verb\2]
@="&Open"

[HKEY_CLASSES_ROOT\AVIFile\RIFFHandlers]
[HKEY_CLASSES_ROOT\AVIFile\RIFFHandlers\AVI]
@="{00020000-0000-0000-C000-000000000046}"
[HKEY_CLASSES_ROOT\AVIFile\RIFFHandlers\WAVE]
@="{00020003-0000-0000-C000-000000000046}"
[HKEY_CLASSES_ROOT\AVIFile\shell]
[HKEY_CLASSES_ROOT\AVIFile\shell\open]
[HKEY_CLASSES_ROOT\AVIFile\shell\open\command]
@="mplay32.exe /play /close \"%L\""
[HKEY_CLASSES_ROOT\AVIFile\shellex]
[HKEY_CLASSES_ROOT\AVIFile\shellex\PropertySheetHandlers]
@="AviPage"
[HKEY_CLASSES_ROOT\AVIFile\shellex\PropertySheetHandlers\AviPage]
@="{00022613-0000-0000-C000-000000000046}"
[HKEY_CLASSES_ROOT\batfile]
@="MS-DOS Batch File"
"EditFlags"=hex:30,04,00,00
[HKEY_CLASSES_ROOT\batfile\DefaultIcon]
@=hex(2):25,53,79,73,74,65,6d,52,6f,6f,74,25,5c,53,79,73,74,65,6d,33,32,5c,73,68,
65,6c,6c,33,32,2e,64,6c,6c,2c,2d,31,35,33,00
[HKEY_CLASSES_ROOT\batfile\shell]
[HKEY_CLASSES_ROOT\batfile\shell\edit]
@="&Edit"
[HKEY_CLASSES_ROOT\batfile\shell\edit\command]
@=hex(2):25,53,79,73,74,65,6d,52,6f,6f,74,25,5c,53,79,73,74,65,6d,33,32,5c,4e,4f,54,
45,50,41,44,2e,45,58,45,20,25,31,00
[HKEY_CLASSES_ROOT\batfile\shell\open]
"EditFlags"=hex:00,00,00,00
[HKEY_CLASSES_ROOT\batfile\shell\open\command]
@="\"%1\" %*"
[HKEY_CLASSES_ROOT\batfile\shell\print]
[HKEY_CLASSES_ROOT\batfile\shell\print\command]
@=hex(2):25,53,79,73,74,65,6d,52,6f,6f,74,25,5c,53,79,73,74,65,6d,33,32,5c,4e,4f,54,
45,50,41,44,2e,45,58,45,20,2f,70,20,25,31,00
[HKEY_CLASSES_ROOT\batfile\shellex]
[HKEY_CLASSES_ROOT\batfile\shellex\PropertySheetHandlers]
[HKEY_CLASSES_ROOT\batfile\shellex\PropertySheetHandlers\PifProps]
@="{86F19A00-42A0-1069-A2E9-08002B30309D}"
[HKEY_CLASSES_ROOT\Briefcase]
@="Briefcase"
[HKEY_CLASSES_ROOT\Briefcase\CLSID]
@="{85BBD920-42A0-1069-A2E4-08002B30309D}"

[HKEY_CLASSES_ROOT\Briefcase\DefaultIcon]
@=hex(2):25,53,79,73,74,65,6d,52,6f,6f,74,25,5c,73,79,73,74,65,6d,33,32,5c,73,79,
6e,63,75,69,2e,64,6c,6c,2c,30,00
[HKEY_CLASSES_ROOT\Briefcase\shell]
[HKEY_CLASSES_ROOT\Briefcase\shell\open]
[HKEY_CLASSES_ROOT\Briefcase\shell\open\command]
@="explorer.exe %1"
[HKEY_CLASSES_ROOT\cdafile]
@="CD Audio Track"
[HKEY_CLASSES_ROOT\cdafile\DefaultIcon]
@=hex(2):25,53,79,73,74,65,6d,52,6f,6f,74,25,5c,73,79,73,74,65,6d,33,32,5c,63,64,
70,6c,61,79,65,72,2e,65,78,65,2c,31,00
[HKEY_CLASSES_ROOT\cdafile\shell]
[HKEY_CLASSES_ROOT\cdafile\shell\play]
@="&Play"
[HKEY_CLASSES_ROOT\cdafile\shell\play\command]
@=hex(2):25,53,79,73,74,65,6d,52,6f,6f,74,25,5c,73,79,73,74,65,6d,33,32,5c,63,64,
70,6c,61,79,65,72,2e,65,78,65,20,2d,70,6c,61,79,20,25,31,00
[HKEY_CLASSES_ROOT\clpfile]
@="Clipboard Clip"
[HKEY_CLASSES_ROOT\clpfile\DefaultIcon]
@=hex(2):25,73,79,73,74,65,6d,72,6f,6f,74,25,5c,73,79,73,74,65,6d,33,32,5c,63,6c,
69,70,62,72,64,2e,65,78,65,2c,31,00
[HKEY_CLASSES_ROOT\clpfile\shell]
[HKEY_CLASSES_ROOT\clpfile\shell\open]
[HKEY_CLASSES_ROOT\clpfile\shell\open\command]
@="clipbrd.exe %1"
[HKEY_CLASSES_ROOT\CLSID]
@="{009541A4-3B81-101C-92F3-040224009C02}"
[HKEY_CLASSES_ROOT\CLSID\CLSID]
@="{0000031A-0000-0000-C000-000000000046}"
[HKEY_CLASSES_ROOT\CLSID\{00000300-0000-0000-C000-000000000046}]
@="StdOleLink"
[HKEY_CLASSES_ROOT\CLSID\{00000300-0000-0000-C000-
000000000046}\InprocServer32]
@="ole32.dll"
[HKEY_CLASSES_ROOT\CLSID\{00000303-0000-0000-C000-000000000046}]
@="FileMoniker"
[HKEY_CLASSES_ROOT\CLSID\{00000303-0000-0000-C000-
000000000046}\InprocServer32]
@="ole32.dll"
[HKEY_CLASSES_ROOT\CLSID\{00000303-0000-0000-C000-
000000000046}\ProgID]

@="file"
[HKEY_CLASSES_ROOT\CLSID\{00000304-0000-0000-C000-000000000046}]
@="ItemMoniker"
[HKEY_CLASSES_ROOT\CLSID\{00000304-0000-0000-C000-
000000000046}\InprocServer32]
@="ole32.dll"
[HKEY_CLASSES_ROOT\CLSID\{00000305-0000-0000-C000-000000000046}]
@="AntiMoniker"
[HKEY_CLASSES_ROOT\CLSID\{00000305-0000-0000-C000-
000000000046}\InprocServer32]
@="ole32.dll"
[HKEY_CLASSES_ROOT\CLSID\{00000306-0000-0000-C000-000000000046}]
@="PointerMoniker"
[HKEY_CLASSES_ROOT\CLSID\{00000306-0000-0000-C000-
000000000046}\InprocServer32]
@="ole32.dll"
[HKEY_CLASSES_ROOT\CLSID\{00000308-0000-0000-C000-000000000046}]
@="PackagerMoniker"
[HKEY_CLASSES_ROOT\CLSID\{00000308-0000-0000-C000-
000000000046}\InprocServer32]
@="ole32.dll"
[HKEY_CLASSES_ROOT\CLSID\{00000309-0000-0000-C000-000000000046}]
@="CompositeMoniker"
[HKEY_CLASSES_ROOT\CLSID\{00000309-0000-0000-C000-
000000000046}\InprocServer32]
@="ole32.dll"
[HKEY_CLASSES_ROOT\CLSID\{0000030B-0000-0000-C000-000000000046}]
@="DfMarshal"
[HKEY_CLASSES_ROOT\CLSID\{0000030B-0000-0000-C000-
000000000046}\InprocServer32]
@="ole32.dll"
[HKEY_CLASSES_ROOT\CLSID\{00000315-0000-0000-C000-000000000046}]
@="Picture (Metafile)"
[HKEY_CLASSES_ROOT\CLSID\{00000315-0000-0000-C000-
000000000046}\AuxUserType]
[HKEY_CLASSES_ROOT\CLSID\{00000315-0000-0000-C000-
000000000046}\AuxUserType\2]
@="Picture"
[HKEY_CLASSES_ROOT\CLSID\{00000315-0000-0000-C000-
000000000046}\Conversion]
[HKEY_CLASSES_ROOT\CLSID\{00000315-0000-0000-C000-
000000000046}\Conversion\Readable]

[HKEY_CLASSES_ROOT\CLSID\{00000315-0000-0000-C000-
000000000046}\Conversion\Readable\Main]
@="3,MSDraw"
[HKEY_CLASSES_ROOT\CLSID\{00000315-0000-0000-C000-
000000000046}\DataFormats]
[HKEY_CLASSES_ROOT\CLSID\{00000315-0000-0000-C000-
000000000046}\DataFormats\DefaultFile]
@="3"
[HKEY_CLASSES_ROOT\CLSID\{00000315-0000-0000-C000-
000000000046}\DataFormats\GetSet]
[HKEY_CLASSES_ROOT\CLSID\{00000315-0000-0000-C000-
000000000046}\DataFormats\GetSet\0]
@="3,1,32,3"
[HKEY_CLASSES_ROOT\CLSID\{00000315-0000-0000-C000-
000000000046}\InprocServer32]
@="ole32.dll"
[HKEY_CLASSES_ROOT\CLSID\{00000315-0000-0000-C000-
000000000046}\MiscStatus]
@="536"
[HKEY_CLASSES_ROOT\CLSID\{00000315-0000-0000-C000-
000000000046}\ProgID]
@="StaticMetafile"
[HKEY_CLASSES_ROOT\CLSID\{00000316-0000-0000-C000-000000000046}]
@="Picture (Device Independent Bitmap)"
[HKEY_CLASSES_ROOT\CLSID\{00000316-0000-0000-C000-
000000000046}\AuxUserType]
[HKEY_CLASSES_ROOT\CLSID\{00000316-0000-0000-C000-
000000000046}\AuxUserType\2]
@="Picture"
[HKEY_CLASSES_ROOT\CLSID\{00000316-0000-0000-C000-
000000000046}\Conversion]
[HKEY_CLASSES_ROOT\CLSID\{00000316-0000-0000-C000-
000000000046}\Conversion\Readable]
[HKEY_CLASSES_ROOT\CLSID\{00000316-0000-0000-C000-
000000000046}\Conversion\Readable\Main]
@="8,PBrush"
[HKEY_CLASSES_ROOT\CLSID\{00000316-0000-0000-C000-
000000000046}\DataFormats]
[HKEY_CLASSES_ROOT\CLSID\{00000316-0000-0000-C000-
000000000046}\DataFormats\DefaultFile]
@="8"
[HKEY_CLASSES_ROOT\CLSID\{00000316-0000-0000-C000-
000000000046}\DataFormats\GetSet]

[HKEY_CLASSES_ROOT\CLSID\{00000316-0000-0000-C000-000000000046}\DataFormats\GetSet\0]
@="8,1,1,3"
[HKEY_CLASSES_ROOT\CLSID\{00000316-0000-0000-C000-000000000046}\InprocServer32]
@="ole32.dll"
[HKEY_CLASSES_ROOT\CLSID\{00000316-0000-0000-C000-000000000046}\MiscStatus]
@="536"
[HKEY_CLASSES_ROOT\CLSID\{00000316-0000-0000-C000-000000000046}\ProgID]
@="StaticDib"
[HKEY_CLASSES_ROOT\CLSID\{00000319-0000-0000-C000-000000000046}]
@="Picture (Enhanced Metafile)"
[HKEY_CLASSES_ROOT\CLSID\{00000319-0000-0000-C000-000000000046}\AuxUserType]
[HKEY_CLASSES_ROOT\CLSID\{00000319-0000-0000-C000-000000000046}\AuxUserType\2]
@="Picture"
[HKEY_CLASSES_ROOT\CLSID\{00000319-0000-0000-C000-000000000046}\Conversion]
[HKEY_CLASSES_ROOT\CLSID\{00000319-0000-0000-C000-000000000046}\Conversion\Readable]
[HKEY_CLASSES_ROOT\CLSID\{00000319-0000-0000-C000-000000000046}\Conversion\Readable\Main]
@=""
[HKEY_CLASSES_ROOT\CLSID\{00000319-0000-0000-C000-000000000046}\DataFormats]
[HKEY_CLASSES_ROOT\CLSID\{00000319-0000-0000-C000-000000000046}\DataFormats\DefaultFile]
@="14"
[HKEY_CLASSES_ROOT\CLSID\{00000319-0000-0000-C000-000000000046}\DataFormats\GetSet]
[HKEY_CLASSES_ROOT\CLSID\{00000319-0000-0000-C000-000000000046}\DataFormats\GetSet\0]
@="14,1,64,3"
[HKEY_CLASSES_ROOT\CLSID\{00000319-0000-0000-C000-000000000046}\InprocServer32]
@="ole32.dll"
[HKEY_CLASSES_ROOT\CLSID\{00000319-0000-0000-C000-000000000046}\MiscStatus]
@="536"

[HKEY_CLASSES_ROOT\CLSID\{00000319-0000-0000-C000-
000000000046}\ProgID]
@="StaticEnhancedMetafile"
[HKEY_CLASSES_ROOT\CLSID\{0000031A-0000-0000-C000-000000000046}]
@="ClassMoniker"
[HKEY_CLASSES_ROOT\CLSID\{0000031A-0000-0000-C000-
000000000046}\InprocServer32]
@="ole32.dll"
[HKEY_CLASSES_ROOT\CLSID\{0000031A-0000-0000-C000-
000000000046}\ProgID]
@="clsid"
[HKEY_CLASSES_ROOT\CLSID\{00000320-0000-0000-C000-000000000046}]
@="oleprx32_PSFactory"
[HKEY_CLASSES_ROOT\CLSID\{00000320-0000-0000-C000-
000000000046}\InprocServer32]
@="ole32.dll"
[HKEY_CLASSES_ROOT\CLSID\{00020000-0000-0000-C000-000000000046}]
@="Microsoft AVI Files"
[HKEY_CLASSES_ROOT\CLSID\{00020000-0000-0000-C000-
000000000046}\AVIFile]
@="7"
[HKEY_CLASSES_ROOT\CLSID\{00020000-0000-0000-C000-
000000000046}\InprocServer]
@="avifile.dll"
[HKEY_CLASSES_ROOT\CLSID\{00020000-0000-0000-C000-
000000000046}\InprocServer32]
@="avifil32.dll"
"ThreadingModel"="Both"
[HKEY_CLASSES_ROOT\CLSID\{00020001-0000-0000-C000-000000000046}]
@="AVI Compressed Stream"
[HKEY_CLASSES_ROOT\CLSID\{00020001-0000-0000-C000-
000000000046}\InprocServer]
@="avifile.dll"
[HKEY_CLASSES_ROOT\CLSID\{00020001-0000-0000-C000-
000000000046}\InprocServer32]
@="avifil32.dll"
"ThreadingModel"="Both"
[HKEY_CLASSES_ROOT\CLSID\{00020003-0000-0000-C000-000000000046}]
@="Microsoft Wave File"
[HKEY_CLASSES_ROOT\CLSID\{00020003-0000-0000-C000-
000000000046}\AVIFile]
@="7"

[HKEY_CLASSES_ROOT\CLSID\{00020003-0000-0000-C000-000000000046}\InprocServer32]
@="avifil32.dll"
"ThreadingModel"="Both"
[HKEY_CLASSES_ROOT\CLSID\{0002000D-0000-0000-C000-000000000046}]
@="IAVIStream & IAVIFile Proxy"
[HKEY_CLASSES_ROOT\CLSID\{0002000D-0000-0000-C000-000000000046}\InprocServer]
@="avifile.dll"
[HKEY_CLASSES_ROOT\CLSID\{0002000D-0000-0000-C000-000000000046}\InprocServer32]
@="avifil32.dll"
"ThreadingModel"="Both"
[HKEY_CLASSES_ROOT\CLSID\{0002000F-0000-0000-C000-000000000046}]
@="ACM Compressed Audio Stream"
[HKEY_CLASSES_ROOT\CLSID\{0002000F-0000-0000-C000-000000000046}\InprocServer]
@="avifile.dll"
[HKEY_CLASSES_ROOT\CLSID\{0002000F-0000-0000-C000-000000000046}\InprocServer32]
@="avifil32.dll"
"ThreadingModel"="Both"
[HKEY_CLASSES_ROOT\CLSID\{00020344-0000-0000-C000-000000000046}]
@="MAPILogonRemote"
[HKEY_CLASSES_ROOT\CLSID\{00020344-0000-0000-C000-000000000046}\LocalServer32]
@="mapisrvr.exe"
[HKEY_CLASSES_ROOT\CLSID\{00020420-0000-0000-C000-000000000046}]
@="PSDispatch"
[HKEY_CLASSES_ROOT\CLSID\{00020420-0000-0000-C000-000000000046}\InprocServer]
@="ole2disp.dll"
[HKEY_CLASSES_ROOT\CLSID\{00020420-0000-0000-C000-000000000046}\InprocServer32]
@="oleaut32.dll"
"ThreadingModel"="Apartment"
[HKEY_CLASSES_ROOT\CLSID\{00020421-0000-0000-C000-000000000046}]
@="PSEnumVARIANT"
[HKEY_CLASSES_ROOT\CLSID\{00020421-0000-0000-C000-000000000046}\InprocServer]
@="ole2disp.dll"

[HKEY_CLASSES_ROOT\CLSID\{00020421-0000-0000-C000-000000000046}\InprocServer32]
@="oleaut32.dll"
"ThreadingModel"="Apartment"
[HKEY_CLASSES_ROOT\CLSID\{00020422-0000-0000-C000-000000000046}]
@="PSTypeInfo"
[HKEY_CLASSES_ROOT\CLSID\{00020422-0000-0000-C000-000000000046}\InprocServer]
@="ole2disp.dll"
[HKEY_CLASSES_ROOT\CLSID\{00020422-0000-0000-C000-000000000046}\InprocServer32]
@="oleaut32.dll"
"ThreadingModel"="Apartment"
[HKEY_CLASSES_ROOT\CLSID\{00020423-0000-0000-C000-000000000046}]
@="PSTypeLib"
[HKEY_CLASSES_ROOT\CLSID\{00020423-0000-0000-C000-000000000046}\InprocServer]
@="ole2disp.dll"
[HKEY_CLASSES_ROOT\CLSID\{00020423-0000-0000-C000-000000000046}\InprocServer32]
@="oleaut32.dll"
"ThreadingModel"="Apartment"
[HKEY_CLASSES_ROOT\CLSID\{00020424-0000-0000-C000-000000000046}]
@="PSOAInterface"
[HKEY_CLASSES_ROOT\CLSID\{00020424-0000-0000-C000-000000000046}\InprocServer]
@="ole2disp.dll"
[HKEY_CLASSES_ROOT\CLSID\{00020424-0000-0000-C000-000000000046}\InprocServer32]
@="oleaut32.dll"
"ThreadingModel"="Apartment"
[HKEY_CLASSES_ROOT\CLSID\{00020425-0000-0000-C000-000000000046}]
@="PSTypeComp"
[HKEY_CLASSES_ROOT\CLSID\{00020425-0000-0000-C000-000000000046}\InprocServer]
@="ole2disp.dll"
[HKEY_CLASSES_ROOT\CLSID\{00020425-0000-0000-C000-000000000046}\InprocServer32]
@="oleaut32.dll"
"ThreadingModel"="Apartment"
[HKEY_CLASSES_ROOT\CLSID\{00020C01-0000-0000-C000-000000000046}]
@="Sound (OLE2)"

"AppID"="{00020C01-0000-0000-C000-000000000046}"
[HKEY_CLASSES_ROOT\CLSID\{00020C01-0000-0000-C000-000000000046}\AuxUserType]
[HKEY_CLASSES_ROOT\CLSID\{00020C01-0000-0000-C000-000000000046}\AuxUserType\2]
@="Sound Recorder Document"
[HKEY_CLASSES_ROOT\CLSID\{00020C01-0000-0000-C000-000000000046}\AuxUserType\3]
@="Microsoft Sound Recorder Server"
[HKEY_CLASSES_ROOT\CLSID\{00020C01-0000-0000-C000-000000000046}\DataFormats]
[HKEY_CLASSES_ROOT\CLSID\{00020C01-0000-0000-C000-000000000046}\DataFormats\DefaultFile]
@="12"
[HKEY_CLASSES_ROOT\CLSID\{00020C01-0000-0000-C000-000000000046}\DataFormats\DefaultSet]
@="SoundRec"
[HKEY_CLASSES_ROOT\CLSID\{00020C01-0000-0000-C000-000000000046}\DataFormats\GetSet]
[HKEY_CLASSES_ROOT\CLSID\{00020C01-0000-0000-C000-000000000046}\DataFormats\GetSet\0]
@="3,1,32,1"
[HKEY_CLASSES_ROOT\CLSID\{00020C01-0000-0000-C000-000000000046}\DataFormats\GetSet\1]
@="8,-1,1,3"
[HKEY_CLASSES_ROOT\CLSID\{00020C01-0000-0000-C000-000000000046}\InprocHandler32]
@="ole32.dll"
[HKEY_CLASSES_ROOT\CLSID\{00020C01-0000-0000-C000-000000000046}\Insertable]
@=""
[HKEY_CLASSES_ROOT\CLSID\{00020C01-0000-0000-C000-000000000046}\LocalServer]
@="sndrec32.exe"
[HKEY_CLASSES_ROOT\CLSID\{00020C01-0000-0000-C000-000000000046}\LocalServer32]
@="sndrec32.exe"
[HKEY_CLASSES_ROOT\CLSID\{00020C01-0000-0000-C000-000000000046}\MiscStatus]
@="0"
[HKEY_CLASSES_ROOT\CLSID\{00020C01-0000-0000-C000-000000000046}\ProgID]
@="SoundRec"

[HKEY_CLASSES_ROOT\CLSID\{00020C01-0000-0000-C000-000000000046}\verb]
[HKEY_CLASSES_ROOT\CLSID\{00020C01-0000-0000-C000-000000000046}\verb\0]
@="&Play,0,3"
[HKEY_CLASSES_ROOT\CLSID\{00020C01-0000-0000-C000-000000000046}\verb\1]
@="&Edit,0,2"
[HKEY_CLASSES_ROOT\CLSID\{00020C01-0000-0000-C000-000000000046}\verb\2]
@="&Open,0,2"
[HKEY_CLASSES_ROOT\CLSID\{00020D05-0000-0000-C000-000000000046}]
@="Inserted File"
[HKEY_CLASSES_ROOT\CLSID\{00020D05-0000-0000-C000-000000000046}\AuxUserType]
[HKEY_CLASSES_ROOT\CLSID\{00020D05-0000-0000-C000-000000000046}\AuxUserType\2]
@="File"
[HKEY_CLASSES_ROOT\CLSID\{00020D05-0000-0000-C000-000000000046}\AuxUserType\3]
@="Windows Messaging"
[HKEY_CLASSES_ROOT\CLSID\{00020D05-0000-0000-C000-000000000046}\InprocServer32]
@="wmsui32.dll"
[HKEY_CLASSES_ROOT\CLSID\{00020D05-0000-0000-C000-000000000046}\ProgID]
@="MailFileAtt"
[HKEY_CLASSES_ROOT\CLSID\{00020D05-0000-0000-C000-000000000046}\Verb]
[HKEY_CLASSES_ROOT\CLSID\{00020D05-0000-0000-C000-000000000046}\Verb\0]
@="&Open, 0, 2"
[HKEY_CLASSES_ROOT\CLSID\{00020D05-0000-0000-C000-000000000046}\Verb\1]
@="P&rint, 0, 2"
[HKEY_CLASSES_ROOT\CLSID\{00020D05-0000-0000-C000-000000000046}\Verb\2]
@="&Quick View, 0, 2"
[HKEY_CLASSES_ROOT\CLSID\{00020D05-0000-0000-C000-000000000046}\Verb\3]
@="&Save As, 0, 2"

[HKEY_CLASSES_ROOT\CLSID\{00020D05-0000-0000-C000-
000000000046}\Verb\4]
@="Re&name, 0, 2"
[HKEY_CLASSES_ROOT\CLSID\{00020D09-0000-0000-C000-000000000046}]
@="Inserted Message"
[HKEY_CLASSES_ROOT\CLSID\{00020D09-0000-0000-C000-
000000000046}\AuxUserType]
[HKEY_CLASSES_ROOT\CLSID\{00020D09-0000-0000-C000-
000000000046}\AuxUserType\2]
@="Message"
[HKEY_CLASSES_ROOT\CLSID\{00020D09-0000-0000-C000-
000000000046}\AuxUserType\3]
@="Windows Messaging"
[HKEY_CLASSES_ROOT\CLSID\{00020D09-0000-0000-C000-
000000000046}\InprocServer32]
@="wmsui32.dll"
[HKEY_CLASSES_ROOT\CLSID\{00020D09-0000-0000-C000-
000000000046}\ProgID]
@="MailMsgAtt"
[HKEY_CLASSES_ROOT\CLSID\{00020D09-0000-0000-C000-
000000000046}\Verb]
[HKEY_CLASSES_ROOT\CLSID\{00020D09-0000-0000-C000-
000000000046}\Verb\0]
@="&Open, 0, 2"
[HKEY_CLASSES_ROOT\CLSID\{00020D30-0000-0000-C000-000000000046}]
@="IPM"
[HKEY_CLASSES_ROOT\CLSID\{00020D30-0000-0000-C000-
000000000046}\InprocHandler32]
@="mapi32.dll"
[HKEY_CLASSES_ROOT\CLSID\{00020D30-0000-0000-C000-
000000000046}\LocalServer32]
@="C:\\Program Files\\Windows NT\\Windows Messaging\\exchng32.exe"
[HKEY_CLASSES_ROOT\CLSID\{00020D31-0000-0000-C000-000000000046}]
@="IPM.Note"
[HKEY_CLASSES_ROOT\CLSID\{00020D31-0000-0000-C000-
000000000046}\InprocHandler32]
@="mapi32.dll"
[HKEY_CLASSES_ROOT\CLSID\{00020D31-0000-0000-C000-
000000000046}\LocalServer32]
@="C:\\Program Files\\Windows NT\\Windows Messaging\\exchng32.exe"
[HKEY_CLASSES_ROOT\CLSID\{00020D32-0000-0000-C000-000000000046}]
@="IPM.Document"

[HKEY_CLASSES_ROOT\CLSID\{00020D32-0000-0000-C000-000000000046}\InprocHandler32]
@="mapi32.dll"
[HKEY_CLASSES_ROOT\CLSID\{00020D32-0000-0000-C000-000000000046}\LocalServer32]
@="C:\\Program Files\\Windows NT\\Windows Messaging\\exchng32.exe"
[HKEY_CLASSES_ROOT\CLSID\{00020D33-0000-0000-C000-000000000046}]
@="IPM.Resend"
[HKEY_CLASSES_ROOT\CLSID\{00020D33-0000-0000-C000-000000000046}\InprocHandler32]
@="mapi32.dll"
[HKEY_CLASSES_ROOT\CLSID\{00020D33-0000-0000-C000-000000000046}\LocalServer32]
@="C:\\Program Files\\Windows NT\\Windows Messaging\\exchng32.exe"
[HKEY_CLASSES_ROOT\CLSID\{00020D34-0000-0000-C000-000000000046}]
@="Report.Any"
[HKEY_CLASSES_ROOT\CLSID\{00020D34-0000-0000-C000-000000000046}\InprocHandler32]
@="mapi32.dll"
[HKEY_CLASSES_ROOT\CLSID\{00020D34-0000-0000-C000-000000000046}\LocalServer32]
@="C:\\Program Files\\Windows NT\\Windows Messaging\\exchng32.exe"
[HKEY_CLASSES_ROOT\CLSID\{00020D35-0000-0000-C000-000000000046}]
@="IPM.POST"
[HKEY_CLASSES_ROOT\CLSID\{00020D35-0000-0000-C000-000000000046}\InprocHandler32]
@="mapi32.dll"
[HKEY_CLASSES_ROOT\CLSID\{00020D35-0000-0000-C000-000000000046}\LocalServer32]
@="C:\\Program Files\\Windows NT\\Windows Messaging\\exchng32.exe"
[HKEY_CLASSES_ROOT\CLSID\{00020D75-0000-0000-C000-000000000046}]
@="Inbox"
[HKEY_CLASSES_ROOT\CLSID\{00020D75-0000-0000-C000-000000000046}\DefaultIcon]
@="C:\\Program Files\\Windows NT\\Windows Messaging\\exchng32.exe"
[HKEY_CLASSES_ROOT\CLSID\{00020D75-0000-0000-C000-000000000046}\InProcServer32]
@="C:\\Program Files\\Windows NT\\Windows Messaging\\mlshext.dll"
"ThreadingModel"="Apartment"
[HKEY_CLASSES_ROOT\CLSID\{00020D75-0000-0000-C000-000000000046}\Shell]
[HKEY_CLASSES_ROOT\CLSID\{00020D75-0000-0000-C000-000000000046}\Shell\Explore]

[HKEY_CLASSES_ROOT\CLSID\{00020D75-0000-0000-C000-000000000046}\Shell\Explore\Command]
@="\"C:\\Program Files\\Windows NT\\Windows Messaging\\exchng32.exe\" /j"
[HKEY_CLASSES_ROOT\CLSID\{00020D75-0000-0000-C000-000000000046}\Shell\Open]
[HKEY_CLASSES_ROOT\CLSID\{00020D75-0000-0000-C000-000000000046}\Shell\Open\Command]
@="\"C:\\Program Files\\Windows NT\\Windows Messaging\\exchng32.exe\" /i"
[HKEY_CLASSES_ROOT\CLSID\{00020D75-0000-0000-C000-000000000046}\shellex]
[HKEY_CLASSES_ROOT\CLSID\{00020D75-0000-0000-C000-000000000046}\shellex\PropertySheetHandlers]
[HKEY_CLASSES_ROOT\CLSID\{00020D75-0000-0000-C000-000000000046}\shellex\PropertySheetHandlers\{00020D75-0000-0000-C000-000000000046}]
@=""
[HKEY_CLASSES_ROOT\CLSID\{00020D75-0000-0000-C000-000000000046}\ShellFolder]
"Attributes"=hex:50,00,00,00
[HKEY_CLASSES_ROOT\CLSID\{00021400-0000-0000-C000-000000000046}]
@="Desktop"
[HKEY_CLASSES_ROOT\CLSID\{00021400-0000-0000-C000-000000000046}\InProcServer32]
@="shell32.dll"
"ThreadingModel"="Apartment"
[HKEY_CLASSES_ROOT\CLSID\{00021401-0000-0000-C000-000000000046}]
@="Shortcut"
[HKEY_CLASSES_ROOT\CLSID\{00021401-0000-0000-C000-000000000046}\InProcServer32]
@="shell32.dll"
"ThreadingModel"="Apartment"
[HKEY_CLASSES_ROOT\CLSID\{00021401-0000-0000-C000-000000000046}\shellex]
[HKEY_CLASSES_ROOT\CLSID\{00021401-0000-0000-C000-000000000046}\shellex\MayChangeDefaultMenu]
[HKEY_CLASSES_ROOT\CLSID\{00022601-0000-0000-C000-000000000046}]
@="Media Clip"
"AppID"="{00022601-0000-0000-C000-000000000046}"
[HKEY_CLASSES_ROOT\CLSID\{00022601-0000-0000-C000-000000000046}\AuxUserType]

[HKEY_CLASSES_ROOT\CLSID\{00022601-0000-0000-C000-
000000000046}\AuxUserType\2]
@="Media Clip"
[HKEY_CLASSES_ROOT\CLSID\{00022601-0000-0000-C000-
000000000046}\DataFormats]
[HKEY_CLASSES_ROOT\CLSID\{00022601-0000-0000-C000-
000000000046}\DataFormats\DefaultSet]
@="MPlayer"
[HKEY_CLASSES_ROOT\CLSID\{00022601-0000-0000-C000-
000000000046}\DataFormats\GetSet]
[HKEY_CLASSES_ROOT\CLSID\{00022601-0000-0000-C000-
000000000046}\DataFormats\GetSet\0]
@="Embed Source,1,8,1"
[HKEY_CLASSES_ROOT\CLSID\{00022601-0000-0000-C000-
000000000046}\DataFormats\GetSet\1]
@="3,1,32,1"
[HKEY_CLASSES_ROOT\CLSID\{00022601-0000-0000-C000-
000000000046}\DataFormats\GetSet\2]
@="8,1,1,1"
[HKEY_CLASSES_ROOT\CLSID\{00022601-0000-0000-C000-
000000000046}\DefaultIcon]
@="mplay32.exe,1"
[HKEY_CLASSES_ROOT\CLSID\{00022601-0000-0000-C000-
000000000046}\InprocHandler32]
@="ole32.dll"
[HKEY_CLASSES_ROOT\CLSID\{00022601-0000-0000-C000-
000000000046}\Insertable]
@=""
[HKEY_CLASSES_ROOT\CLSID\{00022601-0000-0000-C000-
000000000046}\LocalServer]
@="mplay32.exe"
[HKEY_CLASSES_ROOT\CLSID\{00022601-0000-0000-C000-
000000000046}\LocalServer32]
@="mplay32.exe"
[HKEY_CLASSES_ROOT\CLSID\{00022601-0000-0000-C000-
000000000046}\MiscStatus]
@="0"
[HKEY_CLASSES_ROOT\CLSID\{00022601-0000-0000-C000-
000000000046}\ProgID]
@="MPlayer"
[HKEY_CLASSES_ROOT\CLSID\{00022601-0000-0000-C000-
000000000046}\verb]

[HKEY_CLASSES_ROOT\CLSID\{00022601-0000-0000-C000-000000000046}\verb\0]
@="&Play,0,3"
[HKEY_CLASSES_ROOT\CLSID\{00022601-0000-0000-C000-000000000046}\verb\1]
@="&Edit,0,2"
[HKEY_CLASSES_ROOT\CLSID\{00022601-0000-0000-C000-000000000046}\verb\2]
@="&Open,0,2"
[HKEY_CLASSES_ROOT\CLSID\{00022602-0000-0000-C000-000000000046}]
@="Video Clip"
"AppID"="{00022601-0000-0000-C000-000000000046}"
[HKEY_CLASSES_ROOT\CLSID\{00022602-0000-0000-C000-000000000046}\AuxUserType]
[HKEY_CLASSES_ROOT\CLSID\{00022602-0000-0000-C000-000000000046}\AuxUserType\2]
@="Video Clip"
[HKEY_CLASSES_ROOT\CLSID\{00022602-0000-0000-C000-000000000046}\DataFormats]
[HKEY_CLASSES_ROOT\CLSID\{00022602-0000-0000-C000-000000000046}\DataFormats\DefaultSet]
@="AVIFile"
[HKEY_CLASSES_ROOT\CLSID\{00022602-0000-0000-C000-000000000046}\DataFormats\GetSet]
[HKEY_CLASSES_ROOT\CLSID\{00022602-0000-0000-C000-000000000046}\DataFormats\GetSet\0]
@="Embed Source,1,8,1"
[HKEY_CLASSES_ROOT\CLSID\{00022602-0000-0000-C000-000000000046}\DataFormats\GetSet\1]
@="3,1,32,1"
[HKEY_CLASSES_ROOT\CLSID\{00022602-0000-0000-C000-000000000046}\DataFormats\GetSet\2]
@="8,1,1,1"
[HKEY_CLASSES_ROOT\CLSID\{00022602-0000-0000-C000-000000000046}\DefaultIcon]
@="mplay32.exe,3"
[HKEY_CLASSES_ROOT\CLSID\{00022602-0000-0000-C000-000000000046}\InprocHandler32]
@="ole32.dll"
[HKEY_CLASSES_ROOT\CLSID\{00022602-0000-0000-C000-000000000046}\Insertable]
@=""

[HKEY_CLASSES_ROOT\CLSID\{00022602-0000-0000-C000-000000000046}\LocalServer]
@="mplay32.exe /avi"
[HKEY_CLASSES_ROOT\CLSID\{00022602-0000-0000-C000-000000000046}\LocalServer32]
@="mplay32.exe /avi"
[HKEY_CLASSES_ROOT\CLSID\{00022602-0000-0000-C000-000000000046}\MiscStatus]
@="0"
[HKEY_CLASSES_ROOT\CLSID\{00022602-0000-0000-C000-000000000046}\ProgID]
@="AVIFile"
[HKEY_CLASSES_ROOT\CLSID\{00022602-0000-0000-C000-000000000046}\verb]
[HKEY_CLASSES_ROOT\CLSID\{00022602-0000-0000-C000-000000000046}\verb\0]
@="&Play,0,3"
[HKEY_CLASSES_ROOT\CLSID\{00022602-0000-0000-C000-000000000046}\verb\1]
@="&Edit,0,2"
[HKEY_CLASSES_ROOT\CLSID\{00022602-0000-0000-C000-000000000046}\verb\2]
@="&Open,0,2"
[HKEY_CLASSES_ROOT\CLSID\{00022603-0000-0000-C000-000000000046}]
@="MIDI Sequence"
"AppID"="{00022601-0000-0000-C000-000000000046}"
[HKEY_CLASSES_ROOT\CLSID\{00022603-0000-0000-C000-000000000046}\AuxUserType]
[HKEY_CLASSES_ROOT\CLSID\{00022603-0000-0000-C000-000000000046}\AuxUserType\2]
@="MIDI Sequence"
[HKEY_CLASSES_ROOT\CLSID\{00022603-0000-0000-C000-000000000046}\DataFormats]
[HKEY_CLASSES_ROOT\CLSID\{00022603-0000-0000-C000-000000000046}\DataFormats\DefaultSet]
@="MIDFile"
[HKEY_CLASSES_ROOT\CLSID\{00022603-0000-0000-C000-000000000046}\DataFormats\GetSet]
[HKEY_CLASSES_ROOT\CLSID\{00022603-0000-0000-C000-000000000046}\DataFormats\GetSet\0]
@="Embed Source,1,8,1"
[HKEY_CLASSES_ROOT\CLSID\{00022603-0000-0000-C000-000000000046}\DataFormats\GetSet\1]

@="3,1,32,1"
[HKEY_CLASSES_ROOT\CLSID\{00022603-0000-0000-C000-
000000000046}\DataFormats\GetSet\2]
@="8,1,1,1"
[HKEY_CLASSES_ROOT\CLSID\{00022603-0000-0000-C000-
000000000046}\DefaultIcon]
@="mplay32.exe,5"
[HKEY_CLASSES_ROOT\CLSID\{00022603-0000-0000-C000-
000000000046}\InprocHandler32]
@="ole32.dll"
[HKEY_CLASSES_ROOT\CLSID\{00022603-0000-0000-C000-
000000000046}\Insertable]
@=""
[HKEY_CLASSES_ROOT\CLSID\{00022603-0000-0000-C000-
000000000046}\LocalServer]
@="mplay32.exe /mid"
[HKEY_CLASSES_ROOT\CLSID\{00022603-0000-0000-C000-
000000000046}\LocalServer32]
@="mplay32.exe /mid"
[HKEY_CLASSES_ROOT\CLSID\{00022603-0000-0000-C000-
000000000046}\MiscStatus]
@="0"
[HKEY_CLASSES_ROOT\CLSID\{00022603-0000-0000-C000-
000000000046}\ProgID]
@="MIDFile"
[HKEY_CLASSES_ROOT\CLSID\{00022603-0000-0000-C000-
000000000046}\verb]
[HKEY_CLASSES_ROOT\CLSID\{00022603-0000-0000-C000-
000000000046}\verb\0]
@="&Play,0,3"
[HKEY_CLASSES_ROOT\CLSID\{00022603-0000-0000-C000-
000000000046}\verb\1]
@="&Edit,0,2"
[HKEY_CLASSES_ROOT\CLSID\{00022603-0000-0000-C000-
000000000046}\verb\2]
@="&Open,0,2"
[HKEY_CLASSES_ROOT\CLSID\{00022613-0000-0000-C000-000000000046}]
@="Multimedia File Property Sheet"
[HKEY_CLASSES_ROOT\CLSID\{00022613-0000-0000-C000-
000000000046}\InProcServer32]
@="mmsys.cpl"
"ThreadingModel"="Apartment"

[HKEY_CLASSES_ROOT\CLSID\{00030007-0000-0000-C000-000000000046}]
@="Microsoft Drawing"
[HKEY_CLASSES_ROOT\CLSID\{00030007-0000-0000-C000-000000000046}\MiscStatus]
@="512"
[HKEY_CLASSES_ROOT\CLSID\{00030007-0000-0000-C000-000000000046}\Ole1Class]
@="MSDraw"
[HKEY_CLASSES_ROOT\CLSID\{00030007-0000-0000-C000-000000000046}\ProgID]
@="MSDraw"
[HKEY_CLASSES_ROOT\CLSID\{0003000a-0000-0000-C000-000000000046}]
@="Paintbrush Picture"
[HKEY_CLASSES_ROOT\CLSID\{0003000a-0000-0000-C000-000000000046}\Conversion]
[HKEY_CLASSES_ROOT\CLSID\{0003000a-0000-0000-C000-000000000046}\Conversion\Readable]
[HKEY_CLASSES_ROOT\CLSID\{0003000a-0000-0000-C000-000000000046}\Conversion\Readable\Main]
@="8"
[HKEY_CLASSES_ROOT\CLSID\{0003000a-0000-0000-C000-000000000046}\MiscStatus]
@="512"
[HKEY_CLASSES_ROOT\CLSID\{0003000a-0000-0000-C000-000000000046}\Ole1Class]
@="PBrush"
[HKEY_CLASSES_ROOT\CLSID\{0003000a-0000-0000-C000-000000000046}\ProgID]
@="PBrush"
[HKEY_CLASSES_ROOT\CLSID\{0003000a-0000-0000-C000-000000000046}\TreatAs]
@="{D3E34B21-9D75-101A-8C3D-00AA001A1652}"
[HKEY_CLASSES_ROOT\CLSID\{0003000C-0000-0000-C000-000000000046}]
@="Package"
[HKEY_CLASSES_ROOT\CLSID\{0003000C-0000-0000-C000-000000000046}\Ole1Class]
@="Package"
[HKEY_CLASSES_ROOT\CLSID\{0003000C-0000-0000-C000-000000000046}\ProgID]
@="Package"
[HKEY_CLASSES_ROOT\CLSID\{0003000D-0000-0000-C000-000000000046}]
@="Sound"

[HKEY_CLASSES_ROOT\CLSID\{0003000D-0000-0000-C000-000000000046}\Insertable]
@=""
[HKEY_CLASSES_ROOT\CLSID\{0003000D-0000-0000-C000-000000000046}\Ole1Class]
@="SoundRec"
[HKEY_CLASSES_ROOT\CLSID\{0003000D-0000-0000-C000-000000000046}\ProgID]
@="SoundRec"
[HKEY_CLASSES_ROOT\CLSID\{0003000D-0000-0000-C000-000000000046}\TreatAs]
@="{00020C01-0000-0000-C000-000000000046}"
[HKEY_CLASSES_ROOT\CLSID\{0003000E-0000-0000-C000-000000000046}]
@="Media Clip"
[HKEY_CLASSES_ROOT\CLSID\{0003000E-0000-0000-C000-000000000046}\Insertable]
@=""
[HKEY_CLASSES_ROOT\CLSID\{0003000E-0000-0000-C000-000000000046}\Ole1Class]
@="MPlayer"
[HKEY_CLASSES_ROOT\CLSID\{0003000E-0000-0000-C000-000000000046}\ProgID]
@="MPlayer"
[HKEY_CLASSES_ROOT\CLSID\{0003000E-0000-0000-C000-000000000046}\TreatAs]
@="{00022601-0000-0000-C000-000000000046}"
[HKEY_CLASSES_ROOT\CLSID\{009541A0-3B81-101C-92F3-040224009C02}]
@="Wang Image Admin Control"
[HKEY_CLASSES_ROOT\CLSID\{009541A0-3B81-101C-92F3-040224009C02}\Control]
@=""
[HKEY_CLASSES_ROOT\CLSID\{009541A0-3B81-101C-92F3-040224009C02}\InprocServer32]
@="C:\\WINNT\\System32\\IMGADMIN.OCX"
[HKEY_CLASSES_ROOT\CLSID\{009541A0-3B81-101C-92F3-040224009C02}\MiscStatus]
@="0"
[HKEY_CLASSES_ROOT\CLSID\{009541A0-3B81-101C-92F3-040224009C02}\MiscStatus\1]
@="132241"
[HKEY_CLASSES_ROOT\CLSID\{009541A0-3B81-101C-92F3-040224009C02}\ProgID]
@="WangImage.AdminCtrl.1"

[HKEY_CLASSES_ROOT\CLSID\{009541A0-3B81-101C-92F3-040224009C02}\ToolboxBitmap32]
@="C:\\WINNT\\System32\\IMGADMIN.OCX, 1"
[HKEY_CLASSES_ROOT\CLSID\{009541A0-3B81-101C-92F3-040224009C02}\TypeLib]
@="{009541A3-3B81-101C-92F3-040224009C02}"
[HKEY_CLASSES_ROOT\CLSID\{009541A0-3B81-101C-92F3-040224009C02}\Version]
@="1.0"
[HKEY_CLASSES_ROOT\CLSID\{009541A4-3B81-101C-92F3-040224009C02}]
@="Wang Image Admin Property Page"
[HKEY_CLASSES_ROOT\CLSID\{009541A4-3B81-101C-92F3-040224009C02}\InprocServer32]
@="C:\\WINNT\\System32\\IMGADMIN.OCX"
[HKEY_CLASSES_ROOT\CLSID\{02B01C80-E03D-101A-B294-00DD010F2BF9}]
@="Image Document"
[HKEY_CLASSES_ROOT\CLSID\{02B01C80-E03D-101A-B294-00DD010F2BF9}\AuxUserType]
@=""
[HKEY_CLASSES_ROOT\CLSID\{02B01C80-E03D-101A-B294-00DD010F2BF9}\AuxUserType\2]
@="Image Document"
[HKEY_CLASSES_ROOT\CLSID\{02B01C80-E03D-101A-B294-00DD010F2BF9}\AuxUserType\3]
@="Imaging"
[HKEY_CLASSES_ROOT\CLSID\{02B01C80-E03D-101A-B294-00DD010F2BF9}\DefaultIcon]
@="C:\\Program Files\\Windows NT\\Accessories\\ImageVue\\WangImg.Exe,0"
[HKEY_CLASSES_ROOT\CLSID\{02B01C80-E03D-101A-B294-00DD010F2BF9}\InprocHandler32]
@="ole32.dll"
[HKEY_CLASSES_ROOT\CLSID\{02B01C80-E03D-101A-B294-00DD010F2BF9}\Insertable]
@=""
[HKEY_CLASSES_ROOT\CLSID\{02B01C80-E03D-101A-B294-00DD010F2BF9}\LocalServer32]
@="C:\\Program Files\\Windows NT\\Accessories\\ImageVue\\WangImg.Exe"
[HKEY_CLASSES_ROOT\CLSID\{02B01C80-E03D-101A-B294-00DD010F2BF9}\MiscStatus]
@="32"

[HKEY_CLASSES_ROOT\CLSID\{02B01C80-E03D-101A-B294-00DD010F2BF9}\ProgID]
@="WangImage.Document"
[HKEY_CLASSES_ROOT\CLSID\{02B01C80-E03D-101A-B294-00DD010F2BF9}\Verb]
@=""
[HKEY_CLASSES_ROOT\CLSID\{02B01C80-E03D-101A-B294-00DD010F2BF9}\Verb\0]
@="&Edit,0,2"
[HKEY_CLASSES_ROOT\CLSID\{02B01C80-E03D-101A-B294-00DD010F2BF9}\Verb\1]
@="&Open,0,2"
[HKEY_CLASSES_ROOT\CLSID\{02B01C80-E03D-101A-B294-00DD010F2BF9}\Verb\2]
@="&Print,0,2"
[HKEY_CLASSES_ROOT\CLSID\{1B53F360-9A1B-1069-930C-00AA0030EBC8}]
@="HyperTerminal Connection Page Ext"
[HKEY_CLASSES_ROOT\CLSID\{1B53F360-9A1B-1069-930C-00AA0030EBC8}\InProcServer32]
@="C:\\WINNT\\System32\\hypertrm.dll"
"ThreadingModel"="Apartment"
[HKEY_CLASSES_ROOT\CLSID\{1D3ECD40-C835-11CE-9888-00608CC22020}]
@="Wang Image Shell Extension"
[HKEY_CLASSES_ROOT\CLSID\{1D3ECD40-C835-11CE-9888-00608CC22020}\InProcServer32]
@="wangshl.dll"
"ThreadingModel"="Apartment"
[HKEY_CLASSES_ROOT\CLSID\{1F2E5C40-9550-11CE-99D2-00AA006E086C}]
@="Security Shell Extension"
[HKEY_CLASSES_ROOT\CLSID\{1F2E5C40-9550-11CE-99D2-00AA006E086C}\InProcServer32]
@="rshx32.dll"
"ThreadingModel"="Apartment"
[HKEY_CLASSES_ROOT\CLSID\{208D2C60-3AEA-1069-A2D7-08002B30309D}]
@="Network Neighborhood"
[HKEY_CLASSES_ROOT\CLSID\{208D2C60-3AEA-1069-A2D7-08002B30309D}\DefaultIcon]
@=hex(2):25,53,79,73,74,65,6d,52,6f,6f,74,25,5c,73,79,73,74,65,6d,33,32,5c,73,\
  68,65,6c,6c,33,32,2e,64,6c,6c,2c,31,37,00

[HKEY_CLASSES_ROOT\CLSID\{208D2C60-3AEA-1069-A2D7-
08002B30309D}\InProcServer32]
@="shell32.dll"
"ThreadingModel"="Apartment"
[HKEY_CLASSES_ROOT\CLSID\{208D2C60-3AEA-1069-A2D7-
08002B30309D}\shell]
[HKEY_CLASSES_ROOT\CLSID\{208D2C60-3AEA-1069-A2D7-
08002B30309D}\shell\find]
@="&Find Computer..."
[HKEY_CLASSES_ROOT\CLSID\{208D2C60-3AEA-1069-A2D7-
08002B30309D}\shell\find\command]
@=hex(2):25,53,79,73,74,65,6d,52,6f,6f,74,25,5c,45,78,70,6c,6f,72,65,72,2e,65,\
  78,65,00
[HKEY_CLASSES_ROOT\CLSID\{208D2C60-3AEA-1069-A2D7-
08002B30309D}\shell\find\ddeexec]
@="[FindFolder(\"%l\", %I)]"
[HKEY_CLASSES_ROOT\CLSID\{208D2C60-3AEA-1069-A2D7-
08002B30309D}\shell\find\ddeexec\application]
@="Folders"
[HKEY_CLASSES_ROOT\CLSID\{208D2C60-3AEA-1069-A2D7-
08002B30309D}\shell\find\ddeexec\topic]
@="AppProperties"
[HKEY_CLASSES_ROOT\CLSID\{20D04FE0-3AEA-1069-A2D8-
08002B30309D}]
@="My Computer"
[HKEY_CLASSES_ROOT\CLSID\{20D04FE0-3AEA-1069-A2D8-
08002B30309D}\DefaultIcon]
@=hex(2):25,53,79,73,74,65,6d,52,6f,6f,74,25,5c,45,78,70,6c,6f,72,65,72,2e,65,\
  78,65,2c,30,00
[HKEY_CLASSES_ROOT\CLSID\{20D04FE0-3AEA-1069-A2D8-
08002B30309D}\InProcServer32]
@="shell32.dll"
"ThreadingModel"="Apartment"
[HKEY_CLASSES_ROOT\CLSID\{20D04FE0-3AEA-1069-A2D8-
08002B30309D}\shell]
[HKEY_CLASSES_ROOT\CLSID\{20D04FE0-3AEA-1069-A2D8-
08002B30309D}\shell\find]
[HKEY_CLASSES_ROOT\CLSID\{20D04FE0-3AEA-1069-A2D8-
08002B30309D}\shell\find\command]
@=hex(2):25,53,79,73,74,65,6d,52,6f,6f,74,25,5c,45,78,70,6c,6f,72,65,72,2e,65,78,65,
00

[HKEY_CLASSES_ROOT\CLSID\{20D04FE0-3AEA-1069-A2D8-08002B30309D}\shell\find\ddeexec]
@="[FindFolder(\"%l\", %I)]"
[HKEY_CLASSES_ROOT\CLSID\{20D04FE0-3AEA-1069-A2D8-08002B30309D}\shell\find\ddeexec\application]
@="Folders"
[HKEY_CLASSES_ROOT\CLSID\{20D04FE0-3AEA-1069-A2D8-08002B30309D}\shell\find\ddeexec\topic]
@="AppProperties"
[HKEY_CLASSES_ROOT\CLSID\{217FC9C0-3AEA-1069-A2DB-08002B30309D}]
@="Shell Copy Hook"
[HKEY_CLASSES_ROOT\CLSID\{217FC9C0-3AEA-1069-A2DB-08002B30309D}\InProcServer32]
@="shell32.dll"
"ThreadingModel"="Apartment"
[HKEY_CLASSES_ROOT\CLSID\{21B22460-3AEA-1069-A2DC-08002B30309D}]
@="File system attributes"
[HKEY_CLASSES_ROOT\CLSID\{21B22460-3AEA-1069-A2DC-08002B30309D}\InProcServer32]
@="shell32.dll"
"ThreadingModel"="Apartment"
[HKEY_CLASSES_ROOT\CLSID\{21EC2020-3AEA-1069-A2DD-08002B30309D}]
@="Control Panel"
[HKEY_CLASSES_ROOT\CLSID\{21EC2020-3AEA-1069-A2DD-08002B30309D}\DefaultIcon]
@=hex(2):25,53,79,73,74,65,6d,52,6f,6f,74,25,5c,53,79,73,74,65,6d,33,32,5c,73,\
  68,65,6c,6c,33,32,2e,64,6c,6c,2c,2d,31,33,37,00
[HKEY_CLASSES_ROOT\CLSID\{21EC2020-3AEA-1069-A2DD-08002B30309D}\InProcServer32]
@="shell32.dll"
"ThreadingModel"="Apartment"
[HKEY_CLASSES_ROOT\CLSID\{2227A280-3AEA-1069-A2DE-08002B30309D}]
@="Printers"
[HKEY_CLASSES_ROOT\CLSID\{2227A280-3AEA-1069-A2DE-08002B30309D}\DefaultIcon]
@=hex(2):25,53,79,73,74,65,6d,52,6f,6f,74,25,5c,53,79,73,74,65,6d,33,32,5c,73,\
  68,65,6c,6c,33,32,2e,64,6c,6c,2c,2d,31,33,38,00

[HKEY_CLASSES_ROOT\CLSID\{2227A280-3AEA-1069-A2DE-08002B30309D}\InProcServer32]
@="shell32.dll"
"ThreadingModel"="Apartment"
[HKEY_CLASSES_ROOT\CLSID\{2227A280-3AEA-1069-A2DE-08002B30309D}\ShellFolder]
"Attributes"=hex:04,00,00,20
[HKEY_CLASSES_ROOT\CLSID\{3EA48300-8CF6-101B-84FB-666CCB9BCD32}]
@="OLE Docfile Property Page"
[HKEY_CLASSES_ROOT\CLSID\{3EA48300-8CF6-101B-84FB-666CCB9BCD32}\InProcServer32]
@="docprop.dll"
"ThreadingModel"="Apartment"
[HKEY_CLASSES_ROOT\CLSID\{3FA7DEB3-6438-101B-ACC1-00AA00423326}]
@="MAPI 1.0 Session (v1.0)"
[HKEY_CLASSES_ROOT\CLSID\{3FA7DEB3-6438-101B-ACC1-00AA00423326}\LocalServer32]
@="MDISP32.EXE /Automation"
[HKEY_CLASSES_ROOT\CLSID\{3FA7DEB3-6438-101B-ACC1-00AA00423326}\ProgID]
@="MAPI.Session"
[HKEY_CLASSES_ROOT\CLSID\{3FA7DEB4-6438-101B-ACC1-00AA00423326}]
@="MAPI 1.0 Message (v1.0)"
[HKEY_CLASSES_ROOT\CLSID\{3FA7DEB4-6438-101B-ACC1-00AA00423326}\LocalServer32]
@="MDISP32.EXE /Automation"
[HKEY_CLASSES_ROOT\CLSID\{3FA7DEB4-6438-101B-ACC1-00AA00423326}\ProgID]
@="MAPI.Message"
[HKEY_CLASSES_ROOT\CLSID\{3FA7DEB5-6438-101B-ACC1-00AA00423326}]
@="MAPI 1.0 Folder (v1.0)"
[HKEY_CLASSES_ROOT\CLSID\{3FA7DEB5-6438-101B-ACC1-00AA00423326}\LocalServer32]
@="MDISP32.EXE /Automation"
[HKEY_CLASSES_ROOT\CLSID\{3FA7DEB5-6438-101B-ACC1-00AA00423326}\ProgID]
@="MAPI.Folder"
[HKEY_CLASSES_ROOT\CLSID\{40dd6e20-7c17-11ce-a804-00aa003ca9f6}]
@="Shell extensions for sharing"

[HKEY_CLASSES_ROOT\CLSID\{40dd6e20-7c17-11ce-a804-00aa003ca9f6}\InProcServer32]
@="ntshrui.dll"
"ThreadingModel"="Apartment"
[HKEY_CLASSES_ROOT\CLSID\{41E300E0-78B6-11ce-849B-444553540000}]
@="PlusPack CPL Extension"
[HKEY_CLASSES_ROOT\CLSID\{41E300E0-78B6-11ce-849B-444553540000}\InProcServer32]
@="plustab.dll"
"ThreadingModel"="Apartment"
[HKEY_CLASSES_ROOT\CLSID\{47D4D946-62E8-11cf-93BC-444553540000}]
@="DirectSound Object"
[HKEY_CLASSES_ROOT\CLSID\{47D4D946-62E8-11cf-93BC-444553540000}\InprocServer32]
@="dsound.dll"
[HKEY_CLASSES_ROOT\CLSID\{4d2f086c-6ea3-101b-a18a-00aa00446e07}]
@="MAPIPSFactory"
[HKEY_CLASSES_ROOT\CLSID\{4d2f086c-6ea3-101b-a18a-00aa00446e07}\InprocServer]
@="mapi.dll"
[HKEY_CLASSES_ROOT\CLSID\{4d2f086c-6ea3-101b-a18a-00aa00446e07}\InprocServer32]
@="mapi32.dll"
[HKEY_CLASSES_ROOT\CLSID\{56117100-C0CD-101B-81E2-00AA004AE837}]
@="Shell Scrap DataHandler"
[HKEY_CLASSES_ROOT\CLSID\{56117100-C0CD-101B-81E2-00AA004AE837}\InProcServer32]
@="shscrap.dll"
"ThreadingModel"="Apartment"
[HKEY_CLASSES_ROOT\CLSID\{59099400-57FF-11CE-BD94-0020AF85B590}]
@="Disk Copy Extension"
[HKEY_CLASSES_ROOT\CLSID\{59099400-57FF-11CE-BD94-0020AF85B590}\InProcServer32]
@="diskcopy.dll"
"ThreadingModel"="Apartment"
[HKEY_CLASSES_ROOT\CLSID\{593817A0-7DB3-11CF-A2DE-00AA00B93356}]
@="DirectDraw Clipper Object"
[HKEY_CLASSES_ROOT\CLSID\{593817A0-7DB3-11CF-A2DE-00AA00B93356}\InprocServer32]
@="ddraw.dll"

[HKEY_CLASSES_ROOT\CLSID\{59be4990-f85c-11ce-aff7-00aa003ca9f6}]
@="Shell extensions for Microsoft Windows Network objects"
[HKEY_CLASSES_ROOT\CLSID\{59be4990-f85c-11ce-aff7-
00aa003ca9f6}\InProcServer32]
@="ntlanui2.dll"
"ThreadingModel"="Apartment"
[HKEY_CLASSES_ROOT\CLSID\{61E218E0-65D3-101B-9F08-
061CEAC3D50D}]
@="ShellFind"
[HKEY_CLASSES_ROOT\CLSID\{61E218E0-65D3-101B-9F08-
061CEAC3D50D}\InProcServer32]
@="shell32.dll"
"ThreadingModel"="Apartment"
[HKEY_CLASSES_ROOT\CLSID\{64455860-5153-101C-816F-0E6013114B7F}]
@="Image Property Page"
[HKEY_CLASSES_ROOT\CLSID\{64455860-5153-101C-816F-
0E6013114B7F}\InProcServer32]
@="C:\\WINNT\\System32\\IMGSCAN.OCX"
[HKEY_CLASSES_ROOT\CLSID\{645FF040-5081-101B-9F08-00AA002F954E}]
@="Recycle Bin"
[HKEY_CLASSES_ROOT\CLSID\{645FF040-5081-101B-9F08-
00AA002F954E}\DefaultIcon]
@=hex(2):25,53,79,73,74,65,6d,52,6f,6f,74,25,5c,53,79,73,74,65,6d,33,32,5c,73,68,
65,6c,6c,33,32,2e,64,6c,6c,2c,33,31,00
"Empty"=hex(2):25,53,79,73,74,65,6d,52,6f,6f,74,25,5c,53,79,73,74,65,6d,33,32,5c,
73,68,65,6c,6c,33,32,2e,64,6c,6c,2c,33,31,00
"Full"=hex(2):25,53,79,73,74,65,6d,52,6f,6f,74,25,5c,53,79,73,74,65,6d,33,32,5c,73,
68,65,6c,6c,33,32,2e,64,6c,6c,2c,33,32,00
[HKEY_CLASSES_ROOT\CLSID\{645FF040-5081-101B-9F08-
00AA002F954E}\InProcServer32]
@="shell32.dll"
"ThreadingModel"="Apartment"
[HKEY_CLASSES_ROOT\CLSID\{645FF040-5081-101B-9F08-
00AA002F954E}\shellex]
[HKEY_CLASSES_ROOT\CLSID\{645FF040-5081-101B-9F08-
00AA002F954E}\shellex\ContextMenuHandlers]
[HKEY_CLASSES_ROOT\CLSID\{645FF040-5081-101B-9F08-
00AA002F954E}\shellex\ContextMenuHandlers\{645FF040-5081-101B-9F08-
00AA002F954E}]
[HKEY_CLASSES_ROOT\CLSID\{645FF040-5081-101B-9F08-
00AA002F954E}\shellex\PropertySheetHandlers]

[HKEY_CLASSES_ROOT\CLSID\{645FF040-5081-101B-9F08-00AA002F954E}\shellex\PropertySheetHandlers\{645FF040-5081-101B-9F08-00AA002F954E}]
[HKEY_CLASSES_ROOT\CLSID\{645FF040-5081-101B-9F08-00AA002F954E}\ShellFolder]
"Attributes"=hex:40,01,00,20
[HKEY_CLASSES_ROOT\CLSID\{69E2DD40-5321-101C-96BF-040224009C02}]
@="Wang Image Admin Help Page"
[HKEY_CLASSES_ROOT\CLSID\{69E2DD40-5321-101C-96BF-040224009C02}\InProcServer32]
@="C:\\WINNT\\System32\\IMGADMIN.OCX"
[HKEY_CLASSES_ROOT\CLSID\{6D940280-9F11-11CE-83FD-02608C3EC08A}]
@="Wang Image Edit Control"
[HKEY_CLASSES_ROOT\CLSID\{6D940280-9F11-11CE-83FD-02608C3EC08A}\Control]
@=""
[HKEY_CLASSES_ROOT\CLSID\{6D940280-9F11-11CE-83FD-02608C3EC08A}\InprocServer32]
@="C:\\WINNT\\System32\\IMGEDIT.OCX"
[HKEY_CLASSES_ROOT\CLSID\{6D940280-9F11-11CE-83FD-02608C3EC08A}\MiscStatus]
@="0"
[HKEY_CLASSES_ROOT\CLSID\{6D940280-9F11-11CE-83FD-02608C3EC08A}\MiscStatus\1]
@="197009"
[HKEY_CLASSES_ROOT\CLSID\{6D940280-9F11-11CE-83FD-02608C3EC08A}\ProgID]
@="WangImage.EditCtrl.1"
[HKEY_CLASSES_ROOT\CLSID\{6D940280-9F11-11CE-83FD-02608C3EC08A}\ToolboxBitmap32]
@="C:\\WINNT\\System32\\IMGEDIT.OCX, 1"
[HKEY_CLASSES_ROOT\CLSID\{6D940280-9F11-11CE-83FD-02608C3EC08A}\TypeLib]
@="{6D940288-9F11-11CE-83FD-02608C3EC08A}"
[HKEY_CLASSES_ROOT\CLSID\{6D940280-9F11-11CE-83FD-02608C3EC08A}\Version]
@="1.0"
[HKEY_CLASSES_ROOT\CLSID\{6D940284-9F11-11CE-83FD-02608C3EC08A}]
@="Wang Image Edit Property Page"

[HKEY_CLASSES_ROOT\CLSID\{6D940284-9F11-11CE-83FD-
02608C3EC08A}\InprocServer32]
@="C:\\WINNT\\System32\\IMGEDIT.OCX"
[HKEY_CLASSES_ROOT\CLSID\{6D940285-9F11-11CE-83FD-
02608C3EC08A}]
@="Wang Image Annotation Control"
[HKEY_CLASSES_ROOT\CLSID\{6D940285-9F11-11CE-83FD-
02608C3EC08A}\Control]
@=""
[HKEY_CLASSES_ROOT\CLSID\{6D940285-9F11-11CE-83FD-
02608C3EC08A}\InprocServer32]
@="C:\\WINNT\\System32\\IMGEDIT.OCX"
[HKEY_CLASSES_ROOT\CLSID\{6D940285-9F11-11CE-83FD-
02608C3EC08A}\MiscStatus]
@="0"
[HKEY_CLASSES_ROOT\CLSID\{6D940285-9F11-11CE-83FD-
02608C3EC08A}\MiscStatus\1]
@="131473"
[HKEY_CLASSES_ROOT\CLSID\{6D940285-9F11-11CE-83FD-
02608C3EC08A}\ProgID]
@="WangImage.AnnotationCtrl.1"
[HKEY_CLASSES_ROOT\CLSID\{6D940285-9F11-11CE-83FD-
02608C3EC08A}\ToolboxBitmap32]
@="C:\\WINNT\\System32\\IMGEDIT.OCX, 2"
[HKEY_CLASSES_ROOT\CLSID\{6D940285-9F11-11CE-83FD-
02608C3EC08A}\TypeLib]
@="{6D940288-9F11-11CE-83FD-02608C3EC08A}"
[HKEY_CLASSES_ROOT\CLSID\{6D940285-9F11-11CE-83FD-
02608C3EC08A}\Version]
@="1.0"
[HKEY_CLASSES_ROOT\CLSID\{6D940289-9F11-11CE-83FD-
02608C3EC08A}]
@="Wang Image Annotation Property Page"
[HKEY_CLASSES_ROOT\CLSID\{6D940289-9F11-11CE-83FD-
02608C3EC08A}\InprocServer32]
@="C:\\WINNT\\System32\\IMGEDIT.OCX"
[HKEY_CLASSES_ROOT\CLSID\{73FDDC80-AEA9-101A-98A7-
00AA00374959}]
@="WordPad Document"
[HKEY_CLASSES_ROOT\CLSID\{73FDDC80-AEA9-101A-98A7-
00AA00374959}\AuxUserType]

[HKEY_CLASSES_ROOT\CLSID\{73FDDC80-AEA9-101A-98A7-
00AA00374959}\AuxUserType\2]
@="WordPad Document"
[HKEY_CLASSES_ROOT\CLSID\{73FDDC80-AEA9-101A-98A7-
00AA00374959}\AuxUserType\3]
@="WordPad"
[HKEY_CLASSES_ROOT\CLSID\{73FDDC80-AEA9-101A-98A7-
00AA00374959}\DataFormats]
[HKEY_CLASSES_ROOT\CLSID\{73FDDC80-AEA9-101A-98A7-
00AA00374959}\DataFormats\PriorityCacheFormats]
"Rich Text Format"=""
[HKEY_CLASSES_ROOT\CLSID\{73FDDC80-AEA9-101A-98A7-
00AA00374959}\DefaultIcon]
@="C:\\Program Files\\Windows NT\\Accessories\\WORDPAD.EXE,1"
[HKEY_CLASSES_ROOT\CLSID\{73FDDC80-AEA9-101A-98A7-
00AA00374959}\InprocHandler32]
@="ole32.dll"
[HKEY_CLASSES_ROOT\CLSID\{73FDDC80-AEA9-101A-98A7-
00AA00374959}\Insertable]
@=""
[HKEY_CLASSES_ROOT\CLSID\{73FDDC80-AEA9-101A-98A7-
00AA00374959}\LocalServer32]
@="C:\\Program Files\\Windows NT\\Accessories\\WORDPAD.EXE"
[HKEY_CLASSES_ROOT\CLSID\{73FDDC80-AEA9-101A-98A7-
00AA00374959}\MiscStatus]
@="0"
[HKEY_CLASSES_ROOT\CLSID\{73FDDC80-AEA9-101A-98A7-
00AA00374959}\ProgId]
@="WordPad.Document.1"
[HKEY_CLASSES_ROOT\CLSID\{73FDDC80-AEA9-101A-98A7-
00AA00374959}\verb]
[HKEY_CLASSES_ROOT\CLSID\{73FDDC80-AEA9-101A-98A7-
00AA00374959}\verb\0]
@="&Edit,0,2"
[HKEY_CLASSES_ROOT\CLSID\{73FDDC80-AEA9-101A-98A7-
00AA00374959}\verb\1]
@="&Open,0,2"
[HKEY_CLASSES_ROOT\CLSID\{764BF0E1-F219-11ce-972D-00AA00A14F56}]
@="Shell extensions for file compression"
[HKEY_CLASSES_ROOT\CLSID\{764BF0E1-F219-11ce-972D-
00AA00A14F56}\InProcServer32]
@="shcompui.dll"
"ThreadingModel"="Apartment"

[HKEY_CLASSES_ROOT\CLSID\{7D252A20-A4D5-11CE-8BF1-00608C54A1AA}]
@="Wang Image Viewer 1.0"
[HKEY_CLASSES_ROOT\CLSID\{7D252A20-A4D5-11CE-8BF1-00608C54A1AA}\LocalServer32]
@="C:\\Program Files\\Windows NT\\Accessories\\ImageVue\\WangImg.Exe"
[HKEY_CLASSES_ROOT\CLSID\{7D252A20-A4D5-11CE-8BF1-00608C54A1AA}\ProgId]
@="WangImage.Application.1"
[HKEY_CLASSES_ROOT\CLSID\{7D252A20-A4D5-11CE-8BF1-00608C54A1AA}\VersionIndependentProgId]
@="WangImage.Application"
[HKEY_CLASSES_ROOT\CLSID\{84926CA0-2941-101C-816F-0E6013114B7F}]
@="Wang Image Scan Control"
[HKEY_CLASSES_ROOT\CLSID\{84926CA0-2941-101C-816F-0E6013114B7F}\Control]
@=""
[HKEY_CLASSES_ROOT\CLSID\{84926CA0-2941-101C-816F-0E6013114B7F}\InprocServer32]
@="C:\\WINNT\\System32\\IMGSCAN.OCX"
[HKEY_CLASSES_ROOT\CLSID\{84926CA0-2941-101C-816F-0E6013114B7F}\Insertable]
@=""
[HKEY_CLASSES_ROOT\CLSID\{84926CA0-2941-101C-816F-0E6013114B7F}\MiscStatus]
@="0"
[HKEY_CLASSES_ROOT\CLSID\{84926CA0-2941-101C-816F-0E6013114B7F}\MiscStatus\1]
@="132497"
[HKEY_CLASSES_ROOT\CLSID\{84926CA0-2941-101C-816F-0E6013114B7F}\ProgID]
@="WangImage.ScanCtrl.1"
[HKEY_CLASSES_ROOT\CLSID\{84926CA0-2941-101C-816F-0E6013114B7F}\ToolboxBitmap32]
@="C:\\WINNT\\System32\\IMGSCAN.OCX, 1"
[HKEY_CLASSES_ROOT\CLSID\{84926CA0-2941-101C-816F-0E6013114B7F}\TypeLib]
@="{84926CA3-2941-101C-816F-0E6013114B7F}"
[HKEY_CLASSES_ROOT\CLSID\{84926CA0-2941-101C-816F-0E6013114B7F}\Version]
@="1.0"
[HKEY_CLASSES_ROOT\CLSID\{84926CA4-2941-101C-816F-0E6013114B7F}]
@="Wang Image Scan Property Page"

[HKEY_CLASSES_ROOT\CLSID\{84926CA4-2941-101C-816F-0E6013114B7F}\InprocServer32]
@="C:\\WINNT\\System32\\IMGSCAN.OCX"
[HKEY_CLASSES_ROOT\CLSID\{85BBD920-42A0-1069-A2E4-08002B30309D}]
@="Briefcase"
[HKEY_CLASSES_ROOT\CLSID\{85BBD920-42A0-1069-A2E4-08002B30309D}\DefaultIcon]
@=hex(2):25,53,79,73,74,65,6d,52,6f,6f,74,25,5c,73,79,73,74,65,6d,33,32,5c,73,79,
6e,63,75,69,2e,64,6c,6c,2c,30,00
[HKEY_CLASSES_ROOT\CLSID\{85BBD920-42A0-1069-A2E4-08002B30309D}\InProcServer32]
@="syncui.dll"
"ThreadingModel"="Apartment"
[HKEY_CLASSES_ROOT\CLSID\{85BBD920-42A0-1069-A2E4-08002B30309D}\shellex]
[HKEY_CLASSES_ROOT\CLSID\{85BBD920-42A0-1069-A2E4-08002B30309D}\shellex\PropertySheetHandlers]
[HKEY_CLASSES_ROOT\CLSID\{85BBD920-42A0-1069-A2E4-08002B30309D}\shellex\PropertySheetHandlers\{1F2E5C40-9550-11CE-99D2-00AA006E086C}]
[HKEY_CLASSES_ROOT\CLSID\{85BBD920-42A0-1069-A2E4-08002B30309D}\ShellFolder]
"Attributes"=hex:36,01,00,40
[HKEY_CLASSES_ROOT\CLSID\{86747AC0-42A0-1069-A2E6-08002B30309D}]
@="Shell Moniker"
[HKEY_CLASSES_ROOT\CLSID\{86747AC0-42A0-1069-A2E6-08002B30309D}\InProcServer32]
@="shell32.dll"
"ThreadingModel"="Apartment"
[HKEY_CLASSES_ROOT\CLSID\{86F19A00-42A0-1069-A2E9-08002B30309D}]
@=".PIF file property pages"
[HKEY_CLASSES_ROOT\CLSID\{86F19A00-42A0-1069-A2E9-08002B30309D}\InProcServer32]
@="shell32.dll"
"ThreadingModel"="Apartment"
[HKEY_CLASSES_ROOT\CLSID\{86F19A00-42A0-1069-A2EB-08002B30309D}]
@=".PIF file handler"
[HKEY_CLASSES_ROOT\CLSID\{86F19A00-42A0-1069-A2EB-08002B30309D}\InProcServer32]
@="shell32.dll"
"ThreadingModel"="Apartment"

[HKEY_CLASSES_ROOT\CLSID\{88895560-9AA2-1069-930E-00AA0030EBC8}]
@="HyperTerminal Icon Ext"
[HKEY_CLASSES_ROOT\CLSID\{88895560-9AA2-1069-930E-00AA0030EBC8}\InProcServer32]
@="C:\\WINNT\\System32\\hticons.dll"
"ThreadingModel"="Apartment"
[HKEY_CLASSES_ROOT\CLSID\{a4d92740-67cd-11cf-96f2-00aa00a11dd9}]
@="Dial-Up Networking"
[HKEY_CLASSES_ROOT\CLSID\{a4d92740-67cd-11cf-96f2-00aa00a11dd9}\DefaultIcon]
@=hex(2):25,53,79,73,74,65,6d,52,6f,6f,74,25,5c,73,79,73,74,65,6d,33,32,5c,72,61,
73,73,68,65,6c,6c,2e,64,6c,6c,2c,30,00
[HKEY_CLASSES_ROOT\CLSID\{a4d92740-67cd-11cf-96f2-00aa00a11dd9}\InProcServer32]
@="rasshell.dll"
"ThreadingModel"="Apartment"
[HKEY_CLASSES_ROOT\CLSID\{a4d92740-67cd-11cf-96f2-00aa00a11dd9}\shell]
[HKEY_CLASSES_ROOT\CLSID\{a4d92740-67cd-11cf-96f2-00aa00a11dd9}\shell\Open]
[HKEY_CLASSES_ROOT\CLSID\{a4d92740-67cd-11cf-96f2-00aa00a11dd9}\shell\Open\command]
@=hex(2):25,53,79,73,74,65,6d,52,6f,6f,74,25,5c,73,79,73,74,65,6d,33,32,5c,72,61,
73,70,68,6f,6e,65,2e,65,78,65,00
[HKEY_CLASSES_ROOT\CLSID\{a4d92741-67cd-11cf-96f2-00aa00a11dd9}]
@="Dial-Up Shortcut"
[HKEY_CLASSES_ROOT\CLSID\{a4d92741-67cd-11cf-96f2-00aa00a11dd9}\AuxUserType]
[HKEY_CLASSES_ROOT\CLSID\{a4d92741-67cd-11cf-96f2-00aa00a11dd9}\AuxUserType\2]
@="Dial-Up Shortcut"
[HKEY_CLASSES_ROOT\CLSID\{a4d92741-67cd-11cf-96f2-00aa00a11dd9}\AuxUserType\3]
@="Dial-Up Networking"
[HKEY_CLASSES_ROOT\CLSID\{a4d92741-67cd-11cf-96f2-00aa00a11dd9}\InprocServer32]
@="rasshell.dll"
"ThreadingModel"="Apartment"
[HKEY_CLASSES_ROOT\CLSID\{a4d92742-67cd-11cf-96f2-00aa00a11dd9}]
@="Dial-Up Phonebook"
[HKEY_CLASSES_ROOT\CLSID\{a4d92742-67cd-11cf-96f2-00aa00a11dd9}\AuxUserType]

[HKEY_CLASSES_ROOT\CLSID\{a4d92742-67cd-11cf-96f2-00aa00a11dd9}\AuxUserType\2]
@="Dial-Up Phonebook"
[HKEY_CLASSES_ROOT\CLSID\{a4d92742-67cd-11cf-96f2-00aa00a11dd9}\AuxUserType\3]
@="Dial-Up Networking"
[HKEY_CLASSES_ROOT\CLSID\{B7711240-A7D0-11CE-83FD-02608C3EC08A}]
@="Annotation Property Page"
[HKEY_CLASSES_ROOT\CLSID\{B7711240-A7D0-11CE-83FD-02608C3EC08A}\InProcServer32]
@="C:\\WINNT\\System32\\IMGEDIT.OCX"
[HKEY_CLASSES_ROOT\CLSID\{B7711241-A7D0-11CE-83FD-02608C3EC08A}]
@="Annotation Button Property Page"
[HKEY_CLASSES_ROOT\CLSID\{B7711241-A7D0-11CE-83FD-02608C3EC08A}\InProcServer32]
@="C:\\WINNT\\System32\\IMGEDIT.OCX"
[HKEY_CLASSES_ROOT\CLSID\{BD84B380-8CA2-1069-AB1D-08000948F534}]
@="Fonts"
[HKEY_CLASSES_ROOT\CLSID\{BD84B380-8CA2-1069-AB1D-08000948F534}\DefaultIcon]
@=hex(2):25,53,79,73,74,65,6d,52,6f,6f,74,25,5c,53,79,73,74,65,6d,33,32,5c,66,6f,6e,
74,65,78,74,2e,64,6c,6c,2c,2d,31,30,31,00
[HKEY_CLASSES_ROOT\CLSID\{BD84B380-8CA2-1069-AB1D-08000948F534}\Hierarchical]
@="0"
[HKEY_CLASSES_ROOT\CLSID\{BD84B380-8CA2-1069-AB1D-08000948F534}\InProcServer32]
@="fontext.dll"
"ThreadingModel"="Apartment"
[HKEY_CLASSES_ROOT\CLSID\{BD84B381-8CA2-1069-AB1D-08000948F534}]
@="PANOSE Core Mapper"
[HKEY_CLASSES_ROOT\CLSID\{BD84B381-8CA2-1069-AB1D-08000948F534}\InProcServer32]
@="panmap.dll"
"ThreadingModel"="Apartment"
[HKEY_CLASSES_ROOT\CLSID\{D3E34B21-9D75-101A-8C3D-00AA001A1652}]
@="Bitmap Image"
"AppID"="{D3E34B21-9D75-101A-8C3D-00AA001A1652}"

[HKEY_CLASSES_ROOT\CLSID\{D3E34B21-9D75-101A-8C3D-
00AA001A1652}\AuxUserType]
[HKEY_CLASSES_ROOT\CLSID\{D3E34B21-9D75-101A-8C3D-
00AA001A1652}\AuxUserType\2]
@="Bitmap Image"
[HKEY_CLASSES_ROOT\CLSID\{D3E34B21-9D75-101A-8C3D-
00AA001A1652}\AuxUserType\3]
@="Paint"
[HKEY_CLASSES_ROOT\CLSID\{D3E34B21-9D75-101A-8C3D-
00AA001A1652}\DataFormats]
[HKEY_CLASSES_ROOT\CLSID\{D3E34B21-9D75-101A-8C3D-
00AA001A1652}\DataFormats\PriorityCacheFormats]
"#8"=""
[HKEY_CLASSES_ROOT\CLSID\{D3E34B21-9D75-101A-8C3D-
00AA001A1652}\DefaultIcon]
@="mspaint.exe, 1"
[HKEY_CLASSES_ROOT\CLSID\{D3E34B21-9D75-101A-8C3D-
00AA001A1652}\InProcHandler32]
@="ole32.dll"
[HKEY_CLASSES_ROOT\CLSID\{D3E34B21-9D75-101A-8C3D-
00AA001A1652}\Insertable]
@=""
[HKEY_CLASSES_ROOT\CLSID\{D3E34B21-9D75-101A-8C3D-
00AA001A1652}\LocalServer32]
@="mspaint.exe"
[HKEY_CLASSES_ROOT\CLSID\{D3E34B21-9D75-101A-8C3D-
00AA001A1652}\MiscStatus]
@="32"
[HKEY_CLASSES_ROOT\CLSID\{D3E34B21-9D75-101A-8C3D-
00AA001A1652}\PersistentHandler]
@="{098F2470-BAE0-11CD-B579-08002B30BFEB}"
[HKEY_CLASSES_ROOT\CLSID\{D3E34B21-9D75-101A-8C3D-
00AA001A1652}\ProgID]
@="Paint.Picture"
[HKEY_CLASSES_ROOT\CLSID\{D3E34B21-9D75-101A-8C3D-
00AA001A1652}\Verb]
[HKEY_CLASSES_ROOT\CLSID\{D3E34B21-9D75-101A-8C3D-
00AA001A1652}\Verb\0]
@="&Edit,0,2"
[HKEY_CLASSES_ROOT\CLSID\{D3E34B21-9D75-101A-8C3D-
00AA001A1652}\Verb\1]
@="&Open,0,2"

[HKEY_CLASSES_ROOT\CLSID\{D7B70EE0-4340-11CF-B063-0020AFC2CD35}]
@="DirectDraw Object"
[HKEY_CLASSES_ROOT\CLSID\{D7B70EE0-4340-11CF-B063-0020AFC2CD35}\InprocServer32]
@="ddraw.dll"
[HKEY_CLASSES_ROOT\CLSID\{DF0B3D60-548F-101B-8E65-08002B2BD119}]
@="PSSupportErrorInfo"
[HKEY_CLASSES_ROOT\CLSID\{DF0B3D60-548F-101B-8E65-08002B2BD119}\InprocServer]
@="ole2disp.dll"
[HKEY_CLASSES_ROOT\CLSID\{DF0B3D60-548F-101B-8E65-08002B2BD119}\InprocServer32]
@="oleaut32.dll"
[HKEY_CLASSES_ROOT\CLSID\{E1A6B8A0-3603-101C-AC6E-040224009C02}]
@="Wang Image Thumbnail Control"
[HKEY_CLASSES_ROOT\CLSID\{E1A6B8A0-3603-101C-AC6E-040224009C02}\Control]
@=""
[HKEY_CLASSES_ROOT\CLSID\{E1A6B8A0-3603-101C-AC6E-040224009C02}\InprocServer32]
@="C:\\WINNT\\System32\\IMGTHUMB.OCX"
[HKEY_CLASSES_ROOT\CLSID\{E1A6B8A0-3603-101C-AC6E-040224009C02}\MiscStatus]
@="0"
[HKEY_CLASSES_ROOT\CLSID\{E1A6B8A0-3603-101C-AC6E-040224009C02}\MiscStatus\1]
@="131473"
[HKEY_CLASSES_ROOT\CLSID\{E1A6B8A0-3603-101C-AC6E-040224009C02}\ProgID]
@="WangImage.ThumbnailCtrl.1"
[HKEY_CLASSES_ROOT\CLSID\{E1A6B8A0-3603-101C-AC6E-040224009C02}\ToolboxBitmap32]
@="C:\\WINNT\\System32\\IMGTHUMB.OCX, 1"
[HKEY_CLASSES_ROOT\CLSID\{E1A6B8A0-3603-101C-AC6E-040224009C02}\TypeLib]
@="{E1A6B8A3-3603-101C-AC6E-040224009C02}"
[HKEY_CLASSES_ROOT\CLSID\{E1A6B8A0-3603-101C-AC6E-040224009C02}\Version]
@="1.0"

[HKEY_CLASSES_ROOT\CLSID\{E1A6B8A4-3603-101C-AC6E-040224009C02}]
@="Wang Image Thumbnail Property Page"
[HKEY_CLASSES_ROOT\CLSID\{E1A6B8A4-3603-101C-AC6E-040224009C02}\InprocServer32]
@="C:\\WINNT\\System32\\IMGTHUMB.OCX"
[HKEY_CLASSES_ROOT\CLSID\{E60A7940-4B3E-101C-96BF-040224009C02}]
@="Wang Image Admin Print Page"
[HKEY_CLASSES_ROOT\CLSID\{E60A7940-4B3E-101C-96BF-040224009C02}\InProcServer32]
@="C:\\WINNT\\System32\\IMGADMIN.OCX"
[HKEY_CLASSES_ROOT\CLSID\{F0F08735-0C36-101B-B086-0020AF07D0F4}]
@="SCC Quick Viewer"
[HKEY_CLASSES_ROOT\CLSID\{F0F08735-0C36-101B-B086-0020AF07D0F4}\InProcServer32]
@=hex(2):25,53,79,73,74,65,6d,52,6f,6f,74,25,5c,73,79,73,74,65,6d,33,32,5c,76,69,
65,77,65,72,73,5c,73,63,63,76,69,65,77,2e,64,6c,6c,00
"ThreadingModel"="Apartment"
[HKEY_CLASSES_ROOT\CLSID\{f 81e9010-6ea4-11ce-a7ff-00aa003ca9f6}]
@="Shell extensions for sharing"
[HKEY_CLASSES_ROOT\CLSID\{f 81e9010-6ea4-11ce-a7ff-00aa003ca9f6}\InProcServer32]
@="ntshrui.dll"
"ThreadingModel"="Apartment"
[HKEY_CLASSES_ROOT\CLSID\{FBF23B40-E3F0-101B-8488-00AA003E56F8}]
@="Internet Shortcut"
[HKEY_CLASSES_ROOT\CLSID\{FBF23B40-E3F0-101B-8488-00AA003E56F8}\InProcServer32]
@="url.dll"
"ThreadingModel"="Apartment"
[HKEY_CLASSES_ROOT\CLSID\{FBF23B41-E3F0-101B-8488-00AA003E56F8}]
@="MIME and Internet Property Sheet Hook"
[HKEY_CLASSES_ROOT\CLSID\{FBF23B41-E3F0-101B-8488-00AA003E56F8}\InProcServer32]
@="url.dll"
"ThreadingModel"="Apartment"
[HKEY_CLASSES_ROOT\CLSID\{FBF23B42-E3F0-101B-8488-00AA003E56F8}]
@="Internet Explorer"
[HKEY_CLASSES_ROOT\CLSID\{FBF23B42-E3F0-101B-8488-00AA003E56F8}\DefaultIcon]
@="C:\\Program Files\\Plus!\\Microsoft Internet\\iexplore.exe,0"

[HKEY_CLASSES_ROOT\CLSID\{FBF23B42-E3F0-101B-8488-00AA003E56F8}\InProcServer32]
@="url.dll"
"ThreadingModel"="Apartment"
[HKEY_CLASSES_ROOT\CLSID\{FBF23B42-E3F0-101B-8488-00AA003E56F8}\Shell]
[HKEY_CLASSES_ROOT\CLSID\{FBF23B42-E3F0-101B-8488-00AA003E56F8}\Shell\Open]
[HKEY_CLASSES_ROOT\CLSID\{FBF23B42-E3F0-101B-8488-00AA003E56F8}\Shell\Open\Command]
@="C:\\Program Files\\Plus!\\Microsoft Internet\\iexplore.exe"
[HKEY_CLASSES_ROOT\CLSID\{FBF23B42-E3F0-101B-8488-00AA003E56F8}\ShellEx]
[HKEY_CLASSES_ROOT\CLSID\{FBF23B42-E3F0-101B-8488-00AA003E56F8}\ShellEx\PropertySheetHandlers]
[HKEY_CLASSES_ROOT\CLSID\{FBF23B42-E3F0-101B-8488-00AA003E56F8}\ShellEx\PropertySheetHandlers\{FBF23B42-E3F0-101B-8488-00AA003E56F8}]
@=""
[HKEY_CLASSES_ROOT\CLSID\{FBF23B42-E3F0-101B-8488-00AA003E56F8}\ShellFolder]
@=""
"Attributes"=hex:70,00,00,00
[HKEY_CLASSES_ROOT\cmdfile]
@="Windows NT Command Script"
"EditFlags"=hex:30,04,00,00
[HKEY_CLASSES_ROOT\cmdfile\DefaultIcon]
@=hex(2):25,53,79,73,74,65,6d,52,6f,6f,74,25,5c,53,79,73,74,65,6d,33,32,5c,73,68,
65,6c,6c,33,32,2e,64,6c,6c,2c,2d,31,35,33,00
[HKEY_CLASSES_ROOT\cmdfile\shell]
[HKEY_CLASSES_ROOT\cmdfile\shell\edit]
@="&Edit"
[HKEY_CLASSES_ROOT\cmdfile\shell\edit\command]
@=hex(2):25,53,79,73,74,65,6d,52,6f,6f,74,25,5c,53,79,73,74,65,6d,33,32,5c,4e,4f,54,
45,50,41,44,2e,45,58,45,20,25,31,00
[HKEY_CLASSES_ROOT\cmdfile\shell\open]
"EditFlags"=hex:00,00,00,00
[HKEY_CLASSES_ROOT\cmdfile\shell\open\command]
@="\"%1\" %*"
[HKEY_CLASSES_ROOT\cmdfile\shell\print]
[HKEY_CLASSES_ROOT\cmdfile\shell\print\command]
@=hex(2):25,53,79,73,74,65,6d,52,6f,6f,74,25,5c,53,79,73,74,65,6d,33,32,5c,4e,4f,54,
45,50,41,44,2e,45,58,45,20,2f,70,20,25,31,00

[HKEY_CLASSES_ROOT\cmdfile\shellex]
[HKEY_CLASSES_ROOT\cmdfile\shellex\PropertySheetHandlers]
[HKEY_CLASSES_ROOT\cmdfile\shellex\PropertySheetHandlers\PifProps]
@="{86F19A00-42A0-1069-A2E9-08002B30309D}"
[HKEY_CLASSES_ROOT\comfile]
@="MS-DOS Application"
"EditFlags"=hex:30,00,00,00
[HKEY_CLASSES_ROOT\comfile\DefaultIcon]
@=hex(2):25,53,79,73,74,65,6d,52,6f,6f,74,25,5c,53,79,73,74,65,6d,33,32,5c,73,68,
65,6c,6c,33,32,2e,64,6c,6c,2c,32,00
[HKEY_CLASSES_ROOT\comfile\shell]
[HKEY_CLASSES_ROOT\comfile\shell\open]
"EditFlags"=hex:00,00,00,00
[HKEY_CLASSES_ROOT\comfile\shell\open\command]
@="\"%1\" %★"
[HKEY_CLASSES_ROOT\comfile\shellex]
[HKEY_CLASSES_ROOT\comfile\shellex\PropertySheetHandlers]
[HKEY_CLASSES_ROOT\comfile\shellex\PropertySheetHandlers\PifProps]
@="{86F19A00-42A0-1069-A2E9-08002B30309D}"
[HKEY_CLASSES_ROOT\cplfile]
@="Control Panel extension"
[HKEY_CLASSES_ROOT\cplfile\DefaultIcon]
@=hex(2):25,53,79,73,74,65,6d,52,6f,6f,74,25,5c,53,79,73,74,65,6d,33,32,5c,73,68,
65,6c,6c,33,32,2e,64,6c,6c,2c,2d,31,35,34,00
[HKEY_CLASSES_ROOT\cplfile\shell]
[HKEY_CLASSES_ROOT\cplfile\shell\cplopen]
@="Open with Control Panel"
[HKEY_CLASSES_ROOT\cplfile\shell\cplopen\command]
@="rundll32.exe shell32.dll,Control_RunDLL %1,%★"
[HKEY_CLASSES_ROOT\curfile]
@="Cursor"
[HKEY_CLASSES_ROOT\curfile\DefaultIcon]
@="%1"
[HKEY_CLASSES_ROOT\DCXImage.Document]
@="DCX Image Document"
[HKEY_CLASSES_ROOT\DCXImage.Document\CLSID]
@="{02B01C80-E03D-101A-B294-00DD010F2BF9}"
[HKEY_CLASSES_ROOT\DCXImage.Document\DefaultIcon]
@="C:\\Program Files\\Windows NT\\Accessories\\ImageVue\\WangImg.Exe,1"
[HKEY_CLASSES_ROOT\DCXImage.Document\shell]
[HKEY_CLASSES_ROOT\DCXImage.Document\shell\open]
[HKEY_CLASSES_ROOT\DCXImage.Document\shell\open\command]
@="C:\\Program Files\\Windows NT\\Accessories\\ImageVue\\WangImg.Exe\
"%1\""

[HKEY_CLASSES_ROOT\DCXImage.Document\shell\print]
[HKEY_CLASSES_ROOT\DCXImage.Document\shell\print\command]
@="C:\\Program Files\\Windows NT\\Accessories\\ImageVue\\WangImg.Exe
/p\"%1\""
[HKEY_CLASSES_ROOT\DCXImage.Document\shell\printto]
[HKEY_CLASSES_ROOT\DCXImage.Document\shell\printto\command]
@="C:\\Program Files\\Windows NT\\Accessories\\ImageVue\\WangImg.Exe
/pt\"%1\" \"%2\" \"%3\" \"%4\" "
[HKEY_CLASSES_ROOT\DCXImage.Document\shellex]
@=""
[HKEY_CLASSES_ROOT\DCXImage.Document\shellex\PropertySheetHandlers]
@=""
[HKEY_CLASSES_ROOT\DCXImage.Document\shellex\PropertySheetHandlers\
{1D3ECD40-C835-11CE-9888-00608CC22020}]
@=""
[HKEY_CLASSES_ROOT\DirectDraw]
@="DirectDraw Object"
[HKEY_CLASSES_ROOT\DirectDraw\CLSID]
@="{D7B70EE0-4340-11CF-B063-0020AFC2CD35}"
[HKEY_CLASSES_ROOT\DirectDrawClipper]
@="DirectDraw Clipper Object"
[HKEY_CLASSES_ROOT\DirectDrawClipper\CLSID]
@="{593817A0-7DB3-11CF-A2DE-00AA00B93356}"
[HKEY_CLASSES_ROOT\Directory]
@="File Folder"
"EditFlags"=hex:02,00,00,00
"AlwaysShowExt"=""
[HKEY_CLASSES_ROOT\Directory\DefaultIcon]
@=hex(2):25,53,79,73,74,65,6d,52,6f,6f,74,25,5c,53,79,73,74,65,6d,33,32,5c,73,68,
65,6c,6c,33,32,2e,64,6c,6c,2c,33,00
[HKEY_CLASSES_ROOT\Directory\shell]
[HKEY_CLASSES_ROOT\Directory\shell\find]
[HKEY_CLASSES_ROOT\Directory\shell\find\command]
@=hex(2):25,53,79,73,74,65,6d,52,6f,6f,74,25,5c,45,78,70,6c,6f,72,65,72,2e,65,78,65,
00
[HKEY_CLASSES_ROOT\Directory\shell\find\ddeexec]
@="[FindFolder(\"%l\", %I)]"
[HKEY_CLASSES_ROOT\Directory\shell\find\ddeexec\application]
@="Folders"
[HKEY_CLASSES_ROOT\Directory\shell\find\ddeexec\topic]
@="AppProperties"
[HKEY_CLASSES_ROOT\Directory\shellex]
[HKEY_CLASSES_ROOT\Directory\shellex\ContextMenuHandlers]

[HKEY_CLASSES_ROOT\Directory\shellex\ContextMenuHandlers\
ExplorerCompressionMenu]
@="{764BF0E1-F219-11ce-972D-00AA00A14F56}"
[HKEY_CLASSES_ROOT\Directory\shellex\CopyHookHandlers]
[HKEY_CLASSES_ROOT\Directory\shellex\CopyHookHandlers\FileSystem]
@="{217FC9C0-3AEA-1069-A2DB-08002B30309D}"
[HKEY_CLASSES_ROOT\Directory\shellex\CopyHookHandlers\Sharing]
@="{40dd6e20-7c17-11ce-a804-00aa003ca9f6}"
[HKEY_CLASSES_ROOT\Directory\shellex\PropertySheetHandlers]
[HKEY_CLASSES_ROOT\Directory\shellex\PropertySheetHandlers\{1F2E5C40-
9550-11CE-99D2-00AA006E086C}]
[HKEY_CLASSES_ROOT\DirectSound]
@="DirectSound Object"
[HKEY_CLASSES_ROOT\DirectSound\CLSID]
@="{47D4D946-62E8-11cf-93BC-444553540000}"
[HKEY_CLASSES_ROOT\dllfile]
@="Application Extension"
"AlwaysShowExt"=""
"EditFlags"=hex:01,00,00,00
[HKEY_CLASSES_ROOT\dllfile\DefaultIcon]
@=hex(2):25,53,79,73,74,65,6d,52,6f,6f,74,25,5c,53,79,73,74,65,6d,33,32,5c,73,68,
65,6c,6c,33,32,2e,64,6c,6c,2c,2d,31,35,34,00
[HKEY_CLASSES_ROOT\DocShortcut]
@="Shortcut into a document"
"IsShortcut"=""
"NeverShowExt"=""
[HKEY_CLASSES_ROOT\DocShortcut\DefaultIcon]
@=hex(2):25,53,79,73,74,65,6d,52,6f,6f,74,25,5c,53,79,73,74,65,6d,33,32,5c,73,68,
73,63,72,61,70,2e,64,6c,6c,2c,2d,31,30,30,00
[HKEY_CLASSES_ROOT\DocShortcut\shell]
[HKEY_CLASSES_ROOT\DocShortcut\shell\open]
[HKEY_CLASSES_ROOT\DocShortcut\shell\open\command]
@=hex(2):72,75,6e,64,6c,6c,33,32,20,25,53,79,73,74,65,6d,52,6f,6f,74,25,5c,53,79,
73,74,65,6d,33,32,5c,73,68,73,63,72,61,70,2e,64,6c,6c,2c,4f,70,65,6e,53,63,72,61,70,
5f,52,75,6e,44,4c,4c,20,2f,72,20,2f,78,20,25,31,00
[HKEY_CLASSES_ROOT\DocShortcut\shellex]
[HKEY_CLASSES_ROOT\DocShortcut\shellex\DataHandler]
@="{56117100-C0CD-101B-81E2-00AA004AE837}"
[HKEY_CLASSES_ROOT\Drive]
@="Drive"
"EditFlags"=hex:02,00,00,00

[HKEY_CLASSES_ROOT\Drive\DefaultIcon]
@=hex(2):25,53,79,73,74,65,6d,52,6f,6f,74,25,5c,53,79,73,74,65,6d,33,32,5c,73,68,
65,6c,6c,33,32,2e,64,6c,6c,2c,38,00
[HKEY_CLASSES_ROOT\Drive\shell]
[HKEY_CLASSES_ROOT\Drive\shell\find]
[HKEY_CLASSES_ROOT\Drive\shell\find\command]
@=hex(2):25,53,79,73,74,65,6d,52,6f,6f,74,25,5c,45,78,70,6c,6f,72,65,72,2e,65,78,65,
00
[HKEY_CLASSES_ROOT\Drive\shell\find\ddeexec]
@="[FindFolder(\"%l\", %I)]"
[HKEY_CLASSES_ROOT\Drive\shell\find\ddeexec\application]
@="Folders"
[HKEY_CLASSES_ROOT\Drive\shell\find\ddeexec\topic]
@="AppProperties"
[HKEY_CLASSES_ROOT\Drive\shellex]
[HKEY_CLASSES_ROOT\Drive\shellex\ContextMenuHandlers]
[HKEY_CLASSES_ROOT\Drive\shellex\ContextMenuHandlers\
ExplorerCompressionMenu]
@="{764BF0E1-F219-11ce-972D-00AA00A14F56}"
[HKEY_CLASSES_ROOT\Drive\shellex\ContextMenuHandlers\{59099400-57FF-
11CE-BD94-0020AF85B590}]
[HKEY_CLASSES_ROOT\Drive\shellex\PropertySheetHandlers]
[HKEY_CLASSES_ROOT\Drive\shellex\PropertySheetHandlers\{1F2E5C40-9550-
11CE-99D2-00AA006E086C}]
[HKEY_CLASSES_ROOT\drvfile]
@="Device driver"
"EditFlags"=hex:01,00,00,00
"AlwaysShowExt"=""
[HKEY_CLASSES_ROOT\drvfile\DefaultIcon]
@=hex(2):25,53,79,73,74,65,6d,52,6f,6f,74,25,5c,53,79,73,74,65,6d,33,32,5c,73,68,
65,6c,6c,33,32,2e,64,6c,6c,2c,2d,31,35,34,00
[HKEY_CLASSES_ROOT\exefile]
@="Application"
"EditFlags"=hex:38,07,00,00
[HKEY_CLASSES_ROOT\exefile\DefaultIcon]
@="%1"
[HKEY_CLASSES_ROOT\exefile\shell]
[HKEY_CLASSES_ROOT\exefile\shell\open]
"EditFlags"=hex:00,00,00,00
[HKEY_CLASSES_ROOT\exefile\shell\open\command]
@="\"%1\" %*"
[HKEY_CLASSES_ROOT\exefile\shellex]
[HKEY_CLASSES_ROOT\exefile\shellex\PropertySheetHandlers]

[HKEY_CLASSES_ROOT\exefile\shellex\PropertySheetHandlers\PifProps]
@="{86F19A00-42A0-1069-A2E9-08002B30309D}"
[HKEY_CLASSES_ROOT\file]
"EditFlags"=hex:02,00,00,00
"URL Protocol"=""
[HKEY_CLASSES_ROOT\file\CLSID]
@="{00000303-0000-0000-C000-000000000046}"
[HKEY_CLASSES_ROOT\file\DefaultIcon]
@="C:\\WINNT\\System32\\url.dll,0"
[HKEY_CLASSES_ROOT\file\shell]
[HKEY_CLASSES_ROOT\file\shell\open]
[HKEY_CLASSES_ROOT\file\shell\open\command]
@="rundll32.exe url.dll,FileProtocolHandler %l"
[HKEY_CLASSES_ROOT\fndfile]
@="Saved Search"
[HKEY_CLASSES_ROOT\fndfile\DefaultIcon]
@=hex(2):25,53,79,73,74,65,6d,52,6f,6f,74,25,5c,53,79,73,74,65,6d,33,32,5c,73,68,
65,6c,6c,33,32,2e,64,6c,6c,2c,2d,31,33,33,00
[HKEY_CLASSES_ROOT\fndfile\shell]
[HKEY_CLASSES_ROOT\fndfile\shell\open]
[HKEY_CLASSES_ROOT\fndfile\shell\open\command]
@=hex(2):25,53,79,73,74,65,6d,52,6f,6f,74,25,5c,45,78,70,6c,6f,72,65,72,2e,65,78,65,
00
[HKEY_CLASSES_ROOT\fndfile\shell\open\ddeexec]
@="[OpenFindFile(\"%1\", %I)]"
[HKEY_CLASSES_ROOT\fndfile\shell\open\ddeexec\application]
@="Folders"
[HKEY_CLASSES_ROOT\fndfile\shell\open\ddeexec\topic]
@="AppProperties"
[HKEY_CLASSES_ROOT\Folder]
@="Folder"
"EditFlags"=hex:02,00,00,00
[HKEY_CLASSES_ROOT\Folder\DefaultIcon]
@=hex(2):25,53,79,73,74,65,6d,52,6f,6f,74,25,5c,53,79,73,74,65,6d,33,32,5c,73,68,
65,6c,6c,33,32,2e,64,6c,6c,2c,33,00
[HKEY_CLASSES_ROOT\Folder\shell]
[HKEY_CLASSES_ROOT\Folder\shell\explore]
[HKEY_CLASSES_ROOT\Folder\shell\explore\command]
@=hex(2):25,53,79,73,74,65,6d,52,6f,6f,74,25,5c,45,78,70,6c,6f,72,65,72,2e,65,78,65,
20,2f,65,2c,2f,69,64,6c,69,73,74,2c,25,49,2c,25,4c,00
[HKEY_CLASSES_ROOT\Folder\shell\explore\ddeexec]
@="[ExploreFolder(\"%l\", %I, %S)]"
"NoActivateHandler"=""

[HKEY_CLASSES_ROOT\Folder\shell\explore\ddeexec\application]
@="Folders"
[HKEY_CLASSES_ROOT\Folder\shell\explore\ddeexec\ifexec]
@="[]"
[HKEY_CLASSES_ROOT\Folder\shell\explore\ddeexec\topic]
@="AppProperties"
[HKEY_CLASSES_ROOT\Folder\shell\open]
[HKEY_CLASSES_ROOT\Folder\shell\open\command]
@=hex(2):25,53,79,73,74,65,6d,52,6f,6f,74,25,5c,45,78,70,6c,6f,72,65,72,2e,65,78,65,
20,2f,69,64,6c,69,73,74,2c,25,49,2c,25,4c,00
[HKEY_CLASSES_ROOT\Folder\shell\open\ddeexec]
@="[ViewFolder(\"%l\", %I, %S)]"
"NoActivateHandler"=""
[HKEY_CLASSES_ROOT\Folder\shell\open\ddeexec\application]
@="Folders"
[HKEY_CLASSES_ROOT\Folder\shell\open\ddeexec\ifexec]
@="[]"
[HKEY_CLASSES_ROOT\Folder\shell\open\ddeexec\topic]
@="AppProperties"
[HKEY_CLASSES_ROOT\Folder\shellex]
[HKEY_CLASSES_ROOT\Folder\shellex\ContextMenuHandlers]
[HKEY_CLASSES_ROOT\Folder\shellex\ContextMenuHandlers\BriefcaseMenu]
@="{85BBD920-42A0-1069-A2E4-08002B30309D}"
[HKEY_CLASSES_ROOT\Folder\shellex\ContextMenuHandlers\
ExplorerCompressionMenu]
@="{764BF0E1-F219-11ce-972D-00AA00A14F56}"
[HKEY_CLASSES_ROOT\Folder\shellex\ContextMenuHandlers\Sharing]
@="{f 81e9010-6ea4-11ce-a7ff-00aa003ca9f6}"
[HKEY_CLASSES_ROOT\Folder\shellex\PropertySheetHandlers]
[HKEY_CLASSES_ROOT\Folder\shellex\PropertySheetHandlers\BriefcasePage]
@="{85BBD920-42A0-1069-A2E4-08002B30309D}"
[HKEY_CLASSES_ROOT\Folder\shellex\PropertySheetHandlers\Sharing]
@="{f 81e9010-6ea4-11ce-a7ff-00aa003ca9f6}"
[HKEY_CLASSES_ROOT\fonfile]
@="Font file"
[HKEY_CLASSES_ROOT\fonfile\DefaultIcon]
@=hex(2):25,53,79,73,74,65,6d,52,6f,6f,74,25,5c,53,79,73,74,65,6d,33,32,5c,73,68,
65,6c,6c,33,32,2e,64,6c,6c,2c,2d,31,35,35,00
[HKEY_CLASSES_ROOT\fonfile\shell]
[HKEY_CLASSES_ROOT\fonfile\shell\open]
[HKEY_CLASSES_ROOT\fonfile\shell\open\command]
@=hex(2):25,53,79,73,74,65,6d,52,6f,6f,74,25,5c,53,79,73,74,65,6d,33,32,5c,66,6f,6e,
74,76,69,65,77,2e,65,78,65,20,25,31,00

[HKEY_CLASSES_ROOT\fonfile\shell\print]
[HKEY_CLASSES_ROOT\fonfile\shell\print\command]
@=hex(2):25,53,79,73,74,65,6d,52,6f,6f,74,25,5c,53,79,73,74,65,6d,33,32,5c,66,6f,6e,
74,76,69,65,77,2e,65,78,65,20,2f,70,20,25,31,00
[HKEY_CLASSES_ROOT\ftp]
@="URL:File Transfer Protocol"
"EditFlags"=hex:02,00,00,00
"URL Protocol"=""
[HKEY_CLASSES_ROOT\ftp\DefaultIcon]
@="C:\\WINNT\\System32\\url.dll,0"
[HKEY_CLASSES_ROOT\ftp\shell]
[HKEY_CLASSES_ROOT\ftp\shell\open]
[HKEY_CLASSES_ROOT\ftp\shell\open\command]
@="\"C:\\Program Files\\Plus!\\Microsoft Internet\\IExplore.exe\" -nohome"
[HKEY_CLASSES_ROOT\ftp\shell\open\ddeexec]
@="\"%1\",,-1,,,,,"
[HKEY_CLASSES_ROOT\ftp\shell\open\ddeexec\Application]
@="IExplore"
[HKEY_CLASSES_ROOT\ftp\shell\open\ddeexec\Topic]
@="WWW_OpenURL"
[HKEY_CLASSES_ROOT\giffile]
@="GIF Image"
[HKEY_CLASSES_ROOT\giffile\DefaultIcon]
@="C:\\Program Files\\Plus!\\Microsoft Internet\\IExplore.exe,8"
[HKEY_CLASSES_ROOT\giffile\shell]
[HKEY_CLASSES_ROOT\giffile\shell\open]
[HKEY_CLASSES_ROOT\giffile\shell\open\command]
@="\"C:\\Program Files\\Plus!\\Microsoft Internet\\IExplore.exe\" -nohome"
[HKEY_CLASSES_ROOT\giffile\shell\open\ddeexec]
@="\"file:%1\",,-1,,,,,"
[HKEY_CLASSES_ROOT\giffile\shell\open\ddeexec\Application]
@="IExplore"
[HKEY_CLASSES_ROOT\giffile\shell\open\ddeexec\Topic]
@="WWW_OpenURL"
[HKEY_CLASSES_ROOT\gopher]
@="URL:Gopher Protocol"
"EditFlags"=hex:02,00,00,00
"URL Protocol"=""
[HKEY_CLASSES_ROOT\gopher\DefaultIcon]
@="C:\\WINNT\\System32\\url.dll,0"
[HKEY_CLASSES_ROOT\gopher\shell]
[HKEY_CLASSES_ROOT\gopher\shell\open]

[HKEY_CLASSES_ROOT\gopher\shell\open\command]
@="\"C:\\Program Files\\Plus!\\Microsoft Internet\\IExplore.exe\" -nohome"
[HKEY_CLASSES_ROOT\gopher\shell\open\ddeexec]
@="\"%1\",,-1,,,,,"
[HKEY_CLASSES_ROOT\gopher\shell\open\ddeexec\Application]
@="IExplore"
[HKEY_CLASSES_ROOT\gopher\shell\open\ddeexec\Topic]
@="WWW_OpenURL"
[HKEY_CLASSES_ROOT\helpfile]
@="Help File"
[HKEY_CLASSES_ROOT\helpfile\shell]
[HKEY_CLASSES_ROOT\helpfile\shell\open]
[HKEY_CLASSES_ROOT\helpfile\shell\open\command]
@="winhlp32.exe %1"
[HKEY_CLASSES_ROOT\hlpfile]
@="Help File"
[HKEY_CLASSES_ROOT\hlpfile\DefaultIcon]
@=hex(2):25,53,79,73,74,65,6d,52,6f,6f,74,25,5c,53,79,73,74,65,6d,33,32,5c,73,68,
65,6c,6c,33,32,2e,64,6c,6c,2c,32,33,00
[HKEY_CLASSES_ROOT\hlpfile\shell]
[HKEY_CLASSES_ROOT\hlpfile\shell\open]
[HKEY_CLASSES_ROOT\hlpfile\shell\open\command]
@=hex(2):25,53,79,73,74,65,6d,52,6f,6f,74,25,5c,53,79,73,74,65,6d,33,32,5c,77,69,
6e,68,6c,70,33,32,2e,65,78,65,20,25,31,00
[HKEY_CLASSES_ROOT\htfile]
@="HyperTerminal File"
[HKEY_CLASSES_ROOT\htfile\DefaultIcon]
@="%1"
[HKEY_CLASSES_ROOT\htfile\shell]
[HKEY_CLASSES_ROOT\htfile\shell\open]
[HKEY_CLASSES_ROOT\htfile\shell\open\command]
@="C:\\Program Files\\Windows NT\\HYPERTRM.EXE %1"
[HKEY_CLASSES_ROOT\htfile\shellex]
[HKEY_CLASSES_ROOT\htfile\shellex\IconHandler]
@="{88895560-9AA2-1069-930E-00AA0030EBC8}"
[HKEY_CLASSES_ROOT\htfile\shellex\PropertySheetHandlers]
[HKEY_CLASSES_ROOT\htfile\shellex\PropertySheetHandlers\TermPagc]
@="{1B53F360-9A1B-1069-930C-00AA0030EBC8}"
[HKEY_CLASSES_ROOT\htmlfile]
@="Internet Document (HTML)"
[HKEY_CLASSES_ROOT\htmlfile\DefaultIcon]
@="C:\\Program Files\\Plus!\\Microsoft Internet\\IExplore.exe,1"

[HKEY_CLASSES_ROOT\htmlfile\shell]
[HKEY_CLASSES_ROOT\htmlfile\shell\open]
[HKEY_CLASSES_ROOT\htmlfile\shell\open\command]
@="\"C:\\Program Files\\Plus!\\Microsoft Internet\\IExplore.exe\" -nohome"
[HKEY_CLASSES_ROOT\htmlfile\shell\open\ddeexec]
@="\"file:%1\",,-1,,,,,"
[HKEY_CLASSES_ROOT\htmlfile\shell\open\ddeexec\Application]
@="IExplore"
[HKEY_CLASSES_ROOT\htmlfile\shell\open\ddeexec\Topic]
@="WWW_OpenURL"
[HKEY_CLASSES_ROOT\http]
@="URL:HyperText Transfer Protocol"
"EditFlags"=hex:02,00,00,00
"URL Protocol"=""
[HKEY_CLASSES_ROOT\http\DefaultIcon]
@="C:\\WINNT\\System32\\url.dll,0"
[HKEY_CLASSES_ROOT\http\shell]
[HKEY_CLASSES_ROOT\http\shell\open]
[HKEY_CLASSES_ROOT\http\shell\open\command]
@="\"C:\\Program Files\\Plus!\\Microsoft Internet\\IExplore.exe\" -nohome"
[HKEY_CLASSES_ROOT\http\shell\open\ddeexec]
@="\"%1\",,-1,,,,,"
[HKEY_CLASSES_ROOT\http\shell\open\ddeexec\Application]
@="IExplore"
[HKEY_CLASSES_ROOT\http\shell\open\ddeexec\Topic]
@="WWW_OpenURL"
[HKEY_CLASSES_ROOT\https]
@="URL:HyperText Transfer Protocol with Privacy"
"EditFlags"=hex:02,00,00,00
"URL Protocol"=""
[HKEY_CLASSES_ROOT\https\DefaultIcon]
@="C:\\WINNT\\System32\\url.dll,0"
[HKEY_CLASSES_ROOT\https\shell]
[HKEY_CLASSES_ROOT\https\shell\open]
[HKEY_CLASSES_ROOT\https\shell\open\command]
@="\"C:\\Program Files\\Plus!\\Microsoft Internet\\IExplore.exe\" -nohome"
[HKEY_CLASSES_ROOT\https\shell\open\ddeexec]
@="\"%1\",,-1,,,,,"
[HKEY_CLASSES_ROOT\https\shell\open\ddeexec\Application]
@="IExplore"
[HKEY_CLASSES_ROOT\https\shell\open\ddeexec\Topic]
@="WWW_OpenURL"

[HKEY_CLASSES_ROOT\icofile]
@="Icon"
[HKEY_CLASSES_ROOT\icofile\DefaultIcon]
@="%1"
[HKEY_CLASSES_ROOT\inffile]
@="Setup Information"
[HKEY_CLASSES_ROOT\inffile\DefaultIcon]
@=hex(2):25,53,79,73,74,65,6d,52,6f,6f,74,25,5c,53,79,73,74,65,6d,33,32,5c,73,68,
65,6c,6c,33,32,2e,64,6c,6c,2c,2d,31,35,31,00
[HKEY_CLASSES_ROOT\inffile\shell]
[HKEY_CLASSES_ROOT\inffile\shell\Install]
@="&Install"
[HKEY_CLASSES_ROOT\inffile\shell\Install\command]
@=hex(2):25,53,79,73,74,65,6d,52,6f,6f,74,25,5c,53,79,73,74,65,6d,33,32,5c,72,75,
6e,64,6c,6c,33,32,2e,65,78,65,20,73,65,74,75,70,61,70,69,2c,49,6e,73,74,61,6c,6c,48,
69,6e,66,53,65,63,74,69,6f,6e,20,44,65,66,61,75,6c,74,49,6e,73,74,61,6c,6c,20,31,33,
32,20,25,31,00
[HKEY_CLASSES_ROOT\inffile\shell\open]
[HKEY_CLASSES_ROOT\inffile\shell\open\command]
@=hex(2):25,53,79,73,74,65,6d,52,6f,6f,74,25,5c,53,79,73,74,65,6d,33,32,5c,4e,4f,54,
45,50,41,44,2e,45,58,45,20,25,31,00
[HKEY_CLASSES_ROOT\inffile\shell\print]
[HKEY_CLASSES_ROOT\inffile\shell\print\command]
@=hex(2):25,53,79,73,74,65,6d,52,6f,6f,74,25,5c,53,79,73,74,65,6d,33,32,5c,4e,4f,54,
45,50,41,44,2e,45,58,45,20,2f,70,20,25,31,00
[HKEY_CLASSES_ROOT\inifile]
@="Configuration Settings"
[HKEY_CLASSES_ROOT\inifile\DefaultIcon]
@=hex(2):25,53,79,73,74,65,6d,52,6f,6f,74,25,5c,53,79,73,74,65,6d,33,32,5c,73,68,
65,6c,6c,33,32,2e,64,6c,6c,2c,2d,31,35,31,00
[HKEY_CLASSES_ROOT\inifile\shell]
[HKEY_CLASSES_ROOT\inifile\shell\open]
[HKEY_CLASSES_ROOT\inifile\shell\open\command]
@=hex(2):25,53,79,73,74,65,6d,52,6f,6f,74,25,5c,53,79,73,74,65,6d,33,32,5c,4e,4f,54,
45,50,41,44,2e,45,58,45,20,25,31,00
[HKEY_CLASSES_ROOT\inifile\shell\print]
[HKEY_CLASSES_ROOT\inifile\shell\print\command]
@=hex(2):25,53,79,73,74,65,6d,52,6f,6f,74,25,5c,53,79,73,74,65,6d,33,32,5c,4e,4f,54,
45,50,41,44,2e,45,58,45,20,2f,70,20,25,31,00
[HKEY_CLASSES_ROOT\Interface]
[HKEY_CLASSES_ROOT\Interface\{00000000-0000-0000-C000-000000000046}]
@="IUnknown"

[HKEY_CLASSES_ROOT\Interface\{00000000-0000-0000-C000-
000000000046}\BaseInterface]
@=""
[HKEY_CLASSES_ROOT\Interface\{00000000-0000-0000-C000-
000000000046}\NumMethods]
@="3"
[HKEY_CLASSES_ROOT\Interface\{00000001-0000-0000-C000-000000000046}]
@="IClassFactory"
[HKEY_CLASSES_ROOT\Interface\{00000001-0000-0000-C000-
000000000046}\NumMethods]
@="5"
[HKEY_CLASSES_ROOT\Interface\{00000001-0000-0000-C000-
000000000046}\ProxyStubClsid32]
@="{00000320-0000-0000-C000-000000000046}"
[HKEY_CLASSES_ROOT\Interface\{00000002-0000-0000-C000-000000000046}]
@="IMalloc"
[HKEY_CLASSES_ROOT\Interface\{00000002-0000-0000-C000-
000000000046}\NumMethods]
@="9"
[HKEY_CLASSES_ROOT\Interface\{00000003-0000-0000-C000-000000000046}]
@="IMarshal"
[HKEY_CLASSES_ROOT\Interface\{00000003-0000-0000-C000-
000000000046}\NumMethods]
@="9"
[HKEY_CLASSES_ROOT\Interface\{00000004-0000-0000-C000-000000000046}]
@="IRpcChannel"
[HKEY_CLASSES_ROOT\Interface\{00000004-0000-0000-C000-
000000000046}\NumMethods]
@="7"
[HKEY_CLASSES_ROOT\Interface\{00000005-0000-0000-C000-000000000046}]
@="IRpcStub"
[HKEY_CLASSES_ROOT\Interface\{00000005-0000-0000-C000-
000000000046}\NumMethods]
@="8"
[HKEY_CLASSES_ROOT\Interface\{00000007-0000-0000-C000-000000000046}]
@="IRpcProxy"
[HKEY_CLASSES_ROOT\Interface\{00000007-0000-0000-C000-
000000000046}\NumMethods]
@="5"
[HKEY_CLASSES_ROOT\Interface\{00000009-0000-0000-C000-000000000046}]
@="IPSFactory"
[HKEY_CLASSES_ROOT\Interface\{00000009-0000-0000-C000-
000000000046}\NumMethods]
@="5"

[HKEY_CLASSES_ROOT\Interface\{0000000a-0000-0000-C000-000000000046}]
@="ILockBytes"
[HKEY_CLASSES_ROOT\Interface\{0000000a-0000-0000-C000-
000000000046}\NumMethods]
@="10"
[HKEY_CLASSES_ROOT\Interface\{0000000a-0000-0000-C000-
000000000046}\ProxyStubClsid32]
@="{00000320-0000-0000-C000-000000000046}"
[HKEY_CLASSES_ROOT\Interface\{0000000b-0000-0000-C000-000000000046}]
@="IStorage"
[HKEY_CLASSES_ROOT\Interface\{0000000b-0000-0000-C000-
000000000046}\NumMethods]
@="18"
[HKEY_CLASSES_ROOT\Interface\{0000000b-0000-0000-C000-
000000000046}\ProxyStubClsid32]
@="{00000320-0000-0000-C000-000000000046}"
[HKEY_CLASSES_ROOT\Interface\{0000000c-0000-0000-C000-000000000046}]
@="IStream"
[HKEY_CLASSES_ROOT\Interface\{0000000c-0000-0000-C000-
000000000046}\NumMethods]
@="14"
[HKEY_CLASSES_ROOT\Interface\{0000000c-0000-0000-C000-
000000000046}\ProxyStubClsid32]
@="{00000320-0000-0000-C000-000000000046}"
[HKEY_CLASSES_ROOT\Interface\{0000000d-0000-0000-C000-000000000046}]
@="IEnumSTATSTG"
[HKEY_CLASSES_ROOT\Interface\{0000000d-0000-0000-C000-
000000000046}\NumMethods]
@="7"
[HKEY_CLASSES_ROOT\Interface\{0000000d-0000-0000-C000-
000000000046}\ProxyStubClsid32]
@="{00000320-0000-0000-C000-000000000046}"
[HKEY_CLASSES_ROOT\Interface\{0000000e-0000-0000-C000-000000000046}]
@="IBindCtx"
[HKEY_CLASSES_ROOT\Interface\{0000000e-0000-0000-C000-
000000000046}\NumMethods]
@="13"
[HKEY_CLASSES_ROOT\Interface\{0000000e-0000-0000-C000-
000000000046}\ProxyStubClsid32]
@="{00000320-0000-0000-C000-000000000046}"
[HKEY_CLASSES_ROOT\Interface\{0000000f-0000-0000-C000-000000000046}]
@="IMoniker"

[HKEY_CLASSES_ROOT\Interface\{0000000f-0000-0000-C000-
000000000046}\BaseInterface]
@="{00000109-0000-0000-C000-000000000046}"
[HKEY_CLASSES_ROOT\Interface\{0000000f-0000-0000-C000-
000000000046}\NumMethods]
@="23"
[HKEY_CLASSES_ROOT\Interface\{0000000f-0000-0000-C000-
000000000046}\ProxyStubClsid32]
@="{00000320-0000-0000-C000-000000000046}"
[HKEY_CLASSES_ROOT\Interface\{00000010-0000-0000-C000-000000000046}]
@="IRunningObjectTable"
[HKEY_CLASSES_ROOT\Interface\{00000010-0000-0000-C000-
000000000046}\NumMethods]
@="10"
[HKEY_CLASSES_ROOT\Interface\{00000010-0000-0000-C000-
000000000046}\ProxyStubClsid32]
@="{00000320-0000-0000-C000-000000000046}"
[HKEY_CLASSES_ROOT\Interface\{00000012-0000-0000-C000-000000000046}]
@="IRootStorage"
[HKEY_CLASSES_ROOT\Interface\{00000012-0000-0000-C000-
000000000046}\NumMethods]
@="4"
[HKEY_CLASSES_ROOT\Interface\{00000012-0000-0000-C000-
000000000046}\ProxyStubClsid32]
@="{00000320-0000-0000-C000-000000000046}"
[HKEY_CLASSES_ROOT\Interface\{00000016-0000-0000-C000-000000000046}]
@="IMessageFilter"
[HKEY_CLASSES_ROOT\Interface\{00000016-0000-0000-C000-
000000000046}\NumMethods]
@="6"
[HKEY_CLASSES_ROOT\Interface\{00000018-0000-0000-C000-000000000046}]
@="IStdMarshalInfo"
[HKEY_CLASSES_ROOT\Interface\{00000018-0000-0000-C000-
000000000046}\NumMethods]
@="4"
[HKEY_CLASSES_ROOT\Interface\{00000019-0000-0000-C000-000000000046}]
@="IExternalConnection"
[HKEY_CLASSES_ROOT\Interface\{00000019-0000-0000-C000-
000000000046}\NumMethods]
@="5"
[HKEY_CLASSES_ROOT\Interface\{00000100-0000-0000-C000-000000000046}]
@="IEnumUnknown"

[HKEY_CLASSES_ROOT\Interface\{00000100-0000-0000-C000-000000000046}\NumMethods]
@="7"
[HKEY_CLASSES_ROOT\Interface\{00000100-0000-0000-C000-000000000046}\ProxyStubClsid32]
@="{00000320-0000-0000-C000-000000000046}"
[HKEY_CLASSES_ROOT\Interface\{00000101-0000-0000-C000-000000000046}]
@="IEnumString"
[HKEY_CLASSES_ROOT\Interface\{00000101-0000-0000-C000-000000000046}\NumMethods]
@="7"
[HKEY_CLASSES_ROOT\Interface\{00000101-0000-0000-C000-000000000046}\ProxyStubClsid32]
@="{00000320-0000-0000-C000-000000000046}"
[HKEY_CLASSES_ROOT\Interface\{00000102-0000-0000-C000-000000000046}]
@="IEnumMoniker"
[HKEY_CLASSES_ROOT\Interface\{00000102-0000-0000-C000-000000000046}\NumMethods]
@="7"
[HKEY_CLASSES_ROOT\Interface\{00000102-0000-0000-C000-000000000046}\ProxyStubClsid32]
@="{00000320-0000-0000-C000-000000000046}"
[HKEY_CLASSES_ROOT\Interface\{00000103-0000-0000-C000-000000000046}]
@="IEnumFORMATETC"
[HKEY_CLASSES_ROOT\Interface\{00000103-0000-0000-C000-000000000046}\NumMethods]
@="7"
[HKEY_CLASSES_ROOT\Interface\{00000103-0000-0000-C000-000000000046}\ProxyStubClsid32]
@="{00000320-0000-0000-C000-000000000046}"
[HKEY_CLASSES_ROOT\Interface\{00000104-0000-0000-C000-000000000046}]
@="IEnumOLEVERB"
[HKEY_CLASSES_ROOT\Interface\{00000104-0000-0000-C000-000000000046}\NumMethods]
@="7"
[HKEY_CLASSES_ROOT\Interface\{00000104-0000-0000-C000-000000000046}\ProxyStubClsid32]
@="{00000320-0000-0000-C000-000000000046}"
[HKEY_CLASSES_ROOT\Interface\{00000105-0000-0000-C000-000000000046}]
@="IEnumSTATDATA"
[HKEY_CLASSES_ROOT\Interface\{00000105-0000-0000-C000-000000000046}\NumMethods]
@="7"

[HKEY_CLASSES_ROOT\Interface\{00000105-0000-0000-C000-
000000000046}\ProxyStubClsid32]
@="{00000320-0000-0000-C000-000000000046}"
[HKEY_CLASSES_ROOT\Interface\{00000109-0000-0000-C000-000000000046}]
@="IPersistStream"
[HKEY_CLASSES_ROOT\Interface\{00000109-0000-0000-C000-
000000000046}\BaseInterface]
@="{0000010C-0000-0000-C000-000000000046}"
[HKEY_CLASSES_ROOT\Interface\{00000109-0000-0000-C000-
000000000046}\NumMethods]
@="8"
[HKEY_CLASSES_ROOT\Interface\{00000109-0000-0000-C000-
000000000046}\ProxyStubClsid32]
@="{00000320-0000-0000-C000-000000000046}"
[HKEY_CLASSES_ROOT\Interface\{0000010a-0000-0000-C000-000000000046}]
@="IPersistStorage"
[HKEY_CLASSES_ROOT\Interface\{0000010a-0000-0000-C000-
000000000046}\BaseInterface]
@="{0000010C-0000-0000-C000-000000000046}"
[HKEY_CLASSES_ROOT\Interface\{0000010a-0000-0000-C000-
000000000046}\NumMethods]
@="10"
[HKEY_CLASSES_ROOT\Interface\{0000010a-0000-0000-C000-
000000000046}\ProxyStubClsid32]
@="{00000320-0000-0000-C000-000000000046}"
[HKEY_CLASSES_ROOT\Interface\{0000010b-0000-0000-C000-000000000046}]
@="IPersistFile"
[HKEY_CLASSES_ROOT\Interface\{0000010b-0000-0000-C000-
000000000046}\BaseInterface]
@="{0000010c-0000-0000-C000-000000000046}"
[HKEY_CLASSES_ROOT\Interface\{0000010b-0000-0000-C000-
000000000046}\NumMethods]
@="9"
[HKEY_CLASSES_ROOT\Interface\{0000010b-0000-0000-C000-
000000000046}\ProxyStubClsid32]
@="{00000320-0000-0000-C000-000000000046}"
[HKEY_CLASSES_ROOT\Interface\{0000010c-0000-0000-C000-000000000046}]
@="IPersist"
[HKEY_CLASSES_ROOT\Interface\{0000010c-0000-0000-C000-
000000000046}\NumMethods]
@="4"
[HKEY_CLASSES_ROOT\Interface\{0000010c-0000-0000-C000-
000000000046}\ProxyStubClsid32]

@="{00000320-0000-0000-C000-000000000046}"
[HKEY_CLASSES_ROOT\Interface\{0000010d-0000-0000-C000-000000000046}]
@="IViewObject"
[HKEY_CLASSES_ROOT\Interface\{0000010d-0000-0000-C000-000000000046}\NumMethods]
@="9"
[HKEY_CLASSES_ROOT\Interface\{0000010d-0000-0000-C000-000000000046}\ProxyStubClsid32]
@="{00000320-0000-0000-C000-000000000046}"
[HKEY_CLASSES_ROOT\Interface\{0000010e-0000-0000-C000-000000000046}]
@="IDataObject"
[HKEY_CLASSES_ROOT\Interface\{0000010e-0000-0000-C000-000000000046}\NumMethods]
@="12"
[HKEY_CLASSES_ROOT\Interface\{0000010e-0000-0000-C000-000000000046}\ProxyStubClsid32]
@="{00000320-0000-0000-C000-000000000046}"
[HKEY_CLASSES_ROOT\Interface\{0000010f-0000-0000-C000-000000000046}]
@="IAdviseSink"
[HKEY_CLASSES_ROOT\Interface\{0000010f-0000-0000-C000-000000000046}\NumMethods]
@="8"
[HKEY_CLASSES_ROOT\Interface\{0000010f-0000-0000-C000-000000000046}\ProxyStubClsid32]
@="{00000320-0000-0000-C000-000000000046}"
[HKEY_CLASSES_ROOT\Interface\{00000110-0000-0000-C000-000000000046}]
@="IDataAdviseHolder"
[HKEY_CLASSES_ROOT\Interface\{00000110-0000-0000-C000-000000000046}\NumMethods]
@="7"
[HKEY_CLASSES_ROOT\Interface\{00000111-0000-0000-C000-000000000046}]
@="IOleAdviseHolder"
[HKEY_CLASSES_ROOT\Interface\{00000111-0000-0000-C000-000000000046}\NumMethods]
@="9"
[HKEY_CLASSES_ROOT\Interface\{00000112-0000-0000-C000-000000000046}]
@="IOleObject"
[HKEY_CLASSES_ROOT\Interface\{00000112-0000-0000-C000-000000000046}\NumMethods]
@="24"
[HKEY_CLASSES_ROOT\Interface\{00000112-0000-0000-C000-000000000046}\ProxyStubClsid32]
@="{00000320-0000-0000-C000-000000000046}"

[HKEY_CLASSES_ROOT\Interface\{00000113-0000-0000-C000-000000000046}]
@="IOleInPlaceObject"
[HKEY_CLASSES_ROOT\Interface\{00000113-0000-0000-C000-
000000000046}\BaseInterface]
@="{00000114-0000-0000-C000-000000000046}"
[HKEY_CLASSES_ROOT\Interface\{00000113-0000-0000-C000-
000000000046}\NumMethods]
@="9"
[HKEY_CLASSES_ROOT\Interface\{00000113-0000-0000-C000-
000000000046}\ProxyStubClsid32]
@="{00000320-0000-0000-C000-000000000046}"
[HKEY_CLASSES_ROOT\Interface\{00000114-0000-0000-C000-000000000046}]
@="IOleWindow"
[HKEY_CLASSES_ROOT\Interface\{00000114-0000-0000-C000-
000000000046}\NumMethods]
@="5"
[HKEY_CLASSES_ROOT\Interface\{00000114-0000-0000-C000-
000000000046}\ProxyStubClsid32]
@="{00000320-0000-0000-C000-000000000046}"
[HKEY_CLASSES_ROOT\Interface\{00000115-0000-0000-C000-000000000046}]
@="IOleInPlaceUIWindow"
[HKEY_CLASSES_ROOT\Interface\{00000115-0000-0000-C000-
000000000046}\BaseInterface]
@="{00000114-0000-0000-C000-000000000046}"
[HKEY_CLASSES_ROOT\Interface\{00000115-0000-0000-C000-
000000000046}\NumMethods]
@="9"
[HKEY_CLASSES_ROOT\Interface\{00000115-0000-0000-C000-
000000000046}\ProxyStubClsid32]
@="{00000320-0000-0000-C000-000000000046}"
[HKEY_CLASSES_ROOT\Interface\{00000116-0000-0000-C000-000000000046}]
@="IOleInPlaceFrame"
[HKEY_CLASSES_ROOT\Interface\{00000116-0000-0000-C000-
000000000046}\NumMethods]
@="15"
[HKEY_CLASSES_ROOT\Interface\{00000116-0000-0000-C000-
000000000046}\ProxyStubClsid32]
@="{00000320-0000-0000-C000-000000000046}"
[HKEY_CLASSES_ROOT\Interface\{00000117-0000-0000-C000-000000000046}]
@="IOleInPlaceActiveObject"
[HKEY_CLASSES_ROOT\Interface\{00000117-0000-0000-C000-
000000000046}\BaseInterface]
@="{00000114-0000-0000-C000-000000000046}"

[HKEY_CLASSES_ROOT\Interface\{00000117-0000-0000-C000-
000000000046}\NumMethods]
@="10"
[HKEY_CLASSES_ROOT\Interface\{00000117-0000-0000-C000-
000000000046}\ProxyStubClsid32]
@="{00000320-0000-0000-C000-000000000046}"
[HKEY_CLASSES_ROOT\Interface\{00000118-0000-0000-C000-000000000046}]
@="IOleClientSite"
[HKEY_CLASSES_ROOT\Interface\{00000118-0000-0000-C000-
000000000046}\NumMethods]
@="9"
[HKEY_CLASSES_ROOT\Interface\{00000118-0000-0000-C000-
000000000046}\ProxyStubClsid32]
@="{00000320-0000-0000-C000-000000000046}"
[HKEY_CLASSES_ROOT\Interface\{00000119-0000-0000-C000-000000000046}]
@="IOleInPlaceSite"
[HKEY_CLASSES_ROOT\Interface\{00000119-0000-0000-C000-
000000000046}\BaseInterface]
@="{00000114-0000-0000-C000-000000000046}"
[HKEY_CLASSES_ROOT\Interface\{00000119-0000-0000-C000-
000000000046}\NumMethods]
@="15"
[HKEY_CLASSES_ROOT\Interface\{00000119-0000-0000-C000-
000000000046}\ProxyStubClsid32]
@="{00000320-0000-0000-C000-000000000046}"
[HKEY_CLASSES_ROOT\Interface\{0000011a-0000-0000-C000-000000000046}]
@="IParseDisplayName"
[HKEY_CLASSES_ROOT\Interface\{0000011a-0000-0000-C000-
000000000046}\NumMethods]
@="4"
[HKEY_CLASSES_ROOT\Interface\{0000011a-0000-0000-C000-
000000000046}\ProxyStubClsid32]
@="{00000320-0000-0000-C000-000000000046}"
[HKEY_CLASSES_ROOT\Interface\{0000011b-0000-0000-C000-000000000046}]
@="IOleContainer"
[HKEY_CLASSES_ROOT\Interface\{0000011b-0000-0000-C000-
000000000046}\BaseInterface]
@="{0000011a-0000-0000-C000-000000000046}"
[HKEY_CLASSES_ROOT\Interface\{0000011b-0000-0000-C000-
000000000046}\NumMethods]
@="6"
[HKEY_CLASSES_ROOT\Interface\{0000011b-0000-0000-C000-
000000000046}\ProxyStubClsid32]
@="{00000320-0000-0000-C000-000000000046}"

[HKEY_CLASSES_ROOT\Interface\{0000011c-0000-0000-C000-000000000046}]
@="IOleItemContainer"
[HKEY_CLASSES_ROOT\Interface\{0000011c-0000-0000-C000-
000000000046}\BaseInterface]
@="{0000011b-0000-0000-C000-000000000046}"
[HKEY_CLASSES_ROOT\Interface\{0000011c-0000-0000-C000-
000000000046}\NumMethods]
@="9"
[HKEY_CLASSES_ROOT\Interface\{0000011c-0000-0000-C000-
000000000046}\ProxyStubClsid32]
@="{00000320-0000-0000-C000-000000000046}"
[HKEY_CLASSES_ROOT\Interface\{0000011d-0000-0000-C000-000000000046}]
@="IOleLink"
[HKEY_CLASSES_ROOT\Interface\{0000011d-0000-0000-C000-
000000000046}\NumMethods]
@="14"
[HKEY_CLASSES_ROOT\Interface\{0000011d-0000-0000-C000-
000000000046}\ProxyStubClsid32]
@="{00000320-0000-0000-C000-000000000046}"
[HKEY_CLASSES_ROOT\Interface\{0000011e-0000-0000-C000-000000000046}]
@="IOleCache"
[HKEY_CLASSES_ROOT\Interface\{0000011e-0000-0000-C000-
000000000046}\NumMethods]
@="8"
[HKEY_CLASSES_ROOT\Interface\{0000011e-0000-0000-C000-
000000000046}\ProxyStubClsid32]
@="{00000320-0000-0000-C000-000000000046}"
[HKEY_CLASSES_ROOT\Interface\{00000121-0000-0000-C000-000000000046}]
@="IDropSource"
[HKEY_CLASSES_ROOT\Interface\{00000121-0000-0000-C000-
000000000046}\NumMethods]
@="5"
[HKEY_CLASSES_ROOT\Interface\{00000122-0000-0000-C000-000000000046}]
@="IDropTarget"
[HKEY_CLASSES_ROOT\Interface\{00000122-0000-0000-C000-
000000000046}\NumMethods]
@="7"
[HKEY_CLASSES_ROOT\Interface\{00000122-0000-0000-C000-
000000000046}\ProxyStubClsid32]
@="{00000320-0000-0000-C000-000000000046}"
[HKEY_CLASSES_ROOT\Interface\{00000124-0000-0000-C000-000000000046}]
@="IDebugStream"

[HKEY_CLASSES_ROOT\Interface\{00000124-0000-0000-C000-
000000000046}\NumMethods]
@="19"
[HKEY_CLASSES_ROOT\Interface\{00000125-0000-0000-C000-000000000046}]
@="IAdviseSink2"
[HKEY_CLASSES_ROOT\Interface\{00000125-0000-0000-C000-
000000000046}\BaseInterface]
@="{0000010f-0000-0000-C000-000000000046}"
[HKEY_CLASSES_ROOT\Interface\{00000125-0000-0000-C000-
000000000046}\NumMethods]
@="9"
[HKEY_CLASSES_ROOT\Interface\{00000125-0000-0000-C000-
000000000046}\ProxyStubClsid32]
@="{00000320-0000-0000-C000-000000000046}"
[HKEY_CLASSES_ROOT\Interface\{00000126-0000-0000-C000-000000000046}]
@="IRunnableObject"
[HKEY_CLASSES_ROOT\Interface\{00000126-0000-0000-C000-
000000000046}\NumMethods]
@="8"
[HKEY_CLASSES_ROOT\Interface\{00000126-0000-0000-C000-
000000000046}\ProxyStubClsid32]
@="{00000320-0000-0000-C000-000000000046}"
[HKEY_CLASSES_ROOT\Interface\{00000127-0000-0000-C000-000000000046}]
@="IViewObject2"
[HKEY_CLASSES_ROOT\Interface\{00000127-0000-0000-C000-
000000000046}\BaseInterface]
@="{0000010d-0000-0000-C000-000000000046}"
[HKEY_CLASSES_ROOT\Interface\{00000127-0000-0000-C000-
000000000046}\NumMethods]
@="10"
[HKEY_CLASSES_ROOT\Interface\{00000127-0000-0000-C000-
000000000046}\ProxyStubClsid32]
@="{00000320-0000-0000-C000-000000000046}"
[HKEY_CLASSES_ROOT\Interface\{00000128-0000-0000-C000-000000000046}]
@="IOleCache2"
[HKEY_CLASSES_ROOT\Interface\{00000128-0000-0000-C000-
000000000046}\BaseInterface]
@="{0000011e-0000-0000-C000-000000000046}"
[HKEY_CLASSES_ROOT\Interface\{00000128-0000-0000-C000-
000000000046}\NumMethods]
@="10"
[HKEY_CLASSES_ROOT\Interface\{00000128-0000-0000-C000-
000000000046}\ProxyStubClsid32]
@="{00000320-0000-0000-C000-000000000046}"

[HKEY_CLASSES_ROOT\Interface\{00000129-0000-0000-C000-000000000046}]
@="IOleCacheControl"
[HKEY_CLASSES_ROOT\Interface\{00000129-0000-0000-C000-
000000000046}\NumMethods]
@="5"
[HKEY_CLASSES_ROOT\Interface\{00000129-0000-0000-C000-
000000000046}\ProxyStubClsid32]
@="{00000320-0000-0000-C000-000000000046}"
[HKEY_CLASSES_ROOT\Interface\{0000012A-0000-0000-C000-000000000046}]
@="IContinue"
[HKEY_CLASSES_ROOT\Interface\{0000012A-0000-0000-C000-
000000000046}\NumMethods]
@="4"
[HKEY_CLASSES_ROOT\Interface\{0000012A-0000-0000-C000-
000000000046}\ProxyStubClsid32]
@="{00000320-0000-0000-C000-000000000046}"
[HKEY_CLASSES_ROOT\Interface\{00000131-0000-0000-C000-000000000046}]
@="IRemUnknown"
[HKEY_CLASSES_ROOT\Interface\{00000131-0000-0000-C000-
000000000046}\ProxyStubClsid32]
@="{00000320-0000-0000-C000-000000000046}"
[HKEY_CLASSES_ROOT\Interface\{00000132-0000-0000-C000-000000000046}]
@="IObjServer"
[HKEY_CLASSES_ROOT\Interface\{00000132-0000-0000-C000-
000000000046}\ProxyStubClsid32]
@="{00000320-0000-0000-C000-000000000046}"
[HKEY_CLASSES_ROOT\Interface\{00000133-0000-0000-C000-000000000046}]
@="IOSCM"
[HKEY_CLASSES_ROOT\Interface\{00000133-0000-0000-C000-
000000000046}\ProxyStubClsid32]
@="{00000320-0000-0000-C000-000000000046}"
[HKEY_CLASSES_ROOT\Interface\{00000134-0000-0000-C000-000000000046}]
@="IRundown"
[HKEY_CLASSES_ROOT\Interface\{00000134-0000-0000-C000-
000000000046}\ProxyStubClsid32]
@="{00000320-0000-0000-C000-000000000046}"
[HKEY_CLASSES_ROOT\Interface\{00000135-0000-0000-C000-000000000046}]
@="IInterfaceFromWindowProp"
[HKEY_CLASSES_ROOT\Interface\{00000135-0000-0000-C000-
000000000046}\ProxyStubClsid32]
@="{00000320-0000-0000-C000-000000000046}"
[HKEY_CLASSES_ROOT\Interface\{00000136-0000-0000-C000-000000000046}]
@="IDSCM"

[HKEY_CLASSES_ROOT\Interface\{00000136-0000-0000-C000-000000000046}\ProxyStubClsid32]
@="{00000320-0000-0000-C000-000000000046}"
[HKEY_CLASSES_ROOT\Interface\{00000138-0000-0000-C000-000000000046}]
@="IPropertyStorage"
[HKEY_CLASSES_ROOT\Interface\{00000138-0000-0000-C000-000000000046}\ProxyStubClsid32]
@="{00000320-0000-0000-C000-000000000046}"
[HKEY_CLASSES_ROOT\Interface\{00000139-0000-0000-C000-000000000046}]
@="IEnumSTATPROPSTG"
[HKEY_CLASSES_ROOT\Interface\{00000139-0000-0000-C000-000000000046}\ProxyStubClsid32]
@="{00000320-0000-0000-C000-000000000046}"
[HKEY_CLASSES_ROOT\Interface\{0000013A-0000-0000-C000-000000000046}]
@="IPropertySetStorage"
[HKEY_CLASSES_ROOT\Interface\{0000013A-0000-0000-C000-000000000046}\ProxyStubClsid32]
@="{00000320-0000-0000-C000-000000000046}"
[HKEY_CLASSES_ROOT\Interface\{0000013B-0000-0000-C000-000000000046}]
@="IEnumSTATPROPSETSTG"
[HKEY_CLASSES_ROOT\Interface\{0000013B-0000-0000-C000-000000000046}\ProxyStubClsid32]
@="{00000320-0000-0000-C000-000000000046}"
[HKEY_CLASSES_ROOT\Interface\{00000140-0000-0000-C000-000000000046}]
@="IClassActivator"
[HKEY_CLASSES_ROOT\Interface\{00000140-0000-0000-C000-000000000046}\NumMethods]
@="4"
[HKEY_CLASSES_ROOT\Interface\{00000140-0000-0000-C000-000000000046}\ProxyStubClsid32]
@="{00000320-0000-0000-C000-000000000046}"
[HKEY_CLASSES_ROOT\Interface\{00000141-0000-0000-C000-000000000046}]
@="IDLLHost"
[HKEY_CLASSES_ROOT\Interface\{00000141-0000-0000-C000-000000000046}\ProxyStubClsid32]
@="{00000320-0000-0000-C000-000000000046}"
[HKEY_CLASSES_ROOT\Interface\{00020020-0000-0000-C000-000000000046}]
@="AVIFile Interface 1.22"
[HKEY_CLASSES_ROOT\Interface\{00020020-0000-0000-C000-000000000046}\ProxyStubClsid]
@="{0002000d-0000-0000-C000-000000000046}"
[HKEY_CLASSES_ROOT\Interface\{00020020-0000-0000-C000-000000000046}\ProxyStubClsid32]
@="{0002000d-0000-0000-C000-000000000046}"

[HKEY_CLASSES_ROOT\Interface\{00020021-0000-0000-C000-000000000046}]
@="AVIStream Interface"
[HKEY_CLASSES_ROOT\Interface\{00020021-0000-0000-C000-
000000000046}\ProxyStubClsid]
@="{0002000d-0000-0000-C000-000000000046}"
[HKEY_CLASSES_ROOT\Interface\{00020021-0000-0000-C000-
000000000046}\ProxyStubClsid32]
@="{0002000d-0000-0000-C000-000000000046}"
[HKEY_CLASSES_ROOT\Interface\{00020300-0000-0000-C000-000000000046}]
@="IMAPISession"
[HKEY_CLASSES_ROOT\Interface\{00020300-0000-0000-C000-
000000000046}\ProxyStubClsid]
@="{4d2f086c-6ea3-101b-a18a-00aa00446e07}"
[HKEY_CLASSES_ROOT\Interface\{00020300-0000-0000-C000-
000000000046}\ProxyStubClsid32]
@="{4d2f086c-6ea3-101b-a18a-00aa00446e07}"
[HKEY_CLASSES_ROOT\Interface\{00020301-0000-0000-C000-000000000046}]
@="IMAPITable"
[HKEY_CLASSES_ROOT\Interface\{00020301-0000-0000-C000-
000000000046}\ProxyStubClsid]
@="{4d2f086c-6ea3-101b-a18a-00aa00446e07}"
[HKEY_CLASSES_ROOT\Interface\{00020301-0000-0000-C000-
000000000046}\ProxyStubClsid32]
@="{4d2f086c-6ea3-101b-a18a-00aa00446e07}"
[HKEY_CLASSES_ROOT\Interface\{00020302-0000-0000-C000-000000000046}]
@="IMAPIAdviseSink"
[HKEY_CLASSES_ROOT\Interface\{00020302-0000-0000-C000-
000000000046}\ProxyStubClsid]
@="{4d2f086c-6ea3-101b-a18a-00aa00446e07}"
[HKEY_CLASSES_ROOT\Interface\{00020302-0000-0000-C000-
000000000046}\ProxyStubClsid32]
@="{4d2f086c-6ea3-101b-a18a-00aa00446e07}"
[HKEY_CLASSES_ROOT\Interface\{00020303-0000-0000-C000-000000000046}]
@="IMAPIProp"
[HKEY_CLASSES_ROOT\Interface\{00020303-0000-0000-C000-
000000000046}\ProxyStubClsid]
@="{4d2f086c-6ea3-101b-a18a-00aa00446e07}"
[HKEY_CLASSES_ROOT\Interface\{00020303-0000-0000-C000-
000000000046}\ProxyStubClsid32]
@="{4d2f086c-6ea3-101b-a18a-00aa00446e07}"
[HKEY_CLASSES_ROOT\Interface\{00020304-0000-0000-C000-000000000046}]
@="IProfSect"

[HKEY_CLASSES_ROOT\Interface\{00020304-0000-0000-C000-
000000000046}\ProxyStubClsid]
@="{4d2f086c-6ea3-101b-a18a-00aa00446e07}"
[HKEY_CLASSES_ROOT\Interface\{00020304-0000-0000-C000-
000000000046}\ProxyStubClsid32]
@="{4d2f086c-6ea3-101b-a18a-00aa00446e07}"
[HKEY_CLASSES_ROOT\Interface\{00020305-0000-0000-C000-000000000046}]
@="IMAPIStatus"
[HKEY_CLASSES_ROOT\Interface\{00020305-0000-0000-C000-
000000000046}\ProxyStubClsid]
@="{4d2f086c-6ea3-101b-a18a-00aa00446e07}"
[HKEY_CLASSES_ROOT\Interface\{00020305-0000-0000-C000-
000000000046}\ProxyStubClsid32]
@="{4d2f086c-6ea3-101b-a18a-00aa00446e07}"
[HKEY_CLASSES_ROOT\Interface\{00020306-0000-0000-C000-000000000046}]
@="IMAPIMsgStore"
[HKEY_CLASSES_ROOT\Interface\{00020306-0000-0000-C000-
000000000046}\ProxyStubClsid]
@="{4d2f086c-6ea3-101b-a18a-00aa00446e07}"
[HKEY_CLASSES_ROOT\Interface\{00020306-0000-0000-C000-
000000000046}\ProxyStubClsid32]
@="{4d2f086c-6ea3-101b-a18a-00aa00446e07}"
[HKEY_CLASSES_ROOT\Interface\{00020307-0000-0000-C000-000000000046}]
@="IMessage"
[HKEY_CLASSES_ROOT\Interface\{00020307-0000-0000-C000-
000000000046}\ProxyStubClsid]
@="{4d2f086c-6ea3-101b-a18a-00aa00446e07}"
[HKEY_CLASSES_ROOT\Interface\{00020307-0000-0000-C000-
000000000046}\ProxyStubClsid32]
@="{4d2f086c-6ea3-101b-a18a-00aa00446e07}"
[HKEY_CLASSES_ROOT\Interface\{00020308-0000-0000-C000-000000000046}]
@="IAttachment"
[HKEY_CLASSES_ROOT\Interface\{00020308-0000-0000-C000-
000000000046}\ProxyStubClsid]
@="{4d2f086c-6ea3-101b-a18a-00aa00446e07}"
[HKEY_CLASSES_ROOT\Interface\{00020308-0000-0000-C000-
000000000046}\ProxyStubClsid32]
@="{4d2f086c-6ea3-101b-a18a-00aa00446e07}"
[HKEY_CLASSES_ROOT\Interface\{00020309-0000-0000-C000-000000000046}]
@="IAddrBook"
[HKEY_CLASSES_ROOT\Interface\{00020309-0000-0000-C000-
000000000046}\ProxyStubClsid]
@="{4d2f086c-6ea3-101b-a18a-00aa00446e07}"

[HKEY_CLASSES_ROOT\Interface\{00020309-0000-0000-C000-
000000000046}\ProxyStubClsid32]
@="{4d2f086c-6ea3-101b-a18a-00aa00446e07}"
[HKEY_CLASSES_ROOT\Interface\{0002030A-0000-0000-C000-000000000046}]
@="IMailUser"
[HKEY_CLASSES_ROOT\Interface\{0002030A-0000-0000-C000-
000000000046}\ProxyStubClsid]
@="{4d2f086c-6ea3-101b-a18a-00aa00446e07}"
[HKEY_CLASSES_ROOT\Interface\{0002030A-0000-0000-C000-
000000000046}\ProxyStubClsid32]
@="{4d2f086c-6ea3-101b-a18a-00aa00446e07}"
[HKEY_CLASSES_ROOT\Interface\{0002030B-0000-0000-C000-000000000046}]
@="IMAPIContainer"
[HKEY_CLASSES_ROOT\Interface\{0002030B-0000-0000-C000-
000000000046}\ProxyStubClsid]
@="{4d2f086c-6ea3-101b-a18a-00aa00446e07}"
[HKEY_CLASSES_ROOT\Interface\{0002030B-0000-0000-C000-
000000000046}\ProxyStubClsid32]
@="{4d2f086c-6ea3-101b-a18a-00aa00446e07}"
[HKEY_CLASSES_ROOT\Interface\{0002030C-0000-0000-C000-000000000046}]
@="IMAPIFolder"
[HKEY_CLASSES_ROOT\Interface\{0002030C-0000-0000-C000-
000000000046}\ProxyStubClsid]
@="{4d2f086c-6ea3-101b-a18a-00aa00446e07}"
[HKEY_CLASSES_ROOT\Interface\{0002030C-0000-0000-C000-
000000000046}\ProxyStubClsid32]
@="{4d2f086c-6ea3-101b-a18a-00aa00446e07}"
[HKEY_CLASSES_ROOT\Interface\{0002030D-0000-0000-C000-000000000046}]
@="IABContainer"
[HKEY_CLASSES_ROOT\Interface\{0002030D-0000-0000-C000-
000000000046}\ProxyStubClsid]
@="{4d2f086c-6ea3-101b-a18a-00aa00446e07}"
[HKEY_CLASSES_ROOT\Interface\{0002030D-0000-0000-C000-
000000000046}\ProxyStubClsid32]
@="{4d2f086c-6ea3-101b-a18a-00aa00446e07}"
[HKEY_CLASSES_ROOT\Interface\{0002030E-0000-0000-C000-000000000046}]
@="IDistList"
[HKEY_CLASSES_ROOT\Interface\{0002030E-0000-0000-C000-
000000000046}\ProxyStubClsid]
@="{4d2f086c-6ea3-101b-a18a-00aa00446e07}"
[HKEY_CLASSES_ROOT\Interface\{0002030E-0000-0000-C000-
000000000046}\ProxyStubClsid32]
@="{4d2f086c-6ea3-101b-a18a-00aa00446e07}"

[HKEY_CLASSES_ROOT\Interface\{0002031B-0000-0000-C000-000000000046}]
@="IMAPIControl"
[HKEY_CLASSES_ROOT\Interface\{0002031B-0000-0000-C000-
000000000046}\ProxyStubClsid]
@="{4d2f086c-6ea3-101b-a18a-00aa00446e07}"
[HKEY_CLASSES_ROOT\Interface\{0002031B-0000-0000-C000-
000000000046}\ProxyStubClsid32]
@="{4d2f086c-6ea3-101b-a18a-00aa00446e07}"
[HKEY_CLASSES_ROOT\Interface\{0002031C-0000-0000-C000-000000000046}]
@="IProfAdmin"
[HKEY_CLASSES_ROOT\Interface\{0002031C-0000-0000-C000-
000000000046}\ProxyStubClsid]
@="{4d2f086c-6ea3-101b-a18a-00aa00446e07}"
[HKEY_CLASSES_ROOT\Interface\{0002031C-0000-0000-C000-
000000000046}\ProxyStubClsid32]
@="{4d2f086c-6ea3-101b-a18a-00aa00446e07}"
[HKEY_CLASSES_ROOT\Interface\{0002031D-0000-0000-C000-000000000046}]
@="IMsgServiceAdmin"
[HKEY_CLASSES_ROOT\Interface\{0002031D-0000-0000-C000-
000000000046}\ProxyStubClsid]
@="{4d2f086c-6ea3-101b-a18a-00aa00446e07}"
[HKEY_CLASSES_ROOT\Interface\{0002031D-0000-0000-C000-
000000000046}\ProxyStubClsid32]
@="{4d2f086c-6ea3-101b-a18a-00aa00446e07}"
[HKEY_CLASSES_ROOT\Interface\{0002031E-0000-0000-C000-000000000046}]
@="IMAPISpoolerService"
[HKEY_CLASSES_ROOT\Interface\{0002031E-0000-0000-C000-
000000000046}\ProxyStubClsid]
@="{4d2f086c-6ea3-101b-a18a-00aa00446e07}"
[HKEY_CLASSES_ROOT\Interface\{0002031E-0000-0000-C000-
000000000046}\ProxyStubClsid32]
@="{4d2f086c-6ea3-101b-a18a-00aa00446e07}"
[HKEY_CLASSES_ROOT\Interface\{0002031F-0000-0000-C000-000000000046}]
@="IMAPIProgress"
[HKEY_CLASSES_ROOT\Interface\{0002031F-0000-0000-C000-
000000000046}\ProxyStubClsid]
@="{4d2f086c-6ea3-101b-a18a-00aa00446e07}"
[HKEY_CLASSES_ROOT\Interface\{0002031F-0000-0000-C000-
000000000046}\ProxyStubClsid32]
@="{4d2f086c-6ea3-101b-a18a-00aa00446e07}"
[HKEY_CLASSES_ROOT\Interface\{00020321-0000-0000-C000-000000000046}]
@="IMAPIViewContext"

[HKEY_CLASSES_ROOT\Interface\{00020321-0000-0000-C000-000000000046}\ProxyStubClsid]
@="{4d2f086c-6ea3-101b-a18a-00aa00446e07}"
[HKEY_CLASSES_ROOT\Interface\{00020321-0000-0000-C000-000000000046}\ProxyStubClsid32]
@="{4d2f086c-6ea3-101b-a18a-00aa00446e07}"
[HKEY_CLASSES_ROOT\Interface\{00020322-0000-0000-C000-000000000046}]
@="IMAPIFormMgr"
[HKEY_CLASSES_ROOT\Interface\{00020322-0000-0000-C000-000000000046}\ProxyStubClsid]
@="{4d2f086c-6ea3-101b-a18a-00aa00446e07}"
[HKEY_CLASSES_ROOT\Interface\{00020322-0000-0000-C000-000000000046}\ProxyStubClsid32]
@="{4d2f086c-6ea3-101b-a18a-00aa00446e07}"
[HKEY_CLASSES_ROOT\Interface\{00020324-0000-0000-C000-000000000046}]
@="IMAPIFormInfo"
[HKEY_CLASSES_ROOT\Interface\{00020324-0000-0000-C000-000000000046}\ProxyStubClsid]
@="{4d2f086c-6ea3-101b-a18a-00aa00446e07}"
[HKEY_CLASSES_ROOT\Interface\{00020324-0000-0000-C000-000000000046}\ProxyStubClsid32]
@="{4d2f086c-6ea3-101b-a18a-00aa00446e07}"
[HKEY_CLASSES_ROOT\Interface\{00020325-0000-0000-C000-000000000046}]
@="IMAPIRegistrySup"
[HKEY_CLASSES_ROOT\Interface\{00020325-0000-0000-C000-000000000046}\ProxyStubClsid]
@="{4d2f086c-6ea3-101b-a18a-00aa00446e07}"
[HKEY_CLASSES_ROOT\Interface\{00020325-0000-0000-C000-000000000046}\ProxyStubClsid32]
@="{4d2f086c-6ea3-101b-a18a-00aa00446e07}"
[HKEY_CLASSES_ROOT\Interface\{00020326-0000-0000-C000-000000000046}]
@="IMAPIFormRegistry"
[HKEY_CLASSES_ROOT\Interface\{00020326-0000-0000-C000-000000000046}\ProxyStubClsid]
@="{4d2f086c-6ea3-101b-a18a-00aa00446e07}"
[HKEY_CLASSES_ROOT\Interface\{00020326-0000-0000-C000-000000000046}\ProxyStubClsid32]
@="{4d2f086c-6ea3-101b-a18a-00aa00446e07}"
[HKEY_CLASSES_ROOT\Interface\{00020327-0000-0000-C000-000000000046}]
@="IMAPIForm"
[HKEY_CLASSES_ROOT\Interface\{00020327-0000-0000-C000-000000000046}\ProxyStubClsid]
@="{4d2f086c-6ea3-101b-a18a-00aa00446e07}"

[HKEY_CLASSES_ROOT\Interface\{00020327-0000-0000-C000-
000000000046}\ProxyStubClsid32]
@="{4d2f086c-6ea3-101b-a18a-00aa00446e07}"
[HKEY_CLASSES_ROOT\Interface\{0002032A-0000-0000-C000-000000000046}]
@="IPersistMessage"
[HKEY_CLASSES_ROOT\Interface\{0002032A-0000-0000-C000-
000000000046}\ProxyStubClsid]
@="{4d2f086c-6ea3-101b-a18a-00aa00446e07}"
[HKEY_CLASSES_ROOT\Interface\{0002032A-0000-0000-C000-
000000000046}\ProxyStubClsid32]
@="{4d2f086c-6ea3-101b-a18a-00aa00446e07}"
[HKEY_CLASSES_ROOT\Interface\{0002032B-0000-0000-C000-000000000046}]
@="IMAPIViewAdviseSink"
[HKEY_CLASSES_ROOT\Interface\{0002032B-0000-0000-C000-
000000000046}\ProxyStubClsid]
@="{4d2f086c-6ea3-101b-a18a-00aa00446e07}"
[HKEY_CLASSES_ROOT\Interface\{0002032B-0000-0000-C000-
000000000046}\ProxyStubClsid32]
@="{4d2f086c-6ea3-101b-a18a-00aa00446e07}"
[HKEY_CLASSES_ROOT\Interface\{0002032E-0000-0000-C000-000000000046}]
@="IMAPIFormContainer"
[HKEY_CLASSES_ROOT\Interface\{0002032E-0000-0000-C000-
000000000046}\ProxyStubClsid]
@="{4d2f086c-6ea3-101b-a18a-00aa00446e07}"
[HKEY_CLASSES_ROOT\Interface\{0002032E-0000-0000-C000-
000000000046}\ProxyStubClsid32]
@="{4d2f086c-6ea3-101b-a18a-00aa00446e07}"
[HKEY_CLASSES_ROOT\Interface\{0002032F-0000-0000-C000-000000000046}]
@="IMAPIFormAdviseSink"
[HKEY_CLASSES_ROOT\Interface\{0002032F-0000-0000-C000-
000000000046}\ProxyStubClsid]
@="{4d2f086c-6ea3-101b-a18a-00aa00446e07}"
[HKEY_CLASSES_ROOT\Interface\{0002032F-0000-0000-C000-
000000000046}\ProxyStubClsid32]
@="{4d2f086c-6ea3-101b-a18a-00aa00446e07}"
[HKEY_CLASSES_ROOT\Interface\{00020346-0000-0000-C000-000000000046}]
@="IMAPILogonRemote"
[HKEY_CLASSES_ROOT\Interface\{00020346-0000-0000-C000-
000000000046}\ProxyStubClsid]
@="{4d2f086c-6ea3-101b-a18a-00aa00446e07}"
[HKEY_CLASSES_ROOT\Interface\{00020346-0000-0000-C000-
000000000046}\ProxyStubClsid32]
@="{4d2f086c-6ea3-101b-a18a-00aa00446e07}"

[HKEY_CLASSES_ROOT\Interface\{00020349-0000-0000-C000-000000000046}]
@="IMAPIProfAdminRemote"
[HKEY_CLASSES_ROOT\Interface\{00020349-0000-0000-C000-
000000000046}\ProxyStubClsid]
@="{4d2f086c-6ea3-101b-a18a-00aa00446e07}"
[HKEY_CLASSES_ROOT\Interface\{00020349-0000-0000-C000-
000000000046}\ProxyStubClsid32]
@="{4d2f086c-6ea3-101b-a18a-00aa00446e07}"
[HKEY_CLASSES_ROOT\Interface\{00020350-0000-0000-C000-000000000046}]
@="IMAPIFormFactory"
[HKEY_CLASSES_ROOT\Interface\{00020350-0000-0000-C000-
000000000046}\ProxyStubClsid]
@="{4d2f086c-6ea3-101b-a18a-00aa00446e07}"
[HKEY_CLASSES_ROOT\Interface\{00020350-0000-0000-C000-
000000000046}\ProxyStubClsid32]
@="{4d2f086c-6ea3-101b-a18a-00aa00446e07}"
[HKEY_CLASSES_ROOT\Interface\{00020370-0000-0000-C000-000000000046}]
@="IMAPIMessageSite"
[HKEY_CLASSES_ROOT\Interface\{00020370-0000-0000-C000-
000000000046}\ProxyStubClsid]
@="{4d2f086c-6ea3-101b-a18a-00aa00446e07}"
[HKEY_CLASSES_ROOT\Interface\{00020370-0000-0000-C000-
000000000046}\ProxyStubClsid32]
@="{4d2f086c-6ea3-101b-a18a-00aa00446e07}"
[HKEY_CLASSES_ROOT\Interface\{00020400-0000-0000-C000-000000000046}]
@="IDispatch"
[HKEY_CLASSES_ROOT\Interface\{00020400-0000-0000-C000-
000000000046}\NumMethods]
@="7"
[HKEY_CLASSES_ROOT\Interface\{00020400-0000-0000-C000-
000000000046}\ProxyStubClsid]
@="{00020420-0000-0000-C000-000000000046}"
[HKEY_CLASSES_ROOT\Interface\{00020400-0000-0000-C000-
000000000046}\ProxyStubClsid32]
@="{00020420-0000-0000-C000-000000000046}"
[HKEY_CLASSES_ROOT\Interface\{00020401-0000-0000-C000-000000000046}]
@="ITypeInfo"
[HKEY_CLASSES_ROOT\Interface\{00020401-0000-0000-C000-
000000000046}\NumMethods]
@="22"
[HKEY_CLASSES_ROOT\Interface\{00020401-0000-0000-C000-
000000000046}\ProxyStubClsid]
@="{00020422-0000-0000-C000-000000000046}"

[HKEY_CLASSES_ROOT\Interface\{00020401-0000-0000-C000-000000000046}\ProxyStubClsid32]
@="{00020422-0000-0000-C000-000000000046}"
[HKEY_CLASSES_ROOT\Interface\{00020402-0000-0000-C000-000000000046}]
@="ITypeLib"
[HKEY_CLASSES_ROOT\Interface\{00020402-0000-0000-C000-000000000046}\NumMethods]
@="13"
[HKEY_CLASSES_ROOT\Interface\{00020402-0000-0000-C000-000000000046}\ProxyStubClsid]
@="{00020423-0000-0000-C000-000000000046}"
[HKEY_CLASSES_ROOT\Interface\{00020402-0000-0000-C000-000000000046}\ProxyStubClsid32]
@="{00020423-0000-0000-C000-000000000046}"
[HKEY_CLASSES_ROOT\Interface\{00020403-0000-0000-C000-000000000046}]
@="ITypeComp"
[HKEY_CLASSES_ROOT\Interface\{00020403-0000-0000-C000-000000000046}\NumMethods]
@="5"
[HKEY_CLASSES_ROOT\Interface\{00020403-0000-0000-C000-000000000046}\ProxyStubClsid]
@="{00020425-0000-0000-C000-000000000046}"
[HKEY_CLASSES_ROOT\Interface\{00020403-0000-0000-C000-000000000046}\ProxyStubClsid32]
@="{00020425-0000-0000-C000-000000000046}"
[HKEY_CLASSES_ROOT\Interface\{00020404-0000-0000-C000-000000000046}]
@="IEnumVARIANT"
[HKEY_CLASSES_ROOT\Interface\{00020404-0000-0000-C000-000000000046}\NumMethods]
@="7"
[HKEY_CLASSES_ROOT\Interface\{00020404-0000-0000-C000-000000000046}\ProxyStubClsid]
@="{00020421-0000-0000-C000-000000000046}"
[HKEY_CLASSES_ROOT\Interface\{00020404-0000-0000-C000-000000000046}\ProxyStubClsid32]
@="{00020421-0000-0000-C000-000000000046}"
[HKEY_CLASSES_ROOT\Interface\{00020405-0000-0000-C000-000000000046}]
@="ICreateTypeInfo"
[HKEY_CLASSES_ROOT\Interface\{00020405-0000-0000-C000-000000000046}\NumMethods]
@="26"
[HKEY_CLASSES_ROOT\Interface\{00020406-0000-0000-C000-000000000046}]
@="ICreateTypeLib"

[HKEY_CLASSES_ROOT\Interface\{00020406-0000-0000-C000-
000000000046}\NumMethods]
@="13"
[HKEY_CLASSES_ROOT\Interface\{0C733A30-2A1C-11CE-ADE5-
00AA0044773D}]
@="ISequentialStream"
[HKEY_CLASSES_ROOT\Interface\{0C733A30-2A1C-11CE-ADE5-
00AA0044773D}\NumMethods]
@="5"
[HKEY_CLASSES_ROOT\Interface\{0C733A30-2A1C-11CE-ADE5-
00AA0044773D}\ProxyStubClsid32]
@="{00000320-0000-0000-C000-000000000046}"
[HKEY_CLASSES_ROOT\Interface\{4a8df970-8d9a-11cf-8827-00aa00b569f5}]
@="IDocfileAsyncConnectionPoint"
[HKEY_CLASSES_ROOT\Interface\{4a8df970-8d9a-11cf-8827-
00aa00b569f5}\ProxyStubClsid32]
@="{00000320-0000-0000-C000-000000000046}"
[HKEY_CLASSES_ROOT\Interface\{99caf010-415e-11cf-8814-00aa00b569f5}]
@="IFillLockBytes"
[HKEY_CLASSES_ROOT\Interface\{99caf010-415e-11cf-8814-
00aa00b569f5}\ProxyStubClsid32]
@="{00000320-0000-0000-C000-000000000046}"
[HKEY_CLASSES_ROOT\Interface\{a9d758a0-4617-11cf-95fc-00aa00680db4}]
@="IProgressNotify"
[HKEY_CLASSES_ROOT\Interface\{a9d758a0-4617-11cf-95fc-
00aa00680db4}\ProxyStubClsid32]
@="{00000320-0000-0000-C000-000000000046}"
[HKEY_CLASSES_ROOT\Interface\{B196B284-BAB4-101A-B69C-
00AA00341D07}]
@="IConnectionPointContainer"
[HKEY_CLASSES_ROOT\Interface\{B196B284-BAB4-101A-B69C-
00AA00341D07}\NumMethods]
@="5"
[HKEY_CLASSES_ROOT\Interface\{B196B284-BAB4-101A-B69C-
00AA00341D07}\ProxyStubClsid32]
@="{00000320-0000-0000-C000-000000000046}"
[HKEY_CLASSES_ROOT\Interface\{B196B285-BAB4-101A-B69C-
00AA00341D07}]
@="IEnumConnectionPoints"
[HKEY_CLASSES_ROOT\Interface\{B196B285-BAB4-101A-B69C-
00AA00341D07}\NumMethods]
@="7"

[HKEY_CLASSES_ROOT\Interface\{B196B285-BAB4-101A-B69C-00AA00341D07}\ProxyStubClsid32]
@="{00000320-0000-0000-C000-000000000046}"
[HKEY_CLASSES_ROOT\Interface\{B196B286-BAB4-101A-B69C-00AA00341D07}]
@="IConnectionPoint"
[HKEY_CLASSES_ROOT\Interface\{B196B286-BAB4-101A-B69C-00AA00341D07}\NumMethods]
@="8"
[HKEY_CLASSES_ROOT\Interface\{B196B286-BAB4-101A-B69C-00AA00341D07}\ProxyStubClsid32]
@="{00000320-0000-0000-C000-000000000046}"
[HKEY_CLASSES_ROOT\Interface\{B196B287-BAB4-101A-B69C-00AA00341D07}]
@="IEnumConnections"
[HKEY_CLASSES_ROOT\Interface\{B196B287-BAB4-101A-B69C-00AA00341D07}\NumMethods]
@="7"
[HKEY_CLASSES_ROOT\Interface\{B196B287-BAB4-101A-B69C-00AA00341D07}\ProxyStubClsid32]
@="{00000320-0000-0000-C000-000000000046}"
[HKEY_CLASSES_ROOT\Interface\{D2A2F5F2-EBA6-11CD-AF37-02608CA1D0B7}]
@="_DVBScript"
[HKEY_CLASSES_ROOT\Interface\{D2A2F5F2-EBA6-11CD-AF37-02608CA1D0B7}\BaseInterface]
@="{00020400-0000-0000-C000-000000000046}"
[HKEY_CLASSES_ROOT\Interface\{D2A2F5F2-EBA6-11CD-AF37-02608CA1D0B7}\NumMethod]
@="6"
[HKEY_CLASSES_ROOT\Interface\{D2A2F5F2-EBA6-11CD-AF37-02608CA1D0B7}\ProxyStubClsid32]
@="{00020420-0000-0000-C000-000000000046}"
[HKEY_CLASSES_ROOT\Interface\{D2A2F5F2-EBA6-11CD-AF37-02608CA1D0B7}\TypeLib]
@="{D2A2F5F0-EBA6-11CD-AF37-02608CA1D0B7}"
[HKEY_CLASSES_ROOT\Interface\{D5F569D0-593B-101A-B569-08002B2DBF7A}]
@="IPSFactoryBuffer"
[HKEY_CLASSES_ROOT\Interface\{D5F569D0-593B-101A-B569-08002B2DBF7A}\NumMethods]
@="5"

[HKEY_CLASSES_ROOT\Interface\{D5F56A34-593B-101A-B569-08002B2DBF7A}]
@="IRpcProxyBuffer"
[HKEY_CLASSES_ROOT\Interface\{D5F56A34-593B-101A-B569-08002B2DBF7A}\NumMethods]
@="5"
[HKEY_CLASSES_ROOT\Interface\{D5F56AFC-593B-101A-B569-08002B2DBF7A}]
@="IRpcStubBuffer"
[HKEY_CLASSES_ROOT\Interface\{D5F56AFC-593B-101A-B569-08002B2DBF7A}\NumMethods]
@="10"
[HKEY_CLASSES_ROOT\Interface\{D5F56B60-593B-101A-B569-08002B2DBF7A}]
@="IRpcChannelBuffer"
[HKEY_CLASSES_ROOT\Interface\{D5F56B60-593B-101A-B569-08002B2DBF7A}\NumMethods]
@="8"
[HKEY_CLASSES_ROOT\Interface\{de2eacd0-9c9d-11cf-882a-00aa00b569f5}]
@="IFIllInfo"
[HKEY_CLASSES_ROOT\Interface\{de2eacd0-9c9d-11cf-882a-00aa00b569f5}\ProxyStubClsid32]
@="{00000320-0000-0000-C000-000000000046}"
[HKEY_CLASSES_ROOT\Interface\{DF0B3D60-548F-101B-8E65-08002B2BD119}]
@="ISupportErrorInfo"
[HKEY_CLASSES_ROOT\Interface\{DF0B3D60-548F-101B-8E65-08002B2BD119}\NumMethods]
@="4"
[HKEY_CLASSES_ROOT\Interface\{DF0B3D60-548F-101B-8E65-08002B2BD119}\ProxyStubClsid]
@="{DF0B3D60-548F-101B-8E65-08002B2BD119}"
[HKEY_CLASSES_ROOT\Interface\{DF0B3D60-548F-101B-8E65-08002B2BD119}\ProxyStubClsid32]
@="{DF0B3D60-548F-101B-8E65-08002B2BD119}"
[HKEY_CLASSES_ROOT\Interface\{F4F569D0-593B-101A-B569-08002B2DBF7A}]
@="IServerHandler"
[HKEY_CLASSES_ROOT\Interface\{F4F569D0-593B-101A-B569-08002B2DBF7A}\ProxyStubClsid32]
@="{00000320-0000-0000-C000-000000000046}"

[HKEY_CLASSES_ROOT\Interface\{F4F569D1-593B-101A-B569-08002B2DBF7A}]
@="IClientSiteHandler"
[HKEY_CLASSES_ROOT\Interface\{F4F569D1-593B-101A-B569-08002B2DBF7A}\ProxyStubClsid32]
@="{00000320-0000-0000-C000-000000000046}"
[HKEY_CLASSES_ROOT\InternetShortcut]
@="Internet Shortcut"
"EditFlags"=hex:02,00,01,00
"IsShortcut"=""
"NeverShowExt"=""
[HKEY_CLASSES_ROOT\InternetShortcut\ClsID]
@="{FBF23B40-E3F0-101B-8488-00AA003E56F8}"
[HKEY_CLASSES_ROOT\InternetShortcut\DefaultIcon]
@="C:\\WINNT\\System32\\url.dll,0"
[HKEY_CLASSES_ROOT\InternetShortcut\shell]
[HKEY_CLASSES_ROOT\InternetShortcut\shell\open]
[HKEY_CLASSES_ROOT\InternetShortcut\shell\open\command]
@="rundll32.exe url.dll,OpenURL %l"
[HKEY_CLASSES_ROOT\InternetShortcut\shellex]
[HKEY_CLASSES_ROOT\InternetShortcut\shellex\IconHandler]
@="{FBF23B40-E3F0-101B-8488-00AA003E56F8}"
[HKEY_CLASSES_ROOT\InternetShortcut\shellex\PropertySheetHandlers]
[HKEY_CLASSES_ROOT\InternetShortcut\shellex\PropertySheetHandlers\InternetShortcutProperties]
@="{FBF23B40-E3F0-101B-8488-00AA003E56F8}"
[HKEY_CLASSES_ROOT\JobObject]
@="Scheduler Job Object"
[HKEY_CLASSES_ROOT\JobObject\CLSID]
@="{148BD520-A2AB-11CE-B11F-00AA00530503}"
[HKEY_CLASSES_ROOT\jpegfile]
@="JPEG Image"
[HKEY_CLASSES_ROOT\jpegfile\DefaultIcon]
@="C:\\Program Files\\Plus!\\Microsoft Internet\\IExplore.exe,9"
[HKEY_CLASSES_ROOT\jpegfile\shell]
[HKEY_CLASSES_ROOT\jpegfile\shell\open]
[HKEY_CLASSES_ROOT\jpegfile\shell\open\command]
@="\"C:\\Program Files\\Plus!\\Microsoft Internet\\IExplore.exe\" -nohome"
[HKEY_CLASSES_ROOT\jpegfile\shell\open\ddeexec]
@="\"file:%1\",,-1,,,,,"
[HKEY_CLASSES_ROOT\jpegfile\shell\open\ddeexec\Application]
@="IExplore"

[HKEY_CLASSES_ROOT\jpegfile\shell\open\ddeexec\Topic]
@="WWW_OpenURL"
[HKEY_CLASSES_ROOT\lnkfile]
@="Shortcut"
"EditFlags"=hex:01,00,00,00
"IsShortcut"=""
"NeverShowExt"=""
[HKEY_CLASSES_ROOT\lnkfile\shellex]
[HKEY_CLASSES_ROOT\lnkfile\shellex\ContextMenuHandlers]
[HKEY_CLASSES_ROOT\lnkfile\shellex\ContextMenuHandlers\{00021401-0000-
0000-C000-000000000046}]
[HKEY_CLASSES_ROOT\lnkfile\shellex\DropHandler]
@="{00021401-0000-0000-C000-000000000046}"
[HKEY_CLASSES_ROOT\lnkfile\shellex\IconHandler]
@="{00021401-0000-0000-C000-000000000046}"
[HKEY_CLASSES_ROOT\MailFileAtt]
[HKEY_CLASSES_ROOT\MailFileAtt\CLSID]
@="{00020D05-0000-0000-C000-000000000046}"
[HKEY_CLASSES_ROOT\MailMsgAtt]
[HKEY_CLASSES_ROOT\MailMsgAtt\CLSID]
@="{00020D09-0000-0000-C000-000000000046}"
[HKEY_CLASSES_ROOT\mailto]
@="URL:MailTo Protocol"
"EditFlags"=hex:02,00,00,00
"URL Protocol"=""
[HKEY_CLASSES_ROOT\mailto\DefaultIcon]
@="C:\\WINNT\\System32\\url.dll,0"
[HKEY_CLASSES_ROOT\mailto\shell]
[HKEY_CLASSES_ROOT\mailto\shell\open]
[HKEY_CLASSES_ROOT\mailto\shell\open\command]
@="rundll32.exe url.dll,MailToProtocolHandler %l"
[HKEY_CLASSES_ROOT\MAPI.Folder]
@="MAPI 1.0 Folder "
[HKEY_CLASSES_ROOT\MAPI.Folder\CLSID]
@="{3FA7DEB5-6438-101B-ACC1-00AA00423326}"
[HKEY_CLASSES_ROOT\MAPI.Folder\CurVer]
@="MAPI.Folder.1"
[HKEY_CLASSES_ROOT\MAPI.Folder.1]
@="MAPI 1.0 Folder (v1.0)"
[HKEY_CLASSES_ROOT\MAPI.Folder.1\CLSID]
@="{3FA7DEB5-6438-101B-ACC1-00AA00423326}"
[HKEY_CLASSES_ROOT\MAPI.Message]
@="MAPI 1.0 Message"

[HKEY_CLASSES_ROOT\MAPI.Message\CLSID]
@="{3FA7DEB4-6438-101B-ACC1-00AA00423326}"
[HKEY_CLASSES_ROOT\MAPI.Message\CurVer]
@="MAPI.Message.1"
[HKEY_CLASSES_ROOT\MAPI.Message.1]
@="MAPI 1.0 Message (v1.0)"
[HKEY_CLASSES_ROOT\MAPI.Message.1\CLSID]
@="{3FA7DEB4-6438-101B-ACC1-00AA00423326}"
[HKEY_CLASSES_ROOT\MAPI.Session]
@="MAPI 1.0 Session"
[HKEY_CLASSES_ROOT\MAPI.Session\CLSID]
@="{3FA7DEB3-6438-101B-ACC1-00AA00423326}"
[HKEY_CLASSES_ROOT\MAPI.Session\CurVer]
@="MAPI.Session.1"
[HKEY_CLASSES_ROOT\MAPI.Session.1]
@="MAPI 1.0 Session (v1.0)"
[HKEY_CLASSES_ROOT\MAPI.Session.1\CLSID]
@="{3FA7DEB3-6438-101B-ACC1-00AA00423326}"
[HKEY_CLASSES_ROOT\MIDFile]
@="MIDI Sequence"
"EditFlags"=hex:00,00,01,00
[HKEY_CLASSES_ROOT\MIDFile\CLSID]
@="{00022603-0000-0000-C000-000000000046}"
[HKEY_CLASSES_ROOT\MIDFile\DefaultIcon]
@="mplay32.exe,5"
[HKEY_CLASSES_ROOT\MIDFile\Insertable]
@=""
[HKEY_CLASSES_ROOT\MIDFile\protocol]
[HKEY_CLASSES_ROOT\MIDFile\protocol\StdExecute]
[HKEY_CLASSES_ROOT\MIDFile\protocol\StdExecute\server]
@="mplay32.exe /mid"
[HKEY_CLASSES_ROOT\MIDFile\protocol\StdFileEditing]
[HKEY_CLASSES_ROOT\MIDFile\protocol\StdFileEditing\Handler]
@="mciole16.dll"
[HKEY_CLASSES_ROOT\MIDFile\protocol\StdFileEditing\Handler32]
@="mciole32.dll"
[HKEY_CLASSES_ROOT\MIDFile\protocol\StdFileEditing\PackageObjects]
@=""
[HKEY_CLASSES_ROOT\MIDFile\protocol\StdFileEditing\server]
@="mplay32.exe /mid"
[HKEY_CLASSES_ROOT\MIDFile\protocol\StdFileEditing\verb]
[HKEY_CLASSES_ROOT\MIDFile\protocol\StdFileEditing\verb\0]
@="&Play"

[HKEY_CLASSES_ROOT\MIDFile\protocol\StdFileEditing\verb\1]
@="&Edit"
[HKEY_CLASSES_ROOT\MIDFile\protocol\StdFileEditing\verb\2]
@="&Open"
[HKEY_CLASSES_ROOT\MIDFile\shell]
[HKEY_CLASSES_ROOT\MIDFile\shell\open]
[HKEY_CLASSES_ROOT\MIDFile\shell\open\command]
@="mplay32.exe /play /close \"%L\""
[HKEY_CLASSES_ROOT\MIDFile\shellex]
[HKEY_CLASSES_ROOT\MIDFile\shellex\PropertySheetHandlers]
@="MidPage"
[HKEY_CLASSES_ROOT\MIDFile\shellex\PropertySheetHandlers\MidPage]
@="{00022613-0000-0000-C000-000000000046}"
[HKEY_CLASSES_ROOT\MIME]
[HKEY_CLASSES_ROOT\MIME\Database]
[HKEY_CLASSES_ROOT\MIME\Database\Content Type]
[HKEY_CLASSES_ROOT\MIME\Database\Content Type\application/fractals]
"Extension"=".fif"
[HKEY_CLASSES_ROOT\MIME\Database\Content Type\application/mac-
binhex40]
"Extension"=".hqx"
[HKEY_CLASSES_ROOT\MIME\Database\Content Type\application/postscript]
"Extension"=".ps"
[HKEY_CLASSES_ROOT\MIME\Database\Content Type\application/x-compress]
"Extension"=".z"
[HKEY_CLASSES_ROOT\MIME\Database\Content Type\application/
x-compressed]
"Extension"=".tgz"
[HKEY_CLASSES_ROOT\MIME\Database\Content Type\application/x-gzip]
"Extension"=".gz"
[HKEY_CLASSES_ROOT\MIME\Database\Content Type\application/x-latex]
"Extension"=".latex"
[HKEY_CLASSES_ROOT\MIME\Database\Content Type\application/x-stuffit]
"Extension"=".sit"
[HKEY_CLASSES_ROOT\MIME\Database\Content Type\application/x-tar]
"Extension"=".tar"
[HKEY_CLASSES_ROOT\MIME\Database\Content Type\application/x-troff-man]
"Extension"=".man"
[HKEY_CLASSES_ROOT\MIME\Database\Content Type\application/
x-zip-compressed]
"Extension"=".zip"
[HKEY_CLASSES_ROOT\MIME\Database\Content Type\audio/aiff]
"Extension"=".aiff"

[HKEY_CLASSES_ROOT\MIME\Database\Content Type\audio/basic]
"Extension"=".au"
[HKEY_CLASSES_ROOT\MIME\Database\Content Type\audio/wav]
"Extension"=".wav"
[HKEY_CLASSES_ROOT\MIME\Database\Content Type\audio/x-aiff]
"Extension"=".aiff"
[HKEY_CLASSES_ROOT\MIME\Database\Content Type\audio/x-wav]
"Extension"=".wav"
[HKEY_CLASSES_ROOT\MIME\Database\Content Type\image/gif]
"Extension"=".gif"
[HKEY_CLASSES_ROOT\MIME\Database\Content Type\image/jpeg]
"Extension"=".jpeg"
[HKEY_CLASSES_ROOT\MIME\Database\Content Type\image/tiff]
"Extension"=".tiff"
[HKEY_CLASSES_ROOT\MIME\Database\Content Type\image/x-xbitmap]
"Extension"=".xbm"
[HKEY_CLASSES_ROOT\MIME\Database\Content Type\image/xbm]
"Extension"=".xbm"
[HKEY_CLASSES_ROOT\MIME\Database\Content Type\text/html]
"Extension"=".html"
"Encoding"=hex:08,00,00,00
[HKEY_CLASSES_ROOT\MIME\Database\Content Type\text/plain]
"Extension"=".txt"
"Encoding"=hex:07,00,00,00
[HKEY_CLASSES_ROOT\MIME\Database\Content Type\video/avi]
"Extension"=".avi"
[HKEY_CLASSES_ROOT\MIME\Database\Content Type\video/mpeg]
"Extension"=".mpeg"
[HKEY_CLASSES_ROOT\MIME\Database\Content Type\video/quicktime]
"Extension"=".qt"
[HKEY_CLASSES_ROOT\MIME\Database\Content Type\video/x-msvideo]
"Extension"=".avi"
[HKEY_CLASSES_ROOT\MIME\Database\Content Type\video/x-sgi-movie]
"Extension"=".movie"
[HKEY_CLASSES_ROOT\MPlayer]
@="Media Clip"
"EditFlags"=hex:00,00,01,00
[HKEY_CLASSES_ROOT\MPlayer\CLSID]
@="{00022601-0000-0000-C000-000000000046}"
[HKEY_CLASSES_ROOT\MPlayer\DefaultIcon]
@="mplay32.exe,1"
[HKEY_CLASSES_ROOT\MPlayer\Insertable]
@=""

[HKEY_CLASSES_ROOT\MPlayer\protocol]
[HKEY_CLASSES_ROOT\MPlayer\protocol\StdExecute]
[HKEY_CLASSES_ROOT\MPlayer\protocol\StdExecute\server]
@="mplay32.exe"
[HKEY_CLASSES_ROOT\MPlayer\protocol\StdFileEditing]
[HKEY_CLASSES_ROOT\MPlayer\protocol\StdFileEditing\Handler]
@="mciole16.dll"
[HKEY_CLASSES_ROOT\MPlayer\protocol\StdFileEditing\Handler32]
@="mciole32.dll"
[HKEY_CLASSES_ROOT\MPlayer\protocol\StdFileEditing\PackageObjects]
@=""
[HKEY_CLASSES_ROOT\MPlayer\protocol\StdFileEditing\server]
@="mplay32.exe"
[HKEY_CLASSES_ROOT\MPlayer\protocol\StdFileEditing\verb]
[HKEY_CLASSES_ROOT\MPlayer\protocol\StdFileEditing\verb\0]
@="&Play"
[HKEY_CLASSES_ROOT\MPlayer\protocol\StdFileEditing\verb\1]
@="&Edit"
[HKEY_CLASSES_ROOT\MPlayer\protocol\StdFileEditing\verb\2]
@="&Open"
[HKEY_CLASSES_ROOT\MPlayer\shell]
[HKEY_CLASSES_ROOT\MPlayer\shell\open]
[HKEY_CLASSES_ROOT\MPlayer\shell\open\command]
@="mplay32.exe /play /close \"%L\""
[HKEY_CLASSES_ROOT\MPlayer\shellex]
[HKEY_CLASSES_ROOT\MPlayer\shellex\PropertySheetHandlers]
@="MediaPage"
[HKEY_CLASSES_ROOT\MPlayer\shellex\PropertySheetHandlers\MediaPage]
@="{00022613-0000-0000-C000-000000000046}"
[HKEY_CLASSES_ROOT\msgfile]
@="Mail Message"
[HKEY_CLASSES_ROOT\msgfile\DefaultIcon]
@="wmsui32.dll,-1000"
[HKEY_CLASSES_ROOT\msgfile\shell]
[HKEY_CLASSES_ROOT\msgfile\shell\open]
[HKEY_CLASSES_ROOT\msgfile\shell\open\command]
@="\"C:\\Program Files\\Windows NT\\Windows Messaging\\exchng32.exe\" /f %1"
[HKEY_CLASSES_ROOT\msgfile\shell\print]
[HKEY_CLASSES_ROOT\msgfile\shell\print\command]
@="\"C:\\Program Files\\Windows NT\\Windows Messaging\\exchng32.exe\" /p %1"

[HKEY_CLASSES_ROOT\MSProgramGroup]
@="Microsoft Program Group"
[HKEY_CLASSES_ROOT\MSProgramGroup\Shell]
[HKEY_CLASSES_ROOT\MSProgramGroup\Shell\Open]
[HKEY_CLASSES_ROOT\MSProgramGroup\Shell\Open\Command]
@="C:\\WINNT\\system32\\grpconv.exe %1"
[HKEY_CLASSES_ROOT\Network]
[HKEY_CLASSES_ROOT\Network\SharingHandler]
@="ntshrui.dll"
[HKEY_CLASSES_ROOT\Network\Type]
[HKEY_CLASSES_ROOT\Network\Type\2]
@="Microsoft Windows Network shell extensions"
[HKEY_CLASSES_ROOT\Network\Type\2\shellex]
[HKEY_CLASSES_ROOT\Network\Type\2\shellex\PropertySheetHandlers]
[HKEY_CLASSES_ROOT\Network\Type\2\shellex\PropertySheetHandlers\
Microsoft Windows Network objects]
@="{59be4990-f85c-11ce-aff7-00aa003ca9f6}"
[HKEY_CLASSES_ROOT\news]
@="URL:News Protocol"
"EditFlags"=hex:02,00,00,00
"URL Protocol"=""
[HKEY_CLASSES_ROOT\news\DefaultIcon]
@="C:\\WINNT\\System32\\url.dll,0"
[HKEY_CLASSES_ROOT\news\shell]
[HKEY_CLASSES_ROOT\news\shell\open]
[HKEY_CLASSES_ROOT\news\shell\open\command]
@="rundll32.exe url.dll,NewsProtocolHandler %l"
[HKEY_CLASSES_ROOT\Package]
@="Package"
[HKEY_CLASSES_ROOT\Package\CLSID]
@="{0003000C-0000-0000-C000-000000000046}"
[HKEY_CLASSES_ROOT\Package\protocol]
[HKEY_CLASSES_ROOT\Package\protocol\StdFileEditing]
[HKEY_CLASSES_ROOT\Package\protocol\StdFileEditing\server]
@="packager.exe"
[HKEY_CLASSES_ROOT\Package\protocol\StdFileEditing\verb]
[HKEY_CLASSES_ROOT\Package\protocol\StdFileEditing\verb\0]
@="&Activate Contents"
[HKEY_CLASSES_ROOT\Package\protocol\StdFileEditing\verb\1]
@="&Edit Package"
[HKEY_CLASSES_ROOT\Paint.Picture]
@="Bitmap Image"

[HKEY_CLASSES_ROOT\Paint.Picture\CLSID]
@="{D3E34B21-9D75-101A-8C3D-00AA001A1652}"
[HKEY_CLASSES_ROOT\Paint.Picture\DefaultIcon]
@="mspaint.exe, 1"
[HKEY_CLASSES_ROOT\Paint.Picture\Insertable]
@=""
[HKEY_CLASSES_ROOT\Paint.Picture\protocol]
[HKEY_CLASSES_ROOT\Paint.Picture\protocol\StdFileEditing]
[HKEY_CLASSES_ROOT\Paint.Picture\protocol\StdFileEditing\server]
@="mspaint.exe"
[HKEY_CLASSES_ROOT\Paint.Picture\protocol\StdFileEditing\verb]
[HKEY_CLASSES_ROOT\Paint.Picture\protocol\StdFileEditing\verb\0]
@="&Edit"
[HKEY_CLASSES_ROOT\Paint.Picture\shell]
[HKEY_CLASSES_ROOT\Paint.Picture\shell\open]
[HKEY_CLASSES_ROOT\Paint.Picture\shell\open\command]
@="mspaint.exe %1"
[HKEY_CLASSES_ROOT\Paint.Picture\shell\print]
[HKEY_CLASSES_ROOT\Paint.Picture\shell\print\command]
@="mspaint.exe /p %1"
[HKEY_CLASSES_ROOT\Paint.Picture\shell\printto]
[HKEY_CLASSES_ROOT\Paint.Picture\shell\printto\command]
@="mspaint.exe /pt %1 %2 %3 %4"
[HKEY_CLASSES_ROOT\pbkfile]
@="Dial-Up Phonebook"
[HKEY_CLASSES_ROOT\pbkfile\CLSID]
@="{a4d92742-67cd-11cf-96f2-00aa00a11dd9}"
[HKEY_CLASSES_ROOT\pbkfile\DefaultIcon]
@=hex(2):25,53,79,73,74,65,6d,52,6f,6f,74,25,5c,73,79,73,74,65,6d,33,32,5c,72,61,
73,73,68,65,6c,6c,2e,64,6c,6c,2c,30,00
[HKEY_CLASSES_ROOT\pbkfile\shell]
[HKEY_CLASSES_ROOT\pbkfile\shell\Open]
[HKEY_CLASSES_ROOT\pbkfile\shell\Open\command]
@=hex(2):25,53,79,73,74,65,6d,52,6f,6f,74,25,5c,73,79,73,74,65,6d,33,32,5c,72,61,
73,70,68,6f,6e,65,2e,65,78,65,20,2d,66,20,22,25,31,22,00
[HKEY_CLASSES_ROOT\PBrush]
@="Paintbrush Picture"
[HKEY_CLASSES_ROOT\PBrush\CLSID]
@="{0003000a-0000-0000-C000-000000000046}"
[HKEY_CLASSES_ROOT\PBrush\protocol]
[HKEY_CLASSES_ROOT\PBrush\protocol\StdFileEditing]
[HKEY_CLASSES_ROOT\PBrush\protocol\StdFileEditing\server]
@="mspaint.exe"

[HKEY_CLASSES_ROOT\PBrush\protocol\StdFileEditing\verb]
[HKEY_CLASSES_ROOT\PBrush\protocol\StdFileEditing\verb\0]
@="Edit"
[HKEY_CLASSES_ROOT\PBrush\shell]
[HKEY_CLASSES_ROOT\PBrush\shell\open]
[HKEY_CLASSES_ROOT\PBrush\shell\open\command]
@="pbrush.exe %1"
[HKEY_CLASSES_ROOT\PBrush\shell\print]
[HKEY_CLASSES_ROOT\PBrush\shell\print\command]
@="pbrush.exe /p %1"
[HKEY_CLASSES_ROOT\PCXImage.Document]
@="PCX Image Document"
[HKEY_CLASSES_ROOT\PCXImage.Document\CLSID]
@="{02B01C80-E03D-101A-B294-00DD010F2BF9}"
[HKEY_CLASSES_ROOT\PCXImage.Document\DefaultIcon]
@="C:\\Program Files\\Windows NT\\Accessories\\ImageVue\\WangImg.Exe,1"
[HKEY_CLASSES_ROOT\PCXImage.Document\shell]
[HKEY_CLASSES_ROOT\PCXImage.Document\shell\open]
[HKEY_CLASSES_ROOT\PCXImage.Document\shell\open\command]
@="C:\\Program Files\\Windows NT\\Accessories\\ImageVue\\
WangImg.Exe \"%1\""
[HKEY_CLASSES_ROOT\PCXImage.Document\shell\print]
[HKEY_CLASSES_ROOT\PCXImage.Document\shell\print\command]
@="C:\\Program Files\\Windows NT\\Accessories\\ImageVue\\WangImg.Exe/p\
"%1\""
[HKEY_CLASSES_ROOT\PCXImage.Document\shell\printto]
[HKEY_CLASSES_ROOT\PCXImage.Document\shell\printto\command]
@="C:\\Program Files\\Windows NT\\Accessories\\ImageVue\\WangImg.Exe/pt\
"%1\" \"%2\" \"%3\" \"%4\" "
[HKEY_CLASSES_ROOT\PCXImage.Document\shellex]
@=""
[HKEY_CLASSES_ROOT\PCXImage.Document\shellex\PropertySheetHandlers]
@=""
[HKEY_CLASSES_ROOT\PCXImage.Document\shellex\PropertySheetHandlers\
{1D3ECD40-C835-11CE-9888-00608CC22020}]
@=""
[HKEY_CLASSES_ROOT\PerfFile]
@="Performance Monitor File"
[HKEY_CLASSES_ROOT\PerfFile\shell]
[HKEY_CLASSES_ROOT\PerfFile\shell\open]
[HKEY_CLASSES_ROOT\PerfFile\shell\open\command]
@=hex(2):25,53,79,73,74,65,6d,52,6f,6f,74,25,5c,73,79,73,74,65,6d,33,32,5c,70,65,
72,66,6d,6f,6e,2e,65,78,65,20,25,31,00

[HKEY_CLASSES_ROOT\pfmfile]
@="Type 1 Font file"
[HKEY_CLASSES_ROOT\pfmfile\DefaultIcon]
@=hex(2):25,53,79,73,74,65,6d,52,6f,6f,74,25,5c,73,79,73,74,65,6d,33,32,5c,73,68,
65,6c,6c,33,32,2e,64,6c,6c,2c,2d,31,37,33,00
[HKEY_CLASSES_ROOT\pfmfile\shell]
[HKEY_CLASSES_ROOT\pfmfile\shell\open]
[HKEY_CLASSES_ROOT\pfmfile\shell\open\command]
@=hex(2):25,53,79,73,74,65,6d,52,6f,6f,74,25,5c,53,79,73,74,65,6d,33,32,5c,66,6f,6e,
74,76,69,65,77,2e,65,78,65,20,25,31,00
[HKEY_CLASSES_ROOT\pfmfile\shell\print]
[HKEY_CLASSES_ROOT\pfmfile\shell\print\command]
@=hex(2):25,53,79,73,74,65,6d,52,6f,6f,74,25,5c,53,79,73,74,65,6d,33,32,5c,66,6f,6e,
74,76,69,65,77,2e,65,78,65,20,2f,70,20,25,31,00
[HKEY_CLASSES_ROOT\piffile]
@="Shortcut to MS-DOS Program"
"EditFlags"=hex:01,00,00,00
"IsShortcut"=""
"NeverShowExt"=""
[HKEY_CLASSES_ROOT\piffile\shell]
[HKEY_CLASSES_ROOT\piffile\shell\open]
[HKEY_CLASSES_ROOT\piffile\shell\open\command]
@="\"%1\" %*"
[HKEY_CLASSES_ROOT\piffile\shellex]
[HKEY_CLASSES_ROOT\piffile\shellex\IconHandler]
@="{00021401-0000-0000-C000-000000000046}"
[HKEY_CLASSES_ROOT\piffile\shellex\PropertySheetHandlers]
[HKEY_CLASSES_ROOT\piffile\shellex\PropertySheetHandlers\PifProps]
@="{86F19A00-42A0-1069-A2E9-08002B30309D}"
[HKEY_CLASSES_ROOT\pnffile]
@="Precompiled Setup Information"
"AlwaysShowExt"=""
"EditFlags"=hex:01,00,00,00
[HKEY_CLASSES_ROOT\pnffile\DefaultIcon]
@=hex(2):25,53,79,73,74,65,6d,52,6f,6f,74,25,5c,73,79,73,74,65,6d,33,32,5c,73,68,
65,6c,6c,33,32,2e,64,6c,6c,2c,2d,31,35,34,00
[HKEY_CLASSES_ROOT\QueueObject]
@="Scheduler Queue Object"
[HKEY_CLASSES_ROOT\QueueObject\CLSID]
@="{255b3f60-829e-11cf-8d8b-00aa0060f5bf}"
[HKEY_CLASSES_ROOT\QuickView]
@="Quick View File"

[HKEY_CLASSES_ROOT\QuickView*]
@="Default Viewers"
[HKEY_CLASSES_ROOT\QuickView*\{F0F08735-0C36-101B-B086-0020AF07D0F4}]
@="SCC Quick Viewer"
[HKEY_CLASSES_ROOT\QuickView\.ASC]
@="ASCII File"
[HKEY_CLASSES_ROOT\QuickView\.ASC\{F0F08735-0C36-101B-B086-0020AF07D0F4}]
@="SCC Quick Viewer"
[HKEY_CLASSES_ROOT\QuickView\.BMP]
@="Windows Bitmap Graphics File"
[HKEY_CLASSES_ROOT\QuickView\.BMP\{F0F08735-0C36-101B-B086-0020AF07D0F4}]
@="SCC Quick Viewer"
[HKEY_CLASSES_ROOT\QuickView\.CDR]
@="Corel Draw v 4,5 Files"
[HKEY_CLASSES_ROOT\QuickView\.CDR\{F0F08735-0C36-101B-B086-0020AF07D0F4}]
@="SCC Quick Viewer"
[HKEY_CLASSES_ROOT\QuickView\.DIB]
@="Windows Bitmap Graphics File (DIB)"
[HKEY_CLASSES_ROOT\QuickView\.DIB\{F0F08735-0C36-101B-B086-0020AF07D0F4}]
@="SCC Quick Viewer"
[HKEY_CLASSES_ROOT\QuickView\.DLL]
@="Dynamic Link Libraries"
[HKEY_CLASSES_ROOT\QuickView\.DLL\{F0F08735-0C36-101B-B086-0020AF07D0F4}]
@="SCC Quick Viewer"
[HKEY_CLASSES_ROOT\QuickView\.DOC]
@="Any of a number of word processing file formats"
[HKEY_CLASSES_ROOT\QuickView\.DOC\{F0F08735-0C36-101B-B086-0020AF07D0F4}]
@="SCC Quick Viewer"
[HKEY_CLASSES_ROOT\QuickView\.DRW]
@="Micrographix Draw File"
[HKEY_CLASSES_ROOT\QuickView\.DRW\{F0F08735-0C36-101B-B086-0020AF07D0F4}]
@="SCC Quick Viewer"
[HKEY_CLASSES_ROOT\QuickView\.EPS]
@="Encapsulated PostScript Files"

[HKEY_CLASSES_ROOT\QuickView\.EPS\{F0F08735-0C36-101B-B086-0020AF07D0F4}]
@="SCC Quick Viewer"
[HKEY_CLASSES_ROOT\QuickView\.EXE]
@="Executable Files"
[HKEY_CLASSES_ROOT\QuickView\.EXE\{F0F08735-0C36-101B-B086-0020AF07D0F4}]
@="SCC Quick Viewer"
[HKEY_CLASSES_ROOT\QuickView\.GIF]
@="Compuserve GIF File"
[HKEY_CLASSES_ROOT\QuickView\.GIF\{F0F08735-0C36-101B-B086-0020AF07D0F4}]
@="SCC Quick Viewer"
[HKEY_CLASSES_ROOT\QuickView\.INF]
@="Setup Files"
[HKEY_CLASSES_ROOT\QuickView\.INF\{F0F08735-0C36-101B-B086-0020AF07D0F4}]
@="SCC Quick Viewer"
[HKEY_CLASSES_ROOT\QuickView\.INI]
@="Configuration Files"
[HKEY_CLASSES_ROOT\QuickView\.INI\{F0F08735-0C36-101B-B086-0020AF07D0F4}]
@="SCC Quick Viewer"
[HKEY_CLASSES_ROOT\QuickView\.MOD]
@="Multiplan v 3, 4.0, 4.1 File"
[HKEY_CLASSES_ROOT\QuickView\.MOD\{F0F08735-0C36-101B-B086-0020AF07D0F4}]
@="SCC Quick Viewer"
[HKEY_CLASSES_ROOT\QuickView\.PPT]
@="PowerPoint, v 4 Files"
[HKEY_CLASSES_ROOT\QuickView\.PPT\{F0F08735-0C36-101B-B086-0020AF07D0F4}]
@="SCC Quick Viewer"
[HKEY_CLASSES_ROOT\QuickView\.RLE]
@="Bitmap Files (RunLengthEncoding)"
[HKEY_CLASSES_ROOT\QuickView\.RLE\{F0F08735-0C36-101B-B086-0020AF07D0F4}]
@="SCC Quick Viewer"
[HKEY_CLASSES_ROOT\QuickView\.RTF]
@="Rich Text Format File"
[HKEY_CLASSES_ROOT\QuickView\.RTF\{F0F08735-0C36-101B-B086-0020AF07D0F4}]
@="SCC Quick Viewer"

[HKEY_CLASSES_ROOT\QuickView\.TIF]
@="Tiff File"
[HKEY_CLASSES_ROOT\QuickView\.TIF\{F0F08735-0C36-101B-B086-0020AF07D0F4}]
@="SCC Quick Viewer"
[HKEY_CLASSES_ROOT\QuickView\.TXT]
@="Text File"
[HKEY_CLASSES_ROOT\QuickView\.TXT\{F0F08735-0C36-101B-B086-0020AF07D0F4}]
@="SCC Quick Viewer"
[HKEY_CLASSES_ROOT\QuickView\.WB1]
@="Quattro Pro for Windows File"
[HKEY_CLASSES_ROOT\QuickView\.WB1\{F0F08735-0C36-101B-B086-0020AF07D0F4}]
@="SCC Quick Viewer"
[HKEY_CLASSES_ROOT\QuickView\.WDB]
@="Works Database Files"
[HKEY_CLASSES_ROOT\QuickView\.WDB\{F0F08735-0C36-101B-B086-0020AF07D0F4}]
@="SCC Quick Viewer"
[HKEY_CLASSES_ROOT\QuickView\.WK1]
@="Lotus 1-2-3 v 1'n'2 Files"
[HKEY_CLASSES_ROOT\QuickView\.WK1\{F0F08735-0C36-101B-B086-0020AF07D0F4}]
@="SCC Quick Viewer"
[HKEY_CLASSES_ROOT\QuickView\.WKS]
@="Lotus 1-2-3 File or MS Works v 3 File"
[HKEY_CLASSES_ROOT\QuickView\.WKS\{F0F08735-0C36-101B-B086-0020AF07D0F4}]
@="SCC Quick Viewer"
[HKEY_CLASSES_ROOT\QuickView\.WMF]
@="Windows Metafile"
[HKEY_CLASSES_ROOT\QuickView\.WMF\{F0F08735-0C36-101B-B086-0020AF07D0F4}]
@="SCC Quick Viewer"
[HKEY_CLASSES_ROOT\QuickView\.WPD]
@="Word Perfect Demo Files"
[HKEY_CLASSES_ROOT\QuickView\.WPD\{F0F08735-0C36-101B-B086-0020AF07D0F4}]
@="SCC Quick Viewer"
[HKEY_CLASSES_ROOT\QuickView\.WPS]
@="Works Word Processing Files"

[HKEY_CLASSES_ROOT\QuickView\.WPS\{F0F08735-0C36-101B-B086-0020AF07D0F4}]
@="SCC QuickViewer"
[HKEY_CLASSES_ROOT\QuickView\.WQ1]
@="Quattro Pro for MS-DOS File"
[HKEY_CLASSES_ROOT\QuickView\.WQ1\{F0F08735-0C36-101B-B086-0020AF07D0F4}]
@="SCC QuickViewer"
[HKEY_CLASSES_ROOT\QuickView\.WQ2]
@="Quattro Pro v 5 for MS-DOS File"
[HKEY_CLASSES_ROOT\QuickView\.WQ2\{F0F08735-0C36-101B-B086-0020AF07D0F4}]
@="SCC QuickViewer"
[HKEY_CLASSES_ROOT\QuickView\.WRI]
@="Windows 3.x WRITE Files"
[HKEY_CLASSES_ROOT\QuickView\.WRI\{F0F08735-0C36-101B-B086-0020AF07D0F4}]
@="SCC QuickViewer"
[HKEY_CLASSES_ROOT\QuickView\.XLC]
@="Excel 4 Chart File"
[HKEY_CLASSES_ROOT\QuickView\.XLC\{F0F08735-0C36-101B-B086-0020AF07D0F4}]
@="SCC QuickViewer"
[HKEY_CLASSES_ROOT\QuickView\.XLS]
@="Excel 4 and 5 Spreadsheet Files"
[HKEY_CLASSES_ROOT\QuickView\.XLS\{F0F08735-0C36-101B-B086-0020AF07D0F4}]
@="SCC QuickViewer"
[HKEY_CLASSES_ROOT\QuickView\shell]
[HKEY_CLASSES_ROOT\QuickView\shell\open]
[HKEY_CLASSES_ROOT\QuickView\shell\open\command]
@=hex(2):25,53,79,73,74,65,6d,52,6f,6f,74,25,5c,73,79,73,74,65,6d,33,32,5c,76,69,
65,77,65,72,73,5c,71,75,69,6b,76,69,65,77,2e,65,78,65,00
[HKEY_CLASSES_ROOT\QuickView\{F0F08735-0C36-101B-B086-0020AF07D0F4}]
@="SCC QuickViewer"
[HKEY_CLASSES_ROOT\regedit]
@="Registration Entries"
[HKEY_CLASSES_ROOT\regedit\shell]
[HKEY_CLASSES_ROOT\regedit\shell\open]
[HKEY_CLASSES_ROOT\regedit\shell\open\command]
@="regedit.exe %1"

[HKEY_CLASSES_ROOT\regfile]
@="Registration Entries"
[HKEY_CLASSES_ROOT\regfile\DefaultIcon]
@=hex(2):25,53,79,73,74,65,6d,52,6f,6f,74,25,5c,72,65,67,65,64,69,74,2e,65,78,65,
2c,31,00
[HKEY_CLASSES_ROOT\regfile\shell]
[HKEY_CLASSES_ROOT\regfile\shell\edit]
@="&Edit"
[HKEY_CLASSES_ROOT\regfile\shell\edit\command]
@=hex(2):25,53,79,73,74,65,6d,52,6f,6f,74,25,5c,73,79,73,74,65,6d,33,32,5c,4e,4f,54,
45,50,41,44,2e,45,58,45,20,25,31,00
[HKEY_CLASSES_ROOT\regfile\shell\open]
@="Mer&ge"
[HKEY_CLASSES_ROOT\regfile\shell\open\command]
@="regedit.exe \"%1\""
[HKEY_CLASSES_ROOT\regfile\shell\print]
[HKEY_CLASSES_ROOT\regfile\shell\print\command]
@=hex(2):25,53,79,73,74,65,6d,52,6f,6f,74,25,5c,73,79,73,74,65,6d,33,32,5c,4e,4f,54,
45,50,41,44,2e,45,58,45,20,2f,70,20,25,31,00
[HKEY_CLASSES_ROOT\rlogin]
@="URL:RLogin Protocol"
"EditFlags"=hex:02,00,00,00
"URL Protocol"=""
[HKEY_CLASSES_ROOT\rlogin\DefaultIcon]
@="C:\\WINNT\\System32\\url.dll,0"
[HKEY_CLASSES_ROOT\rlogin\shell]
[HKEY_CLASSES_ROOT\rlogin\shell\open]
[HKEY_CLASSES_ROOT\rlogin\shell\open\command]
@="rundll32.exe url.dll,TelnetProtocolHandler %l"
[HKEY_CLASSES_ROOT\rnkfile]}
@="Dial-Up Shortcut"
[HKEY_CLASSES_ROOT\rnkfile\CLSID]
@="{a4d92741-67cd-11cf-96f2-00aa00a11dd9}"
[HKEY_CLASSES_ROOT\rnkfile\DefaultIcon]
@=hex(2):25,53,79,73,74,65,6d,52,6f,6f,74,25,5c,73,79,73,74,65,6d,33,32,5c,72,61,
73,73,68,65,6c,6c,2e,64,6c,6c,2c,31,00
[HKEY_CLASSES_ROOT\rnkfile\shell]
[HKEY_CLASSES_ROOT\rnkfile\shell\Dial]
@="&Dial"
[HKEY_CLASSES_ROOT\rnkfile\shell\Dial\command]
@=hex(2):25,53,79,73,74,65,6d,52,6f,6f,74,25,5c,73,79,73,74,65,6d,33,32,5c,72,61,
73,70,68,6f,6e,65,2e,65,78,65,20,2d,6c,74,20,22,25,31,22,00

[HKEY_CLASSES_ROOT\rnkfile\shell\Edit entry and modem settings]
@="&Edit entry and modem settings"
[HKEY_CLASSES_ROOT\rnkfile\shell\Edit entry and modem settings\command]
@=hex(2):25,53,79,73,74,65,6d,52,6f,6f,74,25,5c,73,79,73,74,65,6d,33,32,5c,72,61,
73,70,68,6f,6e,65,2e,65,78,65,20,2d,76,20,2d,6c,65,20,22,25,31,22,00
[HKEY_CLASSES_ROOT\rnkfile\shell\Hang Up]
@="Hang &up"
[HKEY_CLASSES_ROOT\rnkfile\shell\Hang Up\command]
@=hex(2):25,53,79,73,74,65,6d,52,6f,6f,74,25,5c,73,79,73,74,65,6d,33,32,5c,72,61,
73,70,68,6f,6e,65,2e,65,78,65,20,2d,6c,68,20,22,25,31,22,00
[HKEY_CLASSES_ROOT\rnkfile\shellex]
[HKEY_CLASSES_ROOT\rnkfile\shellex\PropertySheetHandlers]
[HKEY_CLASSES_ROOT\rnkfile\shellex\PropertySheetHandlers\{a4d92741-67cd-
11cf-96f2-00aa00a11dd9}]
[HKEY_CLASSES_ROOT\rtffile]
@="Rich Text Document"
[HKEY_CLASSES_ROOT\rtffile\CLSID]
@="{73FDDC80-AEA9-101A-98A7-00AA00374959}"
[HKEY_CLASSES_ROOT\rtffile\DefaultIcon]
@="C:\\Program Files\\Windows NT\\Accessories\\WORDPAD.EXE,1"
[HKEY_CLASSES_ROOT\rtffile\shell]
[HKEY_CLASSES_ROOT\rtffile\shell\open]
[HKEY_CLASSES_ROOT\rtffile\shell\open\command]
@="\"C:\\Program Files\\Windows NT\\Accessories\\WORDPAD.EXE\"\
"%1\""
[HKEY_CLASSES_ROOT\rtffile\shell\print]
[HKEY_CLASSES_ROOT\rtffile\shell\print\command]
@="C:\\Program Files\\Windows NT\\Accessories\\WORDPAD.EXE /p\"%1\""
[HKEY_CLASSES_ROOT\rtffile\shell\printto]
[HKEY_CLASSES_ROOT\rtffile\shell\printto\command]
@="C:\\Program Files\\Windows NT\\Accessories\\WORDPAD.EXE/pt\"%1\
"\"%2\" \"%3\" \"%4\" "
[HKEY_CLASSES_ROOT\scrfile]
@="Screen Saver"
[HKEY_CLASSES_ROOT\scrfile\shell]
[HKEY_CLASSES_ROOT\scrfile\shell\config]
@="C&onfigure"
[HKEY_CLASSES_ROOT\scrfile\shell\config\command]
@="%1"
[HKEY_CLASSES_ROOT\scrfile\shell\install]
@="&Install"
[HKEY_CLASSES_ROOT\scrfile\shell\install\command]

@="rundll32.exe desk.cpl,InstallScreenSaver %l"
[HKEY_CLASSES_ROOT\scrfile\shell\open]
@="T&est"
[HKEY_CLASSES_ROOT\scrfile\shell\open\command]
@="\"%1\" /S"
[HKEY_CLASSES_ROOT\ShellScrap]
@="Scrap object"
"NeverShowExt"=""
[HKEY_CLASSES_ROOT\ShellScrap\DefaultIcon]
@=hex(2):25,53,79,73,74,65,6d,52,6f,6f,74,25,5c,73,79,73,74,65,6d,33,32,5c,73,68,
73,63,72,61,70,2e,64,6c,6c,2c,2d,31,30,30,00
[HKEY_CLASSES_ROOT\ShellScrap\shell]
[HKEY_CLASSES_ROOT\ShellScrap\shell\open]
[HKEY_CLASSES_ROOT\ShellScrap\shell\open\command]
@=hex(2):72,75,6e,64,6c,6c,33,32,20,25,53,79,73,74,65,6d,52,6f,6f,74,25,5c,73,79,
73,74,65,6d,33,32,5c,73,68,73,63,72,61,70,2e,64,6c,6c,2c,4f,70,65,6e,53,63,72,61,70
,5f,52,75,6e,44,4c,4c,20,25,31,00
[HKEY_CLASSES_ROOT\ShellScrap\shellex]
[HKEY_CLASSES_ROOT\ShellScrap\shellex\DataHandler]
@="{56117100-C0CD-101B-81E2-00AA004AE837}"
[HKEY_CLASSES_ROOT\SoundRec]
@="Wave Sound"
"EditFlags"=hex:00,00,01,00
[HKEY_CLASSES_ROOT\SoundRec\CLSID]
@="{00020C01-0000-0000-C000-000000000046}"
[HKEY_CLASSES_ROOT\SoundRec\DefaultIcon]
@="sndrec32.exe,1"
[HKEY_CLASSES_ROOT\SoundRec\protocol]
[HKEY_CLASSES_ROOT\SoundRec\protocol\StdExecute]
[HKEY_CLASSES_ROOT\SoundRec\protocol\StdExecute\server]
@="sndrec32.exe"
[HKEY_CLASSES_ROOT\SoundRec\protocol\StdFileEditing]
[HKEY_CLASSES_ROOT\SoundRec\protocol\StdFileEditing\server]
@="sndrec32.exe"
[HKEY_CLASSES_ROOT\SoundRec\protocol\StdFileEditing\verb]
[HKEY_CLASSES_ROOT\SoundRec\protocol\StdFileEditing\verb\0]
@="&Play"
[HKEY_CLASSES_ROOT\SoundRec\protocol\StdFileEditing\verb\1]
@="&Edit"
[HKEY_CLASSES_ROOT\SoundRec\protocol\StdFileEditing\verb\2]
@="&Open"

[HKEY_CLASSES_ROOT\SoundRec\shell]
@="play"
[HKEY_CLASSES_ROOT\SoundRec\shell\open]
@="&Open"
[HKEY_CLASSES_ROOT\SoundRec\shell\open\command]
@="sndrec32.exe \"%L\""
[HKEY_CLASSES_ROOT\SoundRec\shell\play]
@="&Play"
[HKEY_CLASSES_ROOT\SoundRec\shell\play\command]
@="mplay32.exe /play /close \"%L\""
[HKEY_CLASSES_ROOT\SoundRec\shellex]
[HKEY_CLASSES_ROOT\SoundRec\shellex\PropertySheetHandlers]
@="WavPage"
[HKEY_CLASSES_ROOT\SoundRec\shellex\PropertySheetHandlers\WavPage]
@="{00022613-0000-0000-C000-000000000046}"
[HKEY_CLASSES_ROOT\StaticDib]
@="Picture (Device Independent Bitmap)"
[HKEY_CLASSES_ROOT\StaticEnhancedMetafile]
@="Picture (Enhanced Metafile)"
[HKEY_CLASSES_ROOT\StaticMetafile]
@="Picture (Metafile)"
[HKEY_CLASSES_ROOT\sysfile]
@="System file"
"AlwaysShowExt"=""
"EditFlags"=hex:01,00,00,00
[HKEY_CLASSES_ROOT\sysfile\DefaultIcon]
@=hex(2):25,53,79,73,74,65,6d,52,6f,6f,74,25,5c,73,79,73,74,65,6d,33,32,5c,73,68,
65,6c,6c,33,32,2e,64,6c,6c,2c,2d,31,35,34,00
[HKEY_CLASSES_ROOT\telnet]
@="URL:Telnet Protocol"
"EditFlags"=hex:02,00,00,00
"URL Protocol"=""
[HKEY_CLASSES_ROOT\telnet\DefaultIcon]
@="C:\\WINNT\\System32\\url.dll,0"
[HKEY_CLASSES_ROOT\telnet\shell]
[HKEY_CLASSES_ROOT\telnet\shell\open]
[HKEY_CLASSES_ROOT\telnet\shell\open\command]
@="rundll32.exe url.dll,TelnetProtocolHandler %l"
[HKEY_CLASSES_ROOT\TIFImage.Document]
@="TIF Image Document"
[HKEY_CLASSES_ROOT\TIFImage.Document\CLSID]
@="{02B01C80-E03D-101A-B294-00DD010F2BF9}"

[HKEY_CLASSES_ROOT\TIFImage.Document\DefaultIcon]
@="C:\\Program Files\\Windows NT\\Accessories\\ImageVue\\WangImg.Exe,1"
[HKEY_CLASSES_ROOT\TIFImage.Document\shell]
[HKEY_CLASSES_ROOT\TIFImage.Document\shell\open]
[HKEY_CLASSES_ROOT\TIFImage.Document\shell\open\command]
@="C:\\Program Files\\Windows NT\\Accessories\\ImageVue\\WangImg.Exe \"
%1\""
[HKEY_CLASSES_ROOT\TIFImage.Document\shell\print]
[HKEY_CLASSES_ROOT\TIFImage.Document\shell\print\command]
@="C:\\Program Files\\Windows NT\\Accessories\\ImageVue\\WangImg.Exe/p\
"%1\""
[HKEY_CLASSES_ROOT\TIFImage.Document\shell\printto]
[HKEY_CLASSES_ROOT\TIFImage.Document\shell\printto\command]
@="C:\\Program Files\\Windows NT\\Accessories\\ImageVue\\WangImg.Exe /pt\
"%1\" \"%2\" \"%3\" \"%4\" "
[HKEY_CLASSES_ROOT\TIFImage.Document\shellex]
@=""
[HKEY_CLASSES_ROOT\TIFImage.Document\shellex\PropertySheetHandlers]
@=""
[HKEY_CLASSES_ROOT\TIFImage.Document\shellex\PropertySheetHandlers\
{1D3ECD40-C835-11CE-9888-00608CC22020}]
@=""
[HKEY_CLASSES_ROOT\tn3270]
@="URL:TN3270 Protocol"
"EditFlags"=hex:02,00,00,00
"URL Protocol"=""
[HKEY_CLASSES_ROOT\tn3270\DefaultIcon]
@="C:\\WINNT\\System32\\url.dll,0"
[HKEY_CLASSES_ROOT\tn3270\shell]
[HKEY_CLASSES_ROOT\tn3270\shell\open]
[HKEY_CLASSES_ROOT\tn3270\shell\open\command]
@="rundll32.exe url.dll,TelnetProtocolHandler %l"
[HKEY_CLASSES_ROOT\ttffile]
@="TrueType Font file"
[HKEY_CLASSES_ROOT\ttffile\DefaultIcon]
@=hex(2):25,53,79,73,74,65,6d,52,6f,6f,74,25,5c,73,79,73,74,65,6d,33,32,5c,73,68,
65,6c,6c,33,32,2e,64,6c,6c,2c,2d,31,35,36,00
[HKEY_CLASSES_ROOT\ttffile\shell]
[HKEY_CLASSES_ROOT\ttffile\shell\open]
[HKEY_CLASSES_ROOT\ttffile\shell\open\command]
@=hex(2):25,53,79,73,74,65,6d,52,6f,6f,74,25,5c,53,79,73,74,65,6d,33,32,5c,66,6f,6e,
74,76,69,65,77,2e,65,78,65,20,25,31,00
[HKEY_CLASSES_ROOT\ttffile\shell\print]

[HKEY_CLASSES_ROOT\ttffile\shell\print\command]
@=hex(2):25,53,79,73,74,65,6d,52,6f,6f,74,25,5c,53,79,73,74,65,6d,33,32,5c,66,6f,6e,
74,76,69,65,77,2e,65,78,65,20,2f,70,20,25,31,00
[HKEY_CLASSES_ROOT\txtfile]
@="Text Document"
[HKEY_CLASSES_ROOT\txtfile\DefaultIcon]
@=hex(2):25,53,79,73,74,65,6d,52,6f,6f,74,25,5c,73,79,73,74,65,6d,33,32,5c,73,68,
65,6c,6c,33,32,2e,64,6c,6c,2c,2d,31,35,32,00
[HKEY_CLASSES_ROOT\txtfile\shell]
[HKEY_CLASSES_ROOT\txtfile\shell\open]
[HKEY_CLASSES_ROOT\txtfile\shell\open\command]
@=hex(2):25,53,79,73,74,65,6d,52,6f,6f,74,25,5c,73,79,73,74,65,6d,33,32,5c,4e,4f,54,
45,50,41,44,2e,45,58,45,20,25,31,00
[HKEY_CLASSES_ROOT\txtfile\shell\print]
[HKEY_CLASSES_ROOT\txtfile\shell\print\command]
@=hex(2):25,53,79,73,74,65,6d,52,6f,6f,74,25,5c,73,79,73,74,65,6d,33,32,5c,4e,4f,54,
45,50,41,44,2e,45,58,45,20,2f,70,20,25,31,00
[HKEY_CLASSES_ROOT\TypeLib]
@="{E1A6B8A3-3603-101C-AC6E-040224009C02}"
[HKEY_CLASSES_ROOT\TypeLib\{00020430-0000-0000-C000-000000000046}]
[HKEY_CLASSES_ROOT\TypeLib\{00020430-0000-0000-C000-
000000000046}\1.0]
@="OLE Automation"
[HKEY_CLASSES_ROOT\TypeLib\{00020430-0000-0000-C000-
000000000046}\1.0\0]
[HKEY_CLASSES_ROOT\TypeLib\{00020430-0000-0000-C000-
000000000046}\1.0\0\win16]
@="stdole.tlb"
[HKEY_CLASSES_ROOT\TypeLib\{00020430-0000-0000-C000-
000000000046}\1.0\0\win32]
@="stdole32.tlb"
[HKEY_CLASSES_ROOT\TypeLib\{00020430-0000-0000-C000-
000000000046}\1.0\HELPDIR]
@=""
[HKEY_CLASSES_ROOT\TypeLib\{009541A3-3B81-101C-92F3-
040224009C02}]
@="1.0"
[HKEY_CLASSES_ROOT\TypeLib\{009541A3-3B81-101C-92F3-
040224009C02}\1.0]
@="Wang Image Admin Control"
[HKEY_CLASSES_ROOT\TypeLib\{009541A3-3B81-101C-92F3-
040224009C02}\1.0\0]
@="win32"

[HKEY_CLASSES_ROOT\TypeLib\{009541A3-3B81-101C-92F3-040224009C02}\1.0\0\win32]
@="C:\\WINNT\\System32\\IMGADMIN.OCX"
[HKEY_CLASSES_ROOT\TypeLib\{009541A3-3B81-101C-92F3-040224009C02}\1.0\FLAGS]
@="0"
[HKEY_CLASSES_ROOT\TypeLib\{009541A3-3B81-101C-92F3-040224009C02}\1.0\HELPDIR]
@="C:\\WINNT\\System32"
[HKEY_CLASSES_ROOT\TypeLib\{6D940288-9F11-11CE-83FD-02608C3EC08A}]
@="1.0"
[HKEY_CLASSES_ROOT\TypeLib\{6D940288-9F11-11CE-83FD-02608C3EC08A}\1.0]
@="Wang Image Edit Control"
[HKEY_CLASSES_ROOT\TypeLib\{6D940288-9F11-11CE-83FD-02608C3EC08A}\1.0\0]
@=""
[HKEY_CLASSES_ROOT\TypeLib\{6D940288-9F11-11CE-83FD-02608C3EC08A}\1.0\0\win32]
@="C:\\WINNT\\System32\\IMGEDIT.OCX"
[HKEY_CLASSES_ROOT\TypeLib\{6D940288-9F11-11CE-83FD-02608C3EC08A}\1.0\FLAGS]
@="0"
[HKEY_CLASSES_ROOT\TypeLib\{6D940288-9F11-11CE-83FD-02608C3EC08A}\1.0\HELPDIR]
@="C:\\WINNT\\System32"
[HKEY_CLASSES_ROOT\TypeLib\{84926CA3-2941-101C-816F-0E6013114B7F}]
[HKEY_CLASSES_ROOT\TypeLib\{84926CA3-2941-101C-816F-0E6013114B7F}\1.0]
@="Wang Image Scan Control"
[HKEY_CLASSES_ROOT\TypeLib\{84926CA3-2941-101C-816F-0E6013114B7F}\1.0\0]
@=""
[HKEY_CLASSES_ROOT\TypeLib\{84926CA3-2941-101C-816F-0E6013114B7F}\1.0\0\win32]
@="C:\\WINNT\\System32\\IMGSCAN.OCX"
[HKEY_CLASSES_ROOT\TypeLib\{84926CA3-2941-101C-816F-0E6013114B7F}\1.0\FLAGS]
@="0"
[HKEY_CLASSES_ROOT\TypeLib\{84926CA3-2941-101C-816F-0E6013114B7F}\1.0\HELPDIR]

@="C:\\WINNT\\System32"
[HKEY_CLASSES_ROOT\TypeLib\{E1A6B8A3-3603-101C-AC6E-040224009C02}]
[HKEY_CLASSES_ROOT\TypeLib\{E1A6B8A3-3603-101C-AC6E-040224009C02}\1.0]
@="Wang Image Thumbnail Control"
[HKEY_CLASSES_ROOT\TypeLib\{E1A6B8A3-3603-101C-AC6E-040224009C02}\1.0\0]
@=""
[HKEY_CLASSES_ROOT\TypeLib\{E1A6B8A3-3603-101C-AC6E-040224009C02}\1.0\0\win32]
@="C:\\WINNT\\System32\\IMGTHUMB.OCX"
[HKEY_CLASSES_ROOT\TypeLib\{E1A6B8A3-3603-101C-AC6E-040224009C02}\1.0\FLAGS]
@="0"
[HKEY_CLASSES_ROOT\TypeLib\{E1A6B8A3-3603-101C-AC6E-040224009C02}\1.0\HELPDIR]
@="C:\\WINNT\\System32"
[HKEY_CLASSES_ROOT\Unknown]
"AlwaysShowExt"=""
[HKEY_CLASSES_ROOT\Unknown\shell]
[HKEY_CLASSES_ROOT\Unknown\shell\openas]
[HKEY_CLASSES_ROOT\Unknown\shell\openas\command]
@=hex(2):25,53,79,73,74,65,6d,52,6f,6f,74,25,5c,73,79,73,74,65,6d,33,32,5c,72,75,
6e,64,6c,6c,33,32,2e,65,78,65,20,25,53,79,73,74,65,6d,52,6f,6f,74,25,5c,73,79,73,74,74,
65,6d,33,32,5c,73,68,65,6c,6c,33,32,2e,64,6c,6c,2c,4f,70,65,6e,41,73,5f,52,75,6e,44,
4c,4c,20,25,31,00
[HKEY_CLASSES_ROOT\vxdfile]
"EditFlags"=hex:01,00,00,00
@="Virtual device driver"
"AlwaysShowExt"=""
[HKEY_CLASSES_ROOT\vxdfile\DefaultIcon]
@=hex(2):25,53,79,73,74,65,6d,52,6f,6f,74,25,5c,73,79,73,74,65,6d,33,32,5c,73,68,
65,6c,6c,33,32,2e,64,6c,6c,2c,2d,31,35,34,00
[HKEY_CLASSES_ROOT\WangImage.AdminCtrl.1]
@="Wang Image Admin Control"
[HKEY_CLASSES_ROOT\WangImage.AdminCtrl.1\CLSID]
@="{009541A0-3B81-101C-92F3-040224009C02}"
[HKEY_CLASSES_ROOT\WangImage.AnnotationCtrl.1]
@="Wang Image Annotation Control"
[HKEY_CLASSES_ROOT\WangImage.AnnotationCtrl.1\CLSID]
@="{6D940285-9F11-11CE-83FD-02608C3EC08A}"
[HKEY_CLASSES_ROOT\WangImage.Application]

@="Wang Image Viewer"
[HKEY_CLASSES_ROOT\WangImage.Application\CLSID]
@="{7D252A20-A4D5-11CE-8BF1-00608C54A1AA}"
[HKEY_CLASSES_ROOT\WangImage.Application.1]
@="Wang Image Viewer 1.0"
[HKEY_CLASSES_ROOT\WangImage.Application.1\CLSID]
@="{7D252A20-A4D5-11CE-8BF1-00608C54A1AA}"
[HKEY_CLASSES_ROOT\WangImage.Document]
@="Image Document"
[HKEY_CLASSES_ROOT\WangImage.Document\CLSID]
@="{02B01C80-E03D-101A-B294-00DD010F2BF9}"
[HKEY_CLASSES_ROOT\WangImage.Document\DefaultIcon]
@="C:\\Program Files\\Windows NT\\Accessories\\ImageVue\\WangImg.Exe,1"
[HKEY_CLASSES_ROOT\WangImage.Document\Insertable]
@=""
[HKEY_CLASSES_ROOT\WangImage.Document\protocol]
[HKEY_CLASSES_ROOT\WangImage.Document\protocol\StdFileEditing]
[HKEY_CLASSES_ROOT\WangImage.Document\protocol\StdFileEditing\server]
@="C:\\Program Files\\Windows NT\\Accessories\\ImageVue\\WangImg.Exe"
[HKEY_CLASSES_ROOT\WangImage.Document\protocol\StdFileEditing\verb]
[HKEY_CLASSES_ROOT\WangImage.Document\protocol\StdFileEditing\verb\0]
@="&Edit"
[HKEY_CLASSES_ROOT\WangImage.Document\shell]
[HKEY_CLASSES_ROOT\WangImage.Document\shell\open]
[HKEY_CLASSES_ROOT\WangImage.Document\shell\open\command]
@="C:\\Program Files\\Windows NT\\Accessories\\ImageVue\\WangImg.Exe\
"%1\""
[HKEY_CLASSES_ROOT\WangImage.Document\shell\print]
[HKEY_CLASSES_ROOT\WangImage.Document\shell\print\command]
@="C:\\Program Files\\Windows NT\\Accessories\\ImageVue\\WangImg.Exe /p\
"%1\""
[HKEY_CLASSES_ROOT\WangImage.Document\shell\printto]
[HKEY_CLASSES_ROOT\WangImage.Document\shell\printto\command]
@="C:\\Program Files\\Windows NT\\Accessories\\ImageVue\\WangImg.Exe /pt\
"%1\" \"%2\" \"%3\" \"%4\" "
[HKEY_CLASSES_ROOT\WangImage.Document\shellex]
@=""
[HKEY_CLASSES_ROOT\WangImage.Document\shellex\PropertySheetHandlers]
@=""
[HKEY_CLASSES_ROOT\WangImage.Document\shellex\PropertySheetHandlers\
{1D3ECD40-C835-11CE-9888-00608CC22020}]
@=""
[HKEY_CLASSES_ROOT\WangImage.EditCtrl.1]

@="Wang Image Edit Control"
[HKEY_CLASSES_ROOT\WangImage.EditCtrl.1\CLSID]
@="{6D940280-9F11-11CE-83FD-02608C3EC08A}"
[HKEY_CLASSES_ROOT\WangImage.ScanCtrl.1]
@="Wang Image Scan Control"
[HKEY_CLASSES_ROOT\WangImage.ScanCtrl.1\CLSID]
@="{84926CA0-2941-101C-816F-0E6013114B7F}"
[HKEY_CLASSES_ROOT\WangImage.ThumbnailCtrl.1]
@="Wang Image Thumbnail Control"
[HKEY_CLASSES_ROOT\WangImage.ThumbnailCtrl.1\CLSID]
@="{E1A6B8A0-3603-101C-AC6E-040224009C02}"
[HKEY_CLASSES_ROOT\Wordpad.Document.1]
@="WordPad Document"
[HKEY_CLASSES_ROOT\Wordpad.Document.1\CLSID]
@="{73FDDC80-AEA9-101A-98A7-00AA00374959}"
[HKEY_CLASSES_ROOT\Wordpad.Document.1\DefaultIcon]
@="C:\\Program Files\\Windows NT\\Accessories\\WORDPAD.EXE,1"
[HKEY_CLASSES_ROOT\Wordpad.Document.1\Insertable]
@=""
[HKEY_CLASSES_ROOT\Wordpad.Document.1\Protocol]
@=""
[HKEY_CLASSES_ROOT\Wordpad.Document.1\Protocol\StdFileEditing]
@=""
[HKEY_CLASSES_ROOT\Wordpad.Document.1\Protocol\StdFileEditing\Server]
@="C:\\Program Files\\Windows NT\\Accessories\\WORDPAD.EXE"
[HKEY_CLASSES_ROOT\Wordpad.Document.1\Protocol\StdFileEditing\Verb]
@=""
[HKEY_CLASSES_ROOT\Wordpad.Document.1\Protocol\StdFileEditing\Verb\0]
@="&Edit"
[HKEY_CLASSES_ROOT\Wordpad.Document.1\shell]
[HKEY_CLASSES_ROOT\Wordpad.Document.1\shell\open]
[HKEY_CLASSES_ROOT\Wordpad.Document.1\shell\open\command]
@="\"C:\\Program Files\\Windows NT\\Accessories\\WORDPAD.EXE\" \
"%1\""
[HKEY_CLASSES_ROOT\Wordpad.Document.1\shell\print]
[HKEY_CLASSES_ROOT\Wordpad.Document.1\shell\print\command]
@="C:\\Program Files\\Windows NT\\Accessories\\WORDPAD.EXE /p\
"%1\""
[HKEY_CLASSES_ROOT\Wordpad.Document.1\shell\printto]
[HKEY_CLASSES_ROOT\Wordpad.Document.1\shell\printto\command]
@="C:\\Program Files\\Windows NT\\Accessories\\WORDPAD.EXE /pt \"%1\|
" \"%2\" \"%3\" \"%4\" "
[HKEY_CLASSES_ROOT\wrifile]

@="Write Document"
[HKEY_CLASSES_ROOT\wrifile\CLSID]
@="{73FDDC80-AEA9-101A-98A7-00AA00374959}"
[HKEY_CLASSES_ROOT\wrifile\DefaultIcon]
@="C:\\Program Files\\Windows NT\\Accessories\\WORDPAD.EXE,2"
[HKEY_CLASSES_ROOT\wrifile\shell]
[HKEY_CLASSES_ROOT\wrifile\shell\open]
[HKEY_CLASSES_ROOT\wrifile\shell\open\command]
@="\"C:\\Program Files\\Windows NT\\Accessories\\WORDPAD.EXE\" \
"%1\""
[HKEY_CLASSES_ROOT\wrifile\shell\print]
[HKEY_CLASSES_ROOT\wrifile\shell\print\command]
@="C:\\Program Files\\Windows NT\\Accessories\\WORDPAD.EXE /p \
"%1\""
[HKEY_CLASSES_ROOT\wrifile\shell\printto]
[HKEY_CLASSES_ROOT\wrifile\shell\printto\command]
@="C:\\Program Files\\Windows NT\\Accessories\\WORDPAD.EXE /pt \"%1\" \
"%2\" \"%3\" \"%4\" "
[HKEY_CLASSES_ROOT\xbmfile]
@="XBM Image"
[HKEY_CLASSES_ROOT\xbmfile\DefaultIcon]
@="C:\\Program Files\\Plus!\\Microsoft Internet\\IExplore.exe,8"
[HKEY_CLASSES_ROOT\xbmfile\shell]
[HKEY_CLASSES_ROOT\xbmfile\shell\open]
[HKEY_CLASSES_ROOT\xbmfile\shell\open\command]
@="\"C:\\Program Files\\Plus!\\Microsoft Internet\\IExplore.exe\" -nohome"
[HKEY_CLASSES_ROOT\xbmfile\shell\open\ddeexec]
@="\"file:%1\",,-1,,,,,"
[HKEY_CLASSES_ROOT\xbmfile\shell\open\ddeexec\Application]
@="IExplore"
[HKEY_CLASSES_ROOT\xbmfile\shell\open\ddeexec\Topic]
@="WWW_OpenURL"
[HKEY_CLASSES_ROOT\XIFImage.Document]
@="XIF Image Document"
[HKEY_CLASSES_ROOT\XIFImage.Document\CLSID]
@="{02B01C80-E03D-101A-B294-00DD010F2BF9}"
[HKEY_CLASSES_ROOT\XIFImage.Document\DefaultIcon]
@="C:\\Program Files\\Windows NT\\Accessories\\ImageVue\\WangImg.Exe,1"
[HKEY_CLASSES_ROOT\XIFImage.Document\shell]
[HKEY_CLASSES_ROOT\XIFImage.Document\shell\open]
[HKEY_CLASSES_ROOT\XIFImage.Document\shell\open\command]
@="C:\\Program Files\\Windows NT\\Accessories\\ImageVue\\WangImg.Exe \
"%1\""

[HKEY_CLASSES_ROOT\XIFImage.Document\shell\print]
[HKEY_CLASSES_ROOT\XIFImage.Document\shell\print\command]
@="C:\\Program Files\\Windows NT\\Accessories\\ImageVue\\WangImg.Exe
/p \"%1\""
[HKEY_CLASSES_ROOT\XIFImage.Document\shell\printto]
[HKEY_CLASSES_ROOT\XIFImage.Document\shell\printto\command]
@="C:\\Program Files\\Windows NT\\Accessories\\ImageVue\\WangImg.Exe
/pt \"%1\" \"%2\" \"%3\" \"%4\" "
[HKEY_CLASSES_ROOT\XIFImage.Document\shellex]
@=""
[HKEY_CLASSES_ROOT\XIFImage.Document\shellex\PropertySheetHandlers]
@=""
[HKEY_CLASSES_ROOT\XIFImage.Document\shellex\PropertySheetHandlers\
{1D3ECD40-C835-11CE-9888-00608CC22020}]
@=""

HKEY_CURRENT_CONFIG Subkeys and Their Values

[HKEY_CURRENT_CONFIG]
[HKEY_CURRENT_CONFIG\Software]
[HKEY_CURRENT_CONFIG\System]
[HKEY_CURRENT_CONFIG\System\CurrentControlSet]
[HKEY_CURRENT_CONFIG\System\CurrentControlSet\Control]
[HKEY_CURRENT_CONFIG\System\CurrentControlSet\Control\Class]
[HKEY_CURRENT_CONFIG\System\CurrentControlSet\Enum]
[HKEY_CURRENT_CONFIG\System\CurrentControlSet\Services]
[HKEY_CURRENT_CONFIG\System\CurrentControlSet\Services\cirrus]
[HKEY_CURRENT_CONFIG\System\CurrentControlSet\Services\cirrus\
Device0]
"DefaultSettings.BitsPerPel"=dword:00000008
"DefaultSettings.XResolution"=dword:00000280
"DefaultSettings.YResolution"=dword:000001e0
"DefaultSettings.VRefresh"=dword:0000003c
"DefaultSettings.Flags"=dword:00000000
"DefaultSettings.XPanning"=dword:00000000
"DefaultSettings.YPanning"=dword:00000000

HKEY_CURRENT_USER Subkeys and Their Values

[HKEY_CURRENT_USER]
[HKEY_CURRENT_USER\AppEvents]
"Migrated Schemes"="1"
[HKEY_CURRENT_USER\AppEvents\EventLabels]
[HKEY_CURRENT_USER\AppEvents\EventLabels\.Default]
@="Default Beep"
[HKEY_CURRENT_USER\AppEvents\EventLabels\AppGPFault]
@="Program error"
[HKEY_CURRENT_USER\AppEvents\EventLabels\Close]
@="Close program"
[HKEY_CURRENT_USER\AppEvents\EventLabels\EmptyRecycleBin]
@="Empty Recycle Bin"
[HKEY_CURRENT_USER\AppEvents\EventLabels\MailBeep]
@="New Mail Notification"
[HKEY_CURRENT_USER\AppEvents\EventLabels\Maximize]
@="Maximize"
[HKEY_CURRENT_USER\AppEvents\EventLabels\MenuCommand]
@="Menu command"
[HKEY_CURRENT_USER\AppEvents\EventLabels\MenuPopup]
@="Menu popup"
[HKEY_CURRENT_USER\AppEvents\EventLabels\Minimize]
@="Minimize"
[HKEY_CURRENT_USER\AppEvents\EventLabels\Open]
@="Open program"
[HKEY_CURRENT_USER\AppEvents\EventLabels\RestoreDown]
@="Restore Down"
[HKEY_CURRENT_USER\AppEvents\EventLabels\RestoreUp]
@="Restore Up"
[HKEY_CURRENT_USER\AppEvents\EventLabels\RingIn]
@="Incoming Call"
[HKEY_CURRENT_USER\AppEvents\EventLabels\RingOut]
@="Outgoing Call"
[HKEY_CURRENT_USER\AppEvents\EventLabels\SystemAsterisk]
@="Asterisk"
[HKEY_CURRENT_USER\AppEvents\EventLabels\SystemExclamation]
@="Exclamation"
[HKEY_CURRENT_USER\AppEvents\EventLabels\SystemExit]
@="Exit Windows"
[HKEY_CURRENT_USER\AppEvents\EventLabels\SystemHand]
@="Critical Stop"

[HKEY_CURRENT_USER\AppEvents\EventLabels\SystemQuestion]
@="Question"
[HKEY_CURRENT_USER\AppEvents\EventLabels\SystemStart]
@="Start Windows"
[HKEY_CURRENT_USER\AppEvents\Schemes]
@=".Current"
[HKEY_CURRENT_USER\AppEvents\Schemes\Apps]
[HKEY_CURRENT_USER\AppEvents\Schemes\Apps\.Default]
@="Windows"
[HKEY_CURRENT_USER\AppEvents\Schemes\Apps\.Default\.Default]
[HKEY_CURRENT_USER\AppEvents\Schemes\Apps\.Default\.Default\.Current]
@="C:\\WINNT\\media\\ding.wav"
[HKEY_CURRENT_USER\AppEvents\Schemes\Apps\.Default\.Default\.Default]
@="C:\\WINNT\\media\\ding.wav"
[HKEY_CURRENT_USER\AppEvents\Schemes\Apps\.Default\.Default\Jungle0]
@="C:\\WINNT\\media\\Jungle Default.wav"
[HKEY_CURRENT_USER\AppEvents\Schemes\Apps\.Default\.Default\Musica0]
@="C:\\WINNT\\media\\Musica Default.wav"
[HKEY_CURRENT_USER\AppEvents\Schemes\Apps\.Default\.Default\
Robotz0]
@="C:\\WINNT\\media\\Robotz Default.wav"
[HKEY_CURRENT_USER\AppEvents\Schemes\Apps\.Default\.Default\Utopia0]
@="C:\\WINNT\\media\\Utopia Default.wav"
[HKEY_CURRENT_USER\AppEvents\Schemes\Apps\.Default\AppGPFault]
[HKEY_CURRENT_USER\AppEvents\Schemes\Apps\.Default\AppGPFault\
.Current]
@=""
[HKEY_CURRENT_USER\AppEvents\Schemes\Apps\.Default\AppGPFault\
.Default]
@=""
[HKEY_CURRENT_USER\AppEvents\Schemes\Apps\.Default\AppGPFault\
Jungle0]
@="C:\\WINNT\\media\\Jungle Error.wav"
[HKEY_CURRENT_USER\AppEvents\Schemes\Apps\.Default\AppGPFault\
Musica0]
@="C:\\WINNT\\media\\Musica Error.wav"
[HKEY_CURRENT_USER\AppEvents\Schemes\Apps\.Default\AppGPFault\
Robotz0]
@="C:\\WINNT\\media\\Robotz Error.wav"
[HKEY_CURRENT_USER\AppEvents\Schemes\Apps\.Default\AppGPFault\
Utopia0]
@="C:\\WINNT\\media\\Utopia Error.wav"
[HKEY_CURRENT_USER\AppEvents\Schemes\Apps\.Default\Close]

[HKEY_CURRENT_USER\AppEvents\Schemes\Apps\.Default\Close\.Current]
@=""
[HKEY_CURRENT_USER\AppEvents\Schemes\Apps\.Default\Close\.Default]
@=""
[HKEY_CURRENT_USER\AppEvents\Schemes\Apps\.Default\Close\Jungle0]
@=""
[HKEY_CURRENT_USER\AppEvents\Schemes\Apps\.Default\Close\Musica0]
@=""
[HKEY_CURRENT_USER\AppEvents\Schemes\Apps\.Default\Close\Robotz0]
@=""
[HKEY_CURRENT_USER\AppEvents\Schemes\Apps\.Default\Close\Utopia0]
@=""
[HKEY_CURRENT_USER\AppEvents\Schemes\Apps\.Default\MailBeep]
[HKEY_CURRENT_USER\AppEvents\Schemes\Apps\.Default\MailBeep\
.Current]
@="C:\\WINNT\\media\\ding.wav"
[HKEY_CURRENT_USER\AppEvents\Schemes\Apps\.Default\MailBeep\
.Default]
@="C:\\WINNT\\media\\ding.wav"
[HKEY_CURRENT_USER\AppEvents\Schemes\Apps\.Default\Maximize]
[HKEY_CURRENT_USER\AppEvents\Schemes\Apps\.Default\Maximize\
.Current]
@=""
[HKEY_CURRENT_USER\AppEvents\Schemes\Apps\.Default\Maximize\
.Default]
@=""
[HKEY_CURRENT_USER\AppEvents\Schemes\Apps\.Default\Maximize\
Jungle0]
@="C:\\WINNT\\media\\Jungle Maximize.wav"
[HKEY_CURRENT_USER\AppEvents\Schemes\Apps\.Default\Maximize\
Musica0]
@="C:\\WINNT\\media\\Musica Maximize.wav"
[HKEY_CURRENT_USER\AppEvents\Schemes\Apps\.Default\Maximize\
Robotz0]
@="C:\\WINNT\\media\\Robotz Maximize.wav"
[HKEY_CURRENT_USER\AppEvents\Schemes\Apps\.Default\Maximize\
Utopia0]
@="C:\\WINNT\\media\\Utopia Maximize.wav"
[HKEY_CURRENT_USER\AppEvents\Schemes\Apps\.Default\MenuCommand]
[HKEY_CURRENT_USER\AppEvents\Schemes\Apps\.Default\MenuCommand\
.Current]
@=""
[HKEY_CURRENT_USER\AppEvents\Schemes\Apps\.Default\MenuCommand\

.Default]
@=""
[HKEY_CURRENT_USER\AppEvents\Schemes\Apps\.Default\MenuCommand\
Jungle0]
@="C:\\WINNT\\media\\Jungle Menu Command.wav"
[HKEY_CURRENT_USER\AppEvents\Schemes\Apps\.Default\MenuCommand\
Musica0]
@="C:\\WINNT\\media\\Musica Menu Command.wav"
[HKEY_CURRENT_USER\AppEvents\Schemes\Apps\.Default\MenuCommand\
Robotz0]
@="C:\\WINNT\\media\\Robotz Menu Command.wav"
[HKEY_CURRENT_USER\AppEvents\Schemes\Apps\.Default\MenuCommand\
Utopia0]
@="C:\\WINNT\\media\\Utopia Menu Command.wav"
[HKEY_CURRENT_USER\AppEvents\Schemes\Apps\.Default\MenuPopup]
[HKEY_CURRENT_USER\AppEvents\Schemes\Apps\.Default\MenuPopup\
.Current]
@=""
[HKEY_CURRENT_USER\AppEvents\Schemes\Apps\.Default\MenuPopup\
.Default]
@=""
[HKEY_CURRENT_USER\AppEvents\Schemes\Apps\.Default\MenuPopup\
Jungle0]
@="C:\\WINNT\\media\\Jungle Menu Popup.wav"
[HKEY_CURRENT_USER\AppEvents\Schemes\Apps\.Default\MenuPopup\
Musica0]
@="C:\\WINNT\\media\\Musica Menu Popup.wav"
[HKEY_CURRENT_USER\AppEvents\Schemes\Apps\.Default\MenuPopup\
Robotz0]
@="C:\\WINNT\\media\\Robotz Menu Popup.wav"
[HKEY_CURRENT_USER\AppEvents\Schemes\Apps\.Default\MenuPopup\
Utopia0]
@="C:\\WINNT\\media\\Utopia Menu Popup.wav"
[HKEY_CURRENT_USER\AppEvents\Schemes\Apps\.Default\Minimize]
[HKEY_CURRENT_USER\AppEvents\Schemes\Apps\.Default\Minimize\
.Current]
@=""
[HKEY_CURRENT_USER\AppEvents\Schemes\Apps\.Default\Minimize\
.Default]
@=""
[HKEY_CURRENT_USER\AppEvents\Schemes\Apps\.Default\Minimize\
Jungle0]
@="C:\\WINNT\\media\\Jungle Minimize.wav"

[HKEY_CURRENT_USER\AppEvents\Schemes\Apps\.Default\Minimize\Musica0]
@="C:\\WINNT\\media\\Musica Minimize.wav"
[HKEY_CURRENT_USER\AppEvents\Schemes\Apps\.Default\Minimize\Robotz0]
@="C:\\WINNT\\media\\Robotz Minimize.wav"
[HKEY_CURRENT_USER\AppEvents\Schemes\Apps\.Default\Minimize\
Utopia0]
@="C:\\WINNT\\media\\Utopia Minimize.wav"
[HKEY_CURRENT_USER\AppEvents\Schemes\Apps\.Default\Open]
[HKEY_CURRENT_USER\AppEvents\Schemes\Apps\.Default\Open\.Current]
@=""
[HKEY_CURRENT_USER\AppEvents\Schemes\Apps\.Default\Open\.Default]
@=""
[HKEY_CURRENT_USER\AppEvents\Schemes\Apps\.Default\Open\Jungle0]
@=""
[HKEY_CURRENT_USER\AppEvents\Schemes\Apps\.Default\Open\Musica0]
@=""
[HKEY_CURRENT_USER\AppEvents\Schemes\Apps\.Default\Open\Robotz0]
@=""
[HKEY_CURRENT_USER\AppEvents\Schemes\Apps\.Default\Open\Utopia0]
@=""
[HKEY_CURRENT_USER\AppEvents\Schemes\Apps\.Default\RestoreDown]
[HKEY_CURRENT_USER\AppEvents\Schemes\Apps\.Default\RestoreDown\
.Current]
@=""
[HKEY_CURRENT_USER\AppEvents\Schemes\Apps\.Default\RestoreDown\
.Default]
@=""
[HKEY_CURRENT_USER\AppEvents\Schemes\Apps\.Default\RestoreDown\
Jungle0]
@="C:\\WINNT\\media\\Jungle Restore Down.wav"
[HKEY_CURRENT_USER\AppEvents\Schemes\Apps\.Default\RestoreDown\
Musica0]
@="C:\\WINNT\\media\\Musica Restore Down.wav"
[HKEY_CURRENT_USER\AppEvents\Schemes\Apps\.Default\RestoreDown\
Robotz0]
@="C:\\WINNT\\media\\Robotz Restore Down.wav"
[HKEY_CURRENT_USER\AppEvents\Schemes\Apps\.Default\RestoreDown\
Utopia0]
@="C:\\WINNT\\media\\Utopia Restore Down.wav"
[HKEY_CURRENT_USER\AppEvents\Schemes\Apps\.Default\RestoreUp]
[HKEY_CURRENT_USER\AppEvents\Schemes\Apps\.Default\RestoreUp\
.Current]
@=""

[HKEY_CURRENT_USER\AppEvents\Schemes\Apps\.Default\RestoreUp\
.Default]
@=""
[HKEY_CURRENT_USER\AppEvents\Schemes\Apps\.Default\RestoreUp\
Jungle0]
@="C:\\WINNT\\media\\Jungle Restore Up.wav"
[HKEY_CURRENT_USER\AppEvents\Schemes\Apps\.Default\RestoreUp\
Musica0]
@="C:\\WINNT\\media\\Musica Restore Up.wav"
[HKEY_CURRENT_USER\AppEvents\Schemes\Apps\.Default\RestoreUp\
Robotz0]
@="C:\\WINNT\\media\\Robotz Restore Up.wav"
[HKEY_CURRENT_USER\AppEvents\Schemes\Apps\.Default\RestoreUp\
Utopia0]
@="C:\\WINNT\\media\\Utopia Restore Up.wav"
[HKEY_CURRENT_USER\AppEvents\Schemes\Apps\.Default\RingIn]
[HKEY_CURRENT_USER\AppEvents\Schemes\Apps\.Default\RingIn\.Current]
@=""
[HKEY_CURRENT_USER\AppEvents\Schemes\Apps\.Default\RingOut]
[HKEY_CURRENT_USER\AppEvents\Schemes\Apps\.Default\RingOut\.Current]
@=""
[HKEY_CURRENT_USER\AppEvents\Schemes\Apps\.Default\SystemAsterisk]
[HKEY_CURRENT_USER\AppEvents\Schemes\Apps\.Default\SystemAsterisk\
.Current]
@="chord.wav"
[HKEY_CURRENT_USER\AppEvents\Schemes\Apps\.Default\SystemAsterisk\
.Default]
@="C:\\WINNT\\media\\chord.wav"
[HKEY_CURRENT_USER\AppEvents\Schemes\Apps\.Default\SystemAsterisk\
Jungle0]
@="C:\\WINNT\\media\\Jungle Asterisk.wav"
[HKEY_CURRENT_USER\AppEvents\Schemes\Apps\.Default\SystemAsterisk\
Musica0]
@="C:\\WINNT\\media\\Musica Asterisk.wav"
[HKEY_CURRENT_USER\AppEvents\Schemes\Apps\.Default\SystemAsterisk\
Robotz0]
@="C:\\WINNT\\media\\Robotz Asterisk.wav"
[HKEY_CURRENT_USER\AppEvents\Schemes\Apps\.Default\SystemAsterisk\
Utopia0]
@="C:\\WINNT\\media\\Utopia Asterisk.wav"
[HKEY_CURRENT_USER\AppEvents\Schemes\Apps\.Default\
SystemExclamation]
[HKEY_CURRENT_USER\AppEvents\Schemes\Apps\.Default\

SystemExclamation\.Current]
@="chord.wav"
[HKEY_CURRENT_USER\AppEvents\Schemes\Apps\.Default\
SystemExclamation\.Default]
@="C:\\WINNT\\media\\chord.wav"
[HKEY_CURRENT_USER\AppEvents\Schemes\Apps\.Default\
SystemExclamation\Jungle0]
@="C:\\WINNT\\media\\Jungle Exclamation.wav"
[HKEY_CURRENT_USER\AppEvents\Schemes\Apps\.Default\
SystemExclamation\Musica0]
@="C:\\WINNT\\media\\Musica Exclamation.wav"
[HKEY_CURRENT_USER\AppEvents\Schemes\Apps\.Default\
SystemExclamation\Robotz0]
@="C:\\WINNT\\media\\Robotz Exclamation.wav"
[HKEY_CURRENT_USER\AppEvents\Schemes\Apps\.Default\
SystemExclamation\Utopia0]
@="C:\\WINNT\\media\\Utopia Exclamation.wav"
[HKEY_CURRENT_USER\AppEvents\Schemes\Apps\.Default\SystemExit]
[HKEY_CURRENT_USER\AppEvents\Schemes\Apps\.Default\SystemExit\
.Current]
@="Windows NT Logoff Sound.wav"
[HKEY_CURRENT_USER\AppEvents\Schemes\Apps\.Default\SystemExit\
.Default]
@="C:\\WINNT\\media\\tada.wav"
[HKEY_CURRENT_USER\AppEvents\Schemes\Apps\.Default\SystemExit\
Jungle0]
@="C:\\WINNT\\media\\Jungle Windows Exit.wav"
[HKEY_CURRENT_USER\AppEvents\Schemes\Apps\.Default\SystemExit\
Musica0]
@="C:\\WINNT\\media\\Musica Windows Exit.wav"
[HKEY_CURRENT_USER\AppEvents\Schemes\Apps\.Default\SystemExit\
Robotz0]
@="C:\\WINNT\\media\\Robotz Windows Exit.wav"
[HKEY_CURRENT_USER\AppEvents\Schemes\Apps\.Default\SystemExit\
Utopia0]
@="C:\\WINNT\\media\\Utopia Windows Exit.wav"
[HKEY_CURRENT_USER\AppEvents\Schemes\Apps\.Default\SystemHand]
[HKEY_CURRENT_USER\AppEvents\Schemes\Apps\.Default\SystemHand\
.Current]
@="chord.wav"
[HKEY_CURRENT_USER\AppEvents\Schemes\Apps\.Default\SystemHand\
.Default]
@="C:\\WINNT\\media\\chord.wav"

[HKEY_CURRENT_USER\AppEvents\Schemes\Apps\.Default\SystemHand\
Jungle0]
@="C:\\WINNT\\media\\Jungle Critical Stop.wav"
[HKEY_CURRENT_USER\AppEvents\Schemes\Apps\.Default\SystemHand\
Musica0]
@="C:\\WINNT\\media\\Musica Critical Stop.wav"
[HKEY_CURRENT_USER\AppEvents\Schemes\Apps\.Default\SystemHand\
Robotz0]
@="C:\\WINNT\\media\\Robotz Critical Stop.wav"
[HKEY_CURRENT_USER\AppEvents\Schemes\Apps\.Default\SystemHand\
Utopia0]
@="C:\\WINNT\\media\\Utopia Critical Stop.wav"
[HKEY_CURRENT_USER\AppEvents\Schemes\Apps\.Default\SystemQuestion]
[HKEY_CURRENT_USER\AppEvents\Schemes\Apps\.Default\SystemQuestion\
.Current]
@="chord.wav"
[HKEY_CURRENT_USER\AppEvents\Schemes\Apps\.Default\SystemQuestion\
.Default]
@="C:\\WINNT\\media\\chord.wav"
[HKEY_CURRENT_USER\AppEvents\Schemes\Apps\.Default\SystemQuestion\
Jungle0]
@="C:\\WINNT\\media\\Jungle Question.wav"
[HKEY_CURRENT_USER\AppEvents\Schemes\Apps\.Default\SystemQuestion\
Musica0]
@="C:\\WINNT\\media\\Musica Question.wav"
[HKEY_CURRENT_USER\AppEvents\Schemes\Apps\.Default\SystemQuestion\
Robotz0]
@="C:\\WINNT\\media\\Robotz Question.wav"
[HKEY_CURRENT_USER\AppEvents\Schemes\Apps\.Default\SystemQuestion\
Utopia0]
@="C:\\WINNT\\media\\Utopia Question.wav"
[HKEY_CURRENT_USER\AppEvents\Schemes\Apps\.Default\SystemStart]
[HKEY_CURRENT_USER\AppEvents\Schemes\Apps\.Default\SystemStart\
.Current]
@="Windows NT Logon Sound.wav"
[HKEY_CURRENT_USER\AppEvents\Schemes\Apps\.Default\SystemStart\
.Default]
@="Windows NT Logon Sound.wav"
[HKEY_CURRENT_USER\AppEvents\Schemes\Apps\.Default\SystemStart\
Jungle0]
@="C:\\WINNT\\media\\Jungle Windows Start.wav"
[HKEY_CURRENT_USER\AppEvents\Schemes\Apps\.Default\SystemStart\
Musica0]

@="C:\\WINNT\\media\\Musica Windows Start.wav"
[HKEY_CURRENT_USER\AppEvents\Schemes\Apps\.Default\SystemStart\
Robotz0]
@="C:\\WINNT\\media\\Robotz Windows Start.wav"
[HKEY_CURRENT_USER\AppEvents\Schemes\Apps\.Default\SystemStart\
Utopia0]
@="C:\\WINNT\\media\\Utopia Windows Start.wav"
[HKEY_CURRENT_USER\AppEvents\Schemes\Apps\Explorer]
@="Windows Explorer"
HKEY_CURRENT_USER\AppEvents\Schemes\Apps\Explorer\
EmptyRecycleBin]
[HKEY_CURRENT_USER\AppEvents\Schemes\Apps\Explorer\
EmptyRecycleBin\.Current]
@="ding.wav"
[HKEY_CURRENT_USER\AppEvents\Schemes\Apps\Explorer\
EmptyRecycleBin\.Default]
@="C:\\WINNT\\media\\ding.wav"
[HKEY_CURRENT_USER\AppEvents\Schemes\Apps\Explorer\
EmptyRecycleBin\Jungle0]
@="C:\\WINNT\\media\\Jungle Recycle.wav"
[HKEY_CURRENT_USER\AppEvents\Schemes\Apps\Explorer\
EmptyRecycleBin\Musica0]
@="C:\\WINNT\\media\\Musica Recycle.wav"
[HKEY_CURRENT_USER\AppEvents\Schemes\Apps\Explorer\
EmptyRecycleBin\Robotz0]
@="C:\\WINNT\\media\\Robotz Recycle.wav"
[HKEY_CURRENT_USER\AppEvents\Schemes\Apps\Explorer\
EmptyRecycleBin\Utopia0]
@="C:\\WINNT\\media\\Utopia Recycle.wav"
[HKEY_CURRENT_USER\AppEvents\Schemes\Apps\MPlay32]
@="Media Player"
[HKEY_CURRENT_USER\AppEvents\Schemes\Apps\MPlay32\Close]
[HKEY_CURRENT_USER\AppEvents\Schemes\Apps\MPlay32\Close\.Current]
@=""
[HKEY_CURRENT_USER\AppEvents\Schemes\Apps\MPlay32\Close\.Default]
@=""
[HKEY_CURRENT_USER\AppEvents\Schemes\Apps\MPlay32\Open]
[HKEY_CURRENT_USER\AppEvents\Schemes\Apps\MPlay32\Open\.Current]
@=""
[HKEY_CURRENT_USER\AppEvents\Schemes\Apps\MPlay32\Open\.Default]
@=""
[HKEY_CURRENT_USER\AppEvents\Schemes\Apps\SndRec32]
@="Sound Recorder"

[HKEY_CURRENT_USER\AppEvents\Schemes\Apps\SndRec32\Close]
[HKEY_CURRENT_USER\AppEvents\Schemes\Apps\SndRec32\Close\.Current]
@=""
[HKEY_CURRENT_USER\AppEvents\Schemes\Apps\SndRec32\Open]
[HKEY_CURRENT_USER\AppEvents\Schemes\Apps\SndRec32\Open\.Current]
@=""
[HKEY_CURRENT_USER\AppEvents\Schemes\Names]
[HKEY_CURRENT_USER\AppEvents\Schemes\Names\.Default]
@="Windows NT Default"
[HKEY_CURRENT_USER\AppEvents\Schemes\Names\.None]
@="No Sounds"
[HKEY_CURRENT_USER\AppEvents\Schemes\Names\Jungle0]
@="Jungle Sound Scheme"
[HKEY_CURRENT_USER\AppEvents\Schemes\Names\Musica0]
@="Musica Sound Scheme"
[HKEY_CURRENT_USER\AppEvents\Schemes\Names\Robotz0]
@="Robotz Sound Scheme"
[HKEY_CURRENT_USER\AppEvents\Schemes\Names\Utopia0]
@="Utopia Sound Scheme"
[HKEY_CURRENT_USER\AppEvents\Schemes\NewSchemes]
[HKEY_CURRENT_USER\AppEvents\Schemes\NewSchemes\Jungle]
@=""
[HKEY_CURRENT_USER\AppEvents\Schemes\NewSchemes\Musica]
@=""
[HKEY_CURRENT_USER\AppEvents\Schemes\NewSchemes\Robotz]
@=""
[HKEY_CURRENT_USER\AppEvents\Schemes\NewSchemes\Utopia]
@=""
[HKEY_CURRENT_USER\Console]
"InsertMode"=dword:00000000
"QuickEdit"=dword:00000000
"FullScreen"=dword:00000000
"FaceName"=""
"FontFamily"=dword:00000000
"FontSize"=dword:00000000
"FontWeight"=dword:00000000
"CursorSize"=dword:00000019
"PopupColors"=dword:000000f5
"NumberOfHistoryBuffers"=dword:00000004
"ScreenColors"=dword:00000007
"HistoryBufferSize"=dword:00000032
"ScreenBufferSize"=dword:00190050
"WindowSize"=dword:00190050

```
"ColorTable00"=dword:00000000
"ColorTable01"=dword:00800000
"ColorTable02"=dword:00008000
"ColorTable03"=dword:00808000
"ColorTable04"=dword:00000080
"ColorTable05"=dword:00800080
"ColorTable06"=dword:00008080
"ColorTable07"=dword:00c0c0c0
"ColorTable08"=dword:00808080
"ColorTable09"=dword:00ff0000
"ColorTable10"=dword:0000ff00
"ColorTable11"=dword:00ffff00
"ColorTable12"=dword:000000ff
"ColorTable13"=dword:00ff00ff
"ColorTable14"=dword:0000ffff
"ColorTable15"=dword:00ffffff
[HKEY_CURRENT_USER\Control Panel]
[HKEY_CURRENT_USER\Control Panel\Accessibility]
[HKEY_CURRENT_USER\Control Panel\Accessibility\Keyboard Response]
"AutoRepeatDelay"="1000"
"AutoRepeatRate"="500"
"BounceTime"="0"
"DelayBeforeAcceptance"="1000"
"Flags"="82"
[HKEY_CURRENT_USER\Control Panel\Accessibility\MouseKeys]
"Flags"="18"
"MaximumSpeed"="80"
"TimeToMaximumSpeed"="3000"
[HKEY_CURRENT_USER\Control Panel\Accessibility\ShowSounds]
"On"="0"
[HKEY_CURRENT_USER\Control Panel\Accessibility\SoundSentry]
"Flags"="2"
"FSTextEffect"="0"
"WindowsEffect"="0"
[HKEY_CURRENT_USER\Control Panel\Accessibility\StickyKeys]
"Flags"="466"
[HKEY_CURRENT_USER\Control Panel\Accessibility\TimeOut]
"Flags"="2"
"TimeToWait"="300000"
[HKEY_CURRENT_USER\Control Panel\Accessibility\ToggleKeys]
"Flags"="18"
[HKEY_CURRENT_USER\Control Panel\Appearance]
"Brick"=hex:
```

"Maple"=hex:
"Spruce"=hex:
"Teal (VGA)"=hex:
"Red, White, and Blue (VGA)"=hex:
"Pumpkin (large)"=hex:
"Eggplant"=hex:
"Rainy Day"=hex:
"Desert"=hex:
"Marine (high color)"=hex:
"Windows Standard (extra large)"=hex:
"Storm (VGA)"=hex:
"Windows Standard"=hex:
"Windows Standard (large)"=hex:
"Rose"=hex:
"High Contrast Black (large)"=hex:
"High Contrast Black (extra large)"=hex:
"High Contrast White (large)"=hex:
"High Contrast White (extra large)"=hex:
"Rose (large)"=hex:
"Lilac"=hex:
"Lilac (large)"=hex:
"Slate"=hex:
"High Contrast Black"=hex:
"High Contrast White"=hex:
[HKEY_CURRENT_USER\Control Panel\Cache]
[HKEY_CURRENT_USER\Control Panel\Colors]
"Background"="0 128 128"
"AppWorkSpace"="128 128 128"
"Window"="255 255 255"
"WindowText"="0   0   0"
"Menu"="192 192 192"
"MenuText"="0   0   0"
"ActiveTitle"="0   0 128"
"InactiveTitle"="128 128 128"
"TitleText"="255 255 255"
"ActiveBorder"="192 192 192"
"InactiveBorder"="192 192 192"
"WindowFrame"="0   0   0"

Author Note

The values under this key contain long listings of hexadecimal numbers. These numbers are not reproduced here but may be seen by viewing the value setting with a registry editor.

"Scrollbar"="192 192 192"
"ButtonFace"="192 192 192"
"ButtonShadow"="128 128 128"
"ButtonText"="0   0   0"
"GrayText"="128 128 128"
"Hilight"="0   0 128"
"HilightText"="255 255 255"
"InactiveTitleText"="192 192 192"
"ButtonHilight"="255 255 255"
"InfoText"="0   0   0"
"InfoWindow"="255 255 225"
"ButtonLight"="192 192 192"
"ButtonDkShadow"="0   0   0"
[HKEY_CURRENT_USER\Control Panel\Current]
"Color Schemes"="Windows Default"
[HKEY_CURRENT_USER\Control Panel\Cursors]
[HKEY_CURRENT_USER\Control Panel\Cursors\Schemes]
"Windows Default"=",,,,,,,,,,,,,"

"Windows Animated"="C:\\WINNT\\Cursors\\rainbow.ani,,C:\\WINNT\\Cursors\\
appstart.ani,C:\\WINNT\\Cursors\\hourglas.ani,C:\\WINNT\\Cursors\\cross
.cur,,,,C:\\WINNT\\Cursors\\sizens.ani,C:\\WINNT\\Cursors\\sizewe.ani,C:\\
WINNT\\Cursors\\sizenwse.ani,C:\\WINNT\\Cursors\\sizenesw.ani,,"

"3D-White"="C:\\WINNT\\Cursors\\3dwarro.cur,,C:\\WINNT\\Cursors\\
appstar3.ani,C:\\WINNT\\Cursors\\hourgla3.ani,C:\\WINNT\\Cursors\\cross.
cur,,,C:\\WINNT\\Cursors\\3dwno.cur,C:\\WINNT\\Cursors\\3dwns.cur,C:\\
WINNT\\Cursors\\3dwwe.cur,C:\\WINNT\\Cursors\\3dwnwse.cur,C:\\
WINNT\\Cursors\\3dwnesw.cur,C:\\WINNT\\Cursors\\3dwmove.cur,"

"Hands 1"="C:\\WINNT\\Cursors\\harrow.cur,,C:\\WINNT\\Cursors\\
handapst.ani,C:\\WINNT\\Cursors\\hand.ani,C:\\WINNT\\Cursors\\hcross.
cur,C:\\WINNT\\Cursors\\hibeam.cur,,C:\\WINNT\\Cursors\\hnodrop.cur,C:\\
WINNT\\Cursors\\hns.cur,C:\\WINNT\\Cursors\\hwe.cur,C:\\WINNT\\
Cursors\\hnwse.cur,C:\\WINNT\\Cursors\\hnesw.cur,C:\\WINNT\\Cursors\\
hmove.cur,"

"Hands 2"="C:\\WINNT\\Cursors\\harrow.cur,,C:\\WINNT\\Cursors\\
handapst.ani,C:\\WINNT\\Cursors\\handwait.ani,C:\\WINNT\\Cursors\\hcross
.cur,C:\\WINNT\\Cursors\\hibeam.cur,,C:\\WINNT\\Cursors\\handno.ani,C:\\
WINNT\\Cursors\\handns.ani,C:\\WINNT\\Cursors\\handwe.ani,C:\\WINNT\\
Cursors\\handnwse.ani,C:\\WINNT\\Cursors\\handnesw.ani,C:\\WINNT\\
Cursors\\hmove.cur,"

"Dinosaur"="C:\\WINNT\\Cursors\\3dgarro.cur,,C:\\WINNT\\Cursors\\
dinosaur.ani,C:\\WINNT\\Cursors\\dinosau2.ani,C:\\WINNT\\Cursors\\cross
.cur,,,C:\\WINNT\\Cursors\\banana.ani,C:\\WINNT\\Cursors\\3dsns.cur,C:\\
WINNT\\Cursors\\3dgwe.cur,C:\\WINNT\\Cursors\\3dsnwse.cur,C:\\WINNT\\
Cursors\\3dgnesw.cur,C:\\WINNT\\Cursors\\3dsmove.cur,"

"Old Fashioned"="C:\\WINNT\\Cursors\\harrow.cur,,C:\\WINNT\\Cursors\\
horse.ani,C:\\WINNT\\Cursors\\barber.ani,C:\\WINNT\\Cursors\\hcross.cur,C:\\
WINNT\\Cursors\\hibeam.cur,,C:\\WINNT\\Cursors\\coin.ani,C:\\WINNT\\
Cursors\\3dgns.cur,C:\\WINNT\\Cursors\\3dgwe.cur,C:\\WINNT\\Cursors\\
3dgnwse.cur,C:\\WINNT\\Cursors\\3dgnesw.cur,C:\\WINNT\\Cursors\\
3dgmove.cur,"

"Conductor"="C:\\WINNT\\Cursors\\harrow.cur,,C:\\WINNT\\Cursors\\
drum.ani,C:\\WINNT\\Cursors\\metronom.ani,C:\\WINNT\\Cursors\\hcross
.cur,C:\\WINNT\\Cursors\\hibeam.cur,,C:\\WINNT\\Cursors\\piano.ani,C:\\
WINNT\\Cursors\\hns.cur,C:\\WINNT\\Cursors\\hwe.cur,C:\\WINNT\\
Cursors\\hnwse.cur,C:\\WINNT\\Cursors\\hnesw.cur,C:\\WINNT\\Cursors\\
hmove.cur,"

"Magnified"="C:\\WINNT\\Cursors\\larrow.cur,,C:\\WINNT\\Cursors\\
lappstrt.cur,C:\\WINNT\\Cursors\\lwait.cur,C:\\WINNT\\Cursors\\lcross.cur,C:\\
WINNT\\Cursors\\libeam.cur,,C:\\WINNT\\Cursors\\lnodrop.cur,C:\\WINNT\\
Cursors\\lns.cur,C:\\WINNT\\Cursors\\lwe.cur,C:\\WINNT\\Cursors\\lnwse
.cur,C:\\WINNT\\Cursors\\lnesw.cur,C:\\WINNT\\Cursors\\lmove.cur,"

"Variations"="C:\\WINNT\\Cursors\\fillitup.ani,,C:\\WINNT\\Cursors\\
raindrop.ani,C:\\WINNT\\Cursors\\counter.ani,C:\\WINNT\\Cursors\\cross
.cur,,,C:\\WINNT\\Cursors\\wagtail.ani,C:\\WINNT\\Cursors\\sizens.ani,C:\\
WINNT\\Cursors\\sizewe.ani,C:\\WINNT\\Cursors\\sizenwse.ani,C:\\WINNT\\
Cursors\\sizenesw.ani,"

"3D-Bronze"="C:\\WINNT\\Cursors\\3dgarro.cur,,C:\\WINNT\\Cursors\\
appstar2.ani,C:\\WINNT\\Cursors\\hourgla2.ani,C:\\WINNT\\Cursors\\cross
.cur,,,C:\\WINNT\\Cursors\\3dgno.cur,C:\\WINNT\\Cursors\\3dgns.cur,C:\\
WINNT\\Cursors\\3dgwe.cur,C:\\WINNT\\Cursors\\3dgnwse.cur,C:\\WINNT\\
Cursors\\3dgnesw.cur,C:\\WINNT\\Cursors\\3dgmove.cur,"

[HKEY_CURRENT_USER\Control Panel\Custom Colors]
"ColorA"="FFFFFF"
"ColorB"="FFFFFF"
"ColorC"="FFFFFF"

"ColorD"="FFFFFF"
"ColorE"="FFFFFF"
"ColorF"="FFFFFF"
"ColorG"="FFFFFF"
"ColorH"="FFFFFF"
"ColorI"="FFFFFF"
"ColorJ"="FFFFFF"
"ColorK"="FFFFFF"
"ColorL"="FFFFFF"
"ColorM"="FFFFFF"
"ColorN"="FFFFFF"
"ColorO"="FFFFFF"
"ColorP"="FFFFFF"
[HKEY_CURRENT_USER\Control Panel\Desktop]
"CoolSwitch"="1"
"CoolSwitchRows"="3"
"CoolSwitchColumns"="7"
"CursorBlinkRate"="530"
"ScreenSaveTimeOut"="900"
"ScreenSaveActive"="0"
"SCRNSAVE.EXE"="(NONE)"
"ScreenSaverIsSecure"="0"
"Pattern"="(None)"
"Wallpaper"="(None)"
"TileWallpaper"="0"
"GridGranularity"="0"
"IconSpacing"="75"
"IconTitleWrap"="1"
"IconTitleFaceName"="MS Sans Serif"
"IconTitleSize"="9"
"IconTitleStyle"="0"
"DragFullWindows"="1"
"HungAppTimeout"="5000"
"WaitToKillAppTimeout"="20000"
"AutoEndTasks"="0"
"FontSmoothing"="0"
"MenuShowDelay"="400"
"DragHeight"="2"
"DragWidth"="2"
"WheelScrollLines"="3"
[HKEY_CURRENT_USER\Control Panel\Desktop\WindowMetrics]
"BorderWidth"="1"
[HKEY_CURRENT_USER\Control Panel\International]

"Locale"="00000409"
"sLanguage"="ENU"
"sCountry"="United States"
"iCountry"="1"
"sList"=","
"iMeasure"="1"
"sDecimal"="."
"sThousand"=","
"iDigits"="2"
"iLZero"="1"
"sCurrency"="$"
"iCurrDigits"="2"
"iCurrency"="0"
"iNegCurr"="0"
"sDate"="/"
"sTime"=":"
"sShortDate"="M/d/yy"
"sLongDate"="dddd, MMMM dd, yyyy"
"iDate"="0"
"iTime"="0"
"iTLZero"="0"
"s1159"="AM"
"s2359"="PM"
[HKEY_CURRENT_USER\Control Panel\International\Sorting Order]
[HKEY_CURRENT_USER\Control Panel\IOProcs]
"MVB"="mvfs32.dll"
[HKEY_CURRENT_USER\Control Panel\Keyboard]
"KeyboardSpeed"="31"
"KeyboardDelay"="1"
"InitialKeyboardIndicators"="0x80000000"
[HKEY_CURRENT_USER\Control Panel\MMCPL]
[HKEY_CURRENT_USER\Control Panel\Mouse]
"SwapMouseButtons"="0"
"DoubleClickSpeed"="500"
"DoubleClickHeight"="4"
"DoubleClickWidth"="4"
"MouseThreshold1"="6"
"MouseThreshold2"="10"
"MouseSpeed"="1"
"SnapToDefaultButton"="0"
"ActiveWindowTracking"=dword:00000000
[HKEY_CURRENT_USER\Control Panel\Patterns]
"(None)"="(None)"

"Boxes"="127 65 65 65 65 65 127 0"
"Paisley"="2 7 7 2 32 80 80 32"
"Weave"="136 84 34 69 136 21 34 81"
"Waffle"="0 0 0 0 128 128 128 240"
"Tulip"="0 0 84 124 124 56 146 124"
"Spinner"="20 12 200 121 158 19 48 40"
"Scottie"="64 192 200 120 120 72 0 0"
"Critters"="0 80 114 32 0 5 39 2"
"50% Gray"="170 85 170 85 170 85 170 85"
"Quilt"="130 68 40 17 40 68 130 1"
"Diamonds"="32 80 136 80 32 0 0 0"
"Thatches"="248 116 34 71 143 23 34 113"
"Pattern"="224 128 142 136 234 10 14 0"
[HKEY_CURRENT_USER\Control Panel\Screen Saver.3DFlyingObj]
[HKEY_CURRENT_USER\Control Panel\Screen Saver.3DPipes]
[HKEY_CURRENT_USER\Control Panel\Screen Saver.Bezier]
[HKEY_CURRENT_USER\Control Panel\Screen Saver.Marquee]
"Font"="Times New Roman"
"Size"="24"
"Text"="Your text goes here."
"TextColor"="255 0 255"
"BackgroundColor"="0 0 128"
"Mode"="1"
"Speed"="14"
"CharSet"="0"
[HKEY_CURRENT_USER\Control Panel\Screen Saver.Mystify]
"Clear Screen"="1"
"Active1"="1"
"WalkRandom1"="1"
"Lines1"="7"
"StartColor1"="0 0 0"
"EndColor1"="255 255 255"
"Active2"="1"
"WalkRandom2"="1"
"Lines2"="12"
"StartColor2"="0 0 0"
"EndColor2"="255 255 255"
[HKEY_CURRENT_USER\Control Panel\Screen Saver.Stars]
"Density"="50"
"WarpSpeed"="10"
[HKEY_CURRENT_USER\Control Panel\Sound]
"Beep"="yes"
"ExtendedSounds"="yes"

[HKEY_CURRENT_USER\Control Panel\Sounds]
"SystemDefault"=","
[HKEY_CURRENT_USER\Environment]
"TEMP"=hex(2):25,53,79,73,74,65,6d,44,72,69,76,65,25,5c,54,45,4d,50,00
"TMP"=hex(2):25,53,79,73,74,65,6d,44,72,69,76,65,25,5c,54,45,4d,50,00
[HKEY_CURRENT_USER\Keyboard Layout]
[HKEY_CURRENT_USER\Keyboard Layout\Preload]
"1"="00000409"
[HKEY_CURRENT_USER\Keyboard Layout\Substitutes]
[HKEY_CURRENT_USER\Software]
[HKEY_CURRENT_USER\Software\Microsoft]
[HKEY_CURRENT_USER\Software\Microsoft\Clock]
"iFormat"="1"
[HKEY_CURRENT_USER\Software\Microsoft\Command Processor]
"EnableExtensions"=dword:00000001
"DefaultColor"=dword:00000000
"CompletionChar"=dword:00000000
[HKEY_CURRENT_USER\Software\Microsoft\File Manager]
[HKEY_CURRENT_USER\Software\Microsoft\File Manager\Settings]
[HKEY_CURRENT_USER\Software\Microsoft\Internet Explorer]
[HKEY_CURRENT_USER\Software\Microsoft\Internet Explorer\
Document Windows]
"width"=hex:00,00,00,80
"height"=hex:00,00,00,00
"x"=hex:00,00,00,80
"y"=hex:00,00,00,00
"Maximized"="no"
[HKEY_CURRENT_USER\Software\Microsoft\Internet Explorer\Main]
"Check_Associations"="yes"
"Show_ToolBar"="yes"
"Show_URLToolBar"="yes"
"Show_StatusBar"="yes"
"Show_URLinStatusBar"="yes"
"Show_FullURL"="no"
"Use_DlgBox_Colors"="yes"
"Display Inline Images"="yes"
"Anchor Underline"="yes"
"Save_Session_History_On_Exit"="no"
"Start Page"="file:C:\\Program Files\\Plus!\\Microsoft Internet\\docs\\home.htm"
"Search Page"="http://www.msn.com/access/allinone.htm"
"Cache_Update_Frequency"="Once_Per_Session"
[HKEY_CURRENT_USER\Software\Microsoft\Internet Explorer\Security]
"Sending_Security"="Medium"

"Viewing_Security"="Low"
[HKEY_CURRENT_USER\Software\Microsoft\Internet Explorer\Services]
@=""
[HKEY_CURRENT_USER\Software\Microsoft\Internet Explorer\Settings]
"Anchor Color"="0,0,255"
"Anchor Color Visited"="128,0,128"
"Background Color"="192,192,192"
"Text Color"="0,0,0"
[HKEY_CURRENT_USER\Software\Microsoft\Internet Explorer\Styles]
"Default_Style_Sheet"="SerifMedium"
[HKEY_CURRENT_USER\Software\Microsoft\Internet Explorer\TypedURLs]
"url1"="file:C:\\WINNT/itgfile.htm"
[HKEY_CURRENT_USER\Software\Microsoft\NetDDE]
[HKEY_CURRENT_USER\Software\Microsoft\NetDDE\DDE Trusted Shares]
[HKEY_CURRENT_USER\Software\Microsoft\NetDDE\
DDE Trusted Shares\DDEDBi3B690712]
[HKEY_CURRENT_USER\Software\Microsoft\NetDDE\
DDE Trusted Shares\DDEDBi3B690712\Chat$]
"SerialNumber"=hex:05,00,00,09,00,00,00,01
"StartApp"=dword:00000001
"InitAllowed"=dword:00000001
[HKEY_CURRENT_USER\Software\Microsoft\NetDDE\
DDE Trusted Shares\DDEDBi3B690712\CLPBK$]
"SerialNumber"=hex:05,00,00,09,00,00,00,01
"StartApp"=dword:00000001
"InitAllowed"=dword:00000001
[HKEY_CURRENT_USER\Software\Microsoft\NetDDE\
DDE Trusted Shares\DDEDBi3B690712\Hearts$]
"SerialNumber"=hex:05,00,00,09,00,00,00,01
"StartApp"=dword:00000001
"InitAllowed"=dword:00000001
[HKEY_CURRENT_USER\Software\Microsoft\Ntbackup]
[HKEY_CURRENT_USER\Software\Microsoft\RegEdt32]
[HKEY_CURRENT_USER\Software\Microsoft\RegEdt32\Settings]
"AutoRefresh"="1"
"ReadOnly"="0"
"RemoteAccess"="0"
"ConfirmOnDelete"="1"
"SaveSettings"="1"
[HKEY_CURRENT_USER\Software\Microsoft\Schedule+]
[HKEY_CURRENT_USER\Software\Microsoft\Schedule+\Microsoft Schedule+]
"MigrateIni"="1"
"MigrateIniPrint"="1"

[HKEY_CURRENT_USER\Software\Microsoft\Windows]
[HKEY_CURRENT_USER\Software\Microsoft\Windows\CurrentVersion]
[HKEY_CURRENT_USER\Software\Microsoft\Windows\CurrentVersion\Applets]
[HKEY_CURRENT_USER\Software\Microsoft\Windows\CurrentVersion\
Applets\SysTray]
[HKEY_CURRENT_USER\Software\Microsoft\Windows\CurrentVersion\Explorer]
[HKEY_CURRENT_USER\Software\Microsoft\Windows\CurrentVersion\
Explorer\CabinetState]
"Settings"=hex:0c,00,01,00,2a,01,00,00,60,00,00,00
[HKEY_CURRENT_USER\Software\Microsoft\Windows\CurrentVersion\
Explorer\DesktopStreamMRU]
[HKEY_CURRENT_USER\Software\Microsoft\Windows\CurrentVersion\
Explorer\NewShortcutHandlers]
"{FBF23B40-E3F0-101B-8488-00AA003E56F8}"=""
[HKEY_CURRENT_USER\Software\Microsoft\Windows\CurrentVersion\
Explorer\RecentDocs]
"a"=hex:48,00,4b,00,45,00,59,00,5f,00,43,00,4c,00,41,00,53,00,53,00,45,00,53,00,5f,
00,52,00,4f,00,4f,00,54,00,2e,00,72,00,65,00,67,00,00,00,25,00,30,00,00,00,00,00,
00,00,00,00,00,48,4b,45,59,5f,43,4c,41,53,53,45,53,5f,52,4f,4f,54,2e,6c,6e,6b,00,00,
00,00
"MRUList"="a"
[HKEY_CURRENT_USER\Software\Microsoft\Windows\CurrentVersion\
Explorer\RunMRU]
"a"="regedit\\1"
"MRUList"="a"
[HKEY_CURRENT_USER\Software\Microsoft\Windows\CurrentVersion\
Explorer\Shell Folders]
"SendTo"="C:\\WINNT\\Profiles\\Administrator\\SendTo"
"Recent"="C:\\WINNT\\Profiles\\Administrator\\Recent"
"Desktop"="C:\\WINNT\\Profiles\\Administrator\\Desktop"
"Programs"="C:\\WINNT\\Profiles\\Administrator\\Start Menu\\Programs"
"Start Menu"="C:\\WINNT\\Profiles\\Administrator\\Start Menu"
"Startup"="C:\\WINNT\\Profiles\\Administrator\\Start
Menu\\Programs\\Startup"
[HKEY_CURRENT_USER\Software\Microsoft\Windows\CurrentVersion\
Explorer\Tips]
"DisplayInitialTipWindow"=dword:00000000
[HKEY_CURRENT_USER\Software\Microsoft\Windows\CurrentVersion\
Explorer\User Shell Folders]
"AppData"=hex(2):25,55,53,45,52,50,52,4f,46,49,4c,45,25,5c,41,70,70,6c,69,63,\
  61,74,69,6f,6e,20,44,61,74,61,00
"Desktop"=hex(2):25,55,53,45,52,50,52,4f,46,49,4c,45,25,5c,44,65,73,6b,74,6f,70,00
"Favorites"=hex(2):25,55,53,45,52,50,52,4f,46,49,4c,45,25,5c,46,61,76,6f,72,69,74,

65,73,00
"NetHood"=hex(2):25,55,53,45,52,50,52,4f,46,49,4c,45,25,5c,4e,65,74,48,6f,6f,
64,00
"Personal"=hex(2):25,55,53,45,52,50,52,4f,46,49,4c,45,25,5c,50,65,72,73,6f,6e,61,6c,00
"PrintHood"=hex(2):25,55,53,45,52,50,52,4f,46,49,4c,45,25,5c,50,72,69,6e,74,48,6f,
6f,64,00
"Recent"=hex(2):25,55,53,45,52,50,52,4f,46,49,4c,45,25,5c,52,65,63,65,6e,74,00
"SendTo"=hex(2):25,55,53,45,52,50,52,4f,46,49,4c,45,25,5c,53,65,6e,64,54,6f,00
"Start Menu"=hex(2):25,55,53,45,52,50,52,4f,46,49,4c,45,25,5c,53,74,61,72,74,20,
4d,65,6e,75,00
"Programs"=hex(2):25,55,53,45,52,50,52,4f,46,49,4c,45,25,5c,53,74,61,72,74,20,
4d,65,6e,75,5c,50,72,6f,67,72,61,6d,73,00
"Startup"=hex(2):25,55,53,45,52,50,52,4f,46,49,4c,45,25,5c,53,74,61,72,74,20,4d,65,
6e,75,5c,50,72,6f,67,72,61,6d,73,5c,53,74,61,72,74,75,70,00
[HKEY_CURRENT_USER\Software\Microsoft\Windows\CurrentVersion\
GrpConv]
"Log"="Uninit Application."
[HKEY_CURRENT_USER\Software\Microsoft\Windows\CurrentVersion\
GrpConv\MapGroups]
"Games"="Accessories\\Games"
"System Tools"="Accessories\\System Tools"
"Desktop"="..\\..\\Desktop"
"Hyperterminal"="Accessories\\Hyperterminal"
"SendTo"="..\\..\\SendTo"
"Multimedia"="Accessories\\Multimedia"
[HKEY_CURRENT_USER\Software\Microsoft\Windows\CurrentVersion\
Internet Settings]
"EnableAutodisconnect"=hex:01,00,00,00
"DisconnectIdleTime"=hex:14,00,00,00
"EnableSecurityCheck"=hex:01,00,00,00
[HKEY_CURRENT_USER\Software\Microsoft\Windows\CurrentVersion\
Multimedia]
[HKEY_CURRENT_USER\Software\Microsoft\Windows\CurrentVersion\
Multimedia\MIDIMap]
"CurrentScheme"="Default"
"CurrentInstrument"=""
"UseScheme"=dword:00000000
"AutoScheme"=dword:00000001
"ConfigureCount"=dword:00000001
"DriverList"="9:05:09 AM, 1, "
[HKEY_CURRENT_USER\Software\Microsoft\Windows\CurrentVersion\Policies]
[HKEY_CURRENT_USER\Software\Microsoft\Windows\CurrentVersion\
Policies\Explorer]

"NoDriveTypeAutoRun"=dword:00000095
[HKEY_CURRENT_USER\Software\Microsoft\Windows\CurrentVersion\
Telephony]
[HKEY_CURRENT_USER\Software\Microsoft\Windows\CurrentVersion\
Telephony\HandoffPriorities]
"RequestMakeCall"="dialer.exe"
[HKEY_CURRENT_USER\Software\Microsoft\Windows Help]
"Xl"="166"
"Yu"="120"
"Xr"="474"
"Yd"="444"
"Maximized"="0"
[HKEY_CURRENT_USER\Software\Microsoft\Windows Messaging Subsystem]
[HKEY_CURRENT_USER\Software\Microsoft\Windows Messaging Subsystem\
PleaseUpgrade]
@=""
[HKEY_CURRENT_USER\Software\Microsoft\Windows NT]
[HKEY_CURRENT_USER\Software\Microsoft\Windows NT\CurrentVersion]
[HKEY_CURRENT_USER\Software\Microsoft\Windows NT\CurrentVersion\
Devices]
[HKEY_CURRENT_USER\Software\Microsoft\Windows NT\CurrentVersion\
Extensions]
"txt"="notepad.exe ^.txt"
"wtx"="notepad.exe ^.wtx"
"ini"="notepad.exe ^.ini"
[HKEY_CURRENT_USER\Software\Microsoft\Windows NT\CurrentVersion\
Network]
[HKEY_CURRENT_USER\Software\Microsoft\Windows NT\CurrentVersion\
Network\Event Viewer]
"SaveSettings"="1"
[HKEY_CURRENT_USER\Software\Microsoft\Windows NT\CurrentVersion\
Network\Persistent Connections]
"SaveConnections"="yes"
[HKEY_CURRENT_USER\Software\Microsoft\Windows NT\CurrentVersion\
Network\Server Manager]
"SaveSettings"="1"
[HKEY_CURRENT_USER\Software\Microsoft\Windows NT\CurrentVersion\
Network\User Manager]
"SaveSettings"="1"
[HKEY_CURRENT_USER\Software\Microsoft\Windows NT\CurrentVersion\
Network\User Manager for Domains]
"SaveSettings"="1"
[HKEY_CURRENT_USER\Software\Microsoft\Windows NT\CurrentVersion\

PrinterPorts]
[HKEY_CURRENT_USER\Software\Microsoft\Windows NT\CurrentVersion\
Program Manager]
[HKEY_CURRENT_USER\Software\Microsoft\Windows NT\CurrentVersion\
Program Manager\Common Groups]
[HKEY_CURRENT_USER\Software\Microsoft\Windows NT\CurrentVersion\
Program Manager\Restrictions]
"NoRun"=dword:00000000
"NoClose"=dword:00000000
"EditLevel"=dword:00000000
"Restrictions"=dword:00000000
"NoFileMenu"=dword:00000000
"NoSaveSettings"=dword:00000000
[HKEY_CURRENT_USER\Software\Microsoft\Windows NT\CurrentVersion\
Program Manager\Settings]
"MinOnRun"=dword:00000000
"AutoArrange"=dword:00000001
"SaveSettings"=dword:00000001
"display.drv"="vga.drv"
"Window"="68 63 636 421 1"
"CheckBinaryType"=dword:00000001
"CheckBinaryTimeout"=dword:000001f4
[HKEY_CURRENT_USER\Software\Microsoft\Windows NT\CurrentVersion\
Program Manager\UNICODE Groups]
[HKEY_CURRENT_USER\Software\Microsoft\Windows NT\CurrentVersion\
TrueType]
"TTEnable"="1"
"TTonly"="0"
[HKEY_CURRENT_USER\Software\Microsoft\Windows NT\CurrentVersion\
Windows]
"load"=""
"run"=""
"NullPort"="None"
"Programs"="com exe bat pif cmd"
"Documents"=""
"DosPrint"="no"
"NetMessage"="no"
"DebugOptions"="2048"
[HKEY_CURRENT_USER\Software\Microsoft\Windows NT\CurrentVersion\
Windows Messaging Subsystem]
[HKEY_CURRENT_USER\Software\Microsoft\Windows NT\CurrentVersion\
Windows Messaging Subsystem\Profiles]
[HKEY_CURRENT_USER\Software\Microsoft\Windows NT\CurrentVersion\

Winlogon]
"BuildNumber"=dword:00000565
"ParseAutoexec"="1"
"RunLogonScriptSync"=dword:00000000
[HKEY_CURRENT_USER\UNICODE Program Groups]

HKEY_USERS Subkeys and Their Values

[HKEY_USERS]
[HKEY_USERS\.DEFAULT]
[HKEY_USERS\.DEFAULT\AppEvents]
[HKEY_USERS\.DEFAULT\AppEvents\EventLabels]
[HKEY_USERS\.DEFAULT\AppEvents\EventLabels\AppGPFault]
@="Program error"
[HKEY_USERS\.DEFAULT\AppEvents\EventLabels\Close]
@="Close program"
[HKEY_USERS\.DEFAULT\AppEvents\EventLabels\EmptyRecycleBin]
@="Empty Recycle Bin"
[HKEY_USERS\.DEFAULT\AppEvents\EventLabels\MailBeep]
@="New Mail Notification"
[HKEY_USERS\.DEFAULT\AppEvents\EventLabels\Maximize]
@="Maximize"
[HKEY_USERS\.DEFAULT\AppEvents\EventLabels\MenuCommand]
@="Menu command"
[HKEY_USERS\.DEFAULT\AppEvents\EventLabels\MenuPopup]
@="Menu popup"
[HKEY_USERS\.DEFAULT\AppEvents\EventLabels\Minimize]
@="Minimize"
[HKEY_USERS\.DEFAULT\AppEvents\EventLabels\Open]
@="Open program"
[HKEY_USERS\.DEFAULT\AppEvents\EventLabels\RestoreDown]
@="Restore Down"
[HKEY_USERS\.DEFAULT\AppEvents\EventLabels\RestoreUp]
@="Restore Up"
[HKEY_USERS\.DEFAULT\AppEvents\EventLabels\SystemAsterisk]
@="Asterisk"
[HKEY_USERS\.DEFAULT\AppEvents\EventLabels\SystemDefault]
@="Default sound"
[HKEY_USERS\.DEFAULT\AppEvents\EventLabels\SystemExclamation]
@="Exclamation"
[HKEY_USERS\.DEFAULT\AppEvents\EventLabels\SystemExit]
@="Exit Windows NT"
[HKEY_USERS\.DEFAULT\AppEvents\EventLabels\SystemHand]

@="Critical Stop"
[HKEY_USERS\.DEFAULT\AppEvents\EventLabels\SystemQuestion]
@="Question"
[HKEY_USERS\.DEFAULT\AppEvents\EventLabels\SystemStart]
@="Start Windows NT"
[HKEY_USERS\.DEFAULT\AppEvents\Schemes]
[HKEY_USERS\.DEFAULT\AppEvents\Schemes\Apps]
[HKEY_USERS\.DEFAULT\AppEvents\Schemes\Apps\.Default]
@="Windows NT"
[HKEY_USERS\.DEFAULT\AppEvents\Schemes\Apps\.Default\.Default]
[HKEY_USERS\.DEFAULT\AppEvents\Schemes\Apps\.Default\.Default\.Current]
@="C:\\WINNT\\media\\ding.wav"
[HKEY_USERS\.DEFAULT\AppEvents\Schemes\Apps\.Default\.Default\.Default]
@="C:\\WINNT\\media\\ding.wav"
[HKEY_USERS\.DEFAULT\AppEvents\Schemes\Apps\.Default\.Default\Jungle0]
@="C:\\WINNT\\media\\Jungle Default.wav"
[HKEY_USERS\.DEFAULT\AppEvents\Schemes\Apps\.Default\.Default\Musica0]
@="C:\\WINNT\\media\\Musica Default.wav"
[HKEY_USERS\.DEFAULT\AppEvents\Schemes\Apps\.Default\.Default\Robotz0]
@="C:\\WINNT\\media\\Robotz Default.wav"
[HKEY_USERS\.DEFAULT\AppEvents\Schemes\Apps\.Default\.Default\Utopia0]
@="C:\\WINNT\\media\\Utopia Default.wav"
[HKEY_USERS\.DEFAULT\AppEvents\Schemes\Apps\.Default\AppGPFault]
[HKEY_USERS\.DEFAULT\AppEvents\Schemes\Apps\.Default\AppGPFault\.
Current]
@=""
[HKEY_USERS\.DEFAULT\AppEvents\Schemes\Apps\.Default\AppGPFault\
.Default]
@=""
[HKEY_USERS\.DEFAULT\AppEvents\Schemes\Apps\.Default\AppGPFault\
Jungle0]
@="C:\\WINNT\\media\\Jungle Error.wav"
[HKEY_USERS\.DEFAULT\AppEvents\Schemes\Apps\.Default\AppGPFault\
Musica0]
@="C:\\WINNT\\media\\Musica Error.wav"
[HKEY_USERS\.DEFAULT\AppEvents\Schemes\Apps\.Default\AppGPFault\
Robotz0]
@="C:\\WINNT\\media\\Robotz Error.wav"
[HKEY_USERS\.DEFAULT\AppEvents\Schemes\Apps\.Default\AppGPFault\
Utopia0]
@="C:\\WINNT\\media\\Utopia Error.wav"
[HKEY_USERS\.DEFAULT\AppEvents\Schemes\Apps\.Default\Close]
[HKEY_USERS\.DEFAULT\AppEvents\Schemes\Apps\.Default\Close\.Current]

@=""

[HKEY_USERS\.DEFAULT\AppEvents\Schemes\Apps\.Default\Close\.Default]
@=""

[HKEY_USERS\.DEFAULT\AppEvents\Schemes\Apps\.Default\Close\Jungle0]
@=""

[HKEY_USERS\.DEFAULT\AppEvents\Schemes\Apps\.Default\Close\Musica0]
@=""

[HKEY_USERS\.DEFAULT\AppEvents\Schemes\Apps\.Default\Close\Robotz0]
@=""

[HKEY_USERS\.DEFAULT\AppEvents\Schemes\Apps\.Default\Close\Utopia0]
@=""

[HKEY_USERS\.DEFAULT\AppEvents\Schemes\Apps\.Default\MailBeep]
[HKEY_USERS\.DEFAULT\AppEvents\Schemes\Apps\.Default\MailBeep\
.Current]
@="C:\\WINNT\\media\\ding.wav"

[HKEY_USERS\.DEFAULT\AppEvents\Schemes\Apps\.Default\MailBeep\.Default]
@="C:\\WINNT\\media\\ding.wav"

[HKEY_USERS\.DEFAULT\AppEvents\Schemes\Apps\.Default\Maximize]
[HKEY_USERS\.DEFAULT\AppEvents\Schemes\Apps\.Default\Maximize\
.Current]
@=""

[HKEY_USERS\.DEFAULT\AppEvents\Schemes\Apps\.Default\Maximize\.Default]
@=""

[HKEY_USERS\.DEFAULT\AppEvents\Schemes\Apps\.Default\Maximize\Jungle0]
@="C:\\WINNT\\media\\Jungle Maximize.wav"

[HKEY_USERS\.DEFAULT\AppEvents\Schemes\Apps\.Default\Maximize\
Musica0]
@="C:\\WINNT\\media\\Musica Maximize.wav"

[HKEY_USERS\.DEFAULT\AppEvents\Schemes\Apps\.Default\Maximize\
Robotz0]
@="C:\\WINNT\\media\\Robotz Maximize.wav"

[HKEY_USERS\.DEFAULT\AppEvents\Schemes\Apps\.Default\Maximize\
Utopia0]
@="C:\\WINNT\\media\\Utopia Maximize.wav"

[HKEY_USERS\.DEFAULT\AppEvents\Schemes\Apps\.Default\MenuCommand]
[HKEY_USERS\.DEFAULT\AppEvents\Schemes\Apps\.Default\MenuCommand\
.Current]
@=""

[HKEY_USERS\.DEFAULT\AppEvents\Schemes\Apps\.Default\MenuCommand\
.Default]
@=""

[HKEY_USERS\.DEFAULT\AppEvents\Schemes\Apps\.Default\MenuCommand\
Jungle0]

@="C:\\WINNT\\media\\Jungle Menu Command.wav"
[HKEY_USERS\.DEFAULT\AppEvents\Schemes\Apps\.Default\MenuCommand\
Musica0]
@="C:\\WINNT\\media\\Musica Menu Command.wav"
[HKEY_USERS\.DEFAULT\AppEvents\Schemes\Apps\.Default\MenuCommand\
Robotz0]
@="C:\\WINNT\\media\\Robotz Menu Command.wav"
[HKEY_USERS\.DEFAULT\AppEvents\Schemes\Apps\.Default\MenuCommand\
Utopia0]
@="C:\\WINNT\\media\\Utopia Menu Command.wav"
[HKEY_USERS\.DEFAULT\AppEvents\Schemes\Apps\.Default\MenuPopup]
[HKEY_USERS\.DEFAULT\AppEvents\Schemes\Apps\.Default\MenuPopup\
.Current]
@=""
[HKEY_USERS\.DEFAULT\AppEvents\Schemes\Apps\.Default\MenuPopup\
.Default]
@=""
[HKEY_USERS\.DEFAULT\AppEvents\Schemes\Apps\.Default\MenuPopup\
Jungle0]
@="C:\\WINNT\\media\\Jungle Menu Popup.wav"
[HKEY_USERS\.DEFAULT\AppEvents\Schemes\Apps\.Default\MenuPopup\
Musica0]
@="C:\\WINNT\\media\\Musica Menu Popup.wav"
[HKEY_USERS\.DEFAULT\AppEvents\Schemes\Apps\.Default\MenuPopup\
Robotz0]
@="C:\\WINNT\\media\\Robotz Menu Popup.wav"
[HKEY_USERS\.DEFAULT\AppEvents\Schemes\Apps\.Default\MenuPopup\
Utopia0]
@="C:\\WINNT\\media\\Utopia Menu Popup.wav"
[HKEY_USERS\.DEFAULT\AppEvents\Schemes\Apps\.Default\Minimize]
[HKEY_USERS\.DEFAULT\AppEvents\Schemes\Apps\.Default\Minimize\
.Current]
@=""
[HKEY_USERS\.DEFAULT\AppEvents\Schemes\Apps\.Default\Minimize\.Default]
@=""
[HKEY_USERS\.DEFAULT\AppEvents\Schemes\Apps\.Default\Minimize\Jungle0]
@="C:\\WINNT\\media\\Jungle Minimize.wav"
[HKEY_USERS\.DEFAULT\AppEvents\Schemes\Apps\.Default\Minimize\
Musica0]
@="C:\\WINNT\\media\\Musica Minimize.wav"
[HKEY_USERS\.DEFAULT\AppEvents\Schemes\Apps\.Default\Minimize\
Robotz0]
@="C:\\WINNT\\media\\Robotz Minimize.wav"

[HKEY_USERS\.DEFAULT\AppEvents\Schemes\Apps\.Default\Minimize\Utopia0]
@="C:\\WINNT\\media\\Utopia Minimize.wav"
[HKEY_USERS\.DEFAULT\AppEvents\Schemes\Apps\.Default\Open]
[HKEY_USERS\.DEFAULT\AppEvents\Schemes\Apps\.Default\Open\.Current]
@=""
[HKEY_USERS\.DEFAULT\AppEvents\Schemes\Apps\.Default\Open\.Default]
@=""
[HKEY_USERS\.DEFAULT\AppEvents\Schemes\Apps\.Default\Open\Jungle0]
@=""
[HKEY_USERS\.DEFAULT\AppEvents\Schemes\Apps\.Default\Open\Musica0]
@=""
[HKEY_USERS\.DEFAULT\AppEvents\Schemes\Apps\.Default\Open\Robotz0]
@=""
[HKEY_USERS\.DEFAULT\AppEvents\Schemes\Apps\.Default\Open\Utopia0]
@=""
[HKEY_USERS\.DEFAULT\AppEvents\Schemes\Apps\.Default\RestoreDown]
[HKEY_USERS\.DEFAULT\AppEvents\Schemes\Apps\.Default\RestoreDown\
.Current]
@=""
[HKEY_USERS\.DEFAULT\AppEvents\Schemes\Apps\.Default\RestoreDown\
.Default]
@=""
[HKEY_USERS\.DEFAULT\AppEvents\Schemes\Apps\.Default\RestoreDown\
Jungle0]
@="C:\\WINNT\\media\\Jungle Restore Down.wav"
[HKEY_USERS\.DEFAULT\AppEvents\Schemes\Apps\.Default\RestoreDown\
Musica0]
@="C:\\WINNT\\media\\Musica Restore Down.wav"
[HKEY_USERS\.DEFAULT\AppEvents\Schemes\Apps\.Default\RestoreDown\
Robotz0]
@="C:\\WINNT\\media\\Robotz Restore Down.wav"
[HKEY_USERS\.DEFAULT\AppEvents\Schemes\Apps\.Default\RestoreDown\
Utopia0]
@="C:\\WINNT\\media\\Utopia Restore Down.wav"
[HKEY_USERS\.DEFAULT\AppEvents\Schemes\Apps\.Default\RestoreUp]
[HKEY_USERS\.DEFAULT\AppEvents\Schemes\Apps\.Default\RestoreUp\
.Current]
@=""
[HKEY_USERS\.DEFAULT\AppEvents\Schemes\Apps\.Default\RestoreUp\
.Default]
@=""
[HKEY_USERS\.DEFAULT\AppEvents\Schemes\Apps\.Default\RestoreUp\
Jungle0]

@="C:\\WINNT\\media\\Jungle Restore Up.wav"
[HKEY_USERS\.DEFAULT\AppEvents\Schemes\Apps\.Default\RestoreUp\Music
a0]
@="C:\\WINNT\\media\\Musica Restore Up.wav"
[HKEY_USERS\.DEFAULT\AppEvents\Schemes\Apps\.Default\RestoreUp\
Robotz0]
@="C:\\WINNT\\media\\Robotz Restore Up.wav"
[HKEY_USERS\.DEFAULT\AppEvents\Schemes\Apps\.Default\RestoreUp\
Utopia0]
@="C:\\WINNT\\media\\Utopia Restore Up.wav"
[HKEY_USERS\.DEFAULT\AppEvents\Schemes\Apps\.Default\SystemAsterisk]
[HKEY_USERS\.DEFAULT\AppEvents\Schemes\Apps\.Default\SystemAsterisk\
.Current]
@="chord.wav"
[HKEY_USERS\.DEFAULT\AppEvents\Schemes\Apps\.Default\SystemAsterisk\
.Default]
@="C:\\WINNT\\media\\chord.wav"
[HKEY_USERS\.DEFAULT\AppEvents\Schemes\Apps\.Default\SystemAsterisk\
Jungle0]
@="C:\\WINNT\\media\\Jungle Asterisk.wav"
[HKEY_USERS\.DEFAULT\AppEvents\Schemes\Apps\.Default\SystemAsterisk\
Musica0]
@="C:\\WINNT\\media\\Musica Asterisk.wav"
[HKEY_USERS\.DEFAULT\AppEvents\Schemes\Apps\.Default\SystemAsterisk\
Robotz0]
@="C:\\WINNT\\media\\Robotz Asterisk.wav"
[HKEY_USERS\.DEFAULT\AppEvents\Schemes\Apps\.Default\SystemAsterisk\
Utopia0]
@="C:\\WINNT\\media\\Utopia Asterisk.wav"
[HKEY_USERS\.DEFAULT\AppEvents\Schemes\Apps\.Default\SystemDefault]
[HKEY_USERS\.DEFAULT\AppEvents\Schemes\Apps\.Default\SystemDefault\
.Current]
@="ding.wav"
[HKEY_USERS\.DEFAULT\AppEvents\Schemes\Apps\.Default\SystemDefault\
.Default]
@="ding.wav"
[HKEY_USERS\.DEFAULT\AppEvents\Schemes\Apps\.Default\
SystemExclamation]
[HKEY_USERS\.DEFAULT\AppEvents\Schemes\Apps\.Default\
SystemExclamation\.Current]
@="chord.wav"
[HKEY_USERS\.DEFAULT\AppEvents\Schemes\Apps\.Default\
SystemExclamation\.Default]

@="C:\\WINNT\\media\\chord.wav"
[HKEY_USERS\.DEFAULT\AppEvents\Schemes\Apps\.Default\SystemExclamatio
n\Jungle0]
@="C:\\WINNT\\media\\Jungle Exclamation.wav"
[HKEY_USERS\.DEFAULT\AppEvents\Schemes\Apps\.Default\
SystemExclamation\Musica0]
@="C:\\WINNT\\media\\Musica Exclamation.wav"
[HKEY_USERS\.DEFAULT\AppEvents\Schemes\Apps\.Default\
SystemExclamation\Robotz0]
@="C:\\WINNT\\media\\Robotz Exclamation.wav"
[HKEY_USERS\.DEFAULT\AppEvents\Schemes\Apps\.Default\
SystemExclamation\Utopia0]
@="C:\\WINNT\\media\\Utopia Exclamation.wav"
[HKEY_USERS\.DEFAULT\AppEvents\Schemes\Apps\.Default\SystemExit]
[HKEY_USERS\.DEFAULT\AppEvents\Schemes\Apps\.Default\SystemExit\
.Current]
@="Windows NT Logoff Sound.wav"
[HKEY_USERS\.DEFAULT\AppEvents\Schemes\Apps\.Default\SystemExit\
.Default]
@="C:\\WINNT\\media\\tada.wav"
[HKEY_USERS\.DEFAULT\AppEvents\Schemes\Apps\.Default\SystemExit\
Jungle0]
@="C:\\WINNT\\media\\Jungle Windows Exit.wav"
[HKEY_USERS\.DEFAULT\AppEvents\Schemes\Apps\.Default\SystemExit\
Musica0]
@="C:\\WINNT\\media\\Musica Windows Exit.wav"
[HKEY_USERS\.DEFAULT\AppEvents\Schemes\Apps\.Default\SystemExit\
Robotz0]
@="C:\\WINNT\\media\\Robotz Windows Exit.wav"
[HKEY_USERS\.DEFAULT\AppEvents\Schemes\Apps\.Default\SystemExit\
Utopia0]
@="C:\\WINNT\\media\\Utopia Windows Exit.wav"
[HKEY_USERS\.DEFAULT\AppEvents\Schemes\Apps\.Default\SystemHand]
[HKEY_USERS\.DEFAULT\AppEvents\Schemes\Apps\.Default\SystemHand\
.Current]
@="chord.wav"
[HKEY_USERS\.DEFAULT\AppEvents\Schemes\Apps\.Default\SystemHand\
.Default]
@="C:\\WINNT\\media\\chord.wav"
[HKEY_USERS\.DEFAULT\AppEvents\Schemes\Apps\.Default\SystemHand\
Jungle0]
@="C:\\WINNT\\media\\Jungle Critical Stop.wav"
[HKEY_USERS\.DEFAULT\AppEvents\Schemes\Apps\.Default\SystemHand\

Musica0]
@="C:\\WINNT\\media\\Musica Critical Stop.wav"
[HKEY_USERS\.DEFAULT\AppEvents\Schemes\Apps\.Default\SystemHand\
Robotz0]
@="C:\\WINNT\\media\\Robotz Critical Stop.wav"
[HKEY_USERS\.DEFAULT\AppEvents\Schemes\Apps\.Default\SystemHand\
Utopia0]
@="C:\\WINNT\\media\\Utopia Critical Stop.wav"
[HKEY_USERS\.DEFAULT\AppEvents\Schemes\Apps\.Default\SystemQuestion]
[HKEY_USERS\.DEFAULT\AppEvents\Schemes\Apps\.Default\SystemQuestion\
.Current]
@="chord.wav"
[HKEY_USERS\.DEFAULT\AppEvents\Schemes\Apps\.Default\SystemQuestion\
.Default]
@="C:\\WINNT\\media\\chord.wav"
[HKEY_USERS\.DEFAULT\AppEvents\Schemes\Apps\.Default\SystemQuestion\
Jungle0]
@="C:\\WINNT\\media\\Jungle Question.wav"
[HKEY_USERS\.DEFAULT\AppEvents\Schemes\Apps\.Default\SystemQuestion\
Musica0]
@="C:\\WINNT\\media\\Musica Question.wav"
[HKEY_USERS\.DEFAULT\AppEvents\Schemes\Apps\.Default\SystemQuestion\
Robotz0]
@="C:\\WINNT\\media\\Robotz Question.wav"
[HKEY_USERS\.DEFAULT\AppEvents\Schemes\Apps\.Default\SystemQuestion\
Utopia0]
@="C:\\WINNT\\media\\Utopia Question.wav"
[HKEY_USERS\.DEFAULT\AppEvents\Schemes\Apps\.Default\SystemStart]
[HKEY_USERS\.DEFAULT\AppEvents\Schemes\Apps\.Default\SystemStart\
.Current]
@="Windows NT Logon Sound.wav"
[HKEY_USERS\.DEFAULT\AppEvents\Schemes\Apps\.Default\SystemStart\
.Default]
@="Windows NT Logon Sound.wav"
[HKEY_USERS\.DEFAULT\AppEvents\Schemes\Apps\.Default\SystemStart\
Jungle0]
@="C:\\WINNT\\media\\Jungle Windows Start.wav"
[HKEY_USERS\.DEFAULT\AppEvents\Schemes\Apps\.Default\SystemStart\
Musica0]
@="C:\\WINNT\\media\\Musica Windows Start.wav"
[HKEY_USERS\.DEFAULT\AppEvents\Schemes\Apps\.Default\SystemStart\
Robotz0]
@="C:\\WINNT\\media\\Robotz Windows Start.wav"

[HKEY_USERS\.DEFAULT\AppEvents\Schemes\Apps\.Default\SystemStart\
Utopia0]
@="C:\\WINNT\\media\\Utopia Windows Start.wav"
[HKEY_USERS\.DEFAULT\AppEvents\Schemes\Apps\Explorer]
@="Windows Explorer"
[HKEY_USERS\.DEFAULT\AppEvents\Schemes\Apps\Explorer\EmptyRecycleBin]
[HKEY_USERS\.DEFAULT\AppEvents\Schemes\Apps\Explorer\
EmptyRecycleBin\.Current]
@="ding.wav"
[HKEY_USERS\.DEFAULT\AppEvents\Schemes\Apps\Explorer\
EmptyRecycleBin\.Default]
@="C:\\WINNT\\media\\ding.wav"
[HKEY_USERS\.DEFAULT\AppEvents\Schemes\Apps\Explorer\
EmptyRecycleBin\Jungle0]
@="C:\\WINNT\\media\\Jungle Recycle.wav"
[HKEY_USERS\.DEFAULT\AppEvents\Schemes\Apps\Explorer\
EmptyRecycleBin\Musica0]
@="C:\\WINNT\\media\\Musica Recycle.wav"
[HKEY_USERS\.DEFAULT\AppEvents\Schemes\Apps\Explorer\
EmptyRecycleBin\Robotz0]
@="C:\\WINNT\\media\\Robotz Recycle.wav"
[HKEY_USERS\.DEFAULT\AppEvents\Schemes\Apps\Explorer\
EmptyRecycleBin\Utopia0]
@="C:\\WINNT\\media\\Utopia Recycle.wav"
[HKEY_USERS\.DEFAULT\AppEvents\Schemes\Apps\MPlay32]
@="Media Player"
[HKEY_USERS\.DEFAULT\AppEvents\Schemes\Apps\MPlay32\Close]
[HKEY_USERS\.DEFAULT\AppEvents\Schemes\Apps\MPlay32\Close\.Current]
@=""
[HKEY_USERS\.DEFAULT\AppEvents\Schemes\Apps\MPlay32\Close\.Default]
@=""
[HKEY_USERS\.DEFAULT\AppEvents\Schemes\Apps\MPlay32\Open]
[HKEY_USERS\.DEFAULT\AppEvents\Schemes\Apps\MPlay32\Open\.Current]
@=""
[HKEY_USERS\.DEFAULT\AppEvents\Schemes\Apps\MPlay32\Open\.Default]
@=""
[HKEY_USERS\.DEFAULT\AppEvents\Schemes\Apps\SndRec32]
@="Sound Recorder"
[HKEY_USERS\.DEFAULT\AppEvents\Schemes\Apps\SndRec32\Close]
[HKEY_USERS\.DEFAULT\AppEvents\Schemes\Apps\SndRec32\Close\.Current]
@=""
[HKEY_USERS\.DEFAULT\AppEvents\Schemes\Apps\SndRec32\Open]
[HKEY_USERS\.DEFAULT\AppEvents\Schemes\Apps\SndRec32\Open\.Current]

@=""
[HKEY_USERS\.DEFAULT\AppEvents\Schemes\Names]
[HKEY_USERS\.DEFAULT\AppEvents\Schemes\Names\.Default]
@="Windows NT Default"
[HKEY_USERS\.DEFAULT\AppEvents\Schemes\Names\.None]
@="No Sounds"
[HKEY_USERS\.DEFAULT\AppEvents\Schemes\Names\Jungle0]
@="Jungle Sound Scheme"
[HKEY_USERS\.DEFAULT\AppEvents\Schemes\Names\Musica0]
@="Musica Sound Scheme"
[HKEY_USERS\.DEFAULT\AppEvents\Schemes\Names\Robotz0]
@="Robotz Sound Scheme"
[HKEY_USERS\.DEFAULT\AppEvents\Schemes\Names\Utopia0]
@="Utopia Sound Scheme"
[HKEY_USERS\.DEFAULT\AppEvents\Schemes\NewSchemes]
[HKEY_USERS\.DEFAULT\AppEvents\Schemes\NewSchemes\Jungle]
@=""
[HKEY_USERS\.DEFAULT\AppEvents\Schemes\NewSchemes\Musica]
@=""
[HKEY_USERS\.DEFAULT\AppEvents\Schemes\NewSchemes\Robotz]
@=""
[HKEY_USERS\.DEFAULT\AppEvents\Schemes\NewSchemes\Utopia]
@=""
[HKEY_USERS\.DEFAULT\Console]
"InsertMode"=dword:00000000
"QuickEdit"=dword:00000000
"FullScreen"=dword:00000000
"FaceName"=""
"FontFamily"=dword:00000000
"FontSize"=dword:00000000
"FontWeight"=dword:00000000
"CursorSize"=dword:00000019
"PopupColors"=dword:000000f5
"NumberOfHistoryBuffers"=dword:00000004
"ScreenColors"=dword:00000007
"HistoryBufferSize"=dword:00000032
"ScreenBufferSize"=dword:00190050
"WindowSize"=dword:00190050
"ColorTable00"=dword:00000000
"ColorTable01"=dword:00800000
"ColorTable02"=dword:00008000
"ColorTable03"=dword:00808000
"ColorTable04"=dword:00000080

```
"ColorTable05"=dword:00800080
"ColorTable06"=dword:00008080
"ColorTable07"=dword:00c0c0c0
"ColorTable08"=dword:00808080
"ColorTable09"=dword:00ff0000
"ColorTable10"=dword:0000ff00
"ColorTable11"=dword:00ffff00
"ColorTable12"=dword:000000ff
"ColorTable13"=dword:00ff00ff
"ColorTable14"=dword:0000ffff
"ColorTable15"=dword:00ffffff
[HKEY_USERS\.DEFAULT\Control Panel]
[HKEY_USERS\.DEFAULT\Control Panel\Accessibility]
[HKEY_USERS\.DEFAULT\Control Panel\Accessibility\Keyboard Response]
"AutoRepeatDelay"="1000"
"AutoRepeatRate"="500"
"BounceTime"="0"
"DelayBeforeAcceptance"="1000"
"Flags"="82"
[HKEY_USERS\.DEFAULT\Control Panel\Accessibility\MouseKeys]
"Flags"="18"
"MaximumSpeed"="80"
"TimeToMaximumSpeed"="3000"
[HKEY_USERS\.DEFAULT\Control Panel\Accessibility\ShowSounds]
"On"="0"
[HKEY_USERS\.DEFAULT\Control Panel\Accessibility\SoundSentry]
"Flags"="2"
"FSTextEffect"="0"
"WindowsEffect"="0"
[HKEY_USERS\.DEFAULT\Control Panel\Accessibility\StickyKeys]
"Flags"="466"
[HKEY_USERS\.DEFAULT\Control Panel\Accessibility\TimeOut]
"Flags"="2"
"TimeToWait"="300000"
[HKEY_USERS\.DEFAULT\Control Panel\Accessibility\ToggleKeys]
"Flags"="18"
[HKEY_USERS\.DEFAULT\Control Panel\Appearance]
[HKEY_USERS\.DEFAULT\Control Panel\Appearance\Schemes]
"Brick"=hex:
"Maple"=hex:
"Spruce"=hex:
"Teal (VGA)"=hex:
"Red, White, and Blue (VGA)"=hex:
```

"Wheat"=hex:
"Pumpkin (large)"=hex:
"Eggplant"=hex:
"Rainy Day"=hex:
"Desert"=hex:
"Marine (high color)"=hex:
"Windows Standard (extra large)"=hex:
"Storm (VGA)"=hex:
"Windows Standard"=hex:
"Windows Standard (large)"=hex:
"Rose"=hex:
"High Contrast Black (large)"=hex:
"High Contrast Black (extra large)"=hex:
"High Contrast White (large)"=hex:
"High Contrast White (extra large)"=hex:
"Rose (large)"=hex:
"Lilac"=hex:
"Lilac (large)"=hex:
"Slate"=hex:
"Plum (high color)"=hex:
"High Contrast Black"=hex:
"High Contrast White"=hex:
[HKEY_USERS\.DEFAULT\Control Panel\Colors]
"Background"="0 128 128"
"AppWorkSpace"="128 128 128"
"Window"="255 255 255"
"WindowText"="0   0   0"
"Menu"="192 192 192"
"MenuText"="0   0   0"
"ActiveTitle"="0   0 128"
"InactiveTitle"="128 128 128"
"TitleText"="255 255 255"
"ActiveBorder"="192 192 192"
"InactiveBorder"="192 192 192"
"WindowFrame"="0   0   0"
"Scrollbar"="192 192 192"
"ButtonFace"="192 192 192"
"ButtonShadow"="128 128 128"

Author Note

The values under the Appearance key contain long listings of hexadecimal numbers. These numbers are not reproduced here but may be seen by viewing the value setting with a registry editor.

"ButtonText"="0   0   0"
"GrayText"="128 128 128"
"Hilight"="0   0 128"
"HilightText"="255 255 255"
"InactiveTitleText"="192 192 192"
"ButtonHilight"="255 255 255"
"InfoText"="0   0   0"
"InfoWindow"="255 255 225"
"ButtonLight"="192 192 192"
"ButtonDkShadow"="0   0   0"
[HKEY_USERS\.DEFAULT\Control Panel\Current]
"Color Schemes"="Windows Default"
[HKEY_USERS\.DEFAULT\Control Panel\Cursors]
[HKEY_USERS\.DEFAULT\Control Panel\Cursors\Schemes]
"Windows Default"=",,,,,,,,,,,,,"

"Windows Animated"="C:\\WINNT\\Cursors\\rainbow.ani,,C:\\WINNT\\
Cursors\\appstart.ani,C:\\WINNT\\Cursors\\hourglas.ani,C:\\WINNT\\Cursors\\
cross.cur,,,,C:\\WINNT\\Cursors\\sizens.ani,C:\\WINNT\\Cursors\\sizewe.ani,C:\\
WINNT\\Cursors\\sizenwse.ani,C:\\WINNT\\Cursors\\sizenesw.ani,,"

"3D-White"="C:\\WINNT\\Cursors\\3dwarro.cur,,C:\\WINNT\\Cursors\\
appstar3.ani,C:\\WINNT\\Cursors\\hourgla3.ani,C:\\WINNT\\Cursors\\
cross.cur,,,C:\\WINNT\\Cursors\\3dwno.cur,C:\\WINNT\\Cursors\\
3dwns.cur,C:\\WINNT\\Cursors\\3dwwe.cur,C:\\WINNT\\Cursors\\
3dwnwse.cur,C:\\WINNT\\Cursors\\3dwnesw.cur,C:\\WINNT\\Cursors\\
3dwmove.cur,"

"Hands 1"="C:\\WINNT\\Cursors\\harrow.cur,,C:\\WINNT\\Cursors\\
handapst.ani,C:\\WINNT\\Cursors\\hand.ani,C:\\WINNT\\Cursors\\
hcross.cur,C:\\WINNT\\Cursors\\hibeam.cur,,C:\\WINNT\\Cursors\\
hnodrop.cur,C:\\WINNT\\Cursors\\hns.cur,C:\\WINNT\\Cursors\\hwe.cur,C:\\
WINNT\\Cursors\\hnwse.cur,C:\\WINNT\\Cursors\\hnesw.cur,C:\\WINNT\\
Cursors\\hmove.cur,"

"Hands 2"="C:\\WINNT\\Cursors\\harrow.cur,,C:\\WINNT\\Cursors\\
handapst.ani,C:\\WINNT\\Cursors\\handwait.ani,C:\\WINNT\\Cursors\\
hcross.cur,C:\\WINNT\\Cursors\\hibeam.cur,,C:\\WINNT\\Cursors\\
handno.ani,C:\\WINNT\\Cursors\\handns.ani,C:\\WINNT\\Cursors\\
handwe.ani,C:\\WINNT\\Cursors\\handnwse.ani,C:\\WINNT\\Cursors\\
handnesw.ani,C:\\WINNT\\Cursors\\hmove.cur,"

"Dinosaur"="C:\\WINNT\\Cursors\\3dgarro.cur,,C:\\WINNT\\Cursors\\
dinosaur.ani,C:\\WINNT\\Cursors\\dinosau2.ani,C:\\WINNT\\Cursors\\
cross.cur,,,C:\\WINNT\\Cursors\\banana.ani,C:\\WINNT\\Cursors\\
3dsns.cur,C:\\WINNT\\Cursors\\3dgwe.cur,C:\\WINNT\\Cursors\\
3dsnwse.cur,C:\\WINNT\\Cursors\\3dgnesw.cur,C:\\WINNT\\Cursors\\
3dsmove.cur,"

"Old Fashioned"="C:\\WINNT\\Cursors\\harrow.cur,,C:\\WINNT\\Cursors\\
horse.ani,C:\\WINNT\\Cursors\\barber.ani,C:\\WINNT\\Cursors\\hcross.cur,C:\\
WINNT\\Cursors\\hibeam.cur,,C:\\WINNT\\Cursors\\coin.ani,C:\\WINNT\\
Cursors\\3dgns.cur,C:\\WINNT\\Cursors\\3dgwe.cur,C:\\WINNT\\Cursors\\
3dgnwse.cur,C:\\WINNT\\Cursors\\3dgnesw.cur,C:\\WINNT\\Cursors\\3dgmove
.cur,"

"Conductor"="C:\\WINNT\\Cursors\\harrow.cur,,C:\\WINNT\\Cursors\\drum.
ani,C:\\WINNT\\Cursors\\metronom.ani,C:\\WINNT\\Cursors\\hcross.cur,C:\\
WINNT\\Cursors\\hibeam.cur,,C:\\WINNT\\Cursors\\piano.ani,C:\\WINNT\\
Cursors\\hns.cur,C:\\WINNT\\Cursors\\hwe.cur,C:\\WINNT\\Cursors\\
hnwse.cur,C:\\WINNT\\Cursors\\hnesw.cur,C:\\WINNT\\Cursors\\hmove.cur,"
"Magnified"="C:\\WINNT\\Cursors\\larrow.cur,,C:\\WINNT\\Cursors\\
lappstrt.cur,C:\\WINNT\\Cursors\\lwait.cur,C:\\WINNT\\Cursors\\lcross.cur,C:\\
WINNT\\Cursors\\libeam.cur,,C:\\WINNT\\Cursors\\lnodrop.cur,C:\\WINNT\\
Cursors\\lns.cur,C:\\WINNT\\Cursors\\lwe.cur,C:\\WINNT\\Cursors\\
lnwse.cur,C:\\WINNT\\Cursors\\lnesw.cur,C:\\WINNT\\Cursors\\lmove.cur,"

"Variations"="C:\\WINNT\\Cursors\\fillitup.ani,,C:\\WINNT\\Cursors\\
raindrop.ani,C:\\WINNT\\Cursors\\counter.ani,C:\\WINNT\\Cursors\\
cross.cur,,,C:\\WINNT\\Cursors\\wagtail.ani,C:\\WINNT\\Cursors\\
sizens.ani,C:\\WINNT\\Cursors\\sizewe.ani,C:\\WINNT\\Cursors\\
sizenwse.ani,C:\\WINNT\\Cursors\\sizenesw.ani,"

"3D-Bronze"="C:\\WINNT\\Cursors\\3dgarro.cur,,C:\\WINNT\\Cursors\\
appstar2.ani,C:\\WINNT\\Cursors\\hourgla2.ani,C:\\WINNT\\Cursors\\
cross.cur,,,C:\\WINNT\\Cursors\\3dgno.cur,C:\\WINNT\\Cursors\\
3dgns.cur,C:\\WINNT\\Cursors\\3dgwe.cur,C:\\WINNT\\Cursors\\3dgnwse.cur,
C:\\WINNT\\Cursors\\3dgnesw.cur,C:\\WINNT\\Cursors\\3dgmove.cur,"

[HKEY_USERS\.DEFAULT\Control Panel\Custom Colors]
"ColorA"="FFFFFF"
"ColorB"="FFFFFF"
"ColorC"="FFFFFF"
"ColorD"="FFFFFF"
"ColorE"="FFFFFF"

"ColorF"="FFFFFF"
"ColorG"="FFFFFF"
"ColorH"="FFFFFF"
"ColorI"="FFFFFF"
"ColorJ"="FFFFFF"
"ColorK"="FFFFFF"
"ColorL"="FFFFFF"
"ColorM"="FFFFFF"
"ColorN"="FFFFFF"
"ColorO"="FFFFFF"
"ColorP"="FFFFFF"
[HKEY_USERS\.DEFAULT\Control Panel\Desktop]
"CoolSwitch"="1"
"CoolSwitchRows"="3"
"CoolSwitchColumns"="7"
"CursorBlinkRate"="530"
"ScreenSaveTimeOut"="900"
"ScreenSaveActive"="1"
"SCRNSAVE.EXE"="logon.scr"
"ScreenSaverIsSecure"="0"
"Pattern"="(None)"
"Wallpaper"="(Default)"
"TileWallpaper"="0"
"GridGranularity"="0"
"IconSpacing"="75"
"IconTitleWrap"="1"
"IconTitleFaceName"="MS Sans Serif"
"IconTitleSize"="9"
"IconTitleStyle"="0"
"DragFullWindows"="2"
"HungAppTimeout"="5000"
"WaitToKillAppTimeout"="20000"
"AutoEndTasks"="0"
"FontSmoothing"="0"
"MenuShowDelay"="400"
"DragHeight"="2"
"DragWidth"="2"
"WheelScrollLines"="3"
[HKEY_USERS\.DEFAULT\Control Panel\Desktop\WindowMetrics]
"BorderWidth"="1"
[HKEY_USERS\.DEFAULT\Control Panel\International]
"Locale"="00000409"
"sLanguage"="ENU"

"sCountry"="United States"
"iCountry"="1"
"sList"=","
"iMeasure"="1"
"sDecimal"="."
"sThousand"=","
"iDigits"="2"
"iLZero"="1"
"sCurrency"="$"
"iCurrDigits"="2"
"iCurrency"="0"
"iNegCurr"="0"
"sDate"="/"
"sTime"=":"
"sShortDate"="M/d/yy"
"sLongDate"="dddd, MMMM dd, yyyy"
"iDate"="0"
"iTime"="0"
"iTLZero"="0"
"s1159"="AM"
"s2359"="PM"
[HKEY_USERS\.DEFAULT\Control Panel\International\Sorting Order]
[HKEY_USERS\.DEFAULT\Control Panel\IOProcs]
"MVB"="mvfs32.dll"
[HKEY_USERS\.DEFAULT\Control Panel\Keyboard]
"KeyboardSpeed"="31"
"KeyboardDelay"="1"
"InitialKeyboardIndicators"="0x80000000"
[HKEY_USERS\.DEFAULT\Control Panel\MMCPL]
[HKEY_USERS\.DEFAULT\Control Panel\Mouse]
"SwapMouseButtons"="0"
"DoubleClickSpeed"="500"
"DoubleClickHeight"="4"
"DoubleClickWidth"="4"
"MouseThreshold1"="6"
"MouseThreshold2"="10"
"MouseSpeed"="1"
"SnapToDefaultButton"="0"
"ActiveWindowTracking"=dword:00000000
[HKEY_USERS\.DEFAULT\Control Panel\Patterns]
"(None)"="(None)"
"Boxes"="127 65 65 65 65 65 127 0"
"Paisley"="2 7 7 2 32 80 80 32"

"Weave"="136 84 34 69 136 21 34 81"
"Waffle"="0 0 0 0 128 128 128 240"
"Tulip"="0 0 84 124 124 56 146 124"
"Spinner"="20 12 200 121 158 19 48 40"
"Scottie"="64 192 200 120 120 72 0 0"
"Critters"="0 80 114 32 0 5 39 2"
"50% Gray"="170 85 170 85 170 85 170 85"
"Quilt"="130 68 40 17 40 68 130 1"
"Diamonds"="32 80 136 80 32 0 0 0"
"Thatches"="248 116 34 71 143 23 34 113"
"Pattern"="224 128 142 136 234 10 14 0"
[HKEY_USERS\.DEFAULT\Control Panel\Screen Saver.3DFlyingObj]
[HKEY_USERS\.DEFAULT\Control Panel\Screen Saver.3DPipes]
[HKEY_USERS\.DEFAULT\Control Panel\Screen Saver.Bezier]
[HKEY_USERS\.DEFAULT\Control Panel\Screen Saver.Marquee]
"Font"="Times New Roman"
"Size"="24"
"Text"="Your text goes here."
"TextColor"="255 0 255"
"BackgroundColor"="0 0 128"
"Mode"="1"
"Speed"="14"
"CharSet"="0"
[HKEY_USERS\.DEFAULT\Control Panel\Screen Saver.Mystify]
"Clear Screen"="1"
"Active1"="1"
"WalkRandom1"="1"
"Lines1"="7"
"StartColor1"="0 0 0"
"EndColor1"="255 255 255"
"Active2"="1"
"WalkRandom2"="1"
"Lines2"="12"
"StartColor2"="0 0 0"
"EndColor2"="255 255 255"
[HKEY_USERS\.DEFAULT\Control Panel\Screen Saver.Stars]
"Density"="50"
"WarpSpeed"="10"
[HKEY_USERS\.DEFAULT\Control Panel\Sound]
"Beep"="yes"
[HKEY_USERS\.DEFAULT\Environment]
"TEMP"=hex(2):25,53,79,73,74,65,6d,44,72,69,76,65,25,5c,54,45,4d,50,00
"TMP"=hex(2):25,53,79,73,74,65,6d,44,72,69,76,65,25,5c,54,45,4d,50,00

[HKEY_USERS\.DEFAULT\Keyboard Layout]
[HKEY_USERS\.DEFAULT\Keyboard Layout\Preload]
"1"="00000409"
[HKEY_USERS\.DEFAULT\Keyboard Layout\Substitutes]
[HKEY_USERS\.DEFAULT\Software]
[HKEY_USERS\.DEFAULT\Software\Microsoft]
[HKEY_USERS\.DEFAULT\Software\Microsoft\Clock]
"iFormat"="1"
[HKEY_USERS\.DEFAULT\Software\Microsoft\Command Processor]
"EnableExtensions"=dword:00000001
"DefaultColor"=dword:00000000
"CompletionChar"=dword:00000000
[HKEY_USERS\.DEFAULT\Software\Microsoft\File Manager]
[HKEY_USERS\.DEFAULT\Software\Microsoft\File Manager\Settings]
[HKEY_USERS\.DEFAULT\Software\Microsoft\Internet Explorer]
[HKEY_USERS\.DEFAULT\Software\Microsoft\Internet Explorer\
Document Windows]
"width"=hex:00,00,00,80
"height"=hex:00,00,00,00
"x"=hex:00,00,00,80
"y"=hex:00,00,00,00
"Maximized"="no"
[HKEY_USERS\.DEFAULT\Software\Microsoft\Internet Explorer\Main]
"Check_Associations"="yes"
"Show_ToolBar"="yes"
"Show_URLToolBar"="yes"
"Show_StatusBar"="yes"
"Show_URLinStatusBar"="yes"
"Show_FullURL"="no"
"Use_DlgBox_Colors"="yes"
"Display Inline Images"="yes"
"Anchor Underline"="yes"
"Save_Session_History_On_Exit"="no"
"Start Page"="file:C:\\Program Files\\Plus!\\Microsoft Internet\\docs\\home.htm"
"Search Page"="http://www.msn.com/access/allinone.htm"
"Cache_Update_Frequency"="Once_Per_Session"
[HKEY_USERS\.DEFAULT\Software\Microsoft\Internet Explorer\Security]
"Sending_Security"="Medium"
"Viewing_Security"="Low"
[HKEY_USERS\.DEFAULT\Software\Microsoft\Internet Explorer\Services]
@=""
[HKEY_USERS\.DEFAULT\Software\Microsoft\Internet Explorer\Settings]
"Anchor Color"="0,0,255"

"Anchor Color Visited"="128,0,128"

"Background Color"="192,192,192"

"Text Color"="0,0,0"

[HKEY_USERS\.DEFAULT\Software\Microsoft\Internet Explorer\Styles]

"Default_Style_Sheet"="SerifMedium"

[HKEY_USERS\.DEFAULT\Software\Microsoft\Internet Explorer\TypedURLs]

"url1"="file:C:\\WINNT/itgfile.htm"

[HKEY_USERS\.DEFAULT\Software\Microsoft\NetDDE]

[HKEY_USERS\.DEFAULT\Software\Microsoft\NetDDE\DDE Trusted Shares]

[HKEY_USERS\.DEFAULT\Software\Microsoft\NetDDE\DDE Trusted Shares\
DDEDBi3B690712]

[HKEY_USERS\.DEFAULT\Software\Microsoft\NetDDE\DDE Trusted Shares\
DDEDBi3B690712\Chat$]

"SerialNumber"=hex:05,00,00,09,00,00,00,01

"StartApp"=dword:00000001

"InitAllowed"=dword:00000001

[HKEY_USERS\.DEFAULT\Software\Microsoft\NetDDE\DDE Trusted Shares\
DDEDBi3B690712\CLPBK$]

"SerialNumber"=hex:05,00,00,09,00,00,00,01

"StartApp"=dword:00000001

"InitAllowed"=dword:00000001

[HKEY_USERS\.DEFAULT\Software\Microsoft\NetDDE\DDE Trusted Shares\
DDEDBi3B690712\Hearts$]

"SerialNumber"=hex:05,00,00,09,00,00,00,01

"StartApp"=dword:00000001

"InitAllowed"=dword:00000001

[HKEY_USERS\.DEFAULT\Software\Microsoft\Ntbackup]

[HKEY_USERS\.DEFAULT\Software\Microsoft\RegEdt32]

[HKEY_USERS\.DEFAULT\Software\Microsoft\RegEdt32\Settings]

"AutoRefresh"="1"

"ReadOnly"="0"

"RemoteAccess"="0"

"ConfirmOnDelete"="1"

"SaveSettings"="1"

[HKEY_USERS\.DEFAULT\Software\Microsoft\Schedule+]

[HKEY_USERS\.DEFAULT\Software\Microsoft\Schedule+\Microsoft Schedule+]

"MigrateIni"="1"

"MigrateIniPrint"="1"

[HKEY_USERS\.DEFAULT\Software\Microsoft\Windows]

[HKEY_USERS\.DEFAULT\Software\Microsoft\Windows\CurrentVersion]

[HKEY_USERS\.DEFAULT\Software\Microsoft\Windows\CurrentVersion\Explorer]

[HKEY_USERS\.DEFAULT\Software\Microsoft\Windows\CurrentVersion\
Explorer\NewShortcutHandlers]

"{FBF23B40-E3F0-101B-8488-00AA003E56F8}"=""
[HKEY_USERS\.DEFAULT\Software\Microsoft\Windows\CurrentVersion\
Explorer\Shell Folders]
"SendTo"="C:\\WINNT\\Profiles\\Default User\\SendTo"
"Recent"="C:\\WINNT\\Profiles\\Default User\\Recent"
"Desktop"="C:\\WINNT\\Profiles\\Default User\\Desktop"
"Programs"="C:\\WINNT\\Profiles\\Default User\\Start Menu\\Programs"
[HKEY_USERS\.DEFAULT\Software\Microsoft\Windows\CurrentVersion\
Explorer\User Shell Folders]
"AppData"=hex(2):25,55,53,45,52,50,52,4f,46,49,4c,45,25,5c,41,70,70,6c,69,63,61,
74,69,6f,6e,20,44,61,74,61,00
"Desktop"=hex(2):25,55,53,45,52,50,52,4f,46,49,4c,45,25,5c,44,65,73,6b,74,6f,70,00
"Favorites"=hex(2):25,55,53,45,52,50,52,4f,46,49,4c,45,25,5c,46,61,76,6f,72,69,74,
65,73,00
"NetHood"=hex(2):25,55,53,45,52,50,52,4f,46,49,4c,45,25,5c,4e,65,74,48,6f,6f,64,00
"Personal"=hex(2):25,55,53,45,52,50,52,4f,46,49,4c,45,25,5c,50,65,72,73,6f,6e,61,6c,00
"PrintHood"=hex(2):25,55,53,45,52,50,52,4f,46,49,4c,45,25,5c,50,72,69,6e,74,48,6f,
6f,64,00
"Recent"=hex(2):25,55,53,45,52,50,52,4f,46,49,4c,45,25,5c,52,65,63,65,6e,74,00
"SendTo"=hex(2):25,55,53,45,52,50,52,4f,46,49,4c,45,25,5c,53,65,6e,64,54,6f,00
"Start Menu"=hex(2):25,55,53,45,52,50,52,4f,46,49,4c,45,25,5c,53,74,61,72,74,20,
4d,65,6e,75,00
"Programs"=hex(2):25,55,53,45,52,50,52,4f,46,49,4c,45,25,5c,53,74,61,72,74,20,4d,6
5,6e,75,5c,50,72,6f,67,72,61,6d,73,00
"Startup"=hex(2):25,55,53,45,52,50,52,4f,46,49,4c,45,25,5c,53,74,61,72,74,20,4d,65,
6e,75,5c,50,72,6f,67,72,61,6d,73,5c,53,74,61,72,74,75,70,00
[HKEY_USERS\.DEFAULT\Software\Microsoft\Windows\CurrentVersion\
GrpConv]
"Log"="Uninit Application."
[HKEY_USERS\.DEFAULT\Software\Microsoft\Windows\CurrentVersion\
GrpConv\MapGroups]
"Games"="Accessories\\Games"
"System Tools"="Accessories\\System Tools"
"Desktop"="..\\..\\Desktop"
"Hyperterminal"="Accessories\\Hyperterminal"
"SendTo"="..\\..\\SendTo"
"Multimedia"="Accessories\\Multimedia"
[HKEY_USERS\.DEFAULT\Software\Microsoft\Windows\CurrentVersion\
Internet Settings]
"EnableAutodisconnect"=hex:01,00,00,00
"DisconnectIdleTime"=hex:14,00,00,00
"EnableSecurityCheck"=hex:01,00,00,00
[HKEY_USERS\.DEFAULT\Software\Microsoft\Windows\CurrentVersion\

Multimedia]
[HKEY_USERS\.DEFAULT\Software\Microsoft\Windows\CurrentVersion\
Multimedia\MIDIMap]
"CurrentScheme"="Default"
"CurrentInstrument"=""
"UseScheme"=dword:00000000
"AutoScheme"=dword:00000001
"ConfigureCount"=dword:00000002
"DriverList"="9:26:58 AM, 2, "
[HKEY_USERS\.DEFAULT\Software\Microsoft\Windows\CurrentVersion\Policies]
[HKEY_USERS\.DEFAULT\Software\Microsoft\Windows\CurrentVersion\
Policies\Explorer]
"NoDriveTypeAutoRun"=dword:00000095
[HKEY_USERS\.DEFAULT\Software\Microsoft\Windows\CurrentVersion\
Telephony]
[HKEY_USERS\.DEFAULT\Software\Microsoft\Windows\CurrentVersion\
Telephony\HandoffPriorities]
"RequestMakeCall"="dialer.exe"
[HKEY_USERS\.DEFAULT\Software\Microsoft\Windows Help]
"Xl"="166"
"Yu"="120"
"Xr"="474"
"Yd"="444"
"Maximized"="0"
[HKEY_USERS\.DEFAULT\Software\Microsoft\Windows Messaging Subsystem]
[HKEY_USERS\.DEFAULT\Software\Microsoft\Windows Messaging Subsystem\
PleaseUpgrade]
@=""
[HKEY_USERS\.DEFAULT\Software\Microsoft\Windows NT]
[HKEY_USERS\.DEFAULT\Software\Microsoft\Windows NT\CurrentVersion]
[HKEY_USERS\.DEFAULT\Software\Microsoft\Windows NT\CurrentVersion\
Devices]
[HKEY_USERS\.DEFAULT\Software\Microsoft\Windows NT\CurrentVersion\
Extensions]
"txt"="notepad.exe ^.txt"
"wtx"="notepad.exe ^.wtx"
"ini"="notepad.exe ^.ini"
[HKEY_USERS\.DEFAULT\Software\Microsoft\Windows NT\CurrentVersion\
Network]
[HKEY_USERS\.DEFAULT\Software\Microsoft\Windows NT\CurrentVersion\
Network\Event Viewer]
"SaveSettings"="1"
[HKEY_USERS\.DEFAULT\Software\Microsoft\Windows NT\CurrentVersion\

Network\Persistent Connections]
"SaveConnections"="yes"
[HKEY_USERS\.DEFAULT\Software\Microsoft\Windows NT\CurrentVersion\
Network\Server Manager]
"SaveSettings"="1"
[HKEY_USERS\.DEFAULT\Software\Microsoft\Windows NT\CurrentVersion\
Network\User Manager]
"SaveSettings"="1"
[HKEY_USERS\.DEFAULT\Software\Microsoft\Windows NT\CurrentVersion\
Network\User Manager for Domains]
"SaveSettings"="1"
[HKEY_USERS\.DEFAULT\Software\Microsoft\Windows NT\CurrentVersion\
PrinterPorts]
[HKEY_USERS\.DEFAULT\Software\Microsoft\Windows NT\CurrentVersion\
Program Manager]
[HKEY_USERS\.DEFAULT\Software\Microsoft\Windows NT\CurrentVersion\
Program Manager\Common Groups]
[HKEY_USERS\.DEFAULT\Software\Microsoft\Windows NT\CurrentVersion\
Program Manager\Restrictions]
"NoRun"=dword:00000000
"NoClose"=dword:00000000
"EditLevel"=dword:00000000
"Restrictions"=dword:00000000
"NoFileMenu"=dword:00000000
"NoSaveSettings"=dword:00000000
[HKEY_USERS\.DEFAULT\Software\Microsoft\Windows NT\CurrentVersion\
Program Manager\Settings]
"MinOnRun"=dword:00000000
"AutoArrange"=dword:00000001
"SaveSettings"=dword:00000001
"display.drv"="vga.drv"
"Window"="68 63 636 421 1"
"CheckBinaryType"=dword:00000001
"CheckBinaryTimeout"=dword:000001f4
[HKEY_USERS\.DEFAULT\Software\Microsoft\Windows NT\CurrentVersion\
Program Manager\UNICODE Groups]
[HKEY_USERS\.DEFAULT\Software\Microsoft\Windows NT\CurrentVersion\
TrueType]
"TTEnable"="1"
"TTonly"="0"
[HKEY_USERS\.DEFAULT\Software\Microsoft\Windows NT\CurrentVersion\
Windows]
"load"=""

"run"=""
"NullPort"="None"
"Programs"="com exe bat pif cmd"
"Documents"=""
"device"=""
"DosPrint"="no"
"NetMessage"="no"
"DebugOptions"="2048"
[HKEY_USERS\.DEFAULT\Software\Microsoft\Windows NT\CurrentVersion\
Windows Messaging Subsystem]
[HKEY_USERS\.DEFAULT\Software\Microsoft\Windows NT\CurrentVersion\
Windows Messaging Subsystem\Profiles]
[HKEY_USERS\.DEFAULT\Software\Microsoft\Windows NT\CurrentVersion\
Winlogon]
"BuildNumber"=dword:00000565
[HKEY_USERS\.DEFAULT\UNICODE Program Groups]
[HKEY_USERS\S-1-5-21-861491223-464875664-709122288-500]

Author Note

The subkeys and values under this key are the same as the [HKEY_CURRENT_USER] key and are not
shown here.

B

Windows NT Server
Registry Issues

This appendix describes the differences between the Windows NT Server and Windows NT Workstation registries. Although you might think that these two products are vastly different, in reality, they are almost identical at the Registry level. These Registry differences are concerned with the way the NT Kernel reads the Registry to determine certain parameters. It is these Registry parameters that cause the operating system to boot as a server or workstation. These parameters are found through the following keys and values:

```
[HKEY_LOCAL_MACHINE\SYSTEM\CurrentControlSet\Control\ProductOptions]
ProductType          Product
REG_DWORD
```

This value can have the following product values:

WINNT	Setting for Windows NT 4.0 Workstation
SERVERNT	Setting for Windows NT 4.0 Server
LANMANNT	Setting for Windows NT 4.0 Advanced Server

```
[HKEY_LOCAL_MACHINE\SYSTEM\CurrentControlSet\Control\
Session Manager\Executive]

AdditionalCriticalWorkerThreads              0 - 16
REG_DWORD
AdditionalDelayedWorkerThreads               0 - 16
REG_DWORD
```

Both of the previous values determine the responsiveness of the Windows NT *worker threads* that control multiple processes per thread, as opposed to *single threads* that control only one process. For NT Server, an idle worker thread's stack remains in memory; an NT Workstation's worker thread can be paged to the disk drive. The ways that these threads are interpreted depend on the setting for the ProductType value, listed previously. The settings for these values are higher for Windows NT Server than for Windows NT Workstation.

Author Note

If you try to manipulate the Registry values under Windows NT Workstation to convert it into a server, you will notice that these values cannot be changed one at a time with a Registry editor. These values must be changed simultaneously, usually by writing a program, or else you receive a blue screen showing this error: SYSTEM_LICENSE_VIOLATION.

Index

Numbers

A

ARP (Address Resolution Protocol)
RAS (Remote Access Service), 321
TCP/IP, configuring, 331

AsyncMac key, 308

ATAPI zip drives, 109-110

AttributeMemory1 (PC cards), 116

AttributeMemorySize (PC cards), 116

audio
16-bit drivers, configuring, 63
32-bit drivers, configuring, 62-63
devices
installing, 55-57
recordings, 58-59
sound cards
disabling, 55
installing, 53-55
wave channels, 63-64

auditing
NetBIOS gateways, 305
RAS (Remote Access Service), 320

authentication
Dial-Up Networking, 245
logons, 208

AuthRestrictions value (Dial-Up Networking), 245

Autocheck application (AUTOCHK.EXE), booting, 136

AutoDial (Dial-Up Networking), 250-251

AutoLogon, 138
Dial-Up Networking, 245

automatic disconnection
RAS (Remote Access Service), 320
Server service, 273

automatic services (Windows NT Services), 262
Alerter Service, 263
backup period, 264
Browser Service, 264
cache hit limit, 264
cache response size, 264
categories, 266
category message file, 267
direct host binding, 264

event log, 266
event message file, 267
log file values, 267-268
maintain server list, 265
Master Browser value, 265
master period, 266
maximum log file size, 267
Netlogon service, 268
query driver, 266
record management, 267

automatically downloading policies, 181-183

autorun (CD-ROM drives), 9

AUTORUN.INF file, 9

AutoShare for servers/ workstations, 273

B

Back off rate (Workstation service), 289

backgrounds, hiding, 186

backup period
Master Browser, 264
Windows NT Services (automatic services), 264

BACKUP.EXE, 105

backups
ERDs (Emergency Repair Disks), 106-107
periods, *see* backup period
tape, 105
Sytos Plus, 107-108
troubleshooting, 106-107
verifying, 105-106

base addresses
MIDI, 57
SCSI adapter cards, 103

Batfile key (file extensions), 161-162

BDC wait period (Netlogon service), 270

BeepEnabled0 (Print key), 95

Beeper, setting up printers, 95

Bézier dialog box (screen savers), 24-25

D

L

S

X-Z

New Riders Professional Library

Windows NT TCP/IP

By Karanjit Siyan
1st Edition Summer 1998
500 pages, $29.99
ISBN 1-56205-887-8

If you're still looking for good documentation on Microsoft TCP/IP, then look no further — this is your book. *Windows NT TCP/IP* cuts through the complexities and provides the most informative and complete reference book on Windows-based TCP/IP. Concepts essential to TCP/IP administration are explained thoroughly, then related to the practical use of Microsoft TCP/IP in a real-world networking environment. The book begins by covering TCP/IP architecture, advanced installation and configuration issues, then moves on to routing with TCP/IP, DHCP Management, and WINS/DNS Name Resolution.

Windows NT DNS

By Michael Masterson & Herman L. Knief
1st Edition Summer 1998
325 pages, $29.99
ISBN 1-56205-943-2

Have you ever opened a Windows NT book looking for detailed information about DNS only to discover that it doesn't even begin to scratch the surface? DNS is probably one of the most complicated subjects for NT administrators, and there are few books on the market that really address it in detail. This book answers your most complex DNS questions, focusing on the implementation of the Domain Name Service within Windows NT, treating it thoroughly from the viewpoint of an experienced Windows NT professional. Many detailed, real-world examples illustrate further the understanding of the material throughout. The book covers the details of how DNS functions within NT, then explores specific interactions with critical network components. Finally, proven procedures to design and set up DNS are demonstrated. You'll also find coverage of related topics, such as maintenance, security, and troubleshooting.

Exchange Server Implementation and Administration

By Doug Hauger, Wynne Leon, Bill Wade
1st Edition Fall 1998
450 pages, $29.99
ISBN 1-56205-931-9

If you're interested in connectivity and maintenance issues for Exchange Server, then this book is for you. Exchange's power lies in its ability to be connected to multiple email subsystems to create a "universal email backbone." It's not unusual to have several different and complex systems all connected via email gateways, including Lotus Notes or cc:Mail, Microsoft Mail, legacy mainframe systems, and Internet mail. This book covers all of the problems and issues associated with getting an integrated system running smoothly, and addresses troubleshooting and diagnosis of email problems, with an eye towards prevention and best practices.

Windows NT Performance Monitoring

By Mark Edmead
1st Edition Fall 1998
400 pages, $29.99
ISBN 1-56205-942-4

Performance monitoring is a little like preventative medicine for the administrator: no one enjoys a checkup, but it's a good thing to do on a regular basis. This book helps you focus on the critical aspects of improving the performance of your NT system, showing you how to monitor the system, implement benchmarking, and tune your network. The book is organized by resource components, which makes it easy to use as a reference tool.

SQL Server System Administration

By Sean Baird, Chris Miller et al.
1st Edition Fall 1998
400 pages, $29.99
1-56205-955-6

How often does your SQL Server go down during the day when everyone wants to access the data? Do you spend most of your time being a "report monkey" for your co-workers and bosses? *SQL Server System Administration* helps you keep data consistently available to your users. This book omits the introductory information. The authors don't spend time explaining queries and how they work. Instead they focus on the information that you can't get anywhere else, like how to choose the correct replication topology and achieve high availability of information.

Windows NT Thin Clients
Building Enterprise Solutions with Microsoft Terminal Server & Citrix Picasso

By Ted Harwood
1st Edition Winter 1998
500 pages, $29.99
ISBN 1-56205-944-0

It's no surprise that most administration headaches revolve around integration with other networks and clients. This book addresses these types of real-world issues on a case-by-case basis, giving tools and advice on solving each problem. If you use Citrix Picasso in your heterogeneous networking environment, this book is for you. The author also offers the real nuts and bolts of thin client administration on multiple systems, covering such relevant issues as installation, configuration, network connection, management, and application distribution.

Windows NT Technical Support

By Brendan McTague & George Neal
1st Edition Winter 1998
300 pages, $29.99
ISBN 1-56205-927-0

Well, you did it. You finally migrated your Enterprise network to Windows NT. Now what you need is a methodology, a logical way you can rigorously approach any problem, whether it's server or workstation related, and quickly get to it's root. That's what we asked Brendan and George, part of the group responsible for supporting Swiss Bank's worldwide NT enterprise, to put together for you. These guys have to support thousands of users on three continents - so they understand what technical support is. So why don't you read through their methodology, practice it on several of the sample work tickets included in the book, then go out and try it yourself?

Windows NT Security

By Richard Puckett
1st Edition Winter 1998
600 pages, $29.99
ISBN 1-56205-945-9

Swiss cheese. That's what some people say Windows NT security is like. And they may be right, because they only know what the NT documentation says about implementing security. Who has the time to research alternatives, play around with the features, service packs, hot fixes and add-on tools, and figure out what makes NT rock solid? Well, Richard Puckett does. He's been researching Windows NT Security for the University of Virginia for a while now, and he's got pretty good news. He's going to show you how to make NT secure in your environment, and we mean really secure.

Windows NT Administration Handbook

By Eric Svetcov
1st Edition Winter 1998
400 pages, $29.99
ISBN 1-56205-946-7

Administering a Windows NT network is kind of like trying to herd cats - an impossible task characterized by constant motion, exhausting labor and lots of hairballs. Author Eric Svetcov knows all about it - he's administered NT networks for some of the fastest growing companies around Silicon Valley. So we asked Eric to put together a concise manual of best practices, a book of tools and ideas that other administrators can turn to again and again in administering their own NT networks. Eric's experience shines through as he shares his secrets for administering users, for getting domain and groups set up quickly and for troubleshooting the thorniest NT problems. Daily, weekly and monthly task lists help organize routine tasks and preventative maintenance.

MCSE Core Essential Reference

By Matthew Shepker
1st Edition Fall 1998
500 pages, $19.99
ISBN 0-7357-0006-0

You're sitting in the first session of your Networking Essentials class and the instructor starts talking about "*RAS*" and you have no idea what that means. You think about raising your hand to ask about *RAS*, but you reconsider—you'd feel pretty foolish asking a question in front of all these people. You turn to your handy *MCSE Core Essential Reference* and find a quick summary on *Remote Access Services*. Question answered. It's a couple months later and you're taking your Networking Essentials exam the next day. You're reviewing practice tests and you keep forgetting the maximum lengths for the various commonly used cable types. Once again, you turn to the *MCSE Core Essential Reference* and find a table on cables including all of the characteristics you need to memorize in order to pass the test.

Lotus Notes & Domino Essential Reference

By Dave Hatter & Tim Bankes
1st Edition Winter 1998
500 pages, $19.99
ISBN 0-7357-0007-9

You're in a bind because you've been asked to design and program a new database in Notes for an important client that will keep track of and itemize a myriad of inventory and shipping data. The client wants a user-friendly interface, without sacrificing speed or functionality. You are experienced (and could develop this app in your sleep), but feel that you need to take your talents to the next level. You need something to facilitate your creative and technical abilities, something to perfect your programming skills. Your answer is waiting for you: *Lotus Notes and Domino Essential Reference.* It's compact and simply designed. It's loaded with information. All of the objects, classes, functions and methods are listed. It shows you the object hierarchy and the overlaying relationship between each one. It's perfect for you. Problem solved.

Linux System Administration

By James T. Dennis
1st Edition Winter 1998
450 pages, $29.99
ISBN 1-56205-934-3

As an administrator, you probably feel that most of your time and energy is spent in endless firefighting. If your network has become a fragile quilt of temporary patches and workarounds, then this book is for you. For example, have you had trouble sending or receiving your email lately? Are you looking for a way to keep your network running smoothly with enhanced perfor-

mance? Are your users always hankering for more storage, more services, and more speed? *Linux System Administration* advises you on the many intricacies of maintaining a secure, stable system. In this definitive work, the author addresses all the issues related to system administration from adding users and managing files permission to internet services and Web hosting to recovery planning and security. This book fulfills the need for expert advice that will ensure a trouble-free Linux environment.

Domino System Administration

By Rob Kirkland
1st Edition Winter 1998
500 pages, $29.99
ISBN 1-56205-948-3

Your boss has just announced that you will be upgrading to the newest version of Notes and Domino when it ships. As a Premium Lotus Business Partner, Lotus has offered a substantial price break to keep your company away from Microsoft's Exchange Server. How are you supposed to get this new system installed, configured, and rolled out to all of your end users? You understand how Lotus Notes works — you've been administering it for years. What you need is a concise, practical explanation about the new features, and how to make some of the advanced stuff really work. You need answers and solutions from someone who's been in the trenches; someone like you, who has worked with the product for years, and understands what it is you need to know. *Domino System Administration* is the answer — the first book on Domino that attacks the technology at the professional level, with practical, hands-on assistance to get Domino running in your organization.

We want to know what you think

To better serve you, we would like your opinion on the content and quality of this book. Please complete this card and mail it to us or fax it to 317-581-4663.

Name _____

Address _____

City _____ State _____ Zip _____

Phone _____

Email Address _____

Occupation _____

Operating System(s) that you use _____

What influenced your purchase of this book?
- ❏ Recommendation
- ❏ Table of Contents
- ❏ Magazine Review
- ❏ Reputation of New Riders
- ❏ Cover Design
- ❏ Index
- ❏ Advertisement
- ❏ Author Name

How would you rate the contents of this book?
- ❏ Excellent
- ❏ Good
- ❏ Below Average
- ❏ Very Good
- ❏ Fair
- ❏ Poor

How do you plan to use this book?
- ❏ Quick reference
- ❏ Classroom
- ❏ Self-training
- ❏ Other

What do you like most about this book?
Check all that apply.
- ❏ Content
- ❏ Accuracy
- ❏ Listings
- ❏ Index
- ❏ Price
- ❏ Writing Style
- ❏ Examples
- ❏ Design
- ❏ Page Count
- ❏ Illustrations

What do you like least about this book?
Check all that apply.
- ❏ Content
- ❏ Accuracy
- ❏ Listings
- ❏ Index
- ❏ Price
- ❏ Writing Style
- ❏ Examples
- ❏ Design
- ❏ Page Count
- ❏ Illustrations

What would be a useful follow up book to this one for you? _____

Where did you purchase this book? _____

Can you name a similar book that you like better than this one, or one that is as good? Why? _____

_____

_____

How many New Riders books do you own? _____

What are your favorite computer books? _____

_____

What other titles would you like to see us develop? _____

_____

Any comments for us? _____

_____

_____

_____

_____

Windows NT Registry 1-56205-941-6

Fold here and scotch tape to mail

- -

Place
Stamp
Here

New Riders
201 W. 103rd St.
Indianapolis IN 46290